An outline of Old Testament theology

Th. C. Vriezen

Professor in the University of Utrecht

An outline of
Old Testament
theology

Second edition / *revised and enlarged*

1970

Charles T. Branford Company ⟩ Newton ⟩ Massachusetts 02159

SBN 8231-1011-7

© H. Veenman & Zonen nv, Wageningen, The Netherlands

No part of this book may be reproduced in any form, by print, photoprint, micro-
film or any other means without written permission from the publisher

First published in The Netherlands in 1949: 'Hoofdlijnen der theologie van het
Oude Testament'. Second edition, 1954. Third edition, 1966

German edition, 1956: 'Theologie des Alten Testaments in Grundzügen'
The second edition is now being revised
Agents for the Bundesrepublik Deutschland: Neukirchener Verlag des Erziehungs-
vereins GmbH, Neukirchen-Vluyn (Kreis Moers)

First English edition, 1958
Reprinted 1960, 1961, 1962, 1966
Second edition, 1970
Basil Blackwell, Oxford (for the British Empire)
Charles T. Branford, Newton, Massachusetts 02159 (for the U.S.A.)

Spanish edition, 'Introducción al Antiguo Testamento', 1970
by Editorial y Libreria La Aurora s.r.l., Buenos Aires, Argentina

Japanese edition, 1969: 旧約聖書神学概説
by the Board of Publications, The United Church of Christ in Japan, Tokyo

Printed in the Netherlands by H. Veenman & Zonen nv at Wageningen

Contents

Preface

TO THE FIRST EDITION

This book was written during the years following the Second World War to meet the demand of young theologians, undergraduates as well as clergymen, for a theological Introduction to the Old Testament. It was first published in 1949, and in 1954 a second, enlarged edition came out.

Soon after the appearance of the first edition, Prof. H. H. Rowley of Manchester and Prof. N. W. Porteous of Edinburgh were so kind as to suggest that the book should also be brought out in an English translation. The difficulties that arose held up the execution of this plan considerably, so that it was decided to await the publication of the second Dutch edition and to use that as the basis for the English translation. Unlike the German translation published last year, which was, in places, abridged and adapted to the specific needs of German theologians in the last few years, the English edition is a complete and exact rendering of the second Dutch edition, except for the bibliographies, where some less important Dutch titles were dropped and some recent works included.

The work distinguishes itself from most other Theologies in that its first part goes into the important theological problems with which the Old Testament confronts the Christian theologian, and the second, material part attempts to answer, in terms of the Christian faith and with the aid of all the results made available by modern scholarship, the question of the meaning and value of the message of the Old Testament for the Christian theologian.

I want to render my best thanks to Prof. H. H. Rowley and Prof. N. W. Porteous for the interest shown in this book, and especially to Prof. F. F. Bruce of Sheffield for his actual cooperation in reading through and revising the English text and the first proofs.

Den Dolder, Holland
February 1958

TH. C. VRIEZEN

TO THE SECOND EDITION

The third Dutch edition (1966) of which this book is a translation was revised and partly rewritten for the following two reasons. The realisation that the central point of faith in the Old Testament testimonies, which was expounded in chapter VI, should now dominate the second part of the book (content of Old Testament Theology) more than in the last edition was the first reason. The second was that after the appearance of the former edition discussion concerning the character of Old Testament Theology revived so strongly, especially in Germany, that it was impossible to ignore either the discussion or the book that came so much to be the centre of the discussion, namely G. von Rad's *Old Testament Theology*. In the new edition, therefore, not only is the new literature considered, but a rewriting has also taken place which tries to stress more firmly the unity of the whole.

This rewriting becomes apparent at the following points: in the first part (the prolegomena, chapters I–V) only a few additions are made, but two of these are rather extensive. They are: a criticism of the latest attempts to establish the connection between Old and New Testaments (pp. 96ff.), and a paragraph devoted to the relation of contents between both Testaments (pp. 104ff.).

The original second part (chapters VI–XI) has undergone an important transformation in form, since I have attempted to establish the 'communion' which is central to chapter VI as the centre of all the expositions.

Because of this, 'The intercourse between God and man' which was chapter IX in the first edition now follows directly after chapter VI. Materially this chapter, which is now chapter VII, has been revised because of special attention paid to the questions of God's self-revelation and the revelation throughout history (pp. 182ff.); several parts have been revised and rewritten (e.g. *Ruach*, pp. 211ff.) and others added (The wise men, pp. 242ff., and The place of revelation, pp. 245ff.).

The community of God and its partners is considered fully in the new chapter VIII in four separate parts: i. Yahweh, the God of community (the former chapter VII: God); ii. The forms of this community, a practically new part in which its historical points, the amphictyony, the kingship, are given special attention; iii. The rules of community (formerly chapter X on Ethics); iv. Man in the community of God (nearly identical with the old chapter VIII).

Finally, as in the first edition the last chapter (chapter XI), now chapter IX, discusses the expectations of the kingdom of God in Israel.

Only selected corrections and additions to the literature published after 1966 have been included in this edition.

To conclude, I would like to express my thanks to the critics and readers whose kind interest very much encouraged me to continue working on this book; and especially once more to Mr. S. Neuijen, English master at the 'Baudartius Lyceum' at Zutphen, who, after the work of translation some twelve years ago and in spite of his busy schedule, took upon himself the exacting task of this revision; and, last but not least, to the publishers Messrs. Veenman and their staff, for their sympathetic co-operation in the completion of the book.

Den Dolder, Holland

TH. C. VRIEZEN

August 1969

Abbreviations

A.A.B.	Abhandlungen der Deutschen (till 1944: Preußischen) Akademie der Wissenschaften zu Berlin	*N.T.T.*	Nederlands Theologisch Tijdschrift
A.A.S.	Acta Apostolicae Sedis	*O.L.Z.*	Orientalistische Literaturzeitung
A.N.E.T.	Ancient Near Eastern Texts relating to the Old Testament	*O.T.S.*	Oudtestamentische Studiën
		R.A.C.	Reallexikon für Antike und Christentum
A.O.T.	Altorientalische Texte	*R.B.*	Revue Biblique
Ar.Or.	Archiv Orientalni	*R.H.Ph.R.*	Revue d'Histoire et de Philosophie Religieuses
A.R.W.	Archiv für Religionswissenschaft	*R.H.R.*	Revue de l'Histoire des Religions
A.T.D.	Das Alte Testament Deutsch	*R.L.V.*	Reallexikon der Vorgeschichte
B.H.Th.	Beiträge zur historischen Theologie	*R.S.Ph.Th.*	Revue des Sciences Philosophiques et Théologiques
Bi.OR.	Bibliotheca Orientalis	*R.Thom.*	Revue Thomiste
B.J.R.L.	The Bulletin of the John Rylands Library	*R.Th.Ph.*	Revue de Théologie et de Philosophie
B.W.A.T.	Beiträge zur Wissenschaft vom Alten Testament	*S.J.Th.*	The Scottish Journal of Theology
B.Z.A.W.	Beihefte zur Zeitschrift für die alttestamentliche Wissenschaft	*St.C.*	Studia Catholica
D.B.S.	Dictionnaire de la Bible, Supplément	*S.Th.U.*	Schweizerische Theologische Umschau
D.S.D.	Manual of Discipline (1QS)	*St.OR.*	Studia Orientalia
E.Jud.	Encyclopaedia Judaica	*St.Th.*	Studia Theologica
E.Th.L.	Ephemerides Theologicae Lovanienses	*St.Z.*	Stimmen der Zeit
		Suppl.V.T.	Supplements to Vetus Testamentum
Ev.Th.	Evangelische Theologie	*Sv.T.K.*	Svensk Teologisk Kvartalskrift
G.B.	W. Gesenius – F. Buhl, Hebräisches und Aramäisches Handwörterbuch	*Te.U.*	Tekst en Uitleg
		Th.Bl.	Theologische Blätter
G.G.A.	Göttingische Gelehrte Anzeigen	*Th.Ex.*	Theologische Existenz heute
G.Th.T.	Gereformeerd Theologisch Tijdschrift	*Th.L.Z.*	Theologische Literaturzeitung
		Th.R.	Theologische Rundschau
H.A.T.	Handbuch zum Alten Testament, hg. v. O. Eißfeldt	*Th.St.Kr*	Theologische Studien und Kritiken
H.U.C.A.	Hebrew Union College Annual	*Th.T.*	Theologisch Tijdschrift
J.B.L.	Journal of Biblical Literature and Exegesis	*Th.W.*	Theologisches Wörterbuch zum Neuen Testament
I.C.C.	The International Critical Commentary of the Holy Scriptures of the Old and New Testament	*Th.Z.*	Theologische Zeitschrift
		T.Th.	Tijdschrift voor Theologie
J.E.O.L.	Jaarbericht Ex Oriente Lux	*Vox.Th.*	Vox Theologica
J.N.E.S.	Journal of Near Eastern Studies	*V.T.*	Vetus Testamentum
J.R.	Journal of Religion	*W.O.*	Die Welt des Orients
J.Th.S.	The Journal of Theological Studies	*Z.A.W.*	Zeitschrift für die alttestamentliche Wissenschaft
K.Th.	Kerk en Theologie		
K.u.D.	Kerygma und Dogma	*Z.D.M.G.*	Zeitschrift der deutschen Morgenländischen Gesellschaft
M.S.L.	J. P. Migne, Patrologiae cursus completus, series Latina	*Z.D.PV.*	Zeitschrift des Deutschen Palästinavereins
N.K.Z.	Neue kirchliche Zeitschrift	*Z.M.*	Zeitschrift für Missionskunde
N.R.Th.	Nouvelle Revue Théologique	*Z.S.Th.*	Zeitschrift für systematische Theologie
N.Th.S.	Nieuwe Theologische Studiën		
N.T.S.	New Testament Studies	*Z.Th.K.*	Zeitschrift für Theologie und Kirche

A Theology of the Old Testament will have to be rewritten in each generation, for each has different needs and each will interpret the past in its own characteristic way. But it will have its inevitable poles around which all else turns. Over against each other are God and man, and all that lies between can be conceived as belonging to the Kingdom, the active kingly rule, of God.

H. WHEELER ROBINSON
Inspiration and Revelation in the
Old Testament

CHAPTER I

The Christian Church and the Old Testament

Historically and spiritually Christianity stands upon the shoulders of Judaism. Like St. Paul and almost all the authors of the New Testament, Jesus Christ was an Israelite. He lived by the Hebrew holy Scriptures which were, for Him as well as for His disciples, the Word of God. During His life He drew the strength for His work from the sacred books of his people. When temptations assail Him, He drives the tempter away with words from the Torah (Deut.viii.3; vi.16; vi.13; x.20); at the hour of His death He prays in the words of Psalm xxii. He argues with the Jewish leaders on the meaning of the scriptures of the Old Testament, which both He and His spiritual opponents take as their starting-point. When it was apparently held against Him that He invalidated the law, He stated expressly that He would not give up one jot or tittle of it; He only wanted to reveal the law by word and action in all its fulness and gravity.[1]

Because of His spiritual understanding of the law He again and again contradicts the Judaic theology of His days derived from it ('them of old time', i.e. tradition, Matt.v; Mark vii), and even repeatedly contradicts certain words of the law (Matt.v.38ff.; xix.1ff.). Sometimes Christ used the traditional text freely, and in doing so He showed Himself superior to all bondage to the letter (in Luke iv.18ff., Isa.lxi.2 is quoted without the words 'the day of vengeance of our

---

[1] The best illustration from the Old Testament of the meaning of the word 'to fulfil' in Matt.v.17 is 1 Kings i.14, where Nathan promises Bathsheba to fulfil her words when he goes to David. 'To fulfil' here means to give effect to her words by his action. See Gesenius, *H.W.B.*, on this text: to complete and confirm; LXX: πληροῦν, like Matt.v.17. Cf. also *Th.W.*, IV, pp.1053ff. (s.v. νόμος), IV, p.872 (s.v. Μωυσης); H.N.Ridderbos, *The Coming of the Kingdom*, 1962, pp.294ff.; A.A.van Ruler, *De Vervulling der Wet*, 1947, pp.327ff.; K.E.Skydsgaard in *Th. L. Haitjema Festschrift, Schrift en Kerk*, 1953, p.80, and *Sc.J. Th.* 1956. See on Jesus and the Law: H.Conzelmann, 'Jesus Christus', *R.G.G.* III³, pp.633ff.; O.Bauernfeind, 'Gesetz IV, im N.T.', *R.G.G.* II³, pp.1517ff.

God'). He even dared to preach in a critical manner[1] and in this He

[1] This critical attitude does not spring from lack of belief in the Old Testament, but from a true understanding of the heart of the Old Testament message (the love of the Holy God as the only foundation of life) and from living by this message. On the attitude of Jesus towards the Old Testament opinions differ widely among Old Testament and New Testament scholars and dogmaticians. It is not surprising therefore that this view of Jesus' critical attitude towards the law is contested both from right and left; so also the views we shall develop later on (pp.13f.), that Jesus rose above the Scriptures and that a critical attitude towards the Old Testament can be taken up in imitation of Christ, share the same fate. It is surprising, however, that the above should have been taken to mean that Jesus was 'critical of the Bible' in our sense of the word. A few words, therefore, in explanation.

Two reasons are often adduced for denying the critical element in the preaching of Jesus: first, the dogmatic thesis that the Scriptures were as authoritative for Christ as for later Hebrew and Christian orthodoxy, and second, the *a priori* argument of the history of religion that the Old Testament was such an unassailable 'coagulated Word of God' in the Hebrew world of the first century that both Judaism and the early Christian Church could do nothing with it but interpret it (see the discussion between P.A.H.de Boer and Th.C.Vriezen in *N.T.T.*, 1951, pp.2ff, and 90ff.). Three things may be considered established facts: that at the beginning of the first century the canonical limits of the Old Testament were as yet by no means rigidly fixed (Diestel, *Geschichte des A.T.*, 1869, p.10; G.Wildeboer, *Het ontstaan van de Kanon des Ouden Verbonds*, 1900, p.5), that in the Judaism of later days a great distinction was felt to exist between the three parts of the (later) canon (H.L.Strack and P.Billerbeck, *Kommentar z. N.T.* IV, 1928, pp.433ff,), and, thirdly, that generally speaking a rather free use of the Bible existed in Judaism (cf. the way in which the Bible was employed in the Judean Rolls found recently and the free use of the Biblical text in the Septuagint and the Midrashim; on the latter see the conclusion of I.L.Seeligmann, 'Voraussetzungen der Midrašexegese', *Suppl. V. T.* I, 1953, p.181. Judaism long kept an open mind with respect to the text, and, until circa A.D. 90, with respect tot the canon as such. An interesting example of the hesitant attitude towards the canonization of the Scriptures taken up by the orthodox Palestinian Jews (in later times) is to be found in the appreciation of Jesus Sirach in rabbinical circles. Cf. M.Haran, *Problems of the Canonization of Scripture*, Tarbiz, XXV, pp.245ff., who rightly observes that this canonization is the result of a process of evaluation taking place in Jewish devotion rather than a decision imposed from above. Fundamentally this is also true of the more extensive forms taken by the Christian canon, see p. 15 n. 5.

The attitude of Jesus Christ and the early Christian Church (St. Paul), is different again: in spite of the fact that the Holy Scriptures are admitted to be the Word of God there is a strong sense of freedom, which springs from the certainty of speaking and acting under the guidance of the Spirit of God. Jesus, and later St. Paul, expressed ideas in which the critical element is unmistakable – besides the texts mentioned above we may also refer to St. Paul's contesting the notion of law as a means of salvation (cf. the Epistle to the Galatians), to the latitude he allows in respect of the Sabbath (Rom.xiv), and his emphasis on Abraham's faith over against the justification attained by the fulfilment of the law (Rom.iv). In this connection the negative datum that nowhere in the N.T. is mention made of Jesus offering sacrifices may be considered important. It is remarkable that Jewish scholars, who are on the one hand strongly inclined to bring out clearly the complete dependence of the N.T. of the O.T., do not express any doubt in respect of the peculiar and critical nature of certain elements in the work of Jesus (cf. J.Klausner, Jesus van Nazareth, E. Jud., XI, pp.70f.; M.Buber, *Two Types of Faith*, 1951, pp.59ff.; H.J.Schoeps, *Aus frühchristlicher Zeit*, 1950, pp.212ff.; *Jesus und das jüdische Gesetz*, pp.271ff.: *Restitutio principii als kritisches Prinzip der Nova lex Jesu*; H.J.Schoeps, *Theologie und Geschichte des Judenchristentums*, 1949, pp.145f., cf. also the book quoted by Schoeps in his *Aus frühchr. Zeit*, p.273, *Jesus and the law of Moses*, by B.H.Branscomb, who supposes that Christ made no distinction between oral and written law but between the primary will of God and the secondary laws.

followed the ancient prophets (cf. Hosea's criticism of Jacob in ch. xii).
He also shows in other respects His spiritual independence of the law
and especially of the verbalism of His theological, orthodox contemporaries. He is Lord even of the sabbath day (Matt. xii. 8) and as
such He gives a new interpretation of the way in which this day should
be celebrated.[1] As the Son of Man He knows that He is called to preach
the Word of God with a new, more profoundly spiritual understanding,[2] and from the awareness of His messianic vocation He speaks as
one greater than Moses.[3] That in doing so Jesus breaks away from
tradition and sometimes even rises above the Holy Scriptures by no
means signifies that those Scriptures had lost their value for Him. On
the contrary: the word of the Law, the Prophets, and the Psalms is His
starting-point; in it He finds the Word of God, from it God speaks to
Him and His people. The authority of Holy Scripture was an incontestable fact for Him, and yet He did not feel committed to its letter.[4]

The Jewish Christians at the beginning of the apostolic age also lived
fully by the Old Testament, on which they drew to prove to the Jews
the legality of Jesus' activity and the fact that in Him the Old Testament prophecies were fulfilled.

As a result of the missionary activity of the Church the critical element soon begins to come to the fore because Gentile Christian circles
opposed the acceptance of various customs which were prescribed by
the Old Testament but felt to be typically Jewish. In the earliest periods
of the Church it is St. Paul, who, as the apostle of the Gentiles, understands these objections and subjects them to theological examination.
He comes to the conclusion that the influence on the world of the
preaching of Jesus Christ must not be curbed by these typically Jewish
customs – however much they might be sanctified by the law,[5] and

---

[1] Cf. W. Rordorf, *Der Sonntag*, 1962, pp. 70f.
[2] From Christ's preaching and from the preaching about Him there arose later the
New Testament, which came to take its place beside the Old Testament and attained
an authority equal to that of the O.T. Here the two aspects of the attitude of the early
Christian Church towards the O.T. come out clearly. This development within the
Christian Church would certainly have been impossible without fundamentally new
starting-points at the time when this Church came into being.
[3] Cf. E. Käsemann, 'Das Problem des historischen Jesus', in his collection *Exegetische
Versuche und Besinnungen* I, 1960, pp. 26off.
[4] On this relation cf. also C. Kuhl, *Die Entstehung des A. T.*, 1953, pp. 6ff.; on the problem as a whole; G. Kittel, 'Judentum und Christentum', *R.G.G.*, III², pp. 492ff. and
now *R.G.G.* II³, pp. 1517f. and III³, pp. 633f.
[5] St. Paul's solution of the problem of the relationship between the law and the
revelation of God is that the law was 'added' (cf. Gal. iii. 19; Rom. v. 20), in order to
keep the congregation together and to prepare it for the coming of Christ (Gal. iii.
15–29; Rom. iv–vii). St. Paul takes up the same attitude towards the Mosaic
revelation as the Jews towards the Prophets and the Writings (Strack-Billerbeck, op.
cit., 435). In his own way St. Paul has given a continuation of what H. J. Schoeps in

even though, in the period when Judaism had had to shake off pagan influences, they had been of very great importance and had therefore been recognized as commandments of God,[1] and been found acceptable as such. In imitation of Christ St. Paul recognized that there were commandments of God that were significant only in a certain age and a certain situation, as well as others that always remained valid because of their purely moral and religious character. The old Jewish Christian congregation, assembled at the apostolic convention of A.D. 48, followed him only reluctantly in this, admitting, at least that the external cultic demands of the Old Testament did not apply to the Gentile Christians. Only four commandments which were considered Noachian, i.e. given by God to Noah for all nations, were maintained (Acts xv). Such a decision is only conceivable when the idea of a canon in the later strict sense of the word either does not yet exist or has been broken down. It is the latter which is the case there, since it was a question of the pre-scriptions of the *Torah*, which were declared not to apply to Gentile Christians.[2]

This victory of St. Paul was one of the most important strides forward for Christianity; it gave the Church the opportunity of dissociating itself in practical life from those elements in the Old Testa-

Aus frühchristlicher Zeit called the 'restitutio principii als kritisches Prinzip der Nova lex Jesu'.

Yet St. Paul (if we may reckon 2 Timothy among the Pauline Epistles; if not, this applies to the early Christian Church) considered and recognized the Old Testament as the Holy Scripture (2 Tim. iii. 16), to which the qualification 'theopneustic', i.e. inspired by God, is applicable ('every passage from the Scriptures given by inspiration from God is also profitable for instruction', on this translation cf. J. de Zwaan, *Inleiding tot het N.T.*, 1942, p. 156). It should be borne in mind, however, that a canon in the sense of a definitely fixed list of writings in the Church was not yet known (the Old Testament canon had not yet been fixed; in the N.T., texts from apocryphal writings are still quoted as authoritative, cf. 1 Cor. ii. 9; Jude 14ff.; 2 Tim. iii. 8; Heb. xi. 35ff.). Only the Torah was canonical in our sense of the word (and also the Prophets, cf. below n. 2). Cf. on the problem of the canon J. de Zwaan, op. cit., pp. 148ff., and especially Fr. Horst's excellent article, 'Das A.T. als Heilige Schrift und als Kanon', *Th. Bl.*, XI, 1932, pp. 161ff., W. Staerk, 'Schrift- und Kanonbegriff der jüdischen Bibel', *Z. S. Th.*, VI, 1929, pp. 101ff. and E. Dinkler, 'Bibelautorität und Bibelkritik', *Z. Th. K.* 1950, pp. 71–79.

[1] We might think here of the reserve with which the Sabbath-commandment is treated (Rom. 14) and of the origin of the Sunday, which developed on entirely novel grounds, see W. A. Rordorf, *op. cit.*

[2] For the Jews the canon really consists of the Torah (Strack-Billerbeck, *loc. cit.*); it is pre-existent and eternal, so that it will continue to exist in the age to come. God Himself studies the Law and so does the Messiah, see *R.G.G.*[3] II. 'Gesetz' III. pp. 1515ff. and W. D. Davies, *Tora in the Messianic Age and the Age to come*, 1952. But in religious practice the second part of the canon (the prophetic books) was practically placed on a level with the Torah (see G. Gerleman, *Synoptic Studies in the O.T.*, 1948, pp. 6ff., where it is proved, on the ground of linguistic differences in the texts, that the line of demarcation between canonical and less authoritative writings is drawn between the Prophets and the Writings); among the sects we find the same attitude, cf. R. H. Charles, *Apocrypha and Pseudepigrapha of the O.T.*, II, 1913, p. 789 with regard to the Damascus Writing.

14

ment that were only of a temporary nature, thus enabling it to become a missionary and world-wide Church. The antithesis, called into existence by the anti-Pauline Jewish Christians of the first centuries (the Nazarenes and the Ebionites),[1] is a most important, though only too often a much neglected testimony to this, though only little is known about these movements.

For the Gentile Christian world from which the world-wide Church sprang, the preaching of the Gospel was and remained the central element, as the preaching of the risen and glorified Lord, Jesus Christ, the Saviour of the world. The message of His life and work, as recorded in the Gospels, became the starting-point and foundation of faith and of life. The Old Testament, it is true, was also accepted as the Word of God and was recognized as canonical, but, in fact, as compared with the apostolic witness to Jesus Christ, it fell into the background (though psychologically rather than theologically).[2] In the Christian Church of the second century some (Marcion, for instance) even made a stand against the Old Testament; Marcion went so far in his criticism that he broke with the Church and had to be looked upon as a heretic.[3]

In the catholic (i.e. universal, Gentile Christian) Church which sprang up all over the Graeco-Roman world, the Old Testament was upheld as the revelation of God all through this struggle and gained still greater authority, even if it could only be made acceptable to the Gentile Christians by typological and allegorical interpretations.[4]

This attitude became of the greatest importance for the Church in her struggle against gnosticism, which gained a great deal of influence in the second century owing to its strongly syncretist character. The belief in God as the Creator of heaven and earth, so strongly proclaimed throughout the Old Testament, was a strong support for Christian preaching.

Owing to these various struggles the Church was compelled to establish her own canon; in the process the sacred scriptures of the Old Testament were accepted,[5] and, besides, a number of writings were

---

[1] See, e.g., G. Krüger, *Handbuch der Kirchengeschichte I, Das Altertum*[3], 1932, p. 71, and H. J. Schoeps, *Theologie und Geschichte des Judenchristentums*, 1949, pp. 117ff.
[2] The best way to mark this difference may be to point to the two oldest creeds, that of the Jewish-Christian congregation: Jesus Christ = Jesus is the Messiah, and that of the later Church: *Christos Kurios* = Christ is the Lord.
[3] A. von Harnack, *Marcion*, 1921 (2nd edition, 1924).
[4] See Dr. J. L. Koole, *De overname van het O.T. door de christelijke Kerk*, Hilversum 1938; L. H. K. Bleeker, *Hermeneutiek van het O.T.*, Haarlem 1948, p. 86ff. We should not forget, however, that allegory was a generally accepted method of exegesis in those days (cf. Philo of Alexandria for Jewish theology, and the interpretation of Homer in the classical world). On the history of exegesis see O. Procksch, *Theologie des A.T.*, 1950, pp. 21ff.
[5] In several ecclesiastical provinces the Old Testament canon of the Christian Church was more extensive than the Jewish canon of Jamnia, because a greater or

recognized that became the nucleus of the New Testament as the apostolic canon. In this way the Old and the New Testament were placed side by side as two canonical series and together they came to form the Bible.[1] In this way the original bond between the earliest Christian congregations and the Old Testament was done full justice, and the critical attitude towards the Old Testament, which had existed from the earliest days, gradually fell into the background.

In a way, however, there has always remained some tension in the World Church concerning the meaning of the Old Testament.[2] As we observed above, it had, since its origin, contained elements of varying degrees of canonicity; this was already evident to the Jews, and it was certainly no less apparent to the Christian Church. The fact that, for instance, neither the Song of Songs, nor Ecclesiastes nor Esther is quoted in the New Testament, did not remain unobserved.[3] The Early Church never reached complete agreement on the Old Testament canon, but resigned herself to the existence of different traditions.

In fact, not until the struggle about the Bible at the time of the Reformation did this problem become the centre of interest, and even then it was not solved really. At the Council of Trent the Roman Catholic Church came to a decision by placing the apocryphal books of the Old Testament on a level with the canonical books,[4] whereas the Churches of the Reformation fell back on the Jewish tradition and in various respects, including exegetical method, associated themselves more and more with Hebrew scholarship. The Reformers themselves

smaller number that were considered of great spiritual value in the first half of the 1st century A.D. but had not been accepted as canonical by the Jewish synod of Jamnia, were indeed accepted as sacred writings in the earliest Jewish-Christian and the later Graeco-Christian churches (the apocryphal books, as they came to be called afterwards). It is not always clear on what grounds certain books were accepted or rejected. Generally speaking we may say that the early Church with her mostly more extensive canon preserved an older and less strict Jewish tradition prevailing before Jamnia. So the Church did follow the Jewish tradition but developed it in her own way. In various churches there arose different traditions concerning the extent of the Old Testament canon: sometimes we find a list of canonical books shorter than the Jewish canon (in which cases such books as Esther are omitted); mostly, however, we find a tendency to conform to the official Jewish canon (this would apply, for instance, to Hieronymus during his Bethlehem period). See A. C. Sundberg, *The O.T. of the early Church*, 1964, pp. 129ff., and Jepsen, *R.G.G.*[3] I, p. 1125.

[1] See below p. 121f. and the article by F. Horst mentioned above; W. G. Kümmel, 'Bibel' II B, *R.G.G.* I[3], pp. 1131ff.

[2] Cf. e.g., the description of this in D. Lerch, *Isaaks Opferung, christlich gedeutet*, 1950, esp. pp. 112–115.

[3] Cf., for example, the criticism of Theodorus of Mopsuestia, who rejected several writings – Job, the Song of Songs, the Epistle of James and the headings of the Psalms – as being unhistorical (see, for example, P. J. Maan, 'Alexandrië en Antiochië', *N.T.T.*, V, p. 206; L. Diestel, *op. cit.*, pp. 129ff.); on his exegetical method (literal sense and exact philological method) see R. Devreesse, 'La méthode exégétique de Théodore de Mopsueste', *R.B.* 1946, pp. 207–241.

[4] See p. 15 n. 5.

did not as yet go so far. In spite of the fact that he contrasted[1] the Old and the New Testament as Law and Gospel, Luther[2] sought the unity of the two Testaments in the revelation of Christ which he did find in the Old Testament: he could call Abraham and Moses Christians. Though there were certain writings or parts of them within the Old Testament (as within the New) that he would, in fact, rather have removed from the canon[3] (especially the book of Esther, which 'judaized' too much in his opinion) he accepted the canon of the Old Testament as a whole. The fact that he did not, as might be expected from his theological criticism, take up a directly critical attitude[4] may probably be accounted for partially by the stand the Reformation had taken up against the Roman Catholic Church with its Scriptural evidence. Luther's work, at any rate, again demonstrates some of the tension that had existed in the Early Church with respect to the relationship between the two Testaments. In Calvin's writings the ideas of Law and Gospel were not applied to the Old and the New Testament, and the connection between the two Testaments is considered wholly organical.[5] In this way the historical point of view in the relationship between the Old Testament and the New Testament can be emphasized more strongly. In the Reformed Churches, unlike the Lutheran Church, the two Testaments were put entirely on a level. No wonder that this in its turn often led to a strongly typological or allegorical interpretation of the text. How the Song of Songs has suffered in the practice of Reformed preaching because of this tendency!

In the second and subsequent generations of the Reformation a type of exegesis came into prominence that often reverted to rabbinical traditions (Buxtorf and others). As a result theologians clung more and more to the literal text. This fact and the controversy with Rome brought about an increasingly stringent conception of inspiration, resulting in the doctrine of the infallibility of the Bible, the canon and the text: the doctrine of the literal inspiration of the original text was even applied to the Hebrew vowel-signs.

[1] Cf. E. Wolf, 'Gesetz' V, *R.G.G.*[3] II, pp. 1523f.
[2] Cf. H. Bornkamm, *Luther und das A.T.*, 1948, esp. pp. 158ff., but also G. Gloege, *Mythologie und Judentum*, 1952, p. 42; H. J. Kraus, *Geschichte der hist.-krit. Erforschung des A.T.*, 1956, pp. 15ff.; R. H. Bainton, 'The Bible in the Reformation', *The Cambridge History of the Bible*, 1963, pp. 1–37.
[3] On Luther and Esther also: H. Bardtke, *Luther und das Buch Esther*, 1964, from which it appears that Luther also had something positive to say of the book, whereas it seems Calvin never mentioned it and so ignored it.
[4] Cf. on this: E. Brunner, *Revelation and Reason*, Eng. Tr., 1947, pp. 275f.; the same inconsistency is also found in Calvin's works: Brunner, *op. cit.*, p. 275 n. 6, and J. A. Cramer, *De Heilige Schrift bij Calvijn*, 1926.
[5] Though Calvin was also distinctly aware of the differences, cf. R. Bijlsma, *Schriftuurlijk Schriftgezag* 1959, pp. 358f.

But at the same time when dogma had made the Bible (including the Old Testament) unassailable and placed it outside history, modern literary-historical and critical research sprang up with irresistible force in reaction to this attitude, and attempted to arrive at a factual understanding of the Old Testament in the light of its own period of origin, starting from certain internal criteria. As one of the first attempts we must mention here Spinoza's *Theologico-Political Treatise*. Accepting and applying this method carried with it the danger that the great spiritual message of the Old Testament was pushed into the background because it was viewed from a purely cultural angle and represented as a mere anthology of ancient Hebrew or ancient Israelite literature. Of course the Old Testament is all this, but we must recognize that it is a very special part of this literature, for it is neither more nor less than that part which was accepted both by the Jews and by the Christian Church as the Holy Scriptures, in which the Word of God spoken by the prophets had been recorded.

In the last century this special character of the Old Testament was sometimes lost sight of completely, owing to the development referred to above. Even at that time objections were raised in various quarters against this negative interpretation, and since the 1920's theologians have again begun to realize that there is another side to the question. There is one lesson which this critical period has taught us for good and all, viz. that the Old Testament really is an ancient oriental book and should be read as such. This is no small gain, for only in this way can it appeal to us as a truly human work. Such a human and historical point of view may also lead to a better understanding of the special character of the Old Testament. It is true that many of the supposed results of the various schools of historical criticism and history of religion of the last century and the early years of this century will have to be abandoned, and that objections must be raised against a good many fundamental (evolutionist[1]) ideas in the field of the philosophy of religion and of general philosophy, which often dominated this criticism. Yet we owe a great debt of gratitude to the leading men of this modern critical and scholarly Bible-research of the last two centuries for their application of philological method and the techniques of historical criticism to the study of the Old and the New Testament. In spite of its sometimes negative views it has been, and still is, invaluable for a new understanding of the Old Testament, not only in the field of literature and the history of religion, but also in that of historical

---

[1] See for example Pedersen's criticism of the historical and critical research in *Z.A.W.* 1931, pp. 161ff., under the title *Die Auffassung vom A.T.*; although this does not apply to Wellhausen to such an extent as Pederson supposes, cf. R. Smend, 'Universalismus und Partikularismus', *Ev. Th.*, 1962, pp. 169ff., esp. 175ff., and L. Perlitt, *Vatke und Wellhausen, BZAW* 94, 1965.

theology. It will be impossible ever to abandon the method of historical criticism.

The negative criticism and (in certain circles) rejection of the Old Testament of the first half in this century[1] brought on another reaction: the revival of the study of Old Testament theology. In the period between the two world-wars the opposition against and the ensuing struggle about the Old Testament arose especially in the German-speaking countries, and led to a new awareness of the theological importance of the Old Testament to the Christian Church and of the necessity of a scholarly approach to this question.

A Christian theology which clings to the revelatory character of the Gospel and recognizes Jesus Christ as its Lord cannot but maintain the revelatory character of the Old Testament, not only because He has accepted this Old Testament as revelation of God and because His preaching is inconceivable without the Old Testament message concerning God, but especially because Christ's Messianic office cannot be confessed and maintained without the Old Testament.

For the theologian who starts from the revelation of God in Jesus Christ and who wants to read the Old Testament in a scholarly fashion, there are nowadays not only many difficulties but also many possibilities. On the one hand he must take seriously research in the fields of philology, archaeology, literature, history and the history of religion; on the other hand he must also take seriously the demand of theology to understand the Old Testament as the Christian Church has understood it from the beginning, as the Word of God. A critical examination of the text may be completely in agreement with this fundamental idea of the theological view of the Old Testament and it will often corroborate this underlying idea; but the theologian must also be willing to do truly critical work, he must attempt to abandon all *a priori* thinking in his scholarly research; he must be willing to listen to the testimony of the Old Testament independently and with an open mind. If he does, he may be a witness of the encounter between man and God in Israel's world and history. This critical research can help him to arrive at a truer understanding of the original message of God, by showing him how to distinguish between essential and peripheral, original and secondary elements.[2] It may help him to discover the fundamental spiritual effects of the encounter between God and man in Israel which remained a living and active influence until they were embodied anew in Jesus Christ. A critical study of the Old Testament will help us to

[1] We need only refer to Fr. Delitzsch, '*Babel and Bible*', *E.T.*, 1903, and his *Die grosse Täuschung*, and to the German Christians during the national-socialist period.
[2] Cf. now W. Zimmerli, 'Die historisch-kritische Bibelwissenschaft und die Verkündigungsaufgabe der Kirche', *Ev. Th.* 1963, pp. 17ff.

come into contact with men of like passions with ourselves, men who know that God has spoken to them, who have come to know Him in His holiness as the God who governs their lives, the life of their people and the future new world. For it is these people who have come to know Him and have heard His word, who bear testimony to Him.

Scholarly research using the methods of historical criticism offers a chance of arriving at an integration of the two Testaments without forcing an apparent unity by false exegesis and spiritual imperialism.[1]

This integration cannot be attained without paying close attention to theological developments in Israel, not without venturing to make theological evaluations in the light of the Gospel.

As in any study in the field of the humanities, it is inevitable that 'subjective' judgments should creep in.[2] It will, therefore, take a long time for Christendom to reach full agreement in this domain. This does not, however, release us from the obligation of striving after this agreement with patience and faith.

Some further literature:

L. Diestel, *Geschichte des A. T.*, 1869. This very detailed and well-documented history of the Old Testament in the Christian Church we mention again here because of its almost classical importance.

G. E. Phillips, *The Old Testament in the World Church*, 1941 (popular).

E. G. Kraeling, *The Old Testament since the Reformation*, Lutterworth Library XLVII, 1955.

H. J. Kraus, *Geschichte der historisch-kritischen Erforschung des Alten Testaments von der Reformation bis zur Gegenwart*, 1956. See also the critical notes on this of W. Baumgartner, 'Eine altt. Forschungsgeschichte', *Th. R.* 1959, pp. 93ff.

H. J. Kraus, 'Zur Geschichte des Überlieferungsbegriffs in der alttestamentlichen Wissenschaft', *Ev. Th.* 1956, pp. 371ff.

S. Amsler, *L'Ancien Testament dans l'Eglise*, 1960.

The Cambridge History of the Bible, the West from the Reformation to the present day, ed. by S. L. Greenslade, 1963.

G. H. Box, 'The value and significance of the Old Testament in relation to the New', in A. S. Peake, *The People and the Book*, 1925, pp. 433ff.

S. A. Cook, *The Old Testament, A reinterpretation*, 1936, ch. XII.

W. F. Lofthouse, 'The Old Testament and Christianity', in H. Wheeler Robinson, *Record and Revelation*, 1938, pp. 458ff.

O. Procksch, *Theologie des A. T.*, 1950, pp. 7ff., 19ff.

P. Auvray *et al.*, *L'Ancien Testament et les Chrétiens*, 1951.

M. Kähler, *Jesus und das A. T.*, 1896.

J. Hänel, *Der Schriftbegriff Jesu*, 1919.

---

[1] See also D. Lerch, *op. cit.*, p. 276; H. H. Rowley, *The Unity of the Bible*, 1953.
[2] We should keep in mind A. Kuenen's comment regarding literary critical research, that there is always a *subjective factor* in historiography (see K. Budde, *Gesammelte Abhandlungen zur biblischen Wissenschaft von Dr. A. Kuenen*, 1894, p. 44).

J. Hempel, 'Der synoptische Jesus und das A.T.', *Z.A.W.*, 1938, pp. 1ff.
C. H. Dodd, *According to the Scriptures*, 1952, pp. 61ff., The Bible of the Early Church.
C. H. Dodd, *The Authority of the Bible*.
G. Schrenk, 'γραφη', *Th. W.*, I, p. 760.
E. Hühn, *Die alttestamentl. Citate und Reminiszenzen im N.T.*, 1900.
A. Vis, *Messianic Psalm-quotations in the New Testament*, (Leiden thesis), 1936.
N. P. Bratsiotis, 'Das A.T. in der Griechisch-Orthodoxen Kirche', *Kyrios* I, 1906/61, pp. 59ff.

CHAPTER II

The historical character of the Old Testament revelation; fundamental and factual observations

General observations

This problem, which we have already touched upon, is the most difficult and the most disputed question of present-day theology[1] and must be dealt with in greater detail.

There are two sides to the problem. On the one hand the Old Testament was secularized and humanized (represented as the result of circumstance and psychological development) by an interpretation of the spiritual life of Israel rising from the study of the history of culture and religion. These views originated in the rationalism of the eighteenth and following centuries, were corroborated by the evolutionism of the last century (strongly supported by the science of archaeology, which made available the literature of the Near East and made possible the comparative history of the religions of the Near East), and have since been worked out in greater detail by psychological research. In consequence the religion of Israel came to be considered purely as a product of the human mind and completely lost its character as a religion of revelation in the theological sense of the word. Moreover, the Old Testament, which was looked upon as the record of this religion, was stripped of all spiritual authority.[2]

On the other hand, because the nature of Christian theology is determined by the affirmation of the revelation of God in Israel, it asserted (and still asserts) the peculiar character of the Old Testament message. This is not merely meant in the sense of the phenomenology of religion, admitting that it has quite distinctive features of its own, or even that it is of the highest importance among many others. It means that the Old Testament is recognized fully as the testimony to the revelation of the living God.[3] In the Old Testament He reveals Himself by entering into an immediate relationship with Israel, His

---

[1] Cf., for instance, M. Noth, 'Die Vergegenwärtigung des A.T. in der Verkündigung', *Ev. Th.*, 1952/3, pp. 6ff.
[2] See Pedersen, loc. cit.
[3] Cf., Joh. de Groot en A.R. Hulst, *Macht en Wil*, 1952, pp. 13ff.; F. Horst, loc. cit.

people, as the God of Salvation, and, as such, as the Creator, Sustainer and Recreator of the world. In Jesus Christ, whom the New Testament affirms to be the Way, the Truth and the Life, God proceeds with His work in Israel. The revelation of God in Jesus Christ is so closely linked with the prophetic testimony of the Old Testament, not only historically but also intrinsically and fundamentally, that when the Christian Church proclaims Jesus of Nazareth to be the Messiah she cannot do without the Old Testament revelation.

This attitude could only result in a war to the death between theology and mere historicism, for the latter essentially denies that there is an element of revelation in the Old Testament testimony, and completely humanizes Israelite religion. The refusal to reject this denial of God's work in Israel would mean no less than the self-destruction of theology.

Because of this struggle, however, the element of truth always implicit even in a 'lie' (for without this it could not even endure for a single day, let alone become a widely held theory) and also present in the historicizing process has, unfortunately, often been ignored by the theologians (at any rate by some schools of theology). Greatly to the detriment of theology, however, for this attitude forces the hand of theology and results in a tendency to make light of everything that comes from historicizing quarters, or even to ignore it completely, and to spiritualize certain passages in the Old Testament by allegorical or typological interpretation (as has again become customary in various sections of present-day dogmatic and exegetical theology). Some theologians, with extreme consistency, even go so far as to deny any historical development in the religion of Israel, though the Old Testament bears obvious traces of it. This persistent denial does not do honour to theology but leads to an attitude of anxious and one-sided resistance. As a result, the clarity of theological distinctions is sometimes obscured and the danger arises of the results of scientific, historical and phenomenological research being ignored and of theology withdrawing into an unassailable tradition or an essentially gnostic form of religion, so that it becomes a pseudo-science rather than knowledge ennobled by the Christian faith.

If theology is to find a truly scholarly approach to the problem of revelation in the Old Testament it must not only consider the data provided by historical sources and fully accept the *facts* that have been brought to light but also admit quite frankly the historical character of the history of Israel, and of the Old Testament which is rooted in this religion. It must admit unconditionally that there are various conceptions and presuppositions linking Israel's religion in various ways with those of the ancient eastern world; a connection which also makes itself felt in the Old Testament. We shall have to review thoroughly the relationship between the ancient oriental religious world, the religion of Israel, and the Old Testament. If the problem is to be stated correctly, both the connections and the distinctions between them must be acknowledged.[1]

At times the ancient oriental world, the Israelite world and the Old Testament are interwoven and interlap, sometimes, however, there is a clear break. The relation between connection and contrast is, however, a fluid one, and cannot be expressed in a symbol that remains constant in every period and in every religious field: the historical element is of the utmost importance. The relation might be illustrated by the image of three rings, linked so that they may be put down in such a way as almost to cover each other or else so that they have only points of contact. Viewed from one angle the former may seem to be the case, from another angle the latter.

First of all the religion of Israel and those of the surrounding ancient eastern world have a great deal in common[2], so much, even, that we might try to make them overlap (which tempts some theologians to represent the religion of Israel as a particular kind of ancient eastern religion) but such attempts have never succeeded completely. The reason is that in the course of its history Israel has received from God experiences that are exclusively her own and that from the outset its particular moral and spiritual elements have left their mark upon this religion, a mark that has never disappeared.[3]

The relation between the religion of Israel and the Old Testament may be expressed in a similar though slightly different way. In Chapter III we shall go further into this matter, but we may here already state that the Old Testament is not merely a collection of ancient Israelite religious texts, but is the book of the religion of Israel as it was reformed in the period of the exile under the influence of the prophets whose critical insight was formed under the guidance of the Spirit of God in times of great distress. Here again there is on the one hand a

[1] See now also the notes of K. Koch in 'Der Tod des Religionsstifters', *K. u. D.* 1962, 100ff., esp. pp. 103, 112ff.

[2] Nearly all ancient Eastern religious institutions are also found in Israel, and vice versa, even prophecy, which until recently was often claimed to be peculiar to Israel; see for instance F. M. Th. de Liagre Böhl, 'Profetisme en Plaatsvervangend Lijden in Israel', *N.T.T.* 1949/50, pp. 81ff., 161ff.; M. Noth, 'History and the Word of God in the Old Testament', in *The Laws in the Pentateuch and other Essays*, transl. by D. R. Ap-Thomas, 1966; W. von Soden, 'Verkündung des Gotteswillens durch prophetisches Wort in den altbabylonischen Briefen aus Mari', *Die Welt des Orients*, 1950, pp. 397ff.; and A. Lods, 'Une Tablette inédite de Mari, intéressante pour l'histoire ancienne du prophétisme sémitique', in *Studies in Old Testament Prophecy* (T. H. Robinson *Festschrift*), 1950, pp. 103ff.; C. Westermann, *Basic forms of Prophetic Speech*, 1967; A. Malamat: New Documents, *S.V.T.* xv, 1965, 207ff.

[3] Cf. my *The Religion of Ancient Israel*, 1967, pp. 22ff., 71ff.

very close connection between the Old Testament and the religion of Israel, yet on the other hand the Old Testament can by no means be identified completely with this religion in its historical development.

We may, therefore, call the Old Testament an oriental book, but only if we realize that this statement does not express the essential quality of the Old Testament. We may also call it an Israelite book, but again we must admit that this is not all there is to be said about it.

After this brief survey of the connection between the three entities – the Old Testament, the religion of Israel and ancient Eastern civilization – and also of the complicated nature of this connection, we must now deal at greater length with the latter of these problems.

Connection implies dependence, derivation, symbiosis, growth, but also resistance, antithesis, increasing tension, separation and the springing up of new forms.

The growth of Israel's religion is influenced by its contact with the ancient oriental civilized world; the development of universalism in the religion of Israel, also apparent in the Old Testament, is certainly to be associated with the fact that relations between Israel and the other peoples of the Near East were being extended in the days of David and Solomon, in the time of Isaiah this universalism was strengthened again by the appearance of the Assyrians. But this contact also brought with it the danger of syncretism, which we hear of so often in the period of the kings. It was the prophetic movement that opposed syncretism and splendidly assimilated and deepened universalism, so that, in fact, within the eastern world only the Old Testament arrived at a truly religious universalism, and that only in some few utterances of some of the great prophets (see the last two chapters).

This also proves that neither the borrowings from and contact with the ancient eastern world, nor the historical development of the Israelite religion are sufficient to account fully for the message of the Old Testament, but that there was another peculiar spiritual factor, which again and again interfered decisively in the life of Israel, and that it was this factor that gave the Old Testament to the world in its present form.

We need not deny, therefore, either the connection between Israel or the Old Testament and the oriental world, or the importance of the cultural and political development of Israel to the range of ideas of the Old Testament, if only we are willing to admit that these are not the only factors in the origin of the Old Testament, and not even the most important factor. There was a spiritual force at work in all this, a force peculiar to Israel that always made its influence felt as a critical principle and was experienced in the communion with Yahweh through history and the operation of the spirit. Again and again this communion proved decisive for Israel's spiritual development and shone through the teaching of those who contributed to the shaping of Israel's religion and the creation of the Old Testament.

There is a spiritual growth from Moses (or Abraham)[1] to Deutero-Isaiah[2], the last of the great prophets in whom the knowledge of God was deepened and broadened, with whom, in fact, Jesus Christ links up directly and to whom St. Paul goes back again and again in his Epistles. This progress of the knowledge of God from Abraham to Christ is expressed in the New Testament in such texts as Hebr. i. 1; ii. 2a, 3a. So in the New Testament this continuous history of revelation is already presupposed[3].

As a result of the historical research of this century and the last our insight into this progress of revelation has increased and deepened. In reaction against 'mere historicism', which is not to be blindly accepted as a solution to all problems, theology must not, therefore, allow itself to shut its eyes to this renewal of Israel's faith in God, ever-recurring in the history of the people.[4] If the history of revelation is acknowledged, theology will become aware of God's coming into the world of Israel and have a ready ear for the testimony to this coming in the prophetic teaching of the Old Testament. The fact that the knowledge of God is a life-giving influence becomes clearer and clearer so that to an ever-growing extent God reveals Himself as the living God in His concern with the world of man. Like an artist who

[1] The present writer takes the historical line to begin with Moses, not because he denies the possibility of a pre-Mosaic revelation to Abraham, but because, in his opinion, a scholarly historical approach is possible to a certain extent with respect to Moses but not with respect to Abraham. See also p. 39f. The apposite view is held by M. Noth, *History of Israel*, 1958, ³1965 (cf. A. Alt, 'The God of the Fathers' in *Essays on O.T. History and Religion*, 1966), but against this see O. Eissfeldt, 'Israel und seine Geschichte', *Th. L. Z.*, 1951, 6, pp. 335–340; cf. also J. J. Stamm in *Bi. Or.*, 1953, p. 195a. On the history of the patriarchal period see now H. H. Rowley, 'Recent discovery and the patriarchal age', in *The Servant of the Lord*, 1952, pp. 271ff., *From Joseph to Joshua*, 1950; Albright, *From the Stone Age*; R.T. O'Callaghan S.J., *Aram Naharaim*, 1948; Böhl, *Das Zeitalter Abrahams*, 1930; B. Gemser, *Vragen rondom de patriarchenreligie*, 1958; Vriezen, *The Religion*, Ch. 4.

[2] See Ch. III, pp. 71, 76f.

[3] That this growth is not an evolution (cf. for instance also A. Bentzen in *Hervormd Teologiese Studies*, Pretoria, VII. 1950/1, p. 7 n. 2) will be clear to everybody; in the way along which God leads Israel there are various catastrophic breaks, and the only reason why this way leads upwards is that the Spirit of God again and again pressed new men into His service; see the quotation from G. W. Anderson, *inf.*, p. 44, n. 1.

[4] We should mention here Von Rad, who in his *O.T. Theology* discovers a close relationship between history and faith in Israel. The point at issue here is, however, a quite different aspect of this relationship. Von Rad frowns upon the idea of a renewal of Israel's faith taking place in history, but looks upon the different traditions as the *vestigia Dei* in history recognized by Israel. These do not lead to a renewal of the knowledge of God; in so far as such knowledge had sprung up it was destroyed by the prophets who proclaimed entirely new actions of God, whose fulfilment is known to God alone.

26

works on his intractable material with this chisel and a steady hand and who sees the image slowly take shape and emerge from the shapeless mass of stone, God has worked on the 'image of God' in mankind. In the Old Testament it emerges rather in the manner of some of Rodin's sculptures where the work of art is still interfused with the material from which it has been created. In the New Testament the creation is completed and the conceptions that God has of and for man, stands out clearly in Jesus Christ, the man of God.

The Bible shows us how through the history of Israel God has entered into the world as the Living God who seeks communion with man. Both the Old Testament and the New bear witness to this desire of God to reveal Himself further to His people.

In this development two lines go together: one divine, the other human[1]; man is initiated further and further into the knowledge of God and so he gains an ever more profound spiritual understanding of God, enabling him to speak of God in new terms and purer forms. The way in which God's love is depicted becomes more subtle and more powerful; at first it is Israel as a people, then also Israel in its defection and sinfulness, and finally it is the man who is broken in spirit. Or, at first Yahweh, the God of Israel, is no more than the supreme ruler over the other gods, the nations, and nature; afterwards He is the Almighty and the only God – the other gods have paled before Him. The history of Israel's syncretism, its religious decadence, political downfall, its contact with other peoples, etc., has in its variety contributed to a greater profundity; even in times of decadence, He created new life and a fierce, but purging opposition sprang up against 'paganism' in its naturalistic forms (vegetative as well as astral). This struggle made the prophets more conscious of the nature of the spiritual gifts Israel had received and thus it resulted in a knowledge of the Nature of God more clearly pronounced than before; formulations such as the deuteronomistic confession of the uniqueness of God (ch. vi) and of the demand to love with all one's heart are cases in point.

Although God reveals Himself to Moses as the exclusive ('jealous') God who is intimately concerned with Israel, who intervenes in its history, the God who is righteous and demands righteousness, the knowledge of God regarding these points of faith is deepened by the prophets under the guidance of the Spirit of God.

Israel's faith in God was never static and grew in the course of history under the constantly renewed leadership of the prophets. A spiritual understanding of God's intentions as taught by Deutero-

[1] Cf., for instance, T.H.Robinson, Hebrew Myths, p. 194 in S.H.Hooke, *Myth and Ritual*, 1933; and A.Guillaume, *Prophecy and Divination*, p. 359.

Isaiah, viz. that God wants to use Israel to bring to the nations the knowledge of His Torah (ch. xlii) and that He wishes to be glorified by His servant in his suffering for the sake of sin (ch. lii f.) was achieved only through exile and suffering. Jesus Christ came to fulfil this highest spiritual purpose of God with Israel, seen and depicted in visions by the prophets (Isa. liii), and thus He accomplished Israel's task. He fully actualized God's purpose with Israel and in doing this He fulfilled 'the law and the prophets' (Matt. v. 17). In His life, death and resurrection He fully actualized the revelation of God as it grew all through the Old Testament. Thus Jesus Christ is the end of God's self-disclosure to Israel and at the same time He is the man through whom God made the world share in His redeeming work in Israel.

Here the unity of the Old and the New Testament becomes evident. The New Testament is the confirmation and the crowning of the Old. They are essentially one, but this unity can be seen only when the revelation of God is admitted to be continuous and the existence of the line of historical development is recognized. Otherwise the danger arises of identifying Christ with the Torah and of failing to see how God patiently builds His temple of salvation; this would mean over-burdening the Old Testament and reading truths into it that are not really there, interpreting texts incorrectly, or even allowing the Old Testament to dominate the New. For in that case Jesus' words on the love of one's neighbour are explained in terms of Old Testament particularism, so that this text no longer applies absolutely to all those whom God places in our way, even our enemies, but is made to apply only to the brethren of the faith[1]; and, as happened during the German occupation of the Netherlands some decades ago, Jael's deed is re-presented as examplary for the relationship between a man and his enemy even in the contemporary Christian world, in spite of the fact that Jesus Christ strongly objected to arbitrary human judgment (Luke ix. 54).

For that reason it is indispensable for our practical moral life as well as for a true understanding of the Christian faith in God that theology should be clearly conscious of the historical nature of the organic relationship between the Old and the New Testament and of the historical element in God's revelation to Israel. But this is no less necessary for the understanding of the Bible itself, from a theological as well as from a spiritual or cultural and historical point of view.

Some facts

After this fundamental exposition we shall have to discuss the facts themselves in order to make it clear that they cannot but lead to the

[1] Cf., Van Ruler, *De vervulling der wet*, 1947, p. 313.

28

thoughts developed in the preceding pages. Moreover, it is desirable to give some striking examples because otherwise the theological exposition of the content of the Old Testament message would be overburdened with historical facts[1] or it could be reproached for being biased in a rendering of the data based on the later prophetic teaching[2].

That the Old Testament is imbued with various general ancient eastern conceptions and even with so-called 'primitive' elements cannot and need not be denied or glossed over from a theological point of view, for the Old Testament is an ancient eastern book in the full sense of the word and possesses all kinds of qualities that are characteristic of its age. It is, however, most necessary to make a clear distinction between two elements: on the one hand, being *burdened with* ancient conceptions that have had their day, but on the other hand *making use of* certain ancient ideas, a habit attributable to the 'imperialism of the Yahwistic mind'.[3] In the former case the ancient conceptions are taken quite seriously and received in the range of ideas of the authors themselves, in the latter these ways of thought, e.g. mythical images and reminiscences, are rather included for the sake of illustration or on aesthetic grounds.[4] The failure to make this distinction has often led to incorrect exegetical conclusions.[5] Many mythical conceptions lost their mythical character,[6] some others were preserved (the conception of chaos, cf. pp. 30, 329, 333).[7]

Truly ancient oriental conceptions are found in the ideas concerning

[1] Sellin rightly divided his theology into two parts: the *Israelitisch-Jüdische Religionsgeschichte* and the *Theologie des A.T.;* Procksch includes the history of religion in his *Theologie,* of which it forms the first section, and Eichrodt worked it into his *Theologie.* The latter method is not impossible, but lays rather much stress on the historical element. In this chapter I shall confine myself to indicating a few lines of development; in my opinion the historical development must be taken into account in a theology, but it should be elaborated in an independent history of religion, in its own context; see Ch. V.

[2] Cf., for instance for many other examples, Thesis V of Prof. M.A.Beek's doctorate thesis in 1935 (although this thesis no longer reflects his present views): 'The attempts made to attain a summarizing "theology of the O.T.", springing from an obvious reaction against historicism, is none the less premature and involves danger to scholarly historical research, in so far as it leads to a forced unity of the Old Testament ideas, which actually does not exist.'

[3] See for instance M.Noth, *op. cit.* 'History and the Word' and B.S.Childs, *Myth and Reality in the O.T.,* 1957.

[4] Cf., for instance, the remarks made rightly by Joh. Lindblom (*The Servant Songs in Deutero-Isaiah,* 1951, pp. 75ff., 104) about the symbolical character of the language of the Old Testament writers.

[5] I have in mind, for instance, all sorts of 'literal' interpretations of figurative expressions, given by Eerdmans in his commentary on the Psalms.

[6] See a.o. the book of Childs.

[7] Cf. further J.Hempel, Glaube, Mythos und Geschichte im A.T., $Z.A.W.$, 1953, pp. 109ff. and B.J.van der Merwe, *Pentateuchtradisies in die prediking van Deuterojesaja,* 1955, pp. 205ff.

the power of words. Here not only the words of God are considered to have power, but also the human word sworn in the name of God, such as curse and blessing. In the 'Code of Holiness' (Lev. xix. 14) we read: 'Thou shalt not curse the deaf'. Behind these words lies a conception of the curse as an active power that cannot be undone by the deaf man because he is deaf; when Isaac gives his son Jacob the blessing due to the first-born, this word, once spoken, cannot be taken back; it remains effective and Esau can only receive a different blessing.[1]

Yet this does not mean that Yahweh is tied down to the word spoken by Him to such an extent that He could not withdraw it; on the contrary, Yahweh is greater than His own powerful word, compare for instance Isa. xvi. 13 and 2 Sam. xvi. 12. From this it appears that magic thought was fundamentally overcome by Israel by virtue of its faith in God (cf. Fensham, loc. cit., pp. 173ff.).

Belief in other magical forces is presupposed in the Old Testament again and again. Even if Israel is forbidden to have anything to do with magic, divination and the consultation of the dead, these things are accepted as real: we must keep in mind the stories of 1 Sam. xxviii and the Egyptian sorcerers who could also change staffs into snakes; the magic power of relics such as the bones of Elijah (2 Kings xiii. 21), etc. The belief in the activity of other gods and in the efficacy of sacrifices offered up to them is certainly connected with this, too, as is evident from the end of 2 Kings 3.

It appears from Gen. i. 2 and ii. 4b ff. that Israel in its outlook on life (its world-picture need not be discussed here as it is wholly ancient and oriental) retained its connection with the ancient eastern world; here it becomes plain that Israel did not succeed in surmounting the difficulty of the conception of chaos. It is true that Israel placed the chaos before the existence of the world in a light other than that in which it was seen by the oriental peoples who attributed divine power to it and looked upon it as a power opposed to the deity, whereas Israel only saw the chaos as mere material existence before the creation. Yet Israel did not arrive at a complete theoretical abandonment of the conception of chaos. This is true even of the comparatively late account of the Creation in Gen. i, for though the Creation narrative is meant to teach the creation of the world by the word of God alone, in reality the activity of this word is at least as much regulating as creative in character; in other words, a material substratum of the world is presupposed before God speaks His creative word. So difficult

[1] Cf., S. Mowinckel, *Psalmenstudien* I and V; Pedersen, *Israel* I–II, pp. 411ff.; J. Hempel, 'Die israelitischen Anschauungen von Segen und Fluch', *Z̧.D.M.G.* 1925, pp. 40ff., now also *Apoxysmata*, 1961, pp. 30ff.; F. Horst, 'Segen und Segenhandlungen in der Bibel,' *Ev. Th.* 1947, pp. 23ff.; F. C. Fensham, 'Curses and Maledictions', *Z̧.A.W.* 1963, pp. 155ff.

it was the Israelite mind to abandon the ancient eastern conceptions and to come to an absolutely new structure of its outlook on life[1]; not until the later apocryphal books and the New Testament is the creation considered entirely as God's work and the last remnant of the idea of primordial material existence abandoned.[2]

In the idea of sin, too, the continued existence of the typical ancient oriental dynamistic conception is evident.[3] Although on the one hand the consciousness of sin is spiritual in nature in the Old Testament, as appears from the terminology (sin is either an error or wrongness or defect), and although sin and guilt are looked upon as closely connected, yet on the other hand a connection is perceived again and again between sin and uncleanness (whether ceremonial uncleanness or the uncleanness of disease, etc.), evident from the purification laws (e.g. Lev. xii ff.), which declare a woman after childbirth, a leper, and even the 'leprous' house unclean, and demand a sin-offering, with or without a guilt-offering for all these cases. At such a sacrifice ritual acts are performed which take away the sin of uncleanness (though of as material): one of two birds is killed while the other is sent away laden with sin. The clearest example is that even a house – a material object – may be purged (Lev. xiv. 49ff.). Behind the laws concerning food and purification there lie, therefore, all kinds of notions about sin which show that the word 'sin' does not always denote a spiritual and moral conception but that it may also mean something like 'contagion'.

Connected with this is also the nature of the act of purification accomplished by guilt-offerings and sin-offerings; the term 'redemption' used in this connection is often to some extent dynamistic in character. The ritual has preserved these very ancient notions, and this is not surprising when we consider that ritual acts may remain unchanged for centuries even when the spiritual conceptions that were formerly connected with them change. It is, therefore, by no means certain that in the period when these ritual texts were adopted or made canonical the same primitive conceptions prevailed as the texts themselves indicate if they are read literally or explained with the help of etymology.[4]

These survivals in the religion of Israel must not, however, be underestimated; for they were preserved in the sacred writings of the *Torah* itself which were compiled so critically, and thus they could exert a

---

[1] In Greek philosophy a parallel phenomenon presents itself where a 'primitive' dynamism survived a long time in the hylozoism of the earliest natural philosophy.
[2] Cf. now H. Junker, 'Die theologische Behandlung der Chaosvorstellung' (*Mélanges bibliques en l'honneur de A. Robert*), 1957, pp. 27ff.
[3] See now 'Sünde und Schuld im A.T.', *R.G.G.*[3], VI, pp. 479ff.
[4] See for example p. 267f. on *reach nichoach*.

great influence for centuries. The teaching of the prophets or of Jesus Christ Himself about sin, e.g. concerning cleanness and uncleanness, which are confirmed in the Acts of the Apostles and in the Epistles of St. Paul, are no less than revolutionary in comparison with the conceptions of the ancient Israelite cultic-ritualistic range of ideas. It is necessary to enter into this range of ideas in order to understand the tremendous importance of the prophetic teaching which made the knowledge of God, the humble walking in God's ways, love and righteousness the central religious demands and repeatedly opposed them to cultic purification and redemption.

Two important problems will be discussed at greater length, viz. the *problem of monotheism*[1], i.e. the relation between God and gods, and *the place of the cult in the Old Testament*.

The first problem has been raised over and over again, and will be referred to repeatedly in this book. It offers an excellent illustration of what has been discussed above and is important for a correct understanding of the conception of God in Israel.

The question 'can the Israelite belief in God be called monotheistic' does not lend itself to a direct answer; it leads neither to a simple 'no' nor to a wholehearted 'yes'. As far as can be concluded from the texts, Moses did not teach monotheism from the outset for he did not give Israel a conception of God but something else: he proclaimed Yahweh as the God who saves Israel by His intervention in history, as the Living God who as such transcends the nations and the forces of nature, the God who attaches Israel to Himself and therefore demands the exclusive worship of Israel. In other words, he proclaimed Yahweh as the God of Israel's salvation, thus bringing to the fore another element than His uniqueness, an element which, once accepted, could not but lead to the acceptance of Yahweh's absoluteness. For that reason monotheism is the most adequate form in which Israel's faith could express the nature of God in later times, when Israel reached the stage of independent theological thought. Yahweh, God of Salvation, is proclaimed to be unique and exclusive ('I Yahweh, thy God, am a jealous God') and under the guidance of the prophets in the struggle against Baalism this confession led to the belief that there was only

[1] See beside the still important book of W. W. Grafen Bandissin, *Studien zur Religionsgeschichte* I, 1876, pp. 47ff., esp. 146ff. (Die Anschauung des A.T. von den Göttern des Heidentums) for instance W. F. Albright, *From the Stone Age to Christianity*[2], 1946, pp. 196ff.; B. Balscheit, *Alter und Aufkommen des Monotheismus*, 1938; B. D. Eerdmans, *The Religion of Israel*, 1947, pp. 109ff.; 'On the road to Monotheism', *O.T.S.*, I, pp. 105ff.; G. E. Wright, *The O. T. against its environment*, 1950, pp. 30ff.; E. Fascher, 'Gott und die, Götter', *Th. L. Z.* 1956, pp. 279ff.; H. H. Rowley, 'Moses and Monotheism'. *Z.A.W.* 1957, pp. 1ff. (now also in: *From Moses tot Qumran*, 1963, pp. 35ff.).

one God, so that Yahweh was acknowledged as God *kat' exochen*. Thus centuries of spiritual struggle led to an absolute theoretical monotheism. It is impossible to give a detailed account of the stages of this development; we can only indicate some salient points. In doing so, we should, however, bear in mind that there is no simple line connecting these points, as they are not equally important: a word from the Decalogue, spoken by God Himself is, after all, of greater importance than the testimony of a soldier such as we find in 1 Sam. xxvi. 19.

For the earliest period the opening words of the Decalogues are the determining factor; the Decalogues, 'cultic' as well as 'ethical', always start with the demand that Israel shall have no other gods beside Yahweh. This does not mean that there are no other gods anywhere, for here mono-Yahwism is demanded of Israel. In the Psalms we read, for instance, that God has come among the *'elohim* to judge them and that He has passed sentence of death on them (Ps. lxxxii) and that the *bene ha-'elohim* are called upon to praise Yahweh (Ps. xxix. 1; cf. also Ps. lxxxix. 7).

In the remarkable story of Gen. vi, which strikes us as rather mythological, it is said that the *bene-ha-'elohim* came in unto the daughters of men.[1] In Judges xi. 24 the view is ascribed to Jephthah that Chemosh gave the country to the Moabites (cf. also vi. 10). In stories dating from the period of the kings we find such texts as 1 Sam. xxvi. 19 and the closing verses of 2 Kings iii, where the existence of gods of other nations is presumed.[2] In Levit. xxiv. 15 we find a general condemnation of the practice of cursing a god. In spite of the tendency of Yahwism towards monotheism, a tendency that had existed from early times, Israel experienced great difficulty in freeing its conception of life from ideas reminiscent of the surrounding polytheistic religions.

As far as ancient Israel is concerned two things may be regarded as incontestable facts: that Yahweh is *the* God, whose divine power manifests itself in the history of Israel, and also that Yahweh is the *supreme* God. This does not mean, however, that He stands at the head of a pantheon like Re in Egypt, El in Canaan-Phoenicia and Marduk in Babylonia, etc., for beside these gods stand other independent

[1] It is unlikely that the *'elohim* of Exod. xxi. 6 should be looked upon as household gods (as is maintained for instance by Eerdmans cf. *A. T. Studien*, III, 1910, p. 128, and by G. Beer, 'Exodus', in *H. A. T.*, 1939, p. 104) and may be put on a level with the *terafim* and with tutelary images (cf. 1 Sam. xix; Hos. iii). Perhaps we must rather take the word to refer to Israel's God or to a temple dedicated to Him; so Dillmann, Böhl (*T. en U.*), M. David (*O. T. S.* V, 1948, pp. 66–7.) and H. A. Brongers (*N. T. T.*, 3, 1948/9, pp. 321ff.).
[2] On Deut. xxxii. 8b (LXX) see G. F. Moore, *Judaism*, I, pp. 226–7.; the Masoretic text may quite easily be maintained here, for the number of Israel's sons is 70 (Exod. i. 15).

divine figures, mentioned by name, whereas Yahweh is surrounded by *'elohim*, who are not mentioned by name and who may probably be looked upon as some kind of angelic host.[1] The uniqueness of Yahweh, is therefore, even in ancient times, something essentially different even from the uniqueness of Aton in the religion of Ikhnaton; Israelite mono-Yahwism must not be put on a level with the mono-Atonism of that particular Egyptian period.[2]

Strictly speaking, there is nothing more than mono-Yahwism in ancient Israel; yet the term monotheism, applied to this strict exclusive Yahweh-religion, is not to be rejected entirely from a theological and religio-historical point of view. In any case it is already monotheism rather than polytheism; the latter term, for which many people have a predilection, in many instances misrepresents the Biblical testimony. Mono-Yahwism is potential monotheism; the latter is not a chance result of mono-Yahwism, even though it is not until the days of the prophets that it can be shown to exist in a strict form.[3] The first clear pronouncement is probably to be found in 1 Kings xviii. 39: *Yahweh hu ha-'elohim*, Yahweh is God.[4]

The step from mono-Yahwism to monotheism is one rather of speculative theology than of essentially religious character, for this determination of Yahweh's nature has not brought about any change in Yahweh Himself. It is a question of becoming aware of and thinking out in theory the principles of faith that had been the starting-point from the outset. In the first period of its existence Israel, as a small group of tribes, came into contact only with the world immediately surrounding it, so that problems of a cosmic or universalistic nature hardly came to the fore. Already in the Song of Deborah Yahweh is the cosmic ruler, even if He is said to dwell on Mount Sinai[5]. His 'range of action' extends as far as Canaan, and even as far as the stars: He

---

[1] We may note that any supernatural being may be called *'elohim*, even, for instance, the spirit of the dead Samuel in 1 Sam. xxviii; we should, therefore, be careful in using this term and not too lightly assume the existence of polytheism on the evidence of this expression.

[2] Cf., for example W. A. Irwin in *The intellectual adventure of ancient man*, Chicago 1946, p. 225; 'Whatever one is to say of the still unsolved problem of Akhnaton's alleged monotheism, it was at the best quite different from and inferior to Israel's'. Even if one should connect Moses with this Egyptian heresy it would be necessary to conclude 'that he thus brought into being a new thing in human history'. See now S. Morenz, *Ägyptische Religion*, 1960, pp. 154ff. In comparison with this the conception which a scholar like S. Freud arrived at in *Moses and Monotheism*, Eng. trans., 1939, pp. 34ff., is most superficial.

[3] See also G. W. Anderson, 'Hebrew Religion', in *The O.T. and modern Study*, 1951, pp. 287ff., where we also find the most important recent literature discussed.

[4] So O. Procksch, *Theologie*, 443.

[5] It is doubtful to what extent Mount Sinai as 'God's holy Mountain' is already mythical in character in ancient Israel, so that a geographical explanation of the so-called 'volcanic' traits in the account of the theophany of Exod. xix must be considered incorrect.

34

makes the stars in their courses fight for Israel (Judges v. 20). Even the ancient song from the Book of the Just (Joshua x. 12 f.), according to which the sun and the moon stood still at Joshua's command, points in the same cosmic direction. For Israel's faith the exclusiveness of Yahweh implies His cosmic majesty. Although the doctrine of creation is only found in Israel at a rather late date, it was already implicit (and probably not only potentially) in Israel's conception of God. The later fundamental monotheism is therefore a deepening and a purification of the Israelite faith in God, but it is not something essentially new. Hence the term monotheism as a general description of the religion of Israel need not be rejected provided that we do not lose sight of the historical development. Certain terms must be interpreted somewhat liberally; otherwise the Old Testament and the religion of Israel would require a whole terminology of their own.

Generally speaking the application of current theological terminology to the Old Testament is a difficult matter. Take, for example, the idea of 'eschatology'.[1] This also is indispensable in connection with the messianic expectations and the hopes of the future in Israel. Yet it presents difficulties, for the older Israelite eschatology is different in character from that of the beginning of the Christian era. Not until the latest period, in the apocalyptic writings, did Israel have an eschatological conception such as is presupposed in the New Testament where the future world is looked upon as a cosmically changed world. In the Old Testament no distinction is made between the *'olam habba'* and *'olam hazzeh* (cf. p. 454); everything takes place on this earth, including the renewal of the people, and even the restoration of the world of paradise; peace among the animals and paradisaic fertility are seen as new conditions on *this* earth.

The second point we have to deal with is the important changes in the domain of the cult. That objections were raised by the prophets to the sacrificial cult as a redemptive ritual is a matter of common knowledge. For the greater part this is clearly connected with the prevalence of the notion, so obvious in cultic ritual, that it works *ex opere operato*.[2] The prophets oppose this sacrificial ritual with all their might, demanding that Israel shall live truly by God's Covenant, spiritually as well as morally. This demand is also characteristic not only of the later Biblical prophets, for it is already made in the stories

---

[1] On this see e.g. J. Lindblom, *The Servant Songs*, 1951, Ch. vf.; my 'Prophecy and Eschatology', *S.V.T.*, I, 1953, and S. Herrmann: *Die prophetischen Heilserwartungen im A.T.*, 1965.

[2] Cf., the article by Dr. G. C. Berkouwer, 'Ex opere operato' in *G. Th. T.*, 1953, pp. 78ff., 93ff. – The term is used here in a phenomenological, not in a dogmatical sense and has, therefore, a more general meaning.

of Samuel (1 Sam. xiii; xv; cf. Prov. xxi. 3), and hence it represents a fairly ancient and rather widely diffused idea. Some prophets go even further by denying that the sacrifices belonged historically to the earliest Yahwism (Amos v. 25; Jer. vii. 22; Isa. xliii. 23; cf. also Ps. l and li).

How matters stood with the sacrificial cult in the days of Moses cannot be stated with any certainty. What we can do, however, is to point out a few elements in the historical writings; the Yahwist presupposes in the times of Abraham a cult at an altar, but this is apparently used especially for *'olah*-offerings as sacrifices in honour of Yahweh; the author of the primitive stories presumes that the first men already had a cult (Gen. iv) with burnt-offerings; in other words, religion was inconceivable without offerings. In the ancient stories the idea of atonement is not predominant; of the oldest ritual only the Passover offering is to be understood in this sense (at least as a purifying defensive rite). The ancient laws also demand (Exod. xxiii, xxxiv) that people shall not come to Yahweh empty-handed at a feast; they should then offer up their first-fruits. Moreover, we may also consider it an established fact that during the period of the genesis of the people the sacrificial ritual was very sober: the oldest sanctuary is the ark with the tables of the Law, which indicates that the central cultic object was not primarily the place where sacrifices were offered up and blood was shed. So also the earth altar, required in the oldest laws (Exod. xx), while the stonealtar is forbidden, makes it likely that the altars were of occasional rather than central importance; the opposition to the building of the temple in the age of David and Solomon points the same way. This opposition is not to be taken as primarily sociological in character, as though Israel's God were originally a desert-god or migration-god, not bound to any particular place (cf. Buber), but presumes above all a peculiar spiritual atmosphere: God is the Omnipotent God who reveals Himself wherever He wishes and orders an altar to be built there (Gen. xii. 7; Exod. xx. 24).[1]

Taking everything into consideration (especially the fact that from the development of the feasts it becomes quite clear that after the occupation of Canaan the number of feasts was supplemented by harvest festivals, as well as the fact that the sacrificial terminology in particular proves to be closely connected with the general Semitic terminology)[2], the safest course is not to reject the idea of sacrifice

[1] On the cult in Israel see further R. de Vaux, *Les Institutions de l'Ancien Testament* II, 1960, pp. 89ff., H. Ringgren, *Israelite Religion* 1966, I 3c and II 8 and my *The Religion*, pp. 91ff., 148ff., 173ff., 182ff.
[2] R. Dussaud, *Les origines canaéennes du sacrifice israélite*, 1921, pointed out the connection between Punic-Phoenician and Hebrew sacrificial terminology. From the Ras Shamra material J. Gray infers that the differences are more striking than the simila-

entirely in the early stages of the Israelite religion, but to consider it as very restricted in scope. In any case, as we observed in the preceding pages, the idea of the *expiatory* sacrifice was originally bound up with the Passover offering even in pre-Mosaic times[1]; the *šelem*-offerings (sacral offering meals) belong, in their connection with the idea of the Covenant, entirely to the Israelite atmosphere (though they are also common Southern Semitic in nature), and the '*olah* (burnt offering) is universal (as is also the rite of the expiatory offering).[2] So, though it cannot be denied that ancient Israel had several forms of sacrifice, a complete reconstruction of the oldest phases of worship is impossible. Nor is it possible to distinguish clearly between the common Semitic element, and the patriarchal, Mosaic and more recent contributions of the sacrificial cult of Israel.[3] Because the Old Testament sacrificial texts as they have been handed down to us are recent, the whole of the cultic laws as it has reached us lies too much on one plane, and for that reason it is very difficult to see these things in a historical perspective.

But, although sacrifices in various forms were not unknown of old, the sacrificial rites flourished and expanded greatly in Canaan after the Israelite invasion of the country, because under the influence of the Canaanite world new festivals began to be celebrated, including all sorts of *minchah*[4], '*olah* and *šelem*-offerings; at the same time the corporate and individual rites of the *expiatory offering* became of ever increasing importance in the spiritual life of Israel after the rise (and the taking over) of *temples*, especially that in Jerusalem, with a official priesthood.

If this view of the development of the cult is correct, it provides a historical justification of the opposition of Amos and Jeremiah and of their remarks that all these offerings were originally not demanded by Yahweh.

The cult as such may be considered an integral part of the religion

rities (J. Gray, 'Cultic Affinities between Israel and Ras Shamra', *Z.A.W.*, 1949/50, pp. 207ff).). Th. Gaster in *Mélanges Syriens*, II, 1939, pp. 577ff. emphasizes the affinities between the Ugaritic, Hebrew, and Southern Arabic material whereas the connection between the Hebrew and the Assyro-Babylonian material is not nearly so strong.
[1] The Paschal-sacrifice is a sacral repast as well as an act of purification; it is not only *šelem* but also *chaṭṭat* (see below pp. 264f.), cf. G. Beer, *Exodus*, 1939, pp. 62ff., and also especially the report of Nilus (c. 400), see H. Junker, *Prophet und Seher in Israel*, 1927, pp. 96ff.
[2] On '*olah* and *zebach* see W. B. Stevenson in the *Bertholet-Festschrift*, 1950; cf. now N. H. Snaith, Sacrifices in the O.T., *V.T.*, VII, 1957, pp. 308ff.
[3] L. Köhler, *Old Testament Theology*, 1957, § 52, considers the cult a piece of ethnic life, adopted by Israel from heathendom and only modified to a certain extent by Yahwism.
[4] i.e. gift, in olden times used to denote all offerings, in Leviticus only to denote unbloody offerings.

37

of Israel, but its scope and character varied widely in the various periods. For example, the Passover was originally celebrated in the family circle and not at the sanctuaries; the other festivals arose in Canaan; a previously unknown New-Year festival (which was practically completely rejected after the exile) rose to great importance during the Age of the Kings, etc. If the development of the life of the tribe and the people must be thought of as having taken place round a communal central sanctuary (amphictyony), a theory developed by M. Noth[1], the cult must have formed an integral part of the whole life of the people from the very beginning. The rise of the sanctuaries, caused at first by the taking over of existing rural cultic places, afterwards by the foundation of the royal temple at Jerusalem (which eventually, as a result of the Deuteronomic reformation, became the exclusive state sanctuary), brought with it revivals in the domain of the public cult. These revivals often entailed great dangers (especially the custom of sacrificing at the rural sanctuaries), as they promoted syncretism and made the cult more and more ritualistic instead of maintaining it as a cult of the family and the individual. This was also the unintentional result of the Deuteronomic concentration of sacrificial worship at the temple in Jerusalem, although that concentration in itself was only intended as a bulwark against syncretism and should be taken as a restriction rather than an extension of the idea of sacrifice. But after the exile and the restoration of the temple the cult was emphasized strongly and in this way ritualism was unintentionally promoted. For then the priest came to dominate religious life entirely; the holiness of the people was enhanced by the acts of the priest more than by anything else; prophecy, which played a prominent part in ancient Israel, became silent fairly soon after the exile, although it continued to exist until Joel (4th century). The priest and the scribe (the wise man) became the central spiritual figures. Prophecy was replaced by apocalyptic: personal piety was now concerned rather with future than with present life – the priest would take care of the latter. Moreover it is clear that the danger of ritualism was not counterbalanced by apocalyptic and wisdom only, but that certain cultic elements, such as the creed and the hymn of praise, also limited the one-sided ritual character of the sacrificial service, so that in the temple worship singing came to dominate the cult more and more.[2]

So in the cult, too, the historical development of the religion of Israel is unmistakably reflected. Except in the syncretistic period of the kings and the post-exilic period, the cult did not dominate the religion or influence the conception of God: it was an important form

[1] M. Noth, *Das System der zwölf Stämme Israels*, 1930; id., *History of Israel*, 1950.
[2] Cf., A. R. Hulst, *Belijden en Geloven*, 1948, and see *inf.*, p.86.

38

of expression of the Israelite religion, but not the dominating factor. The cult was conservative in effect and because of this it proved a blessing to Israel, but it was hardly an animating influence – except at the great festivals – and it brought no revival at all. In the days of Jesus the priestly groups, the Sadducees, were merely the preservers of all that was old, and for that reason the life of the spirit developed more and more outside the cult and moved along its own uncontrolled channels (except in the synagogue) either in the direction of personal piety (the *chasidim* and the '*anawim*) or in that of apocalyptic adventism (esp. with the Essenes).

In view of the plan of this book it is desirable to conclude this chapter by giving a summary outline of the development of the religion of Israel, in which we shall attempt to sketch the fundamental structure and the direction of this development. It is impossible to give a full history of Israel, especially because we have no reliable historical information on the earliest stages.

The fundamental difference between the religion of Israel and those of the surrounding peoples is expressed in Deut. iv. 7f., 19f. as follows[1]: the other nations have nature-gods, they worship the superhuman in nature in various forms; but Israel has a God who delivered the people at a certain point in its history and adopted it as His own people; the God of the miracle, of history and of the Covenant; the God who is near, who hears those who call upon Him and who has given His word in His law.[2] In these words the theological author of Deut. iv has given a very clear description of the peculiar character of the religion of Israel. In this conception of God, who is the personal living Lord of the Covenant, the God who reveals Himself in history, we have the essence of Israel's faith in God.

Historically speaking only little is known of the development of the revelation of God in the Old Testament in the earliest stages. Of the figure of Abraham and of his knowledge of God we can hardly form a notion[3], because the oldest statements concerning him were written

[1] In their book *Macht en Wil* Dr. Joh. de Groot and Dr. A. R. Hulst begin their discussion of Israel's theological and religious starting-point with Deut. vi. 4f.
[2] See for instance W. Eichrodt, 'Offenbarung und Geschichte im A.T.', *Th. Z.* Basel 1948, pp. 321ff.
[3] Neither the reconstruction of the El-religion which Abraham is supposed to have had (cf. R. Kittel, *Die Religion des Volkes Israel*, 1921; F. M. Th. Böhl, *Das Zeitalter Abrahams*, 1930, see also G. W. Anderson, Hebrew Religion, in Rowley, *O. T. and Modern Study*, on the High-God idea in the patriarchal age), nor the reconstruction of the idea of a personal god as given by Alt in his well-known *The God of the Fathers*, 1929, should be considered final, although there is a strong case for Alt's hypothesis. In my *Religion of Israel* I concurred with Alt with respect to the early patriarchal age, and supposed that in the later patriarchal period the tribes of Israel mostly adopted the El-religion. Cf. now S.V.T. xvii, 1969, 17ff.; further M. Buber, *The prophetic Faith*.

so many centuries later and also because the way in which he is depicted in the ancient passage of Gen. xiv differs so widely from that of the detailed J-source. Of Moses, too, it is impossible for us to form a complete historical picture[1], although the Decalogue in its oldest form may be considered Mosaic and some conclusions as to his teaching concerning God may be drawn from the later living knowledge of God in Israel in the historical writings and laws. But however little may be known historically about the first stages of the development, one thing is an established fact: that in the later period, of which we do have historical knowledge, a deepening of faith in God may be noted (among other things a development from mono-Yahwism to monotheism); this gives us a right to assume a certain spiritual development for the earlier period as well.

In spite of the difficulties with which we are confronted by the sources, we must consider Moses, to whom above all others the Old Testament sources, point, to be the founder of the religion of Israel, the man who gave this religion its form. He receives a revelation from Yahweh, delivers a number of tribes from Egypt and, after the miracle at the Red Sea, leads them through the desert where communion with Yahweh is established, with the Decalogue as its fundamental law.[2]

From the beginning the God of the tribes of Moses' time was a personal, spiritual, living, supreme, redeeming and moral God, so much so that from the outset Israel distinguished Yahweh from the gods of other nations. This is evident from the fact that at a very early moment Israel opposed the nationalist and naturalistic conceptions of the Canaanites.[3]

The origin of this contrast is not to be explained from religio-social motives, from the fact that Yahweh was a desert-God who desired to hold his own in a civilized country, but lies much deeper. From the outset Yahweh in ancient Israel is the same He is afterwards, for example in the history of David (the earliest written historical document in the Old Testament!): He is the God who enters into a personal relationship with man who controls the life of the individual as well

[1] See for example B. Balscheit, op. cit., and M. Noth, *History of Israel* (on this latter book, especially with respect to the figure of Moses, see the observations by W. Zimmerli in the *G. G. A.* of 1953); the books on Moses by Buber and Auerbach go too far in their historical reconstruction.
[2] On the whole of this complicated question see my *The Religion*, Ch. V.
[3] A younger, less civilized people is always willing to adopt the culture and religion of the conquered peoples whose cultural standards are higher. Israel however stood out against the assimilation of its religious life to that of the Canaanites when Israel adopted Canaanite culture. Evidence for this is found not only in the ancient stories, (for instance that of Gideon, Judges vi. 25), but also in recent archaeological data (cf. the interesting account of W. F. Albright in *Archaeology and the religion of Israel*, 2nd ed., 1946, p. 114, who states that thus far no images of Astarte have ever been found in any of the early-Israelite strata in central Palestine).

as that of the people who rules history. For that reason the struggle against the clearly vegetative Baal-cult is inevitable, whereas with the more abstract El-conceptions symbiosis is possible to a certain extent (Gen. xiv. 18ff.). From El, Yahweh takes over various functions, such as the dignity of kingship, so that Yahweh is worshipped as the King of gods and the Lord of lords.[1]

The opposition against Baalism originated with the groups that had experienced the deliverance from Egypt and the establishment of the Yahwistic league in the desert under the leadership of Moses; among them the Levites, Moses' closest adherents, stood out by the ardour of their unflinching devotion to Yahweh. When these spread among the Hebrew tribes already living in Canaan, Yahweh became the God of these older tribal groups as well. They united in a Covenant with Yahweh, which found its centre first in Shechem (Joshua xxiv), afterwards probably in Siloh, where the ark had been placed. The sanctuary of Yahweh was not only a cultic but mainly a political and legal centre; here the divine laws were proclaimed and the renewal of the Covenant was celebrated. Here the people assembled on certain festivals, and to commemorate the great deeds of Yahweh (cf. Deut. xxxi. 10ff.). There, too, justice was administered by the Judges.[2]

Besides these judges who maintained law and justice at the sanctuary to serve the community of the tribes, there were also figures inspired by the Spirit of God who performed special acts of delivery on behalf of one or more tribes or groups (the so-called 'great Judges'). Sometimes they were assisted by prophets who call the people to arms for a holy war (Deborah). Sometimes we find that the prophet and the judge were combined by tradition in one figure (Samuel).

The experience of God's saving activity in history again and again influenced Israel's faith; it confirms and renews the knowledge of Yahweh Israel had received from her God since the desert-days.[3]

[1] See A. Alt, 'Gedanken über das Königtum Jahwes', Kleine Schriften I 1953, pp. 345ff.
[2] Many points in this development are not fully clear yet; see M. Noth, Das System der zwölf Stämme Israels, 1930; History of Israel; 'Das Amt des Richters Israels', Bertholet Festschrift 1950, pp. 404ff.; R. Smend, Yahwekrieg und Stämmebund, 1963; Th. C. Vriezen, The Religion, where much further literature is mentioned. This covenant with Yahweh at Shechem is sometimes taken to be the origin of Israels' religion, but this view makes many things inexplicable, such as the connection between the faith in Yahweh, the Lord of Sinai, and the deliverance of the tribes and the conception of the 'wars of Yahweh'. The Israelite groups that came to Canaan after the flight from Egypt came to know Yahweh in the desert as the God of salvation and may already have developed their cultic forms at Kadesh. Shechem is rather the political and cultic centre of the later groups of tribes in the country of Canaan.
[3] This is the element of truth in the main thesis propounded by K. Koch in his 'Der Tod des Religionsstiftrs', K.u.D., 1962 (who, however, emphatically rejects the idea of Moses as the founder of Israel's religion) and also in the description given by G. Von Rad of the ever-changing ways in which the work of Yahweh is represented in

By the occupation of Palestine and the fight against the Canaanites His domination over other territories than the desert is made plain (cf. the Song of Deborah); He even has power over the stars in the sky and He proves to be a God of battle as well.[1] And after Palestine had become the fixed dwelling-place of Israel He also manifested Himself as the God who granted the gifts of Nature to His people. His uniqueness is more evident as more and more the divine functions which the ancient world distributes among many gods are attributed to Him. After the foundation of the national state under David and Solomon He also became the national God. Thus new 'attributes' were continually being added to His Nature.

In the course of this process the original spiritual character of the conception of Yahweh is threatened from two sides: by naturalism and by nationalism. The former danger is external, it is the danger of syncretism and Baalism which is often brought into relation with Yahweh so that again and again the tendency springs up to worship Yahweh especially as Baal, the god of nature and of the soil. The latter is internal as well as external, so that Yahweh seems to be no more than the God of the state and the people. Time and again, however, the danger is averted by the influence of prophecy, which emphasized the spiritual, personal and moral aspects of the nature of God. This prophecy, beginning with Moses, remains a continually critical and correcting element in the religion of Israel; it always springs from and is supported again and again by the two elements that are most characteristic of Israel's religious life: personal vocation and personal communion with God. For that reason the prophets always had to fight on two fronts: against naturalism and against nationalism. From the days of Solomon these two dangers come to the front more and more and there develops an unceasing struggle against these distortions of the conception of God. Typical of the beginnings of this struggle is the reaction against the institution of kingship, which might be considered an encroachment upon the kingship of Yahweh, and no less typical is the opposition on the part of the prophets (cf. Nathan) to the building of the temple because they feared that Yahweh would come to be limited by His sanctuary and that the active God of spirit and life would become a static God. That this opposition was justified appears

the Old Testament historical testimony. One great objection against this view which I think should be raised here and now, is that variety is emphasized here so strongly that unity is entirely lost sight of; Von Rad in *Th.L.Z̧.* 1963; see also Zimmerli in *V.T.* 1962, and my essay in *K.Th.* 1965; O. Cullman, *Heil als Geschichte,* 1965, pp. 70ff., 104ff.

[1] On Yahweh as a God of war see H. Frederikson, *Jahwe als Krieger,* Lund 1945. On the holy war see, J. Pedersen, *Israel,* III–IV, pp. 1–32; G. von Rad, *Der Heilige Krieg im alten Israel,* 1951; R. Smend, *Jahwehkrieg und Stämmebund,* 1963 and my *The Religion.*

from the subsequent course of the history of the Israelitic religion. Particularly from the time of Elijah onwards there was an uninterrupted succession of prophets who, inspired by the Spirit of Yahweh, joined battle first and foremost against Baalism itself which was completely alien to Israel; this struggle, however, gave nationalism another chance and so made possible the rise of a nationalistic group of prophets (the idea of vocation is transformed into that of election). The views of this group in their turn became a spiritual danger and led to another struggle, this time between the two groups of prophets (under the leadership of the 'classical' prophets). As a result of this spiritual struggle the knowledge of God is deepened, so that the profession of God's supremacy over Nature and the nations becomes a profession of His omnipotence and absolute uniqueness. The moral element is also stressed more strongly as a result of the struggle against the danger of naturalism. The struggle of the prophets against nationalism is also of great importance because it emphasizes the strictly distinctive nature of God, His 'otherness' and holiness as well as His spiritual essence. In this way several components of the conception of God grow stronger and stronger.

The gods of the other nations are disposed of completely, as is already evident from the history of Elijah and even more fromt he words of Jeremiah who states emphatically that the other gods are nonentities (ii. 5; to Jeremiah the first satire on the heathen gods is ascribed, x. 16). Hosea fights for the recognition of Yahweh as the God of Love, Amos and Micha emphasize that Yahweh is the God of Justice, Isaiah, Zephaniah, and Ezekiel stress His Holiness. From the time of the Yahwist onwards, and especially in Isaiah and Deutero-Isaiah, we notice a growing awareness that Yahweh is the God of the nations of the world. In Deuteronomy the theocratical conception, linked on the one hand with the idea of election and on the other with the commandment of the love of God, is impressed upon the people as the absolute demand. Ezekiel's teaching that God grants His grace to the repentant sinner and to His people for the sake of His honour (Ezek. xxxvi) is a piece of extremely strict theocentric theology. Deutero-Isaiah does not abandon this theocentric view but – like the Deuteronomists before him – he balances it with the message of the all-embracing love of God (ch. xlix-li; liv).[1]

We cannot speak of a change in the knowledge of God in Israel, but there is rather a deepening of this knowledge through conflict and suffering. The contact with the pagan world with its tempting nature-worship, the serious political troubles which caused people to put all

[1] R. H. Pfeiffer in his important *Introduction to the O.T.*[5], 1946, even goes so far as to say: 'he seems utterly unaware of the inconsistencies in his notion of the deity'.

43

their hopes in God, the downfall which revealed God's justice, the exile which made Israel acquainted with the world and conscious of its universal missionary vocation (in Deutero-Isaiah) – all these influences contributed towards an ever growing understanding of the glory of God in His revelation of Himself to Israel, so that in the writings of the later prophets before and after the exile His majesty, justice, love, uniqueness and holiness were experienced and professed absolutely, and electing grace and the vocation to a life of holiness were acknowledged to be the foundation stones of spiritual life. A new hope, too, is born in this period, a new expectation of the future reveals itself: that of the Kingdom of God in perfect righteousness under the leadership of the Messiah.

Thus we see how all through the course of history there is continuous guidance by God and an ever-growing revelation of Him. By the influence of His Spirit the creed of Israel is purified and amplified more and more.[1] The highest measure of spiritual insight is received by Deutero-Isaiah, who proclaims a new understanding of the universal vocation of Israel – in a clearer form than the Yahwist's – as a missionary task and reveals the redeeming and vivifying power of suffering for the sake of sinners. Israel is to bring the message of the *Torah* to the world[2]. Deutero-Isaiah's figure of the Servant (ch. xlii, xlix, l and lii, liii) originated during the exile, and it is evident, therefore, that during the Dispersion the idea of suffering had become of great importance for the development of the faith of Israel and for its conception of God. Here the Old Testament revelation of God reached its culminating point, especially in Isa. liii, for here the idea arose that the *Torah* (revelation) not only leads to theocracy, the rule of God over Israel itself, but also to that love which suffers unto death for the sins of others. This is the last new element of the revelation of God given to Israel before the coming of Christ; its depth was not understood fully by Israel; indeed, it hardly found an echo among the people in spite of the fact that the post-exilic prophets now and then revert to this idea

---

[1] This is not understood in the sense of an immanent development, but in the sense in which G.W.Anderson, op. cit., p.309, defines it: 'Hebrew religion cannot be described in terms of a smooth, orderly, historical development. The symmetrical patterns, into which we try to fit it, are shattered time and again by historical crises, changes of cultural environment, and the work of great creative personalities; and when we have done our utmost to find in it factors which are distinctive and constant, it is of the nature of the religion that we are driven back to the actuality of history: for the O.T. does not contain a speculative religion, but bears witness to the acts of the living God'. This is also the reason why the writer of this book ventures to fix a certain distance between the religion of Israel and the message of the O.T.

The same growth is found with respect to the conception of the covenant, e.g. by D.J.McCarthy, *Treaty and Covenant*, 1963, pp. 175ff.

[2] Opposite to this P.A.H.de Boer, Second Isaiah's Message, *O.T.S.* XI, 1956.

(Zechariah may be a case in point[1]). It is from this climax that Jesus Christ starts and in Him this word of Isaiah becomes living reality and an all-important element of the faith. Jesus Christ becomes the fulfilment of this divine vision. In this way the greatest and most profound message of the Old Testament is actualized by Him among men on this earth, and thus the true meaning of the word of God, spoken to Israel, is revealed completely. As regards the history of revelation, Deutero-Isaiah forms the climax of the Old Testament – all that comes after him does not bring anything fundamentally new.[2] It is no longer prophecy that leads the way, but theology. The only progress of spiritual knowledge lies in the domain of individual piety.

After the exile Israel's religion assumed a new form; so that after the rebuilding of the temple it was governed by what may be called a new sacramental theology (for which Ezekiel and the 'Code of Holiness', Lev. xviiff., had prepared the ground) which conformed to the best of the ancient traditions in the whole of the religious field, cultic and ethical as well as social and juridical, and gave a critical and theological interpretation of these ancient traditions in accordance with the religio-ethical message of the prophets; the connection with these ancient elements was, however, maintained as closely as possible, though on some points occasional renovations were introduced.

This led to the formation of the *Torah* as the basis of the whole of the religious and social life of the congregation that gathered round the temple and was sanctified and redeemed by the cult.

In this way the entire people became a congregation[3], not only theoretically but in all its institutions, with a history of salvation, a code of law and a missal (Leviticus) entirely its own, or we might say with a gospel, ethos and cult of its own. The *Torah* embraced all aspects of religious life. The scribes together with the priests saw to it that this law was enforced; there was a discipline which put defection out of the question; the cult maintained the communion with God, sanctified the congregation and was in this manner the intermediary through which salvation was obtained. There was, it is true, great tension between the priests and the group of scribes that had sprung up after the Exile, as well as tension (mostly social though to some extent also theological in character) between the priests and the Levites.

[1] Zech. ix. 9f.; the figures of the shepherd and the stabbed man in the Zechariah-apocalypse, xi–xiii, which are sometimes given a messianic interpretation (as bij C. Brouwer in his Utrecht thesis. *Wachter en Herder*, 1949) are too problematic to give a firm support to such an interpretation; cf. especially the careful attempts at exegesis by F. Horst, 'Die zwölf kleinen Propheten' (*H.A.T.*); cf. p. 453.
[2] Cf., p. 14, n. 2 on the appreciation of the prophetical books among the ancient Jews.
[3] Cf., N. Dahl, *Das Volk Gottes*, 1941, L. Rost, *Die Vorstufen von Kirche und Synagoge im A.T.*, 1938 and from a more sociological point of view A. Causse, *Du groupe ethnique à la communauté religieuse*, 1937.

45

One thing was wanting, or rather came to be wanting: the voice of prophecy, the free word of the Spirit. For it was the sacred tradition that became all-important, and the cult that was the central element of the living religion, and the priests who gave the lead in the congregation. The post-exilic period has only a few 'minor' prophets; whatever is genuine in their words is a revival of the ancient prophecies; the greatest thing this period produced[1] is perhaps the rapture at the future new life in the book of Joel, who looks beyond his own times for the miracle that God will grant: 'And it shall come to pass afterwards, that I will pour out my spirit upon all flesh; and your sons and your daughters shall prophesy, your old men shall dream dreams, your young men shall see visions' (iii. 1; R.V. ii. 28). It is as if – before prophecy falls silent altogether[2] – the grand prophetic vision must make itself heard once more.

What can still be perceived of prophecy after two centuries[3] is the somewhat doubtful apocalyptic – for here individual piety can express itself and realize its longing for the moment when the eschatological events will come to pass.[4]

On the other hand the spirit of prophecy is also to be found in the temple-cult itself: it teaches the (lower) priesthood to sing the praises of God. The prophets are now called 'singers in the temple'[5] (1 Chron. xxv. 1). It is remarkable how in the books of the Chronicles the temple cult is framed and dominated by a liturgy which consists of the singing of Psalms. (This is the reason why, notwithstanding their secondary character, these books deserve their inclusion in the Canon, though they do stand rather 'on the fringe'.) Whole companies of singers spring up, and there comes into being a sacred Book of Psalms which, under the guidance of the singing in the Temple, developed into the Book of Psalms we know (cf. p. 83f.).

Songs very often arising from individual experience (cf. the personal songs of lamentation, penance and thanksgiving in the Book of Psalms) become the last expression of personal communion with God.[6]

[1] The last few chapters of Deutero-Isaiah are left out of consideration here, for in them the spirit of ancient prophecy lives on. Zechariah is another important revelation of the ancient prophetical spirit.
[2] In Zech. xiii. 2–6 all forms of new ecstatic prophetism are rejected as fortune-telling, though canonical prophecy is recognized (cf. the reference to Amos vii. 14).
[3] In another way prophetical piety makes its influence felt in the circles of the simple believers, the 'anawim, but these always remain inconspicuous.
[4] R. H. Charles, *Religious Development between the Old and New Testaments*, Oxford University Press, pp. 16ff.; M. A. Beek, *Inleiding in de Joodse Apocalyptiek*, 1950; H. H. Rowley, *The relevance of apocalyptic*[2], 1947.
[5] See for instance S. Mowinckel, *Psalmenstudien*, V.
[6] There is no denying that many psalms may be of cultic origin, but it is not true that all or most of the psalms have arisen from the cult; cf. on the Psalms the detailed and mature bibliography by A. R. Johnson, 'The Psalms', in H. H. Rowley, *The Old Testament and modern Study*, 1951, pp. 162–207 and of J. J. Stamm in *Th.R.*, 1955.

Besides the temple there was, after the exile, also the synagogue, which was, however, no source of revival: it always established a close and personal connection between the congregation and the Torah, but for the rest, like the post-exilic temple, it was more in the nature of a conservative and educative body.

By the side of the synagogue separate communities[1], or sects, sprang up. Of one of these we have gained a more profound knowledge, because their writings were found at 'Ain Feshka in 1948; it may be identified with the sect of the Essenes.[2] They adhered very faithfully to the *Torah*, but had their own (spiritual) interpretation of the law and especially of the prophets, independent of the official theological interpretation. They believed that their leader, 'the teacher of righteousness', was the man who understood all the secrets of the prophetic revelations (Habakkuk Scroll, vii.4ff.).

In spite of itself the new theology from which the *Torah* arose proved conducive to the arrest of religious development by rendering tradition canonical; notwithstanding its 'reformed' cult and its broad theocratic aims it was ultimately not an unmixed blessing – as we have already seen – because by rendering tradition canonical it subdued and finally silenced the voice of free prophecy.[3] It brought about the preservation of ancient values[4] but the result was traditionalism and observantism.[5]

The *Torah*, which was to enable man to live, came to be a cause of death by this procedure which sacrificed living prophecy to tradition. What all this led to can be seen in the New Testament.

For that reason St. Paul had to give an entirely new interpretation of the law once Christ had waged the struggle. The old sacraments

---

[1] Cf., for instance, J. Thomas, *Le mouvement Baptiste en Palestine et Syrie*, Gembloux 1935; W. Brandt, 'Die jüdischen Baptismen'. *B.Z.A.W.* 18, 1910; M. Friedländer, *Die religiösen Bewegungen innerhalb des Judentums im Zeitalter Jesu*, Berlin, 1905.

[2] There already exists an immense literature on these writings. We only mention here A. Dupont-Sommer, *The dead Sea Scrolls* (Eng. trans. 1952) and *The Jewish Sect of Qumran and the Essenes* (Eng. trans., 1954); H. H. Rowley, *The Zadokite Fragments and the Dead Sea Scrolls*, 1952, and J. van der Ploeg, 'De in 1947 in Juda gevonden handschriften', *J. E.O.L.* 11 and 12. The literature-surveys by W. Baumgartner in the *Th. R.* 1948/9 and 1951 are also most instructive; see now *Revue de Qumran* en Burchard *Bibliographie zu den Handschriften vom Toten Meer*, 1957.

[3] See W. Foerster, 'Der Heilige Geist im sog. Spätjudentum', *De Spiritu Sancto*, 1964, pp. 40ff.; cf. also B. de Vries, *Hoofdlijnen en motieven in de ontwikkeling der Halachah*, 1959, pp. 36ff.

[4] Cf., rightly the positive evaluation by Anderson, op. cit., p. 307 and others. One may realize the value of the canonization of the 'classical sources of religion' but also stress the dangers of canonization, which threaten to make a living religion into a book-religion. This also applies to Christianity; cf. A. Bertholet, 'Die Macht der Schrift im Glauben und Aberglauben', 1948 (*A.A.B.*, No. 1); see also F. Horst, loc. cit. (cf. p. 13f. n. 5).

[5] We speak of traditionalism when the traditional elements, having become historical, dominate religion entirely; of observantism when ritual and law become the dominating factor in religion.

47

(sacrifices and rites) were abandoned, for a new sacrifice had taken their place. This changed the whole aspect of the *Torah* and in this way God finally completed the history of His revelation to Israel. The Bible is, therefore, not merely an enlarged *Torah*, but compared to the *Torah* it is something entirely new.[1] The reconciliation with God which according to the Old Testament could be achieved sacramentally, by the sacrificial acts, was accomplished personally by Jesus Christ as the Mediator. Entirely alone and to the very end He went the way that led to the sanctification of the world, thus actualizing completely the vision of Isaiah liii: 'Wherefore God also hath highly exalted him, and given him the name which is above every name'. His Mediatorship gives us now and for ever the assurance that in Him redemption has been attained. The new Sacrament of Holy Communion does not accomplish this redemption but *celebrates* it, recalls it to mind, makes us acquainted with it; i.e. it makes us experience communion with Him *in faith* by eating the bread and drinking the wine.[2] Considered from the point of view of this avowal many things in the Old Testament are no longer of current interest – they have passed into history; but even so they can still teach us an infinity of lessons, because they belong to the history of the revelation of God, on which we are living.[3]

[1] Cf., also A. G. Hebert, *The Bible from within*, pp. 10, 141ff. For this reason we must disagree both with A. A. van Ruler and with P. A. H. de Boer, who, each in their own way, see the N.T. only as an interpretation or application of the O.T.; Van Ruler in *Vox Th.*, 1942, (see below, p. 120). P. A. H. de Boer in *N.T.T.* 1952/3: 'De functie van de Bijbel'.
[2] I gladly refer to the fine essay by W. Barnard, 'Liturgie en Drama', *Kerk en Eredienst*, 1952/3, pp. 8off.
[3] K. H. Miskotte appears to take exception to this sentence, as witness his reaction in *Als de goden zwijgen*, 1955, p. 91 (Engl. transl. *When the Gods are silent*, 1967); he seems to think that in the early Church the Old Testament was received with unqualified appreciation. The present author fails to see how this view is to be reconciled with Acts xv, Rom. xiv, etc., or with the conflicting views on the Old Testament in the 2nd century and the disappearance of early Jewish Christianity. Full admission of the historical course of the revelation of Yahweh, to which both the Old and the New Testament bear witness, with all its consequences for our appreciation of the Bible (the impossibility of maintaining the view that revelation and canon are to be identified, see below p.148/9), seems to present great difficulties to many people. This divergence of opinion is probably mainly caused by the fact that Miskotte as a dogmatist, especially in this book, *starts from the principle of the unity of the Old Testament* (and the Bible), whereas this chapter is historical and describes the variety that manifests itself so clearly in the history of Israel's religion, and attempts in this last paragraph to recover from that the internal connection between the Old Testament and the New Testament (cf. also p. 133).

Further literature (History of Religion):

E. König, *Geschichte der alttestamentlichen Religion²*, 1915 (detailed).
G. Hölscher, *Geschichte der israelitischen und jüdischen Religion*, 1922.
B. D. Eerdmans, *Religion of Israel*, 1947.
E. O. James, *The Old Testament in the light of anthropology*, 1935.
A. Lods, *La religion d'Israël*, 1939 (for the general public).
id., *Israel from its Beginnings to the Middle of the Eighth Century*, 1932.
id., *The Prophets and the Rise of Judaism*, 1937 (the last two works are detailed).
E. Sellin, *Israelitisch-jüdische Religionsgeschichte*, 1933 (short).
E. Dhorme, *L'Evolution religieuse d'Israël*, I, *La religion des Hebreux nomades*, 1937.
W. O. E. Oesterley and T. H. Robinson, *Hebrew Religion²*, 1937, 1947.
J. Pedersen, *Israel*, III-IV, 1940.
H. H. Rowley, *The rediscovery of the Old Testament*, 1945.
W. A. L. Elmslie, *How came our faith*, 1948.
M. Buber, *The prophetic Faith*.
J. Lindblom, *Israels Religion i gammeltestamentlig tid²*, 1953.
W. Eichrodt, 'Religionsgeschichte Israels', in *Historia Mundi* II, 1953, pp. 377-448.
R. H. Pfeiffer, *Religion in the O.T.*, 1960.
Y. Kaufmann, *The Religion of Israel*, translated and abridged by M. Greenberg, 1960.
H. Renckens, *De godsdienst van Israël²*, 1963.

Of the older works we only mention the authors: A. Kuenen, R. Smend, and K. Marti.

CHAPTER III

The spiritual structure of the Old Testament and of the Old Testament Writings

If we are to outline the basic theological ideas of the Old Testament[1] we must not lose sight of the data which the study of its background provides on its origin and development; there are various literary layers and also different strata of religious and theological thought, especially in the historical books. It is therefore impossible to treat all parts of the Old Testament alike but we must differentiate between the various authors to whom we may ascribe certain parts of these books, such as the author of the history of the earliest times, J, E, D, P, and the Chroniclers[2]; the differences go deeper than the mere literary contents, for we must also recognize that the spiritual viewpoints from which these authors survey history are also widely different. There is a difference in originality and spiritual atmosphere between the historical writings just as there is also a difference between the various Psalms.

[1] Some critics, especially Prof. G. Sevenster in *N.T.T.* 1951/2, p. 170f., have raised objections against my separate treatment of the various sources, with respect to the theological question of the O.T. To state that 'the question of a distinct message of a certain source does not arise' appears to me methodologically incorrect. For this would completely exclude the historical approach, the question of perspective from a theology. We are here not concerned with J, E, D, and P in themselves, for on that question different opinions are possible, but with the question whether the historical course of revelation must appear to full advantage. In my opinion the latter will have to be the case, certainly in an introductory chapter, but also in the principal part. This would be absolutely impossible if Deuteronomy or Deutero-Isaiah or the Isaiah-apocalypse could not be considered with respect to the period in which they originated. Fundamentally this is as true of the sources of the Pentateuch, even if it is clear that opinions differ even more widely on this matter than on the sources in Isaiah. The newest Theology of the O.T., Von Rad's *Old Testament Theology*, Eng. ed. 1962/5, wholly expounds the theological contents of the O.T. with the help of the literary and *traditionsgeschichtliche* analysis of the sources. So Von Rad's views are the exact reverse of those of G. Sevenster; in the former's *Theologie der geschichtlichen* and: *prophetischen Überlieferungen* the theological diversity of the various sources is elaborated to such an extent that there is hardly room, if any, for a common theological starting-point. See his article in *Th.L.Z.* 1963, pp. 402ff: 'Offene Fragen im Umkreis einer Theologie des A.T.'
[2] On the sigla J, E, etc. see any Introduction to the Old Testament. The best book still is O. Eißfeldt, *Einleitung in das A.T.*, of which a third, greatly enlarged edition was published in 1964.

50

This is not to say, however, that the essential internal unity of the Old Testament should or could be denied. There are, it is true, certain differences of vision, and sometimes even contrasts largely connected with the historical situation in which a piece of writing came into existence. But in spite of these differences and contrasts there is not only great unanimity among the different authors but especially a fundamental spiritual agreement, springing from the certainty of being received into living communion with the same living God. For a scholar like Prof. B. D. Eerdmans of Leyden to think that a large part of the Old Testament was clearly polytheistic was one of the major errors in the field of Old Testament studies; there have been, quite rightly, very few scholars who shared this idea.

A strong exaggeration of the actual state of affairs seems to me to be G. von Rad's idea that the respective Old Testament authors represented religions so widely different that even their conceptions of Yahweh could hardly have had any elements in common.

Over against these views, which emphasize the differences, I think I am justified in saying that the Old Testament is dominated by the prophetic testimony, the teaching of those men who left a permanent mark not only on the religion of Israel, but especially on the Old Testament, in the course of two hundred and fifty years of the greatest catastrophes and the most miraculous deliverances, between 750 and 500.[1] I make the distinction between the Old Testament and the religion of Israel because in my opinion the Old Testament cannot simply be called the document of the religion of Israel. The Old Testament is a very special testimony concerning the religion of Israel! Neither is it merely a collection of authors who adapted tradition in their own way. A library of documents about Israel's religion would have been quite a different thing; the Old Testament, however, mainly contains only that part of the Israelite religious writings which could be salvaged from the ruins left by the catastrophe of 586, in terms of the criticism of the prophets, and further the writings of these prophets themselves and those that were written afterwards from the point of view of this prophetical criticism.

Literary and historical criticism will have to take into account the fall of Jerusalem in 586 B.C., much more than it has done hitherto. The destruction of the holy city in A.D. 70 had an enormous influence on

[1] As a matter of fact, it is also true of the earliest elements of the written sources, J and E, that they were written by people closely connected with the prophets (cf. p. 57 and elsewhere). When Von Rad repeatedly points to the framework of election-promise-fulfilment in which the historical traditions of these authors are framed (especially in his article in *Th.L.Z.* 1963, pp. 412ff.), to my mind he only indicates the prophetical character of these writings. See also H. W. Wolff, 'Das Geschichtsverständnis der altt. Prophetie', *Ev. Th.* 1960, pp. 218ff.; W. Richter: *Untersuchungen Richterbuch* 1963, 339ff. See below pp. 101ff.

51

the development of the Jews, on the defining of the canon of Old Testament writings, on the genesis of a *textus receptus* and on theology as a whole (characterized by opposition to further development and by radical and traditionalist tendencies). The same applies to the first destruction of the temple in 586 (including the prelude, the downfall of Samaria in 722, and the subsequent aftermath, the restoration of the religious life of the people after 539).[1] It would be of great importance if the study of background were to pay more regard to these data and thus give a historically more justified insight into the '*Sitz im Leben*' of the writings separately and of the canon as a whole. Even a superficial inspection of the dates of these writings suffices to show how the classical writings of the Old Testament centre round these events.

Around 722 – Amos, Hosea, Isaiah, Micah, as prophetical authors, and as 'historical' authors probably E, who rewrote J's work (or E and RJE); around 586 – Deuteronomy and the deuteronomistic historians; Jeremiah, Zephaniah, (Nahum), Habakkuk, Obadiah, Ezekiel; around 539 – Deutero-Isaiah, Haggai, and Zechariah, the Code of Holiness, and P. A large number of the *Kethubim* might also be included here.[2]

The downfall of Israel, and especially the destruction of the holy city of Jerusalem brought about a spiritual concentration on Israel's own religious and national property, a reflection which was thoroughly and radically in earnest, for Israel was confronted with the catastrophic reality of the destruction of the temple of God, predicted by the prophets. Thus the prophetic word of those men who had thus far been reviled became the criterion of this reflection, both in the ensuing sifting of the ancient religious documents and in recording the collection of writings that had come into being in this way. This sifting and formation took place among the ruins of the temple, in the huts of the exiles, while people were deprived of everything, and mercilessly given over to the reality of the ruthlessness of a world that was, as Israel believed, godless, when they could only trust themselves to the grace of God and were, therefore, before His eyes. In this way there came about the new orientation of religious knowledge, the new insight that sprang up with prophets such as Jeremiah, Ezekiel, and Deutero-Isaiah. Valuation and revaluation took place in the searing light of the divine judgment; only God and His grace remained, and from more than one side prophets proclaimed that Israel existed

[1] On the historical consequences see M. Noth, 'La catastrophe de Jérusalem en l'an 587 avant Jésus Christ et sa signification pour Israël', *R. H. Ph. R.*, 1953, pp. 81ff.
[2] In *Suppl. V.T.* IX, 1963, pp. 250ff. ('The Law and the Prophets') D.N. Freedman even suggested that the entire nucleus of the Old Testament, both the Law and the Prophets, had already developed as a literary unity in the course of the 6th century B. C.

only for the sake of the name of Yahweh. This gave the Old Testament testimony that radical religious quality which is its ineffaceable characteristic. Only those ancient values that proved to be equal to terrible experiences of history and to offer support during the desert journey of the diaspora, were preserved and became a sacred unalienable heritage. In the result only the critical writings of the prophets and of the historians who were influenced or purified by this prophetical criticism, could stand the test.

Thus the word of the classical prophets was revealed to be divine truth. This view is confirmed in Zech. i. 1–6 (esp. 6) where this post-exilic prophet has to remind the people emphatically of the fulfilment of the words of the pre-exilic prophets (cf. also Zech. vii. 1–14).

The Old Testament does possess, therefore, an essential unity, notwithstanding its many books and the differences of conception that exist; for its nucleus (which includes the greater part of the Old Testament) is imbued with one and the same spirit.[1] It is true that 'appendices' were added to this nucleus (and also to the separate writings of the nucleus) in the course of the following centuries (when the canon had not yet been closed), but these do not essentially modify the contents of the central message concerning Yahweh, even if some of these later writings show how the postexilic religious development could not maintain itself on its initial high spiritual plane.

After the formation of the two central collections of authoritative writings, the *Torah* and the *Nebiim* (with the Deuteronomistic historical books Joshua–Kings as connecting link), which afterwards successively gained the dignity of canonicity (first the *Torah*, then the *Nebiim*), one more important event took place, the rise of a third series of authoritative books, the *Kethubim*. These, however, came to be vested with authority only very gradually, and were canonized as a collection at a very late date, viz. during the nineties of the first century A.D., to distinguish them from the literary productions (soon increasing in number and standing) of apocalyptic, the Jewish sects, rising gnosticism and the Christian Church which was then coming into existence. But in comparison with the *Torah* and the *Nebiim* this third group remained in more respects than one canonical in a secondary degree, as we have established above.[2]

After this survey of the Old Testament as a whole we must now

[1] There is, therefore, no real 'duality' of Law and Prophets, as is assumed by A. A. van Ruler, *De Vervulling der Wet*, 1947, p. 343; nor a 'ganze Handvoll Theologien, ...die sich... weit von einander unterscheiden' (Von Rad, *Th.L.Z.*, l.c., pp. 403, 405). Especially the word *weit* should not be used here. Even the conceptions of the creation given in Gen. i and Gen. ii/iii, so widely divergent in their literary and cultural aspects, cannot be said to differ so much in their theological and anthropological views.
[2] See p. 14, n. 2; we should bear in mind the liturgical use of the books in the synagogue.

consider the various books separately; as far as is possible they are discussed from a strictly theological point of view.

The author of the narrative of Gen. ii–xi may, no doubt, be looked upon as the most profound of the Old Testament authors. Though a Yahwist narrator and spiritually related to J he may be regarded as an independent author. In him Israel's faith in Yahweh is confronted with the ancient oriental mythological philosophy of life. That is why so many mythological reminiscences are found in his work.[1] Though there is a close spiritual relationship between him and the great prophets, so that he may perhaps be considered their disciple, it might be better to look upon him as one of the first great authors of the earliest period of the Kings, living before the transition of the semi-nomadic and peasant culture into urban civilization. Sociologically his views are conditioned to a high degree by the life of the small farmers, a life that had hardly outgrown the semi-nomadic stage (cf. p. 55 n. 1). He writes about the destruction of the first world; the judgment comes no fewer than four times: first: man is expelled from Paradise, then Cain is exiled to the desert, then the Deluge, and lastly the confusion of tongues and the dispersion of mankind. Because of his disobedience, man, who originally lived in communion with God in the garden of Eden, is expelled from Paradise to the earth which bears the curse of God. The punishment of the first sin is enmity, suffering, trouble and death. This sin consists fundamentally in the self-exaltation of man who wished to make himself the equal of God and to have divine knowledge (knowledge of good *and* of evil) at his command; man shakes off the Child-Father relation with God and is thrown into the great struggle of life because he wants to take matters into his own hands; *man's self-exaltation, his 'hybris' towards God is sin* (Gen. iii; Gen. vi. 1 ff.; Gen. xi), but sin against God also involves sin against one's fellow-man (Cain, Lamech).

Cast off by God, man reveals his high-handed, sinful nature in the gigantic figures of Cain, Lamech, the giants (ch. vi) and Nimrod. The first of these is Cain, who murders his brother and for that reason is driven away still further, from the arable land to the desert. But he also builds a city;[2] from this earliest primitive culture springs Lamech who introduced blood-revenge and bigamy (in the author's opinion monogamy is, therefore, the original state of things) and becomes the father of the first manual workers. This civilization springs from the sinful self-will of man. In this respect the author's views correspond to

[1] See besides my *Onderzoek naar de paradijsvoorstelling* a.o. B.C. Childs, *Myth and Reality*; now *S.V.T.* xvii, 1969, pp. 20ff.
[2] Probably two Cain-traditions merge at this point.

those of the Rechabites.[1] After the destruction of mankind by the Deluge the process repeats itself, as appears from the story of the tower-building at Babylon (the home of the great Nimrod). This negative appreciation of culture is one of the most important traits distinguishing this author both from the J-author of the history of Abraham and from the great prophets (though in some measure such anticultural tendencies also occur with rustic figures such as Amos and Micah).

The author recognises the general sinfulness of mankind (vi. 5) even after the Deluge (viii. 21), and the fall of Noah and the tower-building at Babylon are to be regarded as connected with this. The general sinfulness of the man is not taught here as a dogma in the sense of dogmas in the Christian Church, according to which mankind is a *massa perditionis:* the author distinguishes two lines in mankind[2], the line of Cain with Lamech and his sons and that of Seth, Enos, Noah (owing to the insertion of Gen. v by P, the original line of Enos cannot be reconstructed completely in the primeval history). He regards sin in the religious sense as revolt against God (*pesha'*), and here he is in agreement with the most profound conception of the Old Testament.

The author does not, however, take all this to mean that God is no longer merciful; He is not a God who destroys completely in His anger. God saves Noah, to whom He grants His grace, and in Noah brings Mankind safely through the judgment of the Deluge. Here a prophetical element emerges again: in His mercy Yahweh saves a remnant. The idea of election, also found in Gen. iv (Abel is accepted, Cain is not) dominates the narrative, although it is not expressed openly (in the history of Noah P lays far more stress on Noah's absolute obedience, Gen. vi. 9, vii. 1b). But in the background of the conception of election there is also the moral point of view, cf. Gen. iv. 7: 'If thou doest well, shalt thou not be accepted?' (i.e. find favour with God). Though the will of God is of prime importance in his idea of election, there is in the background also the moral and religious element.[3] For that matter, the fact that disobedience is looked upon as the original sin (Gen. iii. 17) also shows very clearly that in this author's opinion human action is of crucial importance in God's deciding on man's fate.

[1] The same tendency also manifests itself in the story of Noah's intoxication (Gen. ix. 20ff.) as a result of vine-culture; by this sin Ham comes to commit his ignominious act and Canaan is cursed. Compare also how Abel, the shepherd, and his sacrifice are accepted. The author accepts pastoral life in the *midbar* (steppe), the half-nomadic life. True nomadic life in the desert, however, is considered cursed (Cain, Lamech). The author cannot be called a Rechabite, because agriculture and vine-culture as such are not condemned by him (as the Rechabites do, see Jer. xxxv. 7).
[2] If at any rate Gen. iv. 25f. may be taken to have originally belonged to the narratives of the author of the primeval history.
[3] On election in the O.T. see H. H. Rowley, *The biblical doctrine of election*, 1950.

Closely allied to prophetism is the idea of Gen.iv, that what is demanded of man is not sacrifice but 'doing well'; compare the use of the same word in Isa.i.17 and Jer.vii.5 (see also Amos v.15, Micah vi.8), all in the same context – namely, in a discussion of the value of sacrifices. Gen.viii.21 is the only place which might give us the impression that the author attaches great value to sacrifice, but this may be explained from the fact that he is here dependent on older material (as is evident from a comparison of this passage with that of the Deluge-narrative in the Gilgamesh-epic).

The use of Yahweh as the name of God, even for the earliest period, may be an anachronism, but the author apparently is not conscious of this – he was not writing a study in the history of religion! To him the absoluteness of Yahweh as the God of the world at all times is a definitely established fact, even if he admits the existence of 'sons of gods' and giants (Gen.vi) and even if he is aware of evil powers (e.g. the serpent in Gen.iii, though it is not represented as a demonic figure in opposition to God; there is no trace of dualism to be found). The fact that the Yahwistic authors use the name Yahweh from the very first demonstrates that they do not yet recognize a fundamental difference between Israel and the other nations in their relation to God.[1]

The Yahwist (J).[2] It is this author especially who has left his mark on the great record of Israel's earliest history with the patriarchal narratives, the history of the deliverance from Egypt and the development of Israel into the nation that received the promised land. His book, which probably extends from Gen.xii (xi) to Judgesii, rests on the great conception of the call of the people of Israel by God; He has called Abraham out of his country to become the father of a great people in the country which He promised to him, in order that Abraham might become a blessing for the world. The call of Israel is here placed in its true spiritual light: the idea of nationalism is subordinated to the religious conception and is here already given a universalist outlook, as also afterwards in Isa.ii.1ff. Yahweh is the alpha and the omega of history.[3] By His miracles He has called the people into existence: both Isaac and Jacob are children given by a divine miracle; the sons of Israel were miraculously preserved (Joseph) and delivered

---

[1] Cf. C.Westermann, *Forschung am A.T.*, 1964, pp.47ff.

[2] Next to Von Rad's *The Problem of the Hexateuch and Other Essays*, 1966, G.Hölscher's *Geschichtschreibung in Israel*, 1952, J.Hempel, *Althebräische Literatur*, 1930ff, cf. now H.W.Wolff, 'Das Kerugma des Jahwisten', *Ev. Th.* 1964, pp.73ff. (transl. *Interpretation*, 1966, pp.131ff.) and 'Das A.T. und das Problem der existentialen Interpretation', *Ev. Th.* 1963, pp.10ff.

[3] Against K.Galling, *Erwählungstraditionen*, 1928, who emphasizes the nationalistic element in J too strongly. See also my *Die Erwählung Israels nach dem A.T.*, 1953.

(Moses) in Egypt, and miraculously conducted out of Egypt and through the desert to the promised land. Yahweh led Israel and brought it to its destination notwithstanding the sins of the fathers: the sins even of the patriarch Abraham, the exemplar of the truly believing friend of God, who in his cowardice delivered the ancestress of the people into the hands of the Egyptian Pharaoh, and who could not wait for the fulfilment of God's promises (cf. his marriage to Hagar); of Jacob, who, though bearer of the promise, walked in sinful human ways; of Moses, who showed great hesitation at the time of his call; and especially of the people, who continually rebelled against the will of God.

The call, promises and miracles of God dominate this history entirely, while on the part of mankind obstinacy and unbelief are found again and again. In the course of this history God's blessing and His promise to Abraham is reverted to over and over again, while, moreover, this promise is renewed at the birth of Jacob.[1] In various ways the greatness of God's promise is emphasized (Gen. xiii. 14–17, Gen. xv), and so is the fact that Israel owes its existence solely to the promise of God. The miraculous birth of Isaac especially is adduced to illustrate this.[2] At Jacob's birth, too, the oracle ('The elder shall serve the younger') points to the conception that it was only God's electing grace that guided Israel. This corresponds to the fact that in the history of Joseph (which in its present form must derive from a different author) young Joseph is ranked above his brothers (who refuse to accept this) in order to save the people; this narrative is also evidently sustained by the faith in the guidance of God's providence (Gen. l. 20).[3]

The narrative of the deliverance from Egypt glorifies Yahweh[4] as the God who rules the nations and the forces of nature, including even the sea, and who puts His power at the service of Israel in order to deliver His people and thus to fulfil His promise to Abraham. Here again we find that the stress is laid on God's deeds and His faithfulness, and, on the other hand, on the weakness and misery of the people who groan under their servitude to the Egyptians. This piece of history is not viewed in a nationalistic but in a spiritual light and is intended to evoke belief in the peculiar calling of Israel. This vocation does not

[1] The Word of God, which von Rad proved to be the dominating element in the history of the Deuteronomistic historian (Studies in Deuteronomy, E.T. 1953, pp. 75ff.) is also found as a basic idea in the work of the Yahwist. Cf. Gen. xxii. 17f.; xxiv. 34ff.; xxvi. 24; xxvii. 29; xlviii. 15f.; Num. xxiv. 9b.
[2] For a homiletic elaboration of Gen. xii. 1ff. see W. Eichrodt, Gottes Ruf im A.T., 1951, pp. 35ff., of the rest of the history of Abraham, Postille 1951/52, pp. 134ff.
[3] The narrative is dominated by Chokhmah traditions, see G. von Rad, 'Josephsgeschichte und ältere Chokma', Suppl. V. T., 1953, I, pp. 120ff.
[4] See J. Pedersen, 'Passahfest und Passahlegende', Z.A.W., 1934, pp. 161ff., esp. pp. 167f.; M. Buber, Moses, 1947; E. Auerbach, Moses, 1953.

rest on Israel's special spiritual status; on the contrary, again and again the people manifest their disloyalty and unbelief. In the centre of the history of redemption, between the narratives dealing with the deliverance from Egypt and the desert journey, stands the narrative of the revelation of God on Mount Sinai and the divine covenant. From the outset this moment was one of the focal points of Israelite historiography, and more and more it became the point on which earlier and later traditions were concentrated. These traditions were interwoven to such an extent that a literary analysis is now hardly possible any more, even if at certain points the complexity of the stories is abundantly clear.

At the beginning of the story of the entrance into the promised land stands the well-known story of Balaam, who was called upon by the king of Moab to curse Israel but who could only bless it; this recalls the promise to the patriarchs (cf. Numb. xxiv. 9 with Gen. xii. 3). Thus the dominating idea of J's teaching proves to be Israel's call to be the people of God, and the fulfilment of this call by the wonderful grace of God alone, who gave this people His promise and Himself fulfilled this promise.

This original narrative of the Yahwist was adapted several times.[1] The first enlarged edition was that produced by the *Elohist*, which in many respects cannot be distinguished from the original narrative of the Yahwist. Where his hand can be recognized clearly it is the spirit of the prophetical movement that finds expression, which developed in North Israel after the struggle against Baal and against intermingling with other nations in the days of Elijah and Elisha. We may say that, more strongly than his predecessor, he emphasized the separation between Israel and the other nations which is implicit in Israel's vocation (involving the element of religious nationalism). He also laid more stress on the prophetical character of the national figures. The fact that *the patriarchs and the people were elected* is stressed more strongly than the vocation by God. This is, for instance, evident from the power that is ascribed to Abraham as a prophet (Gen. xx) and to Jacob as God's wrestler (Israel) (Gen. xxxii. 23 ff.). If we attempted to define this spiritual atmosphere by means of modern ideas we might say that it is related to chassidism or pietism, in which the faithful are made the centre of interest as much as God, while at the same time the faithful are contrasted with the world. To the Yahwist, however, the grace of God is all-important. On the one hand this gives a peculiar warmth to the narratives of E, as is evident from several places where he (or re-

[1] This view has been defended by the present writer in his *De Literatuur van Oud-Israël*, 1962. It is generally supposed that J and E were combined into an independent history by a Redactor, called RJE.

lated authors) are met with in the Old Testament (in our opinion, apart from the Pentateuch, also at the beginning of the books of Samuel). Narratives such as Gen.xx,xxii, Exod.iii, and I Sam.i,iii, ixf. are especially characteristic. On the other hand the danger that the pious man is valued too highly by E is by no means imaginary. The danger of an antithetical piety of religious nationalism which tends to make Israel's election degenerate into a state of being elect (cf.Gen. xx) is also manifest. The great Biblical prophets, beginning with Amos (ix.7) and Hosea(xii), had to oppose this piety as much as the ever-imminent danger of syncretism. It was this kind of piety that found acceptance most widely in the circles of the so-called 'false' (i.e. nationalistic) prophets of Yahweh (cf. the Pharisees in the New Testament who imagined that they and the people were safe because they belonged to 'the people of Yahweh').[1]

On a level with this prophetical criticism is the work of the *Deuteronomic* authors, which we can trace back in several of the historical books, from Genesis to 2 Kings[2], and which find its starting-point in the book of *Deuteronomy*. Its aim was to lead Israel back to the fulfilment of its calling as the chosen people of God; it calls the people to faithful obedience which must reveal itself in pure worship, but also in the circumcision of the heart and in doing well in accordance with God's commandments: love and the fear of God are the supreme commandments. All the beginning of Deuteronomy the people are reminded of God's special electing grace[3] in history and also of the covenant between God and their fathers, and on that ground an appeal is made to Israel to fulfil her duty to keep His commandments, to respond to its great divine calling in everyday life, in order that Israel may truly be what it is: God's holy people. It is the attempt to fix the true religious and ethical (cultic and social) way of life for Israel as the

[1] Cf. G.von Rad, 'Die falschen Propheten', *Z.A.W.*, 1933, pp. 109ff.; also G.Quell, *Wahre und falsche Propheten*, 1952, who emphasizes the inward, spiritual differences between these two 'groups' (between which there are no external differences); the false prophets are the professional ones; now also E.Osswald, *Falsche Prophetie im A.T.*, 1962.
[2] With M.Noth, *Überlieferungsgeschichtliche Studien*, I, 1943, we start from the idea that later Deuteronomistic writers in the days of the exile have edited the great history (in our opinion not from Deut.i, as Noth asserts, but from Gen.ii.f. to 2 Kings xxv). That this assumption is psychologically correct is evident from the fact that especially in times of political distress a nation harks back to its history, as in the Netherlands during the first few years of the German occupation, and in Germany e.g. after the French domination at the beginning of the nineteenth century (Fichte and others).
[3] In Deuteronomy the idea of election is for the first time emphatically associated with the people. The pre-Deuteronomic authors presuppose this conception, but have not yet worked it out as a fundamental theological conception (see *Die Erwählung Israels*); on the theology of Deuteronomy as a whole see H.Breit, *Die Predigt des Dt.*, 1933, and A.R.Hulst, *Het Karakter van de Cultus in Dt.*, 1938 (Doctorate thesis Groningen).

people of God. If we also take into account the meaning of the great Deuteronomic historical work (see p. 59 n. 2) it appears that the accent has shifted from the call to obedience to the warning, to retribution and the call to repentance. Disloyalty provokes God's anger (Judges iii. 10, 2 Kings xxi. 23), but repentance stirs Him to mercy. The all-important thing in history is loyalty to God's will and His work.

The guiding principles underlying Deuteronomy and the Deuteronomic history are fundamentally the same, but the historical background is different, and so, to a certain extent, is the aim of these works. The historical narrative was written after Israel's downfall and teaches many lessons from the historical events which showed the effects of disobedience in the historical catastrophe. Thus the work calls upon the people to repent and reform; the author still sets his hope on Yahweh and His promises.[1] Deuteronomy itself accentuates Israel's election and the covenant as well as its calling: because Israel is the chosen people it is called to actualize theocracy.[2] Being elect must find expression in the awareness of man's responsibility, otherwise it brings down judgment. We may characterize Deuteronomy as the book that thinks in terms of *theocracy* throughout, and proclaims it to the people in its full reality, thus reverting to one of the most important religious conceptions of ancient Israel.[3]

Behind Deuteronomy and the Deuteronomic writings there is a strong tendency to revert to old ideas, to tradition in its best and most radical form. For that reason Deuteronomy subordinates kingship, which indeed only plays a minor part here, very strictly to the will of God; and therefore, too, the standard the Deuteronomic writings apply to each of the kings is whether or not they conform to God's commandments. In the great historical work David is held up again and again as an example of *the* king of Israel; David, the man after God's heart, in whom the Deuteronomic authors see a promise of future salvation (2 Sam. vii). No wonder, then, that Messianic and Davidic, prophetic and theocratic religious conceptions are closely linked in later Deuteronomic theology.[4] The value that is attached to

[1] In his *Überlieferungsgeschichtliche Studien* I, 1943, p. 150, M. Noth, on the other hand, maintains that the Dtn (the Deuteronomic author of the great historical work) saw the downfall of the people as something definitive.
[2] It is most interesting that during the Deuteronomistic reformation the name of Yahweh comes to be used more and more in names of persons, and that also the artisticpictural element is neglected. The Deuteronomic period seems to have brought with it some sort of 'iconoclasm', cf. A. Reifenberg, *Ancient Hebrew Seals*, 1950, pp. 16, 17, 24.
[3] Cf. Chapter IX.
[4] On this see G. von Rad, 'Die deuteronomistische Geschichtstheologie in den Königsbüchern' (*Ges. Stud. z. A.T.*, pp. 189ff., Engl. transl.: *The Problem of the Hexateuch*);

David and Jerusalem with its temple where Yahweh had placed His name clearly expresses the peculiar theocratic way of thought of the Deuteronomic authors; on the other hand, the part played by the prophets and their message in the whole of the 'Deuteronomic history' is a clear indication of the way in which these authors revert to the prophets of the Old Testament.

As much as Deuteronomy the *Priestly Code* (P)[1] takes upon itself the object of reminding Israel that it is God's people. While with D the ritual is merely one of the forms in which the holiness of the people must manifest itself, the cult is of paramount importance in P. This change is due to the historical situation. When the exiles were allowed to return to their country after 539 to rebuild the temple and to restore the worship of Yahweh, a liturgical manual was urgently needed in order to acquaint the post-exilic generation anew with the form and meaning of the cult. The old temple tradition, which had been preserved in priestly circles, was committed to writing, though the early priestly laws were often reworded in a new spirit, under the influence of ancient prophetic criticism.[2]

Beside a liturgical manual, to be found in Leviticus i-vii and concerned with the sacrifices, several other treatises were included, dealing with purifications (Lev. xiff.), ordinations (Lev. viiiff.) and festivals (Lev. xvi), while in a historical introduction (Gen. i; v; xvii, Exod. xxvff.; xxxvff.) the origins of the cult and the earliest forms of ritual in the sanctuary (during the desert period at the tabernacle) are sketched. The description of the cult in Lev. xix–xxvi probably dates back still further. The whole of this compilation was collected mainly in the Priestly Code and is to be found scattered over the books of Leviticus and Numbers.[3] Finally it was integrated in the early great Deuteronomic historical work. This last revision of the ancient traditions led to the realization of the *Torah* (Pentateuch) and may have been accomplished by Ezrah. In this way the worship of God was impressed upon the people.

That it is not merely a question of ritual forms but that moral motives also played a part is evident from the fact that the Code of Holiness is also included in the Priestly Code. In this Code of Holiness moral laws are given as well as instructions concerning purification

Studies in Deuteronomy, 1953, B; *Theology* I, II, c, 6. H. W.Wolff, 'Das Kerugma des dtn. Geschichtswerkes', *Z.A.W.* 1961, pp. 171ff. denies the messianic idea in the Deuteronomistic history. Also Noth, see n. 1, p. 60.
[1] On P cf. G. von Rad, *Die Priesterschrift im Hexateuch*, 1934, and M. Noth, op. cit., pp. 180ff.
[2] See my *Die Erwählung Israels*, p. 82, and below, p. 62 n. 2 and p. 63f.
[3] In P we must distinguish between an older, shorter, and more 'popular' version, and a later, more technical and purely 'priestly' version. It is impossible to go into the details at greater length here.

and the cult (the famous chapter Lev. xix, containing among other things the demand to love one's neighbour as oneself, vs. 18b).[1]

As we mentioned above, the priestly school also contributed to history. Part of this contribution is what we might call 'scholarly': for example P gives a continuous chronology starting from the creation of the world, thus supplementing one of the trends initiated by the Deuteronomist[2] (for Deuteronomic historiography had also given history its place in a definite historical scheme). This historical 'scholarly' element we may pass without comment in our theological study, though its inclusion gives some indication of the line of development followed by Israelite theology: more and more the need was felt to emphasize the historical element.

There is, however, a third element which we must go into here, namely the systematically theological conception of history. The priestly author is no longer a religious narrator but a real theologian. He gives not only a world-picture but also a conception of history. P does not give a continuous narrative but a few main points of history linked, as it were, by dotted lines – the genealogical registers (cf. also the genealogical registers in the book of Chronicles). There are three main periods, marked by a divine Covenant: the Covenant with Noah, with Abraham and with Moses.

Each of these periods has a character of its own. In the pre-historic period man is, indeed, the master of the animal world but he is not allowed to kill animals. The animals are given the plants for food, man is given fruit-trees and grain. So in this first period a state of perfect peace on earth between man and the animals is presupposed as the original situation (we should think here of Isa. xi. 6ff., the future state of grace).

In the period after Noah man is allowed to eat the flesh of animals, but he may not partake of their blood. There is a special injunction not to shed human blood (Gen. ix). God grants His covenant to man and promises not to exterminate mankind by a deluge again.

The third period is inaugurated by the Covenant of God with Abraham, of which circumcision is the token.

The fourth period is that of the full revelation, in which Yahweh makes Himself known as the God of Israel and gives the people His laws and the priestly cult of Aaron through which atonement can be obtained for the sins of the people.

All this implies the universalist conception of God as well as the

[1] Cf. my 'Bubers Auslegung des Liebesgebotes, Lev. 19:18b', *Th.Z.*, 1966, pp. 1–11.
[2] These additions probably go back to ancient documents from the temple records, even if only via oral tradition in the priestly schools. Deuteronomic-prophetical renovations were introduced. See the next pages on the regulations concerning sin- and guilt-offerings.

peculiar relation between Israel and God. God is the God of the world, but He has bound Israel to Himself in a special way. This also applied to mankind in general, for man is the Image of God and that is the token of His intimate relation with God. There is a close relationship between man and God; God even grants him dominion over the world which he must people and rule, but on the other hand true communion with God is only possible in Israel. Besides that, the narrative of the Creation lays great stress on the transcendence of God, who by His word calls the world into existence. This transcendence is also found in the emphasis on the miraculous element that is typical of the stories of the desert journey and the deliverance from Egypt. All the leading ideas of the religion of Israel are found here. Transcendence and communion between God and man, universalism and particularism, prophetical and cultic vision have been balanced. This balance strongly dominates P's conceptions, as is evident particularly in the Creation narrative. God's work of creation above all is creating the world-order. This is also closely connected with a strong ethical trait in his conceptions: we are told emphatically that Noah, who is saved out of the Deluge, is righteous *(saddiq)* and irreproachable *(tamim)* in the midst of a wicked world, and that he walked with God (Gen. vi. 9; vii. 1*b*). These same things God also expects from Abraham before He concludes His covenant with the patriarch (Gen. xvii. 1). The author, therefore, does not assume that election is arbitrary but he thinks man must come up to the standards of the divine will in order to be chosen. In the Mosaic Covenant the cult is the means of restoring the right relation to God again and again. *Ṣedaqah* (righteousness) and the covenant are, therefore, connected (as also in Pss. xv, xxiv; Ezek. xviii); the cult is the means of grace that again and again restores this *ṣedaqah* by redeeming the sins of Israel (*kipper* means to 'smear' and to wipe off) and thus maintains the covenant relation. The cult is, however, not a magical means (*ex opere operato*); the sin- and guilt-offerings can only atone for sins committed *bi-shegagah* (= through ignorance; Lev. iv f.). This condition shows the influence of prophetical criticism on the pre-exilic penitential offerings, and thus the danger of becoming automatic – a danger that threatens every cultic sacrament of penance – is avoided. On the other hand the sacrament also loses its general validity. P cannot simply be called sacramentarian!

The importance of the cult in P is, of course, bound up with the fact that the most characteristic ritual traits of Israel's religion, which were formerly ascribed to Moses (the sabbath, cf. Exod. xx; circumcision, cf. Exod. iv. 24 ff.; eating meat with the blood, see Exod. xxii. 31) were considered by him as ancient institutions established by God Himself. As circumcision is *the* token of the covenant it must *a priori* have been given to Abraham, with whom God made the covenant. As blood is sacred to God alone, the use of blood must *a priori* have been forbidden at the moment when man was allowed to kill animals (Noah). The fact that God sanctified the seventh day at the Creation is to be explained in the same way: God, who appoints the days, months and years, has instituted the Sabbath from the beginning.

On the one hand P is the systematizer who reduces the ancient points of doctrine to a new system, on the other hand he makes the cultic actions come alive again for the people. In so far as he is the transmitter and editor of the ancient cultic laws he is spiritually reliable and of importance, but his treatment of historical events is sometimes fanciful (some of the numbers he uses were arrived at in accordance with a cabbalistic system). His theological conception of history is strongly constructive and anachronistic. The greatest thing he has given (or probably transmitted) is the narrative of the Creation, which so superbly expresses the glory of God. In this chapter the universe is linked with God, and the light of the loving and glorious God of Israel shines upon the whole world. As this chapter stands at the beginning of the whole of the Old Testament, it leaves a very special mark on the canon.

A few more words on the *Torah* as a whole. In the last century it was pulled to pieces to such an extent that there was hardly anything left of its unity, spiritual as well as historical and literary: everything was called primitive, naive, half or wholly polytheistic, monotheistic or sacramentalistic; in this way the differences were vastly exaggerated. We pointed out above (pp. 51 ff.) that there is a very pronounced unity in the writings of the Torah, notwithstanding the variations and tensions it contains, because these writings all speak of the same holy God who enters into communion with man; this holiness and this communion are met with in all these writings, though the manner in which this communion is effected is depicted in different ways, from a very strikingly anthropomorphic to a more spiritual manner. Both universalism and particularism are to be found in all these writings: Yahweh is the Lord of the world but also stands in a special relation to Israel. For all of them the divine calling is an unalterable fact, but the one (the primeval history and J) lays more stress on divine calling and grace, the other (D) on election and faithful obedience (duty), a third (E, P) on righteousness and divine favour. In the primeval history and in J the emphasis falls on the sins of all, others stress rather the piety of the chosen. All the authors consider the cult as the expression of the right relation to God, they all know that the ceremonies in themselves are insufficient to maintain this right relation to God (P too!; cf. the admission that sin- and guilt-offerings can only atone for un-

64

intentional sins), and they all demand righteousness ('doing well') as the condition for communion with God. P emphasizes, it is true, cultic activity as the means of maintaining communion between God and Israel, but this cultic activity is no longer magical and sacramentalistic in character, though a dynamistic trait in the representation of the atonement was not overcome entirely (see p. 31 f.).

Each of these emphases is valuable, and each has its dangerous points. The author of the primeval history has anti-cultural tendencies, E is steeped in an antithetic pietism, D's attitude may lead to moralism when guilt and punishment, obedience and prosperity are dialectically linked in too close a manner (which happens, indeed, in Deuteronomistic historiography), P may lead to sacramentalism, – and all these things have, indeed, occurred in Israel. There are limits to every religious conception! Even the conception of the people of God, professed by all, became a serious spiritual danger – which already becomes manifest in the Old Testament (the false prophets), but even more in the New Testament (the Pharisees). The prophets already realized this; cf. that Amos – though he accepts the special relation in iii, 2 – emphatically rejects the conception that the special favour of God should mean anything else but the fact that Israel received a special task (compare iii. 2 with ix. 7).

We have dealt with the *Torah* rather extensively because many theological lines from widely different periods come together here. With the other *historical books (nebiim rishonim)* we can, however, deal briefly, because the connection in which these books were included in the Old Testament is in great part determined by the influence of the Deuteronomic authors, on whose theological ideas we already commented in our discussion of Deuteronomy itself (see above, pp. 59ff.).

Apart from the theological framework of the Deuteronomic compilers, the books of *Samuel* and *Kings*, at any rate, are dominated by political rather than theological tendencies. This is certainly true of the former.[1]

These books hinge upon the apology for the house of David (1 Sam. xi to 1 Kings ii, except for certain chapters that were added afterwards). In spite of all his faults David is shown as the man after God's heart, the true king of Israel whom God desired and to whom an eternal kingdom was prophesied in the basic prophecy of Nathan, 2 Sam. vii.[2]

[1] On the books of Samuel see my discussion in *Orientalia Neerlandica*, 1948, pp. 167ff: 'De compositie van de Samuelboeken'; L. Rost, *Die Überlieferung von der Thronnachfolge Davids*, 1926.
[2] See pp. 60f., 60 n. 4; on 2 Sam. vii: M. Noth, 'David u. Israel in 2 Sam. 7', *Robert Festschrift*, pp. 122ff.; E. Kutsch, 'Die Dynastie von Gottes Gnaden', *Z. Th. K.* 1961,

Here lies the origin of the *form* of the later expectation of salvation, which was centred in the house of David. The idea of the Covenant may be considered the deepest foundation of the expectation of salvation.[1] It took the Messianic form, that is, it centres round a definite king who brings salvation, and this is due to Nathan's prophecy concerning the house of David.[2] On that account the expected salvation of Israel is placed in the hands of an anointed king in many circles The figure of David and his dynasty became the starting-point of Israel's expectation and hope, not only in the prophetical books, but also in the Deuteronomic historical books, and especially in Chronicles. For the *Chronicler* the promise of Israel's eternal kingdom is centred in David (not in Abraham); the foundation of the temple is essentially his work and his task is continued in the priestly cult; he is even called the man of God (2 Chron. viii. 14).

This conception is already found in the book of *Kings*, too (cf. 1 Kings xi. 12,36; xv. 4; 2 Kings viii. 19; xviii. 3; xx.5f.; xxi. 7; xxii. 2), though it is there linked with other elements of a historical and didactic nature which remind us of the historiography of the prophets (especially related to E, cf. the stories of Elijah, Hezekiah and Isaiah) and the religious didactics of Deuteronomy (see pp.60f.).

When we compare the *Torah* and the *Nebiim rishonim* (the early prophets, i.e. the historical books from Joshua to Kings), we may say that in the latter the fundamental ideas of the conception of history of the authors of the *Torah* (especially of Deuteronomy) are met with again. The only new element of importance is the figure of David as the king who brings salvation. Judaism has recognized quite rightly that the *Torah* is and remains the central collection of the 'historical' writings. The early prophets became, as it were, an appendix to the *Torah*, closely linked to it by Deuteronomy and the Deuteronomic historical work. One might, therefore, speak with good reason of an *Enneateuch* (a collection of nine books), consisting of the Pentateuch and the *Nebiim rishonim*.[3]

---

pp. 131ff.; A. Caquot, 'La prophétie de Nathan', *Suppl. V.T.* IX, 1963, pp. 213ff. and G. W. Ahlström, 'Der Prophet Nathan und der Tempelbau', *V.T.* 1961, pp. 113ff.

[1] Cf. L. H.K. Bleeker, *Over de betekenis en oorsprong van de israëlitische heilsverwachting*, and A. H. J. Gunneweg, 'Sinaibund und Davidbund', *V.T.* 1960, pp. 335ff.

[2] With the above-mentioned article by Gunneweg (n. 1) we should adhere to the connection between the conceptions of the Sinai-covenant and the David-covenant; cf. also O. Eißfeldt, 'Silo und Jerusalem', *Suppl. V.T.* 1957, pp. 138ff. as opposed to Von Rad, who places the David-Sion tradition as a separate southern tradition by the side of the northern patriarchal and exodus tradition, *O.T. Theology* I, IC 2, 3 and II c 2; cf. on this also E. Rohland, *Die Bedeutung der Erwählungstraditionen Israels für die Eschatologie der alttest. Propheten* (thesis Heidelberg 1956). See also S. Amsler, *David, Roi et Messie*, 1963.

[3] See O. Eißfeldt, *The O.T. An Introduction*, 1965, § 22, 1.

The second important series of Old Testament books, which is essentially on a level with the *Torah*, is the collection of *prophetical books*. In the Hebrew Bible it consists of the three 'major Prophets' (Isaiah, Jeremiah and Ezekiel) and the book of the 'Twelve minor prophets' (Hosea–Malachi). This group of writings was closed and canonized later than the Torah but certainly before 200 B.C.[1] Most of these books were already considered authoritative before 500, but their compilation apparently took a great deal of time: fairly late apocalyptic passages were added to the collections by way of appendices.

This series of prophets[2] whose words have been preserved for us in the Old Testament, may be looked upon as one group, even if a period of 250 years separates the appearance of Amos and Malachi and even if far later additions were incorporated into their work. For, though each of them has his own distinctive characteristics there is a close connection between them; their teaching links up as do the links of a chain; they take over, as it were, each other's message and even each other's words: sometimes the connection is quite evident, as between Jeremiah, Hosea and Micah, between Amos, Isaiah, Micah and Zephaniah, and between Isaiah and Deutero-Isaiah, to mention only some of the most striking instances.[3] After the exile Zechariah deliberately takes the message of the pre-exilic prophets for his starting-point (Zech. i. 1ff.).

The main reason, however, why these prophets may be said to form a group by themselves is that they constitute a peculiar phenomenon within the Israelite religion and even within the world of the Israelite prophets. Sometimes the error is made of attempting a general religio-historical reconstruction of Israelite prophecy on the basis of the type (or types) presented by the prophets whose words were preserved in the Old Testament. Such a reconstruction, however, has little to commend it, for the results of recent research into the origins and forms of prophecy lead more and more to the recognition of the multiplicity of forms in which it manifests itself. These results also justify the conclusion that within the framework of this prophetism the Biblical prophets have a particular place of their own.[4] They have some characteristics in common with other prophets, it is true, but they often stand alone in sharp opposition to their people, and their message differs widely from that of their fellow-prophets.

---

[1] On this see the Introductions to the O.T.
[2] A few summaries may be mentioned here. A.Kuenen, *The prophets and prophecy in Israel*, 1877; B.Duhm, *Die Theologie der Propheten*, 1875, *Israels Propheten*, 1916; J.J.P.Valeton, *Amos en Hosea*, 1894; W.R.Smith, *The Prophets of Israel*[2], 1895; C.H. Cornill, *Der israelitische Prophetismus*, 1896; P.de Buck, *De Profeten van Israel*, (n.d.); A.B.Davidson, *O.T. Prophecy*, 1903; G.Hölscher, *Die Propheten*, 1914; T.H.Robinson, *Prophecy and the Prophets in Ancient Israel*, 1924; J.Ridderbos, *Het Godswoord der Profeten*, I–IV, 1930ff.; J.Keulers, J.Kroon and A.van den Born, *Bijbelse Monographieën, Jeremias, Jesaias, Ezechiël*, 1933ff.; P.Volz, *Prophetengestalten des A.T.*, 1938; J. Paterson, *The Goodly Fellowship of the Prophets*, 1948; J. Hempel, *Worte der Propheten*, 1949; M.Buber, *Der Glaube der Propheten*, 1950; W.Zimmerli, *The law and the prophets*, 1965. For literature on prophecy in general see p. 256f.
[3] See a.o. K.Gross, *Die literarische Verwandtschaft Jeremias mit Hosea*, 1930; J.W.Miller, *Das Verhältnis Jeremias und Hesekiels*, 1955; R.Frey, *Amos und Jesaja*, 1963.
[4] See for instance my *The Religion*, chapter VIII.

There were various kinds of prophets: cultic prophets, attached to the temple, who were at the same time government officials, for temple and state are fundamentally one; there was a highly ecstatic prophetism, which reminds us of pre- and non-Israelite divinational phenomena; there were 'group-prophets' who belonged to mystical communities, and also independent prophets.

The Biblical prophets have many characteristics that remind us strongly of these various forms of prophecy. Some of them have disciples (reminiscent of group-prophecy); some have ecstatic tendencies (Ezekiel), while other apparently reject all fanaticism (Jeremiah); a few may be temple-prophets while the majority show strongly individual characteristics. But though their behaviour often does not differ from that of the other contemporary prophets, their attitude is fundamentally different. Again and again they come into conflict with their people, they stand alone, they are fighters, and sometimes bear the mark of martyrs; the clearest instances of this are Amos (vii), Micah (iii), Jeremiah (passim) and Deutero-Isaiah (l). They are distinguished by their directly personal calling and by the intensity of their preaching. Their message is characterized by the radical terms in which Yahweh is proclaimed (Yahweh alone) and by their *actualization* of faith (at this very moment Yahweh is acting and claiming man). This explains their insistence upon repentance and the severity with which they point out the sins of the people – cultic sins, but especially those in the realm of social and religious ethics. Ultimately the prophetical message is dominated particularly by their application of the eschatological expectations, always current in Israel, (the New Age, the Day of the Lord) to the present and to the immediate future. The realization of this expectation is preached as a severe judgment which will restore only a remnant of the people. The prophets view Israel's salvation in the light of the calling of the people by the Holy God (Amos iii. 2) and the future in the light of the imminent catastrophes of the present. Their radical actualization of Israel's faith leads to the more profound sincerity of inward contrition and also to an 'eschatologization' of spiritual life in its entirety.[1]

These men do not live a mystical life with God, though they are aware of the fact that they see Him working through contemporary events. Here is no mystical vision but the understanding *of faith*, which sees reality as the fulfilment of the will of God. History and life become transparent, because God is quite near, the *auctor primus* of all that happens, pursuing a definite purpose in all that He does.

Therefore everything they see happening is significant. The downfall of Israel and Judah is significant; it is God's judgment, for the course of history is no incomprehensible tragic happening enacted against an obscure background, but these obscure happenings are the footprints of God in His judgment, who in this way prepares the ground for His Kingdom. God, who is a consuming fire, reveals Himself in the sinful world and purges it by fire. The flames and ruins are so many signs that the Holy One rules the world and that He proceeds with His work.

But exactly because the prophets understand this, they have a message for their age: the twofold message of repentance and of future salvation. 'History is no mere story of human activity to be viewed, dissected, and described as one would analyse mathematical statistics. It is the arena of the creative activity of the living, righteous, holy God – a God whose works permit no

[1] This latter aspect is brought into a too one-sided prominence by Von Rad in his *Theology* II.

68

description apart from a clarion call to repentance and conversion.'[1]

In the sight of God, who is approaching with His judgment, the prophets fight for the salvation of their people, to bring them to repentance and renewal of life. But people all follow their own paths, buying and selling, cheating and offering up sacrifices as if nothing much had happened. And thus the prophets had to struggle on for two centuries, until judgment had been consummated and a small remnant woke up to the truth of the prophetic message and then God starts creating a new people from this remnant.

For that reason the prophets stood alone in the midst of their people; they played the same part as St. Francis, Pascal, Bunyan and Kierkegaard in later times.

After this general survey of the elements which these figures have in common we shall now proceed to sketch the individual characteristics of the preaching of each of them.

The message of *Amos*[2], the farmer from Tekoa who was called by God, introduced a new element into the religion of Israel; many scholars have realized this, but it has often been expressed inaccurately, for instance by the statement that Amos introduced moral monotheism[3]; for the faith of Israel knows of Yahweh as a moral as well as absolute God. In Amos's message there is no evidence to show that he realized that he proclaimed God in a new way; on the contrary, he associates himself with the ancient preaching about God and salvation (iii. 2). There might rather be some ground for counting him among the reactionaries, as does J. Pedersen[4], though this is not an adequate characterization of this highly original man of God. For it must be admitted that his preaching does, indeed, introduce a new element into the religion of Israel, from the moment when his eyes were opened to the fact that God will no longer spare His people but will punish them with His judgment (the visions, esp. the third, vii. 7ff., fourth, viii. 1ff., and fifth, ix. 1ff.). He foresees these terrible events, but nobody believes him, for his appearance coincides with the prosperous reign of Jeroboam II of Israel (*c.* 750), when no one could yet suspect what misery Tiglath-Pileser (745–727) was to inflict on Syria and Palestine. These events did not merely dominate Amos's life but also caused a new element in Yahwism to spring up. For from the fire of this judgment the sparks fly all around: the nations all round Israel are to be chastised by God, but, above all things, salvation presents itself in a wholly new light, in the light of responsibility and guilt (iii. 2). For a long time the expectation of the glorious day of Yahweh, an idea

[1] G. E. Wright, *Challenge of Israel's Faith*, 1953, p. 39.
[2] The characteristic features of this prophet are shown extremely well by R. Smend in his 'Das Nein des Amos', *Ev. Th.*, 1963, pp. 404ff.
[3] For example A. Kuenen, *The Religion of Israel* I–III, 1874/5, and, indeed, as recently as R. H. Pfeiffer, *Introduction to the O.T.*, 1941.
[4] Joh. Pedersen, *Israel, its life and culture*, III–IV.

founded on ancient prophecies and on the Psalms used in the cult[1], had already been a living conception among the people, but now this expectation comes to be seen in a new light, too. From now on the whole people fall under this judgment and the sins of the people, especially the social abuses, are laid bare with the utmost severity, while the outward show of religion, promoted by all sorts of sacramental ritual of a cult which developed more and more, is also denounced strongly. When unexpectedly this preaching came to be fulfilled it became a tremendous force strengthening the moral, spiritual, supra-national and directly historical character of faith in Yahweh. Israel had been conscious of this ever since their experience under the leadership of Moses, it is true, but a purification, especially of the element of salvation, had become imperative because the relationship between God and the people was looked upon too much as a matter of course, in imitation of other oriental religions.[2] From now on the element of grace in the deliverance from Egypt is brought out clearly by the prophets. The catastrophes that befell the Northern kingdom in quick succession proved that Amos's prophecies concerning the coming judgment were only too true: an unexpected experience that induced other prophets to speak too, though often with certain changes in emphasis.

The North Israelite prophet *Hosea*[3] came to be involved in the work of God in a most peculiar manner; he is called upon to depict this symbolically in his conjugal life: on the one hand God's incomprehensible love of His unfaithful people, on the other hand God's judgment. While Amos brings the justice of God into prominence, Hosea stresses God's love of Israel (ch. ii and xi) and also demands that Israel should return God's love (vi. 6) instead of being content with offering up sacrifices. In various ways the defection of the people is depicted, especially the cultic infidelity evident from the influence of the worship of Baal, while less attention is paid to social abuses (xii. 8f.). Hosea represents the judgment as a return to the desert period (ch. ii) but he expects it to bring about the conversion of Israel and a propitious restoration (ch. ii; xii. 10f.; xiv). This side of the prophetic message is emphasized more strongly by him than by Amos.

Micah is a slightly younger contemporary; like Amos he came from the South, from Judah. Whereas Hosea addressed his warning in

[1] See Mowinckel, *Psalmenstudien*, II, 1922. I cannot agree with Mowinckel that the disappointment at the delay in the fulfilment of the expectations led to eschatology. Here Mowinckel detracts from the merits of the prophets; see Ch. IX.
[2] See I. L. Seeligmann, 'Phasen uit de Geschiedenis van het Joods historisch bewustzijn', in *Kernmomenten der antieke Beschaving*, 1947, pp. 49ff., esp. p. 56.
[3] H. Wheeler Robinson, *Two Hebrew Prophets* (Hosea, Ezekiel), 1948; cf. *Interpretation,* July 1961, with contributions by W. Eichrodt, H. W. Wolff, D. Ritschl, W. Vischer

particular to Israel and in the second place also to Judah, the exact reverse is found with Micah. He prophesies the fall of Samaria, it is true, but his preaching of repentance is particularly directed against Judah. He is the first prophet to announce directly the fall of Jerusalem and the destruction of the temple (iii. 12); in this respect he is the forerunner of Jeremiah (cf. Jer. xxvi).

In Micah's preaching we find again elements that are familiar to us from Amos and also from Isaiah, such as the denunciation of social abuses, but his criticism is also levelled at false prophets and other leaders (ch. ii f.). As with Amos and Hosea the unfounded reliance on the sacrificial cult is vehemently denounced (vi. 6ff.), and over against the demand to offer up sacrifices the other command is set of the love of God and one's fellow-men. The preaching of Amos and Hosea is, as it were, summed up in Micah vi. 8: 'He hath shewed thee, O man, what is good: and what doth the Lord require of thee, but to do justly, and to love mercy, and to walk humbly with thy God?'[1]

Micah was not only a forceful preacher of penitence but he also saw the coming of better times for Israel after the judgment and repeatedly bears testimony to this. In iv. 1 ff. we find again the well-known idea of universal salvation which appears in Isaiah ii, and in v. 1 ff. he announces the coming of the Messianic kingdom again in words reminiscent of Isaiah (xi).

The greatest of all the prophets of the period of the kings is *Isaiah*, as Deutero-Isaiah may be called the greatest of the post-exilic men of God. He did not confine himself to preaching to the kings of his age, he also wanted to take political action – he understood that faith is not merely a matter of the inner room and of expectation, but that it is of decisive importance for present action.

He proclaims the ancient faith in God's saving power in a new form. It is he who places faith in the foreground (vii. 9; xxviii. 16; xxx. 15), not only in his preaching but also in his actions (vii; x. 5ff.; xxxviff.); he becomes the religious adviser of the young king Hezekiah and to his attitude it is due that Jerusalem was not surrendered to the Assyrian pillagers. His faith in God finds expression in the two names for God, used especially by him: *Yahweh Ṣebaoth*[2], denoting God as the Almighty in the absolute sense of the word (while, on the other hand, in xxxi. 3 man is called flesh, i.e. a transient being), and also *Qedosh Yisra'el* (the Holy One of Israel). The latter name is also found over and over again in Deutero-Isaiah; the emphasis laid by Isaiah on the holiness of

---

[1] Amos does not use the word *chesed*, which dominates the message of Hosea; the most important word in Amos is *mishpat*; in Micah both these words are found together in one verse.
[2] See p. 298.

God originates in the vision of his calling (vi) where Yahweh is celebrated as the Holy One by the Seraphs at His throne; God's holiness is contrasted with human sin and uncleanness, which were also borne in upon him at that moment (vi. 5ff.).[1]

This awareness of God's holiness opens his eye to the sins of the people and to the impending judgment. In Isaiah's prophecies Yahweh now rejects Israel and calls it: *that* people, then again He calls it *my* people, as the God of love who elects His people. On that ground Isaiah prophecies the ultimate universal importance of Sion as well as the fall of Israel and Judah, and even Jerusalem.[2] He knows that the God of Israel uses the power of the Assyrians to chastise His own people, but also that that same God has defined the limits of their power (x. 5ff.); he expects that a small remnant will be saved out of this judgment and that a new people will spring from this remnant[3] (Isa. vii 3, 22; xxviii. 5; cf. viii. 16ff.; xiv. 32; xxviii. 16; also the later x. 20f. and the gloss at the end of vi. 13). In xxix. 1–8 the wonderful acts of this God who performs both these things after His decree and in this way reveals Himself as the Lord, are depicted emphatically (cf. xxviii. 21). Isaiah is the prophet of the strongest contrasts, we might call him the man of the paradox. He always clings to God's love of Israel, even in the midst of judgment; for that reason better times are coming for Israel, and especially for Jerusalem, and therefore he cherishes high hopes of a messianic king from the house of David. In chapter ix the fulfilment of this expectation seems to him to be very near; in xi it is the idea of the remnant, in connection with this expectation, which is stressed more strongly: only the rod out of the stem of Jesse shall come forth and bear fruit (the name of David is avoided here; only the root is left of this royal house); though here, too, the continuity has not been broken entirely (a remnant), the hope of salvation is made conditional on God's intervention, more so than in ch. ix. Isaiah, too, knows a spiritual growth, an ever deepening insight into the work of God. With him, more than with other prophets, hope keeps pace with faith; with him this hope gains wideness of scope: it becomes universal (ii), spiritual (xi. 1ff., ix) and cosmic (xi. 6ff.).

[1] See my 'Essentials of the Theology of Isaiah' in: J. Muilenburg Festschrift: *Israels prophetic heritage*, 1962.
[2] On Isaiah's views with respect to Jerusalem see E. Rohland, *op. cit.*, G. von Rad, *Theology* I, II, J. Schreiner, *Sion-Jerusalem, Jahwes Königssitz* I, 1963; also my *Jahwe en zijn stad*, 1963 and my contribution to Festschrift Muilenburg *Israel's prophetic heritage*, 1962, pp. 128ff.: 'Essentials of the Theology of Isaiah'.
[3] In his *O.T. Theology* II, II B 1., von Rad thinks the idea of the remnant is not theologically relevant in Isaiah; vss. x. 20ff. which are indeed to be considered of early date, and the gloss in vi. 13 prove that Isaiah's disciples were of a different opinion.

With *Zephaniah*, an older contemporary of Jeremiah, the message of Amos seems to take on a new form, as we have also observed with Isaiah and Micah. His prophecy, however, small, and however reminiscent of the message of others, is a pure reflection of the fundamental idea of the Old Testament prophets. His words show how greatly he is moved by the coming judgment; he sees the impending downfall wholly in the light of the Day of the Lord, which is for him, too, the day of judgment (ch. i). There is 'perhaps' a chance of salvation and for that reason he exhorts the people for the last time, as it were, to mend its ways (ii. 1ff.). Like all the other prophets he sees the judgment of God as a world-judgment, which is to fall upon the other nations as well (ii. 4ff.), but for them, too, he sees better times approach; together with Israel they, too, shall be purified and worship the true God (iii. 9f.). Those who escape this catastrophe will be an 'afflicted and poor people'. Apparently, the idea of the remnant still survives with him, and he, too, looks forward to the day when Yahweh, as the God of Zion, will be in its midst and will rejoice over it.

In the book of *Nahum* we hear a prophet who announces the destruction of Nineveh (i. 11-14) and who after the downfall sings the three songs on the destruction of Nineveh (ii; iii. 1–17; iii. 18f.). He has sometimes been considered one of the nationalistic 'false' prophets, but there is no evidence for this. Would not all nations, and all the Judeans have hailed the downfall of this 'bloody city' with grateful joy as well as astonishment? (iii. 19).

The prophecy of *Habakkuk* presents difficulties of interpretation. The somewhat vague form of its message may be the reason why the book was very popular with the sect that dwelt in the Judean desert (the Essenes), who thought the work had particular reference to the events of their days, as appears from a commentary on Habakkuk recently discovered in that area. The prophet, an older contemporary of Jeremiah, wrote during the period of the downfall of Assyria and the rise of the Chaldees. His agonizing problem is how God, who is 'of purer eyes than to behold evil' and who cannot 'look on iniquity', can look 'upon them that deal treacherously' (i. 12–17). The vicissitudes of Fortune which again and again allow the wicked to assume control, confront him with difficult problems. The answer is that the wicked shall perish and that the just shall live by their faith (ii. 1–5). The prophecy gives us an insight into the spiritual struggle of the faithful who witnessed the enormous revolutionary changes of about 612 (the fall of Nineveh). The faith in God's justice survives even this severe test. Theologically the booklet is important because of the well-known words of ii. 4*b*, quoted by St. Paul in Rom. i. 17 and Gal. iii. 11. As a document for the history of religion the book is valuable because it apparently contains a prophecy by a cultic prophet[1], whose preparations for receiving the divine message are described in ii. 1.

In *Jeremiah* many lines converge: the influence of Deuteronomy, Hosea, Micah and Isaiah can be perceived more or less clearly in his work. More than with other prophets we can see from Jeremiah's private life what the consequences of a prophet's office prove to be to an ever-increasing degree; the prophet himself becomes a sacrifice in the struggle for God to save the people even in spite of themselves.[2] Jeremiah's sufferings, described in his Confessions, figure largely in his book. Lamentations iii and perhaps also the description of the suffering Servant of the Lord of Isa. liif. may have been influenced by his life. It is by no means strange that some people identified Jesus with Jeremiah, returned from the dead (Matt. xvi. 14); if any figure of the Old Testament besides the Servant of the Lord can be compared with Christ, it is Jeremiah.

He is a prophet with whom the personal element is of great importance; he does not merely transmit the word of God but he himself wrestles with that word and wrestles with God for his people. In his preaching the destructive element is in the forefront; constructive activity is a secondary consideration (i. 10). This prophet, who, like Hosea, felt God's love of Israel so strongly is used by God as His messenger in the most ruthless age. No wonder that in such an age his message assumes the most radical forms and that he judges all forms of religious life by purely spiritual standards. Like Micah he, too, prophesies the destruction of the temple; like Amos he rejects a sacrificial cult which does not rest on the obedience to God's will, and denies that the earliest laws of Israel referred to sacrifices (Jer. vii, esp. vss. 21ff.). The politico-messianic expectation of salvation does not play a prominent part (xxiii. 5ff.), but the restoration of Israel and Judah is beyond all doubt (xxxf.). He does not expect salvation to spring from a future dispensation of the Spirit (the Spirit does not figure in his life and preaching, probably because his opponents, the false prophets, believed that they possessed the Spirit, cf. xxiii. 9ff.), but rather from a personal relationship between God and the people and from a personal knowledge of God (xxxi. 31–34). He therefore demands again and again the conversion of the heart (iv. 4; ix. 24ff.), and of the people he demands, with Deuteronomy, that they shall live to the glory of God (xiii. 11; cf. Deut. xxvi. 19).

The prophet *Obadiah*, who probably lived immediately after the destruction of Jerusalem, condemns Edom in particular, though the other nations will not escape divine judgment (15). Judgment had

---

[1] Cf. P. Humbert, *Problèmes du livre d'Habacuc*, 1944.
[2] Cf. H. J. Stoebe, 'Prophet und Seelsorger', *Th.Z.*, 1964, pp. 385ff.

already been executed upon Israel, and Obadiah expects the restoration of his people. His prophecy, pervaded by the spirit of the Jewish community of the first years after the destruction of Jerusalem, is full of a firm faith in the coming of the kingdom of God (21).

Ezekiel[1] was a contemporary of Jeremiah. They were both priests and it is therefore very likely that they were acquainted. Yet there is little to show that they quoted each other's prophecies (cf. Jer. xxxi. 29f. and Ezek. xviii. 2). It is not impossible that before he became a prophet Ezekiel was Jeremiah's opponent and after he was called to be a prophet in 593 at Babylon (where he had lived since 597) there was little opportunity for them to come into contact.[2]

After his call (if.) Ezekiel proved to be a powerful and particularly severe prophet. In the vision of his calling he came to know God in His awe-inspiring Majesty so that more than any other Old Testament preacher, he became conscious of the contrast between God and sinful man. Like Hosea (xii. 4) he also proclaims that from the beginning Israel has been a rebellious people (xvi; xx; xxiii), worse even than Sodom (xvi. 46ff.); but, like Hosea and Jeremiah, he also proclaims God's wonderful love of this people (xvi. 4–14), a love that is not only of the past but also of the future, for God does not abandon His people; He may chastise them with great severity but after that punishment He will remember His covenant with Israel and establish an everlasting covenant with His people (xvi. 53–63). These two strands of judgment and salvation are interwoven closely and wonderfully in his preaching. Even in the midst of the worst catastrophe that befell his people he remains confident of God's love and justice; as a judgment the downfall of Israel is inevitable, because God is a just God. He is so convinced of this justice of God that, in the teeth of pessimism and unbelief, he insists that even in the judgment that has come upon Israel God remains absolutely just towards the individual (Ezek. iii. 16ff.; xviii). Yet here, too, he repeats again and again that God has no pleasure at all in the sinner dying, but desires that he should turn from his ways, and live (xviii. 23, 32).

The restoration of Israel, too, announced so emphatically in ch. xxxvi, xxxvii, xl–xlviii is due to nothing but the will of God. Israel had done nothing to deserve this restoration, God only accomplishes it to glorify His Name, desecrated by Israel in the eye of the world (xxxvi. 22ff.). The promises of the new heart and of the Spirit of God within (xxxvi. 26f.) are the greatest that Ezekiel has to offer; the fulfilment of these promises bears out that Yahweh is the God of Israel and that

[1] W. Zimmerli, 'Ezechiel, ein Zeuge der Gerechtigkeit Gottes', in *Das A.T. als Anrede*, 1956, pp. 37ff.
[2] Cf. J. W. Miller, *op. cit.* (above p. 67).

Israel is His people. Ezekiel is also aware of the politico-messianic promise of salvation in the form of the restoration of the house of David (xxxiv. 23f.), and, moreover, he looks forward to a cultic renaissance (xl–xlviii). This prophet remained a priest at heart, as is also evident from the affinity of many of his ideas with the Law of Holiness (Lev. xvii–xxv).[1] He never opposes the sacrificial cult, as Jeremiah does. And here we may have the ultimate reason why these two contemporaries could not go together but went their separate ways, in spite of the fact that their ideas and expectations are fundamentally the same.

Deutero-Isaiah.[2] The chapters xl–lxvi of Isaiah are usually attributed in whole or in part to a second Isaiah, who lived during the Exile. In many respects a close inward resemblance between the two authors becomes apparent, especially in Deutero-Isaiah's very universalistic mode of thought and in the fact that, like the first Isaiah, he thinks of God first and foremost as the Holy One of Israel.

Yet a new spirit also reveals itself in Isa. xlff. The first Isaiah speaks of future downfall and salvation while Jerusalem, the holy city, still stands; Isa. xlff. were written by a man who has passed through the terrible ordeal with his people and who is pining for deliverance; God is the God of Israel, but only because He is the Creator of the world (xl). With the first Isaiah it is, as it were, just the reverse: to him Yahweh is first and foremost the God of Israel and as such He is also the God of the world. There is a definite change of emphasis. Though this does not mean that Deutero-Isaiah was the first universal thinker in Israel, it is clear that universalism is a very prominent element in his work. In this way the Exile tended to enrich the revelation of God in Israel.

The same is true of the experience gained by Deutero-Isaiah with his people in the period of the highest expectations, though the experience was negative and therefore led to altogether different results. For the prophet, who in the greatest exaltation had proclaimed the salvation of Zion, who had praised God's majesty and His love of Israel, who had glorified His power to his people, met with nothing but disappointment on the part of this people. He found little but blunt unbelief and succeeded only very partially in stirring the people to new life and to faith in what God was doing for His people (xlii. 18ff.; xlix. 14; l. 1f. and li. 12ff.). Another idea put forward by this prophet was that God intends to do still greater things for Israel: He will not only save it but above all He will use it as a light to the

---

[1] Cf. R. H. Pfeiffer, *Introduction to the O.T.*[5], pp. 239ff.
[2] For further literature we may refer to the latest commentary: C. R. North, *The second Isaiah*, 1964, to which we may add two publications not mentioned there: J. Hempel, 'Vom irrenden Glauben', reprinted in *Apoxysmata*, *B.Z.A.W.* 81, 1961, and the doctorate thesis by B. J. van der Merwe, see above, p. 29, n. 7.

Gentiles (xlii. 1 ff.; xlix. 1 ff., esp. vs. 6). This conception is repudiated by the people even more emphatically, which caused a conflict within the prophet's life and changed his views on the salvation of his people. It also modified his message concerning the *'Ebed Yahweh:* at first he understands by it his people as such; afterwards, however, he came to see that the *'Ebed* had to suffer in order to save Israel. From l. 4ff. we see how this figure of the suffering Servant is born from the prophet's experience, and in lii. 13 – liii. 12 the picture is completed. The prophet has come to understand that Israel is not to be saved if it is not reconciled to God by this Servant, who will suffer in Israel for Israel's sins and who will in this way lead the people to the glorification of its calling and to victory.

In this manner the new figure of the Saviour arose, from living hope and great disappointment, from the deep distress of the Exile and the new experience of God's mercy. In Deutero-Isaiah's message the universalist traits prevailed, together with the idea of the world-wide mission of Israel, without depriving Israel in the least of the tokens of God's love and salvation. It also shows the victory of faith in God's saving activity in Israel, though it is no longer a fighting and victorious political figure who brings about this salvation, but a suffering and atoning Saviour.

This the suffering Servant of the Lord did, apparently, not appeal strongly to Israel, for only very seldom do we find anything riminiscent of this figure in older Judaism.[1] Yet it seems that a messianic figure who acquired some of the traits of the suffering Servant is to be found in the humble king of salvation depicted in Zech. ix. 9 and in the 'me whom they have pierced' of Zech. xii. 10 f.[2]

The *post-exilic prophets* belong to a distinct type. They mark the transition from ancient prophecy to Judaism. Again and again their message calls to mind the words of ancient prophets upon whom they are largely dependent. They often lack the originality of the 'classic' prophets, but during the hard times immediately after the exile they kept alive the ancient expectation of the kingdom of Grace founded by God in Jerusalem.

Haggai succeeded in inspiring the new community at Jerusalem to rebuild the temple and raised the expectation that in the person of Zerubbabel the house of David had been received back into favour

---

[1] See H. W. Wolff, *Jesaja 53 im Urchristentum*[2], 1950, Chapter III: 'Jes. 53 im Spätjudentum'; on the whole of this problem H. H. Rowley, *The Servant of the Lord*, 1952, pp. 1 ff.; C. R. North, *The suffering Servant in Deutero-Isaiah*, 1948; J. Lindblom, *The Servant Songs in Deutero-Isaiah*, 1951; cf. also below pp. 272f., 451f.; quite otherwise H. M. Orlinsky: *The so-called 'Servant of the Lord'*, S.V.T. xiv, 1967.

[2] See K. Elliger, 'Das Buch der Zwölf kleinen Propheten'[2] (*A.T.D.* 25) 1951, pp. 160ff. Cf. also C. Brouwer, *Wachter en herder*, 1949, pp. 116ff.

(Hag. ii. 24; cf. Jer. xxii. 24; it is not certain that this expectation is really Messianic).

Zechariah (i-viii; chapters ix ff. are largely by a later author and are strongly apocalyptic in character) clearly harks back to the ancient prophets; we are reminded of Jeremiah, Hosea, Deutero-Isaiah, and particularly Ezekiel. He, too, evidently expects the messianic kingdom to come soon, but he utters a warning against the use of force and violence (iv. 6). In his prophecy the messianic dignity is borne not by a temporal ruler alone, but by two complementary figures: a royal and a priestly figure, probably represented respectively by Joshua and Zerubbabel (iii; iv). Zechariah as well as Haggai look upon Jerusalem as the centre of the new world, so much so that all nations shall take their presents to Jerusalem and recognize the God of Israel (Hag. ii. 8 ff.; Zech. viii. 20 ff.). Though this expectation does not entirely lack the universality of Isa. ii, God's grace that is *Israel's* portion is emphasized to such an extent as to foreshadow later Jewish particularism (especially in Haggai).

The foundation of the temple was for him the symbol of the return of God's grace to His people (i. 16 f.); to him (and through his preaching to the whole of the Jewish people afterwards; cf. the theology of the Chroniclers) it became the token that Zion is again the city of God, and as such can be considered the metropolis of the world (Hebr. text ii. 8 ff.; R.V. ii. 4 ff.). In Deutero-Zechariah, however, another destruction of Jerusalem is expected before the kingdom of God on earth is to come (xii; esp. xiv).

The book of *Malachi* continues the line of the two other postexilic prophetical writings: 'the message of the book of Malachi is determined by three basic elements, it has an eschatological trend, it bears the mark of cultic legalism and has tendencies towards national particularism.'[1]

As is evident from ch. i. 2 the book was written to overcome the apathy noticeable in the faith of those days (c. 475) (cf. also iii. 1 ff.). The prophet points out Yahweh's love of Israel, apparent from the destruction of Edom (i. 2 ff.) and, on the other hand, the unbelief in Israel, manifest first of all in the cultic carelessness of the priests (i. 6–ii. 9), but also in conjugal infidelity rampant in Israel (ii. 10 ff.).

With great earnestness the terrible impending Day of the Lord is announced in the true manner of the earlier prophets (ch. iii). A new element is, however, the description of the coming of the herald who will announce the approach of the Lord (iii. 1). Here the apocalyptic trend begins to appear; a tendency that becomes more and more

[1] F. Horst, 'Die zwölf kleinen Propheten', 1938, p. 254 (*H.A.T.*).

78

manifest in its descriptions of the future; in iii. 23 (R.V. iv 5; an addition) this herald is announced as Elijah the prophet.

The latest prophetical writing is *Joel*, probably to be dated about 400 B.C. It already displays a clear apocalyptic trend and we may say it forms the transition between prophecy and apocalyptic. Here, too, the fundamental idea is the announcement that the Day of the Lord is at hand; the occasion for this announcement is the repeated severe locust plagues that afflicted the country and the people. On the one hand the people are called upon to fast (in point of fact there is no question of preaching penance and conversion); on the other hand the imminent destruction and renewal of the world are foretold. The most profound concept of this book is the expectation of the descent of the Spirit of God upon all flesh (iii). The work bears the character of Jewish particularism: salvation is intended for Israel and the divine judgment will overtake the nations that had attacked Israel. The *Isaiah Apocalypse*, on the other hand, which dates approximately from the same period (or a little later), contains both particularist and universalist traits (Isa. xxiv–xxvii).[1]

The book of *Jonah* is not a prophetic book in the true sense of the word (perhaps it was included to round off the number of twelve minor prophets), but a story of a prophet, here and there reminding us of apocryphal writings. Its profound message, like that of Ruth, is that God is the God of the whole world and that He has the fate of the nations outside Israel at heart too. In the figure of the prophet Jonah this book condemns the type of later particularist Jewish piety that developed more and more after Ezra and Nehemiah.

A comparison of the prophets and the *Torah* and an examination of the connection between them shows that there is an essential unity.[2] This is certainly true of those strata in the *Torah* that are usually referred to as J and D. D is dependent upon the preaching of the great prophets and was apparently accepted by Jeremiah (final verses of ch.

---

[1] W. Rudolph, *Jesaja* 24–27, 1933; Joh. Lindblom, *Die Jesaja-Apokalypse*, 1938; M. A. Beek, 'Ein Erdbeben wird zum prophetischen Erleben, Jes. 24–27', *Arch. Orientální*, 1949, pp. 31ff.; E. S. Mulder, *Die Teologie van die Jesaja-Apokalipse*, doctorate thesis, Groningen, 1954; M. L. Henry: *Glaubenskrise Jes. Apocalypse*, 1966.
[2] There is neither a theological nor a historical antithesis between the two: the *Torah* presupposes prophecy (though this is not yet the later classic prophetism), the latter in its turn presupposes the *Torah* (though at this stage not yet as a book). For that reason I cannot possibly agree with Von Rad's assumption that there is a deep-seated difference between the message of the prophets and that of the ancient Israelite traditions: according to Von Rad the prophets only prophesied the downfall and had no hopes for Israel's future in history; cf. also W. Zimmerli, *Das Gesetz und die Propheten*, 1963, pp. 68–93 (cf. The Law and the Prophets, p. 46ff.), who rightly opposes Von Rad's opinion that the prophets had a conception of the Law altogether different from that of their predecessors, because they had turned the Law (*Torah*, the revelation of God's favour) into a series of commandments.

iii and the beginning of ch. iv; ch. xi) with quiet expectation.[1] Several Deuteronomistic coinages, such as the circumcision of the heart and Israel's calling to live to the glory of God, are also found in Jeremiah, even if there are slight differences in phrasing. In Jeremiah we also find again the idea of salvation, much in evidence throughout J: 'in thy seed all the nations of the earth shall be blessed' (or: 'bless each other', Gen. xii. 3, xviii. 18, xxviii. 14, xxii. 18, xxvi. 4; cf. Jer. iv. 2). The idea that Israel is God's people is certainly a prophetic thought as well (Hos. ii, xi; Isa. i. 2 f.; Micah iii. 5 etc., cf. Amos iii. 2, which reminds us to some extent of Gen. xii. 3). But the prophets strongly emphasize the calling that is implied in this. To a certain extent this agrees with the conception of J, for whom calling also means Yahweh's promise and may, therefore, be called more or less 'eschatological' (Gen. xii. 1 ff.)[2]. J also realized clearly that Israel was only seldom aware of all this: he shows plainly how little even the patriarchs and the people in the days of Moses were conscious of their calling. In this respect Hosea and Jeremiah, who speak of the love of youth, are more idealist than J in their conception of the reality of the past. The agreement between the views of the prophets and those of the ancient narrators of tradition is demonstrated most clearly by Von Rad where he emphasizes the fact that election, promise and fulfilment are always closely linked up in the J-narratives.[3] The close relation between these elements is – in my opinion, at any rate – quite characteristic of the religious views of the prophets. From the very first prophet in Israel – whether we call him Moses or, as E does, Abraham – the conception of promise and fulfilment had been characteristic of prophecy.[4]

There is one author in the *Torah* with whom the major prophets do not agree so well, namely E, at any rate if we go by Hosea (ch. xii), who is very critical of Jacob, and even of Jacob's struggle with Elohim. Hosea is more conscious of the sins of the patriarchs than E, who in his pietism (see pp. 58f.) idealizes them too much. There is here a tension between a certain stratum in the *Torah* (E) and the message of the prophets of the crisis who were more aware of the sins of the people than the early prophetic E, who has great sympathy for the patriarchs. Apparently E sprang from an antibaalite background so that there is a rather pronounced nationalist Israelite tendency to be found in his views.

[1] See now, for example, H. H. Rowley, 'The prophet Jeremiah and the book of Dt.', *Studies in O.T. prophecy*, 1950, pp. 157ff. (now also in the collection *From Moses to Qumran*, 1963).
[2] Cf. W. Eichrodt, *Israel in der Weissagung des A.T.*, 1951, pp. 30ff.
[3] See a.o. *Th.L.Z.* 1963, pp. 418ff.
[4] So also rightly H. W. Wolff, 'Das Geschichtsverständnis der alttest. Prophetie', *Ev. Th.* 1960, pp. 218ff.

There is also an element of tension between the P-parts of the Torah and the prophets, namely Amos v.25 and Jeremiah vii.22, who do not look upon the sacrificial cult as an essential element in the religion of Israel and do not recognize it as Mosaic. Nor do the prophets, who actively participate in the life of their times, share the anti-cultural tendencies of the author of the primeval history.

These differences should not, however, be pushed to extremes; this would needlessly exaggerate the differences between the prophets and the authors of the *Torah*. Fundamentally their spiritual basis is the same.

It is remarkable, however, that the prophetical writings refer only to comparatively few parts of the historical and law books. The stories of Paradise and the Deluge are not mentioned in the pre-exilic prophecies – not even the name of Abraham (except in two spurious texts, Micah vii and Isa.xxix). The absence of the name of Abraham is particularly striking. No less striking, however, is the fact that the prophets do not mention and hardly ever allude to what had happened at Mount Sinai. There are allusions to the Ten Commandments (Hos. iv.2; Jer.vii.9) and to the Covenant (Hos.viii.1) but Mount Sinai is not mentioned explicitly. References to the Deuteronomic laws are more frequent in the work of the later prophets (cf. Jer.xxxiv and Deut.xv;[1] Isa.l and Deut.xxiv; Isa lii.12 and Deut.xvi.3).

With the prophets such allusions are mainly focused on the miraculous deliverance from Egypt and the desert. This does not mean that we should come to the conclusion that the early prophets did not know of Abraham; we may reflect that there are no more than two allusions to Moses in the pre-exilic prophecies (Hos.xii where he is called a prophet, and Jer.xv). That Abraham is not mentioned *may* be intentional but it is no evidence that the tradition concerning Abraham was unknown. Something similar can be pointed out in the New Testament Epistles, from which it is impossible to reconstruct the life of Jesus or the Gospel-narratives; only the Cross and the Resurrection are of central importance, like the deliverance from Egypt in the Old Testament!

After all, the prophets have a different end in view from that of the historiographers who wanted to make Israel conscious of its vocation by reminding it of its *history*. The prophets emphasize repentance, in virtue of their message of judgment. On the one hand they had to point out the glorious deeds of God, which explains why they are always harping on the one string of the divine miraculous deliverance from Egypt and the desert journey. On the other hand they had to

[1] See, for instance, M.David, 'The manumission of the slaves under Zedekiah', *O.T.S.*, V, 1948, pp.63ff.

confront the people with their sins, and for that reason they often use narratives that bring out clearly the defection of the people (Hos. xii: Jacob; ix. 10: Baal-Peor). Sodom and Gomorrah are often held up as typical examples of the divine judgment (the history of the Flood, which reached Israel from foreign parts, is not mentioned; that the prophets were aware of the figure of Noah appears, however, from Ezekiel).

The fact that the people finds itself in a great crisis (and the prophets realized perfectly well that this critical moment in history had been decreed by God) is the cause of the struggle of the prophets against the people, for the people; for the prophets know that it is only repentance that will save the people. When their preaching proves ineffective, they keep looking forward to a new future, which would surely come because Israel is God's people and God is a God of life, who remains faithful to all eternity. And therefore, as surely as the Israel of the times of the prophets, the contemporary generation, would perish, so also would God raise a new people from the remnant that would be saved. Every prophet is a prophet of salvation as well as a prophet of woe. The denial of this fact by many has been one of the greatest misunderstandings in the study of the Old Testament.[1] The prophet may proclaim the hope of salvation, and to this hope he himself clings, too, in his struggle for his people. The expectation of salvation is depicted in various ways, in natural forms (great fertility), in political forms (victory over enemies), in the form of a new kingdom of righteousness, and in specific messianic representations (here a king of righteousness is the representative of this kingdom of God); now and then this new kingdom bears universal traits.

The essential difference between the true prophets and the nationalistic 'false' prophets is, that the true prophets expect salvation to come after the judgment, eschatologically (although we must exercise some caution in using this word because the eschatology of the Old Testa-

---

[1] Remarkable is the opinion of Von Rad, who thinks that in their message of judgment the prophets throw overboard all earlier promises of salvation and proclaim a wholly new hope. Though it is true that the prophets frequently proclaim their hopes in forms that are reminiscent of the old promises of salvation, because it was impossible for them to express their hopes differently, yet they are concerned with an activity of God that is wholly new and has essentially nothing in common with the old hopes.

This means that Von Rad does not deny the preaching of salvation, but he is of the opinion that according to this teaching the history of Israel is cut short radically, thus denying that there should be any continuity between the future in the message of the prophets and the present state of the Israel of their days. See Von Rad, *O.T. Theology* I, 1, c, 4, II, 1, G, 2, and W. Zimmerli's criticism in *V.T.* 1963, pp. 106ff. The best refutation of this "überspitzte" point of view is, in my opinion, the message of Deutero-Isaiah and the part that Jerusalem and the house of David keep playing in the expectations of nearly all the prophets.

ment prophets differs to some extent in meaning from eschatology in the apocalyptic writings and in the New Testament, see above, p. 35 and chapter IX). The 'false' prophets, on the contrary, looked upon salvation as Israel's unchanging property, as if Israel might rest assured of salvation. The faithful prophets of Israel were always aware that it depended on God alone, and that it was granted by God only to those who remained faithful to His covenant.

The third group of writings in the Hebrew Bible consists of the *Kethubim*. On p. 53 we have pointed out the secondary canonicity of these books. On p. 51 we opposed the view that the canon (particularly *Torah* and *Nebiim*) had come into being as a kind of anthology of ancient Israelite religious literature; to a certain extent this view may, however, apply to the *Kethubim*. At first sight it is not so evident that these books are the Word of God as it is in the case of the other books. The *Kethubim* contain writings that were used in the cult (Psalms and Megilloth), books of wisdom, an apocalyptic work (Daniel) and lastly a more recent historical work (Chronicles, Ezra, Nehemiah).

They are very different in character. The *Psalms*[1] show the effect of the preaching of Yahweh and His kingdom on religious life, as it manifestst itself on many occasions: at coronation ceremonies (the royal psalms), in disease (individual lamentations), during national disasters (lamentations of the people), in the cult (hymns), to mention only the main types. A discussion of the spiritual content of the Psalms would far exceed the limits of this sketch. In many different ways they give expression to Israel's belief in God. Two things strike us: the absolute uniqueness of the glory of Yahweh as well as the intimate relationship of the faithful with God. Again and again He is addressed as 'my God'[2]; this personal note of confidence, this immediate approach is one of the most characteristic elements of the Psalms; an element which has made them particularly valuable as the expression of personal piety through the ages.

That Jesus Christ died with the words of Psalm xxii on His lips is characteristic of the imperishable value of the Psalms as an expression of faith. The Psalms glorify God as the Lord of the world, as the Saviour of His people, as the Creator; but above all things they give expression to the hope the faithful set on Him in days of distress, personal as well as national. They are also full of inward tension, the 'Why?' and 'How long?' are heard very often; but the assurance of salvation,

[1] H. Ringgren, *The faith of the Psalmists*, 1963.
[2] Cf. O. Eißfeldt, '"Mein Gott" im A.T.', *Z.A.W.*, 1945/48, pp. 3ff.; Eng. trans. '"My God" in the O.T.', *Evangelical Quarterly* XIX (1947), pp. 7ff.

of God's help, is also mentioned again and again. Various religious contrasts such as cultic and anti-cultic attitudes play a part here, as well as in the prophets and the law. A particular motif that Christians often find difficult to understand is the curse against an enemy. Sometimes this curse has an obvious religious background (Ps. cxxxix. 19–22); on other occasions it is rather national or personal (Ps. cxxxvii 8f.); in the latter the idea of revenge is expressed openly and fiercely.[1]

The *Proverbs*, together with *Job* and *Ecclesiastes*, belong to a special form of literature (*chokhmah* or Wisdom-literature); in spite of its broad international background (chapters xxii f., xxx) the first of these books clearly contains a moral and religious conception of the world, in which God occupies a central position. The idea of retribution figures largely here. In the book of Job the holiness of God's deeds – a holiness which transcends our reasoning – is brought out: it seems as if the author of *Job* wants to combat the religious moralism of the Proverbs which often shows strong leanings towards eudaemonism. The creation-motif is strongly predominant,[2] but at the same time this motif is associated with the personal relationship between Yahweh and man[3]; the solution to the problem of this book is to be found in the fact that the two elements merge: God who is the Creator but also communicates with man. *Ecclesiastes*[4], like many other pronouncements in the Old Testament, proclaims most emphatically the mysteriousness of God. He does so, however, in such a one-sided manner that there is practically nothing left of His revelation in word and history. To him God is the Creator, indeed, but He remains hidden behind His creation. The personal relationship is suppressed here. No wonder, then, that the history of the canon shows that Ecclesiastes was always considered a border-line case as regards canonicity. Thus these books of Wisdom, each with its own emphasis, keep each other in equilibrium, as it were.

In *Ruth* (as in Jonah)[5] an anti-particularist tendency comes to the fore. In this respect, too, the tension found in the Law and the Prophets continues in the *Kethubim*. The piety of *Ruth* is focused on faith in God's providence. To the five *Megilloth* (festival rolls) belong three

[1] See below pp. 280f.
[2] Cf. P. Humbert, 'Le modernisme de Job' in Rowley-Festschrift, *Wisdom in Israel and the Ancient Near East*, 1955, pp. 150ff.
[3] As already in Deutero-Isaiah. Cf. A. Lauha, 'Die Krise des religiösen Glaubens bei Kohelet', *Rowley-Festschrift*, pp. 183ff. and G. Fohrer, 'Das Hiobproblem und seine Lösung', *Wiss. Zeitschr. M. Luther Univ. Wittenberg*, 1963; H. H. Rowley, 'The book of Job and its meaning' (*From Moses to Qumran*, 1963, pp. 141ff.).
[4] A. Lauha, op. cit.; J. Pedersen, *Scepticisme israélite;* Th. C. Vriezen, 'Prediker', *N.T.T.* 1946, pp. 1ff.
[5] R. B. Y. Scott, 'The sign of Jonah', *Interpretation*, 1965, pp. 16ff.

other books besides Ruth and Ecclesiastes. The first of these is the *Song of Songs*, a collection of nuptial songs that may be looked upon as an appendix to Proverbs xxxi (in praise of woman). These songs could only be included in the canon on allegorical grounds, by interpreting them as religious songs glorifying the relationship between God and the people. To us these songs are important because they show that in Israel women were not only esteemed as mothers and wives, but also for their own sake.[1]

The book of *Lamentations*[2] reflects the moods prevalent among those who had remained behind after the City of God, Jerusalem, had been destroyed: great spiritual prostration, awareness of judgment, searchings of heart, return to God, and hope that He will intervene on behalf of His people. The prophetic and the deuteronomic message remain in the background.

Lastly comes the book of *Esther*, which was read at Purim. Böhl justly says of it[3] that it is one of the most precious gems of oriental narrative art, but that it is not to be judged by moral or historical standards because the author did not mean to give expression to such standards. The booklet is intended to add to the festive joy of Purim by relating the origin of the feast and humorously exaggerates, even to the point of caricature, the description of characters such as Ahasuerus and Haman, strongly contrasting with the quiet piety and assurance of Mordecai. The underlying fundamental conception, not developed explicitly because of the cheerful nature of the feast, is that of the wisdom of God's rule of the world.

In *Daniel* the assurance of God's redeeming grace for those who keep His commandments is proclaimed to the generation that had experienced the oppression by the Syrians and the war of liberation of the Maccabees. The history of the nations is placed in God's hand. Daniel sees the completion of history in the kingdom of God (ch. vii). Apocalypse, of which the end of this book and some other parts of the Old Testament (Isa. xxiv–xxvii) are examples, represents a more recent form of prophecy; the spirit of prophecy is there, but mingled with various speculative ideas, derived from contemporary notions.[4] In spite of its visionary form, the apocalyptic passages take on much more the character of reflections than does the prophecy which rather

---

[1] H. H. Rowley, 'The Interpretation of the Song of Songs', in *The Servant of the Lord*, pp. 187ff.
[2] See N. K. Gottwald, *Studies in the Book of Lamentations*, 1954; cf. also B. Atbrektson, *Studies in the Text and Theology of the Book of Lamentations*, 1963.
[3] See F. M. Th. de Liagre Böhl, 'Missions- und Erwählungsgedanke', *Bertholet-Fest-schrift*, 1950, p. 94.
[4] See p. 82 and chapter IX. Cf. also M. A. Beek, *Inleiding tot de Joodse Apocalyptiek*, 1950.

85

goes back to an immediate seeing and hearing of the Word of God. The four books *Chronicles, Ezra* and *Nehemiah* form together one great post-exilic historical record[1] which defends the legitimacy of the post-exilic Jewish community in Jerusalem as the representative of the ancient theocratic Israel, on account of the fact that the former Davidic temple was being rebuilt there against the Samaritan community. With great emphasis these books proclaim that David and his house possess the throne of Yahweh; *Israel is the kingdom of God* (cf. especially the alteration of Nathan's prophecy in 1 Chron. xvii. 14; cf. 2 Sam. vii. 16; see also 1 Chron. xxviii. 5 and xxix. 23 and below pp. 438 and 454). David became the central figure in the history of Israel, also because in the messianic prophecies the promise of Israel's salvation rests upon him. From the central position of David and his house as the bearers of God's promises we may conclude that the messianic element forms the background of the conception of history in Chronicles. The miraculous aspect of the work of God in Israel is emphasized more often in these books. Both prophecy and the priesthood (particularly the Levites, who are also looked upon as bearers of the prophetic office) play a great part. On the one hand great stress is laid on the cult (in which, however, not the sacrifice but the praising of God *,toda*, comes into prominence); on the other hand prophets appear by the side of all the kings. In the most recent period cult and law (Ezra) are looked upon as very closely connected.

With the greater part of the *Kethubim* we have come to the borderland of the Old Testament books of revelation; the canonicity of this group of writings is only of a secondary nature, which appears clearly from the fact that in the Septuagint many apocryphal writings were included among the *Kethubim*. In the Hellenistic-Judaic world the border-line between canonical and apocryphal was, therefore, hardly realized so far as the Kethubim are concerned. That a separation of these two groups of writings took place and that it was carried into effect by the rabbinical Jews in this way shows that among the Jews the original spiritual wealth of prophecy was understood.[2] The hesitation as to the Song of Songs, Ecclesiastes and Esther is not devoid of meaning for Christian theological canonicity.

The Old Testament knows all kinds of inward tension; it contains parts that clash with each other (particularly in the *Kethubim*) when

[1] See M. Noth, *Überlieferungsgeschichtliche Studien*, pp. 110ff.; G. von Rad, *Das Geschichtsbild des chronistischen Werkes*, 1930; J. Swart, *De theologie van Kronieken*, 1911.
[2] The first requirement to which a canonical book must conform according to the rabbinical tenets is, as Flavius Josephus tells us, that it should date from the age of the prophets (Moses to Ezra); see W. Staerk, *Der Schrift- und Kanonbegriff der jüdischen Bibel*.

they are considered as pieces of literature that all lie on the same level, and when the actual situation (the *Sitz im Leben*) and the historical background of each of these parts are lost sight of and the connections and relations between these writings are not brought out.[1]

Here we find antagonism towards civilization, and approval of civilization; at one time Israel's election is recognized, at another it is rejected; fragments that preach particularism stand side by side with fragments that repudiate it as the ultimate wisdom. Over against the sacrificial cult as a means of revealing God's grace stands the rejection of the cult; over against the conception of divine rule as a moral scheme of things stands the flat negation of this idea in the later wisdom-literature.

It is necessary to keep both elements in view together, Ezra and Nehemiah together with Ruth and Jonah; Jeremiah as well as the Priestly Code; Job and Ecclesiastes as well as Proverbs. This not only opens our eyes to the tension in the Old Testament, but also shows that even in these antinomies the Old Testament speaks the truth in the form of a divine dialectic.[2] Fundamentally Ezra and Nehemiah share in the truth, so that the antithesis is necessary; but it should not lead to the rejection of the other nations from God's presence. The antithesis has a right to exist for the moment, even in spiritual life, as a means of purging Israel from pagan influences, but it would defeat its object if this necessary means to educate the people in obedience to God were glorified as the ultimate revelation of God – beside it the grace of God for the nations of the world must be preached (Jonah) and the fact that even strangers and Gentiles may be admitted to the covenant must be recognized (Ruth). Together, in their diametrical connectedness, their antinomic relation, they constitute the true divine message. In the Old Testament almost every great spiritual truth is flanked by its opposite, apparently cancelling the former but in fact raising it to a different, a truly spiritual plane.

Indeed, the truth of faith can only be expressed fully in antinomies. Divine reality is so full of life that not only a rational but even a paradoxical judgment cannot exhaust it.[3] A religious truth – and this

---

[1] This is the truth to which an organic conception of the Scriptures adheres. It is a pity that most of the conceptions of the Scriptures that call themselves organic, leave the historical point of view in the history of Old Testament revelation too much out of account.

[2] Cf. A. A. van Ruler, *De Vervulling der Wet*, 1947.

[3] The Old Testament witness concerning God is *dialectical* in the true sense of the word. The word of God's holiness is absolutely related to the God of the Covenant, the God of communion. From communion with God his holiness is known fully (Exod. 33 concluding verses), and conversely (Isa. vi). Thus, for example, Isa. lvii. 15 and Ps. li are also to be understood. Hence the holiness of God could only be professed fully in Israel which was conscious of the God of the Covenant. In this 'ambivalent'

included pronouncements that are looked upon as inspired by the Spirit – is *per se* a one-sided truth, and therefore a misrepresentation of the truth if represented rationally. When considered only by itself, without reference to its context, it is, therefore, an untruth. For instance, the truth of Israel's election is unacceptable if it is rationally understood to mean that *for that reason* God has rejected the nations of the world, that *for that reason* Israel is of more importance to God than those other nations[1], for Israel was only elected in order to serve God in the task of leading those other nations to God. In Israel God sought the world. Israel was God's point of attack on the world. When from the knowledge that it is God's people Israel derived the certainty of its special election, and because of that considered itself to be superior to the other nations, the prophets must contradict this and recall the people to the living God, whose mercy is great for Israel but also for the world. For in His mercy He has called Israel to the service of His kingdom among the nations of the earth.[2]

Another case in point: When Israel thinks it possesses in its sacrificial cult the divine means of grace, the prophets must reject this means of grace and remind the people that God's mercy applies only to those who obey God. From the cult the people is thrown back on the mercy of the living God. Some prophets even go so far in emphasizing God's mercy that they think that they can go no farther than to say: 'If the people comes to repentance, God *may perhaps* repent of His resolve to inflict His judgment upon the people' (Amos, Zephaniah). Even moral repentance does not imply that the punishment will be averted, but only the *possibility* that God may reverse His decision (repent).

In the Old Testament it becomes clear to us how the revelation of the living God can never be contained in dogmatic rules that can be affirmed rationally, but that the living God can only be known truly

nature (cf. A. Bertholet, 'Religionsgeschichtliche Ambivalenzerscheinungen', *Th.Z.*, 1948, pp. 1ff.), which is absolutely and truly genuine in Yahwism, the truth of Israel's religion is revealed. In 'dialectical theology' this element is rightly given great prominence, but in our opinion it not always done justice as the holiness of God is frequently stressed to such an extent that the communion between God and the world is not brought out sufficiently. This applies, for example, when the Word becomes the only point of contact between God and the world, and the Creation and history are left out as possible expressions of Revelation. The *desire for communion* (love) *of the Holy One* means therefore both life and death: life for him who lets himself be loved, death for those who withdraw from the relationship with Him. This came to be revealed in Israel by the O.T. and in the N.T. it was recapitulated again. The splendid study of K. Barth, 'Die Menschlichkeit Gottes' *Theologische Studien* 48, 1956 admirably brings out this message of the scriptures.

[1] Unfortunately some Christian theologians, however strongly they combat the dangers of a mistaken idea of being elect in the Church, cannot refrain even now, in consequence of a religious romanticism, from backing up the Jews in this temptation! In particular the establishment of the State of Israel has increased this danger.

[2] See my *Die Erwählung Israels*.

by a living faith that comes to rest in God and accepts His guidance. Only the living (existential) relationship with God by means of the Spirit is the basis and the object of God's revelation; we may put it differently: His kingship on earth, His kingdom among men is the object of His revelation. This is revealed by the Old Testament as a whole when we examine its fundamental principles.

Fundamentally the Old Testament teaches nothing other than what was taught by Christ, who had learned the purpose of the Father from the Old Testament. Christ's aim was to follow its most profound ideas and to apply them to this life; that is His obedience and also His communion with God – that makes Him the new Adam and the Son of the Father. In this world He lived in the kingdom that God had revealed in the Old Testament by Moses and the prophets. Thus He is the fulfilment of the law, i.e. He actualizes the revelation that had been accorded to Israel, by making the kingship of God the essence and basis of His life.

The true establishment of the Kingdom of God also brings out new things of which the prophets had not yet dreamt. At the actual realization of the Kingdom greater possibilities manifested themselves than even the greatest men of God had expected.[1]

Hence Jesus, when He lays down the constitution of the Kingdom (as we might call the Sermon on the Mount), discovers more and other things in God's Kingdom than had been revealed in the Law and the Prophets.[2] God's Will is not expressed fully in the Decalogue; it means even more to man (Matt. v. 18ff.); God's love *(chesed)* is more than merely the love of the just of which the *Torah* spoke, the law which, for example, only purified the sinner *bi-shegagah* by the sacrament of the guilt- and sin-offering, but God's love includes both the just and the wicked. God's paternal care is so great that He has not only the people of Israel as a whole in mind but is aware of the needs of each individual.

Accepting in this life the promises and the words of God in the Old Testament brings to light even greater, more profound truths and treasures: 'Every scribe which is instructed into the kingdom of heaven is like unto a man that is an householder, which bringeth forth out of his treasure things new and old' (Matt. xiii. 52); that is why Christ teaches 'as one having authority, and not as the scribes'.

In Christ the old has become new, but it has not been rejected, nor

---

[1] Cf. G. A. Barton, *Studies in N.T. Christianity*, 1928, p. 3 (quoted in H. H. Rowley, *The biblical doctrine of election*, 1950, p. 120): 'Fulfilment has always been of a different, a more spiritual, a more glorious character, than anything in the form of prophecy would lead one to guess'.
[2] Cf. also Mat. xi. 11, xiii. 17.

has it been repristinated.[1] We cannot understand Christ without the Old Testament; but neither must we identify the Old Testament with the Gospel. For the very reason that life in the Kingdom, standing in the Kingdom in faith, means that man is accorded the gift of God's Spirit, new things are revealed. When the Word of God is tested, its vitality becomes evident. It is always fulfilled on a higher level than man understands with his reason, or even with his faith, because God is a *living God*, whose strength and glory are always greater than our experience and faith can comprise, and whose nature exceeds all our human knowledge, even the knowledge of human faith.

Some further literature:

Factual surveys of the contents of the books are given in most Introductions to the Old Testament.

The following are more *theological* in character (popular):
B.W.Anderson, *Understanding the O.T.*
A.Schlatter, *Einleitung in die Bibel*[2], 1933.
O.Weber, *Bibelkunde des A.T.* I–II, many ed.
P.Heinisch, *Geschichte des A.T.*, 1950 (R.Catholic).
M.A.Beek, *A Journey through the O.T.*, 1959.
H.Wheeler Robinson, *The religious ideas of the O.T.*, 1913.
A.G.Herbert, *The Bible from within*, 1950.
C.Westermann, *A Thousand Years and a Day*, 1962.
id., *Bibelkunde in Abriß*.

For theological *study:*
Introductions to the books of the Bible in commentaries.
G.von Rad, *O.T. Theology* I–II.
id., *The Problem of the Hexateuch and other Essays*, 1966.
M.Noth, *Überlieferungsgeschichtliche Studien*, 1943.
id., *Überlieferungsgeschichte des Pentateuch*, 1948.

[1] Cf. A.Bertholet, *Biblische Theologie des A.T.*, 2nd vol., 1911, p.496: 'It is in effect a new writing, which is traced over the old written characters'.

CHAPTER IV

The Old Testament as the Word of God, and its use in the Church

In this chapter we shall deal with two closely connected questions; both of which, in principle and in practice alike, focus our attention on the actual meaning of the Old Testament.

First there is the question of *authority*. Can the Old Testament be looked upon as the Word of God in the present-day situation, now that it has become evident that the historical links of the Old Testament with its own period are very strong, and that many of its elements are human – sometimes even all too human?

Secondly there is the question of *the use of the Old Testament* in the Christian Church. How should the Old Testament be read, interpreted, and preached?

The first question particularly is essentially of a dogmatic nature and will have to be dealt with at length in dogmatics; but it should not be neglected in a Theology of the Old Testament if it is to be more than a historical and theological survey of the Old Testament. The Old Testament scholar who approaches his subject in the spirit of the theologian cannot withdraw from his task of advising the dogmatician from his own point of view and with his experience in the Old Testament field, lest the dogmatician, without full knowledge of the facts involved, should arrive at a theoretical scheme which does not fit the facts. It is especially necessary to set the doctrine of the Old Testament as the Word of God in the light of the facts and to confront it with the data found by research in historical and literary criticism.[1]

I. THE OLD TESTAMENT AS THE WORD OF GOD[2]

The tension within the Christian Church about the meaning of the Old Testament, a tension which has existed from the very beginning, has grown stronger during the last few centuries. After all that has been

[1] Subjects like Scripture and tradition, inspiration, etc. are not discussed here.
[2] It would be most instructive to bring in the research in the fields of phenomenology and the history of religion; we only refer to A. Bertholet, 'Die Macht der Schrift im Glauben und Aberglauben', *A.A.B.*, Phil.-hist. Kl. 1948, I, 1949; H. W. Obbink, *Het heilige boek als godsd. hist. verschijnsel*, 1940; id., 'Over de plaats van het heilige boek in de religie', *Vox Th.*, XXIII, 1952/3, pp. 3ff.

said about the history of the Old Testament in the first two chapters we need not dwell on this subject any further.

There are, however, two points that should be touched upon briefly here: in the first place the fact that historical research not only linked up the religion of Israel with many elements of the ancient Oriental religions, but also considered (and had to consider) the Old Testament material itself as closely allied to these religions and dependent upon them in more than one respect. The second point is the severe criticism of the Old Testament that frequently sprang up in the young Eastern Churches in the development of the Christian Church in the last few decades when it spread among many nations of Asia and Africa, especially among the great civilized nations of the Middle and Far East. Here, as it were, we see repeated what happened in the Western Church in the second century. There are many who would agree with the Chinese clergyman who thought that 'reading the Old Testament is like eating a large crab; it turns out to be mostly shell with very little meat in it'.[1] In India many people go even further by accepting only the New Testament as Holy Scripture and replacing the Old Testament by ancient Indian writings.[2] The latter idea has, of course, not only a religious and theological but also a historic and cultural background.

Generally speaking, these doubts as to the value of the Old Testament prove how difficult it is for those who were moved by the message of the Gospel but do not belong to Israel by birth and have, therefore, not received 'the Law and the Prophets' through the ancestral tradition[3], to see the Old Testament as the true message of God.

This hesitation shows, therefore, that the relation between Old Testament and New Testament involves an important problem which forces itself upon each generation and must always be dealt with anew.

This problem is, however, a complex of at least three closely connected questions.

1. The relation between the two Testaments.

[1] G. E. Philips, *The Old Testament in the World Church*, 1942, pp. 22f. We may, indeed, also refer here to the remarks of some German theologians in the discussion on Von Rad's *Theology*, such as F.Hesse (referring to F.Baumgärtel), 'Zur Frage der Wertung und Geltung altt. Texte', *Baumgärtel Festschrift*, 1959, now also in C.Westermann, *Probleme altt. Hermeneutik*, 1960, e.g. pp. 279–283 (transl.: *Essays on O. T. Interpretation*, 1963).
[2] Op. cit., pp. 3, 14ff.; cf. also F.Heiler, *De Openbaring in de godsdiensten van Britsch-Indië en de Christusverkondiging*, 1931, *passim*, esp. pp. 37f., 59f.
[3] The problem is, therefore, typical of the Christians among the Gentiles and did not become acute in the early Christian Church until the mission to the Gentiles started. It became especially pressing for St. Paul, the Pharisee, the Christian from the Jews, who became the Apostle of the Gentiles. So far it has lost none of its interest for the Churches among the non-Christian nations. The Christians in the young African Churches have a strong sense of the close ties that bind them to the Old Testament and they appreciate the element of the Law particularly highly.

2. The spiritual meaning of the material contents of the Old Testament (this question is factually linked very closely with the first).

3. The evaluation of the Old Testament as the Word of God.

The first question is, in fact, decisive; as it cannot be answered without taking into consideration the second question as well, we shall deal with both of them together.

The answer to the third question is fundamentally implicit in that to the first two, and need only be dealt with in its formal aspects.

It is of the utmost importance to see how the problem took a definite and special form from the first moment that Christ was proclaimed to the world though it did not emerge fully until the message was preached to the Gentiles outside the Jewish community. The Pauline epistles bear witness to this on many pages. As soon as Jesus Christ is proclaimed as the central figure of the revelation of God in Israel, the question arises as to the relation of the revelation of God in Jesus Christ and the revelation to the fathers, especially to Moses, i.e. the Torah, 'the Law', which was looked upon as the central and absolute revelation.[1]

With St. Paul, therefore, two lines become clearly visible.[2] The former is that of absolute acceptance of the Old Testament as the revelation of God; St. Paul recognizes the Holy Scriptures of the Old Testament[3] as the Word of God, and from these Scriptures he draws his arguments to corroborate his message concerning Christ.[4] He will not detract in any way from the authority of the Old Testament as the Word of God, and he is second to none of his Jewish and Jewish Christian opponents in recognizing the truth of the revelation of God accorded to Israel before Christ and handed down in the writings of Moses and the prophets.

But there is also another line of thought: that God creates a new relationship to Himself by the revelation in Christ, that He makes Himself known fully in His mercy to sinful men in the death and resurrection of Jesus Christ, so that the Jewish way of salvation, the way of the Law and its works, is superseded. The Law may, therefore, be considered to have been rendered out of date as the way of salvation and to have passed away (Gal. iii. 19–21).[5] (St. Paul means here the

---

[1] On the pre-existence of the *Torah*, by and for which the world is even thought to have been created, see W. D. Davies, *Paul and Rabbinic Judaism*, 1948, pp. 170f., and also Kittel, *Th.W.*, IV, p. 139.

[2] See *Th.W.*, IV, νόμος, pp. 1063ff.; γραφή, pp. 760, 769.

[3] We should not forget the remarks on p. 12 n. 1, 13 n. 5, 14 n. 2 that the Old Testament canon had not yet been fixed definitely at that time.

[4] 'In his Scripture proofs Paul likes to place a quotation from the Law and one from the Prophets alongside each other', *Th.W.*, IV, p. 1062.

[5] Cf. H. M. van Nes in *Tekst en Uitleg*, loc. cit., and Joh. Weiss, *Die Schriften des N. T.*, II, 1917, p. 59.

Torah as the way of salvation, not as the proclamation of the will of God, for as such it was sacred to him.) This means that essentially the Law has been superseded by Jesus Christ as the central point of revelation.[1]

These two lines of thought should both be given full emphasis if we are to do justice to St. Paul; they give his writings a strong tension, according to some even an unbearable tension, which is said to be a sign of absolute confusion.[2] This tension becomes comprehensible and is even removed in part if we bear in mind the difference in appreciation of the Law between St. Paul and the Jews.[3] Whereas the Jews looked upon the law as the means of salvation, St. Paul denied the possibility of justification by the law, because Christ is the only way of life. Thus the law could only give St. Paul knowledge of the demanding will of God and therefore knowledge of sin, but ultimately no deliverance.[4] As a result the law could only have a preparatory function in the light of the revelatory work of Christ. Thus St. Paul's doctrine developed towards what may be called a historical appreciation of the Law[5], without arriving at it.

The Mosaic Law came to be regarded as intermediate in character, while Abraham's faith became the expression of true revelation.[6] This meant a disintegration of the Torah, at any rate a certain reversal of

[1] W. D. Davies, op. cit., pp. 146ff, esp. pp. 172ff.; Kittel, *Th.W.*, IV, p. 139, in connection on with John i.
[2] As one of the most authoritative modern Jewish scholars told me; cf. also the idea of the 'polar character' of St. Paul in J. Klausner, *From Jesus to Paul*, 1943, II 6, XI, and II 7, 1, where St. Paul's inferiority complex, his lack of balance as an epileptic, his cleverness, his mixture of 'diluted' Judaism and 'superficial Hellenism' are described, though in a conciliatory and protective way.
[3] See e.g. J. N. Sevenster in *Het oudste Christendom en de antieke Cultuur*, II, 1951, pp. 277 ff., esp. p. 280; Gutbrod, νόμος, *Th.W.*, IV, p. 1063ff.
[4] Expressed dogmatically, the *usus elenchticus* is given great emphasis, while the *usus didacticus* and *politicus* are accepted, but the *usus salvificus* is denied. In many respects this schematic conception is adequate, but it is not altogether satisfactory because it takes too little account of the living influence of the motif which brings about the change in appreciation, and also because it does not bring out clearly enough the drastic nature of the change which had taken place. In fact, the Law was deprived of its highest religious meaning by the work of Christ; it does retain some of its functions, but not its greatest, it is no longer the means of salvation. What happens here remotely resembles what takes place in a country which changes over from one monetary standard to another, or from one political system to another: all sorts of readjustments become necessary. In the first case some values rise, others are devaluated; in the second new classes come into the limelight while the old classes lose in importance and disappear. Some of the changes are immediately noticeable on the market or in society, others make their penetrating influence felt but slowly. The same applies here. After Christ St. Paul immediately arrives at a revaluation of the Law, but also of the prophetical books: while the Law loses in significance the prophetical books become more important, especially in their eschatological preaching. The same applies to certain parts of the Torah, of the laws and of the narratives.
[5] Cf. Joh. Weiss, op. cit., p. 60.
[6] Something very remotely resembling this may be found in the fact that Islam also appeals to Abraham against Judaism and Christianity; but this is quite different from

94

the order: the patriarchal relationship of faith is represented as the highest and permanent relationship (ultimately restored in Christ), the Law as subsequent[1], temporary and also inferior.[2] In this reversal of the order of the Law and explanation of its temporary meaning and spiritually preparatory function, an internal, material, theological criticism of the Old Testament is implicit, at which Judaism has justly been, and still is, alarmed and because of which it looks upon St. Paul as the greatest enemy of Judaism. The characteristic element of this view is essentially the ambivalence in its appreciation of the Law, and therefore of the Old Testament, which consists in retaining its revelatory character and at the same time abolishing its authority in favour of the Word of God revealed in Christ. The fact that these two relations cannot be separated causes a tension in the Pauline epistles, and also in the life of the Christian Church.[3]

Hence in the ancient Church one side or the other could be emphasized: either the temporary nature at any rate of the ceremonial laws, as in the Epistle to the Hebrews (vii. 18–28; viii. 13), or the absolute general authority of the Holy Scriptures, especially in the later Epistles, mostly held to be non-apostolic (2 Pet. i. 19ff.; 2 Tim. iii. 15f.[4]). From the history of the Church in the second century it becomes evident how this tension continued to dominate the Church and called forth strong contrasts (Judaizers on the one hand, Marcion and Gnosticism on the other). But the Catholic Church had to maintain the unity of the Testaments; as a result, however, the difference between the Testaments fell more and more into the background. At first the episodical character of the Law was still pointed out, in the Pauline sense[5]; afterwards unity was maintained by allegorical and symbolical (and sometimes by the purer form of typological) interpretation of the Scriptures. A rising historicizing view such as that of the Antiochian school, especially of Theodore of Mopsuestia[6] who draws attention to the preparatory theological element in the Old Testament revelation (and prefers the typological exegetical method), cannot attain full development.

St. Paul's reference to the patriarch. In the case of Islam the background is ethnical (Abraham is the progenitor of the Arabs, too) with the result that the holy writings of those who possess the Scriptures are rejected as spurious; St. Paul does *not* reject the Old Testament revelation as spurious, he still recognized it: the Law is called good. For him it had a (spiritually) preparatory function. Cf. O. Schmitz, 'Abraham im Spätjudentum und im Urchristentum', *A. Schlatter-Festschrift*, 1922, pp. 99ff.
[1] See p. 13 n. 5 and 47.
[2] Gal. iii. 19; cf. Van Nes, op. cit.
[3] See the article by G. Schrenk on γραφή in *Th.W.*, I, pp. 76 of.; on St. Paul also: Klausner, op. cit., II 7, XIV 4.
[4] See p. 14.
[5] L. Diestel, *op. cit.*, pp. 41ff.
[6] See p. 16 n. 3; Diestel, *op. cit.*, pp. 130ff.

It was even lost entirely, as other promising scientific tendencies of antiquity were also neglected or denied, not coming to the fore again until the post-Reformation epoch, when the point of view of historical criticism that had sprung up in Renaissance and humanism, also made itself felt in the investigation of the Bible.

The elaboration of this point of view caused great tensions in theology, which have not yet been resolved. On the one hand it paved the way for a more satisfactory and more natural relation between the Old and the New Testament in the field of historical theology, on the other hand it confronted systematical and practical (homiletic) theology with serious problems. Because the historical element was emphasized so strongly, the unity of the Bible was in imminent danger of being lost, at the expense of the absoluteness of the authority of the Scriptures. The ultimate consequence of all this was that the Old Testament lost a great deal of its importance for preaching.

It is not easy to arrive at a completely satisfactory solution for these problems; simple formulas and rigid rules will not do; a more dynamic way of thinking will have to break through in theology, too. It is no use trying to evade the danger of the loss of authority by withdrawing into a massive theology of revelation which sacrifices the historical limitations of the Bible (= books!) to the unity and absolute validity of 'the Scriptures'.

For, on penalty of losing any real basis of faith, it is impossible to neglect the historical limitations of the Bible. Therefore fundamentalism cannot be considered a justified contribution to the solution of these problems, so that we shall pay no further attention to it here. The fact that there are so many sides to the problem led to various other attempts to arrive at a solution. Some of the most important recent attempts must be dealt with here briefly.[1]

Of late these problems have been approached in three different ways:

a. some scholars have tried to reconcile the unity of the Bible and its historical character by reverting to the allegorical and particularly the typological method.[2]

b. Some have tried to ward off the danger of neglecting and disparaging the Old Testament by making it all-important theologically as well as historically.[3]

[1] For the period before 1950 we refer to H.J.Kraus, *Geschichte der historisch-kritischen Forschung*, and to E.G.Kraeling, *op. cit.*, ch. 11–16.
[2] We think here above all of W.Vischer's *Christuszeugnis des A.T.*, of G.A.F.Knight's *A Christian Theology of the O.T.*, of the French Nouvelle Théologie, particularly Daniélou, and also of the second half of Von Rad's *O.T. Theology* II.
[3] Here we should mention K.H.Miskotte, *Als de goden zwijgen* (German translation: *Wenn die Götter schweigen*) and A.A.van Ruler, *Die Christliche Kirche und das A.T.*, 1955, though these two scholars differ in their accentuation of various aspects.

c. Others again have posited the problem of the tension between the two Testaments very drastically by designating the Old Testament in fact as a book of a non-Christian religion.[1]

a) At this point we cannot deal with the return to the typological manner at length, because we shall revert to this subject at a later stage (pp. 136f.). A few remarks may suffice here.

The importance of the typological approach is not to be denied; it rests upon various elements in the Old Testament that correspond with the substance of the New Testament or with a New Testament situation. It should not, however, be developed into a method so that it is applied to all texts like a divining-rod, for as a result the mutual correspondence between the two Testaments would make them seem to be, as it were, reflections of each other.

A relation arrived at in this way no longer convinces the historically well-informed critical modern reader. Quite often the correspondence is based on aesthetic, arbitrary and something wholly fortuitous personal views rather than on internal and therefore spiritually convincing motives.[2]

b) An especially fascinating attempt was made by the two above mentioned Dutch dogmatists. Each of them demonstrated the superiority of the Old Testament in his own way, thus striving against the stream of modern thought. A. A. van Ruler's fundamental tenet is that the Old Testament is the Bible of the early Christian Church, a notion against which we could make some serious objections from a historical point of view (see above, pp. 11–15, especially the notes); in his above-mentioned book he attempts to give new support to the priority of the Old Testament by demonstrating from the content the indispensability and superiority of the Old Testament for Christian thought and for the teaching of the Church. He points to the wide scope of the message of the Old Testament with its theocracy and creation-theology. The New Testament is represented as in fact much more limited because it only developed and elaborated one aspect of the theology of the Old Testament, namely its soteriology. According to Van Ruler this is not a sufficient basis for Christian theology to build on; if it is to give spiritual guidance to the modern world the theocracy and creation-theology of the Old Testament are indispensable.[3]

Like Van Ruler, K. H. Miskotte in his above-mentioned book[4] emphasizes very positively the value of the Old Testament for modern man. He calls attention to four points upon which the New Testament is practically silent: scepticism, revolt, erotics and politics.

Though I admit the comparative truth of these observations on the content of the Old Testament, I must venture to make some objections against the conclusion that the whole of the substance of the Old Testament should be theologically acceptable to the Christian Church without further preface.

[1] F. Hesse, op. cit.; Baumgärtel, Bultmann (see below).
[2] Cf. W. Eichrodt, 'Ist die typologische Exegese sachgemäße Exegese', Suppl. V.T., IV, 1957, pp. 161ff. and H. W. Wolff, Zur Hermeneutik des A.T., but especially the final remarks of his essay 'Der große Jisreeltag' (Hos. ii. 1–3) in his Ges.Studien zum A.T., 1964, pp. 251ff. and 181.
[3] See e.g. my reviews of this book in Ev. Th., 1965, pp. 387ff.; also included in C. Westermann, Probleme altt. Hermeneutik, pp. 181–204 (Engl. transl.: Essays on O.T. Interpretation, 1963).
[4] Cf. also his 'De prediking van het O.T.', in Handboek der Prediking I, pp. 353ff. and Om het levende woord, 1940, pp. 80ff.

In my opinion, any Christian ethics that would simply set up the various aspects of theocracy or erotics and marriage in the Old Testament as the standard to which the modern world or the Church would have to conform without first confronting them with Christ's cross, would fail signally in its duty. The cross is not merely an element of the Biblical message, but a source of light in the centre which casts its rays over all the other elements, and that is the very reason why the gospel must be accounted 'God's last word'.

c) The opposite view was taken by some German theologians, like F. Baumgärtel[1], R. Bultmann[2] and, following in their footsteps, F. Hesse;[3] they do not deny that the Old Testament contains God's word, but they especially emphasize that it is mixed up with error to such an extent that it can only be accepted as such with the greatest reserve.

Baumgärtel states that the true promise given bij God (Verheißung), contained in the words: I am the Lord thy God, is the basis for Israel's faith, but that in the Old Testament this promise is bound up with all kinds of political, material and wordly notions, not only in the historical parts but also in the teaching of the prophets, which therefore gives striking proof of how far Israel's faith had gone astray. It is only in the New Testament that God's promise is understood and actualized spiritually and inwardly by Immanuel, Jesus Christ. F. Hesse especially elaborated the conception that these are due to the chastising hand of God that made Israel harden their hearts (cf. 2 Cor. iii. 14, Rom. ix–xi and Isa. vi). By turning God's word into its opposite, this should teach the Christian to read the Old Testament not only critically but also as a warning directed against himself. In this way the Old Testament can be a dialectical witness to God's activity in Israel, which culminates in Christ's cross.

Though there is much in these views that appeals to us, such as the idea that the Old Testament cannot function theologically in the Church without the New, there are serious objections to be brought against them. The principal of these is that the break in the relation of the two Testaments is widened into such a gulf that the Old Testament could be described as the record of a non-Christian religion. The only thing that still connects them is the promise of the communion between God and man ('I shall be thy God') but the way in which this promise is interpreted and experienced in the two Testaments is so widely different that we can hardly speak of a unity of faith any longer. According to these authors the New Testament faith is spiritual, inward, heavenly, focused on further salvation, whereas the Old Testament faith is worldly-minded, materialistic and nationalistic. It is clear that one cannot but stigmatize the realistic faith of the Old Testament as a perversion of an original promise of God if one thinks in terms of this spiritualized, strongly pietistic hope of salvation which is interpreted dialectically. The question arises, however, whether the standard itself that is being applied here is not wholly false. For it is not the expectation of future salvation that is characteristic of the New Testament hopes, but a hope and assurance of the renewal of this world, and this concerns the people as well as the individual and the nations as well as the Church, it is a question of the present as well as of the future. And for

---

[1] *Verheißung*, 1952, and his criticism of Von Rad's *Theology* in *Th.L.Z.*, 1961, pp. 801ff. and 896ff.
[2] *Weissagung und Erfüllung*, in Westermann, *op. cit.*, pp. 28ff.
[3] E.g. 'Zur Frage der Wertung und Geltung altt. Texte' in Westermann, *op. cit.*, pp. 266ff.

that reason many objections against the teaching of the Old Testament raised by these theologians need not be considered alarming. In the Old Testament itself many things that are too human and could rightly be called 'irrender Glaube' have been rectified (see above pp. 86ff.), though a Christian theologian, taking the message of the Gospel for his starting-point, will certainly not maintain that the Old Testament is faultless in every respect.

On the other hand I must agree with Hesse when he states emphatically that the Old Testament cannot function theologically in the Church without the New Testament. In principle I concur with his objections against Von Rad's theological views, in so far as he accepts and hands on the maximum of the Old Testament in the *Kerygma* of the Scriptures (see his *O.T. Theology* I, p. 108) without any criticism (see also *Theologie* II, p. 10).[1] At this point, too, Hesse oversteps the mark when he pronounces the sharpest theological strictures on the Old Testament on the ground of certain historical data that do not fit the facts[2] and that were worked into the testimony of the Old Testament. Even if we should be prepared to admit frankly that an overwrought historical idea of God's activity (such as, among others, the Deuteronomistic notion of the conquest of the country in the book of Joshua) confuses the testimony and raises expectations that are not in agreement with the gospel, we cannot allow historical accuracy in itself to decide on the theological truth of the Old Testament witness. A historically correct narrative might conceivably contain a less truthful testimony than a story that is non-historical or historically inexact. We might raise all kinds of objections against Nehemiah's message, though his narrative is historically reliable. On the other hand the witness of the first few chapters of Genesis, which are not historical, may be considered the culminating point of the testimony of the Bible, and the same applies to the history of Abraham.

The Bible does not derive its authority from its historical correctness or infallibility, but from its *theological* truth, from the reliability, the trueness to life of its message. The authority of the Bible rests on the spiritual force of the Biblical testimony on God and man, on sin and grace, life and death, world and re-creation.[3]

By this existential conception the problem of the actual authority of the Old Testament is seen in the proper light. For it is authoritative when it shares in the truth revealed in Jesus Christ – in other words, when there is an essential relation between the message of the Old Testament and the New Testament. For Christian theology this is the question regarding the Old Testament: Has the Old Testament mes-

---

[1] The German edition has a Preface missing in the English translation. See my observations in *Theologie en Kerk*, 1965.
[2] Which is still quite often a matter of debate.
[3] This is not the place to discuss the subject of the truth of the Bible itself, for this belongs to the field of dogmatics and the philosophy of religion. We may refer the reader to: J.H.Vrielink, 'Het waarheidskarakter der Heilige Schrift' in: *Schrift en Kerk*, Haitjema Festschrift 1953, pp.29ff.; E.Brunner, *The Divine-Human Encounter*, 1944; M.Buber, *Der Mensch und die jüdische Bibel* 1926, in Buber-Rosenzweig, *Die Schrift und ihre Verdeutschung*, 1963, pp.13ff.; H. von Soden, 'Was ist Wahrheit in Christentum und Geschichte', *Ges. Aufsätze* I, 1951, pp.1ff.

sage anything to do, factually, existentially, spiritually with the Gospel of Jesus Christ, and if so, to what extent? By way of the historical statement of the problem, this has led us back to the original Pauline and (generally speaking) early Christian question.

We cannot give an immediate, one-sided answer to this question, any more than St. Paul could: to us as to him the relationship appeared to be twofold. On the one hand we must admit the *organic* spiritual unity of Old Testament and New Testament because the life of Jesus Christ rested on the foundation of the Old Testament message of the Law and the prophets and because He was sent to the world by the God of truth and righteousness, the God proclaimed by the Old Testament. W. F. Lofthouse says quite rightly: 'If the Christian's faith in the Son of God is an error or delusion, the Old Testament will fall with it'.[1] But on the other hand there is a *historical* relationship; we must admit the difference between some parts of the Old Testament and the message of the Gospel.[2]

There *is* a line that leads from the Old Testament to Christ; this line is not seen with equal clearness everywhere, but it is a very important, central line that runs through the whole of the Law, Prophets, and Writings; *via* the doctrine of sin and grace in Torah and prophets it leads to the profound and all-embracing message of the Servant of the Lord in Deutero-Isaiah.[3] But there are also lines in the Old Testament that lead to Judaism and may draw the reader away from Christ.[4] So much regarding the Old Testament in general.

What is true of the Old Testament as a whole also applies to the individual books of the Old Testament, though – with a few exceptions

[1] W. F. Lofthouse, 'The Old Testament and Christianity', (in H. Wheeler Robinson, *Record and Revelation*, 1938, p. 480).
[2] The well-known book by E. Hirsch, *Das A.T. und die Predigt des Evangeliums*, 1936, speaks only of an essential contrast between Old Testament and New Testament; the tension between the two has become too strong: in the first place because of the Lutheran doctrine of the two kingdoms (13), and secondly because of a wrong evaluation of the prophets (see below p. 101 n.2); cf. also O. Eißfeldt, 'Ist der Gott des A.T. auch der des N.T.?', *Th.St.Kr.*, 109, 2, 1947, pp. 37ff.
[3] See below ch. VII, II c 4, 5, pp. 272f.
[4] See e.g. the quotations from H. W. Obbink and F. Horst, below, p. 121; cf. J. Lindblom, *Israels Religion*[2], 1953, pp. 271ff.: 'the peculiar character of the Old Testament religion as compared with New Testament Christianity is most evident in its religious nationalism, its monarchic and juridical conception of God, its moralism and its material and physical conception of life' (273). We think of the doctrine of sin and grace in the New Testament, which is essentially different from that of the O.T.; remember the continuous protests of M. Buber against this doctrine of the N.T., which according to him and according to all Jewish theologians is unworthy of man, while Judaism comes to man with its demands of the Torah and makes man an independent personality. It is essentially the same opposition as between St. Paul and his Jewish adversaries; cf. also J. Klausner, *op. cit.*, II 7, XIV 4. (Though it is doubtful if the modern Jewish interpretation of this point in the O.T. may be considered correct.)

such as Esther and the Song of Songs – it is very difficult to decide which books can be considered preparatory to the testimony concerning Christ and which cannot. There is a great deal of truth in the words: 'though a qualitive as well as quantitative distinction should be made between the Word of God and the Holy Scriptures, they cannot be separated',[1] because generally speaking the whole of the Old Testament is borne along by one and the same spirit: *the spirit of prophecy which springs from the Spirit of God, the Father of Jesus Christ.*[2] In the next few pages we shall explain this twofold thesis, first of all:

a) *The Old Testament springs from prophecy*

This is the secret of the Old Testament. In a theological inquiry into the essence of the Old Testament it is of decisive importance never to lose sight of this basis of the whole of the Old Testament witness. It does not only apply to the prophetical writings but also to the historical books which are founded on the teaching of the prophets. There is only one thing that will account for the awareness that history is the activity of God: prophetic vision and testimony. Being aware that God is active in the present, the past and the future, living on God's promises and their fulfilment, are typical of the characteristic prophetic witness. In stressing these last two characteristic elements of Old Testament historiography Von Rad clearly demonstrated this prophetic character, though, unlike other theologians[3] he is not prepared to call it by that name.[4]

To say the Old Testament was written with the blood and tears of the people of Israel so that it is a record of the spirit of this people in all its fierceness, variety and sensitiveness, is not to do full justice to the Old Testament; neither would it be the whole truth to explain it from the genius of the Jewish people[5] as many Jewish writers do. For the truth about the Old Testament is that in many respects it is not representative of the spirit of the people of Israel, but of that of the *fools* in Israel, as the message of the gospels and the other New

[1] K. H. Miskotte, *Om het levende Woord*, 1948, p. 74; also A. Weiser, 'Vom Verstehen des A.T.', *Z.A.W.*, 1945/8, p. 21; cf. also above pp. 87ff.
[2] Cf. pp. 43ff. The fact that the Old Testament prophets did not teach the doctrine of the two kingdoms caused Hirsch (*op. cit.*, p. 13) no longer to consider them of particular importance; if we remember, however, how the prophets opposed the people and its nationalism, its hopes, and how they proclaimed a *new kingdom of God* since Isa. ix, xi, ii, we cannot rank the testimony of the Scriptural prophets with that of the nationalistic 'false' prophets (cf. Isa. viii, Amos vii, Mic. iii, Jer., Ezek.). In his remarks on the prophets Von Rad (*Theology* II) defended the opposite view: according to him they are the men who broke through the faith in the old promises of salvation by transforming it into either a law or the proclaiming of an eschatological Kingdom of God.
[3] O. Plöger, 'Geschichte und Geschichtsauffassung', I, im A.T., *R.G.G.*[3] II, pp. 1473ff.; H. W. Wolff, 'Das Geschichtsverständnis der altt. Prophetie', *Ev.Th.*, 1960, pp. 218ff.
[4] *Th.L.Z.* 1963, pp. 412f.
[5] Cf. also M. Noth, 'Von der Knechtsgestalt des A.T.', *Ev.Th.* 1947, p. 306.

Testament writings also sprang from the foolishness of faith. For were not the prophets of the Old Testament derided as fools (2 Kings ix. 11), contradicted (Mic. ii. 6), expelled from the temple and taken for traitors (Jeremiah), maltreated (Isa. l. 4ff.), to mention only a few. Again and again we read how Israel rebelled against Moses who is depicted to us in the historical books. And always the motive for their activity was the fact that God proved the stronger, that they were ordered to speak and to bear witness in spite of themselves. The foundation of the Old Testament is the living God, who gave His Word to His prophets and called upon them to testify.[1] The prophets are the heralds and interpreters of God's message in Israel. So if we say that the secret of the Old Testament is prophecy, that means: the secret of the Old Testament is the Word of God that was entrusted to the prophets in their personal encounter with God (Am. iii. 7). Of this Word the history of Israel is born, by it Israel is governed. It also determines Israel's institutions. It is the secret centre of all Old Testament revelation, elusive and not to be made manageable, neither in the law nor in institutions nor in forms that have become historical like the creed or the covenant or any other theological concept. For all these forms are merely 'answers' to the word of God received by Israel. From the very beginning it came to Israel through the words of the prophets.[2] The history of the patriarchs already bears testimony to this when it speaks of a personal encounter with God, and so does the history of deliverance and victory. Throughout the history of Israel the prophets appear at critical moments as guides in the life of the people. In the vicissitudes of life they guide the people and its leaders by their warnings, their judgments, their directions, as true servants of God. Drastically and decisively they speak God's words to point out the way the people will have to go (in syncretist dangers in the midst of civilized nations, in questions of kingship and temple-building, in the dangers of foreign politics).

This guiding Word of God, that is preached to Israel again and again, dominates the Old Testament. It forced Old Testament Historiography to depict the patriarchs (Abraham at all events) as prophets.[3] It could not but view the whole of Israel's history of salvation in the light of the Word of God that had been revealed.

There are, however, also clear indications proving that these religious ideas dominate tradition and the collection of writings because it was the express intention of the authors to include only those things that were based on the Word of God. The names *Torah* and *Nebiim (rishonim* and *acharonim)* point that way.

A well-known Old Testament scholar rightly made the following statement about the Old Testament: 'Gott allein das Wort zu lassen, alles Übrige, alles Menschliche auszuschalten, das muss die Absicht gewesen sein' ('It must have been the intention to let God speak freely, to eliminate everything else,

---

[1] M. Noth, *op. cit.*, pp. 302ff.
[2] We should not allow our image of the prophet to be determined completely by the Old Testament Scriptural prophets. Essentially the prophet is a 'speaker', see G. v. d. Leeuw, *Phaenomenologie der Religion*, 1933, pp. 204ff. They actualize God's Word and are not merely concerned with the future. A figure like Moses (who is, indeed, repeatedly characterized as a prophet in the Old Testament, cf. Exod. iv, Hos. xii) certainly is entitled to a place among the prophets as a mediator between Yahweh and Israel.
[3] Either explicitly, as in Gen. xx (E), or implicitly, as in the description of the words of God received (in Gen. xv, xvii and xii); cf. also A. Alt, *Der Got der Väter*, who emphasizes the idea of revelation in this type of religion.

everything human'.)[1] The historical data in the writings of the major prophets are to be looked upon as explanatory, or at any rate accompanying descriptions of the prophecies. Here we should keep in mind that autobiographical pieces are practically the only parts that are left of the historical literature on the prophets. Of the biographical pieces only very small parts are left, except in the case of Jeremiah, but his appearance gave so much offence that it immediately led to the apology by Baruch (ch. xxxviff.).

The 'historical books' ('the early prophets') are also essentially prophetical in origin. In my opinion the books of Samuel were written in the spirit of the prophet Nathan, perhaps by his son.[2] The author who is called the Yahwist – though influenced by the wisdom literature[3] – was a kindred spirit to the prophets,[4] like the Elohist, who originated from the north-Israelite world, in which certain characteristic elements of nationalistic prophetism are also to be observed. The Deuteronomistic writings were also influenced by a theology inspired by the prophetism of Isaiah's disciples,[5] and even the writings collected in the so-called Priestly Code felt the effect of a theology influenced by prophetism.[6] From this it is clear that the first two great parts of the Old Testament, the *Torah* and the *Nebiim*, were pervaded and dominated by the spirit of prophetism.

This is not so evident in the case of the later writings, though several of these certainly did not escape this influence: Ruth, many of the Psalms, the apocalyptic book of Daniel, and to a certain extent the Chronicles with Ezrah and Nehemiah, in which the prophetical figures play a very important part, if not a dominating one.[7]

Therefore, together with the Church that has always incorporated the Old Testament into the Holy Scriptures throughout the centuries, we may also testify to the Old Testament Word of God. It is His Spirit that bears these testimonies and gives them life, so that they are still felt to be God's words. For many of them, from the book of Psalms, for instance, are still immediately accepted as of vital importance. The message that comes to us from these writings did not arise in the heart of man but was born of the Spirit. The continuous judgments on the sins of men, even of the best of men, the repudiation of any false heroism and of all demoniacal elements, in short the destruction of everything that might be set up beside God, together

[1] Cf. Budde, 'Eine folgenschwere Redaktion des Zwölfprophetenbuches,' *Z.A.W.* 1921, p. 225.
[2] On this see my essay 'De litteraire samenstelling van de Samuëlboeken', in *Orientalia Neerlandica*, 1948.
[3] Cf. e.g. H. W. Wolff, 'Kerygma des Jahwisten', *Ges. Studien z. A.T.*, 1964, p. 349 (cf. the translation in *Interpretation* 1966, p. 135).
[4] These also show the influence of the *chokmah*, cf. Isaiah and Jeremiah, and even Amos, as has been shown by H. W. Wolff in his *Amos' geistige Heimat*, 1964.
[5] We should think of the part played by the prophets in deuteronomistic historiography and of the 'prophetical style' as it is apparent in such chapters as Judg. iif., x; 1 Sam. ii, xii etc., cf. H. W. Wolff, 'Das Kerygma des Dtn. Geschichtswerks', *op. cit.*, pp. 308ff.
[6] Cf. p. 61.
[7] For Chronicles we should also bear in mind the part played by the temple-songs, rather than the sacrifices. The temple-songs could be looked upon as prophecy.

with the unvarying references to God as the Lord and Saviour, and the complete reliance on His faithfulness and power even in the most desperate situations, all this keeps evoking the firm belief that these testimonies are inspired by the Spirit of God.

We may say this even if there are some occasional human, and even all too human reactions which must be looked upon as rendered out of date in the light of the revelation of God in Christ.[1] But, as we proved at the end of the previous chapter, the Old Testament corrects itself in several respects; it incorporated various critical reactions to certain tendencies, so that *the Old Testament, taken as a whole and as a unity, is a true testimony to God.*

b) *The prophetical message of the Old Testament is continued in the New Testament*

After these general observations on the essence of the Old Testament in which the *R(uach)* (the Spirit) could be looked upon as the *R(edactor)* of the Old Testament (in the manner of Rosenzweig[2], who explained the R. of critical literary history as *Rabbenu* – our Lord, the God of Israel), we must now broach the question of the relation between the content of the message of the two Testaments. Does *the Spirit* that speaks of God in the Old Testament indeed give essentially the same message as the testimony of the New Testament, so that the religious content of the two is fundamentally identical? For on this point Jews and Christians differ, and even the Christians are divided among themselves.

In answering this question we must pay attention to several points, the most important of which are the following:

1) Does the Old Testament preach *the same God* as the New Testament – or is there a fundamental distinction between Yahweh, the God of Israel, and the God and Father of Jesus Christ?

2) Is the *expectation of the Kingdom of God* which dominates the New Testament witness from beginning to end, *essentially the same* as in the Old Testament?

3) Are the *roads that lead to the Kingdom* in the two Testaments *fundamentally the same* or related?

4) Is the *life of faith* in the New Testament essentially the same in character as in the Old Testament, from a material and formal point of view, or is it different so that we should have to speak of two ways of believing?[3] And, closely bound up with the point:

5) Are *ethics* and *religion, religion* and *law* one in their mutual relations,

---

[1] See above, p. 98.
[2] Buber-Rosenzweig, *Die Schrift und ihre Verdeutschung*, 1936, p.47.
[3] Cf. M.Buber, *Zwei Glaubensweisen*, 1950.

or are they so far apart that they must be taken to belong to wholly different systems?

6) Are *the confessions of sin and repentance, the teaching of grace and the love of God,* the inner *strength of faith* and the *future hopes* related or distinct, so that the nature of *piety* in the two Testaments should be looked upon as different?

Before going into these problems in great detail, we may point out that it is not *a priori* to be expected that the New Testament should simply be in an even line with the Old Testament, like the books of the prophets take over and continue each other's message, or like the Deuteronomistic authors treat the witness of the ancient historiographers. There is, and always will be, a wide gap between the two, a gap which cannot be eliminated, but a similar tension exists in the Old Testament between the book of Daniel and the early prophets, as also between Job or Ecclesiastes and the early Wisdom literature, and between the latter and the priestly and prophetical writings.

As regards the relation between Old Testament and New Testament we should not fail to take into account the distance in time and period of culture of the two. Culture and the way of thought in Graeco-Roman Palestine had changed radically from that of the ancient Israelite or even the Persian period.

It is, therefore, of paramount importance that in the Qumranscrolls a literature has come to our knowledge that is contemporary to the New Testament. This literature has convinced many scholars, Christians as well as Jews,[1] of the close spiritual relationship between the early Church and the contemporary Jewish world.

A second preliminary remark is that in our subsequent observations we shall not take into account the tensions between the various elements in the complex of theologies within the Old Testament itself, as they were elaborated by G. von Rad. In his *Theology,* and even more in his own later additional remarks in ThLZ, 1963, pp.401ff., under the title of *Offene Fragen im Umkreis einer Theologie des A. T.,* he defended the thesis that there is not really a theology of the Old Testament, because there are many theologies in the Old Testament.[2] Even if we have to admit that there is some measure of truth in this view, that does not mean that we are presented with an essentially different *kerygma* or testimony concerning God in these various different theological ways of thought. In all of them the God of Israel is fundamentally the same, with the only exception of some ancient petrefacts dating from the pre-Israelite period and hardly integrated in the later historical narratives (e.g. Exod.iv 24–26, see below pp. 303f.).

We shall now answer the question put above as briefly as possible. With regard to the nature of the testimony concerning Israel's God in the Old Testament and the New Testament there can be no doubt, in spite of Marcion and his various disciples, that there is a direct

[1] Cf. e.g. D. Flüsser, *De Joodse oorsprong van het Christendom,* 1964.
[2] Cf. already Zimmerli's remark in *V.T.* 1963, pp. 104f. on the unity in the abundance of theologies in the O.T. In the Christian Church, too, there were many developments of theology round the one centre of the twelve articles of the apostolic creed, which essentially remained their underlying pattern.

internal relationship between the message of the Old Testament and that of the New. The Christian Church derived its *belief in God the Father, the Creator of heaven and earth* through the early Church from the testimony of the Old Testament.[1] Here Yahweh, the God of Israel, is praised as the Redeemer; from the beginning of history, even in the narrative of the creation, paradise and the deluge, He is that God who thinks of man in His love and delivers him. In the traditions of the patriarchs and the deliverance from Egypt He is no less the Saviour of Israel than in the history of the conquest of the country and in the teaching of the prophets. One should read in this connection Hosea, Isaiah, Jeremiah, Ezekiel or Deutero-Isaiah. In the Old Testament, too, God is the Father of His people, in spite of His chastisement of Israel (Hos. xi; Isa. i. 2; Deut. xiv. 1). Man is created in His image, as the son is the image of his father (Gen. i. 26, v. 1–3). Certain elements that have been called demonistic (see pp.300ff.) do not obscure this image of the Father and Saviour, no more than some verses of Hosea (xiii. 7 f.) can detract from the genuineness of the prophetic testimony concerning God as the Loving Husband and Father (Hos. ii, xi).

As regards the second point, the expectation of the Kingdom of God, it has been clear from the earliest preaching of the gospel (Mark i. 2, 14 f.) that it was derived from the Old Testament. Like the Qumran community, John the Baptist and also the messianic community that followed Jesus were dominated by the hope of renewal of the world[2] and the expectation of an early actualization of the prophetic message. There is this main difference – and it is a particularly deep-lying one – that the messianic community was convinced that Jesus of Nazareth constitued a new beginning, that the *New Covenant*[3] (Jer. xxxi. 31 ff.) had now materialized. There is a difference of opinion – and again, the difference is a very radical one – on the actuality of the fulfilment of the hopes and on the *person* of the expected Messiah, but fundamentally all who read the Old Testament as the Word of God are agreed on the expectation itself, on creation and recreation, on the intervention of God who made His world as it is and who placed this man in this relationship to Himself and His creation, and on God's re-creating activity in this world who causes His kingdom to come (think of Deutero-Isaiah, who recognized God's creative activity in the new things that he thought to be close at hand).

---

[1] Cf. R.Bultmann, *Das Urchristentum*, 1949, pp.11ff.; on the whole of the following observations on the New Testament cf. also the article by H.Conzelmann, 'Jesus Christus', *R.G.G.* III[3], pp.633ff.
[2] P.S.Minear, 'New Starting Point', *Interpretation*, 1965, pp.3ff.
[3] See W.C. van Unnik, 'La conception Paulinienne de la Nouvelle Alliance', *Recherches bibliques*, 1960, pp.109ff; id., "Η καινη διαθηκη', *Studia Patristica* IV, 1961, pp.212ff.

In spite of all the differences between Jew and Christian in the practice of their faith in God the Creator and of the messianic teaching of salvation, they have a root in common, from which they both derive their vital strength, founded on the prophetic testimony of the Old Testament.

And therefore both Jew and Christian live by God's promises, by the prophetic Word of God, facing the future, 'zwischen den Zeiten', with this difference that, owing to his belief in the appearance of the Messiah Jesus, the Christian can see the Kingdom of God outlined more clearly than the Jew, who is presented with so many different conceptions by his tradition. Jesus and his community live particularly by the teaching of Deutero-Isaiah and his faith in the Kingdom of God which is being realized (see Ch. IX); their hopes differ from those of Judaism in two aspects, in the first place because they are focused exclusively on the centre of the prophetic message of salvation: full direct communion with God (Jer. xxxi. 33 f.; Ezek. xxxvi. 26 ff.), which means life eternal (John xvii. 3), and second because these hopes were experienced and thought of as being in the process of realization in the appearance and the work of Jesus Christ, in whom and by whom the breakthrough of the Holy Spirit in this world was effected. These two facets belong together and condition the nature of the Christian faith with all its paradox elements, so that there is a direct and full relationship between the present and the future, between life on this earth and life eternal.[1]

The third question is concerned with the connection between the road that leads to the Kingdom in the Old Testament and in the New Testament.

Here we find considerable differences, but also striking parallels, greater in number and more profound than people usually think.

Though the nationalistic, political and particularist hopes that are found so frequently in the Old Testament have been abandoned in the New Testament one cannot simply say that the expectations of the New Testament are exclusively directed towards the world to come. We find that the New Testament hopes are also concerned with the restoration of this world. More expressly than in the Old Testament the road to salvation is conditioned especially by suffering, by the cross. The idea of a battle is still in evidence, but it is no longer a battle fought with arms, as it is waged in the Old Testament and even more clearly in the Essenic community of Qumran ('The Scroll of the War of the Sons of Light with the Sons of Darkness'). Suffering had, however, already been discovered and described in the Old Testament

[1] See beside W. C. van Unnik, 'De Heilige Geest in het N.T.', *De Spiritu Sancto,* 1964, pp. 63ff., also E. Käsemann, 'Geist und Geistesgaben im N.T.', *R.G.G.* II³, pp. 1272ff.

as the road that leads to salvation; this was elaborated most profoundly in the prophecies of Deutero-Isaiah (l;lii–liii), but that is not the only place where we are confronted by it. Deutero-Isaiah's message of suffering is not an erratic boulder transferred to the Old Testament, but it definitely belongs there. For in the lives of the prophets it became more and more manifest that those who proclaimed the Word of God to Israel would also be affected by the guilt and the sin of the people, not only because of the opposition caused by their teaching among their contemporaries, but also because they had to make their message understood by impersonating it symbolically or even in their own lives. From Elijah to Deutero-Zechariah the prophets were persecuted and rejected and many of them had to undergo the sins and the chastisement of the people visibly, in a very real sense; they were set up as examples. A case in point would be Hosea who had to contract a marriage with a woman from the disloyal people, in order to illustrate God's anger with and love of Israel in this way; we should also bear in mind how Isaiah, Micah, Jeremiah and Deutero-Isaiah became involved in the struggle between God and His people, and we should remember how the traditional narrative relates that Moses interceded for his people with God (Exod. xxxii. 31 ff., Ps. cvi. 23). To an ever-increasing extent the road to salvation came to be a way of suffering, of struggle, and of ruin for the faithful witnesses to this salvation. The Old Testament is full of this; less so, indeed, than the New Testament, but so clearly that we may say that the suffering of the 'Ebed Yahweh already began to manifest itself. Cf. H. W. Robinson, The Cross in the O. T., 1955.

It seems to me that this personal way of assimilating and proclaiming the Word of God, in which the messenger himself is involved bodily and spiritually in God's activity in this world, marks an essential feature of the Biblical message concerning the approaching Kingdom of God. For this, too, is one way in which communion with God is actualized. The way of the suffering Christ is the complete actualization of a line of development which, according to the Old Testament, was traced out by God in ancient Israel. The prophets had to go along this road long before one of them (Deutero-Isaiah) came to realize that this was indeed the road decreed by God.

With these observations the other questions (3–6) are also answered in principle: as regards the nature of faith, there is no fundamental difference. Both the Old Testament and the New live by the God who has revealed Himself in the history of Israel by His words and His deeds; they are both based on the true faith in the God of the Covenant to which they bear witness, even if the New Testament, following up the words of Jeremiah (xxxi), rightly testifies to the actualization of a *new* covenant in the person of Jesus Christ.

In the New Testament the relation between ethics and religion is still closer than in the Old Testament, also because the awareness of the absoluteness of the relation between God and man was deepened and widened by the renewal of the covenant in Jesus Christ. Neither does the message of the love of God in Christ detract from the *Torah* as the expression of God's will, though the New Testament recognizes that the Mosaic *Torah* was integrated and glorified in that of Jesus Christ. It was certainly not impaired, for the message of the gospel unites *Torah* and *Kerygma*.[1]

In the New Testament the confession of sin and repentance is heard more clearly, more frankly than in many parts of the Old Testament (cf. the Epistle to the Romans, esp. ch. vii), though the sins of man were already frequently exposed by the holy God (Isa. vi, Ps. li; see also p. 285).

Neither is there an essential difference between the piety of the Old Testament and the New though in some cases there is a difference in practise; the love of God and one's fellow-man, the clinging to the providence of God the Father, the assurance of God's purpose with this world and the life of the community and the individual, the respect for creation and the creature, thankfulness and hope, all these are fundamentally determining factors for both the Old and the New Testament (see further pp. 276 ff. and 333 ff.).

As we said above, there is only one fundamental, deep-lying difference between the two Testaments, and it concerns the recognition of Jesus of Nazareth as the Messiah. And all other points of controversy between Jews and Christians, all other differences between Old Testament and New Testament are closely bound up with it. They are all related to the recognition of Jesus Christ, to His work, His message and His person. None of the points on which Judaism and Christianity differ is fundamentally wanting in the Old Testament. Immediacy, topicality, the personal element, both the individual and the universal aspects of the relationship between God and man, the operation of the Spirit of God, the way of suffering, the coming of the Kingdom, the absoluteness of the communion of the faithful and the love of one's fellowman, all these are elements that are already known in the Old Testament but they are emphasized in the gospel of Jesus Christ. Other aspects of the Old Testament, which had come to the fore in later times, such as the national element (with its territorial and political implications), the institutional and cultic attitude, were thrust into the background.

[1] Cf. W. Zimmerli, *Das Gesetz und die Propheten*, 1963, pp. 144f. (cf. *The Law* etc., pp. 90ff), and the articles on 'Gesetz' and 'Gesetz und Evangelium' in *R.G.G.* II[3].

This change in function of certain elements in Israel's religion brought about the great cleavage in Israel. Judaism, rejecting Jesus as the Messiah, could no longer recognize itself in the renewed form of Israel's faith. Yet the New Testament did not add any foreign elements to Israel's religion (see pp. 12 n. 1, 105, 121 n.2). Nor is it strange from a historical point of view that Israel's faith should have found new forms for its religious life and its theological thought. This had already occurred on several occasions in Old Testament times[1], and in ancient Israel this had also frequently caused great tensions, so that, for example, one prophet opposed another. In the Priestly Code we find three covenants, which could be said to prove that there are in principle three stages to be distinguished in Israel's religion. The renovation that was caused by the appearance of Jesus Christ can be viewed in the same light as the renewals within the Israelite religion. The far-reaching consequences for Israel's religion and the subsequent cleavage were caused by the fact that the form assumed by the Israelite religion among the Jews of the New Testament period was no longer strong enough to stand the radical inward renovation accomplished by Jesus Christ. We should pay some attention to the following data: the ever-increasing transcendentalization of Israel's God in Judaism caused a form of nomism to dominate the religion of Israel[2], but in the message of the gospel a form of religion gained ground in which the nearness of and the communion with God were experienced. In this way the immediate relation between God and man (not merely between God and the people) was restored and the operation of the Spirit was experienced anew, so that the way was cleared for the prophetic element, and above all for the certainty of being a child of God. This immediate experience of communion with God was the reason why the *Torah* could no longer be the only leading spiritual authority it had become in the course of the centuries – contrary to the essence of Israel's religion. For a messianic figure to spring from this process of renewal that was enacted in Jesus Christ Himself, was not essentially foreign to the religion of Israel, though the Jews maintain this persistently. So much, if anything, should be clear that the further one goes back into history, the more frequently we find such figures in Israel's religion: in addition to Moses we could mention the patriarchs who taught their descendants to serve a God who had appeared to them Himself and who was so closely connected with them that He was called by the name of the patriarch 'the God of Abraham', 'the God of my father'. By Jesus Christ the relationship between God and His church was renewed to such an extent that the

[1] Cf. ch. III and G. Von Rad's thesis elaborated in his *Theology* and in *Th.L.Z.* 1963.
[2] Cf. e.g. M. Avi-Yonah, *Geschichte der Juden im Zeitalter der Talmud*, 1962, pp. 1ff.

Church believed in the God and Father of Jesus who, for that reason, was honoured as the Christ. The earliest Judaic-Christian church cannot look upon all it experienced in Jesus as an alienation from the Old Testament and its message, but in this experience it learned to come to a true understanding of the Old Testament in the full glory of God's revelation. The Old Testament became something new, a book different from what it had become for official Judaism. The early Church reads it quite differently and finds other things important in the Old Testament than the Jews do.

With all this it is clear that Christian theology cannot commit itself *unconditionally* to the contents of the Old Testament canon, for the Church itself has not actively co-operated in bringing about this canon but only associated itself afterwards with the decisions that had fallen among the Jews and accepted these decisions from traditional considerations without deciding independently on the formation of the canon.[1] To a certain extent the canon even developed partly as a defence against Christian teaching and the writings that had sprung from this teaching.[2] Various writings that were held in high esteem by the Jews themselves (the so-called Apocrypha) were eliminated, as well as a number of Pseudepigrapha that were apparently considered of heretical origin (apocalyptic).

So theology can, without denying her origins, admit the objections that were repeatedly raised against the Old Testament, such as the objections against certain parts of the Law (the ritual parts) or the *kerygma* of some historical writings (certain parts of the histories of Jacob and Samson), parts of certain Psalms (e.g. the Psalm of innocence Ps. xxvi, the wedding-song of Ps. xlv and the prayers for revenge in Ps. cix and Ps. cxxxvii), certain books (Esther, the Song of Songs, Ecclesiastes), to mention only these few. Here and there other parts could be found in which the Christian can only with great difficulty (or not at all) find the revelation of the Spirit of God, but rather the revelation of the spirit of the age (Ecclesiastes) or of the spirit of the Jewish people (Ps. cxxxvii, Esther). Such objections are not without any foundation or merely the product of a spirit of criticism.[3] On the contrary, one may love such parts of the Bible and admire them as classical monuments. Ps. cxxxvii is, humanly speaking, one of the

[1] This is certainly true of the Old Testament canon of the Reformation churches. The situation is, in fact, that the Roman Catholic Church conformed most closely to the ancient tradition of the early Christian Church, while the Reformation churches conformed to the Jewish decisions concerning the canon taken at the close of the first century A.D.; see also pp. 12ff.
[2] See O. Eißfeldt, *op. cit.*, § 75, 2; Sundberg, *op. cit.*, p. 126.
[3] For that reason Von Rad's remark that 'the kerygmatic picture of the O.T. tends towards a theological maximum' (*Old Testament Theology* I, p. 108) is not to be accepted without more ado; see my criticism in *K. Th.*, 1965, pp. 97ff.

most moving Psalms, Ecclesiastes a pearl of human wisdom, and the Song of Songs a delightful book; we should be loth to miss these elements in the collection of the Old Testament writings, but one cannot call them a message, a revelation of God, or find in them a trace of that activity of the Holy Spirit which was revealed in Jesus Christ.[1]

All this is not a plea for a change in the historical form in which the canon has been handed down to us, but only for the necessity of a theological and critical judgment as a continuation of the process of revaluation, which in principle is already evident in the New Testament; and also for the recognition of a certain measure of fortuitousness in the fixing of the canon, and hence of the fundamental freedom of theological criticism of the Old Testament, when one takes the Gospel of Jesus Christ as a starting-point.

This revaluation does not run parallel to that of scholarly historical criticism and research[2], though the two may go together, as might be maintained in the case of books like Daniel and Esther. But with respect to the truth of a Biblical writing it is fundamentally of no importance whether the date of such a writing is earlier or later than the date attributed to it by the Old Testament tradition or actually coincides with that date. The 'truth' of a Psalm or a prophetic word does not depend on its authorship: a psalm of David is not 'more true' than one by somebody else. Even the historical accuracy of a certain passage, for instance a piece of historical writing, is, as was remarked already (in another connection, see above p. 99), not in itself decisive with regard to its 'truth' – for such a historical narrative was not included first and foremost because of its historical content, but because of its message, or, as we might say, its 'tendency'. Some years ago this view was, rightly, recognized again officially by Roman Catholic theology, in Protestant circles it had already been upheld a very long time ago.[3]

---

[1] One might rejoice in the breadth of vision of those who fixed the Palestinian canon, on the ground that the Song of Songs and Ecclesiastes were included, but for the established fact that the Song of Songs was only included when its spiritual meaning had been fastened down by allegorical interpretation and Ecclesiastes only when it had been made to fit in with the Law by the addition of the last few verses.

[2] In this respect I can agree largely to Von Rad's views as opposed to the criticism of these and others. The modern historical picture of Israel is *not* without further preface a basis for criticism of the testimony of the Old Testament; on the other hand, there may be cases where Israel's kerygmatic picture of history takes such wild forms (cf. the plagues of Egypt, the conquest stories in Joshua) that the relevance of the testimony is obscured by the grotesque composition. See pp. 98f. and 111 n. 3.

[3] See e.g. the encyclical *Divino afflante Spiritu* of Pius XII, 1943 (and the discussion of this by J. Lévie in P. Auvray's 'L'A.T et les Chrétiens', *Rencontres* 36, 1951, pp. 89ff.) and th 'Epistula ad Cardinalem Suhard', *A.A.S.* XL, II, vol. XV, 1948, p. 458, which

The theological evaluation of the Old Testament and its component parts is a question to which it will be hard to find a complete answer to satisfy everyone. Theology has for its task the weighing against each other of the living Word of God and the temporal, human element in the Old Testament. Like all human tasks this one, too, will never reach fulfilment, for again and again new points of view will arise. Theology may gain a deeper insight into the essential meaning of Jesus Christ; it may arrive at a better understanding of the Old Testament, its history, meaning and essence – though the development of theology on this point will certainly not proceed along a straight line towards an ever ripening insight! – but its task will always remain to test the Scriptures in the light of Jesus Christ the Lord, and to know Him and the Father who sent Him by the Scriptures. When the two principal aims of the study of the Scriptures are thus placed side by side we seem to move in a vicious circle – an apparently hopeless undertaking – but when we consider what progress has been made during the past century we may expect to make further progress, and think that there are good hopes for a study of the Bible which is undertaken in true faith, a faith characterized both by loyalty to the Word of God and in honest scholarly work. When we observe how in this respect various Churches in the Christian world have come to gain an ever greater understanding of each other's work, we are led on to hope that the work is under way indeed, and that a sound method has been found.

Our conclusions may, therefore, be stated as follows:

Broadly speaking[1], the Old Testament, in so far as its nature is kerygmatic, may be called truly prophetical in spirit. Its profound testimony concerning God, not only in the prophetical books themselves but also in many historical books, and to a certain extent also in the legal sections and in the Wisdom literature, has become more and more evident owing to research in the fields of literary criticism and the history of religion. A new insight in the Old Testament has been gained and the way has been prepared for a new and positive theological appreciation of the Old Testament by the overthrow of certain

states that the Biblical idea of history should not be judged by the standards of Western scientific views of history; cf. also the various forms of 'historical' narrative style in the O.T., as illustrated in the article on *Bibelwissenschaft* in Haag's *Bibellexicon* (known to me only from *Herders Korrespondenz*, 1953, p. 267ff.). The same view was emphasized recently by G. C. van Niftrik in *Schrift en Kerk*, 1953, pp. 49ff. in his essay 'De verborgen zin der Schrift'. Unfortunately Van Niftrik tries on those grounds to make out a case for the validity of allegorization in the exegesis of the Bible. See also the preceding note.

[1] As we already remarked, the O.T. cannot in all its parts be called kerygmatic, neither should we look upon every form of testimony as prophetic.

traditional positions of literary history (such as the Mosaic origin of the whole of the Pentateuch), by the recently discovered historical and literary connection between various parts of the Pentateuch and the Prophets, between part of the Prophets and Deuteronomy and the Deuteronomic historical writings.[1]

As a prophetic testimony the Old Testament is the authentic record of the history of salvation that God gave to Israel; it makes it possible, as it were, to look into the documents that deal with the work of God in Israel, His concern with man, His deeds in history and His revelation to the prophets through the Word; in the struggle between the prophets and the people it illustrates how by His work, word, and Spirit He was coming to Israel that He had chosen. In a word, it shows God making His Way through Israel to the whole world of mankind. The current of the Spirit flows through both the Old and the New Testament; the revelation granted in Jesus Christ constitutes the last stage in the revelation of God in Israel.[2] In Jesus Christ the new light shines out unexpectedly in the midst of Israel's distress, in Him it becomes clear what freedom and living through the Spirit of the Lord really mean. Here grace and truth have come fully (John i. 17), the grace and truth (*chesed we'emet*) towards which the Old Testament message was always directed (Rom. xv. 8ff.).

There is another very close connection between the message of the Old and the New Testaments – the prospect of the Kingdom of God.[3] That this is the most profound leading motif in the Old Testament is not always equally evident to everybody because of the multitude of historical details and other material that was added in the form of appendices to the Old Testament; yet this motif can be traced through the whole of the Old Testament as a golden thread, e.g. in contrast with the whole of Greek literature.[4] From the connection between the proclaiming of judgment and salvation[5] in the historical and the prophetical books it becomes manifest that for the individual, the people, and the world there is ultimately but *one* hope and *one* certainty that God shall be with them and that they shall live with Him. This complete dependence upon God, this faith in His holy and loving

---

[1] See Ch. III, pp. 53ff.; cf. also my *Die Erwählung Israels nach dem A.T.*, 1953, pp. 81, 82 n. 1, 2. We draw attention to the studies by G. von Rad on Deuteronomy, the Hexateuch, and the Chronicles.
[2] So e.g. also Joh. Lindblom, *Israels Religion i gammeltestamentlig Tid*[2], 1953, p. 271; H. H. Rowley, *The Unity of the Bible*, 1953, and G. E. Wright, *God Who Acts*, 1952.
[3] Cf. W. Eichrodt, 'Les rapports du N. et de l'A.T.', in: *Le problème biblique*, 1955, pp. 105ss.
[4] On this cf. B. A. van Groningen, *In the grip of the past*, 1953, p. 120.
[5] See my 'Prophecy and Eschatology', Suppl. *V.T.*, I, 1953, pp. 199ff.

desire for re-creation is characteristic of the message of both Old and New Testament.[1]

Fundamentally, when we make the New Testament our starting-point, we cannot deny the fact that the message of the Old Testament is derived from the Spirit of God, and we must admit that the Old Testament is authoritative in its preaching, even if this message is wrapped up to a great extent in ancient Oriental material. We cannot agree with the younger churches, therefore, when they allow themselves to be deterred by the somewhat strange and archaic form of the Old Testament message; they will have to gain more practice in the reading and exegesis of the Old Testament.

Historical criticism cannot alter our view of the Old Testament either; it does not do the Old Testament any harm, but can assist in setting off the essential message of the Old Testament to greater advantage as it can render important services by assisting in the historical definition of the sources, thus sifting primary from secondary elements, teaching theological scholarship to distinguish essentials from side-issues, and opening our eye to new spiritual points of view. Indeed, historical criticism reveals the historical relativity of the Old Testament; i.e. it becomes clearer and clearer that the Old Testament originated among men with whom God concerned Himself. That is why the Old Testament does not lose its value as a testimony to God, but, on the contrary, bears witness most clearly to God's work in this world, to the history of salvation, initiated by Him in Israel among men. It is a sign of the true grace of the living God who comes to the world of men.[2] The obvious presence of all kinds of ancient oriental, ancient Israelite and Hebrew elements in the Holy Scriptures of Israel, the recollections of ancient oriental life and thought in the preaching of the Word of God, can indeed strengthen our faith in God's dealings with man and His living approach to him.[3] Unfortunately the point of view of historical criticism has often been set up against the truth of the Old Testament both by champions and opponents, and used by critical scholars as evidence for the unreliability of the Old Testament. We may admit frankly[4], that the Old Testament outlook with regard

[1] Cf. on particulars the above-mentioned essay by W. F. Lofthouse in *Record and Revelation;* see also p. 100.
[2] See *Schrift en Kerk,* 1953 (the essay by P. J. Roscam Abbing, 'De Kerk en het O.T.'), pp. 62ff.
[3] See *Schrift en Kerk,* pp. 23ff.
[4] In this respect we can speak more freely than Roman Catholic theology is as yet allowed to do – cf. the encyclical letter *Divino afflante Spiritu* and the *Epistula ad cardinalem Suhard;* H. Haag, *Bibellexicon,* article on *Bibelwissenschaft,* where the conception of history in the O.T. is discussed, though it is considered there in its dissimilarity rather than in its limitations, Cf. also J. van der Ploeg in *De wereld van de Bijbel,* 1957, pp. 59ff., esp. pp. 64ff., who apparently does admit the existence of errors in certain

to natural science is limited, that the Old Testament contains historical errors and uses sources containing all kinds of legendary material,
but all this detracts in no way from the truth proclaimed by the Old
Testament with respect to the relation between God and man, man
and the world, and man and his fellow-man.[1] We fully recognize this
truth even when we take up a critical attitude, but we shall first have
to arrive at a true theological insight into the Old Testament message.

This leads us on to the last question concerning the authority of the
Old Testament, a question which has now become almost superfluous.
Thus far we have come to the conclusion that in view of the material
contents of Old and New Testaments there is nothing at all strange
even today in sticking to their spiritual unity and maintaining the
religious truth of this unity. The question arises, however, whether the
Old Testament in its complex form, consisting of such widely different
elements, can still be called the Word of God. It is not wrong, or at
any rate, is it not a halting between two opinions, to use this dogmatic
term and to admit at the same time the existence in the Old Testament of so much that is fallible?

This question is essentially formal; in practice it is a matter of
terminology. Yet it must not be neglected, as the traditional associations of the term 'Word of God' are of great importance here. Many
people think that the term 'the Word of God', as used of the Bible,
including the Old Testament, means the literal inspiration of the
Scriptures by the Holy Spirit[2] or (with a definite Jewish conception)
that the Bible is a heavenly book. It is very doubtful, however, if the
term 'Word of God' was taken in this strict sense when it came to be
used of the Biblical writings as a whole. It is more likely that the idea
of verbal inspiration was only formed when the canon was defined
and when the later, stricter views concerning the canon arose. It was

writings, but excuses the biblical authors themselves because in such cases they acted
as compilers and took over elements *which they themselves do not judge* (italics v.d.P.).
On the development and the problems of Roman Catholic exegesis particularly
after 1943, see G. C. Berkouwer, *Vatikaans concilie en nieuwe theologie*, 1964, ch. V, pp.
134ff; H. H. Miskotte: *Sensus spiritualis* (diss. Leiden), 1966.
[1] See above pp. 99f. The Reformers already admitted the existence of certain errors
in Scriptural traditions, *The Cambridge History of the Bible*, 1963, pp. 12ff.
[2] Think of the doctrine of verbal inspiration and its offshoot, fundamentalism. During
the centuries after the Reformation verbal inspiration played an important part; cf.,
e.g., the statement of Hollaz: 'the historical, chronological, genealogical, physical,
and political things, too, were revealed by divine inspiration' (Hollaz, *Examen
theologiae*, p. 83, quoted by E. Brunner, *Die christliche Lehre von Gott*, Dogmatik I, 1946,
p. 117). Such a view far transcends the original conception concerning the Bible as
evident from the textual history of the Bible; cf., e.g., the differences in the 'chronological' data between the Septuagint, the Samaritan and the Massoretic texts.

first applied to the Torah, which was canonized long before Christ[1], secondly to the Prophets and afterwards to the whole of the Holy Scriptures.[2]

First of all we must keep in mind that the term *dabar* in Hebrew is much more dynamic and concrete than its Western equivalent *word*. *Dabar* is something concrete, living, it *'comes to* the prophets' (Jer. i. 2; Ezek. i. 3; Hos. i. 1, etc.; cf. Luke ii. 15); it is used again and again for *revelation* (Isa. ii. 1; Amos i. 1); it *works* (remember the significance of curse and blessing, the significance of the 'name'). Over against the word *torah*, which is the 'divine instruction', it is the 'dynamic, creative or destructive element that comes to the foreground in *dabar*', as Procksch rightly states[3]; this is already found in Sumerian and Babylonian literature; it is also found in the praise of the Law in Ps. cxix (cf. Ps. xixb). The living element in *dabar* is, perhaps, most evident in the fact that the complete term *Word of God* is used in the New Testament only to denote the work and revelation of Jesus Christ[4]; for that reason the Word can become flesh (John i). The background of the expression 'Word of God' is not the cultic word of the oracle in its stern immutability but the Word of God as known to the prophets.[5]

The use of the term 'Word of God' can be traced back practically to its origin.[6] First we meet with the expression to denote a special prophetical message[7] given by God; but it is also used as the superscription of some prophetical books.[8] It is most interesting to see how the collectors hesitated in their terminology, or at any rate how they varied the terms used, for other prophetical writings are headed: 'The words of...' (followed by the name of a prophet).[9]

It seems, then, that the term 'Word of God' was applied originally and fundamentally only to a divine message transmitted directly by

---

[1] See Strack-Billerbeck, op. cit., IV, 1, pp. 435ff.; the Torah is even considered as pre-existent, as created first.
[2] Inspiration is generally taught in Judaism as well as in the New Testament; cf. E. Hühn, *Die alttest. Citate im N.T.*, 1900, p. 272, who draws attention to the way of quoting in the N.T., which corresponds with the Hebrew way of quoting; cf. also Schrenk, s.v. γραφή, *Th. W.*, I, p. 757. It is true that more attention is paid to the historical mediators of the Word of God in the N.T. than among the Jews (Schrenk p. 757) and that the term Holy Scriptures is rarely used in the N.T. (Schrenk, p. 751).
[3] Cf. *Th. W.*, IV, p. 95; cf. also the commentaries by Gunkel and Gemser (Tekst en Uitleg, *De Psalmen* III) on Ps. cxix; cf. L. Dürr, *Die Wertung des göttlichen Wortes im A.T. und im Alten Orient*, 1938.
[4] Kittel in *Th. W.z.N.T.*, IV, pp. 114ff; cf. his interpretation of John i. 14ff., op. cit., p. 138ff.
[5] Cf. *N.T.T.*, 1951/2, pp. 1ff., 102ff.; the discussion between P. A. H. de Boer and myself.
[6] See O. Procksch in *Th. W.z.N.T.*, IV, pp. 95ff., s.v. λόγος.
[7] Also with Ezekiel, Haggai, and Zechariah.
[8] Cf. Hos. i. 1, Joel i. 1, Micah i. 1, Zeph. i. 1 (Mal. i. 1).
[9] Jer. i. 1; Amos i. 1; or also the vision of Isa. i. 1; cf. ii. 1.

the prophets, and that this term was at first only used to denote a collection of such divine messages, containing few, if any, other elements. Exceptions to this rule in the above-mentioned books (see p. 117, n. 8) are Hos. i and iii, Joel ii. 18f.; Micah iii. 1*a*; in the last two of these cases it is most likely[1] that narrative fragments were omitted because the compilers who denoted the books as 'Word of God' did not wish to admit any narratives and additions that were not direct messages from God. This is probably also the reason why the heading 'Word of God' was not chosen for the great prophetical collections, such as Isaiah, Jeremiah and Ezekiel, because it was felt that these collections contained many other things besides divine messages.

It is clear, however, that when, in spite of these objections, the term 'Word of God' was applied to the whole collection of the Old Testament, this term could no longer be taken in this strict sense but in the more general sense of 'Book of Revelation', for many things were included in this book of revelation, looked upon as the Word of God, which originally did not come within the definition 'Word of God' (especially in Isaiah, Jeremiah[2], Ezekiel and Amos).

It is true that the prophetical canon as a whole was afterwards looked upon as verbally inspired[3], but this is a later doctrine, connected with the fact that the conception of the canon grew more and more rigid during the first century, and also with the fact that the term 'Word of God' (originally applied to the whole by metonymy) was afterwards taken literally as a qualification of the whole.[4]

---

[1] As has been demonstrated by Budde in an article in *Z.A.W.*, 1921, p. 218 ('Eine folgenschwere Redaktion des Zwölfprophetenbuchs').

[2] Not only historical narratives added by others, but also additions to the Word of God made by the prophets themselves. Cf., e.g., on Jeremiah: H. Wildberger, *Jahwewort und prophetische Rede bei Jeremia*, doctorate thesis Zürich, 1941; on Amos see the narrative of Amos vii. 10ff.; and e.g. an explanatory addition by the prophet in v. 3 to the divine message of v. 1–2. Cf. also the narrative book of Jonah.

[3] Strack-Billerbeck, IV, p. 443ff.; on this several theories are maintained. First of all there is the simple inspiration theory, also found in 2 Pet. i. 19 (cf. Strack-Billerbeck, op. cit., pp. 450f.); but also the conception that God had already revealed the *Nebi'im* and *Ketubim* to Moses, and that God had revealed the contents of these two collections to the pre-existent souls of the authors at Sinai.

[4] That in the earliest period, before the canon had been fixed, the text was not looked upon to such a degree as might be deduced from the later qualification 'Word of God', is quite evident from what has been said above (p. 12) on the many changes and liberties introduced in translations and interpretations; on the prophetical books cf. P. Kahle, 'Ivans Engnells Text och Tradition', in *Alttest. Studien Fr. Nötscher gewidmet*, 1950; the same author's *Die hebräische Handschriften aus der Höhle*, 1951, pp. 26ff., 43; J. Hempel, 'Über die am Nordwestende des Toten Meeres gefundenen hebräischen Handschriften', *Nachrichten Akad. Göttingen*, 1950, p. 434; W. Baumgartner, 'Der palästinische Handschriftenfund', *Th. R.*, 1951, pp. 144ff.; on the Ketubim: G. Gerlemann, *Synoptic Studies in the O.T.*, 1948. Generally speaking we may say that the issue at stake in the transmission of the Bible is the true sense rather than the literal phrasing (cf. my *De literatuur van Oud-Israël*, 1961, pp. 69ff.).

The expression 'Word of God' developed therefore as follows. Origin ally used only to denote the revelation of the Word, it is afterwards employed for writings that contain (mainly, at any rate) a collection of such inspired divine messages, and later still it is also applied to the whole collection of sacred writings, even if this collection included books containing much more than these divine messages and even if it was originally not called 'Word of God'; but by this application of the qualification 'Word of God' this whole afterwards came to be looked upon as verbally inspired.[1] As a term of literary history the formula 'Word of God' for the Old Testament writings as a whole may, therefore, be called metonymic: a term that was first applied to a part came to be applied to the whole. In theology this view must be taken into account. It is not necessary on the ground of more recent traditional usage to take the expression 'The Bible is the Word of God' in the massive sense that the Bible, including the Old Testament, is to be looked upon as wholly and verbally inspired; nor is it necessary to give up the definition of the Bible as the Word of God because of the strictly limited content of this expression, as this would tend to make us lose sight of the authoritative element of the Bible; the qualification should be restored to its more general sense of *Book of Revelation*.

The statement that the Bible (including the Old Testament) is the Word of God means that it contains the testimony to the revelation of God, objective as well as subjective.[2]

Schrenk[3] is, therefore, right in saying: 'For primitive Christianity Scripture is no longer something merely written down, no longer something merely handed down by tradition, but the dynamic, historically determined proclamation of God, which announces not only His power in general, but in particular His destroying and creating anew; which reaches its height in the revelation of Christ and the revelation of the Spirit through the Risen One. Since the Scripture serves this end and bears this witness, it can include the most diversified elements, even such as overthrow the old idea of authority.'

Summing up, we may say that we must continue to proclaim that the Old Testament is the Word of God, even when we make use of the historical and critical method of Bible study in theology. The term does not clash with a more general, metonymic use, even if it has again and again been interpreted very strictly and connected with a

---

[1] The influence of a certain name on something spiritual is clearly demonstrable in the development of the idea of sacrifice in the early Church and its application to Holy Communion; cf. K. Heussi, *Kompendium der Kirchengeschichte*, 1919, § 21 k.
[2] On the twofold nature of the Torah cf. F. Horst, *Das A. T. als hl. Schrift und als Kanon*, op. cit., pp. 162f.
[3] Op. cit., p. 761.

massive conception of the Bible which does not allow of any gradation in the Scriptures. From a formal point of view we *can* use the term, but in respect of the subject-matter we *must* maintain it in order to state emphatically that the Old Testament is the Book of the revelation of God which is still looked upon as such by Christians, with Christ and St. Paul and the whole of the New Testament, in spite of the scientific criticism that may be brought against it at some points, and certainly in spite of the theological criticism that may be directed against the Old Testament in the light of the New.

II. THE USE OF THE OLD TESTAMENT IN THE CHURCH[1]
(Exegesis and Preaching)

Introductory Remarks

The use of the Old Testament raises special problems for Christian theology; this is evident from the *history* of the Old Testament, which we have touched upon in Ch. I. It also appears from the fact that one of the most urgent contemporary problems concerns the use of the Old Testament in the Church.

On the one hand there are the attempts of W. Vischer who wants the exegesis of the Old Testament to be dominated by the New Testament[2], and of A. A. van Ruler, who thinks the testimony of Old Testament and New Testament identical to such an extent that in his opinion the New Testament is merely the explanatory glossary at the back of the Old Testament.[3] On the other hand there are the words of Von Harnack, that it is a sign of religious paralysis that the Old Testament should still be allowed canonical authority[4] and those of F. Hesse and F. Baumgärtel (see above, pp.97ff.) that the Old Testament 'ein Zeugnis ist aus einer für uns fremden Religion'. These conflicting opinions give us some idea of the ever latent contemporary tensions.

The basic principles involved in this problem have been discussed; the *historical* as well as the *organic* connection between Old Testament

[1] See lit. pp.96f., 125 n.5/6 and the two articles in *R.G.G.*[3]: 'Hermeneutik' by G. Ebeling, and 'Schriftauslegung', by several authors.
[2] Cf. his *Witness of the Old Testament to Christ*, cf. above p.96; see the reviews among others by Bleeker, W.J. de Wilde, and H.W. Obbink, op. cit.; W. Baumgartner, 'Die Auslegung des A.T. im Streit der Gegenwart', *S.Th.U.*, 1941, pp.17ff.
[3] A. A. van Ruler, 'De waarde van het O.T.', *Vox Th.*, 1942, pp.113–117.
[4] *Marcion*, 1st ed., pp.248f. and further p.253: 'To reject the Old Testament in the second century was a mistake which the Great Church rightly refused to make; its retention in the sixteenth century was a fate which the Reformation was not yet able to avoid; but that Protestantism since the nineteenth century should continue to treasure it as a canonical document is the result of religious and ecclesiastical paralysis.' Von Harnack would like the O.T. to be looked upon as the most important apocryphal document – in any case to deprive it of its canonical authority (pp.253f.).

and New Testament were brought out. The *historical* connection implies the admission of the fact that the New Testament originated in the same milieu as the Old Testament (in this sense, however, that the New Testament represents a later phase of Israelite or Jewish spiritual life than the Old Testament), as well as the admission that there is a certain distance between Old Testament and New Testament. The *organic* connection implies the admission of a very close *fundamental spiritual* relation between the two.

Thus the relation between Old Testament and New Testament is depicted as essentially one of great tension: in Christian theology neither the historical and spiritual connection on the one hand, nor the historical and spiritual differences on the other, must be neglected. The Church must always be willing to admit that 'from the historical point of view the Talmud is just as legitimate a continuation of the Old Testament as the Gospel'[1], without admitting, however, that essentially and spiritually the Talmud is the true continuation and the best interpretation of the message of the Old Testament; between Judaism and Christianity there will always remain a fundamental difference of opinion as to the value of the Old Testament. The Christian Church would renounce her true basis if she did not acknowledge Jesus Christ as the author and finisher of faith (faith in the sense of that relation to God which is exemplified in the patriarchs and the prophets).[2]

---

[1] H. W. Obbink in his excellent book, *Theologische Bezinning op het O.T.*, p. 18. Cf. F. Horst, 'Das A.T. als Heilige Schrift und Kanon', *Th.Bl.*, XI, 1932, p. 172: 'The Church desires such a recognition (of the Old Testament as canonical) because she knows that the road from the Old Testament leads to the Church as well as to rabbinical Judaism – because she knows that the unity of the Old and New Testaments is founded alone on the Messiahship of Jesus, which can be acknowledged, but can also be denied.' Now also B. S. Childs in *Interpretation*, 1964, p. 448.

[2] In Jewish quarters the legitimate Jewish character of Christianity is contested again and again, because it is looked upon as the result of a mixture of Judaism and paganism. There (as in certain schools of thought on the left flank of Protestant theology) a distinction is made especially between the Gospel and the Pauline Epistles: the former is considered Judaic, the latter the product of a syncretism with Hellenism (cf. J. Klausner, *Jesus of Nazareth* and *From Jesus to Paul* and M. Buber, *Two Types of Faith*). The discoveries of 'Ain Feshkah make it more and more likely that the element in Christianity which used to be called hellenistic, was already present in the Jewish (gnostic?) sects (cf., e.g., Bultmann, *Theologie des N.T.*, p. 361, n. 1, quoted by W. Baumgartner, 'Der palästinische Handschriftenfund', *Th. R.*, 1951, pp. 97ff.). This would make Christianity Jewish-sectarian and gnostic, but not legitimately Jewish. The opinions of the New Testament scholar D. Flüsser of Jerusalem tend in this direction, cf. his *De Joodse oorsprong van het Christendom*, 1964, p. 17. He recognizes three stages: that of the influence of rabbinism (Jesus and his disciples from Jerusalem), that of Essenism (Paul and John) and that of hellenistic Judaism (the later apologetics). This view can be qualified as a move in the right direction because of its greater differentiation, but the division in historical stages makes the plan of the work too schematic. In more respects than one a close connection between the life and ideas of the sects and those of Christianity cannot be denied (cf. e.g. W. Gros-

For the *practice* of the Church's life this tension between Old Testament and New Testament brings with it a particular problem, which crops up again and again, especially for those who have to preach the Biblical message as the Word of God. For the message of the Christian Church is the Gospel of the Kingdom of God in Jesus Christ. The focal point of preaching lies, therefore, in the New Testament. How can the Old Testament be given a place in Christian teaching without betraying the gospel of Jesus Christ as the central message, without arriving (at best) at a message with two focal points? As we have already said, this is only possible if Old Testament and New Testament are not looked upon as two, but as essentially one; if it is fully admitted that Jesus Christ is the link between the two. For then Jesus

souw, 'The Dead Sea Scrolls and the N.T.', *Studia Catholica* 1951, pp. 289ff., and 1952, pp. 1ff.), but this does not mean that there is such a close relationship between Christianity and the sects (the Essenes) that we might speak of dependence. For in that case we should leave out of account Him who founded Christianity, or we should not do full justice to His 'originality'. The most important point is whether the (Essenic) Jewish sects were indeed dualistic in the gnostic sense of the word (by some it is regarded as an extreme Pharisaic tendency), but immediately after that the question arises whether 'Christian dualism' may be put on a level with that of the sects. In my opinion it is most probable that the relation of Christianity to spiritual tendencies such as evident in this sect may be similar to that of classical Old Testament prophetism to the sect of the Rechabites (on this cf., for instance, my *Hosea, Profeet en Cultuur*, 1941). In that case various affinities are possible, but we need not speak of dependence. From the historical point of view Christianity could thus still be called legitimately Israelite in essence, while at the same time its quite peculiar character could be maintained. Christian theology looks forward to further research eagerly and confidently. Precisely with regard to the real basis of the Christian message, its message of redemption and resurrection, Christianity is essentially and absolutely Israelite, it is indeed the answer to the most profound questions of the O.T., and thus the fulfilment of Old Testament hope. For that reason it fits in really and completely in the line of Israel's hope of salvation. The originality of this message was rashly combated in the works of A. Dupont-Sommer, *The Dead Sea Scrolls* (Eng. trans., 1952) and *The Jewish Sect of Qumran and the Essenes* (Eng. trans., 1954); cf. also Baumgartner, op. cit., pp. 148ff. The final word in regard to this important matter has not yet been spoken: the study of the materials has only just begun and the data are still incomplete, but the results obtained in the last few years are extremely important. Here follows a selection of the most important literature (alphabetical): G. Baumbach, *Qumran und das Johannes-Ev.*, 1957. F. F. Bruce, 'Qumran and early Christianity', *N.T.S.* 1956, pp. 176ff.; cf. also id., *Second Thoughts on the Dead Sea Scrolls*, 1956, pp. 123ff. M. Burrows, *More Light on the Dead Sea Scrolls*, 1958. F. M. Cross, *The ancient library of Qumran and modern biblical studies²*, 1961, pp. 195ff. D. Flüsser, *op. cit.*; id., 'The Dead Sea sect and Pre-Pauline Christianity' in *Scripta Hierosolymitana* IV, 1958, pp. 215ff. H. Kosmala, *Hebräer-Essener-Christen*, 1959. M. Mansoor, *The Dead Sea Scrolls*, 1964, pp. 152ff. R. Mayer und J. Reuss, *Die Qumran-Funde und die Bibel*, 1960. L. Mowry, *The Dead Sea Scrolls*, 1962. J. v. d. Ploeg c.s., *La Secte de Qumran et les origines du Christianisme*. 'Qumran', *R.G.G.³* (several authors). H. H. Rowley, *The Dead Sea Scrolls and the N.T.*, 1957; id., 'The Qumran Sect and Christian Origins', *B.J.R.L.* 1961, pp. 119ff. K. Stendahl (ed.), *The Scrolls and the N.T.*, 1958. Y. Yadin, 'The Dead Sea Scrolls and the Epistle to the Hebrews', *Scripta Hierosolymitana* IV, 1958, pp. 36ff. A. S. van der Woude, 'De theologische betekenis van de rollen van de Dode Zee', *Kerk en Theologie* XIV, 1962, pp. 110ff.

Christ is the incarnate Word of God to Israel, coming to life in Him in its creative impulse and thus bringing new life. He is the Righteous One, springing from the testimony of the Old Testament, the true representative of Israel in His election, His communion with God, His faith and hope, and as such He is the expected Messiah who fully actualized the Kingdom of God in His teaching and His life and death. Like the authors of the apocrypha and of the Qumran-literature, and like John the Baptist, He belongs to the world of the Old Testament[1], and simultaneously He is the creator of the events of which the New Testament is full and thus the head of the new community of the Kingdom of God. In this way there is a fundamental connection between the two Testaments in the person of Jesus Christ. On the one hand this connection could, from a formal point of view, be called one of *perspective;* in a double sense because the teaching and work of Jesus Christ are in an even line with the Old Testament and because Old Testament and New Testament share the same perspective. On the other hand, from a material point of view, this connection may be called *fulfilment.* The Christian faith rightly thinks the appearance of Jesus Christ very closely bound up with the eschatological message of the Old Testament. At the heart of the Old Testament message lies the expectation of the Kingdom of God, and it is the initial *fulfilment* of this expectation in Jesus of Nazareth, who is, for that reason, professed as Christ, that underlies the message of the New Testament. *The true heart of both Old Testament and New Testament is, therefore, the eschatological perspective.*[2] In this connection we may be allowed to quote at length from a book already mentioned above: 'Fulfilment does not mean here a replacement of the Old Testament message by something else; it does not mean that the law is made superfluous by the Gospel and the promise by reality, but it means that the law and the prophets are given a new meaning by Jesus. Neither does fulfilment mean that the time of hoping-without-beholding and of hoping for the future has now come to an end because the reality has become visible and tangible. For the appearance of Jesus also demands faith: the faith that God's

---

[1] This was clearly recognized by the Judaic world, too, see preceding note. From the point of view of the history of religion, it is hardly possible any more to dispute this unity. What *essentially* distinguishes the New Testament from the Old is the confession that Jesus is the Christ; this, too, is the great difference between the primitive church and her Jewish contemporaries, between Judaism and Christianity.

[2] In my opinion Martin Buber (*Two Types of Faith*) is mistaken because he has not seen this common eschatological perspective of O.T. and N.T. clearly enough and has, therefore, arrived at an excessively one-sided notion of the Christian faith as the belief in something that has already been accomplished, thus neglecting the other aspect – the faith of Israel as faith in a God who will act in the future. Cf. now also my *Geloven en vertrouwen,* 1957.

salvation has become manifest in Him whose outward appearance does not give any proof of His mission. Fulfilment does not mean that the promise comes to an end and is replaced by the very thing that was promised, but it means that now the promise itself becomes completely unambiguous, and consequently effective. The coming of Jesus Christ very clearly underlines God's promises; 2 Cor. i. 20: in Him they are 'Yea and Amen'. For the complete *actualization* of those promises Jesus (and, indeed, the whole of the New Testament) points to the end of time. In this respect, however, Old and New Testament are in harmony'.[1] What has been said here about eschatology as the heart of the prophetic message of the Old Testament also applies to other focal points of preaching. The Christian doctrine of the atonement, for instance, is incomprehensible without the Old Testament idea of sacrifice, and especially without the Old Testament message of the absolute sinfulness of man, as taught in Gen. ii-xi, in the whole of the history of the people of Israel, in the Psalms and in the prophetical writings. The New Testament idea of the restoration of communion between God and man is on the one hand purely New Testament, but on the other hand it is also fully based on the Old Testament.

The principal thing is, that the Christian theologian should not strain the Old Testament by neglecting the interval between Old and New Testament, as has happened again and again in the course of the centuries. Theology will have to respect the historical view-point of the interval and difference between Old Testament and New Testament[2]; only this will lead to a truly scholarly and theological attitude towards the Old Testament, and only this can lead to a fruitful discussion with non-Christians, such as for instance the Jews. In principle and in practice, now rudely, now subtly, the Christian Church has too often wiped out the distinction, and thus given just cause for complaints of imperialism; here, perhaps more clearly than anywhere else, it is evident how Christian theology is prone to the sin of anticipation, once

[1] H.W.Obbink, op. cit. pp. 24 and 25; cf. also A.A. van Ruler, *De Vervulling der Wet*, 1947, and W.Zimmerli, 'Verheißung und Erfüllung', *Ev. Th.*, XII, 1952/3, pp. 34ff; R.Bijlsma, *op. cit.*, pp. 332ff. We cannot deal at length here with the discussion that is in full swing in Germany on the use of the words *promise* and *fulfilment*. F.Baumgärtel gives a survey of and criticism on the most important opinions of the last few decads (*Verheißung*, 1952, pp. 86–128), but in spite of some valuable remarks he does not carry the discussion a step further because he contrasts the word promise (Verheissung) *with* prophecy (Weissagung), cf. above p. 98. See among other things L. Köhler's criticism of this book in *Th.Z.*, 1953, G.von Rad, 'Verheißung', *Ev. Th.*, 1953, pp. 406ff. Cf. further especially W.Eichrodt, *Israel in der Weissagung des A.T.*, 1951 and R.Bultmann, 'Weissagung und Erfüllung', *Z. Th. K.*, XLVII, 1950, pp. 360ff; see also above p. 98.

[2] Cf. what G.van der Leeuw (*Phaenomenologie*, 1933, p. 640) writes on the demand of *epochè* which should be kept intact in phenomenological research; the same applies equally to historical theology, especially to its work in the exegetical field.

called by Gunning[1] the real sin of mankind. Instead of taking possession of the Old Testament and interpreting it in its own way, Christian theology must reflect upon the content of the Old Testament most earnestly and critically. The first task of the theologian is, therefore, to make a penetrating study of the language and the spirit of the Old Testament writings in order to arrive at an understanding of the meaning of these writings and to attempt to ascertain their place in the history of revelation. This demands great spiritual restraint[2], a virtue in which, unfortunately, Christian theologians by no means always excel; they often display too much zeal to bring out the unity of the Bible[3], and think there is not better way to attain this result than to maintain the *analogia fidei* without any restriction. This looks like fidelity to the Christian faith, but in reality it is a sign of religious imperialism. If after the victory over the historicism of the last century Christian theology cannot recognize the place of history in the structure of Biblical religion, it does not only depreciate various facts in the history of religion, but also wrongs itself.[4]

Exegesis

It is not our intention to deal exhaustively with hermeneutics at this point. Yet the subject of exegesis must come up for discussion, for it is not a matter of course. In spite of the fact that from Aristotle onwards hermeneutic rules for the interpretation of literary texts have been developed[5], no unanimity has yet been reached on the method of exegesis; people are still groping for the right way of interpretation. It also seems as if every age has its own way of approaching the text.[6]

[1] J.H.Gunning Jr., *Op Nebo's Top* (1879), p.28.
[2] Cf. my article in *J. E.O.L.*, X, 1948, pp.377ff.: 'Bezinning op het O.T.'
[3] This is the important critical element of truth in Von Rad's method, cf. *Th.L.Z.* 1963, pp.401ff., esp. 413f.; though his application of this method is too one-sided, while it is too easily offset by his acceptance of an exegetical method that is essentially typological.
[4] See my 'Schriftgezag en Schriftkritiek', in *Schrift en Kerk*, 1953.
[5] Cf. R.Bultmann, 'Das Problem der Hermeneutik', *Z.K.Th.*, 1950, pp.47ff., esp. p.48 n.1 and the article of Ebeling in *R.G.G.*[3] III, pp.242ff.
[6] Compare what Bultmann writes of Schleiermacher and Dilthey and what he himself believes to be true exegesis (under the influence of existentialism). Interesting in this connection is the rectorial address of R.W.Zandvoort on '*Shakespeare in the Twentieth Century*', 1952, from which it appears that modern literary scholarship is wrestling with the same problems as those met with in theology; a discussion such as that between the two classical scholars W.den Boer and M.Rozelaar in *N.T.T.* 1946/7 and 1947/8 is informative in this connection. On the history of exegesis in theology see besides L. Diestel, *Geschichte des A.T. in der Chr. Kirche*, 1869, also S. Greydanus, *Schriftbeginselen ter Schriftverklaring*, 1946, pp.146ff., L.H.K.Bleeker, *Hermeneutiek van het O.T.*, 1948, but now particularly also D.Lerch, 'Isaaks Opferung, christlich gedeutet' (*B.H.Th.*, 12) 1950 and P.Auvray c.s., *op. cit.* On the earliest times see C.H.Dodd, *The Bible and the Greeks*, 1935, and I.L.Seeligmann, *The Septuagint Version of Isaiah*, 1948.

With gratitude we must admit that by the different ways of approach a clearer insight has been gained in many respects, that more possibilities have come to light, and that people are becoming more and more willing to take up a critical attitude towards what has become their own spiritual property.

It is clear that it is not possible to fix the method of exegesis without further preface; there is more to it than one simple rule, as is sometimes held; for exegesis is often called the interpretation of a piece of writing or a pronouncement, *e mente auctoris*. No one would, of course, abandon this important definition from the school of Schleiermacher and Dilthey[1], but it cannot be accounted final without more ado. The psychological approach demanded here is very difficult and mostly impossible, and more often than not, this definition is too onesided. In the case of a collective work such as the Old Testament, compiled by many successive generation, there is an extra difficulty. Assuming that the various authors are known, we are confronted in principle and in practice with the question: Which author is decisive for the meaning of the story in its context? Remember chapters or pericopes that present difficulties of interpretation such as Jacob at Peniel, or the circumcision of Moses' son[2], or the promise of Nathan which was recast radically by the Deuteronomic compiler. Who is then to be looked upon as the author: the original author of the story or the compiler (R)[3], who has left his mark on the whole? In many cases it is not a matter of 'either – or', but of 'both – and'; in other words, certain parts may have to be interpreted differently, accordingly as they are interpreted in their original form or in their present context after they had been rewritten. Connected with this is the still more difficult question which faces Christian theology: should the Old Testament not be read in the spirit of those who transmitted it to us as an authoritative book – in the spirit of Christ and the earliest Church. It is an established fact that in many respects their way of reading the Old Testament differed from ours.[4] In other words, must we not read the Psalms as prophetical writings – as they did? The latter question has

[1] See Bultmann, op. cit. pp.49ff.
[2] See below pp.303f.
[3] Bear in mind F.Rosenzweig's suggestion that we should interpret R. (Redactor) as Rabbenu ('our Rabbi', in the sense of the real author) ('Die Einheit der Bibel', in M.Buber and F.Rosenzweig, *Die Schrift und ihre Verdeutschung*, 1936, p.47).
[4] An important contribution is made here by C.H.Dodd (*According to the Scriptures*, 1952), who demonstrates that already at an early date *Testimonia*, collections of quotations from the Old Testament, developed within the early Church. These *Testimonia* contained the texts to which the Church referred as evidence for her belief that Jesus was the Messiah. As a matter of fact, such "testimonia" were already discovered among the Qumran-texts (cf. A.S.van der Woude, *Bijbelcommentaren en Bijbelse Verhalen*, 1958, pp.20f. and 81–91). Cf. also R.Bijlsma, *op. cit.*, S.Amsler, *L'A.T. dans l'Eglise*, 1960.

often been answered very positively in the affirmative, and a great many attempts to give an allegorical or christological exegesis are founded on this answer. There is no denying that there is something to be said for this view, which sets aside the author who is to be considered as the original writer and looks upon the party to whose authority *we* owe these writings as the author so far as *we* are concerned.[1]

Although this answer seems to be indisputable it is not quite satisfactory and is, therefore, unacceptable. In the first place because we cannot say without further ado that the New Testament authors really gave an exegesis when they used certain Bible texts in their preaching; they did not merely interpret the text, they employed it in a given situation. Such a use of the text was at that time allowed among the Jews[2], but cannot be looked upon as exegesis, not, at any rate, as exegesis in our modern sense of the word.[3] In the second place it is nowadays impossible to explain a text as the ancient rabbis and the New Testament writers explained it[4], we cannot carry our minds back to the past to such an extent as to think as they did, or to give an exegesis starting from their range of ideas. For this method would not only result in quite mistaken interpretations, it is impossible from the outset. It is remarkable how in his *Encyclopedia* A. Kuyper on the one

---

[1] In fact R. Bijlsma defends this point of view (*op. cit.*, pp. 212ff.), though he abandons the typical Jewish allegorical and symbolical elements as being too closely linked with their period of origin. He applies the demand for an inter-relation between the two Testaments to the exegesis of the whole of the Old Testament – in contrast to the New Testament itself (see Dodd, *op. cit.*, pp. 403f.), so that even allegoresis can be considered legitimate. Our great objection against this book is that it does not distinguish between exegesis and preaching. The effects of this point of view in the Church is clear from history. In principle it led the early and the mediaeval Church through the original sense of the words (the historical meaning) to allegorical or typological exegesis, and ultimately, on those grounds, to the anagogical interpretation, which made the text relevant to the knowledge of the world to come. The second phase could be called characteristic of early Christian theology, particularly that of the second century and afterwards, though there are traces to be found as early as the first century. The third phase is that of the later theologians; the starting-point lies with the Church Fathers, but this application culminates in the Middle Ages (see L. Alonzo-Schökel, in *St.Ƶ.* 1963, pp. 35f.).
[2] Cf. J.W. Doeve, *Jewish hermeneutics in the synoptic Gospels and Acts*, doctorate thesis Leyden; J. Klausner, *From Jesus to Paul*, II 7 n; I.L. Seeligmann, 'Voraussetzungen der Midraschexegese', *Suppl. V.T.*, I, 1953, pp. 150ff., esp. pp. 170ff.
[3] A twofold *exegesis* in our sense of the word – a New Testament and a present-day exegesis – does not really exist, as was assumed to some extent by A.R. Hulst, *Hoe moeten wij het O.T. uitleggen?* 1941, pp. 99f., 120.
[4] The formal agreement of the Jewish and the New Testament use of the Scriptures has not escaped J.L. Koole (*De overname van het O.T. door de Chr. Kerk*, p. 11) either; he comes rightly to the conclusion: 'connected with this is the fact that the New Testament exegesis of the O.T. may be rated highly but that it cannot by any means be considered the absolute standard for our present-day exegesis'. The only things we should like to change are the words New Testament *exegesis* and *absolute:* the first we should like to replace by application, the second could well be omitted.

127

hand demands such a mystical exegesis[1], while on the other hand he practically rejects it because he will not consider the analogy with New Testament exegesis as the determining factor for our exegesis[2] but demands a logical connection between the word of Scripture and its interpretation.[3] From this it is apparent that for present-day exegesis we may start theoretically from the New Testament 'interpretation', but that on further consideration such an interpretation cannot be used as a *method*.

Here we have come down to earth again, which means that twentieth-century theologians must arrive at an exegesis with the aids of the world in which they live and in terms of its insights. One must, of course, guard against accepting such an interpretation as one's method on the strength of a mystical, symbolic or allegorical interpretation of the New Testament, which proclaims rather than giving an exegesis. We must start from the fact that *the Bible as the revelation of God communicates the Word of God in the words of the Scriptures themselves*. We must, therefore, not distinguish between the work of the human writers, the *auctores secundarii*, and the *Auctor primarius*, the Holy Ghost, who is said to have infused a deeper thought into the words than the human authors themselves realized.[4]

We must, therefore, give an obedient exegesis of the Old Testament as it has been transmitted to us. That does not mean that in the light of the New Testament the Old Testament may not come to look quite different from what it seems to be without the revelation of God in Jesus Christ; indeed, the appreciation of some parts changes, as is already evident in the Epistles of St. Paul. This change may even lead

[1] *Encyclopaedie der Heilige Godgeleerdheid*[1], III, 1909, pp. 100ff.
[2] op. cit., p. 121.
[3] op. cit., pp. 103, 120f. The whole principle underlying this point of view is to be rejected, however strongly it was accepted by the Reformed fathers (according to Kuyper) for it is by no means certain that our logical conclusions from a certain text would also be assented to by the original authors (let alone by the Auctor Primarius). More cautious is J.Ridderbos in his contribution to the *Bijbelsch Handboek*, I, 1935, pp. 420ff.: 'De Uitlegging der H.S.'.
[4] As was supposed by Kuyper (op. cit.), and by many with him. The same tendency is found in the attempts to discover in certain texts a 'surplus value' (J.de Zwaan, 'Prolegomena tot Exegese', *N. Th. S.*, XXI, 1938, pp. 2f.; cf. J.de Groot, *Exegese*, 1936, p. 5) or a 'Vollsinn' (J. Coppens, *Les Harmonies des deux Testaments*, 1949, pp. 33ff.; id., *Vom Christlichen Verständniss des A.T.*, 1952, pp. 20ff.; present already in J.T.Beck, see K.H.Miskotte, *Om het Levende Woord*, 1948, p. 82, who concurs with this view). Even if it could be considered psychologically possible it should not be made into an exegetical principle. J.Coppens thinks, therefore, that this exegetical work transcends the normal task of exegesis and can only be accomplished in accordance with 'the teaching office of the Church' (*Vom Chr. Verständniss*, p. 22). For the Roman Catholic there is here a possibility which the Protestant would deny; cf., however, the warnings of J.v.d.Ploeg, who does not call this exegesis but application; 'Profetie en Vervulling', *St.C.*, XXVIII, 1953, pp. 81ff.; see also Berkouwer, *op. cit.*

128

to a difference of opinion on the exegesis of some texts.[1] Yet this does not make a particular Christian method of exegesis justifiable. A difference in the use and appreciation of the text must not lead to a difference in methods of reading the text, which is the task of exegesis.

It is clear that the conception of exegesis advocated here distinguishes materially between exegesis itself and preaching, between the reading and understanding of the text, and propagating. For that reason we have avoided in the first instance the word hermeneutics, which can have both meanings (cf. Ebeling, *op. cit.*). So what we have said here about exegesis itself does not apply without further preface to preaching or the homiletic use of the Old Testament. After a short discussion of the practice of exegesis we shall deal with the homiletic use of the Old Testament separately.

The task of exegesis differs from one branch of scholarship to another.[2] In theology it cannot stop short at a mere literal explanation, such as is sufficient in the case of definite pieces of information or a book containing facts and data. For here exegesis is also concerned with the spiritual background and the deeper meaning of the words; in stories such as, for instance, Gen. ii and iii, the book of Deuteronomy, the book of Ruth, etc., we must not only reach an understanding of the story but we must also get to know the author's meaning, or rather, we must come to grasp a definite reality that was given its spiritual form in a story or a piece of writing. And in this we have not succeeded until we have seen a spiritual pronouncement against the background to which such a pronouncement is directed (the background of the history of religion) *and* until we have come to understand it in relation to the whole of the spiritual movement to which it belongs, that is in the case of the Bible, until we have come to understand its place in the history of revelation. In this respect it is important, therefore, that a pronouncement should be seen in relation to its context, in relation to the whole of the book in which it occurs, and, finally, in relation to the whole of the Old Testament *and* the New Testament.

Theological exegesis, applied to the Old Testament, has, therefore, a threefold task: it undertakes a philological, literary and historical examination of the text; it tries to reach an understanding of the content and aim, in the light of the author's personality, spiritual background and contemporaries; it also attempts to estimate the value of the text in relation to its 'context' (in the widest sense of the

[1] Bear in mind the difference between Jewish and Christian exegesis of texts such as Gen. xv. 6 (where Jewish exegesis explains 'righteousness' as 'merit'), Isa. ix. 5f. (cf., e.g., Buber's exegesis in *Der Glaube der Propheten*, 1950, pp. 202ff.), Isa. liii (cf. the *Targum* on Isaiah, and M. A. Beek, *A Journey through the O.T.* on this text); cf. the basic viewpoint of H. H. Rowley, *The Unity of the Bible*, pp. 94ff.
[2] R. Bultmann, *Das Problem der Hermeneutik*, loc. cit., pp. 55ff.

word, – even, in some cases, as a *Biblical* pronouncement). This is the simplest way of explaining the task of exegesis: it asks three questions in succession:

1) *What* does the text say? – In this question exegesis is concerned with textual criticism, philology, semantics, syntax, literary and historical criticism, literature and history; as such it is known as historico-philological exegesis.

2) What does the text *say;* what does the author want to convey to us? In this question it attempts to approach the text with the mind, to grasp its thought, it aims at an understanding of the author's inner motives for expressing himself; it aims at penetrating into what is *really* important to him. This is the hermeneutical aspect of exegesis; here it arrives at 'interpretation' of the text.[1]

3) What is the connection between the text and the whole message of the Old Testament and the New? This is the specifically theological function of Old Testament exegesis as a branch of theology, and as such it belongs to the realm of the history of religion and phenomenology as well as to that of 'factual' systematic theology.[2]

The distinctions between these three functions are not clear-cut; one leads on to the other automatically. With each of these functions we shall deal briefly.

Ad 1) The philologico-historical and historico-literary examination of the text must be considered the foundation of exegesis.[3] This is fundamentally connected with the fact that theology is convinced that the Bible can only be read and understood correctly in the original text. This principle that was framed for the study of the Bible by Humanism and Reformation, by Reuchlin, Erasmus and Luther[4], has been recognized to an ever-increasing extent by the Roman Catholic Church, too, and has now even been accepted officially.[5] The knowledge of the parent languages of the Bible, Hebrew and Greek at the least, is therefore taken to be the indispensable condition for a scholarly study of the Bible so that the theological students of the Reformation churches are expected to take up these languages as parts of their preliminary studies. This is done in order that the ministers should be able to arrive independently at an exegesis of the Bible and to proclaim

---

[1] Cf. also L.H.K.Bleeker, *Hermeneutiek*, who also makes an emphatic distinction between exegesis and explication.
[2] Cf. with this W.Baumgartner, 'Die Auslegung des A.T. im Streit der Gegenwart', *S.Th.U.*, XI, 1941, pp.36f.
[3] See *Schriftgezag en Schriftkritiek*, cf. above p.125 n.4; G.Ebeling, 'Die Bedeutung der histor.-kritische Methode für die protestantische Theologie und Kirche', *Z.Th.K.*, XLVII, 1950, pp.1–46; E.Dinkler, *Bibelautorität und Bibelkritik*.
[4] Cf. Luther, *An die Ratsherrn aller Städte*, 1523 (cf. ed. Universal Bibl. 2373), p.43: 'Die Sprachen sind die Scheiden, darin dies Messer des Geists stickt'.
[5] Very expressly in *Deo afflante Spiritu*, 1943.

130

the word of God in a justifiable manner. It is their duty to go back to the sources in order to be independent of later traditions or scholastic notions. In this way grammar became, as it were, the symbol of Protestant theology.

One danger arising from this method of exegesis is that the philological approach should come to dominate exegesis. This happened in many ways, in the Protestant orthodoxy of the 17th and 18th centuries as well as in the days of the critical examination of the text in the 19th and early 20th centuries. As early as a hundred years ago A.F.C. Vilmar, a true philologist and theologian[1] protested against what he called 'the Alexandrinism of the Philologists' and pleaded for a way of exegesis that would penetrate to the heart of the matter, to the message of the Old Testament writings, to their value as revelation. Even if we admit that this appeal against the absolute predominance of this exegetical method and especially against its claim to complete open-mindedness[2] is justified, this certainly does not mean that we should underrate the importance of this branch of exegesis or neglect it, for it is simply indispensable. This attempt to begin the work of exegesis as a question of principle and method without any other presuppositions than those that are employed in other branches of scholarship, enables it to attain a certain measure of objectivity and lifts research (in the first instance, at any rate) from the plane of personal convictions or traditional insight to that of sound scholarship. This is already a great advantage in itself, for it ensures at any rate that the analytical examination of the text is carried through as accurately as humanly possible. This analysis must be seen through to the end, even if it leads to complete spiritual understanding of word or writing by itself.

Therefore this form of interpretation of the text needs a complement, in order to enable exegesis to penetrate more deeply into the author's intentions. A synthesis cannot be reached until the next stage of exegesis.

[1] *Theologie der Tatsachen*[3], 1938, pp. 24ff., and since by many others, cf. now e.g. B.S. Childs (see p. 128 n. 1).
[2] If all is well, this method is indeed unbiased in principle, *in so far as it does not attempt to influence the outcome of its research;* but in practice it is not unprejudiced, because each scholar *applies* it in his own way, influenced by his own personal insight; each scholar has his own presuppositions founded on conclusions arrived at previously, and also on personal views that can never be eliminated entirely, and are, indeed, indispensable, in the humanities even more than in science (as to the latter, we may refer to the well-known inaugural address of the famous Dutch chemist J.H. van 't Hoff at Amsterdam in 1877 on the importance of the imagination in science). The great importance of the 'philological' method, however, lies in its fundamental freedom from preconceptions where the outcome of research is concerned. This advantage it has over all methods that stand committed to tradition. And for that reason this method is absolutely indispensable to theology as the initial stage of exegesis.

It is impossible to give here a complete description of the application of this method and of the aids and appliances that are at its service.[1] A few observations may suffice here. Philological and historico-literary research proves to an ever greater degree to be enormously complicated and demands great professional knowledge. After pure morphology, grammar, there are syntax, idiom, the examination of words and style, the literary and historical connections, the history of literary tradition and the literatures of the surrounding nations that draw our attention successively. In the process of this examination we are enabled more or less to relate the text to its original situation and to its context (which may sometimes even be differentiated into different 'layers' or 'sources' that can be distinguished within one textual whole). In this manner the way is paved for the second stage, in which the meaning of the text is examined. The transition from the first stage to the second is marked by a preliminary translation of the examined text. In preparing such a preliminary translation it will repeatedly become evident that various elements have to be re-examined. Quite often the text will prove very refractory so that it is frequently hardly possible to translate it, because it is impossible to give an exact rendering in a modern language of some word, some idiomatic expression or some syntactical form. We shall give one example to make this clear. We refer to the first three verses of the Bible, the translation of which still is a vexed question. What is the syntactic relation between these verses (is vs. 3 the continuation of vs. 1 or vs. 2?; how are the words to be translated that are found, for instance, in vs. 2? What, for example, is *ruach 'elohim* (spirit of God, God's Spirit, wind of God, great wind)? All these translations were proposed in full seriousness by competent scholars. Especially the study of syntax, idiom and style are highly important in this respect. The difficulties involved in the mere study of idiom are not to be under-estimated; various texts have to be compared (with the assistance of a concordance) in order to discover various shades of meaning of a word in different styles of writing. In spite of the enormous amount of trouble taken over this investigation there is still great divergence of opinion among scholars, not only regarding results (the meaning of certain words), but also regarding the methods of research them-selves.[2]

[1] See my contribution in H. van Oyen c.s., *Inleiding in de Studie der Theologie*, 1948, pp. 8–43.
[2] See I. Barr, *The semantics of biblical Language*, 1961, and his criticism of many expla-nations of words in *Theologisches Wörterbuch zum Neuen Testament;* we should also bear in mind the differences between Barr and Pedersen concerning their approach to the language as such. On criticism of Barr's view: N. H. Ridderbos, 'Is het Hebreeuws één van de bronnen der openbaring?' *G. Th. T.* 1964; on the other hand see J. H. Hos-pers, 'Theologie en algemene Taalwetenschap', *Vox Th.*, 1965, pp. 19ff.

No wonder, then, that great differences of opinion already become apparent in this first stage of exegesis. And these often do not diminish when we pass on to the second stage of exegesis and ask after the sense, the meaning of a pericope, a smaller or larger textual unit and finally pass on to the third stage, where an attempt is made to establish the relation of the text to the content of a complete source or a whole book, or even to the concepts or the theology of the whole of the Old Testament or the whole of the Bible. It is certainly possible, though, that further study of a text in the light of the fuller context or in its connection with the purport of the whole piece of writing may advance the solution of a textual problem.

This is not to say that the second, and particularly the third stage of exegesis should in principle be ranked above the first, as some scholars advocate.[1] For the purpose that is discovered in a piece of writing considered as a whole often depends largely on the exegesis of its parts. It is a question of interaction: the two forms of exegesis are both indispensable and complement each other.[2]

There is great hesitation among scholars working on the exegesis of the Bible to allow the overall picture to play an important part in solving the problems raised by the exegesis of minor details. This is easy to understand, because the overall picture has often been influenced by theological and dogmatic notions and is frequently based on scholastic systems and traditional concepts rather than on a conscientious reading of the text. This accounts for the strong and almost unceasing tension to which exegetical studies are exposed, for scholastic influences and personal conviction ('prejudices') make themselves felt again and again even with those who believe they have rid themselves completely of such pre-conceived notions (see above pp. 126ff.). In any case everybody who accepts the overall picture as an element in his exegetical method will have to exercise extreme care to keep his exegesis clear from such influences. The overall picture and the exegesis of details will continuously have to correct each other critically.

The important point in all stages of exegesis is making clear distinctions, a critical examination of the textual, grammatical, literary or theological problems. They are all essential to exegesis, and therefore of equal importance to theology. Many scholars think the performance of this critical historical and literary task irrelevant to

[1] As is done by M. Rozelaar against W. den Boer, see note 6 p. 125. This danger pre-eminently threatens dogmatists, who in many respects have the tendency to start from the overall picture, from the *analogia fidei* or from the unity of the Bible. This becomes apparent repeatedly from exegetical parts of K. Barth's *Dogmatik;* see also my criticism of Miskotte, p. 48 n. 3.
[2] Cf. my article mentioned on p. 25 n. 2.

theology[1] but this view cannot possibly be maintained. The connection between the various branches of theology and the significance of all of them for theology was brought out most clearly by G. Von Rad in his *Theology*, though he himself, quite inconsistently, will not accept the results of the modern historical studies on Israel.[2]

Having said A, however, Reformation will also have to say B and apply this method consistently; only thus can clarity be attained. Those who, like Luther[3] consider the *sensus grammaticus et historicus* the only one that is correct, will have to do full justice to both grammar and history. The historical development of the Bible is of great importance for theology itself. The examination of the Bible in terms of historical criticism fundamentally advances theology by making it definitely conscious of the truly human nature of the form in which the Revelation of God has come to us. This revelation can trace back its authority only to its own truth, which can be taught only by the Spirit of God and can find its certitude in faith alone (Hebr. xi. 1).[4] And in practice it helps theology on by throwing a clearer light on the origin of the Biblical writings and the connection between them. It would not be presumptuous to say that it is to historical and philological research that we owe an insight into the origin of the Biblical writings and the connection between them – an insight that was already lost before the first centuries B.C. Comparative philological research and textual criticism have even shed light on scriptural passages which at the time of origin of the LXX had already become obscure. Although by no means all historical and literary problems have been solved, in many respects we can now see behind the Scriptural data and make them transparent, in so far as general history and the history of religion are concerned.

The philological and historico-critical method is indispensable to exegesis and must always be pursued with the best and most recent means of research, for a really convincing and decisive result has not yet been reached at on all points.

Ad 2) The second stage of exegesis, which we call hermeneutics, aims at the understanding of the *matter;* it is synthetic and asks the question: What does the author mean here? What does he want to convey? A text is placed in its spiritual context, considered from its

[1] Cf., e.g., Th. L. Haitjema, *Het Woord Gods in de moderne cultuur*, 1931, p. 131: '"Historico-critical" and "form-critical" questions concerning the content of the Holy Scriptures are not theological questions'.
[2] See Hesse's criticism of these views, cf. above pp. 97ff. and my article mentioned on p. 99 n. 1.
[3] See Bijlsma, *op. cit.*, p. 398.
[4] See my above-mentioned article 'Schriftgezag en Schriftkritiek', in *Schrift en Kerk*. 1953, and above pp. 101ff.

own milieu, in the light of what we know about a person. It confronts us with the author and leads us to a dialogue in the presence of God, as we might say, on the content of His Word.[1] That which may be called hermeneutics, interpretation, therefore comprises what Schleiermacher wanted to achieve with his psychological and phenomenological research as well as what Bultmann aimed at with his 'factual' *(sachlich)* examination. We are here concerned with the 'understanding', the spiritual 'interpretation' of a passage or a piece of writing; here one tries to grasp the 'meaning' of a literary whole and to find the connection between the literary datum and the reality from which it had sprung. Far more than the philological method this method is threatened by the danger of the influence of personal presuppositions; to a great extent the 'interpretation' depends on personal views. That is why the results achieved in this phase of exegesis especially show such great differences, far greater at any rate than those met with in the first phase, the philological examination of the text. Yet interpretation or hermeneutics cannot be omitted in the study of the humanities in general and of theology in particular; if only it is carried out with great care and all proper reservation. For how easily we may err in ordinary life in ascribing certain utterances to personal motives, even in the case of persons we know well! and how much more easily are such errors committed when we are dealing with the words of those who died centuries ago, of whose language but little is known, and of whose work only little may have come down to us. Plato in his day knew how vulnerable the written word is when its father is not there to protect it.[2] We shall always have to be aware of this at this stage of exegesis.

For this reason the 'interpretation' of the 'sense' always involves an element of subjectivity and therefore of uncertainty, more so than the literal interpretation. It is not such a simple matter – as we remarked above – to satisfy the demand for an exegesis *e mente auctoris*, a demand often made so lightly. It is still more difficult to render the essential matter in one's own words in such a way that full justice is done to it. More than the philological stage it demands continuous willingness to reconsider the results. This implies that – like any other science – theology must be willing to correct itself in each of its branches, even the systematic; this keeps theology alive but also limits its authority. Theology must always be well aware of the brittleness of the earthen vessels in which it keeps its treasures and from which it dispenses them.

Ad 3) To the highest degree this applies, of course, to the third phase of exegesis in which theology, by virtue of its task, attempts to

[1] Cf. H. W. Wolff, *Ges. Studien*, p. 333.
[2] Phaedrus 275 E.

135

give a more systematic insight into the connection and meaning of a certain datum within the framework of the whole Old Testament and even of the whole of the Bible, and tries to arrive at an overall picture of the Biblical message in general. Here the factors we mentioned when dealing with hermeneutics are found again; here even more lines are drawn, even more connections are laid which are only in small part open to historical proof and literary demonstration. Here subjective views play an even greater part.[1]

The connection must, therefore, be judged with great caution. They should certainly not be fixed in one definite scheme, as is done only too often when the Bible is characterized broadly as a unity. For then it becomes difficult to avoid inaccuracy or (even worse) arbitrariness in allowing one or several elements to dominate the whole and suppressing others. One should be conscious of this danger in all theological studies. To mention some examples of the tendency for the scheme to dominate the overall picture, I may refer to J. Kaufman's remarks on the transcendence of God, to M. Buber's observations on the 'dialogical' relation to God, to the views of the early Christian Church on the christocentric meaning of the Old Testament; to the way in which history and the concept of the covenant were made into a scheme in more recent days. Von Rad, the author of the latest Theology to date, represents the Old Testament as a whole without further preface as kerygmatic and referring to Christ throughout. This point of view could not but lead to an essentially typological exegesis. For typology, too, really is a schematic connection imposed upon the history of salvation. We do not deny (see above, pp. 51 f.) that the Old Testament has a character all its own, standing out clearly against the background of the religious literature of the ancient Near-East, nor do we deny (pp. 114f.) that there exists a fundamental, deep-seated unity of the two Testaments, especially concerning the expectation of the Kingdom of God. Yet we have some hesitation in confining the interpretation of the various books of the tremendous, infinitely varied textual material within the bounds of a definite theological ground-plan. In every attempt to view the whole from one single point of view we must beware of wishing to explain every detail in terms of this one aspect and to impose our overall picture upon smaller literary units. Fundamentally we are not justified to allow the *analogia fidei* to predominate in exegesis. The consequence of taking this position is that we must always be conscious of our inability to integrate the exegetical tension ('dualism')[2] in full, for the

---

[1] Cf. what A. Kuenen said on this subject at the time, K. Budde, *Gesammte Abhandlungen* (van Kuenen), 1894, p. 9f.; already quoted in my *The Religion*, pp. 277f.
[2] K. Frör, *Biblische Hermeneutik* 1961, p. 136.

simple and compelling reason that the Bible is a book made up of a series of spiritual testimonies brought together in the course of history; a book in which many voices are heard from many centuries, and all these voices proclaim their testimony concerning God, without, however, blending into harmony.

It is, therefore, equally impossible to apply typology[1] *methodically*, as was done by earlier generations of theologians. Even if it is possible to find all kinds of analogies in the Bible, particularly in the relationship between the two Testaments (see above p. 96) and to accept on these grounds typological references in certain cases, yet one should be on one's guard and not be trapped into applying typology as the methodical basis for exegesis.[2] The Bible is too rich in relations between God and man for it to be confined to this most special and decisive connection. We must leave room for more than one possible way of indicating the connection between Old Testament and New Testament; the most important of these are:

a. typology, which does not only presuppose an organic connection but also *parallelism* between the ideas and the words, though these need not match exactly.

b. preparation, there is an organic connection but the Old Testament idea is present only in part or *in nuce*, and becomes explicit in the New Testament; the New Testament *is in a continuous line with* the Old Testament.

c. similarity, there are religious conceptions which completely correspond or in which the New Testament is entirely dependent on the Old Testament;

[1] Cf. on the N.T. L. Goppelt, *Typos, die typologische Deutung des A.T. im Neuen*, 1939; G. von Rad, 'Typologische Auslegung des A.T.', *Ev. Th.*, XII, 1952/3, pp. 17ff (cf. *Interpretation*, 1961, pp. 174ff.) and his *O.T. Theology II*, III A, B, C; S. Amsler, *op. cit.*; A. M. Brouwer, 'Typologie', *N. Th. S.*, 1941, pp. 98ff. rejects it entirely for present-day theology; Brouwer finds the basis of typology in oriental 'root-thinking', i.e. in the idea that things have been pre-figured in an original pattern which is realized afterwards.

R. Bultmann, who also rejects typology in exegesis finds its root in a cyclical doctrine of repetition ('Wiederholungslehre') ('Ursprung und Sinn der Typologie als hermeneutischer Methode', *Pro Regno et Sanctuario, Festschrift G. van der Leeuw*, 1950, pp. 89ff.).

It seems doubtful to me if either of these ideas *must* form the background of typology and if it is not merely a matter of parallelism. Even if the original situation was as described by Bultmann and Brouwer, we might consider typology justifiable in so far as it seeks out the comparable elements in the two Testaments and tests their fundamental spiritual unity. See especially the cautious remarks on this subject by W. Eichrodt, *Ist die typologische Exegese sachgemäße Exegese*, Suppl. V.T. IV, 1957, p. 161. Von Rad accepts typology as a method on account of the structural analogy of the history of salvation in the Old and the New Testament (*O.T. Theology*, II, III, c).

[2] Cf. also the remark made by H. W. Wolff, *Ev. Th.*, XII, p. 104 (cf. *Interpretation*, 1961, pp. 469ff.).

d. contrast, there are religious conceptions in the New Testament that form a contrast with Old Testament conceptions.

Only by this differentiation is it possible to express the historical and the organic connection without straining the texts.

The homiletic use of the Old Testament

In this section, too, we cannot give a practical application but only indicate some guiding lines.

In virtue of its nature – proclamation of the Word of God, preaching is something else than the interpretation of the Scriptures.

The latter is the theological part of the preacher's task, the former is the prophetical task of the theologian-preacher. There is a prophetical element in preaching, in the sense that the preacher has to pass on the Word of God in a personal, spiritually justifiable manner. This is not to say that he could feel superior to the Word of God of the Bible, for he remains wholly dependent upon it. He is absorbed and inspired by it, in such a way that through his words the Word of God becomes a living testimony to his contemporaries. Like the prophet of olden times, the preacher will have to pass on, as a matter of life and death, as God's concern with this world, the Word that he has come to understand in his living communion with the Bible (Ezek. xxxiii; xxxiv).

For that reason the preacher's attitude is (formally, at any rate) fundamentally different from the standpoint of the exegete.[1] As he is the witness, the preacher stands in an immediate personal relation to what is proclaimed in the Bible and speaks about it from this close relation in spiritual unity with it. The preacher is wholly concerned with what the Bible proclaims to the world. This is his starting-point,

---

[1] Compare Bultmann, *Das Problem der Hermeneutik*, p. 59, on the subject of the *intentio recta* and the *intentio obliqua*, between which F. Blättner makes a distinction in the judgment of religious works of art; by a work of art the faithful are, as it were, brought into immediate contact with the object represented; the art-critic, however, does not see the work of art as a reproduction of the object itself, but as the expression of a creative mind. Thus exegesis is a kind of 'intentio obliqua' owing to its historical element; even if exegesis can really confront man with the matter at issue, the latter exists rather as the object of critical inspection; the *intentio recta* is formed with the naive believer who hears immediately and uncritically the word as the Word of God with which he is confronted, i.e. as the objective divine reality. By the 'prophetic' preacher who has also given a good exegesis, that which he has come to see by critical reflection (*intentio obliqua*) as the factual message of the Scriptures is turned into a *direct message of God* to the congregation. His task is on the one hand to read the Bible critically, on the other to proclaim positively and directly the Word of God. Because he has come to understand the words against their historical background he can present it with even more stress to his audience as the Word of God when he has come to understand it as revelation. In order to be able to do this the preacher must have been touched by the Word of God in the Scriptures and he must go deeply into what it represents in the world.

the subject that he goes into and pursues. The fact that he has been touched by the message of the Bible makes him wholly dependent upon it, but at the same time this obedience to the subject-matter frees him from the letter, from the form in which the message comes to him. He may grasp this message at various points, wherever the discovers it (cf. e.g. the sermon on Faith of Hebr. xi), and by going into the matter itself in all seriousness he may sometimes rise above the historical datum and in this very way proclaim the Word in all plenitude. This must be Christ's intention in Matth. v. 17ff.[1] And thus it must remain in the Christian Church. Again and again the preacher who speaks on behalf of the Church, may and must rise above the historical form in which the Word has come down to us in the Old Testament. In the social and ethical field the Church was compelled in the past to admit the rightness of the abolition of slavery, nowadays the Church finds herself more and more compelled to admit the social equality of man and woman, to mention only some peripheral cases. In the same way the Church will be compelled in the future to draw new, independent conclusions concerning other fields of life not immediately given or foreseen in the Bible.

The purpose of preaching is to bring home the meaning of the biblical message to contemporary man, to make it topical, and for that reason the preacher must always resemble a transformer, he transforms a certain form and style into another, which can touch the contemporary audience. Therefore he must have elbow-room, and not be tied down to traditional schemes. But because the preacher has such a responsible task which allows him so much freedom, he must live and keep living in close contact with the Bible and must let himself be guided by Scripture along the road pointed out to him by exegesis. The very prophetic nature of his work demands a scrupulous theological and exegetical conscience, because otherwise he may easily fall into an unbiblical spirituality, into fanaticism and modernism. The need for a continual training in exegesis can hardly be realized sufficiently, for only in this way can the miracle of the discovery of something new be experienced of which Jesus speaks in Matth. xiii. 52. If in his preaching the minister feels called upon to rise above his text in certain respects, he will have to render an account for this to himself and, as much as possible, to his audience.

We can and may no longer take ingenuous liberties that were taken

---

[1] In this respect K. H. Miskotte rightly speaks of a *perichoresis* of the two Testaments (*Handboek der prediking* I, 1948, pp. 353ff., especially pp. 429f.: *Over de prediking van het O.T.*; cf. also his *Om het levende Woord*, 1948, pp. 8off., 175). This should certainly not be made an exegetical and hermeneutical law, but cannot be called illegitimate in preaching. Splendid instances of this style of preaching are to be found in the volumes of sermons by O. Noordmans, such as *Gestalte en Geest*, 1956.

before the rise of historical thinking, such as are found in the early Church (by allegorization) and in the age of the Reformation (especially by Luther, who, for instance, without further preface called Abraham a Christian), or in the ancient Hebrew world (cf., for example, the commentary on Habakkuk found recently, with its bold exegesis reflecting the views of the commentator's own day) and, in imitation of this, by St. Paul in the New Testament (cf. Gal. iv. 21ff.), and nowadays especially by the sects who without more ado arbitrarily interpret various Biblical texts as if they had direct reference to events of the present day.

The preacher must be critical of the traditional use made of the Bible, but he must be equally critical of a great deal of modern exegesis of the Bible, often dominated by all kinds of dogmatic or philosophical presuppositions; besides dogmatic Christian suppositions we may also find scientific aprioris, aesthetic or dogmatic assumptions! In the post-Reformation period people showed strong leanings towards Jewish exegesis, and nowadays this tendency is remarkably strong again. Neither the dogmatic Christian interpretation (Protestant or Roman' catholic) nor the Jewish interpretation (liberal or orthodox) give any certainty as to a correct understanding of the Word. The preacher must work on the material placed in his hands by arriving at his own exegesis. Such aids as commentaries and dictionaries, ancient writers and modern studies will always be merely *aids* and can never replace his independent examination of the text.

If preaching finds its focal point in the gospel of Jesus Christ, it can never isolate this testimony from the message of the law and the prophets. Neither should it, however, identify the law, the prophets and the gospel, or emphasize the Old Testament to such an extent that the gospel is turned into an appendix, nor should it stress the gospel to such a degree that the Old Testament is looked upon as a thing of the past that has had its day. If all is well, it will be founded on God's work in Israel, or rather, it will, on the ground of the Bible, from Genesis to Revelation, testify to God's communion with the world, from creation to the end of time. This is possible when the message of the Kingdom of God is given the full emphasis it deserves and when it is viewed as described by Dr. H. W. Obbink (see above, pp. 121ff.). This will set us free from a faith centred exclusively on Jesus Christ, a faith which lays too one-sided emphasis on the αὐτοβασιλεία, so that Jesus Christ and the Kingdom of God are identified.[1] It will

---

[1] Marcion; Origen, see K. L. Schmidt, *Th. W.*, I, p. 591; Feine, *Theologie*, p. 99; G. Sevenster, *Christologie*, p. 22. Again and again A. A. van Ruler rightly sounds a warning note against this, cf. now e.g. his *Reformatorische opmerkingen in de ontmoeting met Rome*, 1965, p. 78, though it seems as if he keeps them apart too rigidly. Moreover,

allow us to profess Jesus Christ as the actual revelation in this world of the coming Kingdom of God.

The eschatological motif has been thrust into the background by the soteriological and Christological motif. Fundamentally this means that the Kingdom of God is thrust into the background by the idea of the Church as redeemed humanity. This is the basic error in the Church and in theology; the same pietism that caused the downfall of Israel in its second period after the exile[1] also brought about the decay of the Christian Church from the apostolic congregation to a catholic institute of salvation.

The one thing that can give the Christian faith a new trend, a new vision and a fresh momentum is eschatology in the sense of the preaching of Jesus Christ: 'The Kingdom of Heaven is at hand.'

Without falling into a one-sided view of either the Old Testament or the New Testament, a preaching that serves the Kingdom of God can make Jesus Christ the central figure of the Bible (not of the Old Testament only), or rather, it can see the Gospel of Jesus Christ as the conclusion of the Old Testament and as the heart of the revelation of God in Israel.

Some further literature:

I. The Old Testament as the Word of God:

B. W. Anderson a.o., *The O.T. and Christian Faith*, 1964.
J. Barr, *Old and New in Interpretation*, 1966.
A. Bentzen, 'The O.T. and the New Covenant', *Hervomd Teologiese Studies*, VII, 1950, Pretoria, pp. 1ff.
J. Bright, *The authority of the O.T.*, 1967.
J. Coppens, *Les harmonies des deux Testaments*, 1949.
A. G. Hebert, *The authority of the O.T.*, 1947.
Th. Kampmann, *Das Geheimnis des A.T.*, 1962.
J. Köberle, *Die alttestamentliche Offenbarung*, 1908.
C. G. Montefiore, 'The O.T. and Judaism', in H. Wheeler Robinson: *Record and Revelation*, 1938, pp. 427ff.

he views the Kingdom of God too much in the light of Old Testament theocracy, and too little in the light of the New Testament eschatological perspective; see my criticism of van Ruler's *Die christliche Kirche u. das A.T.*, see above p. 97 n. 3. It is often lost sight of that in the Bible, even in the O.T., too, several figures are identified that must be distinguished but that are also spiritually connected, for instance Israel, Jacob, or Abraham with the people of Israel, the *mal'akh Jahweh* with Yahweh. When identifications are looked upon as complete identity (in accordance with our western scheme of thought) instead of as functional unity, the result can be nothing but wrong conclusions. In her dogmas on the Trinity and the Dual Nature the Church has called this tendency to a halt.

[1] See my *Die Erwählung Israels nach dem A.T.*, p. 110, n. 4.

M. Noth, 'Von der Knechtsgestalt des A.T.', *Ev. Th.*, 1947, pp. 302ff.
A. Richardson and W. Schweitzer, *Biblical Authority to-day*, 1951, pp. 17ff.
H. H. Rowley, 'The unity of the O.T.', *B.J.R.L.*, XXIX, No. 7, 1946.
Id., *The authority of the Bible*, 1949.
G. E. Wright, *The challenge of Israel's Faith*[2], 1946.
Id., *The O.T. against its environment*, 1950, pp. 9ff., 73ff.

II. Exegesis (general):

I. Abrahams, 'Jewish interpretation of the O.T.', in A. S. Peake, *The People and the Book*, 1925, pp. 403ff.
P. Bartel, *Interpretation du langage mythique et Théologie biblique*, 1963 (general remarks on the hermeneutics of the N.T.).
P. A. H. de Boer, 'Methode en mogelijkheden van exegese', in: *Over Bijbel en openbaring*, pp. 23ff.
L. H. K. Bleeker, *Hermeneutiek van het O.T.*, 1948.
B. S. Childs, 'Interpretation in Faith', *Interpretation*, 1964, 432ff. (about the O.T.).
H. Diem. *Grundfragen der biblischen Hermeneutik*, *Th. Ex.*, N.F. 24, 1950.
B. D. Eerdmans, 'Exegese', *Th. T.*, XLIV, 1910, pp. 289ff., 443ff.
W. Eichrodt, 'Zur Frage der theologischen Exegese des A.T.', *Th. Bl.*, 17, 1938, pp. 73ff.
K. Frör, *Biblische Hermeneutik*, 1961.
W. A. Irwin, 'The Interpretation of the O.T.', *Z.A.W.* 1950, pp. 1ff. (criticism on Principles of Interpretation, see Richardson and Wright).
O. Noordmans, 'Licht en donker in de exegese', in *Geestelijke perspectieven*, 1930, pp. 68ff.
A. Oepke, *Geschichtliche und übergeschichtliche Schriftauslegung*[2], 1947.
W. O. E. Oesterley, 'The exegesis of the O.T.', in H. Wheeler Robinson, *Record and Revelation*, 1938, pp. 402ff.
G. von Rad, 'Fragen der Schriftauslegung des A.T.', *Theologia militans*, 20, 1938.
A. Richardson and W. Schweitzer, *Biblical Authority to-day*, 1951, Part III: Principles of Interpretation, pp. 157ff.
G. E. Wright: 'The World Council of Churches and biblical interpretation', *Interpretation* III, 1949, pp. 50ff.
E. Würthwein, 'Vom Verstehen des A.T.', *Festschrift G. Beer*, 1935, pp. 128ff.

On allegorical exegesis:

W. den Boer, *De allegorese in het werk van Clemens Alexandrinus*, doctorate thesis Leyden, 1940.
Dr. G. A. van den Bergh van Eysinga, *Allegorische Interpretatie* (address), 1904.

On typological exegesis:

B. J. Alfrink, *Over typologische exegese van het O.T.* (address), 1945.
F. Baumgärtel, 'Das alttest. Geschehen als heilsgeschichtliches Geschehen', *Geschichte und A.T.* (*Alt-Festschrift*), 1953, pp. 13ff.

Exegesis and Preaching:

M. Noth, 'Die Vergegenwärtigung des A.T. in der Verkündigung', *Ev. Th.*, XII, 1952, pp. 6ff.
W. Rupprecht, *Die Predigt über altt. Texte in den lutherischen Kirchen Deutschlands*, 1962.
W. Vischer, 'Das A.T. und die Verkündigung', *Th. Bl.*, X, 1931, pp. 1ff.

CHAPTER V

Basis, task and method
of Old Testament theology[1]

The term 'theology of the Old Testament' may be called somewhat
ambiguous as the words 'Old Testament' may have the function of a
subjective as well as an objective genitive. We may, therefore, think
of a theology contained in the Old Testament itself or of a theology
which has the Old Testament for its object; a combination of these
two conceptions is also possible. In the first case the 'theology of the
Old Testament' remains limited to an examination of the theological
elements contained in the Old Testament. It is, therefore, a descriptive and historical science, and as such it belongs to the religio-historical and phenomenological study of the religion of Israel, of which
the Old Testament is the most important document.[2] Such an examination of the Old Testament would be possible, for, though we may
not call the Old Testament a theological book, we are justified in
saying that certain theologoumena did, indeed, develop in Israel,
such as the doctrine of election[3] and that of monotheism.[4]

If this historical conception of Old Testament theology is looked

---

[1] On the history of the theology of the O.T. see, besides the wellknown work by
L.Diestel, also O.Procksch, *Theologie des A.T.*, 1950, pp.19ff.; E.König, *Theologie des
A.T.*, 1922, pp.1ff.; and especially the critical survey of the first half of this century by
N.W.Porteous, 'Old Testament Theology', in H.H.Rowley, *The O.T. and modern
study*, pp.311ff. In the following fundamental outline we could not go into all the
latest attempts and expositions, such as G.A.Knight's *A Christian Theology in the O.T.*,
in which the connection between New Testament and Old Testament is elucidated,
and demonstrated in the parallels between their histories, though in many respects
it makes a somewhat artificial impression. Particularly instructive Roman Catholic
contributions are the essays by Alonzo Schökel, *Biblische Theologie des Alten Testaments*,
StZ172, 1963, pp.34–51, and M.L.Ramlot, *Ancien Testament*, R.Thom 1964,pp.65ff.
[2] Something like this seems to be the view of P.A.H.deBoer, in his criticism of the
first edition of this book ('Aantekeningen bij Prof.Vriezen's boek "Hoofdlijnen der
theologie van het O.T."') in *Vox Theologica*, XX, 1949/50, pp.174ff. On the ground of
his restrictive conception of Old Testament theology he disqualifies the Christian-
theological method of the study of the O.T. as unscholarly. Though on wholly
different grounds, G.vonRad *(O.T. Theology)* wants to bring out the theologies
that are found in the various sources and writings of the Old Testament; yet his
exposition rests in principle on a dogmatic Christian basic concept, as appears from
the final chapters of Vol.II (see further pp. 150 n. 4 and 149 n. 2.
[3] See my *Die Erwählung Israels nach dem A.T.*, 1953.
[4] See above, pp.32ff.

upon as being, in the nature of the case, the only possibility, it excludes the second view that Old Testament theology could be that branch of theology which is especially concerned with the Old Testament.[1] It might be looked upon as a one-sidedly consistent continuation of the conception of the 'father of Biblical theology', J. G. Gabler, who in his inaugural address[2] placed Biblical theology beside dogmatic theology as an independent branch of scholarship. The former is historical[3]; it must provide a survey of the various religious concepts of the different Bible authors and starting from this survey it must attempt to develop by comparison an outline of the general Scriptural concepts which is arranged more systematically. This outline could then be passed on to dogmatic theology for further dogmatic elaboration. In Gabler's days biblical theology was still wholly dependent on dogmatic theology, so the introduction of this exegetical and historical branch of study was an indispensable step forward. The two tasks that were entrusted to Biblical theology (collecting the various religious concepts and arranging the general notions into a systematical survey) developed into two separate branches of scholarship: the description of the Biblical religions of Old Testament and New Testament[4] and to the Biblical theologies of the older style.

As the history and the religion of Israel developed from the historical conception of Biblical theology, Biblical theology could set itself especially to the second task assigned to it by Semler: being the link

---

[1] Cf. p. 143 n. 2 This is possible on the ground of a positivist conception of science which as such perceives a strong contrast between science and faith. Cf. against this view W. Eichrodt, 'Hat die alttestamentliche Theologie noch eine selbständige Bedeutung innerhalb der alttestamentischen Wissenschaft?', *Z.A.W.*, 1929, pp.83ff., esp. pp.85ff.; also O. Eissfeldt, 'Israelitisch-jüdische Religionsgeschichte und alttestamentliche Theologie', *Z.A.W.*, 1926, pp. 1ff., but also on the ground of other considerations, as is done by Von Rad, who, strictly speaking, denies the continuity and unity in the theological ways of thought of the Old Testament writers (ThLZ, 1963, pp.403ff.).

[2] *De iusto discrimine theologiae biblicae et dogmaticae, regundisque recte utriusque finibus*, Altorf, 1787, see among others, Herzog-Hauck, *Realencyclopaedie*[3], VI., s.v. Gabler; see now R. Smend, *J. P. Gablers Begründung der biblischen Theologie*, EvTh XXII, 1962, pp. 345ff. We should not forget, though that the term 'Biblical theology' itself is older; it is already used by Calovius in his *Systema locorum theologicorum*, 1655ff., and C. Hagman uses it as the title *('Biblische Theologie')* of such a book containing *loca probantia*, see Dentan, *Preface*[2], pp. 15, 18; Zeller, 1669, employs the term in contrast to 'scholastic' (= dogmatic) theology, see R. Martin-Achard, *Les voies de la Théologie de l'A.T.*, RThPh, 1959, p. 219. Even if pietism toyed with the idea of a Biblical theology of its own, it did not develop as an independent form of Biblical scholarchip until the age of critical theology.

[3] Est theologia biblica *e genere historico*, tradens quid scriptores de rebus divinis *senserint* (Gabler, loc. cit., p.8)

[4] Many people have thought (and many still think) that biblical theology is fundamentally the description of the religion of Israel; cf. E. Kautzsch, *Biblische Theologie des A.T.*, 1911; this is a third conception of the theology of the O.T., a view frequently held but by no means justified.

between dogmatic and historical theology. It collects the materials supplied by the Bible as it has come to understand them in the light of history, so that the dogmatist, engaged in his systematic task, may know what the points at issue in the Bible are[1]. Old Testament theology as a branch of Biblical theology fulfils this task in so far as the Old Testament is concerned.

The question remains in what way this task should be performed. According to Semler the general concepts should be built up from the different views of the biblical writers. Many Biblical theologies have attempted to summarize the Biblical concepts of theology, anthropology, soteriology, eschatology, and others, the themes of which were, in principle, derived from Christian dogmatics. The latest case in point is L. Köhler's *Theologie des A.T.* Radically opposed to this is Steuernagel's view[2], for he thinks it should be a systematic summary of the results of religio-historical research. The great importance of such summaries is evident[3], but they belong to phenomenology and the history of religion rather than to theology. The same applies to such studies as J. Hempel's *Gott und Mensch im A.T.*[4], which, as the sub-title indicates, is a *"Studie zur Geschichte der Frömmigkeit"*, and therefore phenomenological rather than theological: it gives a phenomenological typology.

Eissfeldt[5] has rightly started from theology in setting Old Testament theology its task; he has found its starting-point in the Christian faith. Theology deals with revelation[6], and is concerned with the reality of God and with the faith of the Christian Church; for that reason Old Testament theology has its own place alongside the history of the religion of Israel as a separate branch of scholarship. With Porteous[7] we can only raise this objection against Eissfeldt's view that here the issue is narrowed down in the sense that theology is not concerned with 'the past but with the timeless present'[8], for the theology of the Old Testament cannot simply abstract its content of faith from history. But nevertheless we must be very grateful to Eissfeldt for his sharp methodological distinction between these two branches of study. Only the question of the structure of theology

[1] See G. van der Leeuw, *Inleiding tot de Theologie*, 1935, pp. 180ff.
[2] C. Steuernagel, 'Alttest. Theologie und alttest. Religionsgeschichte' in *Vom Alten Testament, Festschrift Marti, Beih. Z.A.W.*, 41, 1925, pp. 266ff.
[3] Cf. for instance the important essay by Steuernagel, 'Entwicklung der jüdischen Eschatologie', in *Festschrift für Bertholet*, 1950, pp. 479ff.   [4] Second ed., 1936.
[5] Op. cit., see also W. Staerk, 'Religionsphilosophie und alttest. Theologie', *Zeitschrift f. Th. u. K.*, 1924, pp. 289ff.
[6] Th. L. Haitjema's definition of Theology as 'the thought of faith springing from revelation' seems to be quite correct ('Schriftgeloof en Exegese', in *Kerk en Theologie*, 1952, p. 216).
[7] Op. cit. p. 321–2.   [8] Eissfeldt, op. cit., p. 11.

is not solved completely satisfactorily, as the historical element in theology is not given its due.

In this respect Eichrodt's contribution[1] offers a wholly different conception; he contrasts the history of the religion of Israel and the theology of the Old Testament in such a way that in the former 'the genetic understanding of Old Testament religion is emphasized', and in the latter 'the cross-section through what has come to be, by means of which the living contents of the religion may be illustrated in terms of their inner structure.' According to him theology 'has no other material to work with than the history of religion: that is to say, it proceeds from the same subjective presuppositions in an endeavour to classify the empirical facts and in consequence render them intelligible. So its aim, like its method, means that its place lies entirely within the limits of empirico-historical Old Testament study'.

Against this definition, too, some objections can be raised; actually Old Testament theology as defined here is the phenomenological branch of theological study[2]. Eichrodt does, it is true, admit that here and there the research-worker can go further by raising the question of truth, but he does not consider this a method. It is clear that this programme has been elaborated in Eichrodt's *Theology of the O.T.*, though he accentuates more strongly the systematic nature of the Old Testament theology: it has to define the position of the religious concepts of the Old Testament amid the religious life of the nations and of Christianity. He states emphatically that the realm of Old Testament belief must be viewed in its essential coherence with that of the New Testament in Jesus Christ[3]. So with Eichrodt, too, the historical element comes into prominence in Old Testament theology.

The views expressed by Von Rad in his Theology (see I, pp. 7ff.) are radically different. He rejects the structural cross-sections as well as more or less systematic summaries of the religious content of the Old Testament, but wants to give a survey of the credal content of the various separate writings. In this way he hopes to gain a better

[1] Op. cit., p.89.
[2] J. Lindblom also advocates a theology of the Old Testament in the form of a systematical description of the nature of the Old Testament religion, with the Old Testament conception of God as its basic starting-point (SvTK XXXVII, 1961, pp. 73ff.) In the same way but in different terms J. v. d. Ploeg attempts to answer the question: 'Une théologie de l'A.T. est-elle possible? (*E. Th. L* 1962, p.417); in his opinion such a theology is only possible as a summary of religious truths of the Old Testament which constitute and express Israel's religion. In his *Preface*[2], pp. 122ff., R. C. Dentan stresses both the systematical descriptive nature of Old Testament theology and the relation to the New Testament, and to the congeniality of the religious views professed in the two Testaments; he pays attention to ethics and the cult as well as to the conception of God.
[3] W. Eichrodt, op. cit., 1961, pp. 25ff.

insight in the different traditions of Israel which all give a kerygmatic reflection of God's activity in history. These traditions are based on an ancient creed that presents the ground-plan for the religious concepts. Von Rad's *Theology* is therefore in fact the result of his studies in the fields of literature and the history of tradition which caused him to approach the ancient sources and the separate writings (Hexateuch, Deuteronomy and Chronicles) from the angle of their connection with the ancient Israelite creed. Von Rad derived the credal theory as a working hypothesis from the study of the New Testament (cf. his reply to Conzelmann in *Ev.Th.*, 1964); it was first applied by him to the Hexateuch with the aid of the method of the history of tradition. This kerygmatic starting-point gave his historico-literary research, which is wholly dominated by the history of tradition, a historico-literary character, and conversely the theological study of the Old Testament assumes the shape of a history of tradition. This form of research may be useful and correct, but it cannot be looked upon as the only justified or ideal form for a theology of the Old Testament.[1]

In his above-mentioned article in *Th.L.Z.*, 1963 Von Rad admits as much, but he considers it the only scientifically justified method as things are, because in his opinion the Old Testament so clearly contains an abundance of kerygmatic "theologies" that there can be no question of one single Old Testament theology which constitutes a unity. He emphatically extends this view to the belief in Yahweh. This method of study of the history of tradition cannot but lend to such results, for it is concerned with the separate traditions and their "forms", and is, therefore, hardly interested in the common elements that bind these sources together. We may fully recognize its claims as a method, without, however, agreeing where it objects to other important ways of approach, such as the history of religion, phenomenology, the "history of piety", the more systematical summaries or any others that can be distinguished.

In this book we start from the view that *both as to its object and its method Old Testament theology is and must be a Christian theological science.*[2] That does not mean that it denies the empirico-historical, phenomenological or any other results of the other branches of Old Testament study, but that it performs its task independently while taking account of and assimilating the results attained by Old Testament scholarship in all its various aspects – the results, therefore, not only in research in the fields of phenomenology and the history of religion, but also those of archaeology, philology, literature, history, exegesis, etc. It is

[1] See now my criticism in *Kerk en Theologie*, 1965.
[2] Also O. Procksch, *Theologie des A.T.*, 1950; N.W. Porteous, op. cit., *passim*, but esp. p. 343–4.

not correct, therefore, to incorporate the science of religion as such into theology itself, as was done by Procksch in his *Theologie des A.T.*, for in that case the same procedure should be applied in the other branches of scholarship.[1]

It would be preferable to treat the history of religion as an independent parallel science, as was done by E. Sellin in his *Alttestamentliche Theologie auf religionsgeschichtlicher Grundlage*, the first part of which deals with the *Israelitisch-Jüdische Religionsgeschichte* and the second with the *Theologie des A.T.* It is hardly possible, though, to look upon the history of the religion of Israel as the twin brother of Old Testament theology, for the two are indeed too far apart, even if this view is understandable from a historical point of view. Old Testament theology is a form of scholarship differing from the history of Israel's religion in its object as well as in its method. In its object, *because its object is not the religion of Israel but the Old Testament*[2]; in its method *because it is a study of the message of the Old Testament both in itself and in its relation to the New Testament.*[3]

About both these aspects we shall go into more detail. Only when Eissfeldt's line of thought is followed out consistently can we arrive at a definition of Old Testament theology which guarantees a science independent in name and content. Old Testament theology is concerned with the Old Testament; that is to say it is not the religion of Israel in its historical growth and origin, in its development and formation, that is of central importance (so that e.g. Israelite Baalism has as much right to our attention as Yahwism), but it is concerned with the Old Testament as the Holy Scriptures of the Jews, and more especially of the Christians; its task is to define the characteristic features of *the message of the Old Testament*, and for that reason many things can be left out of account which are of more importance in the study of the religion of Israel; as a theological branch of scholarship the theology of the Old Testament seeks *particularly the element of revelation in the message of the Old Testament;* it must work, therefore, with *theological standards* and must give *its own evaluation of the Old Testament message on the ground of its Christian theological starting-point.* In doing so it must guard against the error of tearing apart the *correlation between faith*

---

[1] Nowadays several scholars propose to incorporate the Introduction to the Old Testament into theology, as was already done to a large extent by Von Rad.
[2] On what grounds this distinction can be made is evident from what has been said above on pp. 24ff. and 51ff.
[3] The English works on the theology of the O.T. (A.B. Davidson, *The Theology of the O.T.*, 1911, and H. Wheeler Robinson, see p. 152 n. 1) give us particularly the impression that they start from a synthesis of the theological and the religio-historical methods (e.g. Davidson, p. 6) and that it is this which makes their work so fascinating; cf. also the books by Rowley and North.

and revelation by identifying revelation and canon.[1] From the Christian theological point of view the canon, too, must be submitted to the judgement of the preaching of Jesus Christ. This implies that the method of Old Testament theology is not only purely phenomenological (a reproduction of the Old Testament message in its context), but it also gives the connection with the New Testament message and a judgement from the point of view of that message.[2] So, as a part of Christian theology, Old Testament theology in the full sense of the word gives an insight into the Old Testament message and a judgement of this message from the point of view of the Christian faith. It includes the theological motives found in the Old Testament,[3] but it is also concerned with the whole reality of the revelation of God,[4] as described to us in the historical conceptions and the literary testimony of the Old Testament. In doing this it is not enough to give a general survey of 'sacred history', with a simple rendering of the biblical narrative in the order in which it is given to us in the Canon[5], but it must express the message of God of the Old Testament (using the results of critical research) as it took shape in the various books and sources of the Old Testament during the history which God made Israel pass through until Jesus Christ. All this means complete absorption in the voices which bear witness in the Old Testament to the work of God and so to Him in the course of history and this is not

[1] Cf. Eissfeldt, *op. cit.* p. 3n. (continuation of p. 2, n. 1), who reproaches Barthian theology with this.
[2] The programme unfolded above is an ideal objective, which could only be realized by the close co-operation of theologians in the fields of both the Old and the New Testament. Therefore any Old Testament scholar who devotes himself to this task can achieve no more than patch-work. Von Rad thinks the application of standards so problematical that he prefers to refrain from using them completely, for the present at any rate, and to go no further than allowing the old Testament authors to proclaim their message as objectively as possible (see Th.L.Z. 1963, pp. 407f.). Meanwhile in the latter part of the second volume of his Theology he meets the problem of the relationship between the two Testaments in such a way as to relate the Old Testament typologically to the New Testament. It remains to be seen if in doing so he pays sufficient attention to the critical relationship between the two Testaments and if this kind of methodical search for a solution does not imply a theological conception which does identify canon and revelation after all.
[3] See above p. 153.
[4] Cf. H. Kraemer, 'De theologische studie aan de Universiteit', in H. Kraemer and F. J. Pop, *Gedachten over de vernieuwing der theologische studie*, 1946, p. 7.
[5] As given e.g. by A. C. Welch in his book for religious instruction, *The preparation for Christ*, 1933, or by O. Weber, *Bibelkunde des A.T.*, I, II, 1935, or by P. Heinisch, *Geschichte des A.T.*, 1950, however important this sacred history may be; (cf. that already A. J. C. Vilmar, *Theologie der Tatsachen*, 3rd printing, 1938, p. 33 emphasizes the necessity of a 'special acquaintance with the contents of the whole Bible, which has long since been lost'); the sacred history is an indispensable and *basic* element of all theological study, though one which is all too often lacking. If, however, theology were to stop short here, it would mainly bear witness to only one type of preaching in O.T., viz. that of the last editors of the books, and give us too little insight into the various forms of the message and its spiritual development in Israel.

merely a philological and historical exercise but also a personal exercise in listening and spiritual understanding.

When the question of method is raised we must say first of all that Old Testament theology must first and foremost inquire into the kerugmatic nature[1] of the Old Testament as a whole and of its parts.[2,3] This should really be looked upon as a necessary preliminary. For this reason the outline of the message of the separate writings has been given in the prolegomena (Ch. III). This study must always be continued.

On the ground of the understanding of the message of the books and their authors we can expound the whole body of their testimony concerning God, His work and His relations with man and the world. Fundamentally the witness to the God of Israel, Yahweh, is the central element of the words of the Old Testament authors. There are many voices to be heard in the various writings, but the speakers and singers all want to proclaim one and the same God. He is the one focal point of all the Old Testament writings, whatever their literary character, whatever their period of origin[4]. This leads me to the conclusion that Old Testament theology must centre upon Israel's God as the God of the Old Testament in His relations to the people, man, and the world, and that it must be dependent upon this central element for its structure.

The attempt to understand the Old Testament in this respect demands a continuous intensive contact with the whole of Old Testament scholarship, with its philological and literary aspects as well as

[1] See G. von Rad, 'Grundprobleme einer biblischen Theologie des A.T.', *Theol. Lit. Zt.*, Sept./Oct. 1943, pp. 225ff.
[2] Essentially Von Rad would restrict the task of Old Testament theology to this latter inquiry, for the present anyway. Actually he does not, because he also raises the subject of the relationship between the two Testaments in his *O.T. Theology* (II, pp. 319ff.), where he gives theological directives which make us wonder if they sprang from the study of the tradition-theology, or rather dominate the latter (cf. also the closing remarks of Von Rad's article in ThLZ, 1963, p.416).
[3] This does not mean that all the historical sources of the Old Testament conform to a certain kerygmatic ground-plan (creed), as Von Rad thinks.
[4] Von Rad, too, accepts Yahweh as the element in the Old Testament common to all efforts in the field of historical theology (ThLZ, 1963, p.409); he could hardly do anything else. It is a mystery to me, however, why he should deny that Yahweh is to be looked upon as the central element of the Old Testament. Does this imply a theological conception that makes Christ the 'centre' of the Old Testament? (cf. *O.T. Theology* II, pp. 362ff.). However that may be, I am of the opinion that he lays too much stress upon the divergence between the various testimonies concerning Yahweh to be found in the books of the Old Testament. His point of view is theologically unrealistic when considered in the light of the unity that is a characteristic of the Old Testament witness to God in all its divergent traditions. In *The Meaning of Biblical Theology* (JThS 1955, pp.210ff.) G. Ebeling expresses the view that its task consists in the inquiry into the relations between the variety of testimony and the inner unity of the New Testament.

with its aspects in the field of general history and the history of religion. To demonstrate this connection, this last question was expressly put in Ch. II.

It is, however, neither possible nor necessary in a theology of the Old Testament to deal with all questions concerning the 'religions-geschichtliche' and phenomenological background of the message of the Old Testament. It can only lightly touch on a few very important points, so that the true nature of certain elements can be understood more clearly by a comparison with this background. A synthesis of the material obtained in this way cannot be given without more ado, for the content of the message of several books, even concerning one special aspect, is not always the same; these books will have to be confronted with each other and then with the message of the New Testament, in order that we may form an idea of the deepening or decay of spiritual knowledge by seeing the mutual relations between these different elements, and in order that an impression may be obtained of the guidance of the Spirit in the history of revelation.

It is not really possible to press Old Testament theology into a complete systematical survey, though many have attempted this, including Ludwig Köhler in his well-known *Theologie des A.T.*[1] Porteous is probably right when he remarks that owing to this procedure Köhler has failed to find a satisfactory place in his scheme for the cult so that he came to relegate it to anthropology. At any rate the subjects of the Old Testament always interlock in such a way that a systematic classification of the material implies some measure of arbitrariness. A classification which expresses an existential relationship, such as that between God and people, God and the world, or God and man, attempted by Eichrodt and Procksch, has many advantages but is not wholly satisfactory either.

In view of what we said on p. 150 we shall have to divide up our subject as follows: communion as a relationship and the communion between God and man, communion with Yahweh in history, and the prospects for man and the world. We have always considered these subjects in their connection with each other; this feature is emphasized especially by the first chapter on the content of Old Testament theology – the nature of the Old Testament knowledge of God as a relationship between the holy God and man – in which we have tried to keep the essential characteristic of the Old Testament message to its existential plane; the chapter anticipates the next three: communion between God and man, the communion of faith and the prospects for man and the world and was intended as a summarizing introduction to these chapters.

[1] Third ed. 1953.

In this procedure repetition could not always be avoided. If the various subjects are to be considered in their true connection, certain matters must come up for discussion more than once, though from different points of view.

One thing is certain, though, that the attempt to give a living and true picture of the Old Testament message, on the one hand in its connection with the history of Israel,[1] on the other hand in its perspective in revelation in Jesus Christ, can never succeed fully, not only because our understanding of the Old Testament and the New Testament and of their mutual coherence will always remain imperfect, but above all because God's activity in the history of Israel, the history of salvation (and there is no better name to be found for it), can never be made completely perspicacious to the depths of God Himself, for if we compare this history with a line, there are only certain points of this line that are visible, the line itself cannot be copied by any man, because it is God's secret[2] and He Himself, too, remains a miraculous and essentially hidden God, also in the Old Testament, however much He reveals Himself again and again in history, personal relationship or otherwise.

For *some further literature* see p. 175.

---

[1] This is emphasized by H. Wheeler Robinson in his contributions to the theology of the O.T. in *Record and Revelation*, and in his *Inspiration and Revelation in the O.T.*, 1946. This is done even more strongly by Von Rad, who ranks history, in the form of the traditions concerning God's activity so highly that it becomes the *source* of the knowledge of God and a separate, independent element in Israel's religious life, an element, even, of central importance. Here various objections make themselves felt, i.a. that this view is too one-sided, that it systematizes and abstracts too much ("history" is detached almost completely from the historical facts and, as the central element of the Old Testament message, it is, in fact, as much of a concept as the terms formerly derived from Christian theology). Has 'history' in the Old Testament any other aim than leading man to God and to belief in Him (Exod. xiv. 31)? On this question see also pp. 188ff.

[2] For that reason one must be careful in using the name *historia Revelationis*, which Kuyper (*Encyclopaedie* III, p. 166) wished to give to this subject and especially in using the definition of its task: 'to describe the process of the Revelation of God to mankind and to throw light upon this process both in its parts and in the whole of its progress'. Kraemer rightly remarks (op. cit., p. 23) that the word 'process' is entirely out of place beside the word 'revelation'. On the other hand a Christian need not shrink back from the idea of a line of development which is implicit in the idea of history—for a Christian believes that God has a plan, and he may try to trace this plan, if only he realizes that this plan is fully known only to God.

CHAPTER VI

The nature of the knowledge of God in the Old Testament as an intimate relationship between the Holy God and man

Introductory remarks: knowledge as a relationship

As the Old Testament is not a theological book, but a collection of writings widely differing in their religious character, the elements essential to the construction of an Old Testament theology as described in the previous chapter must be taken from certain tendencies in historical narratives[1], religious utterances, prophecies, cultic or juridical formules, hymns and prayers, sometimes also from creeds, etc., in short from widely different expressions of religious life. There can be no question, therefore, of any direct theological reflection in the Old Testament, apart from a few exceptional cases (as in Deut., e.g. vi. 4, and with some of the prophets). Yet this does not mean that there are no theological main lines of thought to be discovered in the Old Testament. Essentially, indeed, theology is only a more or less systematic exposition of the various religious elements that are to be found in the living religion. If we wish to build up an Old Testament theology, the best plan would be to start by examining the fundamental structure of the knowledge of God as it finds expression in the many testimonies[2].

By way of introduction to this part of theology we shall, therefore, describe the principal characteristics of the knowledge of God in the Old Testament, first as to form, then as to matter.

The Old Testament itself always speaks about *knowing God (da'ath*

---

[1] As against Von Rad I think that the historical literature as a whole was not built up kerygmatically on an ancient creed, though I agree with his view that there is a long theological tradition at the back of the historical writings.
[2] See W. Staerk, op. cit., p. 290.

'*elohim*), without specifying what it fundamentally means, and makes it the first demand of life: Hos. vi. 6, ii. 22 (English versions, ii. 20), iv. 1, v. 4; Isa. i. 3; Jer. ii. 8, iv. 22, xxxi. 34. Deutero-Isaiah is throughout one great appeal to know God and to stand in faith in this world on the ground of this living knowledge of God; in a way this also applies to the other prophets.

This knowledge of God embraces much more than a mere intellectual knowledge, it concerns the whole of human life. It is essentially a communion with God, and it is also faith; it is a knowledge of the heart demanding man's love (Deut. vi); its vital demand is that man should act in accordance with God's will and walk humbly in the ways of the Lord (Micah vi. 8). It is the recognition of God as God, the total surrender to God as the Lord.[1]

Knowledge as a general conception in the Old Testament is quite unlike that of our occidental world,[2] influenced by Greek philosophy. For us knowledge implies grasping things by reason, seeing things in their connection of cause and effect, and the understanding of the component factors of something; the Westerner says that he knows a thing when he has analysed it fully and when he can explain all the factors which it involves or from which it arose, i.e. when he can give it a place in the whole of his range of ideas. In the Old Testament knowledge is living in a close relationship with something or somebody, such a relationship as to cause what may be called communion.[3] For that reason sexual intercourse can be called 'knowing' and *da'ath 'elohim* (the knowledge of God) and *chesed* (solidarity, communion) can be used as parallels, e.g. in Hos. iv. 1 and vi. 6. When Peter denies Jesus and says 'I do not know the man', he denies that there has been any relationship between himself and his Master.

The knowledge of God is something altogether different from having a conception of God, which defines the nature of God. The knowledge

---

[1] H. Kraemer, *The Christian in a non-Christian World*, 1938, p. 64–5.
R. Bultmann (ThW I, p. 696) thinks the original meaning is: to acknowledge; O. Weber (*Grundlagen der Dogmatik* I, 1955, pp. 214ff.) rightly gives the two shades of meaning: acknowledgement, but especially: communion.
[2] In Dutch it is still possible to use the word: '*kennen*' to know in the sense of having a relation with: kennis hebben aan, = to have acquaintance with.
[3] E. Baumann, 'Jada' und seine Derivate', *Z.A.W.*, 1908, pp. 22ff., Procksch, *Theologie*, pp. 614ff.; J. Hänel, *Das Erkennen Gottes bei den Schriftpropheten*, 1923, pp. 223ff.; S. Mowinckel, *Die Erkenntnis Gottes der alttest. Propheten*, 1941; J. Botterweck, *Gott erkennen im Sprachgebrauch des A.T.*, 1951; H. W. Wolff emphasizes rather the 'intellectual' character of the *da'ath 'elohim*, see *Ev. Theol.*, 1952/3, pp. 533ff.: '"Wissen um Gott" bei Hosea als Urform der Theologie'. We must, in fact, admit that the *da'ath 'elohim* starts from the assumption of a revelation of God by word and work (see p. 176). The relationship between God and man in Israel is certainly determined by God's saving work and the tradition concerning it; it is not simply based on faith, as in Buber's somewhat one-sided view in his *Zwei Glaubensweisen*. Important is also E. Brunner, *The Divine-Human Encounter*, Eng. tr., 1944; cf. p. 99 n. 3; cf. p. 320 n. 3.

154

of God does not imply a theory about His nature, it is not ontological, but existential: it is a life in the true relationship to God.[1] In the Old Testament no attempts are made, therefore, to arrive at a theology which defines the Being of God. The Old Testament passes on the testimony concerning God and His work and Word, in order that the man might receive an indication (*torah*) of what God does in the world and of what God requires of man.

The Word of God in the Old Testament starts from God. God is, as it were, behind that word and is described in His activity in history, His desire for men's salvation, His spiritual virtues of goodness, righteousness, truth, mercy, grace (cf. Exod. xxxiv. 6) but not in His Being in itself, which remains hidden. The highest acknowledgement of God is that of His holiness; for that reason we may on the one hand find Him depicted by all kinds of images, from lion and bear (Hosea) to father and saviour, while on the other hand making an image of God is rejected altogether. It is, therefore, possible that the Old Testament speaks anthropomorphically about God and mentions the appearance of the Holy One not only in images of fire and natural phenomena, but even, by way of suggestion, in human form (Isa. vi; Ezek. i; Dan. vii) while on the other hand we repeatedly find the assertion that God is not a man (Hos. xi. 9; Isa. xxxi. 3), that God is invisible (Exod. xxxiii. 18ff., xxxiv. 29ff., Isa. vi. 2), that God is incomparable (Isa. xl. 18; Ps. lxxxix. 7). On the one hand stands the continuous proclaiming of God in His works in nature and history (the historical narratives and the prophets), on the other hand a place is found in the Old Testament even for such a book as Ecclesiastes, in which the impossibility of knowing God is stated so emphatically that there remains no room for the knowledge of His activity in history.

Knowledge of God and communion with Him are possible, but the secret of God's Being is never encroached upon. That the element of the Majesty of God is not injured by communion, is most evident in the word that is pre-eminently the expression for religion in the Old Testament: the fear of the Lord. *The fear of the Lord is the beginning of kwowledge.*[2] It is all-important that man in his life should stand in the right relationship of reverence for the holy God and that he should let himself be guided by this reverence in his heart, his thoughts and his actions. What image is used to denote God is almost immaterial because man can only speak of Him in symbolical forms. And therefore Ecclesiastes, who laid such a one-sided stress on the fear

[1] 'The intimate response of man's whole being to God is what the Bible means by knowledge of God'. N. W. Porteous in *O.T. Theology*, op. cit., p. 343, and in 'Semantics and O.T. Theology', *O.T.S.* VIII, p. 12–3.
[2] Cf. Ps. cxi. 10; Prov. i. 7; Job xxviii. 28, etc.; see p. 161n. 2.

of God, could also be given a place in the canon, although it was done with great hesitation.

Completely alien to the Old Testament, therefore, is the making of an image in the mind. This remains true, even if God is sometimes represented in the Old Testament in terms that tend towards the human (see pp. 155 f.). The Old Testament never attempts to arrive at a doctrine concerning God. Instead it speaks again and again of His activity and His words of revelation, and teaches that God enters into communion with man. But any systematical elaboration of a doctrine concerning God is lacking; all speculation about the Being of God is carefully avoided, though the qualities of God are indeed described (Exod. xxxiv 6 ff)[1]. Later Judaism, too, has always refused to make a confession concerning God the characteristic element of its religion.

It is no wonder, then, that Judaism was looked upon as atheistic when confronted with the Graeco-Roman world, because it rejected all kinds of ancient forms of religion.[2] Though from earlier times no reactions are known we may probably draw the conclusion *per analogiam* on the ground of more recent reactions that the earlier oriental world, too, held this opinion concerning the Israelites and their religion. The absence of images of God, in more recent times (after Josiah) even of altars in the countryside or of care for the dead, all these things must have appeared equally strange to them. The inwardness of this religion was understood as little then as was that of Judaism and Christianity by the Romans. And it is not astonishing that in Israel itself, in spite of all prohibitions, the need of an image of God (Bethel and Dan), of all kinds of altars, of questioning the dead, etc., arose continually, and that syncretism proved to be practically ineradicable.

In Old Testament theology we must, therefore, never lose sight of the fact that any attempt to systematize these testimonies of revelation and of faith involves the danger of twisting the utterances into a form that is not their proper one. Especially any attempt to arrive at a closely reasoned whole, a rationally justified doctrine, is to be avoided radically. One can do no more than give a description of the various "radiations" of God's Being, the several aspects of the revelation of God in the history of the people, in the cult, and in the life of the individual. This is done in the following chapters.

In this chapter we want to determine the *character* of the religion

---

[1] Cf. Num. xiv. 18; Neh. ix. 17; Joel ii. 13; Jonah iv. 2; Ps. lxxxvi. 15; ciii . 8; cxl. 8, See a.o. the essay of Dentan in *V.T.* 1963, pp. 34ff.; see p. 295 n. 1.

[2] Cf. for instance A. G. Roos, 'Joden en Jodenvervolging in het oude Egypte', in *De Gids*, 1947; A. M. A. Hospers-Jansen, *Tacitus over de Joden* (doctorate thesis, Utrecht), 1949, pp. 13, 35ff.

of Israel, so that it can be used as the foundation of the description of the *content* of Israel's knowledge of God.

We saw that the Old Testament esteems the knowledge of God as the the real, decisive element of religion, and that this knowledge can be defined as communion with God, whose Being as such remains a secret and who is holy. *The basis of Israel's conception of God is the reality of an immediate spiritual communion between God, the Holy One, and man and the world*[1]. God is *directly* and personally concerned with the things of this world, first and foremost with Israel as a people, but *by implication* also with the individual Israelite, with the world of nations, and even with man in general and with the world at large. The experience of communion with the Holy One always implies a sense of distance between God and man, which finds expression either in the form of a confession of guilt (Isa. vi) or of fear (Gen. xxviii. 17, Exod. xx. 18ff.) or of wonder (Ps. viii, Isa. xxviiif.).

This certainty of the immediate communion between the Holy God and weak, sinful man may be called the underlying idea of the whole of the Biblical testimony, for in its essence this basic idea is also found in the New Testament.

It is most surprising that this has been denied again and again and that the conception of God in the Old Testament has been set against that of the New Testament, as if the Old Testament spoke of God as a hard despot and the New Testament of a merciful Father in heaven. In this way neither the Old Testament nor the New Testament was done justice: the God and Father revealed in Jesus Christ, who is love (1 John iv. 8b) did not have justice done to His holiness – and Yahweh, who is the God of communion, was denied in His *chesed*, His love. The attempt of M. Buber in his book *Two Types of Faith*, to represent the *relationship to God* in the Old Testament as quite unlike that in the New Testament (in the Old Testament the relation to God rests on an immediate faith, in the New Testament on an intellectual act of faith, namely the affirmation of faith in Jesus Christ) is a misconception, too, for the Old Testament as well as the New Testament demands faith in God's work of salvation to which the prophets revert again and again, and conversely the New Testament also knows the intimate immediate relationship with God based on His work of salvation.[2]

This communion between God and man is given a central position in the historical narratives, prophecies, the psalms and the wisdom-literature as a basic hypothesis or as an explicit testimony and may

---

[1] See also J. Lindblom, 'Vorstellung vom Sprechen Jahwes' in *Z.A.W.* 1963, p. 263 (particularly p. 287), and W. Zimmerli; *Gesetz und Propheten*, p. 93; cf. J. Hempel, *Gott und Mensch*[2], 1936.
[2] See my *Geloven en Vertrouwen*, 1957 (inaugural address Utrecht).

be called the A-B-C- of the Biblical religion and message. It is the spiritual presupposition and the purpose of the cult and of the other institutions of salvation (the monarchy, prophetism), the foundation-stone of creed and hymn, the starting- point of faith, ethics and expectations; it dominates the whole field of Israel's religious life and thought. For a theological interpretation of the Old Testament, not only in its historical and prophetical traditions, but also regarding its inward vital priniple that integrates all the expressions of Israel's faith, we shall have to deal with this fundamental category of the communion between *this* God Yahweh and *this* people of Israel. Here we find the factual content of the Old Testament expressed most profoundly. Times without number the words: "I am Yahweh, thy God" are repeated in the historical and prophetical writings; in the latter it becomes a guiding principle for a hope of salvation in the future.[1]

This does not mean, however, that this communion is a natural assumption in the Old Testament. It is, for instance, not, as Buber assumes,[2] a psychical expression of Judaism, or 'the typical form of the Israelite soul'. In this respect we must also raise objections against Joh. Pedersen's *Israel*, where the communion is considered as inherent to the religion of the people of Israel[3]. As the Old Testament itself bears witness, this communion is abandoned again and again in the religion of Israel just because the people proves not to believe in a God who is near, but thinks Yahweh far off (Exod.xxxii–xxxiv), and continually wishes to replace Him by other, nearer gods; Baals (Hos. ii) or more visible gods, star-gods, or, on the other hand, because it brings Yahweh, the Holy One, too near (Jer.xxiii. 23). The point at issue in the struggle in Israel's religion is always how to hold fast to Yahweh, the Holy One, as the God who is not far-off.

This communion exists as a spiritual knowledge, revealed by God; as something Israel received in a special way in its covenant with Yahweh.

It was revealed more and more clearly to Israel in its history because

---

[1] Cf. Jer.xxxi.33 and elsewhere, Ezek.xi.20, xxxvi.28, xxxvii.27; Zech.viii.9. No wonder that F.Baumgärtel considered these words to be the content of the whole of the Old Testament message (cf. *Verheissung*, 1952).

[2] *Kampf um Israel*, 1932, pp.52ff.; *Two Types of Faith*, passim.

[3] If this psychological conception were to be accepted we should have to see Israel's religion as a sublimation of the mixture of the Semitic desert-religion which imagined God to be far and high, and the Western-Semetic Canaanite religion which experienced the eternal in the vegetative forces of nature. Though there may be a great deal of truth in this when we consider Israel's religion from a genetic and phenomenological point of view (cf. e.g. V.Maag, *Malkut Jhwh*, Suppl. VT VII, 1959, pp.129ff., esp. p.137, and following up his opinions, K.Koch, *Der Tod des Religionsstifters*, KuD, 1962, pp.100ff.), it is no more than a partial truth; from a purely historical point of view the religion of Israel is more complicated; it is certainly not to be explained without the creative work of the prophets, as has been shown e.g. by Staerk, op. cit. Every merely naturalistic, psychological or sociological approach to the religious

the prophets made God's work transparent at every turn. From the earliest times (Abraham or Moses, see p. 26) and up to the end these "men of God", inspired by the Spirit of God and grasped by the "Hand of God", proclaimed the explanatory Word of God all through Israel's history (pp.230ff.). They showed the people how the reality of this earth with its blessings and its curse, its salvation and its judgment was a life in communion with God; both the national existence of Israel and individual life were experienced and proclaimed to be such a communion, and again and again their faith and their message were confirmed.

Again and again, however, in Israel the danger springs up of making this knowledge a natural instead of a revealed truth, so that the communion between God and the people threatens to degenerate into a certainty self-evident for national life instead of being part of the message of salvation, so that the people forgets that it was only God's grace and vocation that placed them in this communion. This danger exists in certain Old Testament testimonies (e.g. in the author E, see pp. 58f., and in the piety of some of the Psalms) but especially in the nationalistic, "false" prophets; the relation between the Holy One and the people then becomes one of a common destiny rather than communion.[1] Amos already objects to this supposition (Amos iii.2; ix.7), and this resistance also lies at the root of the message of judgment of the other prophets (cf. e.g. Jer.vii).

Another misconception leads to a notion found frequently in later Judaism, when it looks upon Israel (not the national Israel as such, but the spiritually-minded Israel, which understands its calling and is faithful to the *Torah*) as necessarily connected with God and represents God and the faithful Israelite as *correlative*. This conception is also to be found in many forms of present-day Judaism.[2]

In his doctorate thesis Miskotte has rightly rejected this Judaic view on the ground of the Old Testament–especially of its proclamation of the Holiness of Yahweh. He thinks it incompatible with the prophetic conception of the Old Testament and he looks upon this controversy as one of the essential contrasts between synagogal and Christian theology.[3]

message of the O.T. detracts particularly original starting-point of Old Testament faith; the realism that is characteristic of it and that leads on to ever new discoveries is based only on a real meeting, confirmed again and again by historical experience.
[1] Seeligmann, *Kernmomenten der antieke beschaving*, 1947, p.56; present author's *Die Erwählung Israels nach dem A.T.*, 1953, *passim*.
[2] See K.H.Miskotte, *Het wezen der Joodse religie*, esp. pp. 448ff.: The doctrine of correlation as a new doctrine of the covenant; cf. also G.F.Moore, *Judaism* I, 1932, p.219–20; and *Die Erwählung Israels*, pp.20ff., 29.
[3] Op. cit., pp.485ff. The fundamental mistake is here that a piestistic attitude is made into a theological and anthropological dogma; cf. *Die Erwählung Israels*, p.110, n.4.

It must remain an established fact that communion between the Holy One and man is the essential root-idea of the Old Testament message, but equally, that the knowledge concerning this relation is only the effect of God's work of revelation and the relation itself was only ordained by God in His grace (Deut. vii; ix)! In this communion man may, on the one hand, realize that he does indeed stand in a personal relationship to God and may speak to God as God speaks to Him[1]; on the other hand this should never make him think that his relation to God is a true "dialogue-situation"[2]. Man cannot keep quarreling with God to the end: even if God does allow man to dispute with Him (cf. Job, Jer. xv)[3], ultimately disputing man is always silenced and condemned (Job. xlii, Jer. xv. 19). The discussion between God and man is never a dialogue pure and simple; the man who speaks must always realize and experience that he is addressing himself to the *Holy One*, and his word or answer spoken to God can fundamentally be a prayer only.

The last word, therefore, never rests with man; even in Gen. xviii. 33 God terminates the discussion with Abraham more or less abruptly; and even Israel's prayers of penitence are not always answered by Yahweh (Jer. xv; Hos. vi).[4] It is for Him to take *the decision* whether or not to accept man's words. Therefore Buber just oversteps the mark when he says that in the dialogue between God and His creature man is a real partner in his own right who can speak his own word independently and of his own free will.[5] This view smacks too much of modern individualism and humanism.

When the communion between the Holy God and man is taken to be the underlying idea of the Old Testament witness concerning God we must always keep in view that there is in this message a strong tension, which for the sake of truth must never be relaxed, between these two elements: the Holiness of God and His communion with man. The fact, already pointed out, that the most fundamental expression for faith or religion in the Old Testament is *yir'ath Yahweh*, the fear of the Lord, speaks for itself;[6] this need not be taken to mean,

[1] J. Muilenburg, *The way of Israel*, 1961, pp. 18ff. rightly points to the frequent use of the vocative where God speaks to man and conversely.
[2] Buber, *Kampf um Israel*, p. 32. This view is connected with the one quoted above, p. 158.
[3] Cf. also M. A. Beek, *Het twistgesprek van de mens met zijn God*, 1946.
[4] Neither does He accept sacrifice – Amos v, Jes. i, Ps. l, Gen. iv, etc.
[5] Buber, op. cit., p. 33. More objections can be raised against some conclusions of P. A. H. de Boer, *De voorbede in het O.T.*, 1943, who ascribes to the intercession too much decisive force, 'actualizing Yahweh'. Thus the word of a prophet or pious person becomes a kind of magical word; for this conception there is no room in the O.T. This does not oppose the view that intercession may be accepted by Him and may be able to influence Him and to make Him change His mind.
[6] Cf., for instance, Isa. xxix. 13c: 'their fear toward me is taught by the precept of

as some commentators think, that Israel never managed to rise above the terror of God,[1] for the word fear also occurs as a synonym for faith and expectation[2]; but the presupposition of the glory and holiness of God is always implicit in the word. When God appears to Israel or to a prophet, the first reaction felt is always that of fear (Exod. xixf.; Isa. vi, Ezek. iff.).

All through the Old Testament we find that man cannot behold God, that man must die after having seen God or one of His messengers. God cannot, therefore, really be seen or described. There are a few exceptions to the former, where God is actually seen, so e.g. Exod. xxiv. 1of., where the elders of Israel see God but the appearance itself is not described; it is, however, stated emphatically that God did not lay His hand upon the 'nobles of the children of Israel', those who had been specially elected for this purpose. In connection with the concluding of the Covenant we are here informed of a most peculiar event (to a certain extent comparable with St. Paul's 'mystical' experience in 2 Cor. xii). Also in connection with the concluding of the Covenant God is said to have spoken to Moses face to face (Exod. xxxiii. 11; Num. xii. 8; Deut. xxxiv. 10) and the appearance of God to Moses is assumed (Exod. xxxiv. 5ff., 29ff.), but on the other hand Exod. xxxiii. 18ff. expressly states that even Moses could not bear to see Yahweh in all His glory; God's face could not be seen, only His back.[3] In later times the appearance of God is beheld, by prophets such as Isaiah (ch. vi) and Ezekiel, but they cannot see, let alone describe, God properly speaking; for in Isaiah's case even the seraphim shroud their faces and figures and encircle the throne of God, while in Ezek. i the prophet can only describe the appearance approximately ('I saw as it were...').

On the other hand the anthropomorphical appearances of God, taking place especially in the stories of the patriarchs, show the other aspect: the communion between God and man. This representation of the appearance of God may be partially due to a more primitive aesthetic way of expression, going back to oral folk-tales, on which the authors draw, it is at any rate also partly due to the tendency of the authors to make the people of Israel participate in the experience of

men'; another possible translation would be: 'their religion is a lesson learnt by heart'.
[1] O. Pfister, *Das Christentum und die Angst*, 1944, pp. 13ff.
[2] Buber, op. cit., pp. 55ff.; B. Gemser, 'Jir'at Jahwe in de Psalmen', *Nieuwe Theol. Studien*, 1939, pp. 140ff.; H. A. Brongers, 'La crainte du Seigneur', *O.T.S.*, V. 1948, pp. 151 ss.; B. J. Oosterhoff, *De vreze des Heren in het O.T.*, doctorate thesis Utrecht, 1949; Procksch, *Theologie*, pp. 610ff.
[3] The end of Exod. xxxiii, from vs. 12 onwards, looks like a discussion on the question of the reality of knowing God face to face (vs. 11) and reminds of a later collection like the midrash; see pp. 186ff.

the original intimacy of the relationship between God and man; this tendency is not primitive, but originates purely in religious Yahwism.[1] Finally we shall point out a few main ideas that dominate Old Testament religion and give expression to various aspects of the leading motif of Israel's religion, namely the direct relationship between the Holy God and man.[2]

a. One of the most fundamental elements of the Old Testament teaching is the great stress laid on *God's activity in history*.[3] The belief in God seems to be wholly based on the experience of this activity. The background against which the image of God stands out in the Old Testament is history.[4] Yahweh is in the Old Testament rather the God of history than the Creator[5] or the God of Nature, though these latter elements are not lacking (cf. pp. 331ff.). This thought was expressed by Pascal in his well-known words: 'Dieu! Dieu d'Abraham, d'Isaac et de Jacob! Dieu de Jésus Christ, non des philosophes et des savants.' Israel derives its knowledge of God from His activity in history on behalf of His people, particularly in Egypt and in the desert. He has intervened in behalf of the oppressed and the forsaken and has thus called Israel into being. This is pointed out continually with great emphasis by the prophets. In history, by His activity for the good of His people, God has revealed Himself as the living God who is near, but who is holy, too.[6] And throughout the course of history God intervenes at critical moments; He follows His people, saving as well as judging them, and He controls their destiny. The whole life of the people passes under His eyes in times of disaster and of prosperity; both are signs of His activity. There are always these two aspects to His activity: it is majestic and inspires confidence, for it is the Supreme God who intervenes, who does as He pleases and who is terrible

[1] F. Michaeli, *Dieu à l'image de l'homme*, 1950; W. Vischer, 'Words and the Word: The anthropomorphisms of the Biblical Revelation', *Interpretation*, 1949, pp. 1ff.; F. Horst 'Face to Face, the Biblical Doctrine of the Image of God', *Interpretation*, 1950, pp. 259ff.; M. A. Beek, 'De vraag naar de mens in de godsdienst van Israel', *Vox Theol.*, XXII, 1952, pp. 69ff. These authors are disposed to look upon the doctrine of the Incarnation in the New Testament as rooted in the anthropomorphic conceptions of God in the O.T. See now also J. Barr, 'Theophany and anthropomorphism in the O.T.', *Supp. V.T.* VII, 1959, pp. 31ff. and below 182ff.
[2] See Lindblom, *l.c.*
[3] See pp. 26ff. and pp. 190ff.
[4] A. Weiser, *Glaube und Geschichte im A.T.*, 1931; C. R. North, *The O.T. interpretation of history*, 1946, pp. 141ff.; H. Wheeler Robinson, 'The Theology of the O.T.', *Record and Revelation*, 1938, pp. 303ff.; id., *Inspiration and Revelation*, 1946, pp. 106ff.; Köhler, *Theologie des A.T.*[3], pp. 77ff.; J. de Groot and A. R. Hulst, op. cit., pp. 213ff.; R. C. Dentan, *The idea of history in the Ancient Near East*, 1955, which the contribution on Ancient Israel by Millar Burrows, pp. 99ff.
[5] See e.g. H. A. Brongers, *De Scheppingstradities bij de profeten*, docorate thesis, 1945; G. Lambert, 'La Création dans la Bible', *Nouvelle Revue Théologique*, 1953, pp. 252ff.; E. Beaucamp, 'Dieu de l'Univers et Dieu de l'histoire', *Studii bibli. Francisc.*, IV, 1953/4, pp. 5ff.   [6] Cf. for example W. J. Phytian-Adams, *The call of Israel*, 1934.

even when He intervenes in behalf of His people; cf. e.g. Exod. xv; Pss. lxviii, cxi, cxiv; Isa. xlv. The works of Yahweh are performed to make His people glorify Him, Pss. xxxiii, xcv–xcix, but also give Israel reason to extol Him because they have thus experienced His faithfulness and love (many Psalms,[1] Deuteronomy, Deutero-Isaiah and Ezekiel).

b. Whereas God's saving activity in history is the general basis for the certainty of the direct relationship between God and man, *prophecy* is the deepest and strongest revelation of the communion between the Holy One and man.[2] It is found throughout the history of Israel and is the most characteristic element of the structure of the Israelite religion. God is not only the God of history, who acts with and on behalf of man, but He is also the God who allows the man whom He has called to share in His activity by His Spirit or Word. God performs nothing without revealing His decree to His servants, the prophets (Amos iii. 7), the prophet is allowed to be a witness to God's work in history and, as it were, "sees reality through God's eyes" (Heschel); that is why he is called a "seer".

It is even possible to speak of a 'pathetic' theology.[3] God's work in history is accompanied by the prophetic revelation, God reveals His mind to man. *There must be an original connection between Israel's belief in God who acts in history and the prophetic experience* expressed so strongly by Amos; for this word is not merely *his* conviction, but it is the testimony of the Old Testament generally[4]. The prophets did not only explain God's work in history, but revealed it, too (often also by foretelling it).

That this certainty is found again and again through the course of the centuries can only be attributed to the fact that this connection between prophetic revelation and God's work in the history of His people formed part of Israel's religious conceptions from the very beginning: the figure of Moses must therefore have been prophetic; it is to him that the religious relationship dates back.[5] For this reason

---

[1] The truly historical Psalms are a typical Israelite genre, see Gunkel-Begrich, *Einleitung in die Psalmen*, 1933, pp. 323ff.
[2] See for example Staerk, op. cit., pp. 291ff.; M. Buber, *Der Glaube der Propheten*, 1950; Procksch, *Theologie*, pp. 128ff., 610f.; see below pp. 230ff.
[3] A. J. Heschel, *Die Prophetie*, Krakow, 1936; *The Prophets*, 1962. It is this reality of the knowledge of God that is denied to man by Ecclesiastes.
[4] Cf. e.g. J. Bright, *Jeremiah*, 1965, pp. xxviiff.
[5] To this K. Koch objects: 'The conception of Moses as a founder of religion is and remains dead', in KuD 1962, pp. 100ff., *Der Tod des Religionsstifters*, opposed by F. Baumgärtel in KuD 1963 under the same title.
The use of the word 'prophetic' in this book to denote the personal and moral character of Israel's religion, is based upon this conviction that the religion of Israel dates back in the first instance to the prophetic work of Moses; besides this general broad use of the word prophetic there is the more limited sense of the word denoting the religious conviction of the classical prophets.

prophecy and history are not to be separated, as some theologians are inclined to do, for that would make the prophets mere interpreters of what has already happened, and history itself would become the medium of revelation.[1]

Hempel rightly says:[2] 'In the origin of the religion of Israel two elements cooperate: the miracle, the exceptional event in nature or history, experienced as a miracle, and the extraordinary man who explains this miracle; revelation and inspiration, to use dogmatic terminology.'

And it is exactly in this prophetic experience focused on the history of today and tomorrow that the two elements of the knowledge of God, the Holy One, *and* of communion with Him are most closely linked; we mention here the figure of Isaiah who comes to know God as the Holy One in the vision of his vocation and announces His judgment with great force, but who on the other hand is the very proclaimer of confidence, or faith, almost more so than any other prophet (cf.Isa.vii.9:'believe',xxx.15:'quietness and confidence'); another such prophetical figure is Deutero-Isaiah, in whose message both elements are found very strongly supplementing each other, compare Isa.xl and xlv with Isa.lv. But with Hosea, too, the preacher of Gods' love, the element of dreadfulness in the Nature of God stands out clearly. He depicts Yahweh as a lion (v.14), or even as a consuming disease (v.12), a lion or a leopard by the way (xiii.7ff.). The same applies to the earliest prophet Amos, who sees God as a destroyer (vii.7ff., viii.1ff., ix.1ff.), and as a roaring lion (i.2, iii.8), but also as saving righteousness. To this experience of communion by the prophets clearly corresponds the message they teach, always ending in the proclamation that Yahweh shall be Israel's God and Israel Yahweh's people (e.g. Hos.ii, xiv; Isa ii; Jer.xxxi; Ezek.xxxvi f.; Isa.xlv; li f.; Zech.viii, etc., see pp. 157f.). The keystone of the message of salvation is always the proclamation of the actualization of communion with God.

c. A third typical characteristic of Israel's religion, connected with the preceding, is *the personal character of religious life.*[3] Like the belief

---

[1] Cf. W.Pannenberg c.s., *Offenbarung als Geschichte*, 1961, particularly the contribution of R.Rendtorff, *Die Offenbarungsvorstellungen im A.T.* and the discussion between W.Zimmerli and R. in *Ev. Th.* 1962, pp.15ff and 621ff. See also J.Hempel, *Geschichten und Geschichte im A.T. bis zur persischen Zeit*, 1963, and my essay 'Geloof, Openbaring en Geschiedenis', *Kerk en Theologie* 1965, and below pp.188ff.
[2] J.Hempel, *Gott und Mensch im A.T.*[2], 1936, p.2 n.2 now also *Geschichten*, p.232. Cf. further Phytian-Adams op. cit., p.42.
[3] D.Klein Wassink, *Persoonlijke religie in Israel tot op Jeremia* (doctorate thesis Groningen), 1918; W.Eichrodt, *Theologie* III,'Gott und Mensch', pp.1ff.; H.Wheeler Robinson, *Inspiration and Revelation*, pp.279ff.; N.W.Pirteous, 'The basis of the ethical teaching of the prophets', in *Studies in O.T. prophecy*, 1950, pp.151ff.

in Yahweh as the God who acts in history, this element of Israel's religion may also be looked upon as closely connected with its prophetic character. Like the two preceding elements this characteristic, too, is of a very early date[1] and it is, as it were, the product of the first two; it stands out clearly in the Yahwistic narratives of the patriarchs in the calling of Abraham and his faithful obedience in the Word of God. We may agree here with A. Alt who discovers evidence of the personal character of the relationship between the patriarchs and their God in names such as "the God of the fathers", "the God of Abraham", "the fear (relation?) of Isaac", "the Mighty One (?) of Jacob".[2] As to the stories concerning Moses, which are highly coloured by later religious conceptions, as are the patriarchal narratives, we may be brief. In Exod. xxxiiif., Numb. xii and Deut. xxxiv the personal relationship is emphasized so strongly, that any sense of distance seems to have disappeared altogether. The same is true of the earliest historical work that has come down to us, the history of David and his succession; for in 2 Sam. xii. 16 we already find how David very personally 'besought God for the child' to which Bathsheba had given birth; this chapter is a profound account of David's spiritual struggle with God to save the child's life. In 1 Sam. xxx. 6 we read that David, in one of the most difficult moments of his life, when he stood all alone during a catastrophic event, 'encouraged himself in the Lord his God'. In the Psalms God is invoked again and again with the simple, direct exclamation: '*Elohai*, my God.,[3] and on comparing this appellation with the many titles and names of deities that we meet with in the initial verses of Accadian psalms it becomes quite apparent that there is a vast difference in distance between gods and men in Babylon and God and man in Israel;[4] the words 'my God' bear witness to the intimacy of the communion between man and God. Many other Psalms (Ps. xxxiii; xvi, the final vss of lxxiii, etc.) testify to the reality of the communion and to the spiritual strength radiating from it. In the prophetic type of piety, especially in Jeremiah's confessions, we are struck by the directness of the relationship between man and God, which is perhaps brought out even more clearly by the way in which Micah (vi. 8) defines religion: 'He hath shewed thee,

---

[1] Cf. J. Hempel, op. cit., pp. 189ff.; W. Eichrodt, *Das Menschenverständnis im A.T.*[2], 1947.
[2] See A. Alt, *Der Gott der Väter*, 1929, pp. 42ff. and 62ff.
[3] See also Hempel, op. cit., pp. 185–6; O. Eissfeldt, '"My God " in the O.T.', *Ev. Quarterly*, XIX, 1947, pp. 7ff. (cf. p. 83, n. 2).
[4] An exception to this is in Mesopotamia the relationship to the personal tutelary deity, a lower deity who must intercede with the mighty gods as an intermediary; see H. Frankfort, *Intellectual adventure*, 1946, pp. 203ff.; J.J.A. van Dijk, *La sagesse suméro-accadienne*, 1953, pp. 13ff.

O man, what is good; and what doth the Lord require of thee but to do justly, and to love mercy, and to walk humbly with thy God?' The simple farmer of Moresheth near Gath must have known a very direct contact with God. The personal relationship to God as the God of history brings with it *faith*, complete reliance on God; this is stressed by the prophet Isaiah, and it is by this faith that Abraham's life is judged in Gen. xv. 6.

The other side to this personal relationship between God and man is the consciousness that all lies exposed before the Holy God, who knows man in all his ways (Ps. cxxxix; Isa. xxix. 15ff.), and calls him to account for all his acts (Amos iii. 2). Moreover, communion with God also leads to the experience of the terribly severe demand which serving God involves. It is precisely the man who has been called personally by God who is led into the fight by Yahweh (Mic iii. 8, Jer. i, viii. 18ff., ix. 1ff., xi. 18ff., xv. 15ff., xvi, xvii. 14ff., xx. 14ff., xxxviff.). The prophet of the exile who experienced this personally (Isa. 1) realized most profoundly how the true Servant of the Lord, the *'ebed Yahweh*, would have to suffer and die for God's people, according to God's will.

d. In the preceding more *general structure forms* of Israel's religion, as depicted in the Old Testament, it becomes quite clear that the relationship between God and man is a communion. The same holds good for the two following important *theological conceptions: the idea of the Covenant* and the doctrine of *man as the image of God*. On closer examination, however, we also see that these, too, are base on the recognition of the fundamental distinction between God and man.

We shall first deal with the *conception of the Covenant*, as this idea was the most influential in the Old Testament writings, especially in and influenced by Deuteronomistic theology.

We cannot dwell at length here on the vexed question (belonging to the history of the religion of Israel) whether the doctrine of the Covenant is early or late, whether it is a late theological scheme or dates back to an early historical fact. Of late the tendency among scholars has been to decide the question in favour of the latter view, particularly since more has become known about the ancient oriental covenants.[1] In our opinion the fact that in this respect the earliest prophetic writings (esp. Hosea, cf. ch. ii; vi. 7; viii. 1; xi.1; xii; xiii. 4f.) agree with the two earliest historical sources (J, E) on the origin of the doctrine of the

---

[1] It is impossible to mention even the most important literature on this subject here. The new investigations began with G. E. Mendenhall's *Law and Covenant in Israel and the ancient Near East*, 1955, and, partly on account of new discoveries, it led to a much more profound knowledge of the background of the concept of Israel's covenant and to a clearer insight into this matter. We shall give only two titles here: J. Begrich, *Berit*, ZAW, 1944, and especially D. J. McCarthy, *Treaty and Covenant*, 1963, containing an extensive reading-list.

Covenant, points to an early date for the emergence of the covenant[1]. We are here concerned with grasping the spiritual conception implicit in this doctrine.

When the Old Testament regards the relationship between God and the people as a covenant-relationship, this means that the relationship is not looked upon as natural but as placed in history by Yahweh. The importance of this doctrine becomes evident only when we see it against the background of the other ancient oriental religions. Often the latter represent the relation between the chief deity and his people as a natural unity: deity, country and people bear the same name (Assur). The gods are even quite frequently looked upon as the physical parents of the nations[2] they have procreated (this phenomenon is found among Arabic tribes). It is likely that in the Old Testament Edom (cf. Obed-Edom) and Seth (Num.xxiv.17; cf. Gen.iv) were originally names of progenitors as well as names of heroes; Cain (Gen.iv.1) may have been looked upon as born from the goddess Chawwah and as the progenitor of the Kenites, etc.; cf. also Jer.ii.26f., Jeremiah's accusation against the pagan ideas of his days. The goddess, as the mother of the people, is often taken to be united with the king in the *hieros gamos*, so that goddess and people share one life[3] (the characteristic of true popular religion). Moreover we usually find in the ancient oriental conceptions, that the national religious institutions are taken to be autochthonous and given at the time of the creation, e.g. the Babylonian temples in the Babylonian Creation-narratives. This fact, too, indicates how the national values were made absolute and is connected with the whole of the apotheosis of the people's national existence.[4]

If we contrast with this conception the doctrine of the Covenant used by the Old Testament to express the relationship between God and the people, we understand how unique a view of this relation is given by the conception of the Covenant.

First of all it proves that Israel's religion, in so far as we find it in the Old Testament, lacks the real characteristic element of the ancient popular religions[5]; from a purely religio-historical point of view, too, Yahwism cannot be called a national religion, though this view has

---

[1] See the Theologies by Eichrodt and Köhler; Hempel, op. cit., p.162; Quell in *Th. Wb.z.N.T.*, II, pp.120ff., and my *Religion of Israel*, 145f.
[2] See many examples in W. Robertson Smith, *The religion of the Semites*[3], 1927, pp.41ff.
[3] Cf. that, on the other hand, the O.T. considers the *connubium* of *bene ha-'elohim* and women as the limit of decadence (Gen. vi. 1ff.), see p. 54f. Literature, e.g., F. M. Th. de Liagre Böhl, *Opera Minora*, 1953, pp.155ff.; H. Frankfort, *Cylinder Seals*, 1939, pp. 75, 77, 97.
[4] Cf. G. E. Wright, *The O.T. against its environment*, 1950, pp.63ff.
[5] Cf. Eichrodt, *Theologie des A.T.*, I, pp.9ff.

often been defended (i.a. by A. Kuenen in his *Godsdienst van Israel*); even regarding the 'theoi patroioi' of the patriarchs it cannot be maintained successfully (the personal relationship with chieftain and tribe does not include a natural relation).

The doctrine of the Covenant presupposes a relationship between Yahweh and Israel which arose in history, not a natural relationship. The Covenant relation was established by Yahweh alone – in the Old Testament Yahweh is always the subject of the verb used to indicate the concluding of the Covenant. This clearly shows that Yahweh and Israel are not co-equal partners: everything originates with Yahweh, it is He who states the terms of the Covenant. The Judaic theological notion of a bi-lateral covenant is hardly supported by the Old Testament data, but rather by a later theological interpretation of these data. It is true, though, that especially in the Deuteronomic works such a tendency is, indeed, to be observed: we see how Israel as a partner to the Covenant confirms it and agrees with it; in this way Israel acknowledges its reponsibility for adhering to the rules of the Covenant decreed by Yahweh (e.g. Deut. xxvi. 16–19; Exod. xix. 7, xxiv. 3ff.)[1].

By concluding the Covenant with Israel Yahweh enters into communion with this people. The Hebrew word *berith* (covenant) means something like 'bond of communion'; by concluding a covenant a connective link is effected[2] (by means of a sacrifice or a meal or both) between the two partners, who thereby enter into an intimate relationship.

Yahweh entered into such a relationship with Israel. To that end he has drawn up the rules that are to obtain, rules which Israel could not but accept if it wanted to be accepted or remain within this circle. Thus Israel was admitted to God's Covenant and thus it was sanctified. By allowing Israel to enter into this Covenant God by no means gives up His holiness, but Israel is admitted to His holy sphere of life (cf. Levit. xix).

The Covenant may be 'transgressed' (*'abar*), 'left' (*'azab*), broken (*hefer*), but Israel cannot meddle with its laws. We must, therefore,

---

[1] Especially in Joshua xxiv the bilateral aspect seems to be emphasized, but the situation is different; this appears to be a description of the historical formation of the Yahweh-amphictyony, in which the ancient pre-Mosaic tribes enter into the Yahweh-religion and join the Yahweh-league. Even here, though, those who enter into the Covenant do not decide on the condition of entering.

[2] According to Buber, *Königtum Gottes*, 1932, pp. 113, 231, *Berith* means 'Umschränkung' ('circumscription', 'confinement'). The word cannot be divorced from the Assyrian *biritu*, intervening space, in the sense of what is common, and unites (*ina birit* = between); cf. B. Landsberger, *Ana ittišu*, MSL 1937, p. 89; W. von Soden, *Akkadisches Handwörterbuch, s.v.* and M. Noth, *Das alttest. Bundschliessen im Licht eines Mari-textes*, Ges. Stud. z.A.T. pp. 142ff.

certainly not represent the Covenant as a 'voluntary agreement' between the two parties[1]. As we said above, and Köhler himself admits (p. 45) God is always the subject when the Covenant is concluded, and in later times He is always said to 'cause the Covenant to exist', 'to establish' (*heqim*), 'found' (*sim*) or 'give' (*nathan*) it!

The Covenant is, therefore, 'unilateral', not bilateral in origin: Israel is expected to obey the rules of the Covenant drawn up by God and by Him alone. After the Deuteronomic reformation Israel was called God's heritage, His own, to the glory of God in the world. Israel is elected by God, and therefore the object of His electing will, committed to this will. As the elected people Israel is the *'ebed*, the *servant*, as Deutero-Isaiah has it.[2]

Though the Covenant is broken by Israel and God punishes His headstrong and wilful people, the Covenant itself is not set aside by God. Even if God rejects the empirical Israel in its entirely for some time, that does not mean that Israel as such is rejected. None of the prophets taught that the judgment of the people in their days implied the lasting rejection of the people as such! Each prophet was, somehow, a prophet of salvation as well as a prophet of evil and hoped that God's Covenant, which owed its existence to His love would also be restored by Him. Israel was never rejected absolutely, a conception which is found with the ancient Orientals, e.g. the Babylonians, who in their Creation-narratives suppose that the wrath of the gods had in view the complete destruction of mankind.[3]

All this points the same way: the *Covenant* between God and the people *did not bring these two 'partners' into a contract-relation, but into a communion, originating with God, in which Israel was bound to Him completely and made dependent on Him.*

The Covenant absolutely obliges Israel to do God's will. Israel cannot remain itself but must let itself be sanctified. Particularly the book of Deuteronomy emphasizes strongly the spiritual obligations while the Priestly Code stresses the fact that God has *made* the Covenant and that Israel is sanctified to the Lord.

---

[1] Köhler, *Theologie*[3], p. 52.
[2] We should not forget that especially to this poet Israel's election was also a sign of God' sfavour and love; see i.a. my *Erwählung Israels.*
[3] The view that the counterpart of the election of Israel in the O.T. is the rejection of Israel (Köhler, *Theologie*, p. 66) cannot be maintained in this general form. It is true that in Ps. lxxviii. 67 the rejection of the northern tribes – because of their idolatry is mentioned, and in Isa. xiv. 1 and Zech. i. 17, ii. 6 (R.V. 12) we read of the *'further'* (Hebr. *'od* is 'anew', or 'further') election of Jerusalem. This implies the continuous faithfulness of the electing God rather than the possibility of definite rejection by God of what He has once elected. In any case rejection is a judgment based on the inconvertibility of man and never founded on the unwillingness of God, as may be found elsewhere, as far as Israel is concerned rejection only exists partially and temporarily as punishment. Cf. my *Die Erwählung Israels*, pp. 98ff.

The priestly author considers all communion between God and man from the angle of the Covenant. In his conception of history (see pp. 62ff.) there are three kinds of covenant: besides the Mosaic Covenant there is the Covenant with Abraham (Gen. xvii), sealed by circumcision, and before that the Covenant with the whole of mankind and, indeed, with all creation–the Noachian Covenant (Gen. ix. 9ff.).

The doctrine of the Covenant implies, therefore: (1) the absolute recognition of the reality of a true *communion* between God and people (man); (2) the absolute recognition of God, the Holy One, the Supreme, who has established and guides this relationship; (3) the absolute acknowledgement of the rules of the Covenant, given by God. Thus the doctrine of the Covenant is the clearest illustration of communion with God, the fundamental idea of the Old Testament message.

The Covenant-relationship is one of the most important forms in which the communion between God and man reveals itself in Israel's religion, but this communion is also expressed by quite different relations, such as those between father and child, husband and wife, lord and servant, king and people. For that reason the present author thinks it preferable, for various reasons, to use the much wider term 'communion' in a theological exposition to denote the relationship between God and man rather than the more definite notion of the 'Covenant'.

e. Finally: *the doctrine of man as the Image of God*[1].

A correct understanding of the doctrine of the Creation, a doctrine which figures especially in the Priestly Code, can only be attained on the basis of the Old Testament belief in Yahweh, the Saviour-God, who stands in a Covenant-relation with His people. For God, the Creator, is the same God whom Israel has come to know in its history as the Saviour. This element also dominates the conception of the relationship between God and man at the Creation. Only seldom does the Old Testament speak of man in general. But when man in general is mentioned (*ha'adam*, the father of men in Gen. iif., or Noah, the progenitor of mankind after the Flood, or also mankind in Gen. i), he is involuntarily considered in the light of Israel's faith, as it was marked by Israel's history of salvation. God is the God of salvation for *ha'adam* of Gen. iif., for Noah in Gen. viff. and for man in general in Gen. i as much as for Abraham and for the Israelite who lived within the Mosaic Covenant. Even though Israelite theology after Deutero-

[1] P. Humbert, *Etudes sur le récit du paradis et de la chute dans la Génèse,* 1940, pp. 153ff.; L. Köhler, 'Die Grundstelle der Imago-Dei Lehre', *Th. Zeitschrift Basel,* 1948, pp. 16ff. F. Horst, *Face to Face,* loc. cit.; M. A. Beek, *De vraag naar de mens* etc., loc. cit.; cf. also note 1 p. 162, and p. 171 n. 3.

nomy emphasized the idea of election, the Old Testament dit not maintain that God was not concerned with mankind outside Israel. 'In virtue of their creation by the one God the nations are numbers of a large family and the list of nations of Gen. x, which stands alone in ancient oriental literature, gives to Israel itself, too, however conscious of its important place in history, its place among mankind in general, and does not claim for Israel a fundamentally different natural ability, a hereditary nobility which would contrast it with all the other nations. The Old Testament will not hear of originally inferior races, nor of a barrier between Hellenes and Barbarians, never quite overcome in the humanism of antiquity, or between masters and slaves'.[1] The Old Testament conception of communion between God and man which is implicit in the doctrine of the Covenant and makes Israelites brothers, applies, in a wider sense, over the borders of Israel (as God is proclaimed as the Lord of the world) : the nations, too, can be called upon to praise God together with Israel, as men in the sight of God (Pss. xcvi, xcviii). But this was only possible because the God of the Covenant, in whose nature it is to seek communion, was confessed as the God of Creation.[2]

The outstanding feature of the conception of man in the Old Testament is the pronouncement of the Priestly Code that man is created *in God's image, after His likeness* (Gen. i. 26f., cf. v. 1, ix. 6; Ps. viii). Like other elements in Gen. i this wording must be considered in the light of the ancient oriental range of ideas: there man is often placed in a directly physical relationship with the deity: man is frequently represented as born from the mother-goddess or as created by the deity from divine blood (partially at least). This view is the expression of an 'idealistic' anthropology[3] namely the conception that man is essentially of divine origin, an idea well-known from Greece (cf. Acts xvii) and inherent in naturalistic paganism which puts cosmogony on a level with theogony. According to Babylonian theology, e.g., man distinguishes himself from the gods by weakness and mortality, but otherwise man and the gods spring from the same stock (men can also be looked upon as deities, as is proved by the Mesopotamian and especially the Egyptian ideology concerning the monarch).[4]

---

[1] W. Eichrodt, *Das Menschenverständnis des A.T.*[2], 1947, p. 35. Whereas in the Old Testament man is thought to have sprung from a father of men (Adam, Noah) and the word man (*adam*) may have a very wide meaning, in Egypt the word 'man' was taken to refer to the Egyptian only, not the foreigner, who is an enemy and a barbarian. Cf. B. H. Stricker, *De brief van Aristeas*, 1956, pp. 36ff.

[2] This connection is established particularly by Deutero-Isaiah, and the Psalms mentioned here were strongly influenced by his teaching.

[3] See *Oudtestamentische Studiën*, II, 1943, pp. 87ff.; Th. C. Vriezen, 'La création de l'homme d'après l'image de Dieu'.

[4] See Wright, op. cit., pp. 63ff., 107f.; H. Frankfort, *Kingship and the Gods*, 1948; I. Engnell, *Studies in Divine Kingship*, 1943; A. Bentzen, *Det Sakrale Kongedømme*, 1945;

This notion is utterly unknown to the Old Testament and this constitutes the essential difference between the Biblical and non-Biblical conceptions of God. In the Bible God and man are absolutely distinct, because God essentially precedes nature and is superior to it[1], however much He many reveal His power in nature.

In spite of the fact that this absolute difference is clearly recognized in the Old Testament, the Old Testament is by no means behind any of the non-Biblical philosophies in its spiritual appreciation of man, as appears from the recognition of the communion between God and man. Whereas there is a great ideological tension in the ancient oriental world concerning the relationship between God and man (on the one hand man is the child of God, or at any rate he shares in the same life with the deity, and on the other hand he is merely a slave used by the deity) which gives rise to the typically naturalistic (ancient oriental and Greek) and tragic view of life, the Old Testament religion is founded upon the certainty of the relationship between the holy God and man.

The representation of man as the *imago Dei* is the symbol of this certainty of the communion of the Holy God who is 'wholly different', with man, the creature of God. This term may be called a 'critico-theological' idea which on the one hand indicates a direct, positive communion, but on the other hand excludes any equality. By this wording, the actual terms of the Father-child relationship are a-voided, but the relation itself is meant, as also in the whole of the Old Testament, to denote the relationship between God and man.

There are only very few texts where this image is used; we mention here Hos. xi. 1 (and Exod. iv. 22) where Israel is called 'my son' (the reading of the Septuagint is 'his [i.e. Israel's] sons', so that here, too, the Father-child image is avoided!); Deut. xiv. 1 ('sons are ye to the Lord your God'; the sentence-construction is very careful here, and avoids the form 'ye are the children of the Lord';[2] and Isa. i. 2 (cf. also xxx. 1, 9 and Jer. iii. 14).

Strictly speaking, the word child is only used in connection with God as a collective to denote Israel, and very rarely, at that, and so it has a symbolical value. There is one other case where a human being is acknowledged to be son of God, and that is the king, whose ascension to the throne involves adoption as son of God (Ps. ii. 7; 2 Sam. vii. 14; Ps. lxxxix. 27f., cx. 3?); we may assume that there is an ancient oriental

C. J. Gadd, *Ideas of divine rule in the Ancient East*, 1948; A. R. Johnson, *Sacral Kingship in Ancient Israel*, 1955, cf. further p.366.
[1] In fact, the *ruach 'Elohim* is said to circle over the waters of the chaos before the creation of the world (Gen. i. 2, see below p.215)
[2] On the sentence-structure, in which the connection is expressed by *lamed*, cf. Gesenius, *Hebr. Gr.*[28], § 129; this construction denotes a close connection but not descent.

court ritual at the bottom of such phrases as 'thou art my son', for as an individual the king is certainly not considered divine in Israel (as he is in Egypt), for neither in life at court nor at his burial do we find any hint of this (see also below n.3).

The Old Testament is as cautious in using the turn of phrase that Yahweh is the Father of man. This term, too, is used occasionally for God as the Father of Israel, Deut.xxxii.6 (cf.Jer.iii.4; Isa.lxiii.16, lxiv.8; Mal.i.6), but the context proves that the word father is here not to be taken in a generative sense; the word is used here to express the intimate confident relationship of the people that realizes and recognizes its complete dependance upon its God, whom it worships as the Creator and Maintainer. For the Israelite can use the term father in widely different aspects of life.[1] (This turn of phrase, too, is used to denote the relationship between God and the king, 2 Sam. vii.14, Ps.lxxxix.27).

Only in a few texts is the ancient oriental image of generation adopted, but then the symbolical meaning is evident; cf. Deut.xxxii. 18 where Yahweh is called the 'Rock that begat thee' and at the same time 'God that formed thee' (= gave birth to thee)! The formula is also used a few times in connection with the king: Ps.ii.7 and perhaps Ps.cx.3 (according to a better reading of the text). Jeremiah thinks that invoking a foreign god (made of wood or stone) as father and procreator is the worst kind of religious decadence (Jer.ii.27).

The image of the relationship between husband and wife is employed *even more sporadically to denote* the communion between God and man than the father-child relationship. It is found with a few prophets only especially with Hosea (Hos.i–iii, Ezek.xvi, Jer.ii.2, xxxi.32?, iii.14?). It is clear that Ezekiel only employs this notion to symbolize the Covenant; in xvi.8 he passes on to the Covenant without more ado. We must, therefore, agree with G.E.Wright[2] where he remarks that this terminology was apparently considered inadequate fairly generally and was no longer used.

If the father-child image was only seldom accepted by the Old Testament authors to denote the relation between God and the people, apparently in protest against pagan influences[3], the expression was not used at all to denote the relationship between God and mankind in

[1] According to P.A.H.deBoer, *De Zoon van God in het Oude Testament*, 1958, there was the notion of consanguinity in earlier times, whereas in later periods the relationship is rather looked upon as the result of belonging to the community of those over whom God asserts His paternal authority and to whom he extends His paternal care.
[2] Cf. G.E.Wright, *The challange of Israels Faith*, 1946, pp. 38ff.
[3] In the period of the earliest Israelite kings names such as Abihu, Abyah, i.e. He or Yahweh is (my) Father, were known, which shows that the idea could even be used to denote the relationship between Yahweh and the individual Israelite.

general.[1] There can hardly be any other explanation for this than the wish to avoid the conception of a natural relationship between God and man.

In this light the wording of the Priestly Code must be viewed which speaks of man as the image of God. The formula that man is the son or child of God is avoided but this same intimate relationship is intended. This becomes evident when we compare Gen. i. 26 with Gen. v. 3, where Adam's son Seth is said to be in the likeness and after the image of his father. In other words, the expressions 'image' and 'likeness' (between which we should not make any fundamental distinction) were chosen to denote on the one hand the absolute difference between God and man, on the other their relationship (see also below p.413).

It would be possible to add many important points to the five already mentioned; we indicate the following, without pursuing the subject further, because they are discussed more or less fully in the factual part of the book; the *cult*, whose main object is the strengthening or restoration of the communion between God and the people (see especially pp. 255ff.); *wisdom* which in its Israelite form fully aims at keeping peace with God and leads to the proclamation of communion with Him, as we see particularly clearly at the end of the book Job[2]; *eschatology*, which proclaims the message of the kingdom of peace between God and man with God as the focal point of this communion (cf. p.204f.); the *Spirit of God* which operates in history and dominates the kingdom of God (cf. p. 211f.), and last but not least the very *name of God* in Israel, *Yahweh*, in which both the idea of nearness, of being present and the idea of mystery are found (cf. pp. 180f.).

Thus the Old Testament is pervaded throughout by the security contained in the name which Isaiah held up to his people: Immanuel, God with us. Right from the start, Gen. i–iii tells us, God had in view life in communion with man. The historians bear testimony to the fact that throughout history, in spite of sin and guilt, transgression and unbelief, God went with His people, to which He revealed His communion. To this the prophets add the message that at the end of time there shall be full *shalom* between God and man. And in the face of death one of the Psalmists sings; 'My flesh and my heart faileth: but God is the strength of my heart and my portion for ever'.

This communion is always experienced in the Old Testament as something miraculous, for God is God and no man; man is on earth, God is in heaven. Yet they belong together, because He willed

[1] In contrast with the Canaanite-Phoenician world; cf. how in the Ras Shamrah texts El is called the *'ab' adam*, the father of men.
[2] See p.84 n.3.

174

it so in His incomprehensible goodness (Ps.viii)[1]. In this fundamental point of faith the New Testament is in complete agreement with the Old. And for that reason the communion between God and man is the best starting-point for a Biblical theology of the Old Testament, and the following chapters will, therefore, be arranged with this aspect in view.

Some further literature to Ch. V (see p. 152):

O.J.Baab, 'O.T. Theology: Its Possibility and Methodology' in H.R. Willoughby, *The Study of the Bible To-day and To-morrow*, 1949, pp.401ff.
O.J.Baab, *Theology of the O.T.*, 1949.
M.Buber, *Der Glaube der Propheten*, 1950.
M.Burrows, *An outline of biblical Theology*, 1946.
R.C.Dentan, *Preface to O.T. Theology*, 1963.
F.V.Filson, 'Biblische Theologie in Amerika', *Th. L.* 1950, pp.71ff. (literature 1945-1950).
P.Heinisch, *Theologie des A.T.*, 1940.
E.Jacob, *Théologie de l'Ancien Testament*, 1955.
J.Muilenburg, *The way of Israel*, 1961.
C.R.North, *The thought of the O.T.*, 1948.
W.J.Phytian-Adams, *The call of Israel*, 1934 and *The fullness of Israel*, 1938.
N.W.Porteous, 'Semantics and O.T. theology', in *O.T.S.* VIII, 1950, pp.1ff.
H. Renckens, *De godsdienst van Israël²*, 1963.
H.H.Rowley, *The unity of the Bible*, 1953 and *The Faith of Israel*, 1956.
A.A.van Ruler, *Das A.T. in der christlichen Kirche*, 1955.
W.Schweitzer, 'Biblical Theology and Ethics to-day, in A.Richardson and W.Schweitzer: *Biblical Authority for to-day*, 1951, p.129ff.
J.D.Smart, 'The death and rebirth of O.T.Theology', *The Journal of Religion*, 1943, pp.1ff., 125ff., with criticism of W.A.Irwin, pp.286ff.
N.H.Snaith, *The distinctive Ideas of the O.T.*, 1944 and next years.
A.Weiser, 'Die theologische Aufgabe der alttest. Wissenschaft', in *Werden und Wesen des A.T.*, Beih. *Z.A.W.*, 66, 1936, pp.207ff.
G.E.Wright, *God Who acts*, 1952. Id., *The rule of God*, 1960.

---

[1] This relationship should never be denoted by the word 'kinship', a supposition which we find all through Pedersen's *Israel*, and in H.Weeler Robinson's well-considered work, *Inspiration and Revelation in the O.T.*, 1946, p.190 ('there is a real kinship between God and man. Man is presented in the O.T. as a spiritual being and as such he is, notwithstanding all limitations, akin to God who is Spirit'). The former places God and man too much in a relationship of natural mysticism, the latter spiritualizes man too much.

175

CHAPTER VII

The Intercourse between God and man

INTRODUCTORY REMARKS

All Old Testament teaching rests, as we explained in the previous chapter, on the certainty of the communion between the Holy God and man, a belief founded on the intercourse between Yahweh and Israel experienced in the history of revelation.

The word 'intercourse' is an excellent rendering of the relationship between God and man; it presupposes a *relationship* between several persons, finding expression in certain mutual actions. It is used in the Old Testament itself (the *hithpa'el* of *halakh*, 'to go', means 'to walk', 'to have intercourse with') to denote the communion of the faithful with God (subjective piety, Gen. v. 24; Mic. vi. 8) as well as for the relationship between God and His people Israel (cf. 2 Sam. vii. 6; Lev. xxvi. 12; Deut. xxiii. 15, A.V. 14). It is certainly no coincidence that in Gen. iii. 8 the verb to walk or have intercourse is also used to denote God's presence in the garden of Eden. The expression is not used often with respect to God but beside it we also find the expression that *God dwells among Israel*. An even more intimate expression of the idea of the intercourse between God and man is found in the term *yada'*, i.e. to know or to have intercourse with, and, connected with this, the idea of the *da 'ath 'elohim* (the knowledge of God, see Ch. VI). This expression is also used to denote both aspects of the relationship between God and man. In Amos iii. 2 we already find that God enters into a special relationship with Israel ('knows' Israel); on the other hand Hosea emphatically demands that man should 'know God', which implies a knowledge of God's revelation.

Finally we may mention the term *sod*, the confidential circle or intercourse, which is used in the Psalms, the Wisdom-literature and the prophets to denote the intimate relationship between God and man: Ps. xxv. 14, cxi. 1, Prov. iii. 32, Jer. xxiii. 18, 22 (cf. Amos iii. 7). What is meant here is also found in the experiences of the prophets (cf. e.g. 1 Kings xxii and Isa. vi).

The intercourse between God and man has many aspects; it proceeds from God, who reveals His presence in many ways: by speaking, by appearances, by tokens; God's actual presence was particularly experienced in history, both by His judgements upon Israel and by His saving activity on behalf of the people. A permanent token of His presence is the cult in the sanctuary and the sanctuary itself. In various ways man in Israel responded to the many signs of God's intervention on behalf of His people, in corporate worship and personal piety. All these relations are bound up together so closely that they should be dealt with in one chapter, to be divided into the following subjects:

I The revelation of God
   A. General remarks
   B. God's self-revelation
   C. Revelation in history
   D. Other ways in which God reveals Himself
   E. Revelation as communication
   F. The intermediaries of revelation
   G. The place of Revelation
II The Cult
III Piety

I. THE REVELATION OF GOD

A. General remarks

In Christian theology the revelation of God in the Old Testament is characterized as revelation by the Word. This description certainly brings out one of the principal elements of the history of revelation.

Yet it is one-sided. For God does not reveal Himself by the Word only, but also in many other ways, especially in history and in nature. Another objection against this one-sided emphasis on the revelation by the Word is that it gives rise to the notion that revelation is, in an intellectual sense, a communication made by God. Of late strong opposition has risen against this view because it is thought that the very idea of a dogmatic pronouncement or anything even remotely resembling a dogmatic element in the Old Testament should be rejected.[1] For that reason some theologians practically restrict the revelation of God to His activity in history. As with many symptoms of reaction, there is a considerable element of truth in this view, yet, on the other hand, the very fact that it is one-sided makes it disputable. Quite rightly the living, dynamic and historical element in the revelation of God in the Old Testament is emphasized, but it would not be right to restrict God's revealing activity to history. If we are to do justice to revelation in the Old Testament we must take all

---

[1] Cf. e.g. G. E. Wright, *God who acts*, and G. von Rad, *O.T. Theology.*

forms of revelation to be found in the Old Testament seriously, and we can only do this by relating them all to the essential purpose of revelation: the *communion between God and man:* I shall be thy God and thou shalt be My people.[1] Throughout the Old Testament this has been considered the *basic element* and *telos* of revelation; we may think of J's words concerning the vocation of Abraham (Gen. xii. 3, xv), of the way in which D (or E?) introduces the Sinaitic revelation (Exod. xix. 3f., xxiv). We should also bear in mind the prophetic message of salvation (Hos. ii. 15, 22, Jer. xxxi. 31ff., Ezek. xxxvi. 23ff.; xxxvii. 26ff., Zech. ii. 9, RV. vs. 5, Zech. viii. 3, 8); the prospect of communion with God is the loftiest expression of personal faith in the Psalms, both in the present (Ps. xvi, xxxiii, xxvii, lxi, lxii) and in the future, after death (Ps. lxxiii. 25ff.); it is the notion impressed upon the faithful by the apocalyptic writings (Isa. xxv. 6–9); it is the essential basis of the ethics of the prophets (Mic. vi. 8) and of the confidence that is characteristic of the wisdom-literature (Prov. iii. 32).

Just as in the New Testament Gospel according to St. John (ch. xvii) word and truth, knowledge and eternal life are connected with the communion which Christ establishes between man and God, so in the Old Testament there is a connection between the speaking of God, the life of man and full communion with God (Isa. lv. 2f.).

The Revelation aims at the knowledge of God, but knowledge taken in the Biblical, Hebrew sense, that is to say, a knowledge which enables man to understand and communicate with God and actualizes this communication. This communion does not, however, do away with the holiness of God, the respect and the distance between God and man. On the contrary, in expressing this communion the faithful come to know all the better that God is divine, that He is different from man and the world. The fact that the faithful become all the more conscious of the distance between God and themselves is an indication of the reality of their communion with God. Jeremiah experienced a most intimate personal relationship to God but he knew, better than his contemporaries did, that Yahweh was not only 'a God at hand' but also 'a God afar off' (Jer. xxiii. 23). Even as the God of the Covenant He remains inscrutable in His holiness for His people. God does not reveal Himself to man in such a way that man could see through Him, that man could enter into His thoughts; on the contrary, when He reveals Himself He rather makes man conscious of His glory and brings him to adoration, not only when He acts in His judgments but also in His work of salvation. His exceptional eternal goodness emphasizes His majesty. In this light we should read

[1] Cf. the main thesis of F. Baumgärtel's book: *Verheißung.*

178

Ps. cxxx. 4: 'But there is forgiveness with Thee, that Thou mayest be feared'.

True knowledge of God never exists in the Old Testament without the fear of the Lord, the *yir'ath Yahweh*[1]; this fear of the Lord even became the standing expression for what we call religion. The ideas *da'ath 'elohim* and *yir'ath Yahweh* do not cancel each other out but rather pervade each other.

The revelation of God's grace serves at the same time to glorify His divinity. Ezekiel even emphasizes this in ch. xxxvi so that he can view God's work of salvation in Israel in the light of the self-glorification of the name of God among the nations of the world (cf. Ezek. xxxvi. 16–37, esp. 21ff.). This double aspect of the revelation stands out quite clearly in the story that relates how God revealed Himself to Moses, Exod. iii. 13ff,[2] and at the same time it brings out the characteristic essence of this revelation, it demonstrates what it means to the Old Testament that God reveals Himself.

Moses asks to be allowed to know God's name so that he may refer to it when confronted with the Israelites. He wants to have a convincing legitimation in case they should not believe him. Then Yahweh says to Moses: 'I am that I am'. And further, 'Thus shalt thou say unto the children of Israel, I am hath sent me unto you'. There are two interpretations that have usually have been applied to these words: the first, that God here reveals His name, His Being, to Moses by calling Himself the One who Is, i.e. the Eternal One, or the Faithful One, or something similar[3]; the second that God here emphatically keeps His name a secret, so that these words would mean 'it does not concern you who I am'.[4]

Yahweh, however, gives Moses not an immediate[5], but certainly

[1] See pp. 155, 161f.
[2] Compare the literature mentioned on p. 343 (see also pp. 318f.); particularly the article by G. J. Thierry in *O. T. S.*, V; M. Buber, *Der Glaube der Propheten*, 1950, pp. 48f.; my "Ehje 'ašer 'ehje' in *Festschrift Bertholet*, 1950, pp. 498ff., for different views e.g. M. Reisel, *'Ehje 'ašer 'ehje*, *HW'H*, 1957 (doctorate thesis); G. Lambert, *Que signifie le nom de Jahweh* (NRTh 1952, pp. 897ff.); J. Lindblom, *Noch einmal die Deutung des Jahwenamens in Ex 3, 14*, in Annual Swedish Theological Institute III, 1964, pp. 4ff., which also gives a large amount of further literature on the subject.
[3] Albright, *From the Stone Age*, p. 198, translates Yahweh by 'the Creator (He who causes to be)'; Bowman, op. cit., by 'He who speaks'; many other translations for example in Albright's work; very interesting is also the latest view of L. Köhler in 'Vom hebräischen Lexicon', *O. T. S.*, VIII, 1950, pp. 153f.: Yahweh is a Hebrew nominal formation with prefixed *jod*, meaning 'life', 'being', 'reality'; see also his *Theologie*[3].
[4] Defended again by Dubarlez in *Revue des Sciences philos. et théol.*, XXXIV, 1951, pp. 1ff. ('le nom suggère l'impossibilité de définir Dieu', p. 20).
[5] This indirect, non-theoretical but practical way of answering we also find in the N.T. The lawyer asks Jesus who is his neighbour. Jesus answers his question in this sense that He shows by the parable how and by whom the neighbour is really known (Luke x. 25ff.).

a conclusive answer, by saying: I Myself am there, count on Me! And if Moses should be asked who had sent him, he is to say that it is 'I am (there)'.[1] On the ground of these and many other texts (cf. Gen. xvi, xvii. 2, xxvi. 23, xxviii. 13; Exod. vi. 1, xx. 2) revelation in the Scriptural sense could be defined as God Himself coming to man, revealing Himself to man as the One who is there for man, anyhow. When God reveals Himself He introduces Himself in the first person singular, and His words point to deeds. These three elements are linked indissolubly. Yet the 'I' of the *'ehje* in Exd. iii and of the words 'I am the Lord thy God' is and remains the starting-point of His speaking, His promises and His threats, and Exod. iii shows that this was realized quite clearly.

In the name 'I am (there)' Yahweh reveals His Being only in its 'formal aspect' by speaking of His *actual* presence. This is not a qualification of Yahweh's Being, for *Yahweh does not mention His name*; but at the same time He does more than this: He gives man the most solemn assurance of His presence. For him who understands this there is no more need to ask about His name. Taken in this way this word of God to Moses typifies as shortly and essentially as possible all that Israel believes and knows concerning God. The name Yahweh, thus taken to mean 'He who is', without any further qualification of His Being, is therefore of fundamental importance. It only denotes God in His 'actuality', not in His Being itself.

This very absence of qualities makes the name of Israel's God something quite *sui generis*, something very peculiar in the ancient Eastern world. For in this sphere the names of God always have a certain meaning and represent a definite element in the world of nature or the world of the spirit (even, for instance, a moral principle). This is not the case with the name Yahweh. And this very fact, together with the functional meaning of the name, makes it into something particular, shows that Israel is conscious of the miracle of God's Being in His unapproachable transcendence and in His presence.

This does not reduce God to a lifeless abstraction, a 'Being' or

[1] The only immediate parallel to this text is Hos. i. 9b (cf. also H. W. Wolff in his commentary on Hosea). There is nothing strange in the assumption that Hosea and the E-author of Exod. iii accepted the same theology concerning the name Yahweh; they were approximately contemporaries and belonged to the same prophetical group. Even if this should be an individual theological interpretation given by E (Von Rad, *Theology* I, p. 181), it is rather improbable that the only foundation of this interpretation should be 'the rhetorical device of playing freely on the derivation of a name' (Von Rad, *loc. cit*). Apart from a possible appeal to Hos. i 9 there is another important fact that we should bear in mind: the ancient oriental names of deities all have, in fact, a meaning, mostly even a very clear meaning, and were never 'no more than a name' (against Von Rad, *Theology I*, p 10).

'eternal Being' in the Greek sense of the word.[1] On the contrary, God is in Israel the One who is always really present! Here we must point to Kraemer's statements on Biblical realism in his *The Christian Message in a Non-Christian World*. This conception of Biblical realism corresponds completely with the name of Israel's God.

This twofold relationship between God and man (the world), a relationship full of tension, comes to light throughout the revelation. It may sometimes seem as if God is identical with the forces of nature in which or through which He works. Hence Western scholars could again and again consider Him a God of nature. On different grounds He has been represented as a popular god (there are in fact, some phenomena that suggest this idea). Yet the people does not stand in a relationship of 'being' to God, even if it lives in communion with Him, nor is it one of the essential traits of Yahweh as He was known to Israel that He should be connected closely with the forces of nature.[2]

This two-fold paradoxical relationship between God and man (in the sense of one that transcends human understanding) must always and in all fields be borne in mind. For instance, when dealing with inspiration, we must always keep in view that God gives His Spirit to man or in man, but this never leads to deification of man; the prophet speaks in God's name in the first person but not because he identifies himself with God in any way! On the contrary, he is merely the messenger who takes a message[3]; man is the *'ebed*, the servant, the slave, and also the one who loves God. Thus the Messiah of God is He who acts in the name of God but always remains of secondary importance in comparison with God. Union *and* subordination go together in this relationship between God and man.

The awareness of a divine revelation in the sense of communion between man and God may not be lacking in any religion, but in the Old Testament it plays a very important part and is, indeed, predominant there; not only because of the frequency of God's active intervention in this world, but particularly because of its directness. In the Old Testament the revelation is only very partially committed to outward ritual means and actions, dreams, *'urim* and *thummim*, etc.; though they do exist, they are not to be compared in number and

[1] The Hebrew verb 'to be' does not have the abstract sense of its Greek or modern Western equivalents; cf. C. H. Ratschow, *Werden und Wirken*, 1941, and Th. Boman, *Das hebräische Denken im Vergleich mit dem Griechischen*, 1952, pp. 27ff.; see below p. 319.
[2] The fact that Yahweh is connected particularly with wind, storm and thunderstorm warrants the supposition, also justifiable on other grounds, that in the pre-Mosaic era Yahweh was worshipped outside Israel (the Kenites) as a mountain-god (and storm-god, perhaps already as a war-god, too), an trait that stuck in the later conception of Yahweh, the God of Israel.
[3] See for example L. Köhler, *Theologie*[3], p. 13, and particularly his *Deuterojesaja stilkritisch untersucht*, 1923, pp. 102ff.

importance to the external media which other oriental peoples can employ, such as omens based on divination, natural phenomena, astral data, chance meetings with animals, etc.

What we do find quite frequently in the Old Testament, however, is the direct revelation, so that even Amos can say: 'Surely the Lord God will do nothing, but he revealeth His secret unto His servants the prophets' (iii. 7).

The question arises if this statement should be taken in a general sense (as is usually done; see also p. 163) or if it should be thought to have a more restricted meaning, in view of the context; in the preceding verse the prophet stated that all evil comes from God (iii. 6) and then goes on (v. 7) to add that He does not bring this evil without first revealing it to His servants (so that they in turn can warn the people by their preaching). Even so it still remains clear how intimately the relationship between God and man could be represented.

Perhaps there is no subject in the Bible more varied than the revelation of God.[1] It may be imparted in many ways: it may manifest itself in nature, history, the word, visions, external means, etc.; this variety of revelation forms demonstrates the fact that Yahweh, unlike most ancient oriental deities, is not committed to any one form or phenomenon.

This multiplicity of forms of revelation, together with the fact that God is not committed to any particular form, indicates God's absolute freedom as the Creator, also in his relations to man and the world, and shows that He is really the Living One; the transcendent God is at the same time the immanent God.

B. The self-revelation of God

All the testimonies concerning God's various acts of revelation are sustained by the certainty that they are directly related to God. It is God who gives Himself by His deeds and His words: the words of God are words from His own lips, guaranteed by His 'I'; they express His love, His anger and His will. They are not merely words predicting His deeds in the future but pronouncements that convey His momentary relations to what happens in the world, words that call to penance and repentance, and that may be withdrawn as warnings when they are heard. Fundamentally they betray the inner motives of the *Deus praesens* rather than the designs cherished by Him from all eternity[2].

That is the reason why the words and deeds of revelation cannot be dissociated from God's relation to man. They constitute a form of

[1] Cf. a.o. W. Eichrodt, 'Offenbarung (im A.T.)', *RGG³*, IV, pp. 1599ff.
[2] Cf. e.g. the above-mentioned book by Herschel: *The Prophets*.

self-revelation and as a matter of principle they cannot, therefore, be separated from Him; in fact, they can sometimes hardly be distinguished from Him[1]. When Hosea announces God's judgment upon Israel (xi. 8ff.) he shows how God is moved by this judgment. Therefore it would not be right to deny the theological qualification of self-revelation to the Old Testament revelation with an appeal to the activity of God in history.

To return from a moment to the 'I' of this God who reveals Himself, we may point out that the narratives concerning the selfrevelation of Yahweh which are given in several ways in the book of Exodus are dominated entirely by this 'I (am)'; in Exod. iii (J, E) Yahweh says in vs. 6: 'I am the God of thy father'; in vs. 14 He reveals the meaning of the name: 'I am that I am'; in Exod. vi. 2 (P) God says to Moses: 'I am Yahweh'; when He makes His law known to the people (Exod. xx) it is introduced by the well-known words: 'I am Yahweh, thy God'. Again and again we find the form of self-introduction employed in Israel's traditions concerning the revelation of Yahweh to introduce the Word of God; the conclusion is, therefore, justifiable that it dominated the entire theological conception of revelation. W. Zimmerli rightly qualifies such formulas as self-introductory[2], though they are not used for this purpose alone, but also to give expression to Yahweh's holiness and majesty[3]. We are not concerned here with the original place ('Sitz im Leben') of this concept (in the cultic or the prophetic sphere)[4], but to Old Testament theology it is especially relevant that this notion came to pervade the structure of the Yahwistic concept of revelation in the Old Testament, as appears from its place in Exodus.

Even the Christian theologian who is willing to concede that a 'full' self-revelation of God in the Old Testament is out of the question, because it could only be expected eschatologically, cannot deny that the Old Testament witness rightly speaks of God's selfrevelation. We might even say that it is the unmistakable starting-point of this testimony that God revealed Himself to the fathers, through Moses and the prophets, though it is also equally clear that there are other testimonies to be found in this same Old Testament which emphasize that God did not allow man to know Him 'fully'. God remains mys-

[1] Against W. Pannenberg c.s., *Offenbarung als Geschichte*, 1961; also particularly Rendtorff's article on the Old Testament.
[2] *'Ich bin Jahwe'*, in Alt Festschrift 1953, pp. 179ff., now also in his Gesammelte Aufsätze, *Gottes Offenbarung*, 1963, pp. 11ff. and *Das Wort des göttlichen Selbsterweises*, *op. cit.*, pp. 120ff.
[3] See K. Elliger, *'Ich bin der Herr, dein Gott'*, Theologie als Glaubenswagnis, Heim Festschrift, 1954, pp. 9ff. and *Das Gesetz, Leviticus 18*, ZWA 1955, pp. 23ff.
[4] See Zimmerli, *op. cit.*, pp. 125ff.; this problem belongs rather to the field of the history of religion or to that of the history of tradition.

terious, and the mystery is not revealed. But the mystery does not nullify the self-revelation, no more than the selfrevelation can remove the mystery.

Those to whom God reveals Himself in the Old Testament are certain of having to do with that God who is present; His words and deeds are ever new proofs and tokens of His living, personal presence. The wisdom-poet can make Job bear witness to that at the end of his book (xlii. 5, cf. also xix. 26 and xxxiii. 26); the prophet knows that Yahweh dwells 'in the high and holy place', but also 'with him that is of a contrite and humble spirit' (Isa. lvii. 15).

The same thing is found with psalmists, cf. xi. 7; lxiii. 3; more emphatically in Ps. xvii. 15 where the Psalmist seems to expect God to appear in the sanctuary. In Ps. xvi.(8) the poet is sustained by his meditation on the presence of God.

What did the authors of all these texts have in mind: seeing God actually with their own eyes (which is most likely in Ps. xvii. 15), or rather a spiritual experience? A clear-cut answer to this question is not to be found, but anyhow their experiences convinced them of the absolute reality of God's presence.[1]

The evidence of the prophets concerning experiences of the self-revelation of God is clearer than that found in the Psalms and the wisdom-literature. From what they have to say in their 'confessions' it appears that these spiritual experiences were of crucial importance in their lives and faith and gave their message a character all its own.

This applies to the farmer of Tekoah, who once saw God standing at the altar (of Bethel?), an experience which transformed him into the prophet Amos, who proclaimed judgment upon the northern kingdom with uncompromising severity. To an even greater extent it is true of Isaiah, who beholds the Holy One among the seraphim and is so deeply impressed by the holiness of Yahweh, the God of the temple of Jerusalem and the Lord of the world (Isa. vi), that he can hardly find any other names to denote Him than 'the Holy One of Israel', 'the Mighty One of Israel', 'the Lord of hosts'. But the influence of the visions of Yahweh accorded to Ezekiel (ch. i and iii) was also so great that they left their mark on the relationship between the Almighty and His messenger. From that moment Ezekiel was addressed only by the name of 'son of man', and he knew God to be the Absolute One, so much so that he became the most consistently theocentric thinker of the Old Testament.

These are three examples of theophanies that appear real to the reader, more real in any case than many others of which we find an account in the Old Testament. They are strongly visionary in charac-

[1] See F. Nötscher, *Das Angesicht Gottes schauen*, 1924, pp. 20ff.

ter, it is true, but the prophets emphatically state that these are things they have seen with their own eyes (Isa. vi. 1; Amos ix. 1; Ezek. i. 4, 15).

Even if the description of the theophanies in the older writings make a much more unreal impression, they are not intended to be less real, cf. 1 Sam. iii. 10, where Yahweh is said to stand near Samuel.[1] We repeatedly find the expression: Yahweh 'appeared to', 'showed Himself' (wajjerah), as with Moses, Exod. vi. 3 and iii. 2 (of the mal'akh Yahweh). In Gen. xii. 7, xvii. 1[b], and xviii. 1 with Abraham; with Isaac: Gen. xxvi. 24; xxxv. 9, xxviii with Jacob. The unconstrained manner in which these things are described and this phrasing is kept up in earlier and later writings is clear evidence of the fact that manifestations of Yahweh were certainly accepted fully in Israel[2] even if they were mainly accorded to exceptionally privileged men.

That prophets and patriarchs were not the only ones to have these encounters with God is apparent from the stories of Hagar (Gen. xvi. 7ff., the mal'akh Yahweh) and Manoah's wife (Judg. xiii. 6). Especially striking are also the stories from Jacob's life (Gen. xxviii and xxxii; on the latter chapter see p. 304).

Most of these theophanies are hardly or not at all described in detail, but are followed by a divine message (Gen. xii. 7; xxviii. 13 and elsewhere) or by the making of a covenant (xv. 17, xvii. 1ff.; Exod. vi. 1ff, xix–xxiv). This was rightly observed by most scholars who dealt with this subject; Rendtorff wrongly infers from it that most of these announcements of a theophany were in fact no more than formal and unimportant introductions to a 'Verheiszungsrede' or a tradition of the foundation of a sanctuary.

Several of these manifestations take the form of an appearance of the mal'akh Yahweh (see below), but repeatedly the theophany is also described as the appearance of a man.[3] J. Barr rightly observes

---

[1] Cf. i.a. J. Barr, Theophany and anthropomorphism, Suppl VT VII 1959 (pp. 30ff., esp. 31).

[2] J. Barr, op. cit., p. 32; also against R. Rendtorff, Die Offenbarungsvorstellungen im alten Israel (in W. Pannenberg, op. cit.) who attempts to make the theophanies irrelevant in favour of the revelation through the word and especially through history. In an article, Theophanies in holy places in Hebrew Religion, HUCA, XXXII, 1961, pp. 91ff. (cf. p. 106) J. Lindblom makes a fundamental distinction between these experiences in extatic visions of the prophets on the one hand, and the theophanies experienced in holy places; of the latter he says that they 'were rather hallucinatory experiences with many analogies at all stages of human life'. It is true that he states that for those who had these experiences 'the reality of Yahweh's presence and appearance in person was of course beyond all doubt'. It seems to me that this also applies to those who transmitted these traditions and incorporated them into their descriptions, so that for them the distinction made by Lindblom did not exist. Cf. J. Jeremias, Theophanie, WMAT 1965.

[3] Judge. xiii. 6; Gen. xviiif., xxxii; Isa. vi; Ezek. 1.26.

185

(p. 34) that the Old Testament emphasizes the fact that seeing God is fatal to man (Judg. xiii. 22; Exod. xxxiii. 20) rather than the fact that God is invisible. God is and remains above all the Holy and Unapproachable One.

Of especial importance in this respect is the passage of Exod. xxxiii. 14–23.

Here the story that Yahweh will not accompany Israel on its wanderings (xxxiii. 1–6) and that He spoke to Moses face to face in the tent (vss. 7ff.) is followed by conflicting traditions (we might perhaps even call this a theological discussion on the possibility of seeing the glory of God, His countenance, God Himself, esp. vss. 18–23). Here the special grace accorded to Moses is emphasized and it is also stated that no man, not even Moses, can see Yahweh and live. This text, or perhaps we could say: this *midrash*, demonstrates the problem confronting Israel in the manifestation of God. On the one hand it was considered a real thing, on the other it was thought impossible that man could survive it, and in this text the two views stand side by side unreconciled.

No wonder, then, that regarding the theophanies there remain many problems. One of the most important of these is whether the stories concerning these manifestations were indeed considered adequate in certain Israelite circles. According to many scholars the appearances of the *mal'akh Yahweh* or the stories that tell how God manifested Himself in a dream are evidence that the direct manifestations of God were no longer accepted in Israel. Against this militates the fact that as late as Isaiah and Ezekiel the appearance of God was still experienced and that even the priestly author allowed the expression to stand: 'God appeared' to Abraham and Moses.

We shall have to tread warily here and must accept both these views. In some of the writings a certain measure of shyness is to be observed concerning the immediacy of God's presence, in others we find the absolute conviction of the reality of these experiences.

Another important problem which has not yet been solved satisfactorily and which we may not be able to solve with the data available, is whether theophanies occur in the cult. At this point we can only touch lightly on the subject.[1]

[1] In his *Psalmenstudien* II, 1922, pp. 114ff. Mowinckel thinks that Yahweh may have sat enthroned on the ark (perhaps as an image), so that the theophany formed a regular element of the cult. In his *The Psalms in Israel's worship* I, 1962, pp. 140ff. he takes the epiphany of Yahweh to be the central element of the New Year festival, but here the reality is 'visibly expressed through the symbols and rites of the feast and the emotional reaction of the congregation' (p. 142). A. R. Johnson, *Sacral Kingship in Ancient Israel*[2], 1955, speaks more or less similarly of the 'actual presence' of God, without using the terms epiphany or theophany. A. Weiser made a strong plea for the theophany as an essential element of the temple-cult, taking it to be a realization

It is even clear that the temple was often looked upon in Israel as the place where Yahweh dwelt[1], though in the deuteronomic literature Yahweh was rather considered to be represented in the temple by 'the Name' than that He was thought to dwell there Himself. From Ezek. x and xliii it appears that the *Kabod* (glory) of Yahweh was looked upon as something visible and concrete, and was taken to be proof of the presence of God Himself.

The Ark, too, was often represented in the Old Testament as an immediate representation of God Himself (Num. x. 35). With respect to the cult in Israel there is, therefore, every reason to speak of the *Deus praesens*. The cultic acts indicate this. It is evident that there is a communion between God and man in the cult; man asks and God replies or God comes to man at certain feasts with His word and man glorifies Him. There are some places in the Psalms that justify the idea of a manifestation of God in the temple: Ps.l. 2ff.; lxxxi; but they do not present us with a clear picture. It is not impossible that theophanies occurred more regularly in the pre-exilic period than afterwards and that for that reason memories of such manifestations faded or were smoothed away. On the available data it is impossible to decide whether theophanies were announced by a cultic prophet or were denoted by certain ceremonies. What we can say is that they were experienced either in the proclamation of the revelation on Mount Sinai (Weiser) or in the course of certain ceremonies (Mowinckel, Johnson) or through the proclamation of a charismatic prophet (Kraus).

Apparently individuals could have such experiences, too, when they prayed for an oracle in the temple and spent the night there (Ps. xvii. 15, 1 Kings iii. 5ff., cf. Gen. xxviii. 10ff. – dreamoracle).[2]

Taking everything into consideration we should certainly take the theophanies in the Old Testament seriously as one of the most fundamental expressions of faith in the communion between the Holy One and man.

The *words* used to denote revelation[3] show that Israel was aware

of the historical tradition of the revelation on Mount Sinai during the covenantal feast of sacral tribalism (cf. his *Psalmen* I, pp. 31–35; but esp. *Theophanie in den Psalmen und im Festkult*, Bertholet Festschrift, 1950; also W. Beyerlin, *Herkunft und Geschichte der ältesten Sinaitraditionen*, 1961, pp. 140ff.). Whereas Weiser strongly emphasizes the cultic ritual, H. J. Kraus, *Gottesdienst im Israel*[2], 1962, pp. 255f., and *Psalmen* I, LXVIff., 373f., thinks of proclamations during the cult by charismatic prophets whc proclaim the presence of God.
[1] See now R. E. Clements, *God and Temple*, 1965.
[2] Cf. E. L. Ehrlich, *Der Traum im A.T.*, 1953, pp. 13ff.; id., *Kultsymbolik im A.T. und im nachbiblischen Judentum*, 1959, pp. 19ff.; he ascribes the outward manifestations of Yahweh to the influence of Cananite religion (pp. 18f.).
[3] On the terminology see, besides the above-mentioned article by Rendtorff, also H. Haag, *Offenbaren in der hebräischen Bibel*, ThZ, 1960, pp. 251 ff. and F. Schnutenhaus *Das Kommen und Erscheinen Gottes im A.T.*, ZAW, 1964, pp. 1ff.

187

of the fact that in this revelation God gave Himself to the people: *He has appeared* (*nir'ah*, 'to show oneself', 'to appear'); *He revealed Himself to* (*niglah*, 'to uncover oneself'); *He has made Himself known to (hithwadda'* and *noda'*)*, *He has come together with (no'ad)* His people; He comes *to (bo')* His people (especially in Deutero-Isaiah). Concerning this last verb we should bear in mind that it does not merely denote 'arriving at' someone's house, but rather 'entering into' and 'dwelling in' it (Isa. lii. 6f.; Zech. ii. 14, cf. vs. 9; in modern translations vss. 10 and 5).

Over and above that, however, the revelation contains in particular the proclamation of His will, His intentions; this becomes evident in such expressions as: *God showed* (*Hiphil* of *ra'ah*, 'to see'), *revealed (galah, Kal* and *Pi'el)*, or *opened the eyes (galah, Pi'el)*, *gave indications* or *taught (Hiphil* of *yarah)*, but in particular *spoke ('amar)* and *said (dibber)*. These last two are used very frequently. The auditive element, rather than the visual, plays an important part, particularly in the prophetic religion; and no wonder, for the prophets appear mainly as messengers who call upon the people to *hear* and to *obey*.[1]

C. Revelation in history

a. General observations

From the preceding section it has become clear that the Old Testament keeps bearing witness to the occurrence of theophanies, both at the beginning of the history of revelation and afterwards. This would bear out the statement, of great theological importance, that Israel's faith is founded upon the certainty of the presence of God and the communion with Him. Again and again God gives evidence of this in the course of history by entering into a relationship Himself, first with each of the patriarchs, then with Moses, and after that with various other groups of men of God, in this way inaugurating a new period in Israel's history. All the historians, both earlier and later, bear testimony to this.[2]

After the announcement of the appearance of God there mostly follows an order and (or) a promise which is always supported by the signs of the presence of God Himself. One should not divorce the revelation through the Word from this presence, nor should the manifestation be looked upon as something formal and unimportant from a theological point of view.[3] Because God Himself appears at

---

[1] Cf. for example C. J. Bleeker, *De godsdienstige betekenis van oog en oor*, (oration), 1964, p. 171.
[2] Cf. xv (JE) and xvii (P), xxvi (JE), xxviii (JE), xxxv (E, P), Exod. iii (JE), vi (P), Josh. 1.5f., I Sam. iii, Isa. vi; xl; lii.
[3] As on p. 183 n. 1.

the beginning of a new historical phase, the whole of the succeeding period is borne by Him. It becomes His work, and is directly related to Him of Whose will it is the expression.

So the theological view in the Old Testament is always that God informs man of His activity in history before interfering in the life of the people and the individual. Man is allowed to know beforehand what God who goes with him is going to do.[1] And therefore Israel's faith is not determined exclusively or even primarily by the historical facts and their interpretation after the event, but God Himself makes 'His secret' known to His people of Israel (Am. iii. 7).

Of late a strong controversy has developed on the relation between revelation and history. No one would deny that revelation comes to Israel in the frame of history, but the relation between these two is a highly controversial issue. In the *Theology* of Von Rad and his school, history is looked upon as the starting-point of faith. In Vol. I p. 106 Von Rad says: 'in principle Israel's faith is grounded in a theology of history. It regards itself as based upon historical acts, and as shaped and re-shaped by factors in which it saw the hand of Jahweh at work'. And elsewhere, II p. 338; 'it is in history that God reveals the secret of his person'. According to Von Rad, the view that Israel's faith is historically determined is confirmed by the kerygmatic histories of the Old Testament that provide him with the material for his theological expositions. The ideas of his disciples (W. Rendtorff e.g.) concerning history as the source of revelation are even more one-sided. These views were rightly opposed by Zimmerli in a criticism of Rendtorff's ideas (in *Ev. Th.* 1962, pp. 15ff.) when he said that history can be regarded as the place of revelation but not as its organ. In a review of Von Rad's *Theology* in *Ev. Th.* 1963, pp. 143ff. M. Honecker (pp. 167f.) rightly observes that Israel's faith is not grounded in the facts of history but in 'the hope of God's faith which can never be proved on historical grounds, a hope proclaimed in the Word spoken to Israel'. Long beforehand, C. Westermann had already pointed out that it is only the connection with the 'proclaiming Word' that makes the historical fact into God's activity, and that it is only in this way that there can be a 'history of the ways of God with His people', cf. Zur Auslegung des A.T. in: *Probleme alttestamentlicher Hermeneutik*, 1960, p. 27. Von Rad and his school paid hardly any attention to this highly important element, though he does mention it on p. 106 of his book. This gave his *Theology* its one-sided historical character.[2]

[1] See J. Barr, *Revelation through history in the Old Testament and in modern Theology*, Interpretation 1963, pp. 197, 201ff.
[2] See i.a. the objections raised by J. Barr, *Revelation through History*, and my above-

God's revelation in history is continually accompanied by the proclaiming word. History is, therefore, not revelatory in itself[1] but is made clear by God in His speaking to the men of God; if God had not spoken in this way Israel would not have understood its history.[2]

The revelatory Word of God made Israel experience the events of history as God's activity. Owing to this experience God became more a living reality to Israel. Israel does not know God as a deity who whispers unintelligibly in the cultic oracle, or as a regularity inherent in the course of events, but as the Lord Who acts and accomplishes His will within the lives of human beings. The life of the people, in which God intervenes again and again, is a life in His presence. The history in which both the people and the individual live runs its course in a direct relationship to Him. There is a correspondence between what happens to Israel and Israel's God. There exists an absolute openness of life towards Him.

No wonder, then, that many great historical facts are described as events at which God is present, in which He takes part.

In the Old Testament we find a remarkable transition from theophany to God's activity in history, especially in the description of the epiphanies. Schnutenhaus[3] was quite right in following C. Westermann[4], who distinguished between the two conceptions: he uses the term theophany to denote the direct encounter between God and man, and epiphany for God's intervention on behalf of His people in their struggle with their enemies. It is not always possible to make a clear distinction between the two: in the stories concerning Mount Sinai the descriptions are closely allied to those of the epiphanies, though these stories are meant to describe theophanies. Yet the distinction is most enlightening. In the epiphanies a very descriptive expression (in the 3rd person!) is given of God's activity in history; from a literary point of view these descriptions are closely related to Babylonian descriptions of manifestations of certain deities. That the epiphanies, which are so closely related to the theophanies, should have been employed in the poetical rendering of historical elements, is of extreme theological importance. It proves that God's intervention in history is taken to mean that God leaves His inaccessible dwelling-place. The researches made by Schnutenhaus demonstrate that

mentioned essay on *Geloof, Openbaring en geschiedenis* in KTh 1965; cf. also F. Mildenberger, *Gottes Tat im Wort*, 1964.

[1] It is, therefore, impossible to conclude from Old Testament evidence that 'revelation through history can be understood by anyone who has eyes to see', that 'it is universal in character', as W. Pannenberg says *(op. cit. p. 98)*.

[2] Mildenberger, *op. cit.*, pp. 37ff., 44ff.

[3] See p. 187 n. 3. J. Jeremias, *op cit.*, neglects this distinction.

[4] *Das Loben Gottes in den Psalmen*, 1954, pp. 65ff.

the verbs *yaṣa'* – to go out – and *yarad* – to descend – are very characteristic of this conception. Such descriptions are found in Deut. xxxiii. 2–5, Judg. v, Ps. xviii; lxviii, Isa. xxx. 27ff., Mic. 1. 3f., Hab. iii (cf. also Exod. xv), in widely different periods of Israelite history, there fore, but for the greater part in the early poetic literature. Here Yahweh is described especially as a military hero. It was the custom for Israel to place itself under the protection of God and to pray for His oracle before battle (Ps. xx, 1 Kings xxii, 2 Kings iii and elsewhere) in order to be certain of His assistance (Exod. xv., Judg. v, etc.). The ark, the earliest symbol of Yahweh, was a warsymbol and accompanied the people into battle (Numb. x. 35f., 1 Sam. iv–vi, 2 Sam. xi. ii). Their experiences of war gave the Israelites their strong faith in God's presence in their midst and made the certainty of God's intervention in history one of the most characteristic elements of their faith.

In later days this way of describing God's activity comes to be used less and less, as appears from the Deuteronomistic and prophetic description of God's intervention in history (see the treatment of the conquest of Canaan in Joshua, the wars of Saul and David and of the later kings, and chapters such as Isa. x. 5ff.). Nevertheless we do find as late as Joshua v. 14 that a man with his sword drawn in his hand and calling himself captain of the host of the Lord appears before Joshua to guide him, and in Isa. lxiii Yahweh is depicted vividly as coming to avenge the wrongs done to Israel by Edom; again and again it is said of David in connection with his voctories that God was with him (1 Sam. xviii. 12, 14, 28; 2 Sam. v. 10).[1] It was in battle that God proved to be near, and that was where Israel felt God's presence, and where Israel's faith in God's activity in history confirmed ever anew.

As Von Rad has demonstrated, this faith even developed into the hope of even greater and even more decisive victories, even the hope of an all-decisive victory of Israel's God when all the enemies were to be destroyed, the *Yom Yahweh*, the Day of the Lord.[2] Originally this day was looked forward to as the great day of salvation, the day when Yahweh was to be victorious over all His enemies on behalf of Israel. When, however, Amos announced that this day would not be a day of salvation but rather a day of darkness and gloom for the people, this was an unprecedented message which was the very opposite of all that Israel had expected up to that time.

From that moment two (or perhaps we had better say three) ways

---

[1] Cf. 2 Sam. v. 17ff., 24; xxii. 30ff.; xxiii. 10, 12, and my article 'Das Lied als historisches Dokument', *Verbum*. H. W. Obbink Festschrift 1964, pp. 112ff., esp. p. 124.
[2] *Theology* II, pp. 119ff.

in which God's activity in history was proclaimed are found side by side. In the former, in accordance with the ancient fathers, God's work is thought to consist in His acts of salvation *(ṣidqoth Yahweh)*, of which we hear in the early historical narratives and to which the words of Jacob (Gen. xlix), Moses (Deut. xxxiii) and Balaam (Numb. xxiif.) bore testimony. In the latter God's activity includes His judgments that were expected to come. This latter message is proclaimed by the so-called prophets of woe, whose prophecies have come down to us in the Bible and who are also called the 'classical' prophets (see below pp.230ff.). But this message of doom is never taken to be final, for the prophets of evil did not believe either that this judgment was to be the end of God's work. From the tension between these two forms of preaching the eschatological hope of salvation springs up.

b. Communion with God revealed in the saving history
It was, indeed, the great acts of salvation experienced by Israel at the outset of its history that forged an inseverable link between Israel and Yahweh. Without these saving acts the message of Moses, the man of God, would have been utterly unfounded: his message of salvation-to-come was confirmed by the deliverance from Egypt. Together with the appearance of the prophets, God's saving activity became the firm foundation-stone of Israel's faith.

Israel's faith in God is characterized by great optimism, or rather by great joy and hope. Again and again God revealed Himself in history as the Saviour-God.

Some scholars have thought that Israel's faith in a redeeming God derived from one single miracle experienced by the Hebrew slaves who had fled from Egypt, namely the passage through the Red Sea, by which the deliverance of the people was achieved.[1] This view does not, however, fit the data of tradition. It is true that this fact plays a part in tradition, in the historical narratives and also in the message of the prophets, but it is not always recorded by any means[2] and should be looked upon as merely one of the elements in the history of deliverance.[3] The pre-exilic prophets hardly ever mention it[4]; they are far more concerned with the deliverance during the desert-journey than with that of the passage through the 'Red Sea'. What we can say is that the deliverance from Egypt (and the sea), the deliv-

---

[1] See M. Noth: *Überlieferungsgeschichte des Pentateuch*, 1948, pp. 52f., G. von Rad, *Theology* I, p. 175f.; and elsewhere; also A. Lauha, *Das Schilfmeermotiv im Alten Testament*, Suppl. VT, IX, 1962, pp. 32ff.
[2] Not by the prophets before Jeremiah, neither in Ps. cv.
[3] So rightly A. Lauha, *op cit.*
[4] Only in a late passage in Jeremiah (xxxii), perhaps in Nahum, and certainly in Hab. iii.

errance from the desert and the conquest of the 'promised land' all together are considered the basis of Israel's history of salvation (cf. pp.335f.). Subsequently the message of the prophets,[1] the Psalms[2] and the deuteronomic literature again and again revert to this body of tradition from Israel's earliest history (or better perhaps: prehistory).

Even if ever new savings acts of God were experienced during the times of the judges and in the period of the Kings, especially in the days of David, these acts could never obscure the Exodus-tradition which expresses the basic pattern[3] of Israel's faith. On the contrary, when the gains of the period of the kings are lost, the Exodus-motif stands out more clearly again (Deuteronomy; the exilic prophets, Ezekiel and Deutero-Isaiah). As the foundation-stone of faith the Exodus-tradition came to be more and more the *pièce de résistance* of the description of the history of salvation in the historical books. It became one of the strongest pillars of Israel's religious life, too, but also of legal and moral thinking, the starting-point of both the message of judgment of the prophets and their message of hope (judgment Am. iii; hope: Deutero-Isaiah).

In the opening words of the Decalogue Yahweh is proclaimed to be the Saviour: 'I am the Lord thy God, which have brought thee out of the land of Egypt, out of the house of bondage', and in this way the whole body of Israelite law, both cultic and moral, is viewed in terms of the revelation of God's saving activity (cf. beside Exod. xx and Deut. v, Levit. xix. 34, 36f., xviii. 3, xx.24ff., xxvi. 13, 45; further the whole of the introduction to the book of Deuteronomy, as well as the ceremony of the offering of the first-fruits in the temple, Deut. xxvi. 5ff.)

Above all other prophets it is Deutero-Isaiah, the prophet of hope, who emphasizes the deliverance from Egypt. In his message, however, it is not only history that bears testimony to Yahweh as the Saviour *(go'el)*, but creation or rather the conception of creation also strengthens Israel's faith in the God of salvation. Because Yahweh the Redeemer is also known to be the Creator, creation is not a 'soullessly

---

[1] Am. ii. 10, iii. 1, v. 25, ix. 7; Hos. ii, xi, xii, xiii (viii. 1); Micah vi (vii. 15); (Isa. x. 24ff., xi. 16, iv. 5); Hab. iii (Nah. i. 4); Jer. ii, vii. 22f., xi, xv. 1, xvi. 15, xxxi. 32, xxxii. 20f.; Ezek. xvi, xx. 5ff., xxiii; Isa. xliii. 16ff., xlviii. 20f., li. 9f., lii. 11f., lxiii. 7ff.; Hag. ii. 5; on Deutero-Isaiah see B. J. van der Merwe, *Pentateuchtradisies in die Prediking van Deuterojesaja*, 1955, pp. 146–246; B. W. Anderson, *Exodus Typology in Second Isaiah*, Muilenburg Festschrift, 1962, pp. 177ff.
[2] E.g. lxxvii. 15f., lxxviii, lxxx, lxxxi, lxxxix. 10, cv, cvi. 7ff., cxiv. 3f., cxxxv. 8f., cxxxvi. 10ff.
[3] See the title of D. Daube's work: *The Exoduspattern in the Bible*, 1963; the elaboration of his idea that the history of redemption is strongly dominated to a large extent by the legal terminology, presents many difficulties.

beautiful and senselessly brutal' nature, but a token of God's majesty and greatness, and man is not a stranger in the world that surrounds him. Because Isaiah knows that God is behind this world, the creation can proclaim salvation (xl.26ff.). Closely bound up with this must be the fact that this prophet thinks in universal terms and therefore believes that the servant of the Lord, the 'ebed Yahweh, is called upon to bring salvation to the world. From this faith have sprung the special songs of the Servant of the Lord, which attribute to the service of Yahweh a power that overcomes the world and even death (ch.xlii. 1ff., xlix, l, lii. 13–liii.12; cf. further also lxi.1ff.).

It was this prophet who by his preaching aroused Israel from its lethargy and made many Israelites return to Jerusalem, in the expectation to receive the Kingdom of God there. We may say, therefore, that – humanly speaking – this champion of the faith, who himself had to bear so many afflictions (Isa.l, liii) was the man to whom Israel owed its revival. From generation to generation his message was handed on to others who, each in his own way, bore testimony to the same expectation: Haggai, Zechariah, Malachi, and in this way many generations were inspired by new hopes.

Deutero-Isaiah did not only remind his people of God's saving activity in the days of Israel's origin, but also of God's deeds in the patriarchal age (ch.li) and in the life of David (Isa.lv.3).[1] Here the prophet merely follows out a line that dominates the whole of Israelite tradition and demonstrates that throughout its existence Israel was conscious of being sustained by the fact that God remained faithful. This becomes evident on going through the various historical books.

The deuteronomic description of the conquest of the promised land in the book of Joshua is a continuous testimony to the miraculous deeds of God in Israel's history. Like the stories of Exod.i–x, those of Josh.i–x have a strong miraculous tendency, which proves that especially in later times the traditions concerning God's saving activity were embellished to the greater glory of Yahweh. Some of the historical narratives are even given a cosmic tendency (Exod.xv[2], Josh.x).

The book of Judges tells us in a historically less elusive manner about God's deeds accomplished by the 'Judges' who were inspired by the Spirit of God. The history of David, too, abounds with proclamations of divine activity accomplished through this 'man after God's heart'; in principle they were ascribed to God Himself, who went out before

---

[1] O. Eißfeldt, *The promises of Grace to David in Isaiah55 : 1–5*, Muilenburg Festschrift, pp. 196ff.
[2] Cf. what Lauha *(op. cit.)* says on the later renderings of the miracle at the Red Sea.

him and was with him (2 Sam. v.20, 1 Sam. xvii, 2 Sam. xxiii. 10 12).[1]
Even long afterwards we find the prophets bearing witness to this
divine activity. It is rather curious that Isaiah, who hardly mentions
the Exodus-traditions at all, should refer to the deliverance through
Gideon (Isa. ix. 3) and repeatedly to the deeds of David (xxviii. 21,
xxix. 1). In my opinion these elements in Isaiah's work do not imply
that we are justified in speaking of a separate Davidic tradition of
salvation peculiar to Jerusalem, to which greater importance was attached in Jerusalem than to the northern tradition of the deliverance
from Egypt.[2] For it was David himself who brought the ark to Jerusalem, and thus laid a connection between Jerusalem and the earliest
history of Israel, the desert period. This made it clear that Yahweh
who had established his dwelling-place in Jerusalem was none other
than the Yahweh who had led his people from Egypt through the
wilderness.[3]

So the historians knew that Israel was guided by God from beginning to end. This theme was elaborated ever anew in the historical
books, from Genesis to 2 Kings. The intention of the authors is not
so much to proclaim various separate deeds of God, but to depict
God's guidance of His people in its history. And in doing so they pay
attention to political, worldly affairs above all. By the earliest prophets
the material aspect of God's redeeming activity is also stressed most
(even in an eschatological connection) Amos (ix, concluding vss.),
Hosea (ii, xiv).

Yet this material and political aspect was not a goal in itself for
Israel either: it was the outward manifestation of a life in peace with
God and in obedience to Him; this, too, is to be found in Hos. ii.

To outline the content of God's redemptive activity as proclaimed
by the Old Testament we may draw upon the words written by H.
Wheeler Robinson as the conclusion of a short study of the meaning
of redemption in the Old Testament[4]: 'The Old Testament idea of
redemption, then, lays emphasis on the divine initiative, comprehends
within itself the deliverance from material as well as from spiritual

[1] See my essay in the Obbink Festschrift, *Verbum*, 1964, mentioned above on p. 191
n. 1.
[2] This view is taken by G. von Rad, *Theology* I, pp. 39ff., esp. p. 46f., and also by
E. Rohland, *Die Bedeutung der Erwählungstraditionen Israels für die Eschatologie der
Propheten*, 1956. Von Rad thinks the traditions of David and Zion to be one and the
same; Rohland demonstrates the divergences between them. Against this see my
Jahweh en zijn stad, 1962, and *Essentials of the Theology of Isaiah*, Muilenburg Festschrift, 1962, pp. 128ff. Cf. also the texts from Amos and Micah mentioned in n. 1
on p. 193.
[3] See also O. Eißfeldt, *Silo und Jerusalem*, VT, 1957, pp. 138ff., and M. Noth, *Jerusalem
und die isr. Tradition*, OTS, 1950, pp. 202ff.
[4] *Redemption and Revelation*, 1944, p. 227.

perils and constraints, and deals primarily with Israel as a people, though growingly concerned with the relation of the individual to God, within that social solidarity'.

Particularly in the prophets' messianic hope of salvation the spiritual renewal of the people is emphasized more and more. They look forward to the righteousness that will prevail everywhere, to the peace and the knowledge of God that will spread all over the earth.[1]

We generally find that the term 'to live' is used, for example in Ezek. xxxiii. 11 : 'I have no pleasure in the death of the wicked; but that the wicked turn from his way and live', but here the word implies more than mere physical subsistence: it must certainly also mean a life in peace with God.[2]

Thus Isa. lv speaks of the repentance of the sinner, to which God responds with *mercy* and *forgiveness*. In Ps. cxxx these two ideas of forgiveness and redemption are also connected (cf. verses 4, 8); the last verse runs: 'He shall redeem Israel from all his iniquities' (cf. also Ps. ciii. 3f.).

Here redemption is therefore understood in a deeper sense, as a deliverance from the spiritual grasp of sin. The Old Testament is conscious of the danger of sin in human life, it is aware of the fact that one sin brings another in its train, and that sin is as it were a chain that winds itself closer and closer round man; think for example of the history of primeval times: Gen. ii–vii (see pp. 413ff.).

Redemption from sin is also brought out in full clarity in Isa. liii; here it appears that the servant of the Lord will reclaim many by his vicarious suffering (cf. vs. 11). In this chapter Israel's hopes concerning God's redeeming activity and the atonement which He brings about flow together. This latter is one of the aspects of God's redemptive work, but is is so important that it deserves separate treatment (pp. 286ff.).

The most important theological terms used in the Old Testament are *padah* (to buy off) and *ga'al* (to ransom).[3] These terms have a symbolical meaning, which appears clearly from the use of *padah*, for only once do we find the price mentioned which God pays for His people Israel whom He redeems (Isa. xliii. 3f.), while in all other places

---

[1] See the last chapter.
[2] Cf. J. Hempel, *Heilung als Symbol*, p. 281.
[3] *Padah* is liberating somebody who is in the possession of somebody else by giving a ransom; *ga'al* is standing up for a nearest relation, either by redeeming his property that had to be sold from necessity or also by avenging his death. On the terminology see J. J. Stamm, *Erlösen und Vergeben im A.T.*, 1940; on *ga'al* in particular also A. R. Johnson, 'The primary meaning of ga'al in *Suppl. to Vetus Testamentum*, I, 1953, pp. 67ff., who reduces the two stems *ga'al* to one, with the general meaning 'to cover'; in the religious sense *go'el* is rather protector than redeemer.

the word is used in the general sense of redeeming and delivering.[1] The verb *ga'al* is also used in a general sense to denote redemption. Both these words are used when it is a question of deliverance from an emergency[2]; they imply the redemption both of the people as a whole and of the individuals, the faithful.

c. Communion with God even in judgment

In spite of its fundamental unity the Old Testament has many controversial traits. Though the preaching of salvation predominates, the Old Testament is full of messages concerning God's judgments. God reveals His presence not only by His activity on behalf of Israel but also by His judgments on the people. The prophets whose words accompany God's deeds, taught the people to see their history in the light of the will of God, the Holy One.

In this way it became possible for Israel to bear the crushing defeats it had to suffer and even the fall of Israel as a state, by its faith in God. Israel found it very hard to integrate its afflictions into its faith, and the same is true of the prophets themselves. This is evident from many places in the various prophetic writings that tell us of their inward and outward difficulties. The announcements that God was preparing His judgments on His people, were received with unbelief, scorn, resentment and enmity. We find a great many examples of this in the Old Testament, such as Am.vii; Mic.ii.6, iii.8; Isa.xxviii. 14ff., xxx. 10f.; Jer.xi. 18–xii.6, xviii. 18f., xxvi, xxviii, xxxviff.; Ezek.iii.4ff., xiii, xiv; Isa.xlii.18ff., xlix.14, l.1ff.; Hag.i.

But it also cost the prophets a great effort to pass on such messages; they could not believe it, they would not hear of it, this task lay heavy upon them. Some cases in point are Am.vii. 1–9 (where in three visions that belong together the spiritual struggle is depicted that Amos has to go through in order to be able to accept the message of judgment); Hos.vi.4f., xi.8f.; Isa.viii. 17f.; Jer.viii. 18ff., ix. 1ff., xiv. 17ff., xv. 1f., 10ff., 15ff., xvi, xx. 7ff.; Ezek.xi. 13, xii. 17, xxi.6. They only shouldered their task because they had been called to it by God (Isa.vi; Jer.i, xx. 7ff.).

Yet God's judgment was not an idea that was altogether alien to Israel's faith. It cannot be maintained that Israel only thought in terms of salvation, as if Yahweh were only a God of promise and favour. From the outset the revelation of Yahweh was partly determined by the proclamation of His will. Though historically we cannot be absolutely certain if this is true of Israel's religion, it is clear that in

[1] See Köhler, *Theologie*, p. 224.
[2] J.J.Stamm, *op. cit.*, p. 147; they are used only occasionally in the meaning of: to forgive, to put away sin: Ps.cxxx.8 (*padah*), Isa.xliv.22 (*ga'al*), Stamm, pp. 142ff.

Israel's faith as unfolded to us in the Old Testament the law, whether it takes the form of the Decalogue or not, is very closely bound up with the revelation of Yahweh[1]; we may even rightly posit that this already applies to the earliest historians, though we cannot reconstruct with certainty in what way. As the inauguration of kings in the ancient Eastern world was attended with the enactment of laws[2], the proclamation of Yahweh as the God of Israel was thought of as involving the proclamation of His will. And proclamations of laws always contain sanctions, too, like treaties, which may perhaps be looked upon as a special kind of legislation. Like treaties, laws are protected by the gods; contempt of these inexorably involves punishment.

This did not only hold good for Israel, but also for the whole of the ancient oriental world. No wonder, then, that several texts were found showing that the ancient eastern nations realized that certain disasters falling upon the royal house or the country were due to the anger of the gods, on whose authority certain laws had been enacted and who therefore were revenged on all those who violated these laws in spite of all their menacing curses.[3]

In the Old Testament we find such threats as that of Exod. xx. 5: 'I the Lord thy God am a jealous God'; those of Levit. xxvi and Deut. xxvi–xxviii are even more far-reaching. We read in the Old Testament that the Israelites kept the truce with the Gibeonites in spite of the fact that they knew themselves to be deceived, for they had sworn to do so, invoking the name of Yahweh and calling down His vengeance upon themselves in case they should not fulfil their pledge. And the fact that Saul had unilaterally broken this treaty was afterwards charged to him and his family as a grave sin (2 Sam. xxi), not only by the Gibeonites but also by David, who was brought to take up this attitude by a divine oracle and judgment.

So divine judgment absolutely forms part of Israelite religious life. Frequently prophets are found to threaten kings with judgment (e.g. Saul: 1 Sam. xiii, xv; David: 2 Sam. xi; Jeroboam: 1 Kings xii. 25ff., xiii; Ahab: 1 Kings xvii, xxi, xxii, and elsewhere). These judgments are, however, due to certain demonstrable sinful acts of kings who dragged down their people into judgment with them.

The prophetic announcements of God's judgments cannot be dissolved from these conceptions, yet they are something novel as

---

[1] Cf. W. Zimmerli, *The Law and the Prophets*, 1965, and *Das Gesetz im A.T.*, ThLZ, 1960, pp. 481ff.

[2] See my article 'Exod. xx. 2', *Recherches bibliques* VIII, pp. 35ff, 1967.

[3] See my *Religion of Israel*, pp. 28ff. and A. Malamat, *Doctrines of causality in historiography*, VT, 1955, pp. 1ff.

well. They involve the people and its life in judgment directly and completely. The divine anger is not only roused by some cultic or social offence, but is directed against the way of life of king and people. In their indictments the prophets from Judah (Amos, Isaiah, Micah, Jeremiah) especially stress the social and political abuses. The only prophet from the North (Hosea) emphasizes rather the cultic betrayal of Yahweh. The prophets from Judah fulminate against injustice, oppression and entering rashly into relations with various other nations. Hosea does mention this latter element, but his criticism is mainly directed against the prevalent Baalworship.

Again and again we find that already in the earlier period the prophets of Israel proclaim judgment as something still to come. We get the impression that among the other ancient-Eastern peoples the anger of the gods is inferred from the disasters themselves, as also in 2 Sam. xxi. In Israel the connection between judgment and sinful act is accentuated much more clearly, so that the relation between the catastrophe and divine anger can be inverted: on the ground of an awakened sense of guilt it is possible to come to the conclusion that God's anger is aroused and that His judgment is imminent.

It is quite clear, at any rate, that with several of the prohets the proclamation of judgment precedes the historical threat, as can be demonstrated from the dates for Amos, Hosea and Isaiah.[1] Amos starts preaching before Tiglath-Pileser appears on the scene, and Isaiah has his vision (ch. vi) before this king has turned towards the West. Hosea's threat against Jizreel (ch. i) can hardly be assigned to any other period than Jeroboam's reign, so before the period of Tiglath-Pileser.[2]

In any case the prophets themselves never take the historical event as such for the starting-point of their message. They always refer to spiritual experiences, granted to them in the vision of their vocation (Amos vii, Isa. vi, Jer. i, Ezek. i, Isa. xl) or otherwise (Hos. i) which gave them a new understanding. These testimonies will have to be taken absolutely seriously. Through a personal encounter with God (Isa. vi, Ezek. i) or by hearing His word the prophets came to realize the immediacy of the relationship between Israel and Yahweh. They learned that Yahweh was the living reality confronting the prophets as well as the people at large, and so life gained a wholly new meaning for them: they came to see the events as immediate acts of God, a

---

[1] This would not apply to Isaiah, if A. Jepsen's chronology *(Die Quellen des Königsbuches,* 1953, p. 43) should be correct.

[2] For that reason the appearance of prophets should not be explained *a priori* from historical events. This seems to be the view of P. A. H. de Boer *(Second Isaiah's Message,* 1956, p. 86) regarding the exilic prophet.

deep consciousness arose that the life of the people was valueless and even doomed in the eyes of the Holy One. From this they gathered that Israel was ripe for judgment. The story of the vision of Isaiah's calling is the classical example of what took place in the spiritual life of the prophet who saw himself confronted ty the Holy One in the full splendour of His glory. From this moment of awakening it became clear to the prophet how far the people had strayed from God's will and from His law, and what divine judgments were threatening Israel.

In this way the prophets became preachers of penitence who viewed the events of their times in terms of judgment. This gave them the certainty that the 'Day of the Lord' would be a day of divine anger (Amos, Isaiah, Zephaniah, Joel). There were two factors, therefore, that moulded the prophets: their personal vocation and the confrontation of the life of the people with the will of the Holy One who had revealed His law to Israel. This latter is a very important factor; in fact it made the proclamation of God's anger fundamentally possible in Israel. We may say, therefore, that essentially this form of the announcement of judgment, quite peculiar to Israel, can only be accounted for on the ground of the knowledge of God's will of which Israel was conscious.

This prophecy of doom has more aspects than one: it is either prophecy of ruin or prophecy of penitence. Research in the history of religious form might lead to even finer distinctions, but these two are the most important. The former aspect is found with Amos and Hosea, though they occasionally call the people to repentance, too (Amos v. 14ff., Hos. ii, xiv). With Isaiah and Jeremiah the latter aspect is found frequently: they try to move their people to repentance (Isa. i. 16ff., 27ff., viii. 16ff., Isa. vii – the name *Shear Yashub*, cf. Isa. x. 20ff., xiv. 32, xxx. 15, Jer. iv. 1ff. 14ff., v. 20ff., vi. 8ff., 16, vii. 3ff. and elsewhere), though they, too, lay the strongest stress on the prediction of a coming catastrophe.

So the prophets cannot be considered as preachers of doom only and it cannot be held that they broke practically with all the ancient religious forms concerning the history of salvation and looked upon salvation as a mere hope for the future.[1] This view is too one-sided, for at certain moments of their activity they represent the conversion of the people as decisive for their own days. From the beginning Isaiah strongly emphasizes the approaching doom (ch. vi), but he also speaks

[1] This one-sided view is maintained by G. von Rad, *Theology* II; according to him the prophets only see salvation in an eschatological perspective. This does not, however, make it clear how Isaiah can predict the downfall of Jerusalem but, on the other hand, also announces to the Assyrian king in 701 that his downfall is imminent.

of salvation; Jeremiah rather proceeds from the preaching of repentance to the prophecy of the complete downfall.

The miraculous element in the preaching of the prophets is that they predict the judgment upon their people without denying the relationship between God and Israel. With Isaiah the disastermotif is predominant; in his prophecies Yahweh condemns His people by calling them: 'this people', but He also frequently calls them 'my people' (cf.vi.9 with i.3); with Jeremiah we find that the latter appellation, 'my people' predominates to such an extent that K. Kutter could publish a book on Jeremiah under the title *Mein Volk* (1929). When the prophets predict God's wrath and judgment and yet cling to His love of Israel they know what they are speaking about. What makes their message so majestic is the fact that they can represent God Himself on the one hand as taking action against His people like a savage wild beast (Hos.xiii. 7f.) or a great warrior (Isa.xxviii. 21, xxix. 1ff.) and on the other hand as appealing to Israel to give Him her love. Fundamentally their message is always paradoxical, and Isaiah realized this very clearly, too (xxviii. 21ff.).

In their witness to God who takes action against Israel in His judgments they also maintain that He is the God of communion with Israel. Even when they predict the downfall of the people and the destruction of Jerusalem and the temple, as Jeremiah did, they do so fully convinced that Yahweh does not reject Israel but stands by His people (Jer.xxxi. 36).

So God's judgment as we find it predicted in the preaching of the prophets does not demonstrate that Yahweh breaks with His chosen people[1]; on the contrary, the prophets deny emphatically the conclusion arrived at by the people on the ground of their chastisement (cf. Jer.xxxiii. 19ff. with xxxi. 36ff., Isa.l. 1ff., Zech.i). Yahweh is incensed against His people, it is true, and He has punished them most severely for their unfaithfulness, but essentially this was only a temporary matter (Isa.xl. 1, l. 1ff.): God did not set out to destroy, but to renovate His people. Even the judgment He executes with His own hand is a token of His communion with Israel.

In the Old Testament the conception that God is a hidden God (a statement formulated clearly in Isa.xlv.15)[2] is not linked directly with the judgment that falls upon Israel[3]; on the contrary: in Isa.xlv this view refers to God's saving activity in the future.

It is clear that, however difficult the prophets must have found it

---

[1] See my *Erwählung des Volkes Israel*, 1953, pp.98ff. The idea of rejection does not play a part in the Old Testament equivalent with that of election.
[2] Cf. also Jer.xxiii. 23.
[3] As is apparently done by G. von Rad, *Theology* II, pp.374f., ThLZ, 1963, pp.405ff.

to integrate the message of judgment into their faith, they managed to do so after a prolonged struggle. It was, and always remained a miraculous activity, but as such it revealed His awe-in-spiring holiness (Isa. xxix). The Old Testament is full of the paradoxical message of the judgment of Israel's God, the God of salvation, and it is the historiographers who bear witness to it, especially the post-prophetic (deteuronomic and later) hisoriographers.

In contrast with the views of the non-Biblical nations, who look upon catastrophes as evidence of the imperfection of the gods (the Greeks) or of their unwillingness (Babylon), the Old Testament proclaims that these disasters arise from the will of the Holy God of grace, who desires to establish His kingdom in Israel and in the world. Generally speaking, human suffering and death may be looked upon as a judgment upon sin. They are neither an 'accident' of creation, nor a matter of chance, or obstinacy or even fate, *heimarmenè*[1], but a judgment of God, which is to restore communion with Him. This is shown very impressively in the Scriptural narrative of the Deluge. This story as it appears in the Old Testament purports to show that this most terrible of all catastrophes that befell mankind in primeval times was to establish a new relationship between God and the remnant of mankind saved by Him. The judgment upon which God had decided pained Him most grievously (Gen. vi. 5ff).

This shows how the Old Testament always presupposes a positive relation of God to the world: there is no contrast but, fundamentally from God's point of view, only a relationship of communion. This relationship is demonstrated very positively by the fact, that the Old Testament accepts a fundamental connection between the judgment and God's redemption[2] – it is often purifying and renewing. This is perhaps expressed most strongly in the Isaiah-apocalypse (xxvi.8ff.): 'When thy judgments are in the earth, the inhabitants of the world will learn righteousness' (verse 9.) Here the judgment has also acquired a pedagogic meaning.

Further the Old Testament always bears testimony to the *justice* of God's judgments. The prophets always attempt to make it clear in their testimony that the punishments inflicted by God completely fit the sins of the people (cf. instance Jer. ii. 5*b*); they also try to convince the people of the *foolishness of sin*, of the fact that it is something *unheard-of* (for example Isa. i. 2f.,; Jer. ii. 10ff.; Hos. xi. 1ff.), which demonstrates most clearly the guilt of the people. Then the

---

[1] To some extent K. Koch's views tend this way, in so far as he will not speak of retribution, but of a calamitous deed; see his *Gibt es ein Vergeltungsdogma im A.T.*, ZThK, 1955, pp. 1ff., also Von Rad, *Theology* I, pp.264ff.
[2] See p.191f.

people is always *warned* by God *beforehand* and is given an opportunity to *repent*.

God's judgment is never so severe that His punishment is fully in accordance with the gravity of the sin committed: He always shows His mercy in one way or another, there always remains a call to repentance and with it the possibility of repentance[1], and there is always a remnant that is saved. Even though some prophets consider the possibility of being saved problematical at a certain moment (Amos v.15, and elsewhere), yet they always keep hoping for a restoration (chapter ix).

At any rate God's judgment is not a sign of unwillingness, but rather of anger; anger does not exlude the possibility that there – still – is a relationship. God's holiness is a consuming fire and cannot bear the existence of sin; yet God desires that the sinner should be *saved*, which is expressed most clearly by Ezekiel (xxxiii. 11; xviii. 2 1ff.), Ezekiel who elsewhere, in order to bring out God's glory as the motive for all His acts, makes bold to say that God does not act thus for the sake of Israel, but to glorify His holy Name (xxxvi). In one of the most profound hymns of the Old Testament, Lamentations iii, written by an author deeply impressed by the exile, we hear the emphatic testimony: 'For He doth not afflict willingly nor grieve the children of men, for though He cause grief, yet will He have compassion according to the multitude of His mercies' (iii. 33 and 32); in other words, God must, in His holiness, intervene in the world with His judgments, but His real activity is the showing of His mercy.

The Old Testament always keeps proclaiming that, even in passing His judgment, God is merciful. This affection of God is expressed most profoundly by the prophet Hosea, who depicts God as divided against Himself, when 'mercy rejoiceth against judgment' and ultimately God's love prevails over His just anger (Hos.xi. 8f.; a related passage is Jer. iii. 19–iv. 4). Hence it is never the judgment that is allowed to have the last word in the prophecies, but always the hope of salvation; and the most critical preachers are also those who emphasize future salvation very strongly (cf. Hos. xiii. 7f. with chapter ii or xi, see Ezek. xvi).

That is why not a trace should be allowed to remain of the conception, or rather misconception, that the teaching of the Old Testament depicts a God quite different from the God of the New Testament. On the contrary, the God of the prophets, who fulminates against sin, but who is also distressed about the people because of the judgment

[1] See for example J. Fichtner, 'Die Umkehrung in der prophetischen Botschaft', *Th. Lit. Zt.*, 1953, pp. 459ff.; compare also H. W. Wolff, 'Das Thema "Umkehr" in der altt. Prophetie', *Zeitschr. f. Th. u. K.*, 1951, pp. 129ff.

He has to inflict upon it, the God of the narratives of primeval history, who deeply regrets His creation of man, this God, who is deeply moved, who as the Holy One proceeds with strict justice against sinful man and in doing so suffers most Himself, this same God sent Jesus Christ into the world to take its sins upon Himself and to suffer for them on the Cross. In the New Testament Jesus Christ attacks the sins of the people as strongly as the prophets had done in the Old Testament. He uses the threat of a coming judgment just as they had done; but to a greater extent than they He ventures personally into the struggle between God and man, so that the judgments falls upon Himself; therefore His death on the Cross is evidence of His never-ceasing love, which again is the sign of God's love. In all this Old Testament and New Testament are essentially one; the actual difference only concerns the way in which salvation is proclaimed, and it is this difference that makes the Christian speak of fulfilment (see above pp. 104ff.).

From this judgment it becomes apparent that God Himself is in this world; in His holiness nothing that happens on this earth eludes His observation (Ps. cxxxix) – and for that reason this glorious God who is Love Itself is also always leading man back to Himself in a true return of love, even by means of His judgments. Finally we should bear in mind the strongly conditional nature of the preaching of judgment, for fundamentally is it a threat to recall man from his evil ways. This conditional elements is illustrated very clearly by the little book of Jonah.[1]

d. God's saving activity in the future: the fulfilment of communion

The prophets whose message of judgment we discussed in the previous section were most deeply convinced of God's activity in history, both in the past in His saving acts on behalf of Israel and in their own days in the judgments which He brought about and which they had to announce. But at the same time they knew that they were called upon to speak of God's saving activity in the future. For the very reason that they believed that God would keep His faith with Israel, even in His chastisement which sometimes bewildered them by its severity, these prophets came to proclaim the hopes of a new Israel, of a new future for the people, a new kingdom of God, a new covenant. In many ways they handed on this message to their disciples.[2] It is inconceivable that they should have been prophets of

[1] See the note on p. 203.
[2] In contrast with the prophecies of doom, which were to be heard by the whole people, the message of hope of the prophets was addressed especially to their disciples,

woe only, for they were far too deeply convinced of the majesty of Israel's God and of the strong bonds linking Him with His people. With none of the prohets the message of salvation is lacking[1]; it cannot be denied, therefore, to the pre-exilic prophets, as is done by some scholars. There exists no inherent contradiction between the prophecies of doom and those of salvation, if we read them correctly. On the contrary, it is impossible to imagine that in Israel, where the relationship between God and the people is dominated to such an extent by a communal sense, any true Israelite believer could have abandoned hope altogether. For hope certainly is one of the vital elements of Israelite faith.[2]

That is why ever new hope springs up in the hearts of the faithful in Israel, even in the greatest tribulations. Yahweh, who determines the course of history, also controls the future and for that reason the future always lies open to Israel. One thing especially is never wanting in this hope of the future: the fulfilment of communion with God. In the New Kingdom man will be led by the Spirit of God to the experience of what living with God really means (Ezek. xxxvi. 26f., cf. Jer. xxxi. 31ff.).

Within the limits of this chapter we cannot attempt to show the great variety of Israel's hopes of the future. In our final chapter we shall revert to this subject and examine it in greater detail.

D. Other ways in which God reveals Himself

a. Introductory remark

God did not only reveal Himself to Israel by His personal presence and by His intervention in the course of historical events, but also in many other ways. The Old Testament speaks of various manifestations of the divine presence which can hardly or not at all be apprehended by us any more. Many of these are typically ancient-oriental in character and show that the Israelite outlook upon life and way of thought was utterly dissimilar from that of present-day man, or at any rate of western man in the twentieth century. Some of these manifestations may be understood more easily in other continents and civilizations. The idea, for instance, that the name is a representation of God is certainly connected with the intrinsic power attributed in the ancient East to the word and especially to the name. The belief that God reveals Himself in certain natural phenomena is to be seen against the background that the ancient Israelite was dependent upon

to the 'remnant that repents'. This should not make us think, however, that the prophets held both an 'esoteric' and an 'exoteric' doctrine.
[1] According to many scholars Amos might be an exception.
[2] J. Moltman, *Theologie der Hoffnung*,[2] 1965.

nature to a far greater extent than modern man is, and therefore felt more at one with the world because he felt that both the world and himself had been created by this God.

In this chapter various ways in which God made His presence known are discussed. They are only partly connected with each other, often not at all. Some of them are closely bound up with the realm of nature, others with personal life, others again with the cult.

There is only one subject regarding God's acts of revelation that will not be discussed here, namely the revelation which God grants by means of His Spirit and His Word to human beings who serve as intermediaries in revelation. For essentially the word revelation is given in this context a different meaning: here the point at issue is rather the content of the act of revelation, the message that is transmitted to man through the Word of God, through visions and oracles. This subject should be dealt with separately.

b. The revelation of God in natural phenomena

One of the forms of revelation that have become quite alien to our western religious ideas and yet play an important part in the Old Testament is that which connects the presence of Yahweh with natural phenomena, in particular with thunder and lightning, with wind and storm (Exod. xixf., Deut. iv, Judg. v. 4f., Pss. xviii, xxix, civ. 2ff., 1 Sam. vii. 10, 1 Kings xix). These and similar texts often serve as descriptions of epiphanies (see above, p. 190) and demonstrate the close link between Israel's God and these natural phenomena. They are not only looked upon as phenomena connected with the appearance of Yahweh, but also as characteristic of His Being, or at any rate of His manifestation of Himself. From 1 Kings xix. 11ff. we get the expression that in later days certain prophetic circles raised objections against such ways of representing God, but nevertheless they continued to influence Israel's faith up to a fairly late date (Hab. iii).

Israel shares these notions with the surrounding nations. In Ugarit and Mesopotamia similar representations are found regarding the appearance of Baal and Hadad. Not unjustly it is supposed (also on linguistic grounds) that Ps. xxix was originally a hymn of praise dedicated to Hadad and that it was taken over by Israel and adapted to the worship of Yahweh.

As a matter of fact, it is not impossible from a historico-religious point of view that in pre-Mosaic times the Kenites worshipped Yahweh as a mountain-, storm- and war-god. After the revelation to Moses and Israel's deliverance from Egypt the image and the nature of Yahweh were changed radically, so that the Yahweh in whom Israel believed in the post-Mosaic period had no more than a few traits in common with the original Yahweh of the Kenites. One of these traits may well have been the way in which Israel's God revealed Himself as the God of storm and lightning.

The fact that Israel held on to this notion for so long is obviously bound up with two things. In the first place there is the fact that to Israel the creation was very closely connected with God (though Israel certainly made a clear distinction between God and the world). The Israelite could think of man as created in the image of God, and conversely he could represent God in human shape; at cultic centres such as Bethel and Dan the image of a bull could be taken to be a divine symbol. No wonder, then, that a direct connection was thought to exist between God and what we call the great forces of nature.

In the second place we should bear in mind that wind, storm and lightning were exceptionally apt illustrations of the majesty and incomparableness of the divine, not only because of their grandeur but also owing to their suddeness. Wind, storm and lightning develop all at once and turn wherever they wish. It is not to be wondered at, therefore, that especially among Israel where the holiness of God's absolutely independent Being was stressed so strongly, these awe-inspiring natural phenomena could remain the symbols of the divine for such a long period, and that these representations were even found in critical prophetic circles.

Apart from these phenomena 'nature' has other means as well to reveal the glory of God. It proclaims the glory of God (Pss. xix, civ; Isa. vi. 3, xl), God's wisdom and His loving care (Job xxxviiiff., Ps. civ, cxlvii). The bond between God's Being and His creation is strong, one might almost say direct; not to such an extent, it is true, that the Israelite should have identified God with the world or with certain forces of nature, but believing that nature bore testimony to the wonders of God and to His love of the world. Wisdom is the foundation-stone of creation (Prov. viii), the world may be looked upon as the expression of the joy of God (Gen. i. 31).[1]

c. The *Kabod*, the glory and the *Shem*, the name, as manifestations of God.

We often find that God is said to manifest Himself in a blaze of fire (cf. Ps. l. 2f., but especially in the description of the theophany in Exod. xixf., Deut. ivf.). Closely connected with this is the notion of Yahweh's *Kabod* or glory. It is 'the radiating power of His Being' (Buber, see also p. 299) which appears as a radiant light. In Isa. vi it is said that the earth is full of His glory (hymn of the seraphim). It

[1] See also G. von Rad, *Aspekte alttestamentlichen Weltverständnisses*, Ev. Th., 1964, pp. 57ff.

seems as if the earth is seen from heaven as bathing in the splendour of His light.

It is especially in the later books that this 'glory' is considered an *independent manifestation* of Yahweh (see Ezek. i, iii. 23, viii. 4, ixff.), representing Him in the same way as other manifestations do (cf. *mal'akh Yahweh*, p. 209). It is one of the outwardly visible aspects of His Being.

It is associated in particular with the temple; it is found in a description of the temple (i Kings viii. 11); Ezekiel experiences in a vision how the *kabod* leaves the temple when the destruction of Jerusalem and the temple is near at hand (ixf.); but it returns when God restores Jerusalem and the temple (xliii. 1ff.). In the Priestly Code the *kabod* is also linked with the tabernacle (Exod. xl. 34); indeed, according to P the glory of God accompanies Israel all through the desert journey in a column of fire and cloud (Exod. xiii. 21ff. and elsewhere); by night it emanates light, by day it can only be distinguished by the cloud surrounding it.

The *kabod* is the symbolical expression of the full glory of God's nearness and at the same time it makes this Glory into something permanent without tying God down to a certain locality. It is a later theological way of representation, particularly in the Priestly Code[1] which expresses the communion of the Holy One with Israel as a people and was chosen on the one hand to maintain the glory of Yahweh fully and to keep Yahweh Himself from an immediate relationship with Israel (the *kabod* is enshrouded in a dark cloud) and on the other hand to be able to express the enduring contact between Yahweh and the people. In any case this view expresses the *praesentia realis* of Yahweh in the temple very directly, much more so than the *shem* (name) theology of Deuteronomy.

In the same way the *shem*, the *name of God*, can occur as something independent representing God, cf. Jer. vii, where the temple is the place that is called by God's name. By giving His name to the sanctuary in Jerusalem, He is there Himself and has made the temple His sanctuary, but this does not mean that He is contained within this temple. Yahweh is in heaven and all over the world, and yet He is in the temple in a particular way. It is especially the Deuteronomist who emphasizes this doctrine that the name of Jahweh dwells in the temple, evidently in order to create a distance between God Himself and the temple in this way.[2]

It is not only on this point that Deuteronomy gives a theological criticism of certain religious nationalistic elements, but also on others, such as the doctrine of ellection. In the days when Deuteronomy

[1] Cf. G. von Rad, *Studies in Deuteronomy* (Eng. trans., 1953), pp. 37ff.
[2] G. von Rad, loc. cit.

originated Israel's faith was based far too much on visible religous
signs, on the possession of the temple of Yahweh, as if this implied
that Yahweh's fate was linked with that of Israel (see Jer. vii. 1ff.).
Therefore the immediate connection between Yahweh and the temple
had to be replaced by a less direct relationship. The word *shem*, the
name, was extremely appropriate for the purpose, in so far as it
covers the person on the one hand but can also be considered distinct
from him on the other. Applied to Yahweh, the *name* can represent
Him fully, but is not to be identified with Him. We may suppose that
the influence of the message of the prophets lies at the bottom of this
subtle 'critical theology'.

d. *Mal'akh Yahweh*, the Messenger of Yahweh, and the
'Countenance of Yahweh'.

The Old Testament calls the *Messenger of Yahweh* (the 'angel of the
Lord') those manifestations or figures that come to human beings in
the name of Yahweh to carry His message or act among men in His
name (Exod. xxxiii). They may be represented as human beings
(Judges xiii), but also as angels (Gen. xxii), sometimes in both ways
within a single story (Judges xiii. 19f.). Whatever their appearance,
-they are God's messengers who as such represent Him, as the messengers in the ancient Eastern world (and ambassadors nowadays)
represent the King who has sent them.[1] In some narratives the names
of Yahweh and the 'Messenger of Yahweh' are used alternately
(Gen. xvi, xxi. 17ff., xxii; Exod. iii), while in other stories a clear distinction is made between Yahweh and His Messenger (Num. xxii;
Judges xiii). As the visible manifestation of God the Messenger may be
looked upon as being one with Him or as clearly distinct.[2] This
seems somewhat baffling to us, but apparently the difficulty was not
so great for the ancient Oriental, who could easily conceive of the
particular manifestation as acting independently and at the same
time maintain the unity of this particularization[3] with the divine
being. This conception may be connected with the fact that in the
Old Testament Yahweh can speak of Himself both in the singular and
in the plural (Isa. vi. 8, Gen. i. 26, iii. 22; as the people do, too: Num.

[1] Compare G. von Rad in *Th. Wb. z. N.T.*, I, pp. 75ff.; F. Stier, *Gott und seine Engel*,
1934; A. R. Johnson, *The one and the many in the Israelite conception of God*, Cardiff,
1942, pp. 8ff.; W. Baumgartner, 'Zum Problem des Jahwe-Engels', *Schweiz. Theol.
Umschau*, 1944, pp. 97ff.; R. Schärf, 'Die Gestalt des Satans im A.T.', in C. G. Jung,
Symbolik des Geistes, 1948, pp. 207ff., 297ff.; A. S. van der Woude, *De mal'ak Jahwe,
een godsbode*, NTT, 1963/4, pp. 1ff., and J. Lindblom, *Theophanies in holy places*, HUCA,
1961, pp. 101ff.
[2] This can lead to a difference in interpretation, see Isa. lxiii. 9 according to the
readings of the Masoretic text and the Septuagint.
[3] *Extensio* (Johnson, H. Wh. Robinson).

xxi. 22). Wheeler Robinson introduced theword *corporate personality* to denote this phenomenon.[1] We may further compare the connection of Yahweh with various localities: Mount Sinai, the temple, heaven; and also the fact that the ark is the symbol of Yahweh's presence and may also be identified with Yahweh (Num. x. 35). This unity of symbol and essence is found in many ways, throughout the Eastern world as well as in Israel, nor is it alien to our outlook upon life, as appears from the celebration of the Lord's Supper in the Christian Churches.

The *mal'akh Yahweh* is distinct from the Spirit *(ruach)* of Yahweh (see below, p.211ff.), because the *mal'akh* is rather a personal representation which proclaims or guides, whereas the Spirit is the power proceeding from Yahweh which takes possession of a man and moves him to action (1 Kings xxii. 21f.).

With the 'Countenance of the Lord' we find a phenomenon similar to what we discovered in the conceptions of the 'Angel of the Lord' and the 'Glory of God', namely that they are on the one hand identified with God, but are on the other hand also considered to be independent of Him. The face is the best means to come to know a person, and therefore it may well be employed to represent that person. This conception is also applied to God: the Countenance of the Lord reveals the essence of His Being and may represent God Himself. As such it may be a token of the revelation of God's merciful nearness, and conversely, to be hid from the face of God means the absence of contact with Him (Gen. iv. 14; cf. also Ps. civ. 29), It may, however, also be represented as an independent manifestation of God, cf. Exod. xxxiii. 14, Isa. lxiii. 9 (emended text).[2]

All things go to show that Israel struggled in many ways to express in a theologically justifiable manner both the real communion between God and man and at the same time the absolute holiness of God's Being.

In Israel's faith the intercourse between God and man is absolutely real; it manifests itself in various ways but it never commits God to man. God manifests Himself in many ways to all kinds of men, in various places, but this does not detract at all from the freedom of His divine Being, which even in these manifestations remains consistent with itself. In this light the various forms of the self-revelations of God in the Old Testament should be considered, both the directly personal and the active and more symbolical manifestations.

---

[1] Compare 'The Hebrew Conception of Corporate Personality', in *Werden und Wesen des Alten Testaments;* further in *Inspiration and Revelation in the O.T.*, 1946, p. 70 and elsewhere, cf. also Johnson, op. cit. Yahweh's arm and hand were also personified (Isa. lxiii. 5b. 12), and even His sword (Jer. l. 35ff.).
[2] Cf. F. Nötscher, *Das Angesicht Gottes schauen*, 1924; P. Dhrome, *L'emploi métaphorique des noms de partie du corps en hébreu et en accadien*, 1963, pp. 42ff.

E. Revelation as communication

Introductory remark

So far the one, divine, side of the self-revelation of God has been the subject of our inquiry. But, as we already observed before (p.177), revelation is viewed in the Old Testament in the light of communion; by revealing Himself God wishes to maintain communion with man and realize it ever more fully. For that reason God does not only show that He exists and is active, that He will come to man and even abide with him symbolically in the sanctuary, but He also enters into a real communion with man by inspiring Him with His Spirit, thus enabling him to do his work by the Spirit, by addressing him and giving him directions, or also by answering his questions.

So there is communication in various ways. The relationship sought after and posited by God is essentially reciprocal: it stirs people to move towards Him, to act for Him. He grants them knowledge of Himself; they are allowed to hear what He has decided on in His divine decrees and may turn to Him with their questions and their problems, their doubts and their hopes.

This is the full purpose of revelation: realizing the intercourse between God and man. God opens the way to Himself by His self-revelation, so that the world should manifest itself fully as His Kingdom. The ways in which God achieves this communication are widely different, and should therefore be discussed separately.

Successively we shall have to deal with:

1 The *ruach* (Spirit)
2a The Word
2b The *Torah*
3a The vision
3b The dream
4 Outward means (see also:– The priests, p.241).

1. The *ruach* (Spirit).[1]

This subject will serve very well as a transition from the theme discussed in the previous paragraphs to that of the subsequent sections. The *Spirit of God* could be discussed separately and given a chapter all to itself, or it might even be included in the foregoing, because the *ruach* has some traits in common with conceptions such as the *mal'akh* or the *shem*, in so far as they may represent Yahweh. On the other

---

[1] See, besides the theologies, P.Volz, *Der Geist Gottes*, 1910; J.H.Scheepers, *Die Gees van God en die gees van die mens in die O.T.*, 1960; D.Lys, *Ruach, Le Souffle dans l' A.T.*, 1962; A.R.Johnson, *The vitality*[2], 1964, pp.32ff.; Th.C.Vriezen, 'De Heilige Geest in het O.T.', in *De Spiritu Sancto*, 1964, pp.7ff.

hand, however, the *ruach* is connected so closely with the intermediaries of revelation dealt with in the next chapter, as well as with the Word, discussed in this section, that the subject demands, as it were, a place at the beginning of this new section. By the *ruach* man is pressed into the service of God and enabled to perform God's work; it prepares him to receive the revelation of God and brings him to appear in the name of God, through his words or his actions.

The *ruach* brings about a direct communion between God and man and this results in human activity authorized by God rather than in co-operation with God. But this communion may be imagined to take place on widely different levels. In the full sense of the word, having the *ruach Yahweh* (or *'Elohim*) may indicate inspiration by God, but it may also be regarded on a biological level. There is also a universal human possession of the *ruach Yahweh*, but in most cases the *ruach* produces a highly personal effect. The Spirit always belongs to God, so that it can never become the property of man, although possession of the *ruach* may sometimes be more than momentary: it may be lasting, which makes the *ruach*, mostly rather transitory in nature, resemble to some extent 'gratia infusa', in which God can allow others to participate as well (Num. xi).

The *ruach* causes a link, a unity, between God and man, without leading to any kind of identification. For that reason the *ruach* can express the paradoxical nature of the communion between God and man better than any other spiritual phenomenon. It can allow the unity of the two partners to function and at the same time keep the two partners separated.

The fact that the *ruach* is 'intermittent' (Eichrodt) or better perhaps, charismatic is always expressed emphatically.

The word *ruach*, which has many secular meanings, such as: wind, breath, passion, thought, the self, (and which may therefore also represent the person) implies this possibility. In daily life *ruach* denotes the *wind* that goes wherever it chooses and no one knows whence it comes (John. iii. 8, Prov. xxx. 4, Eccles. xi. 5, viii. 8, Job xxxviii. 24, Ps. cxxxv. 7b), or the *breath* of the nostrils (the organ of the *ruach* is the *nose*, as is also apparent from the related words *reach*-smell, the verb *heriach* – to smell ond the expression *ruach af* – breath of the nose, so the breath exhaled through the nose), or also the *life* of man, but especially his *emotions*, his *inner self*. It is particularly suited to express the dynamic, the emotional, the will and the personal.

Used with regard to God, either in the form of *ruach Yahweh* or as the *ruach'Elohim* or occasionally as *(ha)ruach*, the dynamic character is emphasized strongly, too, and in widely different ways: as an external force or as a strong inward activity. The *ruach Yahweh* may manifest itself as a violent storm of wind, but also as a seething power inspiring people and prompting them to perform tremendous deeds, or as a power that overwhelms the entire emotional life of man. But the creative activity of the artist and even man's spontaneous life is due to the operation of the Spirit, too.

In many fields of life the Israelite experiences the operation of the *ruach Yahweh*.[1] He knows that he owes his existence as a living being to the Spirit of God; his breath is the *ruach Yahweh*. The cosmos as such is not pervaded by the Spirit of God (for it was not created through the *ruach* but through the word of God). But again and again God demonstrates His active presence through the *ruach* in history and in the lives of human beings, when He imparts His Spirit to man in a special way at difficult moments in the life of the people and fits a man for the task of delivering his people (the 'great' judges), when He inspires prophets with His Spirit to such an extent that they are thrown into ecstasies and see visions, when He makes artists do creative work in His service, and finally when He renovates the heart of man and cleanses it of sin through the Spirit and opens perspectives of a future that will bring God and man together in His kingdom in a perfect communion. The *ruach Yahweh* as an *extensio* of God brings about a unity of God and man without deifying man.

All these various operations of the *ruach Yahweh* (*'Elohim*) did not manifest themselves simultaneously or to the same extent. In the earliest period of Israel's history the powerful aspect of the *ruach* predominates, but in the period of judgment and downfall (exile) it is rather the cleansing aspect that comes into the foreground. Here, too, a spiritual growth manifested itself in the course of history.

The earliest stories concerning the operation of the *ruach*, in the books of Judges and Samuel deal with two things: the activities of the charismatic judges (Othniel: Judges iii. 10; Gideon: vi. 34; Jephthah: xi. 29; Samson: xiii. 25, xiv. 6, 19, xv. 15) and the work of the extatic prophets (1 Sam. x, xix. 18ff., Num. xi. 24ff. and xxiv. 3ff.).

In the books of the 'classical' prophets the operation of the Spirit is only mentioned occasionally (cf. Mic. iii. 8).[2] Ezekiel is the only prophet who mentions the *ruach* distinctly ([ii. 2], iii. 12, 14, 24, viii.

---

[1] Apart from the history of Joseph, the *ruach Yahweh* does not figure in the patriarchal narratives, nor in those parts of the Pentateuch that deal with the laws (except in the data concerning the *building* of the tabernacle). To non-Israelites the *ruach* is not granted (the only exception is Balaam, Num. xxiv. 2, but we should bear in mind the statement of xxiv. 1 that Balaam was guided by what pleased Yahweh); it is not even granted to Cyrus in Deutero-Isaiah, however much Cyrus is looked upon as the deliverer of the people (in spite of 2 Chron. xxxvi. 22 = Ezrah i. 21). Possession of the *ruach* presupposes perfect harmony between man's inner life and God.

[2] If *ruach* is original and not *koach*, which could be considered the alternative reading (in fact superfluous beside *geboera*).

3, xi. 1, xliii. 5) but here the Spirit only brings about the physical displacement of the prohets. It is true that in Hosea ix. 7 the prophet is called pre-eminently 'the spiritual man', but it is not clear whether this expression is only employed to denote the false ecstatic prophets, or (which is more likely) that it is intended to refer to the character of prophets in general.[1] Only once, in Ezekiel xi. 5, do we find the *ruach Yahweh* mentioned in connection with being granted a revelation, but the two latest commentators[2] consider this verse spurious. If this should be the case, the only words of revelation in the pre-exilic books due to the inspiration of the *ruach* would those ascribed to Balaam (Num. xxiv) and to the prophets of Ahab 1 Kings xxii. 19–25).[3]

Quite otherwise in post-exilic books (cf. 2 Chron. xv. 1, xx. 14, xxiv. 20, Neh. ix. 30 and Zech. vii. 2), where the inspiration of the *ruach* and the Word of God are without hesitation immediately connected with each other. In pre-exilic times it was different (except with Micah?), for in those days the operation of the Spirit is connected with ecstasy rather than with speaking the Word of God (false prophets and Balaam). From other utterances, such as Jeremiah's criticism of prophets of his own days (cf. xxiii. 13ff., esp. 23ff.) it has become apparent that 'classical' prophets of Yahweh were very much afraid that what proceeded from the mind of man would be mixed up with what came from the Spirit of God. A *ruach* may also be a *lying Spirit* (1 Kings xxii. 21ff.; cf. a similar criticism in postexilic times in Zech. xiii. 1ff.).

Both in the later historical narratives and by Ezekiel an operation of the *ruach Yahweh* by which a human being is taken up and displaced is mentioned (1 Kings xviii. 12, 2 Kings ii. 16 and the texts from Ezekiel mentioned above); in most of these cases the experience resembles being carried away by a tornado, certainly in 2 Kings ii. 16[4]; in other cases we cannot be certain whether the prophet was suddenly compelled or carried away by violence: Ezekiel iii. 14 reminds us of the former, and this is also possible in the case of 1 Kings xviii. 12.

Texts such as these make it clear that until a late date (Ezekiel) the activity of Yahweh is experienced in what we call the field of nature. Mighty gusts of wind are the result of Yahweh's activity, and even of Yahweh's voice (Ps. xxix). The idea of the appearance of Yahweh in the days of Israel's deliverance is evident not only from Exod. xix but also from 1 Kings xix.[5]

[1] Cf. that the prophet is elsewhere called expressly 'man of God', too (this expression is used only once of a *ma'lakh*, elsewhere always of prophets or of figures looked upon as prophets, cf. e.g. L. Köhler, *Lexicon* s.v. *ish ha'elohim*). [2] W. Zimmerli and G. Fohrer.
[3] Both in 2 Sam. xxiii. 2 and in Ps. xxxiii. 6 the *ruach Yahweh* probably means: the spoken Word of God.
[4] Here *ruach Yahweh* should certainly be translated by 'a whirlwind impelled by Yahweh'; most of the texts in Ezekiel seem to point in the same direction.
[5] Cf. the commentaries of Zimmerli, *Ezekiel* and J. Gray, *Kings*, l.c.

No wonder that the operation of the *ruach Yahweh* is connected with the wind again and again. (Gen. iii. 8, Num. xi. 31, Ps. xviii. 8, 11, 16, civ. 3, Amos iv. 3, Jonah i. 4, iv. 8). The *ruach Yahweh* (*'Elohim*) keeps in check the waters of the *tehom*, the primeval flood (Gen. i. 2, viii. 1 f.; cf. Exod. xv. 8ff.).[1] The *ruach'elohim* does not figure independently at the creation and is not thought to have mingled with the primeval waters. The creation as such is not a mixture of the divine and the natural; the *ruach 'elohim merachephet*, moved upon, circled over the waters of the chaos, to watch them as an eagle would watch the nest with his eaglets. Gen. i. 3ff. does not show any trace of the *ruach 'elohim* in God's creative activity.[2]

Nowhere is the *ruach* found operating independently or hypostacised.[3]

So the *ruach* was not looked upon as independent or creative, nor was it thought to be part of nature as such, but the *ruach Yahweh* is granted by God to men and animals, so to animated nature which can move and act spontaneously; the *ruach* is a divine gift that belongs to men and animals as long as they live; after their death it returns to God (cf. Gen. vi. 3, 17, vii. 15, 22; Job xxxiii. 4, xxvii. 3, cf. xxxii. 8, Ps. civ. 29f., Eccles. xii. 7, cf. iii. 19, 21). *Ruach* has the meaning of vital energy and may be looked upon as something permanent. God is simply *ruach* (Isa. xxxi. 3; the word *ruach* is contrasted here with *basar* the flesh, as something transitory), and for that reason He is the everlasting One. In this participation in the *ruach* of God, manifesting itself in the spontaneous vital force, we find something similar to what we see in the ancient-oriental world, for there, too, both the Babylonians and the Egyptians the vital force is considered to be of divine origin.[4]

[1] In this connection we must, I think, say that by the *ruach'elohim* of Gen. i. 2 is meant the wind that God had sent; compare Job xxvi. 12 (and also *Enuma elish* IV 42ff., 131f.) with Gen. 1. 2, especially Eusebius, *Preparatio Evangelica* I, X, 1, for instance in E. H. Gifford's edition, I, III, Oxonii 1903, where Philo Byblius is quoted who says that in the primeval age there was not only a damp chaos but also wind. The Israelite author supposed God to have been present before the creation and expressed this by means of the *ruach'elohim*.
[2] With respect to the Old Testament the function of the *ruach* is not comparable to that of the *chokhmah*, which was watching at the creation of the world, as Prov. viii has it, and which did not play an active part either! It was not until much later that *ruach* and *chokhmah* were linked as independent entities and identified more or less (Sap. Salomonis i. 6ff., vii. 22ff., xii. 1ff.; we may compare (as H. Gese did, RGG³, VI, 1576) Jesus Sirach xxiv. 3 and Gen. i. 2.
[3] Not even in Isa. lxiii. 10f.; cf. P. van Imschoot, *Théologie de l' A.T.*, I, *loc. cit.*, and elsewhere. See also my essay in *De Spiritu Sancto*, pp. 7ff. With respect to Job. iv, where a *ruach* appears to Eliphaz and speaks a word of revelation, we might think of a substantivation of the *ruach 'elohim*, but the description is doubtful; som escholars translate: 'Hauch' (F. Horst, *loc. cit.*; on the ruach ra'ah me'et Yahweh, 1 Sam. xvi. 14, see below p. 304.
[4] In Ichnathon's hymn to Aton (final verse) the sun is the source of vital energy; in Mesopotamia it is the *sharu*, the wind or breath of one of the gods; cf. J. Hehn, *Zum Problem des Geistes im alten A.T.*, ZAW 1925, pp. 296ff.

Besides power, ecstasy and life the *ruach 'Elohim (Yahweh)* also grants *wisdom*. This emerges most clearly in the later literature. It is true that from early times wisdom in the interpretation of dreams and judicial wisdom had been associated with God (2 Sam. xiv; cf. 1 Kings iii and x, Isa. xxviii. 5 and Gen. xli. 38); explicitly wisdom in connexion with the *ruach Jahweh* is found in the pre-exilic literature only in Isa. xi. 2 and Gen. xxxxi. 38; cf. also Job iv. 15f., xxxii. 8; Neh. ix. 20f., cf. Ps. cxliii. 10; especially clear are the texts Exod. xxxi. 1–6, xxxv. 30ff., cf. xxviii. 3, from the Priestly Code, where *ruach 'Elohim* and wisdom (craft) are associated.[1]

An especially important part is played by the *ruach Yahweh* in the hopes of salvation in the Old Testament, especially with the two Isaiahs, with Ezekiel and with Joel. The time of salvation which they see coming is brought about by the *ruach Yahweh*. It renovates the world, it changes the inner man, makes him share in God's gifts of grace and allows him to experience communion with God. Each of the prophets forms his own idea of the time of salvation. Isaiah looks upon the messianic king as the bearer of the Spirit of Yahweh, which bestows upon him all the gifts that he needs in his high office: wisdom and understanding, counsel and might, knowledge and the fear of the Lord (Isa. xi. 1ff.). Ezekiel depicts the age of salvation as the epoch of the great change in the heart of the people, when the Spirit of God will make man obedient to His will and bring about a lasting communion (xi. 19, xxxvi. 26f., xxxvii. 14); here the spirit is the re-creating vital principle.[2] With Deutero-Isaiah we find both these views: the messianic expected ruler (xlii. 1ff., lxi. 1ff.), who guided by the Spirit of God, will accomplish the kingdom of salvation among those who are afflicted and are looking forward to His kingdom, as well as the personal renovation that will be achieved and will manifest itself in the restoration of communion with God (xliv. 3ff., cf. lix. 21 and xxxii. 15b). Joel proclaims in the exuberant manner of the ecstatic prophets that in the age of salvation the Spirit shall be poured out upon all flesh (cf. Num. xi. 29) and shall grant dreams and visions. However different the manner, it is quite clear that the prophets expect that the intervention of the *ruach Yahweh* will cause a radical change.

Besides ancient salvation-motifs (strength, prosperity, wisdom) two things stand out in these eschatological hopes: the element of communion with God (perhaps recalling ecstatic prophecy) and that of the sanctifying power of the *ruach*. The latter in particular seems to be a new element.

[1] Indeed, the association of the deity with wisdom is a very ancient element in the East. Cf. also Gen. ii, the tree of the knowledge of good and evil (= supreme wisdom) as the divine tree, etc.

[2] In 1 Sam. x. 6 it is said, too, that the Spirit turns Saul into another man.

Outside the prophetic books we find this element expressed quite strongly in Ps. li, where the word *ruach* is used four times (12–14 and 19). The links with the exilic *ruach* – hopes are clear[1], so that this Psalm is rightly assigned to this or the early exilic period.[2] Since the major prophets gave their prophecies of hope, the Spirit of God had been mentioned frequently in post-exilic times, cf. Hag. ii. 4f. (western translations 5f.) and Zech. iv. 6. We already mentioned other texts from Zech. viii, 2 Chronicles and Nehemiah. In this connection Zech. iv. 6 is of especial importance. Here the prophet states emphatically that it is only the Spirit of God that must operate and can achieve renovation – here the Spirit (looked upon as identical with God) is contrasted with force and violence and the older conception, according to which these elements go hand in hand, is broken with.

After a period in which a hesitant attitude was taken up towards the *ruach* (the pre-exilic classical prophets), faith in the *ruach* revived in new forms during and after the catastrophe of the exile. The Spirit is not only experienced as a force proceeding from God that grants might or wisdom, but as a force that re-creates the inner man, and prepares man for life in communion with God. No wonder, then, that we see the hopes of the Spirit of God reviving again and again in later religious revivals among the Jews, such as the apocalyptic movement, the Qumran sect and the earliest Christian community.

2a. The Word

Though we may say that the word most generally used to denote Revelation in the Old Testament is the word *chazon* (i.e. seeing, a vision)[3] we must not conclude that the granting of visions etc. is the proper way of revelation in the Old Testament (see pp. 227f.). On the contrary, the revelation of God in the Old Testament is mainly revelation by the Word. Köhler is quite correct in pointing out in his *Theologie*[4] that all the appearances are speaking appearances; the appearance in itself is therefore never sufficient but it is accompanied by the word. The visual element passes away, the Word is enduring. This revelation by visions is revelation by the Word, too.

The message of the prophets is nearly always introduced by the words: '*Thus saith Yahweh*', or concluded with '*saith the Lord*'. What God gives to the porphet is a *word (dabar* or *'imrah)*.

That the message to the prophet is a word is clearly evident for

[1] Cf. vs. 19 with Isa. lvii. 15, and 12–14 with Ezek. xxxvi. 25f.
[2] see also H. J. Kraus, *Psalmen* I, p. 384.
[3] Cf. Isa. i. 1.
[4] p. 87; this view was developed in a too one-sided manner by Rendtorff in: W. Pannenberg, *Geschichte als Offenbarung*.

instance from Hab. ii. 1–5.[1] Habakkuk is, probably not incorrectly, taken to be a temple-prophet, awaiting the word of God in his 'watch', he will 'watch to see what he will say unto me' (verse 1b), and 'the Lord answered me and said, Write the vision, and make it plain upon tables, that he may run that readeth it'. It is clear that there the vision is a message, a word of God, probably contained in ii. 4 or ii. 4 and 5.

When Ezekiel is told to eat a book-roll (ch. iii) this points to the same verbal character of his vision. Indeed, the prophets nearly always supplement their message of revelation with preaching. In the prophetic writings revelation and preaching are often interwoven (this clearly applies to Ezekiel and Deutero-Isaiah as well as to Jeremiah).[2]

All through the course of history the Word of God accompanies the life of the people. Already in the earliest historical narratives the Word of God intervenes decisively and leads to the knowledge of the will of God. Already in the work of the Yahwist but particularly in deuteronomic historiography the events are always preceded by the Word of God that dominates history.[3] In the ancient stories of David, too, the Word of God plays a decisive part: through the priest (1 Sam. xxiii. 9ff., 2 Sam. v. 18ff.) or the prophet (i.a. Nathan a.o. cf. 2 Sam. vii. 12) the Word of God is communicated to David at important moments. At critical moments the kings can always count on God's guidance through the words of the prophets. The Chronicler develops this conception; according to him there is a prophet standing behind each of the kings, intervening in history by the Word. So from first to last, from Abraham till the foundation of the temple after the exile, the historical narratives of the Old Testament are interwoven with traditions of revelations through the Word that were received. In all the historical sources we are confronted with this same phenomenon, which demonstrates the extreme importance attached in Israel to this form of relationship between God and His people.

That God has always come to His people with His Word shows how He keeps His faith in His intercourse with His people. When He refuses to speak it is a clear sign of His wrath (1 Sam. iii. 1, Ps. lxxiv. 9).

His Word of Revelation always aims at the salvation of man or the people and *can never* be ambiguous, let alone misleading, so as to lead man into uncertainty or even lead him astray, as we do find else-

---

[1] See above p. 73f.
[2] See H. Wildberger, *Jahwewort und prophetische Rede bei Jeremia*, 1942, and B. Gemser, 'Vertraagde openbaringsbewustheid', *N(ed.) Th. T.* XV, 1960–1, pp. 241ff.
[3] G. von Rad, *op. cit.* pp. 52ff., cf. M. Noth, *Überlieferungsgeschichtliche Studien*, 1943, pp. 5f.

where in the ancient world with respect to divine instructions and oracles.[1] The Old Testament contains one text that speaks of a misleading instruction given by God (Ezek.xx.25f.) where the prophet thinks of the demand for the sacrifice of the first-born, even of the first-born child (Exod.xxii.29); he can apparently consider this revelation only as a chastisement by God – so that it must be viewed in the light of stories such as the hardening of the heart of Pharaoh or of Israel, Ps. lxxxi.13, or 2 Sam.xxiv.1, Isa.vi.10, etc.[2] This text of Ezek.xx.25 is, however, also a clear example of a criticism within the Old Testament itself of certain ancient institutions.[3]

But apart from this text in Ezekiel there appears to be a consciousness of the sufficiency and the importance for life of God's revelation in the Old Testament. Israel knew that it was particularly blessed by God's word of revelation over and above the heathen nations all around; we have in mind here a text such as Deut.iv.8: 'And what nation is there so great, that hath statutes and judgments so righteous as all this law which I set before you this day?' or the praise of the law (or, perhaps, rather of the Word of God) in Pss.xix.8ff. and cxix.

This revealing Word does not only proclaim salvation, but also brings it near and actualizes it.[4] The revelation of God is *efficax*, it effects something (Ps.xix.8f.). This is particularly evident from the prophetic words that are followed by their fulfilment, though we must not think that God could not retract His words: God's word may be dynamic but that does not mean that it is magical.

From Deutero-Isaiah we hear the famous words: 'So shall my word be that goeth forth out of my mouth: it shall not return unto me void, but it shall accomplish that which I please, and it shall prosper in the thing whereto I sent it' (lv.11).

The word works among men (cf. Jer.xxviii.17 and all the stories that show how the word of the prophets was fulfilled, for example Isa.xxxvi.ff., the story of Elijah, Ezekiel iv.f., xxiv, xxxiii.21ff.; cf. also Deut.xviii.22, where the actualization of a Word of God is looked upon as the criterion of its truth); being the Word of the Creator, it is connected both with God's creative and with His

[1] Compare the stories of the Greek historians about the obscurity of the oracles of Delphi; and W.Kristensen, *De goddelijke bedrieger*, 1928, and J.P.B. de Josselin de Jong, *De oorsprong van den goddelijken bedrieger*, 1929.
[2] Cf. pp.305ff. The author of Deut.iv.19 (Yahweh gave the nations the gods of nature that are forbidden to Israel) probably did not go so far; he is concerned rather with bringing out the rejection of those nations over against the election of Israel. Compare on this also pp.306ff. and particularly 315f.
[3] For other critical observations see e.g. Amos v.25 and Jer.vii.22.
[4] See also p.20, and cf. the fine essay by W.Barnard on 'Liturgie en Drama', in *Kerk en Eeredienst*, 1952, particularly pp.86ff.

sustaining activity.[1] One should bear in mind here the importance of the Word of God in the history of the partriarchs; there the Word of God again and again precedes the event, introduces it, and even brings it about; cf. Gen.xii. 1ff., xvi. 10ff., xxv. 23, xxxvii. 5ff., etc. And therefore it is heard again and again at decisive moments in history, according to the later historical books of Israel, as was demonstrated by M. Noth.[2]

Where God's acts are announced in prophecy this is done so positively by the prophets that they represent things as if they had already come to pass. Consequently the prophets use the so-called *'prophetic perfect'* for their prophecies – this is actually neither a *perfect* nor a *future*, but an expression of a positive fact.

As we remarked above, this does not mean that the Word of God functions magically and that it is realized without more ado once it has been pronounced. God's Word is never *heimarmenè* or *fatum*, for God always retains control of it. It remains in His power, He can take it back or carry it into effect. God can relent, He can revoke the word of the prophet and answer a prayer. Not because a prayer ot the intercession of someone else could be some kind of counter-force that may be opposed to God's power, but because God is and remains God in this respect too, that even His Word is absolutely dependent upon Him and that He remains completely free to dispose of it as He wishes. God can even 'repent' and 'turn back' (cf. p. 316). This is connected with the fact, already mentioned above several times, that God's Word, God's revelation always has man's salvation in view, that it is meant to bring about communion with man, to renovate and vivify.[3] After all, the issue is not whether the Word is fulfilled literally as it was spoken, but that the higher, more profound aim with which it was spoken, is attained.

The communion between God and man is a living relationship; there is intercourse between God and man, and therefore this relationship remains eternally changeable, even more so, we may say, than a relationship between one man and another. And the living character of this communion makes it necessary that momentary decisions should be renewed again and again, so that God may realize His will by entering into the demands of a new situation and a renewed

---

[1] Cf. for example L. Dürr, *Die Wertung des göttlichen Wortes im Alten Testament und im alten Orient*, 1938.
[2] See *Überlieferungsgeschichtliche Studien*, 1943, p. 5f.; this applies to the deuteronomic historians who have the judge or the prophet address the people with a message from God at critical moments in the history of the people (Deut. 1ff., Josh. i, xxiv, Judges ii, 1 Sam. xii, cf. 1 Kings viii.
[3] Though it is also possible to emphasize, as in Ezekiel xxxvi, God's holiness rather than man's salvation.

relationship with man. Thus God's 'inconstancy' in the Old Testament is a sign of God's love of and fidelity to man, and evidence of His omnipotence to do as He pleases. This 'inconstancy' of God as an expression of His affection and His freedom is the strongest sign of His merciful Majesty. His relationship with man is therefore thoroughly personal.

We must always bear this in mind in connection with the problem of the unfulfilled prophecies[1], it is clear that these exist, and not only in the sense of prophecies that were not fulfilled literally or that have not been realized yet, but also in the sense of prophecies that have not been fulfilled and cannot be fulfilled because the actual course of events proved to be different from what the porphets had predicted[2], for instance Huldah's prophecy about Josiah (2 Kings xxii. 19f.), that by Jeremiah about Jehoiakim (Jer. xxii. 19), and that by Ezekiel about Tyre (cf. Ezek. xxvii ff. and xxix. 17–21).[3] We need not make a long argument about it, as has often been done: people have either hunted diligently for unfulfilled prophecies in order to deny the authority of the prophetic message, or thought they could deny the fact from apologetic considerations in order to maintain the authority of the profetic message. With Volz[4] we must point out that the prophets were the human bearers of the Word of God, who sometimes predicted things in their prophetic teaching which God did not fulfil in that way; in particular we shall have to point out, with W. Eichrodt[5], that the prophets were not, and did not want to be, prophesiers in the proper sense of the word; they could even take back their words (Ezek. xxix. 17ff.; Isa. xvi. 13f.), for first and foremost they were the proclaimers of the Will of God[6], they did not prophesy as soothsayers, but as those who 'had to give an ever clearer picture to the faithful of the end of God's ways, the purpose of all His dealings with His people', and thus they guided 'the people through the mystery of history' (Eichrodt). For that reason neither the fundamental truth nor the untruth of the prophetic message should be made to depend upon its literal fulfilment. Though it is true that in the Old Testament the literal fulfilment of a prophecy is esteemed very highly (see above, p. 219), yet on the other hand it is evident from Deut. xiii. 1f. that the fulfilment of a

[1] See E. Jenni, *Die politischen Voraussagen der Propheten*, 1956.
[2] A. Kuenen, *De profeten en de profetie onder Israel*, I–II, 1875; P. A. Verhoef, *Die vraagstuk van die onvervulde voorzeggingen* (Isa. i-xxxix), doctorate thesis Free University, 1950. See also G. C. Aalders, *De profeten des Ouden Verbonds*, 1918, pp. 34ff., 175ff. and n. 1.
[3] See the commentaries by Hermann, Bertholet, Fohrer, and Zimmerli.
[4] *Prophetengestalten*, 1938, p. 24.
[5] *Israel in der Weissagung des A.T.*, 1951, p. 12; W. Zimmerli in *Ev. Theol.*, 1952, pp. 46f.
[6] Cf. also Wheeler Robinson, *Inspiration*, p. 185.

prophetic message does not always mean that it is also reliable; in other words, the content, too, must demonstrate the reliability of the prophetic message. This is also stated most emphatically by Jeremiah. The standard he applies, apart from the reliability of the men themselves, particularly the question whether they are prepared to place God's name above everything (xxiii. 25ff.), or follow the desires of their own hearts and the wishes of the people; in ch. xxviii. 8ff. this amounts to the question whether they predict judgment or salvation.

It is impossible to establish the truth of the message of the prophets on external grounds[1]; what is essential is the spiritual content of their message, in other words the question whether their teaching is in agreement with God's will and has sprung from His Spirit.

The Word of God may come to the prophets in widely different ways either as the accompaniment of a 'vision' or directly; it may come as the answer to a prophet's prayer or entirely unexpectedly. It is impossible to give a rule for the way in which a prophetic message is received. In the earlier period (as still with Elisha, 2 Kings iii) the revelation apparently comes especially when the prophet has been brought into a kind of trance, though in the case of Nathan, for instance, we do not find anything of the sort. In the case of the later prophets we no longer perceive any signs that they had been brought into a special state of mind. They see something, sometimes something quite ordinary (Am. viii: a basket of summer-fruit; Jer. i: an almond branch in bloom), sometimes also something rather exceptional (Am. vii. 4ff.); but it is always accompanied by an explanatory word. The prophets are quite clearly aware that God has given them a definite message. In what way this was done is not known; it has been assumed that mystical experiences played a part here, either ecstasy of the indwelling of God, but the prophets never mention such supernatural experiences: on the contrary, we find (with the major Scriptural prophets, at any rate) that a clear distinction was made between 'the inspiring divine element and the receiving human subject and the contingent way in which the revelation is communicated'.[2] Man is confronted personally with God, who speaks His word to the prophet. This serves to indicate a most intimate communion between God and His people, of which the Israelite witnesses to God's revelation were conscious.

The word as an element of revelation bears witness to the direct personal relationship between God and man as well as to the spiritual

[1] Compare now also Quell, op. cit., and my 'Die Hoffnung im A.T.', *Th. Lit. Zt.*, 1953, p. 582.
[2] I. P. Seierstad, *Die Offenbarungserlebnisse der Propheten Amos, Jesaja und Jeremia*, Oslo, 1946, p. 195.

nature of this relationship. By the word the deepest feelings of one man can find an echo in the heart of another, even without any physical manifestation or contact,[1] although, of course, a gesture or personal presence may strengthen the impression created by the word. This proof of the spiritual importance of the word, which as a phenomenon is as great a secret as life itself and which may be considered the essential feature of man's spiritual life. To an even greater degree than the modern Westerner the Oriental of ancient times was impressed by the importance of the word; he would never have called the word *'nur Schall und Rauch'* (mere sound and fury); to his mind it is something laden with power. And finally the word allows the possibility of maintaining distance; for the word as a means of conveying spiritual experiences and feelings may be used in any relationship between one spiritual being and another; for the mutual understanding of a word the speaker and the hearer need not have the same status in life; the word as such leaves the difference in level completely intact.

For that reason the word as a means of revelation is in the closest harmony with the spirit of the whole of the Old Testament religion of revelation, which lays equal stress on the communion and the distance between God and man; it is therefore not to be wondered at that it should stand in the focal point of the intercourse between God and man in the Old Testament.

2b. The Torah[2]

The revelation by the Word, like the revelation by the Spirit, is strongly spiritual and personal in character and may come so unexpectedly and vehemently that the prophet Amos (iii.8) could compare it to the roaring of a lion. Besides this, however, there also exists a more continuous contact, in which God replies to a prophet's question, either directly, Jer.xiv.f., or after some delay, Hab.ii.1f., Jer.xlii.7. But over and above this revelation by the word there is also a 'rather more official and formal' relationship between God and man, in which Yahweh expresses His will to man with respect to a particular case of human action. When man is uncertain how to act in things of daily ethical, ritual, or juridical life he can receive 'instructions' *(torah)* from God; for that purpose he goes to the priest or the prophet and asks for a decision in the name of God in a particular matter.

[1] A.Heschel, *Die Propheten*, 1936, and *The Prophets*, 1962, says that the prophets share in God's *pathos*; in fact we need not think here of a mystical relationship, as it can be explained from the revelation by the *word*.
[2] Compare G. F. Moore, *op. cit.*, I, pp. 263ff.; *Th. Wb. z. NT.*, IV, pp. 1029ff; J. Begrich, 'Die priesterliche Thora', in *Werden und Wesen des A.T.*, Beih. *Z.A.W.*, 66, 1936; G. Östborn, *Tora in the O.T.*, Lund, 1945; see also above p. 117.

Such an interrogation of the *torah* is depicted in I Sam. xxiii.9, where David has the priest Abiathar, who has brought the *'efod* with him, consult God. It is true that the giving of *torah* is not mentioned but this case may certainly be included here. In Hag. ii. 12–14, we also find the asking of *torah*, 'Ask now the priests concerning the law' (English versions, verse 11); here *torah* is given directly by the priests.

Torah is the instruction, teaching, given by God to His people through the intermediary of the priests. Very probably *torah* means in the first place 'indication' ('hint'), namely as to what should be done in a particular case; and secondly 'instruction'. *Torah* can be given by the priest with respect to matters of ritual, juridical problems, and historical or personal difficulties; and also, for that matter, by the prophet (Isa. i. 10, viii. 16, 20; xxx. 9). It is also used to denote the instruction given by the teachers of wisdom (Prov. xiii. 14); here the religious background of wisdom is clearly hinted at. That God gives *torah*, i.e. that God is willing to concern Himself with man's personal problems of life or with formal difficulties occurring in the fulfilment of official duties among the people, is an added proof of the communion with God of which people are conscious.

In Israel the *torah* replaces all forms of oracles found among the other nations.[1] While in the world of nations around Israel all kinds of special means were needed to ascertain the will of God (omens, inspection of the liver, astrology, etc.) Yahwism rejected these means. Israel could do this because it was the People of the Covenant and as such was conscious of God's guidance in life and of His revelation when His people needed Him. It is, therefore, impossible to maintain that the Biblical relationship between God and man, brought about by Word and Spirit, is merely like a lightning-flash *(blitzartig)*, that there can only be the jumping over of the fiery spark of the Spirit. Moreover in the Bible a relationship is assumed in which man can also count on his God, can depend upon it that God will hear, answer, and, generally speaking, react; in a word, there exists intercourse and this intercourse is not only personal, with that man whom God chooses at any particular moment, but it also exists permanently; God also wants to act through official representatives. He will not only warn, predict, or aid in a particular situation, He also wishes to teach, to instruct, to educate.

The divine *torah* becomes the starting-point of a sacred tradition which is normative for daily action and which is codified with a view to further use.

[1] Some scholars have attempted to connect *Torah* with the Assyrian *tertu* – command, oracle –, but this etymological connection is uncertain, though in the Assyrian world *tertu* has functionally more or less the same meaning as *torah* in Israel.

It was elaborated into what afterwards became the *Torah par excellence*.

It is impossible to trace this development in detail, particularly as regards its earliest stages. Fairly recently an important discussion on this subject got under way, but it has not nearly been concluded yet. It brought out the view that the *Torah* does not only start from legal precepts derived from the cult, but also from very ancient sanctified traditions in the life of the people. These traditions are closely related to those preserved in the wisdomliterature. Where as A. Alt[1] thought apodictic law to have originated in the cult, and so-called casuist law in the administration of justice at the city-gate, in the last few decades the view has been advanced that the law administered at the amphictyonic sanctuary should be looked upon as the basis of Israelite legal thought and the codification of law.[2] Recently E. Gerstenberger[3] pointed out that wisdom was the most important source of law. These ideas were supported by H. W. Wolff, who thinks 'Sippenweisheit' to be the foundation-stone of Amos' legal tradition.[4] In my *Religion of Israel*[5] I already pointed out that the background of part of the Decalogue is to be found in ancient Kenite tradition. In dealing with the problem of origin we shall have to be on our guard against a one-sided emphasis on either cult or wisdom, for these two fields did not exist independently in ancient oriental life, not at any rate in the earliest period.[6]

Probably Hos. viii. 1 already points to such a codified body of divine instruction, closely linked with the covenant; and there are also other statements of the prophets where we find *torah* mentioned, which might have this summary of doctrine in view (either written down or otherwise). In any case the Deuteronomists frequently meant by *torah* the deuteronomic *code of law* itself (Deut. iv. 44); xvii. 18f.; Joshua viii. 31f.). When the *torah* had been codified it soon came to be looked upon as the summary of the wisdom revealed by God (Deut. iv. 6ff.).

In later times the World is used especially to denote that collection of writings that contain the revelation of God to Israel, which is normative for life: the Pentateuch. It is especially the laws contained in this collective work that have given it the meaning of the Law[7];

---

[1] *Ursprünge des israelitischen Rechts.*
[2] M. Noth, *Die Gesetze im Pentateuch*, W. Zimmerli, op. cit.
[3] *Wesen und Herkunft des sogenannten apodiktischen Rechts im A. T.* (Thesis Bonn, 1961).
[4] *Amos geistige Heimat*, 1964; cf. also G. Fohrer about the Decalogue in *Kerugma und Dogma*, 1965.   [5] 1967, p. 148; cf. Ex. xviii.
[6] We should bear in mind that the tradition of the Kenite origin of the administration of justice in Exod. xviii is linked with Jethro, the *priest*.
[7] The word Law, already used in the Septuagint and the N.T. *(nomos)*, is in itself not a correct translation because it is only an approximate rendering of the content of the original word.

these in particular may be called *Torah* because they are derived from the divine revelation and have therefore divine authority, and moreover because they are looked upon as normative for life, as 'instruction'. Gutbrod's remark in his article in the *Th. Wb. z. Neuen Testament*[1] that the important element in the *Torah* is not its form but its divine authority does not seem to be quite correct; in our opinion we should not neglect the guiding (instructive) tendency a word must have if it to be styled *torah*.

This is also why the *Torah* has never been the only canonical collection of books in the Old Testament. It has never been the only, not even the most original form of revelation. When the Pentateuch was closed and considered as the *Torah par excellence*, the writings of the Prophets had certainly already been recognized as divine revelation and had already become canonical in part, though the collection as such had not yet been definitively and finally established. The connection between *Torah* and *Nebi'im* cannot be broken.[2] From a historical point of view it is understandable that the *Torah* was codified first, because the organization of the life of the people and the state after the exile required something like a spiritual basis, a binding Law, a constitution. The laws included in the Pentateuch gave something to go by; the fact, however that these laws were accepted as Holy Scripture by the priests and the people certainly does not imply that the Prophetic Writings were not admitted to be of divine origin.

But the start the Pentateuch-*Torah* gained in the development of Israel's religion, because it was formally the first to be acknowledged as Holy Scripture, does mean, however, that those elements in the revelation that were directive for the life of Israel came to be considered of paramount importance. Thus the religious - moral and the cultic element, the tendency towards rigidity in Israel's religion of revelation came to be emphasized strongly, so that the nomistic element (as we know it from the New Testament) could develop. This explains why in the New Testament *Torah* is always found defined as *nomos*, 'law', and why the Septuagint also translates the Old Testament *torah* in practically all cases by *nomos* – a practice also adhered to in our Western translations. In its turn it fostered the appreciation of the Pentateuch and of the whole of the Old Testament as *law*.

We should not forget, however, that fundamentally *torah* in the Old Testament denotes God's *revelational decision* and points to the guidance that God would give His people in their every-day life through the intermediary of the official representatives of the people. A translation

---

[1] IV, pp. 1038, 24f.
[2] See above pp. 79f. and particularly W. Zimmerli, *The Law and the Prophets*.

of *torah* by 'word of revelation' would come closer to the original meaning.

3a. The vision

The word has often been used in a general sense to denote *all the revelations* given to prophets, even if there is no question of a visual image (Isa. i. 1). This is possible because in the visual image the revelation by the word is decisive: 'The visual element is transitory, the content of the word is permanent. Revelation by visions is also revelation by the word'.[1]

The word 'vision' denotes a visual image seen by a man when awake, though it can also be used to denote a dream, namely in the expression 'nocturnal vision'. All the prophets may see visions and they are ascribed to both 'true' and 'false' prophets. Yet there is a certain remarkable difference in expression to be observed, emphasized by König[2], that the Biblical prophets themselves never use the word *chazah* for the receiving of their visual experiences, but always use the word *ra'ah* (to see), while they usually call the false prophets 'seers'. They credit their own visions with complete reality but apparently they call in question the reality of the visions of others (Jer. xxiii. 16).

J. Lindblom[3] distinguishes between 'descriptive and dramatic' visions. The former describe an image, the latter an action. These distinctions are of religio-psychological rather than theological importance.

That the prophets often receive the word of God in visual images is evident from the visions of Amos (vii–ix), Isaiah (vi), Jeremiah ei, xxiv), Ezekiel (i–iii), Zechariah (i–vi, nocturnal visions). Some theologians have looked upon this visionary character as an ecstatic phenomenon[4], and therefore rejected it as being unreal.

The prophets apparently did not look upon it in this light, as is manifest from the use of the word 'to see' to denote the receiving of their visions. In the visions of Jeremiah the exstatic visionary element is almost completely absent, but there is no denying that it does occur

---

[1] Köhler, *Theologie*, p. 87.
[2] *Theologie des A. T.*, 1922, pp. 69ff.
[3] *Prophecy*, pp. 122ff.
[4] In the following pages the idea of ecstasy is used in spite of the fact that it is open to fundamental objections as it fits in with the Greek way of thinking rather than with the Hebrew range of ideas. For ecstasy implies the notion that the soul can leave the body; this is not an Israelite conception, for in the Hebrew way of thinking it is the divine spirit that takes possession of man. See Wheeler Robinson, op.cit., p. 181; J. Ridderbos, *Profetie en Ekstase*, J. Lindblom in *Festschrift Bertholet*, pp. 326f. and in *Prophecy*, pp. 32ff., 47ff., 105f., 122ff. By ecstasy we may understand (with Lindblom, p. 106) a state of mind concentrated upon one experience to such an extent that the normal outlook upon life is eliminated.

in the writings of Amos (ix), Isaiah, and Ezekiel.[1] The element of ecstasy need not, however, detract from the reality of the spiritual experience, for Christian theology will always admit the possibility of a spiritual reality of mystical experiences (glossolaly; rapture, 2 Cor. xii) and has therefore no difficulty in acknowledging and accepting the ecstatic element in the visions. In the case of the visually minded Israelite, who, moreover, lived in an atmosphere in which the visionary element played an important part, this element had a psychological background. However much this phenomenon may be psychological, personally or generally, or however closely it may be linked to its age, this need not at all detract from the spiritual importance of the contents of the message received in this way. In religious life human and psychical elements are always interlaced with the activity of the Spirit of God, in the same way as, for instance, social factors also influence certain forms of the spiritual aspect. Therefore it would be wrong to sacrifice the one to the other, to link the problem of the ecstatic element without more ado to the question of truth, and to make the truth of a vision conditional on the question whether it is ecstatic or not.

For the prophets themselves the visionary revelation by the word is an immediate experience of God's presence, so that from a theological point of view it may be equated with the experience of the Theophany.

3*b*. The dream[2]

The dream, too, can have the nature of revelation in the Old Testament. Indeed, this also applies to all the rest of the ancient – Eastern world[3], and we find this exemplified in the Old Testament many times: frequently dreams are said to have been granted to non-Israelites (Gen. xx, xxxi. 24, xlf., Judges vii. 13f., Dan. iiff.)

A fundamental distinction between dream and vision is not always

[1] In the book of Amos we find two types of 'visions' between which Amos does not make any distinction. In the former things are seen, apparently, that are wholly real (vii. 1–3, viii. 1–2; cf. Jer. i. 11ff.), in the latter there is an occurrence of a more particularly visionary character (vii. 4ff., 7ff.). There is apparently a difference between the type of visionary who (like Jeremiah) particularly beholds real things that are given a deeper, symbolical meaning by the word of revelation (Jer. xiii, xviiif., xxiv) and the true visionary who receives 'visions', who sees things that cannot be observed directly with the eye. One of the main representatives of this type is Ezekiel. Amos, on the other hand, receives both types of visions. In the history of religion there are parallels between the former type and certain phenomena in the Arabian world (see Guillaume, op.cit., pp. 145ff.).
[2] E. L. Ehrlich, 'Der Traum im A.T.' (*Beich. Z.A.W.*, 73), 1953; A. Guillaume, *Prophecy and Divination*, 1938, pp. 231ff., who, however, lays too much stress on the importance of the dream ('the importance ascribed to dreams in the O.T. record of revelation cannot be overstated').
[3] On Egypt and Assyria see ANET, pp. 449ff.; on Mari: W. von Soden, *Verkündung des Gotteswillens*, WO, 1950, pp. 397ff.; on Ugarit: the Keret-legend.

made, no more than a distinction between either of these and the nightly vision. In Num.xii.6–8 and Joeliii.1 the words 'dream' and 'vision' are used indifferently; in Dan.vii.1ff. the term 'nightly vision' is used in addition to the word 'dream'. The dream is not only means to receive a Word of God; like the vision it may be an experience of the presence of God (Gen.xxviii.11f.).

Dream-revelations are considered fully legitimate.

A positive appreaciation of the dream is found in some old stories, especially in E (Gen.xx.3, 6; xxviii.12; xxxi.10f., 24; xlvi.1–4; Num.xii.6), further in the stories of Joseph (xxxvii; xl; xli), Gideon (Judges vii.13ff.), Saul (1 Sam.xxviii.6, 15), Solomon (1 Kings iii.5, 15), Job (iv.13; xxxiii.15, a night vision), and not the least frequently in apocalyptic texts: Joeliii.1 (R.V.ii.28) and Daniel (iiiff., vii.1).

Sometimes dream-oracles are sought in sanctuaries (incubation-oracles). In this case a person spends the night in a room near a temple, awaiting the appearance of the deity or hoping to be granted a divine message. This was also done in Israel: with Ehrlich we may look upon the story of Solomon in 1 Kings iii as a case in point, perhaps also the story of Jacob in Gen.xxviii.10ff. (Ps.xvii.15?).

Whereas the dream plays a particularly prominent part in the older narratives and in the apocalyptic writings, the same does not apply to the prophets. We might point to Micahiii.6, where Micah predicts the coming judgment to the prophets: darkness shall come upon them, but they shall not receive visions. Jeremiah does not think much of the gift of receiving dream-oracles; apparently he supposes that it is found especially with false prophets (xxiii.25–32, xxvii.9 and xxix.8) and that may be the reason why he speaks of 'a vision of their (own) heart' (xxiii.16). It is true that in many respects Jeremiah is a radical reformer: he does not believe in spiritualist operations of the spirit, he attacks the sacrificial cult quite sharply and emphatically prophesies the destruction of the temple; though he was a particularly sensitive man he was an out and out realist. Whether he rules out the dream as a means of revelation as a matter of principle cannot be stated with certainty.

This is not done, at all events in Deut.xiii.2–6 (R.V.1–5), and in Deut.xviii.9ff. the dream is not included among the forbidden ways of divination, either. We do find the dream rejected in Zech.x.2. Sometimes the dream is mentioned in the texts without special importance being attached to it; it is considered a terrible nightly experience in Jobvii.14; in Isa.xxix.7f., Ps.lxxiii.20, cxxvi.1, Job xx.28 and Eccles.v.6 the dream is looked upon as something unreal. In Eccles.v.2 it is explained psychologically from the disturbed human mind. In the later wisdomliterature it is condemned on reasonable grounds (Jesus Sirach,xl. 5ff., xxxi. 1ff.). Yet the dream was accepted fairly generally as a means of revelation in other writings in the late Jewish period[1] (for the N.T. cf. i.a. Matth. if., xxvii. 19).

4. External means

The most external means of divination known in the ancient oriental world are rejected in the Old Testament; the most important of these are enumerated in Deut.xviii.9–14. The interrogation of the dead in particular was rejected at an early date (1 Sam.xxviii), though it continued to be resorted to for a long time (Isa.viii. 19).

Only a few forms of mantics in which external means were made use were considered legitimate; compare what has been said on the subject on pp. 241f.

F. The intermediaries of revelation

1. The prophets[2]

The prophet, *nabi* (= speaker)[3] is the typical and most important figure in the Old Testament[4]. The term *'ish ha'elohim*, man of God, is used in the Old Testament especially to denote prophetical figures (apart from a few occasions where it denotes an angel or David). In contrast with the ancient Eastern cultural religions (Babylon

---

[1] See Ehrlich, op. cit., pp. 164ff.
[2] There is an immense amount of literature on the prohets. On p.67 we mentioned the literature on the prophetic books and here we shall add some titles of the principal books (mainly not mentioned above) on prophecy: H.H.Rowley 'The nature of O.T. prophecy in the light of recent study', in *The Servant of the Lord*, 1952, pp.91ff., gives an excellent survey of the problems in question and of the literature on these subjects after 1914; in that same year there appeared the famous book by G.Hölscher, *Die Propheten*, afterwards opposed by Seierstadt's doctorate thesis, mentioned above; F.E.König, *Der Offenbarungsbegriff des A.T.*, I–II, 1882; J.Lindblom, *Die literarische Gattung der proph. Lit.*, 1924, *Hosea, literarisch untersucht*, 1924, cf. also *Festschrift Bertholet*, pp.325ff., Nabi *Prophecy in Israel*, 1962; Max Weber, *Das antike Judentum*; H.W. Hertzberg, *Prophet und Gott*, 1923; E.Fascher, *Prophètes*, 1927; A.Causse, *Les prophètes d'Israël et les religions de l'Orient*, 1913, and *Du groupe ethnique*, 1937; A.Lods, *Les prophètes d'Israël et les débuts du Judaisme*, 1935; J.Skinner, *Prophecy and Religion*, 1926; J.Pedersen, *Israel*, III–IV; F.Häussermann, *Wort und Symbol in der altt. Prophetie*, 1932; Heschel, *Die Prophetie*, 1936, *The Prophets*, 1962; H.W.Wolff, *Das Zitat im Prophetenbuch*, 1937; B.Bendokat, *Die prophetische Botschaft*, 1938; H.Knight, *The Hebrew Prophetic consciousness*, 1947; G.Widengren, *Literary and psychological aspects of the Hebrew prophets*, 1948; A.C.Welch, *Prophet and Priest in Old Israel*, 1936; M.Schmidt, *Prophet und Tempel*, 1948; A.Neher, *Amos*, 1950, *L'essence du prophétisme*, 1955; O.Procksch, *Geschichtsbetrachtung bei den vorexilischen Propheten*, 1902; W.Staerk, *Das assyrische Weltreich im Urteil der Propheten*, 1908; J.M.Powis Smith, *The prophets and their time*[2], *revised by* W.A.Irwin, 1940; C.Westermann, *Grundformen prophetischer Rede*, 1960; R.B.Y.Scott, *The relevance of the prophets*[6], 1959.
[3] The form of the verbal noun may perhaps be considered as a passive; these nominal forms are often used as names of offices, see my *Erwählung*, p.50; perhaps the prophet is he who speaks and is spoken to, cf. Guillaume, op cit., pp.112f.; Albright prefers the passive meaning, *From the Stone Age*, pp.231f., see also Rowley, *Servant*, p.198.
[4] See also Rowley, loc. cit., and particularly Procksch, *Theologie*, pp.128ff.

and Egypt) the prophet plays an important part in Israel; in these former religions there occur a few similar figures, but their place in the whole of the cultic and public life of the people is completely different (with the exception of Mari).[1]

Some scholars have assumed that in Canaanite and Phoenician religious life the *nabi* played an important part as an ecstatic figure. In an ancient Egyptian travel-story (Wen-Amon) we find an exstatic figure who carries a divine message to a Phoenician king.[2] It is, however, not quite clear yet what prophetism meant there. It is true that exstasy certainly played a part in the Canaanite, Phoenician, North-Syrian and Mesopotamian world (cf. for instance the prophets of Baal at Carmel and also the prophets mentioned in the Mari-scrolls) and the ecstatic elements we find in Israelite prophecy in the period of the earlier kings (and also still in a figure like Ezekiel) may certainly be attributed to the influence of this outside world.

All this does not suffice, however, to explain prophecy as it developed in Israel, particularly the appearance of the classical prophets whose words have been handed down to us in the Old Testament. In the first place the ecstatic element is not an essential characteristic of prophecy as it is found in the books of the Scriptural prophets of the Old Testament (see p. 68) and in the second place it is historically most likely that the religion of Israel sprang from the unique prophetic experiences of Moses. There is a fundamental difference between the activity of the major prophets in Israel and that of the ecstatic figures of the ancient Eastern world.[3]

The prophet is the man who speaks, who carries the Word of God. As the messenger of God he speaks the Word of his Lord and delivers his message in the form in which he has received it from His Lord[4] in other words, because the Lord speaks in the first person the prophet-

---

[1] On Babylon and Egypt see, besides the texts in Gressmann, *Altorient. Texte z. A.T.* and Pritchard, *Ancient Near Eastern Texts*, also A. Haldar, *Associations of Cult-Prophets among the ancient Semites*, 1945, and especially the new discoveries on the appearance of prophets in Mari, see Böhl, *Ned. Th. T.*, 1950, pp. 81ff., and W von Soden, 'Verkündung des Gotteswillens' etc., in *W.O.*, 1950, pp. 397ff.; N. H. Ridderbos, *Israëls profetie en 'profetie' buiten Israël*, 1955; A. Malamat in *S. V. T.* XV, 1966, pp. 207ff.
[2] See for example H. Gressmann, *Altorientalische Teste zum A.T.*[2], 1926, p. 72.
[3] In Israelite prophecy various prophetic movements must be distinguished; one of them, apparently strongly represented at the time of Samuel, is ecstatic; these may originally have been the nabis. Besides these there also were prophets of the *ro'eh*-visionary type, as depicted by Guillaume, these belonged rather to a type of nomadic religiosity; it is not certain whether the *chozeh* originally was distinct from these. In Israel several types are found together, and the bond with kingship or sanctuary also differs. The classical prophets have many things in common with these various types, but not all the same traits: they may, however, be taken to consitute a type apart because of their peculiar message (judgment and eschatology). See particularly Procksch, Knight, Eichrodt, *Theology* I, and my *Religion*, pp. 200ff.
[4] Cf. for the rest above, p. 117f. and B. Gemser, *Vertraagde Openbaringsbewustheid*.

231

passes his message on in the first person, too. Formerly it was frequently supposed that the prophetic message in the first person meant that the prophet identified himself with God. Books like Hölscher's *Die Propheten* are based upon this presupposition. This point of view is, however, gradually being abandoned and nowadays it is realized more and more that the Israelite prophet only speaks in this form because he is faithful messenger of God.

The prophets are free men, called by God, who are compelled by Him to speak His Word. Fundamentally prophecy is in complete agreement with the essence of Yahwism. The prophet's activity is an expression, a sign of Yahweh's Nature. Yahweh Himself calls the prophet, whosoever he may be, now a farmer, then a shepherd (Moses), then a priest, without any regard for this original position. Being called by Yahweh is the all-important thing; however much the prophet may attempt to resist (Jer. i; Isa. vi; Exod. iiif.) he cannot but obey (Amos iii. 8). Jer. xx. 7f.). Ezekiel expresses this with the words: 'the hand of Yahweh was upon me' (Ezek. iii. 22; xl. 1). All this is in complete agreement with Yahweh's omnipotence. The prophet is called personally, there is a direct bond between God and His servant (Amos iii. 7; Jer. xxiii. 22; cf. further the lives of Moses, Elijah, Isaiah, Jeremiah, and Ezekiel); if a man has once had to do with God he has been drawn into His service forever. No wonder then that there is a very close communion between God and the prophet; here a conversation is possible, here we find an encounter (Exod. xxxiiif.; Num. xii; Deut. xxxiv. 10; Amos viiff.; 1 Kings xxi; Jer. xv, xvi). This contact is the spritual background and explains the fact that the prophets usually received the Word of God without any further special experiences (cf. above pp. 222f.).[1] It is dictated to them, for God speaks to them.

The task of the prophet is to proclaim the Word of God to the people. This makes them very special figures, not found anywhere in the ancient Eastern world, we might even say, not found anywhere in antiquity, because they are preachers who have a responsibility of their own for the people towards God,[2] and 'guardians' who watch over the people's religious life.[3] In the rest of the ancient world with its polytheism and syncretism such figures are unknown, because people are too tolerant; each man worships his own god or gods and collectively the whole people has its state-religion from which no one

---

[1] This leads Heschel, op. cit., pp. 69ff., to his [view of the *sympatheia* between the prophet and God, in which the prophet also experiences the divine pathos.
[2] Ezek. iii. 16ff; xxxiii; cf. W. Eichrodt, *Theology*, I, pp. 278f.
[3] W. Eichrodt, Das prophetische Wächteramt, Weiser Festschrift, *Tradition und Situation*, 1963, pp. 31ff.

withdraws.[1] Only by doing this last it would be possible to come into conflict with the Eastern world; in Israel, however, people may not worship anyone but the *one and only* God; apostasy from Yahweh is betrayal both of Him and of the people, so that the spiritual struggle remains forever latent and may break out again at any moment.

The prophets also attracted groups of disciples: in the case of Isaiah (viii. 16) we know this for certain; with respect to others it may reasonably be supposed (Uriah, Jer.xxvi); it was probably the disciples who further propagated the words of the prophets and afterwards collected these words in writing (the book-roll of Baruch in Jer.xxxvi); it is mainly to them that we owe the prophetic writings of the Old Testament.

The content of the prophetic message shows that the God of Israel is the Holy One, whose Nature does not depend upon His people or upon the worship He receives. He punishes His people as well as the other nations of the world; He is not dominated by the cultic ceremonies offered by His servants. Yahweh is supra-national, supracultic, for He is holy, but also merciful and just; He also expects these qualities in His people. In spite of His judgement Yahweh remains the God who does not abandon Israel but promises it a new future that shall be realized by the Messiah.

The prophetic message is characterized by judgment and salvation, both of which are announced. The prophets themselves are thrown by God into the struggle for the salvation of the people; they are not merely preachers, but also witnesses, martyrs[2], and for that reason they have to struggle for their people. This becomes evident in figures like Amos (vii. 10), Micah (iii. 8), Isaiah (viii. 11ff.), Jeremiah (xxvi), and also in the various symbolical acts they have to perform (Hos.i–iii; Isa.xx; Ezek.ivf.; xxiv. 15 and elsewhere), where they themselves become the living symbols of their message.[3] They are as it were God's representatives among the people, they are entirely Yahweh's servants. Hence there is no fundamental difference between the work of the prophet and the activity of the servant of the Lord in Isa.xlii, xlix, l, lii (liii). Only too often the prophet is looked upon only as the proclaimer, the preacher; but as the responsible representative of his

---

[1] See H.Kraemer, *De wortelen van het syncretisme* (oration), 1937; F.M.Th. de Liagre Böhl, '*Missions- und Erwählungsglaube*', Festschrift Bertholet, pp.8of. (also in the *Opera Minora*).
[2] For that reason they have also been called tragic figures; though this definition does contain an element of truth it is not correct; see the fine essay by P.Humbert, 'Les prophètes d'Israel ou les Tragiques de la Bible', *Revue de Théologie et de Philosophie*, 1936, pp.209ff.
[3] See A. van den Born, *De symbolische handelingen der O.T. profeten*, doctorate thesis Nijmegen, *Profetie metterdaad*, 1947; G.Fohrer, *Die symbolische Handlungen der altt. Propheten*, 1953.

Lord (cf. Ezek. iii. 17ff., xxxiii) the prophet is the intermediary between Yahweh and Israel.

So the prophets bear personal responsibility and were called to the work of Yahweh Himself. This becomes evident most profoundly in the chapters on the Servant of the Lord in Isa. xliiff., where the nation of Israel as a whole, in so far as it is faithful, is called upon as the servant of Yahweh to perform His will.[1] In this personal activity of the prophets, too, and in this active love of their people and their God, born from the Spirit of God, the nature of Yahwism is revealed, and the nature of Yahweh Himself who desires the salvation of His people. Thus the prophets as the servants of God are the image of Jesus Christ, the Son, who gave Himself completely to restore the communion between God and man.

Once a man comes to see this he understands the immense distance between the Canaanite ecstatic figures and the Israelite prophet. By pointing out the *spiritual* character of prophecy (the prophet is being driven on by the Spirit of God) we have arrived at the *freedom* which is characteristic of prophecy. The nature of Israelite prophecy can only be understood from the activity of God, from the spiritual element. The prophet is driven on by the *Spirit* of God, he is called directly by God Himself. He is called in a special manner, personally; even Jeremiah and Ezekiel, though originally priests, only became prophets by a special call. We should not forget that of several Old Testament prophets, at any rate of the major prophets, we are told the history of their call: Amos, Isaiah, Jeremiah, Ezekiel; further also of Moses and perhaps of Hosea, too. This call-narrative is considered as a kind of 'letter of credence', and the call as the initiation into the function. For that reason the view that the prophets as such (including those whose writings have been handed down to us) had an official function in the cult, that they were a kind of temple servants, a view that has found many adherents of late, must be rejected.[2] It is a fundamental mistake, affecting not only the character of prophecy but also that of the whole of Old Testament religion; we might even say that this question touches the very essence of the Christian church.

Because we think that the freedom of the prophetic office should be fundamentaly maintained we do not deny that in certain periods many

[1] On this see pp. 107f., 194.
[2] One should also bear in mind that the word *bachar*, to choose, is never applied to them, see my *Erwählung*, p. 45; on the ritual character of prophecy see Haldar's work, *Associations of Cult-Prophets;* Welch, *Prophet and Priest;* A. R. Johnson, *The cultic Prophet in ancient Israel,* [2]1966; it is now defended again very strongly by H. Graf Reventlow in several works on Jeremiah, Ezekiel, etc.; a critical discussion of this point of view, which is advocated particularly by Scandinavian scholars, is found i.a. in J. Lindblom, op cit., pp. 327ff., and H. H. Rowley, op. cit., pp. 104ff., together with a great deal of literature on the subject.

234

prophets were connected with the temple (for instance Hananiah, Jer. xxviii; probably Habakkuk[1] and others), but we do deny that the prophets as such were official assistants at the cult. Not only from the character of Elijah, the remark of Amos (vii. 14f.), the figure of Huldah, the wife of a palace official (2 Kings xxii. 14) is it evident that there was no unbreakable connection between prophecy and the priestly office, but also from the general tone of the prophecies of Micah, the activity of Haggai (ii. 12f.) and particularly from the well-known story of Eldad and Medad in Num. xi, the expectation of Joel ii. 28ff., etc.

It is clear that in the period of the kings prophets belonged to a certain group or order (the sons of the prophets) or held a cultic office. We have already pointed out the various forms of prophecy. As long as there were sanctuaries, there were also cultic prophets in Israel; this must have been the case to an ever greater extent under the influence of the Canaanite world and particularly of kingship, which, in accordance with the ancient Eastern tradition tended to co-ordinate all religious and cultic life under the central authority of the king.

That is why we find so many prophets linked with kingship in the Northern Israelite kingdom in the time of Ahab (under the influence of Jezebel). There were apparently only a few prophets left who had resisted this co-ordination: besides Elijah from Transjordania and Micaiah the son of Imlah, 1 Kings xxii, there were still a hundred prophets, hidden by Obadiah (1 Kings xviii. 13).

That the free prophets were occasionally consulted officially is evident, for example, from the questions put to Jeremiah by King Zedekiah (Jer. xxi.). It is very likely that this official appearance of the prophets that was to be found in all periods[2] did indeed promote the obtaining of an official function in the cult. We should further bear in mind the following instances: the consultation of the prophets Samuel (1 Sam. ix), Ahijah (1 Kings xiv), Elisha (2 Kings iii), Isaiah (Isa. xxxviif.), Jeremiah (Jer. xlii). This proves therefore that even when the prophets did not serve in the cult in an official capacity, they could yet enjoy great personal confidence both from the side of the people and from the servants of the crown (cf. for example Jer. xxxvi 12ff.), so that they could have a very influential position (Isaiah).

---

[1] Cf. P. Humbert, *Problèmes du livre d'Habacuc*, 1944, see also above pp. 73f. and 218f.
[2] Compare, for instance, the part played by Elisha in 2 Kings iii; he accompanies the king into battle; like the priests of the oracle in Babylon the prophets were apparently consulted regularly in connection with the military operations the king intended to undertake (1 Kings xxii; cf. 1 Sam. xxiii. 2, where the priest is consulted; cf. Ps. xx). See also M. Weber, op. cit., who considers the prophets as magicians who originally appeared mainly in war, and A. Bentzen, 'The ritual background of Amos i. 2–ii. 6', *O.T.S.*, VIII, 1950.

The classical prophets have often been looked upon as political figures[1]; there is some ground for this view, for in earlier times the prophets did, indeed, concern themselves with politics, internal as well as foreign (Ahijah, Elisha); the prayer for the king in battle is also connected with this (2 Kings iii, cf. Pss. xx, xxi). This was implicit in the religious character of national life. But all this does not apply without more ado to the classical prophets. Their intervention went no further than proclaiming to the people and the kings the Word or God, also with respect to politics. They had especially to hold their contemporaries back from relations with foreigners on the ground of the message that foreign princes, too, are called, used, and punished by Yahweh alone (Isa. x. 5ff.). This gives their message the timeliness and religious strength which still constitute the great significance of of their teaching.[2]

The fact and the nature of the activity of the prophets in Israel reveal God in His personal, loving relationship to the people, they reveal His holiness, which does not spare Israel, and His justice, which causes judgment and future salvation to be proclaimed alike, and finally His love which keeps contending for the conversion of the people. If there is one thing that can convince us of the living communion between God and Israel it is that ever renewed, struggling, purifying, and above all sanctifying activity of His servants, the prophets.[3]

2. The Priests

However important the priestly office may have been in the whole of Israel's religious life, the personal influence of the priests was merely of secondary importance to Israelite theology, at any rate when compared with that of the major prophets. There are only few great priestly figures whose appearance directly influenced the spiritual development of Israel. We might perhaps think of Hilkiah (2 Kings xxiif.) and Joshua (Zech.). This is partly due to the fact that the priests served in the state temples and were in a large measure subjected to the authority of the kings (cf. Amaziah, Am. vii), but even more to the fact that they had only few opportunities to appear personally because they formed part of a collective whole owing to their office. It was their duty to preserve tradition and outward religious forms rather than to renovate them. As anywhere else they were the strongest

[1] See the literature mentioned in H. H. Kraus, 'Prophetie und Politik', Thel. Existenz heute, N.F. 36, 1952.
[2] See now H. Donner, Israel unter den Völkern, Die Stellung der klassischen Profeten des 8. Jhrh. zur Außenpolitik der Könige von Israel und Juda, 1964, especially pp. 168ff.
[3] Cf. M. Noth, The History of Israel, 1960, 255f.

preserving element in religion. When changes were made in the cult, this was done by order of the kings (Solomon, Jerobeam, Ahaz, Josiah); the priests merely carried them into effect. Only once do we get the impression that a priest played an important part, namely Hilkiah in the deuteronomic reformation.

During the period of the kings greater national sanctuaries arose and the priests were the chief functionaries there, yet the priesthood could never develop into an independent power, as it sometimes did in Babylonia and Egypt, because they were far too dependent on the kings. Only after the return from the Exile did the priesthood attain the most important position in the Jewish community. This was the natural consequence of the fact that politically the Judean community formed part of the Persian world-empire (as afterwards again and again of other great powers). No political power that could have overshadowed the priesthood could develop at Jerusalem.

In the Old Testament we find no ancient data about the institution of the priesthood. Yet it is not considered an intruder nor ever condemned in itself. The priestly office is rather looked upon as a specialization of a function originally belonging to the faithful themselves. The work of the priests was originally entrusted to the head of the family who in olden times offered up the Passover, as a means of atonement for his family. The father is the priest of his household, and, conversely, the priest is also called Father in Israel (Judges xvii. 10, xviii. 19); it is also the father who hands on tradition, the ancient religious stories to the children (Deut. vi. 7, xi. 19). When, however, the federation of families, clans and tribes develops into a community, a state, a priesthood springs up quite naturally, interceding for the community. When and how this priesthood consolidated its position can no longer be traced back with certainty. In later Biblical tradition (the Priestly Code) the origin is traced back to the period when the people came into existence, the age of Moses[1], and it should be considered possible that during that period, particularly under the influence of the priesthood at Kadesh, where the Israelites spent a considerable time (Num. xiii. 26, xx. 1ff.; Deut. i. 19, 46), the cult came to be accepted in the sense of an official intercession for the community.

If this view is not correct the origin of the cult must date mainly from the earliest period of the settlement in Canaan, an alternative for which there is supporting evidence. The fact that Yahwism took over Canaanite sanctuaries was the reason why the priests were originally dispersed all over the country and why their sphere of influence

---

[1] On the figure of Aaron, who does not come to occupy a prominent position until the latest tradition, see M. Noth, *Ueberlieferungsgeschichte des Pentateuch*, 1948, pp. 195ff., now also E. Auerbach: Das Aharon-Problem, *S.V.T.* xvii, 1969, pp. 37ff.

was only limited; moreover the danger of syncretism became very great. How far Shechem and (or) Shiloh may have played a part as central sanctuaries is not quite clear yet.

Cultic life in olden times cannot have been very complicated (cf. Amos v. 25; Jer. vii. 22, see pp. 36ff.); the Passover was celebrated and after that the most important offering was that of the first-fruits. How the ceremonial ritual developed is a matter of guess-work rather than of certain knowledge. The Canaanite worship on the heights with its agricultural festivals and afterwards the foreign cult of the Phoenicians (cf. *Hiram*, who assisted Solomon in building the temple) made their influence felt strongly.[1] We need not go further into these problems which belong rather to the field of the history of religion; it is sufficiently clear that especially in this respect Israel adopted many things from the ceremonial of the nations around it, or at least that Israel had many things in common with them. This involved great dangers, especially because the view could arise (strongly opposed by the prophets) that the expiatory offerings worked *ex opere operato*[2] and as such cleansed man from sin, and because people tended to lose sight of the holiness of God owing to the dissoluteness of the ritual practices belonging to the vegetation religion predominent in Canaan. An age-long struggle was needed to deliver Israel from these dangers; the struggle was at its height in the days of Elijah, but afterwards, too, until the days of Manasseh, the prophets had to stand firm against idolatry, libertinism and magical ritualism.

The cultic laws as presented in the books of Exodus – Deuteronomy are the fruit of the spiritual struggle waged for the preservation of true Yahwism. In the course of this struggle much was deepened and renewed of which only the rudiments were found in the earliest stage of Yahwism.

Yet the priests also played an important part in the spiritual guidance of Israel, though outwardly their influence was often not easily noticeable. The *torah* (see pp. 223ff.) was given particularly by the priests. Instruction in the religious laws was entrusted to them. Thus they had to apply Yahweh's work of revelation to everyday life and to educate the people in this tradition. Moreover, they were also mediators between God and man. They offered up the sacrifices in behalf of the people, gave the blessing to the people in the name of God, and, by the sacrifices, made sure of the goodwill of God towards

---

[1] On this subject see, besides my *Religion of Israel*, particularly H. Ringgren, *Israelitische Religion*, 1963, and R. de Vaux, *Les Institutions de l'A.T.*, II, 1960.

[2] This word is used here as a term of the phenomenology of religion. On the correct meaning of this idea in its dogmatical sense see Dr. G. C. Berkouwer, 'Ex Opere Operato', *Geref. Theol. Tijdschrift*, 1953, pp. 78ff., 93ff.

His people. And as such the priesthood, as a permanent institution, was a great support in the practice of the daily life of Israel. As the mediator the priesthood represented the people before God and God before the people. They lived in or near the sanctuary where they alone were allowed to discharge their priestly duties. They alone were allowed to appear before the face of God and imparted to the people decisions on various questions of vital importance. In their performing of the sacramental actions the priests were the guarantee of communion with God. The great danger, actually inherent in the priesthood, was that it made the institutional element of religion into something immutable, something permanent, and that the priesthood tended therefore to make the sanctuary into something absolute as an eternal symbol of God. Jeremiah vii and xxvi are eloquent of the serious consequences of these religious views of the priesthood (cf. also Ps. xlviii).[1]

The prophets could not but protest against this view; a tension between the prophets and the priests is just as necessary in a living, spiritual relationship to God as the going together of these two[2]; in going together the priest must always be willing to follow the advice of the prophet. A priesthood that will not accept this guidance murders its own prophets (Luke xiii. 33), thus cutting off its own roots, because in this way the priesthood destroys the living strength of its own religion. But as soon as the priesthood accepts the inspiration of prophecy, new life springs up and new fruits develop. This is evident the origin of the book of Deuteronomy, which according to the most likely interpretation, was due to the reflection of the priesthood at Jerusalem, under the bracing influence of the disciples of the prophet Isaiah. It may be considered one of the matured products of the whole of the spiritual development of Israel.

That is why the priest must never dominate in the religious community that is called into being by the revelation of the Scriptures and lives by faith in the God who works in the present. He must in particular be willing to serve and to cooperate in transmitting the Word of God to the people. On the other hand, prophecy which springs up fresh and spontaneously from the Spirit, lacks that opportunity to make its spiritual gifts permanently fruitful by institutional forms. So prophecy in its turn needs the priesthood which is conscious of the fact that it must serve God and the people and which is willing to consolidate and elaborate that which has been gained spiritually. The prophet calls for the priest who can take over and continue his work but who must not try to take charge alone. The fact that the

[1] See my *Jahwe en zijn stad*, p. 12, n. 23.
[2] See W. Barnard in *Kerk en Eredienst*, 1952, p. 87.

priesthood has, indeed, done this in Israel, that it finally ranked the *Torah* (the Law) above the *Nebi'im* (the prophetical books) (perhaps not as a matter of theological theory, but certainly in practice, owing to the demands of history gave Israel's religion the conservative and legalistic character that stifled prophecy and silenced the Spirit (see p. 46).

The task of the priests.

The priest is a functionary serving a sanctuary to which he mostly belonged in virtue of family tradition. There he performed the sacred acts, mainly offering up the sacrifices and giving oracles, which were performed there; he also gave instruction and was the guardian of tradition.

Properly speaking the priest is nothing in himself: he is what he is because of the symbols he serves or actualizes, the symbols which he reveals to the people in their power and their meaning. The chief function of the priesthood is not its conserving and instructing activity but rather its mediatorial and particularly its redeeming activity. The latter is to be dealt with in one of the following sections of this chapter, here we are only concerned with the mediatorial function of the priest.

The priest could mediate in the intercourse between God and people because Israel had received a *sanctuary* from God where He would reveal Himself in a particular manner, and because that sanctuary contained the symbols He would make use of to maintain the relationship with His people.[1]

Apparently, in Israel the priest at Yahweh's sanctuary are looked upon first and foremost as the servants at the ark: they surround, as it were, the Ark, which within Israel occupies the place of what among the surrounding nations is the throne of the deity with his symbol, the image (Nm. x. 35f.). As such the Ark plays a part in the period of the Judges and the Kings, cf. the stories of 1 Sam. ivff., 2 Sam. vi, where it becomes clear that the Ark is given divine honour. For that reason it seems to David that the Ark makes the building of the temple necessary (cf. the connection between 2 Sam. vi and vii). But Jeremiah, the iconoclast, has no longings to have it back (Jer. iii. 16); he hopes that in the new, the re-born Israel the Law of God will no longer be taught by one man to another, because it is written in people's hearts (xxxi. 31ff.). Then there will be no need any longer for an Ark where the *autographon* (the original divine manuscript) of the Law is kept.

The priesthood around the Ark does not only guard the tables of the Law in the Ark, it is also, as we saw above (see pp. 223ff., 238f.)

[1] See M. Schmidt, *Prophet und Tempel*, and R. E. Clements, *op. cit.* The sanctuary itself will be discussed in the next section.

the *dispenser* of the *torah*. At the request of the pious who visit the temple, it asks God to grant His instructions *(torah)* for the benefit of the pious (Jdgesxviii.4ff.). Such an oracle was requested by means of external means, the *'urim* and the *thummim*. These symbols are carried in the breast-bag of the priestly *'efod;* what these *'urim* and *thummim* were like and how decisions were obtained by means of them cannot be established with any certainty; probably the one gave a positive, the other a negative answer to a question.[1] They were a kind of lotstones (cf. also 1 Sam.xiv.41 in the reading of the Septuagint; 1 Sam.xxiii.9, xxx.7; Deut.xxxiii.8). The solution of problems by means of these lot-stones is probably the earliest form of *torah;* in the period after the foundation of the temple at Jerusalem this form of giving oracles is no more heard of in the history of Israel.

Even though we do not find this priestly oracle by lot mentioned again after David, the practice of casting lots was still used in Israel outside the temple at a much later date (cf. Actsi)[2], as a means of learning the will of Yahweh. There, too, the choice is given between two alternatives. Thus the sanctuary with the Ark, the priests and the sacred lot-stones is a fixed point for Israel where it can go to be assured of God's guidance.

One may feel inclined to be rather critical about the spiritual importance of these external means of revelation. But when we compare them with the omens, astrology, and other similar means of the heathen nations we may admit that this asking the advice of Yahweh alone is really a great spiritual blessing. In any case man lays his destiny in the hands of no one but Yahweh. This is also true of the *trial by ordeal* (as described in Num.v.11f.), in which the priest must bring out a hidden sin by conditional curses and ceremonies. For that matter, in the daily life of the people other, purely mechanical means of finding out about the future must also have existed; think of the cup-divination of which we read in the story of Joseph (Gen.xliv.4f.) and which is apparently considered as something normal there; further we should remember the difficulty of overcoming spiritism etc. (1 Sam.xxviii). Compared with these means of divination the method of laying down a problem before God and allowing it to be decided by lot stands on a much higher plane. In judging these means we should not forget that casting lots to obtain a decision remained the fashion for a long time in the Christian world (for example among the early Moravian brethren to indicate the woman with whom the pro-

[1] Compare also, for example, H. Wheeler Robinson, *Inspiration and Revelation in the O.T.*, 1946, p. 202, and R. de Vaux, *Institutions.*
[2] It is also mentioned in the *Manual of Discipline*, V, 3, though the expression is used there in a figurative sense; cf. also VI, 16; Damascus document XIII, 4.

spective missionary was to be sent out) and was even used in the matter of ecclesiastical appointments. The more, however, both the omnipotence of God and the moral responsibility of man are taken seriously, the more people try to avoid a decision by lot.[1] Ultimately the Christian cannot but reject the practice of casting lots, as it is a means of extorting a premature decision from God. On the cultic function of the priest see: The cult, pp.263ff.

3. The wise men[2]

Whether the *wise men* could or should be included among the 'mediators of revelation', is still doubtful.

Some scholars emphatically declare themselves willing to do so, such as B. Gemser, who thinks the counsel of the wise men was given on the ground of a 'consciousness of authority based on a higher sanction'.[3] Others, however, equally emphatically reject this view (e.g. W. Zimmerli).[4] This already tends to show that wisdom can be viewed from more aspects than one. It is certain that in the ancient Eastern world Wisdom was associated with the gods. It is equally certain that the quest for wisdom especially serves wordly interests. In Israel human wisdom is not linked so unmistakably with Yahweh. Wisdom belongs to God, it is true, but then, it really and fundamentally belongs to God alone. Unlike primitive man in the Canaanite and Phoenician world, who is 'full of wisdom', man in the Paradise-story of Gen. iif. was forbidden to covet the wisdom that God had reserved to Himself. Human wisdom is ambivalent: on the one hand it may be looked upon as God's gift, especially in the form of practical skills (Exod. xxxvi. 1f.), on the other it is ascribed to the sons of

[1] When H. Wheeler Robinson, op. cit., pp.204f., thinks that in later days 'urim and thummim were condemned as heathen (referring to Deut. xviii.9ff.) and states that 'revelation through personality is potentially as much higher than divination by the sacred lot as the dynamic conception of Yahweh the living God transcends all kinds of necessarily static idolatry' he goes too far in our opinion. Here he pays too little attention to what we pointed out above regarding the true faith that may be at the back of such acts, and overlooks too much the difference between the occult presuppositions of divination and this ritual act.
[2] Literature: W. Baumgartner, *The wisdom literature*, in H.H. Rowley, *O.T. and modern study*, 1951, pp.210ff.; B. Gemser, *Sprüche Salamos*, (HAT), 1963; H. Gese, *Lehre und Wirklichkeit in der alten Weisheit*, 1958, *Weisheit; Weisheitsdichtung*, RGG[3] VI, pp.1574ff., 1962; W.H. Gispen, *De wijze in Israel*, 1956 (oration); J. Fichtner, *Die altorientalische Weisheit in ihrer isr.-jüd. Ausprägung*, 1933; G. von Rad, *O.T. Theology*, I, pp.418ff., 441ff.; O. Rankin, *Israel's Wisdom Literature*[2], 1954; H. Ringgren, *Word and Wisdom*, 1947; H.H. Rowley Festschrift *Wisdom in Israel and in the Ancient Near East*, Suppl VT, III, 1955; J.C. Rijlaarsdam, *Revelation in Jewish Wisdom Literature*, 1946.
[3] B. Gemser, *op. cit.*, p.11.
[4] W. Zimmerli, *Zur Struktur der altt. Weisheit*, ZAW, 1933, pp.177ff., who emphasizes the human and eudaemonistic nature of wisdom, and points to 'höfische Lebensklugheit' as the background of wisdom; cf. M. Noth, *Die Bewährung von Salomos 'Göttlicher Weisheit'*, Suppl. VT, III, pp.225ff.; see also note 4, McKane.

Lamech, the progeny of Cain (Gen. iv. 19ff.). For a long time it remained ambivalent; its influence is found with the prophets[1], yet they, and Jeremiah in particular, see that judgment is to fall upon the wise man (Jer. viii. 8f.).[2]

We may be sure of two things:

a. that in Jer. xviii. 18 the wise men are mentioned by Jeremiah as a third group of spiritual leaders besides the priests and the prophets: the priests have the *torah*, the prophets a Word of God, *dabar*, but the wise men have 'counsel', *'eṣa*. Though it does not appear from this verse, which prophesies judgment upon the wise men, that Jeremiah attributes any spiritual authority to them, his contemporaries apparently do, for in their conflict with the prophet they appeal to these three groups of leaders as authorities of greater prestige than Jeremiah.

b. that in the later Wisdom literature (Prov. i-ix) wisdom is integrated more and more into Israel's faith and, even if it is not considered divine, is looked upon as God's first creation, as His 'delight' (Prov. viii. 22, 30).[3]

So in Israel wisdom is apparently one of those elements of life that are integrated fully slowly but surely. Other cases in point would be kingship in the domain of national life, certain elements like fertility in the conception of Yahweh or urban civilisation in the cultural pattern. We may perhaps say that because wisdom was not received in Israel until a fairly late date it could only be integrated into Yahwism very late.[4] Yet the matter is a little more complicated than that.

Some observations on the history of wisdom in Israel must, therefore, precede a full appreciation of wisdom. To begin with, there is the fact that Israel also had an original form of popular wisdom, as other peoples had; a wisdom of farmers and shepherds, a wisdom very practical in character without, however, neglecting the religious knowledge of life; many sayings that are to be found in the earliest collection of Proverbs (x–xxii) may have been derived from this. In later days the study of wisdom becomes the concern of the official preceptors of princes and sons of high officials, men who derive their knowledge not only from the ancient Israelite wisdom sources, but

[1] J. Lindblom, *Wisdom in the O.T. prophets*, see Suppl. VT, III, pp. 192ff.; J. Fichtner, *Jesaja unter den Weisen*, ThLZ, 1949, pp. 75f; on Amos: H. H. Wolff, *op. cit.*, and S. Terrien, *Amos and Wisdom*, Muilenburg Festschrift, 1962, pp. 108ff.
[2] W. McKane, *Prophets and Wise men* 1965, strongly emphasizes the contrast between the classical prophets and wisdom.
[3] On *'amon* of Prov. viii. 30 see Gemser, *op. cit.*, p. 46; R. B. Y. Scott in VT, 1960, pp. 213ff.; W. Vischer in EvTh, 1962, pp. 309ff.
[4] We should make an exception in that case for the ancient 'Sippenweisheit' which was integrated into Yahwism at an early date (H. W. Wolff, *op. cit.*; Gerstenberger, *op. cit.*).

also from the wisdom literature of the surrounding nations: the Egyptians, Edomites, Phoenicians, and afterwards the Assyrians, too (Achiqar). They must instruct their pupils in the wisdom found at the royal courts. Hence they frequently revert to the wisdom literature of the other nations; no wonder then that a strong foreign influence can be traced in the book of Proverbs and the further wisdom literature (Job, Ecclesiastes). It has been discovered that Prov. xxii–xxiv and xxx contain extensive borrowings from Egyptian and other sources (see the Introductions). It is only to be expected that the study of wisdom in this form and for this purpose should have resulted in a certain spiritual attitude and in new opinions. We therefore find a strong universal human trait in Israelite wisdom, as well as moral conceptions that are in harmony with the range of ideas of foreign wisdom rather than with Israelite faith.[1]

The absorption of these views broadens and humanizes man's outlook upon life. People come to realize the *order* governing life in this world. We might say that 'man' is discovered – nowhere in the Old Testament[2] do we hear so much about 'man' *('adam)* as in the wisdom literature – as well as a certain world-order (an idea such as *ma'at* from Egypt is taken over in a typically Israelite moralized form which gives rise to the idea of 'good and bad' which carry with them their reward, an idea which almost has dogmatic force).[3] Yahweh is its Protector. The wisdom of Proverbs is dominated by a deep-rooted trust in God who maintains the world. Yahweh is here the Preserver of the world-order (see note 3). The Creation-belief plays an important part in the later wisdom literature in particular (Prov. viiif., Job, Eccl. xii).

In the post-exilic period wisdom is integrated theologically; it is fundamentally absorbed into the scheme of things of the Creation (Prov. iii. 19, viiif.) and therefore it is the true preceptor of mankind (i. 20ff.); its starting-point is the *yir'ath Yahweh*, the fear of the Lord (i. 7, ix. 10; cf. also already xv. 33). In Jesus Sirach it is essentially identified with the *Torah*. So in the later book of Proverbs wisdom has acquired some value as revelation and it can be looked upon as a spiritual authority. We does not, however, arrive at a knowledge of God Himself through wisdom, though it does teach us about God's Creation, about the world and the world-order.

For that reason wisdom cannot be considered a direct source of the

[1] Cf. Zimmerli, *op. cit.* The historical tradition plays no role in wisdom. It is true that we find Yahweh mentioned much oftener than Elohim.
[2] Id., p. 179.
[3] It is remarkable, though, that this conception is criticized so sharply in Job and Ecclesiastes and that in the book of Job the idea of the retribution of sin in suffering is put into the mouth of three non-Israelite speakers. Job, a non-Israelite too, becomes as it were the preacher of faith in Yahweh (though it was strongly influenced by the *chokhmah*, cf. the conception of the Creation in xxxviii ff.).

revelation of God in the Old Testament; it speaks only indirectly
of Him in so far as it speaks of the Creation and unfolds the Creation
ordinances. The forces of nature and the grandeur of the Creation
may be viewed as manifestations of God's greatness; Wisdom,
which explains God's Creation, can only show the glory of God indirectly, by teaching us the scheme of things ordained by God.

The insight passed on by the wise men aims first and foremost at
the education of the young Israelite princes who are to become the
future rulers and of the officials, at preparing them for practical life,
at teaching them how to attain a good, happy and long life. Moral
action, spiritual insight into the order of things and reckoning with
God are taught in order to enable man to make a success of life. This
gives the Proverbs a eudaemonistic, anthropocentric tendency, which
in this form is alien to the rest of the Old Testament message.

It is not strange, therefore, that this self-centred form of practical
piety should have broken down on the experience of life itself, so
that new problems arose. The books of Job and Ecclesiastes demonstrate that there were wise men who came to understand the optimism of this moralism was false. While the Job poet was brought very
close to the prophets' confession that God is the Holy and Unsearch-
able God, who yet does not deny His blessing to those who believe in
Him, Ecclesiastes was brought to the verge of a desperate attitude
to life. He was kept from the abyss of a consisted pessimism by a faith in
God, the Creator of the world and the individual, a faith which was
actually quite irrational to his ways of life and thought. It was the
last remnant of the Israelite chokmatic and religious tradition that
spiritually saved him as a human being from chaos. The most important role of wisdom in Israel was that it preserved tradition and gave
Israelite thought a broader view of man and the world. In this way it
helped to reveal the greatness of Yahweh, the God of Israel.

G. The place of revelation

In this chapter we cannot go into details concerning the holy places
available to Israel during its historical existence and the way they
were organized. These points should be dealt with in a biblical ar-
chaelogy and a history of Israelite religion.[1] We shall confine ourselves to the problem of the function of the sanctuary in Israelite
faith; we shall therefore attempt to give what might be called a
'theology of the holy place'.[2]

[1] For this we refer especially to R. de Vaux, *Institutions* II and H. Ringgren, *Israelitische Religion*.
[2] Cf. R. de Vaux, *op. cit.*, p. 166, who speaks of 'La Théologie du Temple', and now
also R. E. Clements, *God and Temple*, 1965.

Fundamentally we may take it that for Israel, as among the other peoples of the Near East, the sanctuary is the place where God is present. This is particularly true of the altar which is above all the symbol of that presence of God – and here again we find that this also applies to the rest of the ancient world.[1] It was erected in the place where Yahweh had once revealed Himself. Ringgren rightly referred to Ps. lxxxiv. 3 and xliif. (xliii. 4), where 'the courts of Yahweh' and 'the living God', 'the altar of God' and 'the God of joy' are looked upon as parallels, as if the Psalmist does not see any essential difference between the two.[2] Consequently it is not surprising that Amos sees Yahweh standing at the altar (ix. 1). The altar is the sanctuary itself *in nuce*.[3] In fact, it is the part of the sanctuary that is erected first and frequently it is the only part that is erected. In the ancient narratives and cultic laws we hear especially of the building of altars (Gen. xii. 7, xxvi. 25, xxxv. 1ff., Judges vi. 24, xiii. 19f., 2 Sam. xxiv. 18ff., Exod. xx. 22ff., cf. Deut. xii. 4ff. and Exod. xxxiv. 13). We sometimes find in the Old Testament that an altar was built before Yahweh had manifested Himself in a certain place (Gen. xxii) and occasionally even without a theophany being mentioned *expressis verbis* (Gen. xiii. 18; xxxiii. 20). Yet in spite of that we are justified in principle to associate the building of an altar with a theophany (whether God appears somewhere Himself or manifests His presence by an act of salvation; apart from the two last-mentioned texts see also Exod. xvii. 15 and 1 Sam. xiv. 35).

This connection is established especially in the earliest altar-text of Exod. xx, as vs. 24b must be read in an immediate connection with 24a. I should translate: An altar of earth thou shalt make unto Me (and shalt sacrifice thereon they burnt-offerings, etc.) in all places where I proclaim My name (come to thee); and I will bless thee'.[4]

Both in the Exodus-text and in that of Deuteronomy[5] the point is that the altar is erected in the place where Yahweh has His name proclaimed (Exod. xx) or establishes His name (Deut. xii). The altar recalls the fact that Yahweh has proclaimed His name in a certain place, that He has manifested His presence there, and thus proclaimed that place to be a holy place.

[1] See G. van der Leeuw, *Phaenomenologie der Religion*, 1933, p. 426, cf. p. 375.
[2] *Op. cit.*, p. 139, see also Gen. xxxiii. 20.
[3] If the horns of the altar were really 'masseben', sacred stones (K. Galling, s.v. *Altar* and *Steine, heilige*, RGG[3] I and II), the altar itself represents the godhead.
[4] The text was clearly revised.
[5] Exod. xx. 24–26 is an altar-commandment, in which two possibilities are posited. Vs. 24 is 'überfüllt' by the parenthetic clause. Deut. xii. 5 is a related younger parallel – also 'überfüllt': 'but unto the place which Yahweh your God shall choose out of all your tribes to put His name there, to dwell, shall ye seek the oracle, and thither thou shalt come'.

A sanctuary, marked by an altar, must therefore be viewed essentially as the place where Yahweh dwells[1], a place where people come to Him to offer up sacrifices to Him and to receive an oracle. When Yahweh manifests Himself in a certain place, this is in fact always done in order to proclaim His Word (see above p. 185). In a temple, a place sanctified forever by His presence, one may expect to receive His Word again and again.

But if a man wants to come to a sanctuary, he must not come empty-handed, because a man may not appear before God's face empty-handed (Exod. xxiii. 14, xxxiv. 20). No man could attempt to contact a superior without honouring him with a present (cf. 1 Sam. xvi. 2off., xxv. 18ff.), no man approaches a servant of God without a gift (1 Sam. ix. 7f.), no man can go to the sanctuary, i.e. to God, without an offering whatever it may be. The altar is the place par excellence where man can dedicate his gifts to God. That God is thought to be present in the temple is quite clear from an ancient legal text such as Exod. xxi. 6, where taking a slave to 'Elohim is considered equivalent to taking him to the sanctuary.[2]

The fact that in the ancient oriental world and in Israel the sanctuary is God's dwelling-place is underlined in many ways by the situation, the construction and the appointments of the temple.[3] But apart from the tradition of the foundation, in which the theophany is narrated, the most important thing is the divine symbol itself that is kept in the temple. In the ancient oriental world it is the image of the deity surrounded by the retinue of minor deities. In Israel, where the image of Yahweh was not accepted, the presence of God is symbolized in the Ark[4], at any rate in the temple at Siloh and afterwards in the temple in Jerusalem. At Bethel and Dan images of bulls (probably originally dedicated to El in olden days) were used as symbols of Yahweh.[5]

The temple in Jerusalem, to which we shall confine ourselves henceforth, as it is the only sanctuary of Israel recognized in the Old Testament, is regularly called 'the house of Yahweh' (e.g. 1 Kings vi. 37), and also 'the house for the name of Yahweh' (1 Kings viii. 20; cf. with this Deut. xii. 5). The name can represent Yahweh. The name-theology (see above, p. 208f.) makes it easier to bridge the distance

[1] Deut. has side by side: 'to put His name there' and 'to dwell'; there are two distinct traditions that underly these expressions. The latter must be older, pre-deuteronomic.
[2] See i. a. A. Dillmann and F. M. Th. Böhl in their Exoduscommentary, M. David, *The manumission of slaves*, OTS, V, 1948, p. 67, and H. A. Brongers, *De betekenis van het substantief 'Elohim*, NTT, III, p. 323.
[3] Ringgren, *op. cit.*, pp. 146ff.; De Vaux, *op. cit.* is even more reserved, pp. 169ff., 289ff.
[4] On the ark see i. a. my *Religion*, pp. 146ff., and De Vaux, *op. cit.*, pp. 127ff.
[5] Cf. also *Religion*, pp. 186f.

between God who dwells in heaven (1 Kings viii. 27) and God who is present in the temple. In olden days the conception that God is associated with certain places seems to have been accepted without any difficulty together with the notion that He also dwells in heaven. The reason was that logical thinking was not yet applied to spatial relations. In the periods after the beginning of kingship these relations were reflected on more deeply. Yet these reflections do not destroy the unity of God in heaven and God on earth. This is apparent from Isaiah vi; Yahweh is enthroned high above the temple and the whole earth; the latter itself is 'the fulness of glory'; here Yahweh's *kabod* is depicted as pervading heaven and earth, so that his presence does not only make itself felt in the temple but everywhere; it is universal, cosmic. How close the relation between Yahweh and the temple was in Isaiah's days for all that, is proved by texts such as Isa. xxxvii. 14f. (2 Kings xix. 14), where it is said of Hizkiah that he spreads out a letter from the Assyrian king 'in the house of the Lord' 'before the countenance of the Lord'. God's reply comes in the form of an oracle which Isaiah passes on to Hizkiah.

So from many things it is clear that Yahweh is thought to be present in the temple: when a man comes to the temple, he appears before God.[1] People wish to go to the temple to receive a word of deliverance from Yahweh who is present there (Ps. iii. 5, v. 8, xx. 3, and elsewhere), to behold His loving countenance (Ps. xxi. 7, xxvii. 7ff., xlii. 3).

It is therefore quite likely that people were granted theophany-experiences in the temple at certain festivals or perhaps on unexpected occasions, though it is not clear in what way these experiences took place[2], a verse such as Ps. xvii. 15 may be a reminiscence of the hope of a divine manifestation felt by an individual praying (see p. 187). There was apparently a definite place where temple-prophets could expect to receive a vision or word of God (Hab. ii. 1f.).

The temple has a two-fold function:

a. it serves as the place where the *torah* is given (see p. 240f.), or divine instruction, or an oracle; these are passed on by priests or temple prophets and serve to teach the people to live before the Lord in the right way (cultic oracles) or to give the King and the people instructions regarding an imminent war (prophecies about acts of war, cf Ps. xx). Generally speaking the task of the priesthood to instruct the people in the law of Yahweh is to be explained from this giving of the *torah*. It was especially the Levites who were afterwards charged with this duty;

b. to mediate in offering up sacrifices to God on the altar. We shall go into this subject at length in the next chapter.

[1] F. Nötscher, *op. cit.*; Exod. xxiii. 15, 17.   [2] See above, pp. 184ff.

So the temple serves wholly to advance the communion between God and man, and is the meeting-place. It was therefore considered an ancient Yahwistic symbol in Israel, which had already been given by Moses in the form of the tabernacle during the desertperiod (especially with P). From a historico-religious point of view it seems that the temple did not become such an important element in the Israelite religion until after the settlement of Palestine.

The prophets, too, accepted the notion that the temple was the token of God's presence, even the prohet Jeremiah who was in many respects so critical. But he opposes a faith that looks upon the temple as a symbol associated with God so closely that it could be eternally unalterable or imperishable. In his opinion the temple can only exist as long as the relationship between God and the people is a living reality. Therefore he says that the temple cannot escape the fate of destruction when God in His judgment must chastise the people with their downfall (vii, xxvi). Indeed, to support this message he can refer to what had happened to Siloh. Micah had given this message before him (iii. 12); Isaiah did predict the fall of Jerusalem, but not *expressis verbis* the destruction of the temple itself. This does not mean, however, that to him the temple could have seemed unassailable.[1] During the last few years before the downfall of the city and the temple Ezekiel associated himself with Jeremiah's prophecies of doom and clearly predicted the destruction of the temple (vii–xii).

The destruction of the temple was such a blow to the Judeans that many people threatened to lose their faith completely, or at any rate to lose their faith of being in a special relationship with Yahweh, their faith in their election (Jer. xxxi final vss and xxxiii) which was held up to them so seriously by the Deuteronomists in order to bring them to reflection and repentance (Deut. vi. f.). The Lamentations bear testimony to the great distress and the struggle brought about by the destruction of Jerusalem and the temple in the minds of the Judeans. Again and again the prophets point out that God does chastise His people severely and that He even brings about his judgment, but that He does not abandon His people to destruction and prepares a new future to them (Jeremiah, Ezekiel, Deutero-Isaiah).

After the exile the first thing to be rebuilt in Jerusalem is the temple. This is done after the decree of Cyrus and after the appeals of the prophets Haggai and Zechariah (Ezrah, Haggai, Zechariah). In this way it could become the centre of the life of the people after the exile.

Here the ancient traditions are put into practise again. Round the

[1] See my *Jahwe en zijn stad;* N. W. Porteous, *Jeruzalem-Zion: The growth of a symbol,* in W. Rudolph Festschrift, *Verbannung und Heimkehr,* 1961, pp. 220ff. (now in *Living the mystery,* 1967, pp. 93ff.); M. Noth: *Jerusalem und die isr. Religion,* O.T.S, VIII, 1950, pp. 220ff. (now in *Gesammelte Studien*); also J. Schreiner, *Sion-Jerusalem, Jahwes Königssitz,* 1963.

temple Israel could recover from the blows of the past and was given the chance to grow into its task of being the people of Yahweh. Even more than before the exile Israel became the people of the temple, a thecratic community. To a certain extent this meant the fulfilment of Ezekiel's vision (Ezek. xl–xlviii). But that was also the very moment when it appeared that a theocracy centred round the temple and a law which rounded off tradition were not the only things that Israel needed. In this age-long practise of tradition in the cultic, ritual and moral field one thing was lost: the operation of the Spirit. This had been mentioned by Ezekiel before the temple as a means to achieve renovation (xxxvi, xxxvii) and was also looked upon as necessary above all things by Zechariah who impressed it upon the priestly and wordly leader of the congregation of his days (iv; cf. also ii. 8f – modern trans. 4f –, vii. 8).

For centuries the temple continued to bear witness to God's faithfulness and communion with Him. Yet, as ritualism and traditionalism came to predominate, the later development of spiritual life in many respects passes by the holy place. The hope of a new experience of communion with God in the Messianic kingdom took on an ever more concrete aspect and largely dominated the spiritual life of the people (apocalyptics). This does not mean that these groups turned their backs on the temple as such, it does mean that they rejected the ruling priesthood and the sacrificial services and festivals as celebrated in practise (the Essenes).

The destruction of the seond temple also sealed the fate of Israel as a people; but faith in the God of Israel and so in Israel's future remained unshaken as it had been at the first downfall. The destruction of the temple did mean the loss of an important point of support, but history and the Word continued to speak of God's faithfulness. The props on which Israel rested were the *Torah*, the *Nebiim* and the *Kethubim*, but these bore witness to more than ritual and cult alone. Yahweh had made use of the temple as a token, but His relationship with Israel was much more comprehensive and rooted far more deeply than what could be experienced in the temple-cult by itself.

II. THE CULT

a. *General Observations* [1]

As in the last section of this chapter we shall understand by the cult the official cult in the sanctuary. We shall not deal with oracles at this

[1] G. B. Gray, *Sacrifice in the O.T.*, 1925; G. van der Leeuw, *op. cit.*, pp. 317ff.; A. J. Wensinck, *Liturgie in het O.T.*, 1937; S. Mowinckel, *Religion und Kultus*, 1953; *The Psalms and Cult*, 2 vols, 1962; E. L. Ehrlich, *Kultsymbolik im A.T. und im nachbiblischen*

place (see above, p. 241), but we shall pay special attention to the service at the altar and the cycle of feasts associated with it.

The place of the cult in religion in general and in Israel in particular is a vexed question indeed. While by some scholars, particularly by the so-called *myth-and-ritual school* [1], a central and even dominating importance is attached to the cult in the Old Testament, there are also others who only allow it a subordinate position. The former do not only consider the cult the predominant element in the priestly parts of the Old Testament only, but also in the Psalms and the Prophets, and even in the historical literature. Thus the prophets come to be looked upon as cultservants[2], but, moreover, the historical books are also taken to consist partly of liturgies recited at cultic feasts[3].

The latter believe that it is only in one of the latest parts of the Old Testament (the Priestly Code in the Pentateuch) that a position of any importance is attributed to the cult, and for that reason they do not look upon the cult as an essential, integral element of the Old Testament teaching, which they think to be essentially prophetic in character and origin; prophetism is simply looked upon as anti-cultic.

Both these conceptions are one-sided, though both can refer to certain elements in the literature of the Old Testament that has come down to us. We do find anti-cultic utterances in the work of the prophets which must not be glossed over (Jer. vii. 22; Amos v. 25), but that does not mean that the prophets may be called anti-cultic

---

Judentum, 1959; H.Ringgren, *op. cit.*; R. de Vaux, *op. cit.*; H.J.Kraus, *Gottesdienst in Israel²*, 1962; A. S. Herbert, *Worship in Ancient Israel*, 1959.
[1] Called by this name after S.H.Hooke's work *Myth and Ritual*, published in 1933. In 1935 a new work of this group was published under the title of *The Labyrinth*. The same scholar published another book in 1958, only partly written by the same contributors, and far less radical in character, under the title of *Myth, ritual and Kingship*. From this book it appeared that a number of English scholars, among whom Hooke himself, rejected the extreme consequences of this 'school' which had been drawn by the so-called Uppsalaschool. Among them we may include A.Haldar with his *Associations of Cultprophets* and J.Engnell, *Studies in Divine Kingship*. Indeed, in Scandinavia too a divergence of opinions arose soon. Though S.Mowinckel's *Psalmstudien* gave a strong impulse to the rise of this school, he dissociated himself from it. An intermediate position was taken up by A.Bentzen, *Det sakrale Kongedømme*, 1945, and *Messias, Moses Redivivus, Menschensohn*, 1948. See also H.H.Rowley, *The O.T. and modern Study*, especially the contributions of A.R.Johnson *(Psalms)* and G.W.Anderson *(Hebrew Religion)*; also the former's *Sacral Kingship in Ancient Israel*, 1955; cf. also the critical article by J.Lindblom in the Bertholet Festschrift.
[2] As we already find with Haldar, and recently with H. Graf Reventlow (see p. 234, n. 1).
[3] For example Joh.Pedersen, *Passahfest und Passahlegende*, ZAW, 1934, pp. 161ff.; A.Bentzen, *The cultic use of the story of the ark in Samuel*, JBL, 1948; *The ritual background of Amos i. ii*, OTS, VIII, 1950, pp. 85ff.; *Daniel, Ein Versuch zur Vorgeschichte der Martyrerlegende*, Bertholet Festschrift, pp. 58ff.; in his *Das formgeschichtliche Problem des Hexateuch*, 1938, G. von Rad sought the basis of the ancient Israelite historiography in cultic legends (see also his *Theology* I).

251

without any further qualification. On the other hand there is something like a 'cultic heart' beating behind the facade of many Psalms, and sometimes behind the message of the prophets, but that again does not mean that all the Psalms should be understood originally in terms of the cult, or that all the prophets were cult-servants. And as regards the historical wirtings, even if certain parts of these (apart from the cultic laws) were used in the cult at certain feasts, that does not mean that the tradition as a whole was determined by the cult. The historical books were influenced by prophetic tendencies in so many respects that it is impossible to dissociate them from these influences.[1]

First of all, we shall have to state things clearly. We may therefore refer first and foremost to an observation made above, that we must distinguish clearly between the facts in the history of the religion of Israel and the approach to these facts in the Old Testament sources, which describe these events from a definite point of view.

Large parts of the Old Testament do not only represent a fairly recent stage of the religion of Israel, but are strongly influenced by the spirit of prophecy in their composition and development. The (late) cultic legislation itself had passed through the criticism of the prophets, and most of the narratives are from quite different hands, date from very different periods and give a strongly varied and very fragmentary picture of cultic life. Only very little is known about the pre-exilic cult[2], and for that reason we shall have to exercise the utmost care in drawing conclusions from the most recent material. The cultic life of Israel in the course of time must in practice always have differed from what we now find in the cultic laws.

After establishing that both for Israel and for the heathen world of nations the cult was the normal means of serving God, Procksch[3] quite rightly remarks that Israel was not an immutable quantity in history, but that it was different in the periods of the desert journey, of the conquest of the promised land, of the judges and the kings, etc. Above all, we must add that the cult, too, in these different periods (or also even in one period in different parts of the country) differed in each case. The cult may form a fairly constant quantity in religious

---

[1] In spite of von Rad's observations on pp.127f. of his *Theology* I; The fact that von Rad cannot accept these prophetic tendencies results from his quite one-sided view of the prophets. In his opinion there can be no organic connection between their message and the ancient Israelite tradition. According to him the prophets had broken with the whole of the ancient Israelite conception of history (cf. above p.200). This view is untenable; moreover it also neglects completely the results of literary-critical research, which prove that the oldest traditions were revised in great par by E and later Yahwist authors.
[2] So rightly J. v. d. Ploeg again in a review of Mowinckel's *The Psalms* in VT, 1964, p.230.
[3] *Theologie*, p.531.

life, but it is not immutable. It is true, however, that the cult has the peculiarity that it does not abandon traditional forms easily; these are kept side by side with new elements, which often give the whole a completely new content; this variation in the cult has often been recognized and taken into account too little. In the desert period the place of the sacrifice may have been (and probably was) quite different from that of the period when the Israelite economy was predominantly agricultural or of the period from which the cultic laws must date that have been handed down to us. During the desert period the tribes probably knew external cultforms in a limited measure, and it is doubtful which of these should be considered as characteristic of that period.[1] The cultforms and their hierarchical order also differed frequently widely in the various successiveperiods, probably they differed from sanctuary to sanctuary as well: in one place the oracle may have predominated, elsewhere the offering or a certain form of sacrifice, elsewhere again the liturgical element. The foundation of the temple at Jerusalem may have had some influence, but it is not certain in what sense it influenced the other sanctuaries. Not until the period of the last kings (Josiah) and the post-exilic period did the temple at Jerusalem become of predominant importance. We know next to nothing about all these developments for the history of religion; a clear idea concerning these things would be most important but to the theology of the Old Testament it is hardly relevant. What is important for theology is the question what the cult of which the Old Testament speaks meant for the faith of Israel.

If we are to answer this question satisfactorily we shall have to distinguish clearly between the cultic laws of the Old Testament as they have been handed down to us, and the cult as it is presupposed in various historical narratives. We shall also have to attempt to find the common elements proper to the Israelite cult as a whole and also to define the difference in character between the Israelite and non-Israelite cults.

For from a literary point of view the cultic laws (Leviticus) are late, though they contain essentially ancient elements; they have passed through the criticism of the prophets, which introduced some elements and removed others[2]; indeed, the Deuteronomic legislator had already made many alterations in the cult (cf. Deut.xii, the sacrificial law; Deut.xvi, the Passover) and Ezekiel had also formed a legislation of his own for cultic reform. Further, in some older narratives certain cultic elements come to the fore which are not found the same way in the cultic laws.

[1] See pp. 35ff.
[2] See my *Erwählung*, p.82.

For a first and correct view of the cult in the Old Testament the best way of approaching it is making a comparison with the cult in other related Semitic religions, in particular the Assyro-Babylonian, about which we are informed best up to the present. Here the position and function of the cult are completely different from those of the Old Testament cult: the creation of man is represented as its leading idea; here man is said to have been created to serve the gods, to enable them to lead a carefree, divine life.[1] In Sumerian mythology man is 'given breath' to look after the sheep-cots and the 'good things' of the gods[2]; in the ancient Mesopotamian world the state is wholly orientated towards the service of the cult as Thorkild Jacobsen has described it[3]: 'By upholding a great god, by providing the economic basis which permits that god to enjoy full and free self-expression, the city-state is upholding some great power of the universe and assuring its freedom to function as it should. And this is the function of the human city-state within the cosmos. In this manner it contributes to maintaining and perpetuating the ordered cosmos and its powers'.

Here the cult is a service for and to the gods in order that this world of which man forms part and this state, so closely linked with these gods, should survive. Here the cult ensures in principle the existence of the gods and therefore of the cosmos and of the state itself. The cult is the all-important means to preserve God, the world, and man.[4] Besides this state-cult there is also the personal cult of each member of the state in behalf of a deity whom he has chosen as his personal god; the cult of this deity has for its object to gain the favour of the deity, particularly in days of distress and illness, days when the anger of the gods manifests itself.[5] This conception of the cult approaches very closely that other conception well-known because of its utility-motif, the *do-ut-des* principle, found principally in the Indian and Roman world.[6]

The conception of the cult in the Old Testament is very remote from these two views. In Yahwism there is no ground at all for such ideas. It would be absurd to say that in the Old Testament the cult

---

[1] *Enuma elish* VI, 8, 34ff., for example Labat's edition, *Le poème babylonien de la création*, 1935, pp. 142ff.; see also my *Paradijsvoorstelling*, pp. 85ff.
[2] See S. N. Kramer: *Sumerian Mythology*, 1944, pp. 72ff.; and my *Paradijsvoorstelling*, pp. 68f.
[3] H. Frankfort, etc., *The intellectual Adventure of Man* (which afterwards appeared under the title of *Before Philosophy*), 1946, p. 191.
[4] An idea which is quite in keeping with the ancient Eastern world outside Israel, where theogony and cosmogony are mingled together, where the gods are really personified forces of nature, etc.
[5] See for example Br. Meissner, *Babylonien und Assyrien*, II, 1925, p. 83; and Frankfort, *op. cit.*, pp. 204ff.
[6] See G. van der Leeuw, p. 328.

'upheld' God or maintained the world; and it would be equally absurd to think that in the Old Testament the cult should be regarded directly in the light of utility (Ps.1, Isa.xl. 16).

The cult is not something man does for God, so that God may profit by it, nor is it performed in order to obtain something from God, so that man may get something out of it, for in Israel God is good to His people. In Israel the cult exists in order to *maintain and purify the communion between man and God: the cult exists as a means to integrate the communion between God and man which God has instituted in His Covenant, in other words, the cult exists for the sake of the atonement.*[1]

The other two conceptions, that man does something for God by means of the cult, and that by it man may achieve something with God, are not quite foreign to the practice of Israelite life and may certainly have played a part in the practice of religion in certain periods. The first idea occurs repeatedly in the Old Testament in a negative form, but only to be contradicted.

This, however, proves that it must have been popular in Israel (Ps.1 ;cf. xl. 7ff., li. 18; Isa. xliii. 22ff.) ;the second idea is no texpressed directly, but it is more or less presupposed in such a text as 1 Sam. xxvi. 19.

But essentially neither of these belongs to the Yahweh-religion as taught by the Old Testament; the rôle of the cult is widely different from that of the cult in the Babylonian world, where the temples were thought to have been created first.[2] In Israel the temple is a late phenomenon, of secondary importance[3]; it is true that the altar is thought to be very early: at all events it was used already by Noach after the Flood and by Abraham after his arrival in the promised land, though it does not yet figure in the narrative of the privemal history of man (sacrifice does figure there in Gen. iv. 1ff. as an offering of first-fruits and calling upon the name of Yahweh, Gen. iv. 26).

On the one hand the cult in the form of sacrificial service was looked upon in Israel as something essentially human and then also as an integral part of Israel's religion, on the other hand it is a late element in the form of the temple-ritual. In Exod. xxiv ff. the cult is represented as having been regulated by covenant and therefore as part of the covenant-relationship. Theologically this is of some importance, for it demonstrates that in the final (though late) form which theology

---

[1] This word taken in a general sense.
[2] See my *Paradijsvoorstelling*, pp. 90f., 97.
[3] Even if there is a tendency for the temple to predominate more and more, particularly when the temple at Jerusalem (in Deut. declared to be the only sanctuary) dominates the whole of religious life in the post-exilic period (the Theology of Chronicles!).

acquired in Israel *the cult is associated with God's Covenant*,[1] and not with the Creation, as in Babylon. In Gen. i. 28 man is given a cultural task at the Creation, not a cultic assignment; Yahweh does not need a cult in the ancient Eastern sense of the word. The cult has no cosmic significance, but has a purely *religious* meaning.

Israel's God does not demand a cult from which He could reap benefit, but on the contrary He gives His people a cult that enables them to maintain communion with Him by means of the atonement. (Lev. xvii. 11). In Israel the cult preserves the communion with God, helps to establish the intercourse between God and man: it ensures, as it were, that this intercourse should continue. The cult is, as it were, a road for two-way traffic: in the cult God comes to man, but man also comes to God.[2] Thus God comes to man as a forgiving God and affords him an opportunity to cleanse himself regularly of his sins; and in the cult man comes to God with his confession of guilt, with his tokens of thankfulness and adoration. God also comes to man in the cult as a revealing God – He makes use of priests, symbols, and the temple to proclaim His will in the Torah; we have already dealt with this subject,[3] so that we shall not enter into it at length here, but mention it only to demonstrate how the cult is a focal point of the intercourse with God, and, as a matter of fact, in either direction.

We may be allowed a slight digression with respect to one point. The cult occupies a central position, but in Israel it is not the only way in which the communion between God and man is effected: inward communion also plays too important a part for that (cf. 1 Sam. xxx. 6; 2 Sam. xii). Indeed, the same might be said of any religion; in his *Phaenomenologie* G. van der Leeuw also admits that religion has an inward as well as an external aspect – though, quite rightly, he immediately adds the remark[4] that the words inward and external do not denote a fundamental distinction, because an external act can only be understood in its relations to the inner man.

One might perhaps try to group the inward action under the word cult as well[1] (in that case cult and religion would be the same thing), but this is not the normal use of the word and would even have to be stigmatized as a linguistic misuse of the word. The cult is the complex of outward forms and acts, in corporate life, through which the inter-

---

[1] See also Ps. l. 5f.: the sacrifice is a token of the Covenant with Yahweh, it is not intended (cf. vs. 8ff.) to provide sustenance for Him.
[2] For that reason I cannot agree with J. v.d. Ploeg, who in his above-mentioned review of Mowinckel's *Psalms* thinks that the cult originates one-sidedly with man.
[3] See above p. 241.
[4] *Op. cit.*, p. 317.
[5] For example if one were to take Mowinckel's description of the cult as 'creation's response to the Eternal' as a definition (see *Religion und Kultus*, p. 13).

course between God and man takes place. Particularly in Israel a personal communion with God is also possible without these external forms, as is especially evident in the figures of the classical prophets; the most remarkable feature is perhaps that the beginning of Israel's religion is described in these few words: 'Now the Lord had said unto Abram' (Gen.xii.1); it was therefore a voice that did it, as also in Isa.xl.6. The prophet Micah even says – when things are going wrong with the external form of religion, the cult – that true religion is something quite different from the cult: it is 'to do justly, and to love mercy, and to walk humbly with thy God' (Mic.vi.6–8). The fact that piety is put on a level with humility, is also quite obvious (the pious man is the 'ani or the 'anaw, the humble man; in Babylon the pious man is the na'idu, he who takes care, the man who maintains the observances with respect to the gods).

If in Israel the cult is not the only 'means of communication' between God and man, it remains an element of central importance; in Israel the pious man who is unable to go to the house of God with the celebrating crowd feels miserable (Ps.xlii.2–6); we should not forget the songs of pilgrimage (Ps.cxxff.). For the sanctuary with its priests, festivals, and ceremonial is the visible token of God's Covenant, of the communion between God and the people or the individual.

Like every cult the cult of Israel is the visible expression of the inner nature of Israel's religion. The close connection between the external and the inward aspects of religion – which G. van der Leeuw emphatically put first and foremost – rules out the assumption that the Israelite cult was fundamentally merely Canaanite, and adapted in some degree to Israelite ideas, as some scholars would have it[1], who would trace back Israel's cult either to Babylon or to the Canaanite, and Phoenician world. Even though it is an established fact that Israel as a young civilized nation associated itself with certain ancient forms of religious life, particularly in the cult, yet on the other hand Israel did not take these over without more ado, but used them quite freely and independently and left its own mark on them; this applies to the use of the Psalms[2] as well as to the adoption of certain cultic schemes such as the celebration of the feast of the New Year[3] etc.

[1] See p.36 n.2 on Dussaud.
[2] On the O.T. Psalms and their connection with the Babylonian see for instance G.Widengren, *The Accadian and Hebrew Psalms of lamentation*, 1936, who emphasizes the dependence very strongly; besides this H.Gunkel and J.Begrich, *Einleitung in die Psalmen*, who, like Zimmern, Landsberger and Driver, strongly oppose the dependence of the Hebrew Psalms on the non-Scriptural Psalms; F.Stummer, *Sumerisch-akkadische Parallelen zum Aufbau alttest. Psalmen*, 1922 (cf. Landsberger's criticism in *OLZ*, 1925); Zimmern in *Alte Orient* VII[3]; Simpson, *The Psalmists*, 1926, with contributions by H.Gressmann, 'The development of Hebrew Psalmody'; and particularly by G.R.Driver, 'The Psalms in the light of Babylonian Research'; C.C.Cum-

The foundations of the Israelite cult are to be found in the religion of Israel and in many respects it presents to us forms that are quite its own, particularly by the historicizing of ancient rites that go back partly to ancestral nomadic observances, partly to Canaanite agricultural feats; by the celebration of the Sabbath which is unique in the East (not only the day itself but also the manner in which it is celebrated); and by the fact that various elements found in other ancient Eastern religions are lacking here, for instance the external inspection of omens in the examination of the liver, in astrology, etc.; the feminine element in the priesthood; the image of the deity, etc. These are only some few factors that stand out clearly and immediately; if we could survey the whole field the difference between the cult in Israel and the cults of the surrounding nations would also become evident in various minor details.

The decisive main characteristic of the religion of Israel as it clearly manifests itself in the Old Testament cult is the strong consciousness of the communion between God and man, of the fact that God is the holy God of the Covenant, and that the people and the individual are in the grip of sin and are again and again in danger of breaking this communion. This gives the cult its permanent tendency to maintain and restore this communion between the holy God and sinful man, both on the national and the individual plane. If we want to gain a correct understanding of the Israelite cult we must therefore see it against the background of the doctrine of the holiness of God, of the sinfulness of man and of the Covenant between this holy God and this sinful man. As this was proclaimed in ever varying keys and the knowledge of God's holiness and that of man's sinfulness have many different aspects, it is no wonder that the representations of the atonement often differ widely, now running parallel, then again diametrically opposed. It makes a lot of difference whether sin is considered concretely and realistically as a taint, or more personally, as guilt, and also whether the holiness of God is depicted in naturalistic or rather in moral tones – all these things have great influence on the practice of the atonement, and consequently the cultic acts in the various periods often differ in the way of their execution. Yet there is also a fundamental connection between various ideas and acts, all

ming, *The Assyrian and Hebrew hymns of praise*, 1934; W.G.Kunstmann, *Die baby-lonische Gebetsbeschwörung*, 1932; A.Falkenstein and W. von Soden, *Sumerische und Akkadische Hymnen und Gebete*, 1953; A.H.Edelkoort, *Het zondebesef in de babylonische boetepsalmen*, 1918 (doctorate thesis Utrecht); F.M. de Liagre Böhl, *Hymnisches und Rhythmisches in den Amarnabriefen aus Kanaan*, Opera Minora, 1953, pp.375ff.; M.A. Beek, *Aan Babylons Stromen*[2], 1951, pp.213ff.
3 On the so-called 'Enthronement festival' see above pp.330f. The time is approaching when an accurate comparison can be made between the Israelite religious festivals, based on agricultural life, and the Phoenician and Canaanite festivals, as soon as further progress has been made with the interpretation of the Ras Shamra texts.

borne by the main characteristic mentioned above. This appears very clearly from the 'sacred times', the *Feasts* and the 'sacred acts', the sacrificial service.

Feasts

The *feasts*[1] were instituted in order to maintain the communion between Yahweh and the people, or, as we may also say, to 'sanctify' life.[2] This sanctification is effected in various ways: in the Passover feast God's redemptive act of the deliverance from Egypt is celebrated by the reiteration of a kind of cultic drama (the only thing of its kind known in Israel) in the form of some actions and the reciting of a festive legend; thus Yahweh is proclaimed as Israel's God of salvation from generation to generation. In the course of time the form of this celebration, which had probably sprung from the ancient Semitic lustral spring-offering festival, was modified extensively; by the process of historicizing it developed from a tribal feast into a temple-feast and family-feast[3]; by its sacrificial ritual, its blood-manipulation and its legend of the origin of the festival it bears the character of a renewal of the relationship between God and the people; the Passover lamb is on the one hand a community-meal (peace-offering), on the other hand a sin-offering (the sprinkling of blood), and by the legend connected with it it was a glorification of Yahweh; viewed in this manner this feast is in itself already representative of the whole of the Israelite cult. From earliest times it had therefore been the central Israelite feast.[4] With this (originally pre-Palestinian) main feast of ancient Israel an agricultural feast (the feast of *Maṣṣoth*) came to be quite closely linked in the course of time, a feast that emphasizes the character of a thanksgiving feast to glorify Yahweh.

Something similar is to be observed in the autumn cycle of feasts; there, however, all was not reduced to one feast, but the various elements were spread out; fundamentally, however, they belong together. On the first day of the 7th month (according to the ancient Israelite calendar originally the beginning of the year) the New-Year's day is celebrated, on which Yahweh is glorified as Creator and King, while the feast-legend was probably formed by the Creation-narrative[5]; the

[1] See Exod.xii, Deut.xvi, Lev.xxiii; xvi; compare archeological works; now also De Vaux, *op. cit.*; Ehrlich, *op. cit.* and Kraus, *op. cit.*
[2] Cf. J.Pedersen, *Israel*, III–IV, 'Passahfest und Passahlegende', *Z.A.W.*, 1934, pp. 161ff. and *R.G.G.*[3] III pp. 177f. s.v. *'Heiligung. Im A.T.'*.
[3] On its origin see pp. 36f. above, G.Beer, *Exodus* on Exod.xii, R.de Vaux, *Les sacrifices de l'A.T.*, 1964, pp. 7ss.: Le sacrifice paschal; on the part of jewish orthodoxy J.B. Segal, *The Hebrew Passover*, 1963.
[4] Compare the way in which Ezekiel (xlv. 18ff.) breaks up the Passover festival into different festivals; cf. my 'Hizza, lustration and consecration', *O.T.S.*, VII, 1950, pp. 201ff., particularly pp. 220f.
[5] See above p. 334.

fire-offering that is offered up (Lev. xxiii. 25) is the burnt-offering that is considered as a gift, an offering to honour Yahweh. On the 10th day the feast of purification and atonement *in optima forma* follows: the Day of Atonement (Lev. xvi), at which the act of expiation for the sins of the people is performed directly before the face of God by the sprinkling in the Holy of Holies.[1] And on the 15th the Feast of Tabernacles follows, a harvest festival, which also serves to renew the Covenant (cf. in Deut. xxxi. 9–13, the command that once every seven years the law should be read officially).[2] In contrast with the spring-feast this autumn cycle of feasts is truly Palestinian in character, both the time of the New-Year's day and the origin of the Day of Atonement, which originally was probably a feast for the purification of the temple, and the Feast of Tabernacles are of Palestinian origin. As we have already observed, the typically Palestinian agricultural feasts (the feasts of *maṣṣoth* and *sukkoth*) were linked with the great feasts; a third feast that did not rise to such great importance was the feast of *shabu 'oth* (the feast of weeks), the later Pentecost, the thanksgiving-feast after the wheat harvest. Like *maṣṣoth* and *sukkoth* this feast, too, was historicized and, in a later period, connected with the giving of the Law on Mount Sinai.[3] In contrast to the Canaanite feasts the harvest festivals are no longer naturalistic in character, no longer devoted to the promotion of fertility, but linked with historical events and, in so far as they remained agricultural feasts, they were stamped as harvest-thanksgiving festivals by the offerings of the first fruits. The character of these agricultural feasts, at any rate as they developed afterwards during the prophetic and Deuteronomic periods, appears most clearly from the liturgy of the offering of the first-fruits, that has been preserved in

[1] See my *Hizza*, pp. 219ff.
[2] On this festival and the whole connection between the three festivals in the 7th (1st) month see the authors mentioned above p. 250 n. 1.
[3] We cannot go further into the problems concerning the background of the Sinai-tradition. The research of von Rad and Noth into the history of tradition has raised two questions: whether there really are historical connections between the Sinai-tradition and the tradition and history of the exodus, and if not, where else they could have originated. Both these scholars reject such a historical connection and suppose that the tradition of the revelation on Mount Sinai arose from a different range of tradition than that from which the tradition of the exodus from Egypt stems. According to them the Sinai-datum belongs to tribal groups that had from of old been familiar with the God of Mount Sinai through pilgrimages. Apparently they suppose that Yahweh was introduced among the tribes of Israel by this group, whereas the stories of the exodus and the desert journey were introduced by tribal groups that invaded the country from the East. An amphictyony established in Palestine around the sanctuary at Shechem apparently linked these traditions with the patriarchal traditions that were familiar to the tribal groups which already inhabited the country. So the Sinai narratives should be explained from cultic connections. Cf. M. Noth, *Geschichte Israels* (many reprints); *Überlieferungsgeschichte des Pentateuch*, 1948; Von Rad, *Hexateuch* see criticism i. a. by J. Bright, *History of Israel; Early History writing in Ancient Israel;* A. S. van der Woude, *Uittocht en Sinaï*, and my *Religion of Israel*, Ch. V.

Deut. xxvi. 1ff.[1] Here it becomes evident how much the historicizing process had already influenced all these feasts.

From these agricultural festivals with their first-fruits it appears, as also, for instance, from the redemption of the first-born sons, that Yahweh is honoured as the giver of all gifts of nature, as the maintainer of His people. By the fact that He is offered the first-fruits of everything all is dedicated to Him *(pars pro toto)*. The same thing obtains for the *Sabbath*, the weekly recurring feast-day, in which Israel gave expression in a very special way to the sacredness of the life received from God, by sanctifying an ever-recurring day to Him.[2]

3. Sacrifies[3]

The three most striking elements of cultic life: the glorification of Yahweh, the maintaining of communion with Him, and the cleansing from sin, which already appeared in our treatment of the feasts, emerge still more clearly in the *sacrificial ceremonies*. The three principal offerings that are distinguished in Lev. i–vii each bring out with particular clarity one of those facets. This does not mean, however, that each of these offerings represents one such facet quite exclusively. Of the burnt-offering, which is first and foremost a gift-offering to glorify God, we read in Lev. i. 4 that it serves to make atonement. Indeed, the whole of the sacrificial cult is dominated by the idea of atonement.[3] It is evident, however, that in this statement, as also in

[1] See G. von Rad, *Das formgeschichtliche Problem des Hexateuchs*, 1938; on the cult in general in Deut., A. R. Hulst, *Het karakter van de cultus in Deut.*, doctorate thesis Groningen, 1938. See the criticism of von Rad's view that Deut. xxvi contains an ancient creed in A. Weiser, *Einleitung* and elsewhere, cf. below p. 296 n. 1.

[2] See below p. 396.

[3] R. de Vaux, *Les sacrifices*; H. Ringgren, *Sacrifice in the Bible*, 1962; R. J. Thompson, *Penitence and sacrifice in Early Israel outside the Levitical Law*, 1963; D. Schötz, *Schuld- und Sündopfer im A.T.*, 1930; A. Wendel, *Das Opfer*, 1927; G. B. Gray, *op. cit.*; R. Hentschke, *Opfer. Im A.T.*, RGG³ IV, 1641ff.

[4] Cf. J. Pedersen, *Israel*, III–IV, p. 399; 'Whatever the view taken of sacrifice, it always contained germs of what developed into the idea of atonement. The worshipper purified himself, and was purified by the sacrifice, he presented a gift to the God and partook of a meal with the God; in all cases a new peace was created for him through the sacrifice, a renewal of harmony. But man could only be in harmony with God when he was 'whole'. The sacrifice removed whatever was wasting away his integrity, what was called sin. This was brought about by man being sanctified while at the same time God was induced to be lenient towards him.'

And similarly H. Wheeler Robinson, *Inspiration and Revelation in the O.T.*, 1946, p. 227: 'The sacrificial act is in miniature the actual renewal of a relation. In the fundamental conception of sacrifice as a gift, seen in the whole burnt-offering, acceptance of it restores some previous relation which has been broken, or reinforces one which exists. The peace offering works to similar ends by different means. Here the meal eaten by the worshippers and the blood poured out for the deity on the altar, coming as they do from the same consecrated animal, realistically unite the worshippers and their God.

The sin-offering with its special manipulation of the blood primarily cancels what the anthropologist would call a broken taboo, figuring as a ritual offence. The guilt-offering centres in the necessity to make reparation for offences of wider range, such

261

Lev. i. 4, the idea of atonement is used in a general sense, namely, in the words of H. Wheeler Robinson, as the *renewal of the relation*. In Christian dogmatic theology a sharp distinction is usually made between reconciliation (*Versöhnung*, καταλλαγή) and expiation (*Sühne*, ἱλασμός); this distinction – and as a matter of fact – others, too (see below), are also to be found in the Old Testament, but the two ideas are no longer clearly distinct. Thus, for instance, the word that was originally used exclusively to denote expiation, *kipper*[1] is used in some texts in the sense of reconciliation or in the meaning of to forgive and to receive forgiveness.[2]

Lev. i–vii together with xvi and xvii give the best insight into the cultic ceremonies and their character, even though these chapters

as theft, in addition to restoration. Yahweh's will as well as man's right has been infringed: the offering, if accepted, restores the broken relation to Him' (cf. Ps.l.5).

[1] The original meaning of *kipper* in the O.T. is probably, like the Akkadian *kuppuru*, 'to smooth', 'to smooth out', 'to spread', and not (as Köhler argues from the Arabic) 'to cover'; this latter is a secondary meaning which also occurs in Hebrew, but the parallelism between *kipper* and *machah* (to put away) and other similar synonyms, as well as other meanings of *kafar*, make us think first and foremost of 'to spread', in various shades of meaning; see besides the Lexica and Theologies especially J. Herrmann, *Die Idee der Sühne im A.T.*, 1905, and *Th. Wb. z. N.T.*, III, pp. 301ff., with literature on the subject, and J.J. Stamm, *Erlösen und Vergeben im A.T.*, 1948. This expiatory conception in its purely lustrative form is not found any more in the O.T. ritual institutions, but it is implied in various expiatory acts.

It is connected with a pre-Israelite conception (still active in Israel!) of sin as a stain, a taint, which endangers the well-being of the individual and the community. That sin is a stain which is wiped off by the *kipper*-act also appears clearly from the prescriptions given in Lev.v. 1 with respect to the 'sins' that make a sin-offering imperative; from the ceremonies of the Day of Atonement. (Lev.xvi), which purify temple and altar as well as the high priest and the people (Lev.xvi. 19f.); and from the consecration of the altar (Lev.viii. 14f.), the atonement for a house, where the word *kipper* is also used (Lev.xiv. 53), and the purification of lepers, for whom a sin-offering must also be offered up to obtain atonement (Lev.xiv. 19). A related idea may be supposed to be the original background of the manipulation of the sacrificial blood at the Passover, namely spreading the blood of the lamb on the door-posts and lintel. All these acts are apotropaic (keeping off demons) or lustrative in character; often these two elements coincide (cf. also the Passover).

In many cases, also in the prophetic books, the verb *kipper* can be translated metaphorically by '*to wipe off*', cf. Isa.vi. 7, xxviii. 18, Jer.xviii. 23, as appears from the parallel ideas used there (Isa.vi. 7, 'taken away'; Isa.xxviii. 18, 'shall not stand'; Jer.xviii. 23, 'to blot out').

One may suppose that the belief in the redeeming power of the bood was one of the main reasons why the ritual of the expiatory sacrifice developed so strongly during the period of the kings. This belief greatly stimulated the readiness to offer up sacrifices. It was this ever growing faith in the (magically) active power of the lustrative

acts that caused the prophets to criticize the whole of the expiatory ritual of their days.

In the cultic laws of the book of Leviticus this idea has been overcome fundamentally: the blood is still used as a purification from sin, but the lustrative ritual is understood to have a purifying function only *because Yahweh was willig to accept it as such* (Lev.xvii. 11).

[2] In Lev.i. 4 the verbs *raṣah* and *kipper* are found side by side; in Gen.xxxii. 21 *kipper* may already mean to atone, cf. also texts such as Prov.xvi.6, Ps.lxv.4, where the best translation is 'to forgive', and Exod.xxxii. 30, where it is best translated by 'to effect forgiveness.'

refer to the cult of the post-exilic temple[1], so that they contain some elements due to later prophetical criticism. One of these elements is the emphatic provision that the cult only obtains for sins committed *bishegagah*, 'in error'; another is the fact that only burnt-offerings and peace-(community-) offerings will serve to placate Yahweh, not sin- and guilt-offerings.[2] These exist in order to atone for sin and to make man pure in the sight of God, thus restoring the communion between the sinner and the Holy God. In other words by the expiatory offerings proper God Himself is not *'umgestimmt'*, God does not change from a wrathful God into a favourably disposed God; this may be connected with the fact that the real reconciliation is said to originate with God Himself (Lev. xvii. 11f., see below).

b. The Sacrificial Laws

The leading ideas of the sacrificial laws may be summed up as follows:

1. The atonement was *instituted by God*, and as such it is His work.
2. This work is performed *as a sacrament by the priests*.
3. The priest makes atonement for sin, or – which is the same thing – reconciles the *sinner* to God. When in Lev. xvii. 11 the blood as such is said to make atonement this statement should be understood symbolically: just as the priest only acts in the name of God the blood is merely the means granted by God. *'Selbst-erlösung'* ('self-atonement') (Köhler) is aboslutely out of the question here.
4. The sacrificer is *active* in so far as he brings the offering with him and, by laying his hands on the animal *(semikhah)* gives evidence of his intention to sacrifice it. Originally at least he also performs the preparatory sacrificial acts (the killing of the animal), but at the act of atonement proper he remains passive, as it is performed for him by the priest, the intermediary between God and man. The figure of the priest makes the offering become a twofold act in which God and man come together in a symbolical and ritual manner.

The main data on the ritual laws can only be given in a few most essential points (Lev. i–v, xvi, xvii).

[1] In its present from the book of Leviticus is late and composite, but as regards its content it often contains elements that are very old. The main elements connected with the cult probably date from the period of the exile (the so-called Law of Holiness, Lev. xviiff.) or from the period immediately after the exile, the period of the restoration of the second temple (thus Lev. i–v, and Lev. xvi, though this last chapter has been handed down to us in a later redaction; cf. my *Hizza*). On these chapters see any of the Introduction, to the O.T.
[2] Only of the former three sacrifices it is said again and again that they serve as *reach nichoach*, a sweet (literally bringing peace) savour, for Yahweh (Lev. i–iii); this expression is not found in the case of sin- and guilt-offerings (Lev. iv.f), except once in a secondary text, Lev. iv. 31, see Herrmann, *Th. Wb. z. N.T.*, loc cit., p. 305, n. 22; see also below p. 264.

As we already remarked above, the introductory verses (Lev. i. 4) more or less ascribe an expiating meaning to the whole of the sacrificial cult, though a distinction (no only as to their origin but also with respect to their essence) should be made between the burnt-, gift- and community-offerings on the one hand and the expiatory offerings, *par excellence* on the other. This appears clearly from various elements, both regarding terminology and ritual: the use of the word *kipper* is limited – except in i. 4. – to the guilt- and sin-offerings (ch. iv, v); whereas the other offerings are said to be performed as a *reach nichoach* for Yahweh (i–iii); moreover the bloodmanipulation of ch. i–iii differs from that of ch. ivf.[1]; it is also remarkable that of the expiatory offerings it is never said that they are *le-raṣon*, agreeable, while these words are used when burnt-offerings and thank-offerings are mentioned (in Lev. i–vii only in i. 3, cf. also *nirṣah* in verse 4; but elsewhere the word is used more often).

We cannot here enter into the other differences in the sacrificial acts, for instance with respect to the dividing of the flesh, the burning of certain parts, the partaking of the offering by the priest etc., as they are of only relatively slight theological importance.

For the sake of further clarity we may discuss two texts here: Lev. i. 3f. and xvii. 11f.

---

[1] In ch. i–iii *zaraq:* the blood is sprinkled against the altar (this pouring of the blood is no lustrative act, though it does have a cultic meaning: in this way the blood is dedicated to God, to whom alone it belongs). The *expiation* or *lustration* is effected (Lev. ivf.) by (a) *splashing* the blood before the face of God *(hizza)*, (b) smearing the blood with the finger *upon the horns of the altar* (the *kipper*-act proper), and (c) by pouring out the rest of the blood at the foot of the altar. The *hizza* ritual has a special meaning; it is only found with sin-offerings, as an introduction to the sacrificial act, and means the *consecration* of the blood of the sacrificial animal, which is brought before God in this way in order that, after having been accepted by God, it may be used for the lustration or expiation proper. This strikes at the root of all notions that the sacrificial act should work *ex opere operato* or should be accomplished by the sinner as a self-redemption. This consecration stamps the following expiation as a sign of Yahweh's mercy; it expresses the same faith as Lev. xvii. 11f. Apparently this act, first found in the sacrificial laws, is a ritual institution due to the new spirit among the priests during and after the exile. On this see my *Hizza*, loc. cit; cf. also below pp. 265f.

From this it follows that in the case of the offerings mentioned in Lev. i and iii all the blood was taken to the altar as a part of the sacrifice; at the expiatory acts proper (Lev. ivf.) the first two sacrificial manipulations of the blood are effected; then the blood is poured out *(shafak)* at the foot of the altar; this could hardly be considered part of the expiatory act itself.

It is also remarkable that in the guilt-offerings (*'asham*) the blood is sprinkled against the altar without any further *kipper*-act taking place (Lev. vii. 2); in other words as regards the blood-manipulation this sacrifice is treated as if it were a burnt- or thank-offering, while as regards the burning the animal is treated again as a sin- offering. The *'asham* is therefore an intermediate form between the expiatory and the burnt-offering; the sins that are atoned by the *'asham* are apparently not such as to separate God and man (this separation was caused by the sins that demanded a *chaṭṭat*-offering). See pp. 265f.

Lev. i. 3f. reads: 'If his offering be a burnt sacrifice he shall offer it of his own voluntary will at the door of the tabernacle of the congregation before the Lord. And he shall put his hand upon the head of the burnt-offering, and it shall be accepted for him to make atonement for him.' Then the altar is sprinkled with the blood[1] to denote that Yahweh, the Lord of all life, is offered the life of the animal sacrifice.

After this 'sprinkling of the blood' the animal itself is offered to Yahweh and to that end it is burnt on His altar. By this process of burning the animal is, therefore, offered up to Yahweh; its odours reach Him and are agreeable to Him, so that by this burnt-offering the relation is strenghtened, as is expressed by the word 'accepted' in verse 3.

This burnt-offering *'olah* is therefore a true 'gift-offering' of animal character, just as the *minchah* (Lev. ii) is a gift offering of a vegetable kind.[2] These offerings were sacrificed particularly *to propitiate Yahweh*, just for instance as presents were used to please the king; originally they were 'honour-offerings' and must have been offered up as a token of gratitude or personal piety in order to glorify God. Generally speaking we may say that these offerings form an expression of *pietas;* God accepts them gladly and they serve to maintain and renew the existing bond between Him and faithful man.

Besides these there are the *shelem*-offerings (Lev. iii) of which the fat of the inner part of the sacrifice is offered up to Yahweh and to some parts of which the priests have a right. These are a quite distinct type of offering; they serve to make a feast in honour of Yahweh possible, in which therefore, as it were, God Himself, the priest, and the sacrificer with his guests take part. This form of sacrificial ritual strenghthens the relation between Yahweh and the faithful by means of a sacramental repast.

The expiatory offerings, on the other hand, are rather the acts that *restore* the bond between God and man when its existence had been endangered. In the first place we must think here of the *sin-offerings* (*chaṭṭaṭ*), as described in Lev. ivf., and also of those of the Day of Atonement, Lev. xvi. This conclusion can be drawn from the way in which the sacrifices are offered up, i.e. from the ritual performed with the blood and the flesh. With the sin-offerings[3] the blood is first of all

[1] See the previous note.
[2] On *'ola* see W. B. Stevenson, 'Hebrew *'olah* and zebach sacrifices', *Festschrift Bertholet*, pp. 488ff.; cf. N. H. Snaith, 'Sacrifices in the O.T.', *V.T.*, VII, 1957, pp. 308ff.
[3] Not the guilt-offerings, see above p. 264 n. 1. It only happens when a priest or the whole people must be atoned for: Lev. iv. 1ff.; xvi. 1ff.; cf. Lev. iv. 22ff. When a sin-offering is offered up in behalf of an individual it was suffcient for the priest to smear the blood upon the horns of the altar. Here the splashing of the bood before

'sprinkled' or rather 'splashed' in the Holy Place, in the direction of the Ark, the place where God sits enthroned. And once a year this blood is taken beyong the veil, and sprinkled (splashed), once on the ark and seven times before it. This ritual, performed at the gravest sin-offerings, can only have the meaning of an act of consecration.[1] Thus the blood is brought before the face of God and sanctified to Him; after it has been accepted by Him the sacrosanct act of atonement can be performed with it: the blood is put upon the horns of the altar.

It may be called remarkable that for guilt-offerings (Lev. vi and vii), according to vii. 2 the ritual of the sin-offering is not required. Apparently the deeds that require a guilt-offering have not such serious consequences and do not bring about such a complete break between Yahweh and the faithful as the deeds for which sin-offerings are demanded. Guilt-offerings are required for sins in the field of property (v. 14ff.) and sin-offerings for defilements that exclude man from the relation with God; from the character of the acts (Lev. v. 1ff.) it appears clearly how strongly ancient ideas survived here in Israel for a long time.

How fundamentally important the blood-manipulation is even in this later sacrificial ritual is evident from the wording of Lev. xvii. 11, where we read with respect to the blood:

'For the life (the vital force) of the flesh is in the blood; and I ('ani) have given it to you upon the altar to make an atonement for your souls (for you): for it is the blood that maketh an atonement by reason of the soul (the vital force)'.

This shows clearly how important the blood-manipulation is considered to be. God has instituted this sacramental act in order that atonement should be effected for man by the soul (the blood, the vital force).

The blood effects the atonement by virtue of the soul (the force of life), namely for the souls of men, i.e. in behalf of man.

This is an important statement that gives occasion to serveral remarks. The first is that here it becomes clear that in the later laws the blood-manipulation is looked upon as the fundamentally decisive sacramental act of expiation *because God wants to use it as such* ('I – with emphatic front-position – give it upon the altar').

The second is that the blood is considered a means of atonement because it is the repository of life.[2] This 'sap of life' ('life-blood')

Yahweh is therefore not executed, apparently because a layman could be purified on the authority of a priest.
[1] Cf. p. 264 n. 1.
[2] So also R. de Vaux, Sacrifices, p. 84.

which, as we know from the whole of the Old Testament but especially from this passage, belongs to God alone, has characteristics, as the repository of life, on the ground of which it belongs to the divine. God is the Lord of life who gives life (Gen.ii.7). Life springs from Him (Ps.civ.29), He is the foundation of life (Ps.xxxvi.10). To Him alone it must return (Eccl.xii.7). The atoning blood-manipulation was designated by God as a sacramental act, so that it effects something on behalf of the sacrificer.

The third element we find in this verse is that by this blood the atonement is effected – i.e. sin is removed, the sinner is sanctified. The sacrificer gives the life of the animal to God and God accepts it. Thus a life-relation, that threatened to be dissolved, or had weakened or broken altogether, is restored or strengthened. Indeed, by the blood-manipulation man is sanctified, just as the altar is also 'sanctified' (Lev.viii.14f.; xvi.16ff.), and just as the priest was ordained (Lev.viii.22f.)! See finally again p.275.

c. The cultic ideas outside the sacrificial laws [1]

The cultic laws bring us into contact with the most exalted and purest form of cultic ideas; in this form they arose under the influence of the personalist ethical devotion of the prophets. In the older histories of the historical writers, and also in more recent narratives of priestly origin there are elements that strike us as less ethical and are dominated by ideas that are more ritualistic and more grossly anthropomorphic such as *placatio* and *satisfactio*.

1. The atonement by *placatio* and *satisfactio*.

There are certain elements in the Old Testament that, quite differently from the later Old Testament message of atonement in the cultic laws, centre upon the idea that atonement is effected *because* God's wrath is allayed.

The most striking example is 1 Sam.xxvi.19, where David says to Saul in his rude soldiers' language: 'If the Lord have stirred thee up against me, let Him accept an offering'. The word atonement is not used in this text, but the idea is present. It is supposed that Yahweh is brought into another, more favourable frame of mind by the *reach nichoach* (viz. in the original meaning of 'a quieting odour'). This idea is not expressed in so many words in Gen.viii.21,[2] though it is suggested by the verse to some extent, for Noah does not offer up a sacrifice in order to allay Yahweh's anger; his sacrifice is no guilt-offering but rather a thank-offering. The expression used in this verse is probably due to the literary background of the story, namely the

[1] See R.J.Thompson, *op. cit.*
[2] Against Köhler, *Theologie.*

267

Babylonian Deluge-narrative: there the deluge-hero Utnapishtim offers up a sacrfice to the gods that comforts them greatly.

The value attached to the offering, mentioned in 2 Kings iii. 27, by Mesha[c], the king of Moab, shows that as late as the period of the Kings such ideas, which remind us strongly of the pagan sacrificial theories, had not yet been wiped out entirely in Israel.

In later periods the only remnant of these ideas was the expression *reach nichoach*, which still occurs again and again in the cultic laws but there it no longer has the original meaning of 'a quieting odour', but means 'a fragrant smell'; for it is clear, as Herrmann says[1], that in the cultic laws the *reach nichoach* originally was not found in connection with the idea of the atonement (nor in connection with the expiatory act of *kipper*, nor in connection with guilt- and sin-offerings). Another example that reminds us of this early range of ideas is the formula, which continued to be used until a late date; '*to soften the countenance of Yahweh*' *(chillah panim)*, to propitiate Yahweh by an offering (1 Sam. xiii. 12) or (elsewhere) by prayer.

The anthropomorphic way of expression found in a large part of the Old Testament made it possible for the *wording*, reminiscent of this way of representing things, to survive even when the idea itself had already been superseded theologically; in such cases the expression must be understood symbolically.

It is certain that in an older period, when people had not yet attained the stage of critical theological reflection concerning the atonement, this atonement was represented too simply, too much on the human plane. At that time the offering was credited with great efficacy and the offering as such was a human achievement or gift, which people thought could be used to influence God. In this spiritual atmosphere it is still possible to agree with Köhler *(Theologie)* in calling the sacrificial cult '*Selbsterlösung*'.

In our opinion no theological dogmas can be derived from these survivals; in fact, they belong to the history of Israel's religion; they hail from a period in this religion which was in many respects precritical and pre-theological. For that reason this range of ideas should not be introduced as evidence of decisive importance in judging the theological thought of the Old Testament, or a Biblical doctrine of the atonement – no more than other concrete anthropomorphisms or representations recalling polytheistic notions should be used uncritically as materials for an Old Testament conception of God.

1a. Another application of this same principle but more juridical and cultic in nature, and therefore better denoted as *satisfactio*, is presented in 2 Sam. xxi, where David has an expiatory act performed

[1] *Theologisches Wörterbuch zum N.T.*, III, p. 305; see also p. 263 n. 2.

by the Gibeonites, because Saul had persecuted and tried to kill them. On that account a blood-guilt had arisen – Israel had admitted the Gibeonites into the Covenant on oath – for which Israel was punished by a three years' famine. David asks the Gibeonites how he must make atonement (verse 3) after the guilt of the house of Saul had been established by means of an oracle. Atonement is made: seven sons and grandsons of Saul are delivered up to the Gibeonites by David, and they are tortured, killed, and hanged by way of blood-revenge.

On the one hand this blood-revenge is an expiatory act, on the other, from the point of view of David, it is an act that placates the Gibeonites (in verse 3 the words have been chosen in such a way that both these interpretations are possible).

From the beginning and the end of the pericope (verses 1 and 14) it appears, however, how God Himself is concerned with this act: Saul's crime has roused His anger; the land that had been drenched by innocent blood (even if it was not the blood of Israelites but of 'allies') has been defiled; and therefore the victims are hanged before the Lord (vss. 6 and 9). To expiate this crime the Gibeonites demand the full price; they will not accept blood money, but the full expiation by the death-penalty for Saul's children. They are probably not allowed to demand less (see Num. xxxv. 31ff.). Here it appears what a penalty or expiation is in the true and strictest sense of the word: giving complete satisfaction to those against whom a crime has been committed.

2. Atonement by personal intercession

In the later period, at any rate where the influence of the prophets made itself felt, the ritualistic and juridical conception of the atonement is supplanted by more moral conceptions. Here the personal element becomes more prominent. – God guides His people by figures of mediators, who because of the special place assigned to them by God, can intercede with Him on behalf of the people and can effect the atonement by their prayers of intercession.

They remain, however, subject to Gods will. For their sake God will pardon and save men – but God does not commit Himself to them. He keeps Himself perfectly free to decide – towards them as well. We frequently find that an intercession is not or not wholly successful: in spite of his intercession and in spite of the fact that God responds to his appeal Abraham could not save the city of Sodom (Gen. xviii); even though he risks his own life Moses cannot obtain full atonement from God (Exod. xxxii. 30ff.), for he himself says: '*peradventure* I shall make an atonement for your sin'; the narrator tells us, in fact (cf., however, verse 35), that God does not appear to be fully placated but that He sends an angel (messenger) who is to represent Him.

In the case of Amos the opposite happens: at first God seems to be willing to listen to him; He answers upon his intercession that the plague shall not come (vii. 1–6), whereas He afterwards proclaims the judgment as inevitable (vii. 7ff.; viii. 1f.). Jeremiah (xivf. and elsewhere) is even no longer allowed to pray for the people.

Besides these examples there are several intercessions that are granted by God: Lot prays that Zoar may be saved (Gen. xix. 20ff.), Abraham prays for Abimelech (Gen. xx. 17), Moses for Pharaoh (Exod. ix. 27ff., x. 16ff.), and for Miriam (Num. xii. 11ff.), for the people (Exod. xxxiv. 9f., Numb. xxi. 7f., Deut. ix. 16ff.), Samuel for the people (1 Sam. vii. 5ff., cf. xii. 19), David for Jerusalem (2 Sam xxiv. 17), Job for his friends (xlii. 8, 10); the intercession may also be performed by a mediator-angel (Job xxxiii. 23ff.).

The mediator addresses himself to God in prayer; in other words, he performs the prayer of intercession.[1] This is not an official act; it does not even have a name of its own in the Old Testament. Various verbs meaning to pray are also used to denote the intercession.

The strongly personal relation with God that underlies this act of intercession and atonement is characteristic of the prophetic religion which springs from a very personal relation with God. It demonstrates to how great an extent Yahweh is known in Israel as a personal God, who wants to avail Himself of the service of men in his intercourse with the world.

3. The religious-moral line

The prophets, however, principally pointed out the necessity of repentance and obedience to attain atonement. The way to the relation of God with the people may be opened again, also by means of mediators, but can only be opened fully by *penitence* and *repentance*.

By way of example we may emphatically call attention to Isa. i. 11 ff., particularly to the verses 18f. After having rejected the sacrifices as an unsuitable means the prophet points out another way, that of obedience to God's commandments, the moral and religious way therefore. And he follows this up with the words: then you must come to Me– then the *lustratio* which you now try so hard to attain by sacrifices will fall to you of its own accord; then the people will no longer need to fear the judgment of Yahweh. He who walks in the ways of obedience shall experience that he is sanctified by God: 'though your sins be as scarlet, they shall be as white as snow; though they be red like crimson, they shall be as wool!' The prophet expresses

---

[1] Cf. P. A. H. de Boer, *De voorbede in het O.T.*, 1943 and F. Hesse, *Die Fürbitte im A.T.*, 1951.

himself forcibly here (and from the point of view of logic even somewhat strangely), but his words are clear: Israel needs a different atonement, a different purification – coming from God alone: and Israel
may attain this by the obedience of faith. This is the only way to salvation indicated by the prophets.

In this way people came to understand that the cultic *expiatio* and
placatio in themselves, however often repeated and reinforced, ultimately left people where they were, and they came to see that purification and atonement could only be effected by God's merciful will.

In this connection we should read the statement of Isa. xliii. 22ff.
where we find quite clearly that Yahweh had neither accepted any
sacrifices from Israel, nor dictated them and (25) that *God* pardoned
sin *only for His own sake*. The passion with which this is expressed is
most striking: '*I, even I, am he that blotteth out thy transgressions for mine
own sake!*'

There is therefore one thing that marks off the later cultic laws
quite clearly from the religious attitude to life before: the emphasis
on God's good pleasure and God's will, on which the whole of the
sacrificial cult hangs! This is expressed particularly in Lev. xvii. 11;
and this formula at the beginning of the 'Code of Holiness' may be
considered to dominate the whole of the later cultic laws. *Lustratio,*
expiatio and *placatio* remain elements of the cult after the exile, but then
they only exist as God's merciful gifts.

3*a*. The prophetical preaching, which stresses the moral-religious
character of the atonement, also brought history, particularly the
judgment that fell upon Israel, within the range of ideas of the atonement. By this it became possible to experience the suffering which men
shared as members of the people of Israel as a penitence inflicted by
God. By this conception suffering became significant and Israel was
given a great spiritual support in the judgment itself: what the people
had to pass through was not caused by chance or fate, but was the
will of God. Suffering was made meaningful by the conviction that it
was a chastisement and judgment, which raised hope of new future
possibilities. In this way it became possible to discern the hand of
God in it and to acknowledge Him as the living God in the present,
too, in spite of the distress. We may deal briefly with this *historical and
pedagogical* approach. It was particularly worked into the conception
of history of the Deuteronomic authors. The word atonement is not
used there, it is true, but the idea can be read between the lines.
It is expressed particularly in the penitential preaching of the book of
Judges, where it forms the groundplan of the historical narrative, cf.
especially Judges ii. 6ff. and x. 6ff. Israel's apostasy arouses the anger
of God, who punishes the people by making others rule them until

they call upon Him. Then Yahweh repents of (ii. 18) or becomes impatient (x. 16) about the distress of the people and sends deliverance. The main point is here the idea of punishment. It leads people back to God because it makes them cry for Him; we may also suppose that at the back of all this there lies the idea of the spiritual, educating, renewing, but especially redeeming power of punishment.

This idea was expressed most clearly in Isa.xl.2: 'Speak ye comfortably to Jerusalem, and cry unto her, that her warfare is accomplished, that *her iniquity is pardoned*, for she hath received of the Lord's hand double for all her sins'.

This idea of the atonement connects the prophetic ideas of penitence and conversion with the more juridical conception of expiating one's guilt by bearing a punishment, which approaches the doctrine of satisfaction, and on the other hand with the 'Wisdom' and pedagogical range of ideas, according to which sorrow is a necessary element of education (Ecclesiastes, Elihu's speech in the book of Job).

4. Isaiah liii

The most exalted spiritual summary of the data on the atonement is presented by Isa.liii; here almost all lines converge and are welded together into a higher unity.

Important is a comparison between the atonement as depicted here and as found in the *Torah*. The following comparison might be drawn: while the ceremonial laws of Leviticus take for their startingpoint the ancient ritual acts and further adapt this material with the aid of prophetical criticism, so that God became the absolute giver of reconciliation (and in this way the idea of *'Selbsterlösung'* was overcome, and also the idea that the atonement existed in order to allay God's anger first) – Deutero-Isaiah's conception of the atonement sprang from exactly the opposite development: the pedagogical and juridical view (bearing the punishment as penitence and therefore as a means to renovation) and the mediatorial view (taking the guilt upon oneself for the sake of others), with the ancient cultic range of ideas of *expiatio* in the background as the frame work within which these concepts are brought together.

The atmosphere is quite different from that of Leviticus, and yet the two approaches of the atonement have several things in common! One point is that neither of them teach any more that God's anger must be allayed. In Isa. liii, too, this idea has disappeared completely – the *placatio* is no more found here, though the *expiatio* pervades it all – sin must be purged, and for that reason it must be expiated with life; the Servant is not only compared to a 'lamb for the slaughter', but his life is also called an offering for sin, an *'asham* (verse 10); this expiation, however, is no cultic act – the blood in itself no longer plays

272

a part-but an ethical and juridical act (the expiation is effected by the bearing of a punishment and even by laying down one's life). It is, in fact, rather a personal mediatorial act with an expiatory effect because sin is expiated by the punishment of an innocent man: the punishment is suffered by a substitute and thus effects expiation. Thus the whole can still be included under the heading of *expiatio*, but only in a formal sense; for the other elements (particularly *mediatio* and *re-conciliatio* and the juridical and pedagogical element) play a decisive part. It might be even better to speak of *expiatio vicaria*, instead of *expiatio*.

In this comprehensive rendering Deutero-Isaiah gives a new view of a purely moral and religious character of the expiatory task of the servant of the Lord, and in it he professes that sin can only be removed by the suffering unto death of the servant of God, who is absolutely obedient. But death does not have the last word here, for God is in and with all this: He has demanded this – even though it is not because of His anger (liii.4*b*), but because of human sin which must be expiated (liii.5); God has laid all the guilt and all the penance for sin upon the shoulders of the servant (6, 7), so that there was no more hope for him (8– 10*a*) – and for that reason God will yet show Himself to him as the God of life and glory: 'he shall see his seed, he shall prolong his days' and save many (10*b*–12) and all the nations and princes shall witness this miracle (liii. 12; lii. 12, 13). That this vision is connected with Israel, and that it depicts the ideal task of Israel in the world (to which it is sent in order to bring the Kingdom of God), detracts nothing from the fact that in this sketch the prophet also reaches beyond the historical Israel to the saviour who shall fulfil the task of redemption in Israel for Israel. This preaching has everything to do with the Old Testament doctrine of the atonement, and yet it is new in this form, both against the cultic and the prophetic teaching (in this profound unity of God's holy judgment and the merciful proclaiming of salvation, of obedience before Him and of the inevitable expiatory suffering of the innocent servant). The author here gave a profound spiritual answer, an answer completely his own, to the question what the issue between God and Israel is, namely to effect the atonement of sin by an innocent person taking the indignity of sin upon himself in such a way that they are really borne and consumed. This task can be effected in no other way than by the personal appearance of him who lives in the favour of God and has been called by Him.[1]

5. The last phase

In the theology of the atonement we see, perhaps better than any-

[1] On Isa. liii see the literature mentioned on p. 77 n. 1.

where else, how again and again the Spirit of God was creatively active in Israel and thus opened up ever new views. Indeed in the whole evolution of cultic life there are elements showing that the teaching of the prophets is taken more and more seriously. What the prophets had proclaimed (cf. Hos. xiv. 3) about thanks to God being the true offering, also becomes more and more real in the Old Testament cult; in the Psalms it was expressed (Ps. l), but in the book of Chronicles it appears most clearly that people understand what the issue between God and Israel is. It is this element of praise in Chronicles that makes it felt how spiritual life in Israel attained a deeper understanding of God, even when the voice of the prophets had fallen silent (though spiritual life was still activated by this voice).

It is true that this growth only manifested itself in some points, for besides greater profundity the opposite phenomenon also occurs: greater superficiality; the laws came to be understood less and less, and they were kept more and more only in slavish obedience to the letter of the law. In this way the cultic ritual gradually gets stuck in mere observance and was looked upon more and more as the highest spiritual achievement, a danger that seems inherent to any legalism and sacramentalism in piety. We must keep in mind, however, that the *rabbinical Jews* often remained conscious of the relativity of the ceremonial ritual; for them it remained a secondary phenomenon while the spiritual penitence remained of primary and dominating importance.

But the message of Deutero-Isaiah was but little understood; at any rate the preaching of atonement by suffering hardly found an echo among the people.[1] If this prophecy were to find response it would first have to be explained intelligibly in a new form. The most exalted message of the Old Testament, to which both cult and prophecy had contributed, could only be understood after its realization.

d. Final remarks

We have tried to give an outline sketch of the teaching of the atonement and to understand its nature. One thing, of great importance for the Christian doctrine of the atonement, has not appeared to full advantage, the question in how far the doctrine of *substitution* figures in it.[2]

With respect to this we may establish the following: in Ancient Israel the idea of substitution in general is found; for example the first-fruit

[1] See also above pp. 44, 77, n. 1 and 452; on Qumran see A. S. van der Woude *Lijden en verzoening in de hss. van de Dode Zee*, NTT, XVI, pp. 81ff.; in connection with the N.T. now F. Hahn, *Christologische Hoheitstitel*, 1963, pp. 54ff., where further literature is discussed.
[2] See C. Lattey, 'Vicarious solidarity in the O.T.', *V.T.*, I, pp. 267ff. and in particular S. H. Hooke, 'The theory and practice of substitution', *V.T.*, II, pp. 2ff.

offering of men could be replaced by sacrificing an animal (Exod. xxii. 29; cf. Exod. xxxiv. 19f. and Gen. xxii), but this sacrifice cannot be considered as an expiatory act; we should rather think of 'ransoming' (*padah*, 1 Sam. xiv. 45), though it is not clear whether an expiatory offering was sacrificed here as a ransom, or only a certain ransom was paid. Cf. also Deut. xxi. 1ff.

The question in how far substitution is found in the cultic expiatory offering is very difficult to answer.

Eichrodt has rightly observed[1] that the idea of *satisfactio vicaria* did not come to dominate the cult; the ritual does not admit of such an interpretation. Yet it is not to be denied that the idea is suggested, at any rate in the wording of Lev. xvii. 11 (in the Code of Holiness), where the blood of the animals (which is said to contain 'the soul', i.e. the vital force) is indicated emphatically as making an atonement for 'your souls'. There is something in this expression that points to the *expiatio vicaria*.

This idea of substitution appears, however, to better advantage in the Old Testament in those places in the prophetic religion where the mediator acts in behalf of his people, see Exod. xxxiii (cf. Ps. cvi. 23 and Ezek. xxii. 30); here at any rate the idea of substitution is very near. The appearance of the servant of the Lord is also represented in accordance with this mediatorial idea of the atonement; in the last few words of Isa. liii it is said that he has made intercession for the transgressors, that he appealed to God in prayer on their behalf. Indeed, the whole of his suffering is characterized by this!

Biblical theology cannot do without the idea of substitution but it is only in the personal sacrifice that it can be found in its fulness, in the mediator's service on behalf of his brethren and to a God who is personally moved with compassion for sinners. Any other doctrine of the Atonement is unbiblical, even if it may be supported by the letter of one or two texts. The atonement that unites God and man is only that which effects something in the world of sin to restore respect for His

---

[1] *O.T. Theology* I, 165. That this idea is even lacking in the expiatory offerings appears from the following reasons: If the sacrificial animal as such were laden with sin it would always be unclean whereas it is in many cases clean; further one would expect that the most important act would be the killing of the animal (the killing of the animal instead of the man who had deserved the death penalty because of his sin).

Moreover the sins atoned for by the sacrifices are no mortal sins at all, but only the sins committed *bishegagah*. The imposition of hands upon the sacrificial animal does not express a symbolical union between the sacrificial animal and man, in which the sacrificer declares that the animal was to take his place, but by this act the animal is declared to be his and indicated as his offering. The fact that the idea of substitution is lacking in the cultic laws (except to a certain extent in Lev. xvii. 11) may rest on a conscious elimination on the ground of the criticism of the prophets.

holiness and to win back sinners for Him, to that end accepting the struggle of love on behalf of the sinners while the mediator's own life is at stake.

III. PIETY

The treatment of 'piety' in theology has for its purpose to reveal something of the reaction in the human soul to the revelation of God. A discussion of this subject belongs as much to theology as the Psalms belong to the Canon or the testimonies of St. Peter and St. Paul belong to the New Testament – even though they are and remain reactions and as such of secondary importance as elements of revelation in comparison with the Word, which is the primary revelation of God. But just as in the New Testament the splendour of Christ's glory becomes evident most clearly in what people say of Him, so in the Old Testament, too, the glory of God becomes evident in a way all its own in human piety, particularly in the piety of the Psalms but also in that of the Books of Wisdom and the later historical writings.

It is centainly one of the most difficult tasks to describe the spiritual experiences of others, especially of an ancient people like Israel, or to value them at their true worth; to estimate, on the ground of the written records that have come down to us, what religion and religious communion meant to them personally. Yet, owing to various very personal remarks, it is possible to gain some idea of this exactly in the case of the Old Testament – though it remains extremely difficult to assess at its right value the 'religious' feeling of life itself, the response aroused by the words of revelation. One thing is, at any rate, an established fact: too often Old Testament piety is seen in the light of the later religion of the Law, which we have come to know so well from the New Testament and which St. Paul opposes – a piety of which we mainly see one side only in the New Testament (as also appears from rabbinical literature), namely its legalistic narrowness and social seclusion and therefore its lack of personal life, its confinement to its own system and therefore its lack of openness to immediate relation with the living God by the Spirit.

But with respect to the Old Testament at any rate we must disabuse ourselves of this idea; in the Old Testament piety is a living, spiritual, personal, joyful thing, while its legalistic element makes itself felt only partially; the development of this latter element only started at a late date.

Old Testament piety is rather characterized in many respects by exuberance. This exuberance becomes evident in many things: we need only think of the splendid praises of God sung in hymns such as the hymn of Deborah, Judges v; Exod. xv; Ps. lxviii; hymns of praise

276

such as Pss.xcii–c, ciii–cxviii, cxlv–cl. Here music and dancing play a part, at any rate in the ancient ritual at the sanctuary in the time of David (2 Sam.vi; cf.also Ps.cl.4). Musical instruments are mentioned in many Psalms, for instance Pss.cviii.3; cxlvii.7; cxlix.3; cl. We may therefore imagine the joy at the temple-cult to have been fairly tumultuous, at any rate very exuberant. We may remind the reader here how particularly in later periods the people came to the temple from many directions, to praise, honour and thank God (see Pss.xliif., cvii, cxviii, etc.) and observe how the sacrifices were sometimes offered up with great shouts (Ps.xxvii.6) and how songs of praise could accompany them (Ps.xxxiii.3).[1]

The pious Israelite was conscious of the fact that in his religion he was confronted with the absolute reality of God. God is the highest reality for him, whose being itself is beyong all dispute; it seems simply absurd to him that the existence of God could be denied, that it could be said 'there is no God' (Pss.xiv; liii); and in Israel the fool is the man who has not only no reason, but whose life is also spiritually empty; this folly leads to an abandoned criminal life.[2]

It is not only that to the Israelite God is the absolute reality, but He is also the One who sees through and experiences human life (Ps.xciv.8ff.: 'He that planted the ear, shall He not hear?', and Ps.cxxxix), who therefore lives in contact with man. This may be awe-inspiring, but it is not terrifying; on the contrary, besides awe it also inspires *the certainty of the relation with Him,* and as such it fills the whole life of the pious Israelite in the Old Testament. The Psalms are full of this, the Book of Psalms might be called one great testimony to devout faith. Of nearly all the Psalms, also those in which individual or national distress are laid before God, this is the central element: the certainty that the holy God hears and saves. We need only glance through the Psalms: Pss.ii.4ff.; iii.4ff.; iv.4, 7ff.; v.12f.; vi.9ff.; ix.5ff.; x.14ff.; xii.6ff.; xiii.6.; xiv.5; xxxi.4ff.; xli.2ff., 13 etc.[3]

The Psalms show clearly therefore that religion gave the pious Israelite comfort and security, because it filled him with a deep and fervent faith in God, a faith that was given a classical expression in

---

[1] See the essay by P.Humbert, *La terou'a,* 1946, and '"Laetari et exultare" dans le vocabulaire religieux de l'Ancien Testament', *Rev. d'hist. et de phil. relig.,* 1942, pp. 185ff.
[2] Pedersen, *Israel,* I–II, pp.429f.
[3] Such confident utterances are already found in the Babylonian Psalms, see especially W.G.Kunstmann, *Die Babylonische Gebetsbeschwörung,* 1932, who rightly opposes J.Begrich, *Die Vertrauensäuszerungen im isr. Klagelied des Einzelnen und in seinem babylonischen Gegenstück,* because Begrich looked upon the Babylonian utterances as flattery. On the Israelite utterances in the Psalms see H.Gunkel, *Einleitung in die Psalmen,* 1933, pp.130f., 232ff., and especially C.Westermann, *Das Loben Gottes in den Psalmen,* 1954.

hymns such as Pss. xvi, xxiii and xxvii, to mention only these. It may, for instance, be considered very remarkable that the tragic idea of life was overcome in the O.T. on the ground of this faith in God, though there were enough elements in the history of Israel that could have given rise to tragic sentiments, and in spite of the fact that the faithful also had to struggle against this sentiment repeatedly.[1]

In the last chapter of his *Religion of Israel*[2] Eerdmans called confidence in God the first characteristic of Israel's religion.[3] Faith is the basis of religious life. This was not only the case with great figures such as Isaiah (vii. 9b; xxx. 15), Micah, Jeremiah, and Deutero-Isaiah, but also with the many nameless Israelites whose hymns have been preserved in the Psalms, read for example Pss. iii. 7; xviii. 30ff.; xxvii; xxxiv; xlvi; lvi; lxii; etc. From these hymns it appears how strongly faith could strengthen personal life.

Generally speaking this personal element is one of the most prominent features of Israel's religion; we have already pointed this out repeatedly and shall therefore not dwell on it at length here.[4] Particularly in the Psalms it emerges splendidly in various situations: the pious Israelite addresses himself to God with his prayers and lamentations, and sometimes also with his accusations (such as, for instance, Ps. xxvi, where the poet protests his innocence; also in Ps. xliv; best-known in this respect are the individual hymns of Jeremiah and Job's complaints against God). It also reveals itself in the directness with which the pious Israelite addresses himself to God with the simple invocation *Yahweh* (Lord) or *'Elohim* (God) or *'Elohai* (my God);[5] such examples are, for instance, hardly known in the Babylonian Psalm-literature; there the deity is addressed with very elaborate and ceremonious forms of address.[6] Thus it becomes evident from personal piety how much the idea of the communion finds an echo in Israelite spiritual life.

In Israel's religion this individual piety has an opportunity to realize itself in a particularly sacred state: the *Nazirate*. Whatever its

[1] See my essay in *Kernmomenten*, 1947 ('De overwinning van het tragische levensgevoel in Israël')

[2] *The Essence of the religion*, 1947, a chapter which gives a good characterization of Israel's religion. The only cause for regret is perhaps that it comes at the end of the book and not at the beginning.

[3] Cf. F. Baumgärtel, *Glaube im A.T.*, RGG³ II, 1588; my *Essentials of the Theology of Isaiah*, J. Muilenburg Festschrift, pp. 128ff., esp. 136ff.; see also above pp. 71f. and 157f. on the connection between 'faith' in the Old and New Testaments. Against J. Barr, *Semantics*, pp. 160ff., I adhere to 'to be firm' as the fundamental meaning of *'mn* (see my *Geloven en Vertrouwen;* Köhler-Baumgärtner, *Lexicon;* Jean Hoftijzer, *Dictionnaire*).

[4] See pp. 164f.

[5] O. Eissfeldt, *Z.A.W.*, 1945–8, pp. 3ff.; *Evangelical Quarterly*, 1947, pp. 7ff.

[6] See J. Begrich, *op. cit.* and W.G. Kunstmann, *op. cit.*

origin[1], in this state everyone can give personal expression to the worship of God by dedicating himself or his children to the service of the Lord. As serving in the sanctuary was the privilege of certain families the Nazirate made a sacred state possible for those who did not belong to the priestly tribe. This Nazirate probably originated in the period when the conflicts about syncretism started. The institution is anti-cultural in character (Nazirites take no wine), which demonstrates the need to maintain a certain traditional style of life. Wearing long hair is another ancient symbol, the meaning of which can, however, no longer be established with certainty. In this case it is the outward sign of the sacred state. A life-long Nazirate is found in the dedication of children by mothers who had at first remained childless but conceived a child after praying for it and dedicated it to God in gratitude (Samuel, Samson).

Under certain circumstances people may commit themselves by vows to fulfil a special obligation towards God. Vows are a special confirmation of prayer; they are made under certain conditions. Originally they consist, therefore, of two parts: the matter which the person who makes the prayer hopes will be fulfilled ('if God...') and the promise (cf. Gen. xxviii. 20ff.; Judges xi. 30f.). Failing to fulfil a vow is looked upon as a grave transgression, as a breach of faith (Deut. xxiii. 22ff.; Num. xxx. 1ff.; Eccles. v. 3f.)[2]

One of the ways in which personal spiritual life can best express itself is *prayer*.[3] In the religion of Israel prayer was not yet bound to definite ceremonies and instructions in the Old Testament period, even though certain forms of prayer did exist (in those times people could prostrate themselves, stand upright, with their hands lifted up towards heaven or not, etc.) but there were no coercive prescriptions as yet: 'The outward attitude had not yet been fixed so as to become mechanical' (Volz).[4] Though people liked to pray in the temple (for instance Hannah, 1 Sam. i), God could be approached anywhere (Gen. xxiv) and at any moment of the day. Apparently prayer was not at all hemmed in yet by rules and prescriptions, as it was in the time of the N.T.

Prayer is spontaneous in character, as appears from invocations made in strongly personal terms, such as: my God. In fact it is always

---

[1] Cf. M. Weber, *op. cit.*, pp. 52, 103ff., where it is seen in the light of the holy war.
[2] A. Wendel, *Das israelitisch-jüdische Gelübde*, 1931. W. H. Gispen, 'De Gelofte', *G. Th. T.* 1961, pp. 4ff., 37ff., 65ff., 93ff.
[3] See now C. Westermann, 'Gebet', *R.G.G*[3]. II, pp. 1213ff., W. H. Gispen, 'Het Gebed', *G. Th. T.* 1958, A. R. Hulst, *Belijden en Leven*, 1948; A. Wendel, *Das freie Laiengebet*, 1931; P. A. H. de Boer, *Voorbede*.
[4] *Die biblischen Altertümer*, 1919, p. 245; Westermann, R.G.G. II, 1213. This, too, may be seen as evidence for the personal character of Israel's religion.

a personal experience that leads to prayer, either illness, or misery or joy. What C. Westermann said of the psalms of praise also applies to prayer: it is 'ein Geschehen vom Menschen zu Gott'.[1]

The prayer proper is usually preceded by a complaint in which the distress is expressed, whether it is caused by other people or by consciousness of guilt.

And so the content of prayer may be the most widely different supplications; there are prayers for aid and deliverance, for forgiveness of the guilt of sin (psalms of penitence), but sometimes also – as we find, for example, in Nehemiah (v. 19; xiii. 14, 22, 31) – prayers to God to recall the good a man has done: prayers therefore for the reward of a good work. Such prayers are clearly stamped by the eudaemonistic and moralist influences of *chokhmah*.

In contrast with this we often find the prayer for revenge on one's enemies, even in the case of such a spiritual figure as Jeremiah (xi. 20; xii. 3; xv. 15; xviii. 19ff.; xx. 12), which returns again and again in the Old Testament in many ways. These Psalms and prayers of revenge bear a strongly human character and do not always convey sanctified thoughts; they are very remote from the prayer Christ uttered on the Cross for his enemies, and very remote, too, from the spirit of the Lord's Prayer.

Apart from personal prayer there is also an official form of prayer, in which a priest or a prophet leads in a prayer of intercession (see above pp. 269f.). This prayer can also be performed by individual prophets, though it is in principle entrusted to the holder of a mediatorial office (Am. vii; Jer. xi. 14, xivf.). Prayer is not merely a personal but also a communal matter in the Old Testament and like official prayer the latter is linked to the place of the communal cult. People like to pray in the sanctuary, as appears from the various psalms. (v. 8; xlii. 5; xliii. 3.; lxxiii. 17[2]; lxxxiv. 11; cxviii; the songs of ascent). From these last hymns it also appears most clearly what the temple and the cult in general meant to the faithful Israelite.

We may say that people lived, as it were, for a year on this spiritual food; the pilgrim to Jerusalem also sings: 'I was glad when they said unto me: Let us go into the house of the Lord' (Ps. cxxii. 1).

This is expressed even more poignantly in the passionate song written in memory of the exile period when the temple had been destroyed:

'If I forget thee, o Jerusalem,
    let my right hand forget her cunning;
    if I do not remember thee,

[1] C. Westermann, *Loben*, p. 113.
[2] Compare for instance the interpretation of this verse by L. H. K. Bleeker in *Onder Eigen Vaandel*, XI, 1936, pp. 101ff.

let my tongue cleave to the roof of my mouth;
if I prefer not Jerusalem above my chief joy.'
(Ps. cxxxvii. 5f.)

The cult was therefore not practised unter the pressure of the law
or as a social and religious act from which there was no escape, but
it was a feast for the individual pious Israelite. It did not only bring
the joy of being able to give God the first-fruits (cf. on the liturgy belonging to it Deut. xxvi. 5) and of being allowed to sacrifice the burnt-
offerings that ensured God's good pleasure (Lev. i) or of the community offerings where the communion with God is celebrated at a
sacrificial repast with one's relatives and friends (Lev. iii), but it also
brought the certainty of reconciliation with God (Lev. i. 4; Job i. 5)
with respect to sin. The cult could take away alarm about guilt and
sin and gave an inward peace when people felt uncertain about themselves or others, like Job. From this we can see that the cult did occupy
a prominent place in the spiritual life of the people. It is often even
considered as working *ex opere operato* (though this is no Old Testament
doctrine!): for that reason Job even expiates in anticipation sins about
which he is not even certain that they have been committed, thus
demonstrating his great piety (i. 5).

In Ps. l. we meet with a singular case: the testimony of a poet who
knows that the congregation in Israel lives by these sacrificial practices
while he himself is convinced that God cannot be honoured with
offerings but only with praise and thanks (verses 14–21). In this psalm
we have apparently a clear echo of the prophetic teaching. The poet
does not simply reject the offerings, but is conscious of something surpassing them. He stands in the transitional phase between the old
and the new appreciation of the offerings and attempts to reconcile
the two views.

At the beginning of this section we pointed out the exuberance of
Israel's piety. About the background of this phenomenon some thing
more should be said, for here spiritual life is made clear to us, and
moreover it gives an indication concerning a use of the Old Testament
with respect to contemporary problems in Reformed theology.

Old Testament piety contains an element of joy of living, of
appreciation of earthly goods which seems most attractive to us
nowadays.[1] There is an air of naive religious joy of living in nearly
all the Old Testament, which reminds us most of Eastern Orthodox
Christianity. In connection with the lack of a fixed theological system
in the Old Testament, a lack caused by the consciousness of the little-
ness of man who cannot describe adequately the fulness of God's

---

[1] K. H. Miskotte, *Als de goden zwijgen* and A. A. van Ruler, *Die christliche Kirche und das A. T.* consider this an advantage of the O.T. over the N.T. (see above p. 97).

Being, Prof. Eerdmans in the above-mentioned final chapter of his *Religion of Israel* pointed to the Eastern Churches of to-day where we also find the same consciousness. An excellent idea, indeed. With respect to the similarity of religious sentiment in Israel and the Eastern Churches, there is, however, something more to be said, in the hope of throwing more light on Old Testament piety from another side. Both in oriental Christendom and in ancient Israel we are struck by a cosmic attitude to life which has disappeared almost completely from the western Christian world, because the moral element came to dominate religious life to such an extent. In spite of the absolute re-cognition of God's transcendence there is in the East a much more direct communion between all life and the spring of life, God.[1] The same is also found in Israel; in the Old Testament the cosmos is sometimes looked upon as a direct revelation of God: 'The heavens

[1] On listening to 'orthodox' Christians or reading such a book as Stefan Zankow's *The Eastern Orthodox Church* (London, 1929) on Eastern Christianity one is impressed by this again and again. One might quote at length from such a work to characterize in this way the religious atmosphere of Israel. One of the most important elements where a relation can be observed is the relationship between God and the world.

On p. 44 of this work Zankow says: 'In spite of our conception of the boundless sublimity of God and the sense of our own nothingness, we orthodox feel God to be truly near, and have a deep confidence in Him.' Here the author sees a distinction between Western and Eastern theology. It is not first and foremost a matter of theoretical insight, but of experiencing the close relationship between God and the world, which is experienced in Eastern theology especially on the ground of the celebration of the sacraments; these are celebrated as 'mysteries', and 'their general meaning is the penetration of all creation by the Spirit of God' (p. 113).

'The mysteries are both symbols and realities, symbols in their externals, realities in the mystical activity of the Grace of God' (p. 113). In this religion unity and communion have become perfectly real, and nature shares in this communion. Hence the well-known words from Dostojewski's *The Brothers Karamazov*, spoken by the staretz Sossima: 'Love the whole of God's creation, the universe and the tiniest grain of sand. Love every leaf-every one of God's sunbeams. Love the animals – the plants – love everything – when you love everything you will understand the Divine secrets hidden in them. Love to throw yourself down upon the earth and kiss it – kiss the earth and love it constantly, insatiably; love everything, love everything, seek such rapture, such exuberance' (p. 133) can be considered as typical of orthodox piety by Zankow.

Humility, love, and a sense of responsibility for others are mentioned as the spiritual fruits of this piety. Love even goes so far as to comprise the sinners, the fallen: 'the criminal is here considered as an unhappy man'.

In this last respect the Israelite world and these Eastern Orthodox views are certainly widely divergent because in the Israelite world he who is evil is looked upon as having been cast out by God. Indeed, in the Israelite world the '*finitum non capax infiniti*' applies; earthly things may be the repository of the divine spirit but they can never be deified themselves; in other words, in Israel the world may be transparent to the divine, but it can never be included in the divine in such a way that earthly things become part of the being of God. And there certainly are other points where the comparison does not hold at all. One finds it difficult to dismiss the idea that the doctrine of the Resurrection and the Incarnation to which Eastern Christendom always refers became the gate through which ancient Greek ideas that man was an organic member of the cosmos could slip in again (Bultmann, *Das Christentum als orientalische Religion*, p. 19; Miskotte, *op. cit.*, p. 386 n. 1).

declare the glory of God; and the firmament showeth His handiwork' (Ps. xix. 1); 'the whole earth is full of His glory' (Isa. vi. 3c). We should also think of Isa. xl, Gen. i, Ps. civ, but above all of the manifestations of God which are depicted in a 'naturalistic' way (Pss. xviii, xxix, etc.): the clouds are God's chariot, the thunder His voice; trees and mountains may be called divine (Pss. lxxx. 11; xxxvi. 7). We must further remember the immediate connection between the work of God and earthly blessings (Hos. ii. 14; Amos ix; etc.).

This is the expression of a piety that links *cosmos* and *theos* closely together[1]; the world is immediately connected with God because it is His creation.[2] This view of life does not predominate in the Old Testament because the teaching of the prophets starts fundamentally rather from the theology of revelation and atonement than from the theology of the Creation (see pp. 162f., 332f.) though the latter does form an integral element in the whole of the Old Testament. We must say[3] that the Old Testament lacks the *unbrokenness* of the real mystical idea of life in the relation between man, the world, and God or perhaps rather that the Old Testament no longer has this unbrokenness. It is very likely that it was still to be found in a very strong degree in the ancient Israelite world as depicted by Pedersen. In that case we should say that in the Old Testament the cosmic view of life stands in the background, it is only present in a broken form; in the Eastern Orthodox world we find it again founded on the preaching of the Resurrection and the Incarnation.[4]

Viewed from the angle of this piety it is no wonder that earthly goods are appreciated highly and looked upon simply as God's gifts; this gives the Old Testament an eudemonistic, '*diesseitige*', at any rate very realistic trait. We may think for example of the end of the book of Job (xlii), or, an even better case in point, of the end of the history of the exodus from Egypt (Exod. xi. 2f.; xii. 35f.).

Owing to this great appreciation of natural things it is easy to understand that in Israel there can be hardly any criticism of or

[1] This aspect of Israel's religiousness is strongly emphasized by Pedersen, *Israel;* in my opinion, however, it is over-emphasized as a characterization of religion as a whole.

[2] Miskotte, *op. cit*, pp 157, 386; Van Ruler, *op. cit.*, p. 82; J. H. Grolle in the *Weekblad der Ned. Hevr. Kerk* dated May 21, 1949, 'The fundamental message of Israel is Unity. The Unity of God, which includes the unity of all opposites, of all nations and of all that exists'.

Finally we may point to G. van der Leeuw, who in his *Inleiding tot de Sacramentstheologie*, 1949, begins by pointing out the same factors which are found again in the existential thought of our days (pp. 6f.).

[3] Cf. pp. 318 n. 3 and 425.

[4] On the problems in the Christian churches in connection with Incarnation and art, see H. van Oyen, 'Zur Frage der christlichen Kunst', *Theol. Zeitschr.*, Basel, 1951, p. 441.

aversion from the gifts of nature, or that, at any rate, these cannot attain predominance. A criticism of the Palestinian agricultural civilization, such as was championed by the Rechabites, was never accepted officially in the Old Testament; it even left hardly any traces,[1] although the danger of wine-drinking (not of vineculture itself) is recognized (for instance in Gen. ix. 20ff.). There is, however, some criticism of cultural institutions, particularly of urban civilization: the prophets protest against militarism, against the building of the gorgeous palaces, against large landownership; and in the earliest periods we must not forget the criticism of kingship, of the building of the temple, and in Gen. ii-xi of the town itself (cf. pp. 371ff.). We must distinguish clearly between this openness to nature and her gifts and a certain reserve towards civilization in its many aspects, and keep both these things in view.

Sometimes a delight in civilization *(Kulturfreudigkeit)* is attributed to the Old Testament too simply and in a too one-sided fashion. It is a fact that the Old Testament ideas on culture are much more varied than would appear from a superficial view. This is evident from the distinction made between city- and country-life (cf. Zech. ii. 8). In this respect the views of the author of the history of primeval times and the ideas of the prophets become rather similar, although they are not exactly identical; there is even no denying that the former show a certain tendency towards the Rechabites, which does not hold good with regard to the prophets.[2]

This criticism of civilisation came from various sides. Most consistent were the so-called Rechabites, a sect that sprang up in the 9th century, in the period when decadence and syncretism were at their worst, and was founded by Jehonadab the son of Rechab (see Jer. xxxv; 2 Kings x. 15ff.), a contemporary (and disciple?) of Elijah and a supporter of Jehu. This sect attempted to counteract the influence of syncretism by preaching the nomadic ideal, the return to the old ways of life in the desert of the original Israel as it had been called by Yahweh. This could best be looked upon as a primitive form of asceticism which rejected the farmer's life (no sowing, no vineculture) as well as the civilization of the cities (no building of houses, but dwelling in tents)[3] and which thus purified Yahwism of all foreign influences.

Less severe were other trends which probably originated among the farmers and already existed before kingship; they rejected kingship (1 Sam. viiiff.; Judges viiif.) and in the first instance condemned the building of the temple (2 Sam. vii. 7). The prophets, however, did not

[1] See above p. 55 and p. 425 n. 1.
[2] Cf. my *Hosea, profeet en cultuur*, 1941; see also below.
[3] Jer. xxxv. 7. Perhaps ancient Kenite influence manifests itself here.

284

agree with this view (in spite of the appearance of Nathan in 2 Sam. vii) and accepted all those elements of civilization that did not clash with the essence of Yahwism and could therefore be reformed and thus assimilated. The above-mentioned objections (against militarism, large landownership, splendid palaces) did not spring from a hostility against civilization itself but from religious and social motives, because the fear of suppression of the poor by the rich dominated the prophets and because they saw the danger that the purity of social relations in the national community, as ordained by God in Israel, might be disturbed; they abhorred militarism as springing from human *hybris*. We may therefore consider it an established fact that the Old Testament does not appreciate civilization for its own sake, and also that kingship in itself is not to be considered sacred but that it is only accepted in so far as it was willing to be guided by the commandments of God. So we may say that the idea of revolution is not simply rejected (Abijah and Jeroboam; the prophets and Jehu; the death of Athaliah), when reigning kings were guilty of despotism and idolatry.

The acceptance of the gifts of nature that we found in the Old Testament does not therefore give cause for severe criticism; this naïve human openness to the value of the gifts of nature, even founded on a truly religious basis, must be appreciated even if the danger of eudemonism cannot be denied altogether.

It is true that in this Old Testament appreciation natural and spiritual life were often linked too closely. This is, however, not due to the theological acknowledgment of God's creation as such (which should find more acceptance in Christian theology!) but rather to the fact that in the Old Testament people were not sufficiently conscious of the brokenness of the Creation. In the Old Testament we find no unequivocal pronouncement on the sinful nature of man which is brought out so severely and emphatically in the N.T.: chapters like Rom. iii, v, or vii, which describe the life of man in his inward revolt against God, are inconceivable in the Old Testament. It is true that there are in the Old Testament *moments* when we hear of such guilt and of a gulf between God and man owing to the effect of sin.[1] But, generally speaking, the consciousness of sin is still too fragmentary: sins exist and people know that these must be put away, but there is no awareness of belonging to the *massa perditionis* because of sin which creates a gulf between God and man.

For the same reason natural relations are but seldom viewed in the light of sin. Only the author of Gen. iif. looked upon death as a punishment, but for the rest 'the worst enemy' is accepted as a natural phenomenon. In later periods, however, the Jews did pay full attention

[1] See pp. 413ff.

to the doctrine of Gen. iif. But natural things are, generally speaking, accepted without criticism in the Old Testament; natural life within the bounds of the Law is looked upon simply as sound.

This is, indeed, a very profound difference between Judaism and Christianity. Judaism has never been able to admit that the will of man is sinful, that sin has affected the essence of human life. It did recognize the tendency in man that may lead to evil, which is called the *yeṣer raʿ;* this is the natural desire, the instinct to live and act, an impulse as necessary for life as it is dangerous, for on the one hand it preserves life but on the other it also threatens again and again to turn itself against the Creator. Judaism teaches that besides this evil inclination there is also a *yeṣer ṭob,* a good inclination that makes man fulfil the Torah; both these inclinations were, however, given by God at the Creation. We may therefore say that Judaism recognized both a natural will of man which is weak and inclined to sin, and a good will which directs itself towards the Law and keeps the natural will under control. It is this difference between Judaism and Christianity that makes the former seek salvation by the Law, the latter by God's act of salvation. In the Old Testament we find the seeds of both these views.[1]

But besides, or rather through this 'this-wordly' *('diesseitige')* optimism about life another element also came to the fore, already in the Old Testament itself. The same prophetic theology which was critical of so many forms of life that had become traditional, and which thought repentance and penitence the only way of salvation, also pointed to the necessity of a complete renewal of life – to a new life that was only possible if man were to receive a new heart (Ezek. xi. 19; xxxvi. 26f.), or by the inward knowledge of the Law of God (Jer. xxxi. 33; cf. xxx. 21). The salvation granted by God, which in the earliest periods was only depicted as concerned with the gifts of nature (Gen. xlix. 8–12) comes to be seen more and more as something spiritual (Isa. xi; Jer. xxiii. 5ff.; Joel ii. 28); and in the Psalms, too, we find this certainty (Pss. xlix. 14ff.; lxxiii. 24–28).

The traditional elements of the hope of salvation, of enormous fertility and paradisiacal beauty are also preserved here, as well as the idea of national restoration, but these ideas no longer predominate. Salvation is considered to consist principally in the fact that God Himself shall be the centre of the new people (cf. Jer. xxiii. 6; Zech. ii. 9, A.V. 10 '... and I will dwell in the midst of thee'); here the earthly

---

[1] On the two *yeṣeroth* see Moore, *Judaism*, I, pp. 479ff.; W. D. Davies, *op. cit.*, pp. 20ff.; Strack-Billerbeck, III, pp. 92ff., IV, pp. 466ff.; P. A. H. de Boer in *Het oudste Christendom en de antieke Cultuur*, I, 1951, pp. 519f.; W. Sjöberg, *Gott und die Sünder*, 1939, pp. 152f.; R. J. Z. Werblowski, 'Das Gewissen in jüdischer Sicht', in: *Das Gewissen, Studien aus dem C. G. Jung-Institut* VII, Zürich 1958, pp. 104ff.

element of salvation, which still remains, is, quite rightly, dominated by the spiritual element, by God's glory, which really brings salvation.

The Old Testament hardly knows the idea of a destruction of the world which is to precede this salvation; such texts as Joel iv. 15ff. (R.V. iii. 13ff.) point in this direction; and especially in Isa. xxivff. the catastrophic destruction of all things earthly is expected to precede God's salvation (cf. Ps. cii. 26f.). These religious ideas are, however, late and did not make their influence felt until afterwards; in the New Testament they form the background of the eschatological hopes.

The whole problem of 'this-worldliness' *('Diesseitigkeit')* returns again with respect to the life on earth of the individual. Here, too, the same three elements are to be found: the earliest conception essentially does not reach beyond life on this earth; the later hope expects that salvation is to be attained with God through death (Ps. lxxiii. 26) – and finally the spiritual *and* material elements are linked together in the resurrection of the body (Isa. xxvi).

Piety is, however, not dominated only by the idea of a communion linking together God, man, and the world, but also by God's holiness, which calls upon man to obey God's will in His commandments and makes man first and foremost God's servant, *'ebed*.[1] This introduces an element of great humility into religiousness; religion is: the fear of the Lord *(yir'ath Yahweh)*. Man knows himself to be entirely unworthy in the sight of God, cf. Isa. vi and also the other narratives of the call of the prophets, such as Jer. i and Exod. iiif. Yet the idea of the *'ebed* is not only the absolute self-rejection of man. In Deutero-Isaiah at any rate the servant of God is also the beloved.[2] And this consciousness of being loved is found again in all the books: in Gen. xviii. 17ff. and Ps. cv. 6ff. Abraham is God's friend; God speaks to Moses face to face (Deut. xxxiv) or mouth to mouth (Num. xii.8; cf. also Ps. cv. 26).

In spite of the idea of the *'ebed*, the predominant characteristic of the relation between God and man, this relation does not become slavish; God's mercy extends so far that man's freedom can also be preserved. We cannot therefore say that submission is typical of Old Testament piety; this becomes evident at once on reading the prophecies of Jeremiah or the spiritual struggles of Job as they are described by the author of the book, or when we think of the intercession of Abraham or Moses (Gen. xviii; Exod. xxxii), or of Elijah's behaviour when he complains of God's acts (even with his head covered!) or of Jonah who resists God with respect to his task and whose

---

[1] W. Zimmerli, 'παῖς θεοῦ' in *Th. Wb.z.N.T.*, V, pp. 653ff.; C. Lindhagen, *The servant motif in the O.T.*, 1950.
[2] P. Volz, *Jesaja*, II, p. 18; Lindhagen, *op. cit.*, pp. 201, 210f.

contradiction is tolerated by God; nor should we forget 1 Sam. xxvi. 19!

All through the Old Testament we find a fresh breeze of spiritual freedom, notwithstanding the awe-inspiring majesty of God. This freedom is a gift of grace from the glorious God who has given man (however small and insignificant he may be) spiritual independence (this, too, is implied in the doctrine of the image of God), and has even clothed him as such with power over God's works on earth. A Psalm such as Ps. viii is one of the finest instances of a deeply human feeling of dependence and unworthiness linked with the consciousness that man has been called to a great, an independent task. These two go together in a striking way in the Old Testament.[1]

Humility, meekness does remain one of the most striking fundamental elements of Israelite piety: man is conscious of being as nothing before the face of God (Pss. viii. 5; cxliv. 3; Job vii. 17f.; xiv.) One of the demands formulated by Micah was to walk humbly with God (vi. 8). This humility appears still more splendidly where the idea of dependence is ennobled and made more profound by consciousness of guilt. Then nothing remains of that which gives Israelite piety a certain self-conciousness, namely the idea of being chosen which makes the Israelite feel superior to the world of nations or the impious in Israel.[2] In the Songs of Penitence, particularly a Psalm such as Ps. li, the poet only knows that God is pleased by brokenness of heart: 'a broken and a contrite heart, O God, thou wilt not despise' (Ps. li. 19 (R.V. 17), cf. Isa. lvii. 15) Then the poet cannot even glorify God of his own accord but must be taught his hymn of praise by God: 'O Lord, open thou my lips; and my mouth shall shew forth thy praise!' Life before the face of God can only be granted by the Spirit of God (Ps. li. 12–17 R.V. 10–15).

When, together with prophecy, spontaneity disappeared more and more from religion and when humble communion gives way to mere subjection, there arises a consciousness of dependence which becomes servile even if it seeks compensation in a strongly developed consciousness of having been called. The balance is lost, the father-child relation in religion is lost, the distance becomes greater, the certainty of contact becomes weaker (Eccles. v). We can trace this process from Ezekiel, who is still addressed from high heaven only as son of man, to Ecclesiastes.[3] In a way it runs parallel to the development of religion in the cultic sense as it was outlined at the end of Ch. II (pp. 38ff.).

Religion is led by theology, cult and pedagogy (the Wisdom of the

[1] B. Gemser, 'Humilitas of Dignitas', *N. Th. T.* XIV, 1959/60, pp. 161ff.
[2] On later Judaism see my *Erwählung*, pp. 18ff.
[3] In rabbinical literature God is not called only the King or the King of kings, but even 'the King of kings of kings'!

Proverbs), but in spite of these supports it sinks away in formalism more and more. This happens notwithstanding the best traditions, collected in the Torah notwithstanding the profound wisdom and the earnestness of theology, notwithstanding the venerableness and impressiveness of the sacramental acts.

It is this religiousness of the Pharisees and the Scribes that is depicted in the New Testament[1] and which must resist from the bottom of its heart the latest and most splendid revelation of Israel's religion in Jesus Christ, for whom complete openness to God and His creation, but also to the sinful world of man, is the predominant trait and who fulfils the Law and the prophets in this respect, too.

[1] On this see also the remark on p. 276.

CHAPTER VIII

The Community of God

In the previous chapters the term 'Communion' was used particularly to denote the relationship between God and man. In this chapter we shall employ the word 'community' in a concrete and historical sense to denote the community that sprang from this communion with God.

We have decided upon the term 'community' in preference to 'covenant' on the strength of considerations advanced above (p.170). For various reasons the word 'congregation' proved not very suitable, in the first place because it could only refer to the human aspect of the communion so that it cannot include God who is the Lord of this community, and secondly because it is conditioned as to place and organization. The word 'people' also presents difficulties, not only because it cannot include God as a partner either, but also because it is too much qualified ethnologically in our western languages[1], because the community of Yahweh existed before Israel had become a people in our sense of the word and also after Israel had lost many of the traits characteristic of a national community. This community of Yahweh can be said to have existed in many forms in succession: first of all as a league of certain clans, then a group of tribes or amphictyony, a people united into a state, a double state, a group without nationality and temple, and finally as a widely dispersed temple congregation dominated by a hierocracy. In all those forms assumed in the course of history the community of Yahweh could maintain its essential traits by its faith in its relationship with Yahweh, the God who had 'called' or 'chosen' it to enter into communion with Him.

Without paying much attention to the historical stages (for which a history of religion should be consulted) we shall deal in this chapter with the partners in this community, so with God and man, with the forms in which it manifests itself and the standards governing it. The subject will be divided into the following principal parts:

I. Yahweh, the God of this community
II. The forms of this community

[1] The most widely used Hebrew equivalent of 'people': '*am* must not as such be considered a religious term for 'God's people' though this is often done. Actually the meaning of '*am* agrees much more closely with our word 'community'.

III. The standards of this community (ethics)
IV. Man in the community of God.
Each of these will be subdivided into several sections, which can easily be found again in the chapter itself or in the table of contents.

I. YAHWEH, THE GOD OF COMMUNITY

A. Introduction

When the Old Testament speaks of the community of God, Yahweh is always taken to be the principal partner, whether the author has in mind a covenant (Gen. xv, Deut. xxvi. 16ff., Josh. xxiv) or a marriage-relationship (Hos. ii, Jer. ii. 2, Ezek. xvi, xxiii) or a family (Hos. xi, Isa. i. 2f.). The Old Testament does not speak of the community of God without thinking of Him who had created it. The people of Israel is unthinkable without Yahweh. Even if the words 'Yahweh thy God' came to be used consciously by the Deuteronomic authors, it had already been employed in the pre-Deuteronomic period, both in narrative and in prophetic literature; in this earlier period these words apparently have a very solemn meaning (Isa. vii. 10).

Even the name of Yahweh by itself is mostly linked with Israel as a matter of course in the Old Testament. Yet the above mentioned pronouncement: 'the people of Israel is unthinkable without Yahweh' cannot simply be complemented by the opposite statement that Yahweh is inconceivable without Israel. I would at any rate hardly call the relationship between Yahweh and Israel as expressed in the latter sentence typical of the Old Testament[1], as many other scholars do[2], because both in the earliest literature (cf. J in Gen. ii–xi and in Gen. xvi) and by the early and later prophets (Am. ix. 7, Isa. xlii, xlix and elsewhere) clear relations between Yahweh and the world of nations are expressed; moreover in the historical narrative of Exodus the Kenites are supposed to have already known Yahweh, and above all, universal and cosmic motifs are frequently used in the descriptions of the hopes of the future.

[1] In his study *Die Bundesformel*, 1963, R. Swend rightly made a stand against Wellhausen in this sense: he admits that Israel acknowledged both Yahweh as its God and itself as the people of Yahweh, but he says that the combination of these two statements is not of a very early date. Though the prophets prepared the way for it, it only started functioning in its twofold form owing to and after the Deuteronomic reformation.
[2] Cf. G. F. Moore, *op. cit.* I, pp. 219f. (above p. 159) who calls the two statements 'correlatively exclusive'. J. Wellhausen considers: 'Jahwe, der Gott Israels und Israel das Volk Jahwes, zu allen Zeiten der Kurze Innbegriff der israelitischen Religion', see his *Israelitisch-jüdische Religion*, now in the edition prepared for the press by R. Smend: Julius Wellhausen, *Grundrisse zum A.T.*, 1965, pp. 72ff. (Theologische Bücherei 27). In orthodox Jewish theology and modern Jewish philosophy we also find this doctrine of correlation.

In spite of the objections that can be raised against a too one-sided characterization of the relationship between Yahweh and Israel, we should not forget that it is a particularly intimate relationship. This may be illustrated most clearly by the example of Amos. On the one hand Amos states (ix. 7) that Yahweh led the other nations to their dwelling-places as well as Israel, yet he does not contest the special relationship between Yahweh and Israel (iii. 2), though the conclusions he draws from it differ from those of his contemporaries. He, who sees Yahweh so clearly as a universal God, also acknowledges the unique relationship between Him and His people and gives expression to it in the word: *to know*, which makes us think of a communion (see above, p.153). Amos recognized this communion as clearly as did his younger contemporaries Hosea and Isaiah (see above).

In the foregoing chapters we have already gone into the nature of this relationship at length; here we are concerned with describing the concrete forms assumed by it.

In our description of the community of God we must speak of God first and foremost, because He is the more important partner in it. His 'figure' (if we may use this word; it is not altogether alien to the Old Testament either, see above pp.184f.[1] dominates the community itself, it determines its standards and to a large extent its form, too, and even the image of man himself presented by the Old Testament.

In spite of all the objections raised on many sides there is no denying that Israel's belief in God was given a definite outline in the Old Testament. Though the Old Testament does not speak independently of God's Being, that is not to say that there are not some prominent traits of this belief in God in the Old Testament which enable us to describe up to a point the way in which the Israelite believer knew God. This admission certainly does not imply at all that the conception of God in Israel or in the message of the Old Testament should have remained unchanged as the years went by (see for instance above, ch. II), but neither does it mean the opposite, that the knowledge of God was so much dependent on momentary interventions in history or life that there is no pattern to be discerned in the image of God in the Old Testament. Notwithstanding many differences in the descriptions of the God in Whom the various authors of the Old Testament books believe, there is such a measure of agreement between them that a number of important aspects of the content of their conception of God can be ascertained. This view can be supported, as will appear from the next section, by several statements in the Old Testa-

[1] We may mention here Ps.xvii.15, whatever our interpretation of the verse; J. van der Ploeg, *Le Psaume XVII et ses problèmes*, OTS, XIV, 1965, pp. 273ff. is inclined to think of beholding God after this life only.

ment that could be looked upon as 'creeds'. Some authors of Old Testament theologies are so apprehensive that the testimony of the Old Testament should be trammelled by dogmatics as to reject any further definition of the image of God in the Old Testament. It seems to me that this rejection springs from a reaction which is indeed justified but which also went too far.

It is clear that, in contrast with the conception of God of the ancient Eastern peoples the Israelite belief in God came to transcendentalize God entirely, though without losing hold of the real and immediate communion of Yahweh with His people and the world. It cannot be said that God is a hidden God in the Old Testament, not that He 'sich von Mal zu Mal in seinen Selbstoffenbarungen vor seinem Volke tiefer und tiefer verbirgt'[1]; it is only possible to say such a thing if one clings to the communion with God and the knowledge of God implied in such a communion and if one sticks to both these concepts as essentially characteristic of the Old Testament. The poetic conclusion of the book of Job (xlii. 1–6) may be considered the most eloquent testimony to this fact. The sublimity and inaccessibility of God is one element, indeed, but is not the ultimate or fundamentally all-important *motif*.

Non-biblical religions also teach the sublimity of the deity, but fundamentally this idea of sublimity rests only on a difference in degree between God, man, and the world, a difference especially in power, knowledge, time, and space. As the idea of the divine always rests on certain natural phenomena in which growth, culmination, and decline, or birth, marriage, and death always have their place, the similarity between God, man and the world is greater than the difference. When, however, on rational grounds the world of the gods becomes transcendent it becomes vague, infinite and unknowable.

In the prophetic religion of the Old Testament God's sublimity stands at the beginning, and Yahweh comes to the world (to Israel) from His secrecy in His revelation of Himself in His words and activity as the ever-present God. The knowledge of Yahweh is, therefore, essentially different from the knowledge of the non-Israelite deities.[2]

Though the Old Testament authors realized the relativity of the knowledge of God, the relationship into which God entered with Israel meant the creation of a communion that gave the Israelite

[1] G. von Rad in ThLZ 1963, p. 406; cf. also his *Theologie* II, pp. 387ff., see Engl. trans. pp. 374ff.
[2] Cf. now also C.J.Labuschane's doctorate thesis: *Die onvergelijkelijkheid van Jahwei n die Ou Testament* (Pretoria, 1961), sec. ed. *The incomparability of Yahweh in the O.T.*, 1966, where the notion of the incomparableness of the Deity in Israel is confronted with the allied conceptions outside Israel.

believer the certainty that he knew God, however relatively and temporarily, and that he had to bear witness to Him. This idea dominates the psalms and the prophetical writings as well as the historical books.

B. CREEDS CONCERNING YAHWEH

In this section we cannot enter into the individual testimonies of the various sources and their authors[1]; in chapter III we attempted to give a brief survey. We shall here be concerned with confessions of faith that are of a more general and clearly theological nature. There are different forms of creeds, some of them very brief, probably dating back to a very early period, others more elaborate and of later date; they all have their own place and origin in the spiritual life of Israel.

a) The words: *Yahweh is our God* may be called one of the very early forms of creed. We may take it that it goes back to the earliest period, either the Mosaic period itself (an idea which may appeal to those who assume that the Sinai-narratives have a nucleus of historical truth), or no further back than the period of the occupation of Canaan (the amphictyony).[2] In its shortest form it is found in Joshua xxiv. 17a and 18b; a more elaborate and more theological formulation is to be found in Joshua xxii. 22: 'God of gods is Yahweh, God of gods is Yahweh', an even clearer one in 1 Kings xviii. 39: 'Yahweh, he is the God, Yahweh, he is the God' (*Yahweh hu'ha'elohim*, where the article with *'elohim* emphasizes the absoluteness of Yahweh's divinity).[3] Closely linked with this creed are the prohibitions in the decalogues of worshipping other gods (Exod. xx.3; xxxiv. 14; Levit. xix.4; see also Exod. xx. 23, Ps. lxxxi. 10).

The well-known *shema'* of Deut. vi.4: 'Hear, o Israel: Yahweh our God, Yahweh is *'echad*' (One; on this see below p.323) may be looked upon as the final stage in the development of this creed. In the later Hebrew world this is considered the creed *par excellence* and together with other texts it is recited twice daily by the believers.[4] Especially in its later forms this creed is clearly polemical in its attitude and bears the marks of Israel's spiritual struggle for the belief in God.

[1] As elaborated in Von Rad's *Old Testament Theology*.
[2] This view is advocated by R. Knierim, *Das erste Gebot*, ZAW 1965, pp. 20ff., esp. 37f., and R. Smend, *op. cit.*
[3] Fohrer, *Elia*, 1957, p. 47, thinks such a formulation Deuteronomic.
[4] The *shema'* consists of the texts Deut. vi.4–9, xi. 13–21 and Num. xv. 37–41; cf. also J. de Groot and A. R. Hulst, *op. cit.*, pp. 41ff. and Strack-Billerbeck, *Kommentar z. N.T.* IV, pp. 189ff.

b) By the side of this creed another and entirely different creed developed in the circles of the teachers of wisdom.[1] The clearest example of this is the creed found in Exod. xxxiv. 6 and also heard in many other places in the Old Testament (cf. Num. xiv. 18, Deut. vii. 9, v. 9f., Exod. xx. 5f. and Jer. xxxii. 18; further Ps. lxxxvi. 15, ciii. 8, cxlv. 8, Nah. i. 3, Neh. ix. 17, Jonah iv. 2, Joel ii. 3).[2] Dentan was the first to point out that this creed was strongly marked by the wisdom-literature; it is not so much concerned with a Kerygma, with the history of Israel, but rather with man as such. For that reason it has universalist and pedagogical traits and its wording is not polemical or eristic, as is the creed mentioned under a). It differs from the latter particularly because it attributes certain qualities to God, so that it is theological and ethical in nature. The way in which the Deuteronomic authors incorporated such a creed in their message may lead to the assumption that it goes back to the pre-Deuteronomic era.[3]

c) Entirely different again is the creed elaborated by Von Rad as the essential Old Testament creed under the name of *Kleines geschichtliches Credo* (Deut. xxvi. 5–10).[4] This confession, too, is much more elaborate than the one mentioned under a). It has a very special *Sitz im Leben*, since it is used as a formulary for the offering of the first-fruits of the land. It is therefore a liturgical text, drawn up for use in the cult. It is intended as an expression of the confession of Yahweh as the Lord of the land and its produce. The text shows how Yahweh had led Israel from its earliest beginnings in the patriarchal era, that He led it into Egypt, made it a great people there, delivered it from Egypt and finally gave it the land of Canaan. In this way the reasons are demonstrated why the first-fruits of the land are dedicated to Yahweh. It might be called a 'thanksgivings day' liturgy.

On the question whether such a liturgical text could be called a creed opinions may differ, but it must be admitted that in its own way it expresses the confession that Yahweh is the Lord, as we stated above. Owing to its historical form it differs widely in character from the creeds we dealt with before, Like the a)-type of creed, it originated from a controversy, from the struggle against the influence of the Baal-religion.[5]

[1] See R. C. Dentan, *The literary affinities of Exodus XXXIV 6f.*, VT 1963, pp. 34ff.
[2] Dentan, *op. cit.* pp. 38f.
[3] Dentan rightly points to the special place taken in the O.T. by the credal tradition of Exod. xxxiv. It is therefore somewhat surprising that these verses hardly play a part in Von Rad's *Theology* (see my essay *Geloof, openbaring en geschiedenis*, KTh 1965, p. 215).
[4] See his *Das formgeschichtliche Problem des Hexateuch*, and his *Theology* I, pp. 129ff.
[5] For Ba'al was worshipped widely in Israel as the Lord of the land and of fertility (cf. especially Hos. ii).

Von Rad pointed out that this type of creed must be the most original; he even thinks it to be the starting-point for the whole of Israelite historiography. Of late strong objections have been raised against this conception, which was accepted by many scholars.[1] The text of Deut. xxvi. 5ff. must be explained in terms of its Deuteronomic framework. It cannot possibly be claimed that it is a very ancient confession on the grounds of its historical character nor on account of its rhythmical composition[2] because it is marked far too clearly by Deuteronomic influences.

Recapitulating we may say that Israel's confessions of faith have taken diverse forms. The polemical forms had apparently existed from the earliest days and developed in various directions: there is not only an 'eristic' but also a thetical form of creed, which sprang from the wisdom-literature. The former emphasize the idea that Yahweh is divine and that He is the Lord; they oppose Baalite influences. The latter emphasizes the 'qualities' of God.

If we were to deal with this subject at greater length we could point out several parallel phenomena in the Old Testament. We might, for instance, wonder if from a formal point of view a text like Isa. vi. 3 might not be compared with Exod. xxxiv. 6f. as well. Both of these texts are in the nature of a proclamation, proclaiming the glory of Yahweh in a descriptive manner.

On account of these and other texts it is not so strange as some scholars would have it that an Old Testament theology should speak of the qualities or virtues of God. We should not do an injustice to the Old Testament if we pay serious attention to a description of these qualities in a theology of the Old Testament.

C. THE MOST IMPORTANT ASPECTS OF THE KNOWLEDGE OF GOD

1. *Introductory remarks*

In the last few years students of the Old Testament theology have shown great reserve in giving a more precise definition of the knowledge of God in Israel. This is due to the complex of problems denoted by the term *Entmythologisierung* (demythologizing),[3] a matter we can-

---

[1] See i. a. A. Weiser, *Einleitung;* C. H. W. Brekelmans, *Het historische Credo van Israel*, TTh, 1963, pp. 1–10; Th. C. Vriezen, *The Credo in the O.T.*, in Studies on the Psalms, papers read at the 6th meeting O.T. Werkgemeenschap in S. Afrika, 1963, pp. 5ff.

[2] Deut. xxvi. 4ff. is indeed typically Deuteronomic as to rhythm and style. On the contemporary historical background of Deut. see now R. Frankena's essay *The vassal treaties of Esarhaddon*, in OTS XIV, 1965, pp. 122ff.

[3] For an introduction to this subject P. Barthel, *Interprétation du langage mythique et Théologie Biblique*, 1963.

not, however, go into here. The problem is a very real one that will (and must) keep arising; in fact, the Old Testament itself points it, as we demonstrated before, see above p.186ff. The possibility of knowing God is affirmed as well as denied (Exod. xxxiii); on the one hand there is the prohibition of making an image of God, on the other we find descriptions or hints at any rate of the appearance of God (though these are never developed). Although He is known to transcend all conceptions man may form of Him, various qualifications of His Being are found.[1] Some of these are clearly functional in meaning; they do not really describe God Himself and are not intended to depict His Being but His relationship with man and the world. They describe His activity rather than Himself. This is especially true when titles such as King, Lord, Saviour, Judge, etc. are attributed to Him (see below p.345). It is otherwise with descriptions in the form of adjectives used predicatively; these describe His Being in terms of His relation to man. When it is said that He is 'holy' (Isa. vi; cf. Levit. xix. 1), when He is called *qanna'*, 'jealous' (Exod. xx. 5 and elsewhere) or 'merciful and gracious' (Exod. xxxiv. 6) these are statements that qualify aspects of His Being though not His Being itself.

A number of these will be discussed below. It is difficult to determine in what order they should be dealt with if we are to give a correct impression of God as He is known and professed in the Old Testament. No wonder that in the various theologies of the Old Testament the elements are arranged in different ways. In our opinion the tension in the message of the Old Testament as witness to the holy God in His communion with man is of central importance in the whole of the Old Testament, and that is why we have decided to start with the discussion of God's holiness, to be followed by the aspects of His Being that reveal how He has turned towards man.

2. *Yahweh is a holy God*

Holiness is the quality most typical of the belief in God in the Old Testament. In Israel the word *qadosh* is used very frequently to denote God and came to occupy a very important place here, though the stem of the word is also found in the other ancient Semitic languages and is frequently used of the gods in the western Semitic world.

Quadosh[2] is God as the '*Wholly Other One*', as appears from Hos. xi. 9:

---

[1] See H. Berkhof, *God voorwerp van wetenschap?*, 1960; H. Gollwitzer, *Gottes Offenbarung und unsere Vorstellung von Gott*, 1964; W. Eichrodt, *Das Gottesbild des A. T.*, 1956; H. M. Kuitert, *De mensvormigheid Gods*, 1962; see above pp.180ff. and below pp.298f.

[2] The etymology is uncertain: the root-meaning is either the idea of brilliance or that of separation, the former after the Babylonian (see W. W. von Baudissin, 'Der Begriff der Heiligkeit im A.T.', in *Studien zur semitischen Religionsgeschichte*, II, 1878, pp. 1ff.; J. Hänel, *Die Religion der Heiligkeit*, 1931; E. Sellin, *Theologie*, pp. 19ff.; H. Ringgren,

'I am God and not man; the Holy One in the midst of thee'. That God is different in nature is stressed in this text by the idea 'holy', which explains why His actions are wonderful, unlike anything man could ever expect. This is especially clear in the prophecies of Isaiah; this prophet, who emphasizes Yahweh's holiness so strongly, again and again speaks of the miracles (*pele'*) performed by God; he even uses the word *strange* to denote God's work.[1]

The content of the word *qadosh* is shown most clearly in Isa. vi. This prophet, whose life was determined by the vision of his vocation, has in this vision come to know God as the Holy One, so that again and again in his preaching God is referred to as the holy God, or the Holy One of Israel.

What God's holiness means, is manifest from the attitude and the singing of the Seraphim. They sing the *trisagion*, 'Holy, holy, holy', covering their faces so that they cannot behold Him, and their 'feet', so that He cannot behold them, and thus they move around His throne, proclaiming to each other the holiness of God. This holiness first of all involves *unapproachableness*, even for the angels around His throne. It is, therefore, comprehensible that many scholars connect the word holy with a stem meaning *to separate*. Yet the meaning of holiness is not restricted to this negative element only. The angels sing: 'Holy, holy, holy, is the Lord of hosts (*Yahweh Ṣeba'oth*); the whole earth is full of his glory!' The name *Yahweh Ṣeba'oth* and the description fill, as it were, the idea of God's holiness. This name has been the subject of much controversy.[2] The best interpretation is to take *Ṣeba'oth* as a plural of intensity, embracing all powers in heaven and on earth, and that is the reason why Isaiah can go on to say 'the whole is full of His glory' (Isa. vi. 3). *Yahweh Ṣeba'oth*[3] is Yahweh the Almighty,

The prophetical conception of Holiness, 1948; N. H. Snaith, *The distinctive Ideas of the O.T.*, 1945, p. 24; Eichrodt, *Theologie; I*, p. 139). The most plausible meaning seems to be 'to be brilliant', so that man cannot behold it. See the articles *Heilig II* and *Heiligung I* in RGG III[3], pp. 148ff. and 177f.; H. Fredriksson, *Jahwe als Krieger*, 1945, p. 114, points out that Yahweh's holiness is deep-rooted in what he calls 'Kriegsfrömmigkeit.' This may be supported by the fact that in Isaiah's work the name *Yahweh Ṣeba'oth* occupies a dominant position as well as the expression *Qedosh Yisrael*. Cf. also that the warriors are called 'sanctified ones', Isa. xiii. 3, and see further Micah iii. 5, Jer. vi. 4, Joel iv. 9. See now also C. J. Labuschagne, *op. cit.*, p. 165.

[1] Cf. Isa. xxviii. 21, 29; xxix. 14, and my 'Prophecy and Eschatology', *Suppl. to V.T.*, I, 1953, pp. 207ff.

[2] Cf., for instance, J. Hehn, *Bibl. und Bab. Gottesidee*, 1931, p. 250; K. Cramer, *Amos*, 1930, pp. 99ff.; H. Fredriksson, *Jahwe als Krieger*, Lund, 1945, pp. 5off.; H. A. Brongers, *De Scheppingstraditie bij de profeten*, 1945, pp. 117ff.; L. Köhler, *Theologie des A.T.*, p. 31; G. v. Rad, *Theologie I*, pp. 27f.

[3] Grammatically *Ṣeba'oth* may be taken to be an attribute: Yahweh (who is) *Ṣeba'oth* cf. Gesenius-Kautzsch, *Gram.* 28, § 131; cf. also an expression used in Ps. cix. 4*b*: I (am) prayer, i.e. I give myself unto prayer. *Yahweh Ṣeba'oth* = Yahweh who reveals Himself as Ṣeba'oth. The hypothesis that this solemn name of God is due to Isaiah

taken in its most intense meaning.[1]

In this text Yahweh's holiness is also linked closely with His glory. This association of *qodesh* and *kabod* (*majestas, gravitas*)[2] is found again and again in the Old Testament. *Kabod* is the radiant power of His Being,[3] as it were the external glorious manifestation of His mysterious holiness,[4] it extends all over the earth.

The original meaning of the word gives holiness both a saving and a destructive aspect. The idea of the terrible splendour of the Majesty of Yahweh probably underlies His *qodesh*. In Assyro-Babylonian the stem *qdsh* has the two meanings of 'to be terrible' and 'to shine brightly'. He is 'glorious in holiness, fearful in praises, doing wonders' (Exod. xv. 11). When God reveals Himself as the Holy One he shows His might among the nations in the salvation of Israel (Ezek. xx. 41, and *passim*).[5] Very clearly the terrible, consuming splendour of God's holiness is described in Lev. x. 1 – 7: when Aaron's sons bring 'strange' fire to the altar a consuming fire goes out from Yahweh and He says: 'I will reveal Myself in holiness in them that come nigh me, so that I may be glorified before all the people'.

God's holiness implies His absolute power over the world, a power that can be like a consuming fire and, therefore, can be terrible. When in 1 Sam. vi. 20 the death of the men of Bethshemesh is related the inhabitants say: 'Who is able to stand before this holy Lord God?' In His terrible deeds His holiness is revealed to them. When Isaiah beholds Yahweh Ṣeba'oth, he, too, is afraid that he will die: 'Woe is me! for I am undone'. God's holiness is the absolute glory of His Being which is so completely different that man cannot stand before it. That God is so often called *terrible* is an immediate consequence of His holiness.

This idea of the holiness of God has great influence on cultic forms. This is shown most clearly in the arrangement of the temple: Yahweh

(Brongers, *op. cit.*) it well-founded in so far that this all-embracing meaning was attributed to the expression by Isaiah; cf. now also B. N. Wambacq, *L'épythète divine Jahwé Sebaoth*, 1947; and particularly the important article by O. Eissfeldt, 'Jahwe Zebaoth' in *Miscellanea Academica Berolinensia*, II, 2, 1950, pp. 128ff. (where much further literature is mentioned, too), who arrives at the same conclusion as we defend here. A wholly different view is held by L. Köhler, *Theologie*[3], pp. 31 ff., who takes Ṣeba'oth in the meaning of 'stars', while V. Maag, 'Jahwes Heerscharen', *Schweizerische Theol. Umschau*, 1950, pp. 27ff. (Köhler-festschrift) finds in Ṣeba'oth 'mythical nature-powers of Canaan deprived of their potency'; when Yahweh is afterwards called God of the Ṣeba'oth, it means that His majesty surpasses that of the Canaanite gods.
[1] In that case the translation of certain texts in the Septuagint, *pantokrator*, the Almighty, was a correct rendering of the meaning.
[2] Cf., for instance, H. Wagenvoort, *Imperium*, 1941, p. 108.
[3] Ezek. i. 28. Cf. also M. Buber, *Königtum Gottes*, 1932, p. 214.
[4] Procksch, *Theologie*, p. 428.
[5] See Frederiksson, *op. cit.* and the articles of *R.G.G.*, mentioned above.

lives in the 'Holy of Holies', the hindmost part of the temple, shut off from all human coming and going. Not even the priests may enter, except the high priest once a year, in order to perform the ceremony of expiation in the presence of God Himself. It is dark inside; it has the shape of a cube, the symbol of perfect space. In the complete seclusion of this divine residence there appears a new element, not to be found elsewhere in the ancient oriental world. In the latter the *cella*, the abode proper of the gods in the temple, also takes up a central position in the building but it is daily accessible to the priests (so that they can provide the gods with food and clothing and can anoint the images). In Israel, it is true, the shewbread (bread of the presence) is offered, this, however, is not placed in the Holy of Holies but in the Holy Place, lying in front of it, on the table of the shewbread. This emphasis on the holiness of God even in the organization of the cult marks the singularity of the transcendent conception of God in Israel.

The holiness of God is not only the central idea of the Old Testament faith in God, but also the continuous background to the message of love in the New Testament. In this respect the two are in complete agreement, and here the Christian faith is based on the revelation of God in the Old Testament.

The charge is frequently made against the Old Testament conception of God that the holiness of God, in the very fact that He is different, bears traits which are demonic, a-moral, from a religious and theological point of view; and demonic traits in Yahweh are also emphasized again and again from the point of view of phenomenology and the history of religion.[1]

Both these points of view should, however, be approached with great caution. In the first place we must tread warily when dealing with the data offered on the ground of the texts by the the the exponents of the history of religion. Volz says, for example, in his book *Das Dämonische in Jahwe*[2] on the ground of 1 Kings xxii. 22 and 2 Kings viii. 10, that Yahweh makes use of lies. From a careful examination of these two cases it appears that this was certainly not intended in the story: in 1 Kings xxii Yahweh makes Micaiah ben Imlah warn Ahab against the lying spirit of the prophets; and in 2 Kings viii. 10 we must certainly distinguish between two different prophecies.[3] With regard to the theological appreciation of the Old Testament

[1] P. Volz, *Das Dämonische in Jahwe*, 1924; cf. also his *Der Geist Gottes*, 1910; N. Söderblom, *Das Werden des Gottesglauben*, 1916, pp. 313ff.; R. Otto, *The Idea of the Holy*, Eng. tr., 1923, pp. 74ff.; G. van der Leeuw, *Phaenomenologie der Religion*, 1933, pp. 604ff., (cf. the French edition *La religion*, 1948, pp. 618ff.).
[2] *Das Dämonische in Jahwe*, p. 9 n. 1; I have quoted two examples at random; cf. now the book of Klopfenstein, see below p. 310.
[3] Cf., for instance, Montgomery-Gehman, 'Kings' in *I.C.C.*, *loc. cit.*, though my opinion is slightly different: Elisha says that Benhadad shall recover, but that he shall die

conception of God, we may first consider the remark of Procksch[1] that there is nothing demonic in Yahweh, because He is a Person and the demonic always has something infra-personal, something neutral; his next remark, however, that Moses' views were already wholly monotheistic is difficult to prove and in any case does not preclude that there are, indeed, stories in the Old Testament which to some degree give a 'dynamistic' impression of Yahweh's activity. It is here the place to recall what has been said in the first few chapters about certain infra-prophetic traits in the Old Testament; they are relevant to a history of religion or a history of the canon, but to a *theology* on a critical basis they just fail to be relevant. We should, therefore, be cautious in our judgment. There are, after all, certain features of God's holiness in the Old Testament which we, Christians of the West, can hardly appreciate any more because in our conception of holiness the moral element has become so preponderant. Most of all this is true of cultic sins in the above-mentioned examples of 1 Sam. vi. 20 and Lev. x. 1ff.[2] The reason is that the idea of a holy object, a concrete thing charged with divine power and essence, no longer conveys anything to Protestants. In the Christian world only the Roman Catholic and Orthodox Churches still know this conception. In Israel there were many cult objects: altar, sacrifice, temple, ark, etc., and also persons and occasions charged, as it were, with holiness. The violation of the cultic order, the desecration, even without evil intent, of cultic objects (1 Sam. vi; 2 Sam. vi) involves death as punishment. That is why in the Elisha legends even little children who had mocked the prophet in his sacred state had to die (2 Kings ii. 23ff.).[3] And for Amos, too, one of the most evil things that throw into high relief the wickedness of Israel is that the Nazirites (people dedicated to God who, among other things, had taken a vow to abstain from wine) were compelled to drink wine (Amos ii. 12). From this point of view a great many texts – often incomprehensible to us – will have to be interpreted. In such cases it is clearly felt that there are some elements in the Old Testament that are strictly limited to their won age, yet this is not a sufficient reason to call them demonic. (For so-called 'demonic' elements cf. also the discussion below of Yahweh's wrath, pp. 305ff., and of religious hatred, pp. 315f.).

by another cause – the former is a message for Benhadad, the latter for Hazael; this latter message need not be taken as an incitement to murder (Ehrlich).
[1] *Theologie* p. 82.
[2] Cf., for instance, also the census in 2 Sam. xxiv; it should be regarded in the light of Exod. xxx. 12. Generally speaking, a census must be accompanied by an expiatory sacrifice in the ancient world.
[3] A fairly clear, though indirect, criticism of the spirit of a story such as 2 Kings i. 10ff. is to be found in Luke ix. 54ff.

The holiness of God does not only imply a consciousness of His un-approachableness, His being completely different, His glory and maj-esty, but also His *self-assertion*. This element is found again and again in earlier as well as in later texts. Yahweh gives His honour (*kabod*) to no one else (Isa.xlii.8, xlviii.11), or, to use the words of the Deca-logue: *Yahweh is a jealous God*, an *'El qanna'*. We must be very accurate in our distinctions regarding this idea: it is not to be identified with what is known in heathenism as the jealousy of the gods which may be revealed not only against other gods but also against man when things are going particularly well with him. The fear of the jealousy of the gods in the higher polytheistic religions is an after-effect of a demonic belief in God, which has been banished in the Old Testa-ment. Applied to Yahweh this word has a shade of meaning different from the one it has when it is applied to men. The verb with which *qanna'* is connected means, besides being jealous, also to maintain one's rights to the exclusion of others (e.g. Num.xi.29; 2Sam.xxi.2). And it is in the latter sense that the word is to be understood in the Deca-logue of Exod.xx and Deut.v, and elsewhere (Exod.xxxiv.14; Deut.iv.24, vi.15) where God is called a jealous God; He is God who will not share His glory with any one else, neither with a man nor with a strange God. He is alone, and demands for Himself alone wor-ship to which, moreover, He has a right. The zeal of Yahweh is, therefore, a conception necessarily connected with Him. That is the reason why in the garden of Eden He does not allow man to eat of the knowledge of good an evil, because by so doing man would become like God; and that also explains why (Gen.xi) He cannot allow people to build a tower 'whose top may reach unto heaven', and why in Gen.vi He cannot tolerate that the *bene ha-'elohim*, the sons of God, the heavenly creatures, should have intercourse with earthly women. And in the same way He will not share His honour with other gods. From the beginning the worship of other gods is forbidden in Yahwism in various ways. He *alone* is to be adored as God and His Name alone is to be used by the servants of Yahweh (Exod.xxiii.13); that is why in the Old Testament various names of strange gods are corrupted: Baal is turned into Bosheth (shame), Ninurta into Nimrod ('we will rebel'), Abednebo into Abednego, often Hadadezer into Hadarezer, etc.[1] The salvation of Israel, too, is seen again and again in the Old Testa-ment in the light of the jealousy of Yahweh, who will renew His people for the honour of His Name (Isa.ix.6, xxxvii.32, lix.17ff.). Ezekiel sees the deliverance of Israel by Yahweh only as the glorification of His holy Name (Ezek.xxxvi.22ff.).

[1] In Prov.xxx.31b 'El Qos (God Qos) was corrupted to *'alqum*, which does not make sense; see my essay *The Edomitic deity Qaus*, OTS XIV, 1965, pp.330f.

This idea of the jealousy of Yahweh is closely connected with the religious exclusiveness of the religion of Israel and must be recognized as inherent in Yahwism; it is the main cause of the development of theoretical monotheism, which does not only forbid the worship of other gods but also denies their existence (of which we read up to the days of David, 1 Sam. xxvi. 19, and even much later, 2 Kings iii. 27).[1]

From this jealousy of God has sprung not only the struggle against polytheism but also that against all sorts of mantic and magic, against witchcraft and divination (Deut. xviii. 9ff.), a struggle that can be traced back to quite ancient times (cf. 1 Sam. xxviii; Exod. xxii. 18, Hebrew text verse 17).[2]

The jealousy of Yahweh may take the form of *wrath*[3], against the heathen (Zeph. iii. 8; Jer. xxv. 15f.) as well as against the people of Israel (Isa. v. 25, ix. 7ff.; Jer. xv. 14; Num. xxv. 11). This wrath is a manifestation of God's holiness as directed against man.[4] The motives given for God's wrath are nearly always of a moral and religious nature.[5] He is wrathful because man opposes His commandments and is disobedient to His holy will. There are, it is true, cases in the Old Testament where no spiritual reasons are given for God's wrath, especially in some stories that bear the stamp of particularly ancient traditions. Very remarkable, for instance, is, in Exod. iv. 24 the unexpected threat of Yahweh, apparently directed against Moses; it is a *torso* among the stories admitting of more than one interpretation.[6]

The attitude of Elohim towards Jacob in the darkness of night (Gen. xxxii) also offers difficulties arising from the mythological character of the original narrative which has here been woven into the history without undergoing a sufficiently clear spiritual adaptation. If we are right in thinking that this story may be considered to be from the pen of E[7], and that we may, therefore, assume a closer relation with such chapters as Gen. xx, where Abraham (in spite of his white lie) is represented as the 'mighty' prophet who can save by his intercession,

[1] See p. 33.
[2] In an article in VT 1963, pp. 269ff., H. A. Brongers maintained that the meaning of *qanna* itself is *angry*. On the other hand B. Renaud, *Je suis un dieu jaloux*, 1963, pp. 71, 153, emphasizes that the jealousy of God in the Old Testament is really due to the notion of outraged love.
[3] Cf. esp. Th. W. z. N.T., V, pp. 392ff. *s.v.* 'οργη; esp. pp. 404, 410.
[4] *Th. W.z.N.T.*, V. p. 409.
[5] In contrast with most non-biblical narratives and histories; see e.g. the unmotivated anger of the gods at the Flood in the Gilgamesh-epic, Tablet XI, and the unmotivated anger of Chemosh against Moab in the Mesha-inscription, line 5; cf. now the new Atrahasis-text.
[6] It may be the oldest narrative of the introduction of circumcision, retained out of 'historical' considerations; at any rate it demonstrates that for Israel the blood-manipulation was of fundamental importance in circumcision and had a sanctifying influence.
[7] See my 'De literatuur van Oud-Israël', 1961, 108.

then something similar must be the case in Gen. xxxii. The patriarch Jacob, who, like Abraham, is a spiritual Father of Israel, is here the man who, because of his piety, is able to wrestle with the Deity and to wring a blessing from Him. The fact that Jacob is the kind of man to gain the victory over God stands in the foreground here. So in spite of everything this story cannot be regarded as concerned with the demonic.[1]

Now that we are dealing with the so-called demonic traits of the Old Testament belief in God we must also go into another aspect of this question: the connection between God and evil which has also been explained by the concept of the demonic. That Yahweh should do evil (cause misfortunes) (Amos iii.6; Job.ii.10; Isa.xlv.7) and should even instigate evil (1 Sam. xxvi. 19; 2 Sam. xxiv. 1)[2] is, however, connected not so much with the fact that there might be a demonic element that had remained in His nature as with the insuperable difficulty the problem of evil presents to any monotheistic religion. For whenever God is regarded as the only God, from whom all action springs, evil must, in the last resort, also be imputed to Him. In Israel this was, indeed, done, as appears from the abovementioned texts.

Side by side with this solution of the problem of evil here is still another: God is surrounded by spirits, angels, and among them there is also the spirit of evil who instigates evil (1 Sam. xvi. 14f.; 1 Kings xxii. 22f.).[3]

Besides this evil spirit of God there is also a spirit (Satan, i.e. the

---

[1] Perhaps it is incorrect not only to call these two narratives demonic, but also to consider them from the point of view of the anger of God. Apart from the religious-historical background (on which see, among others, the essay by P.A.H. de Boer on Gen.xxxii in *Ned. Theol. Tijdschrift*, 1946/7, and the somewhat wild study by F. Sierksma on Exod.iv.24ff. under the title 'La circoncision en Israel', in *O.T.S.*, IX, pp. 136ff.), it is possible to read both Exod.iv.24f and Gen.xxxii.23ff. in connection with their contexts as concrete narratives of an affliction by Yahweh and '*Elohim* (whom E identifies in this story with Israel's God). In that case Yahweh does not really appear as an enemy, but thwarts Moses and Jacob in order to put them to the test, and thus to give to Moses his means of grace (circumcision as a protective sign of the Covenant), and to Jacob His blessing (in the powerful name of Israel). Nowhere in the O.T. does Yahweh appear as the enemy of man, unless His anger has been aroused because sin has been committed, cf. Isa.lxiii.10; Lam.ii.5; also Hos.v.12ff.; cf. now also K. Elliger, 'Der Jakobskampf am Jabbok; Gen.xxxii.33ff. als hermeneutisches Problem', *Z.f.Th. u. Kirche*, 1951, pp. 1ff., and Dillmann's Commentary, *loc. cit.* G.Beer, *Exodus* (Handb. z. A.T.) p.39, says: 'In the context of the whole biography of Moses iv.24–26 denotes a consecration of Moses to his office.' Cf. now B.S.Childs, *Myth and Reality*, pp.58ff. and O.Eissfeldt, 'Jakobs Begegnung mit El und Moses' Begegnung mit Jahwe', *O.L.Z.* 1963, pp.325ff.
[2] The last two of these texts should not be emphasized too strongly from a theological point of view: the former is a sample of crude 'soldiers' theology' (Valeton); while the introduction to 2 Sam.xxiv (a torso) is apparently lacking; moreover 2 Sam.xxiv is clearly a cultic story.
[3] See also Procksch, *Theologie*, p.465.

304

Accuser), who seeks out evil in man in order to be able to accuse him before God (Job if.) and who also takes over the function of the evil spirit of God, thus becoming the Evil One (Satan) himself, in the sense in which the word is used in later Hebrew and in Christian theology, as an Evil Power who does, indeed, occupy a subordinate position but who works independently as long as this world lasts; as such he tempts man to do evil (1 Chron. xxi. 1; and cf. also 2 Sam. xxiv. 1: here it is God who acts in His wrath and causes David to sin in order to punish him). That the doctrine of Satan arose is due to a more profound spiritual understanding of God, who is too holy to countenance sin. In Israel God's Being becomes more and more ethical and transcendental, so that Evil can no longer be regarded as coming from Him, but is detached from God in the figure of Satan.[1]

We must now return to the subject we were dealing with: God's wrath.

Even if God's wrath is not always clearly defined from the moral point of view, yet we may note that the general tendency of the Old Testament certainly is to connect this wrath with religious and moral motives. God's wrath exists because of sin: suffering is the punishment God inflicts because of sin. In Gen. iii death and the suffering of women in pregnancy and childbirth are accounted for as being due to sin. Death does not exist arbitrarily in this world, as the Babylonian Gilgamesh epic would have it, where the gods have kept life for themselves and have prepared death for man. On the contrary, not only the case of exceptional distress of the people but also the general anthropological phenomena of suffering and death are to be explained as the punishment of disobedience and of trespassing against the will of God.

The wrath of God is described in the Old Testament with terrible severity, especially by the prophets. It is remarkable that exactly those prophets who emphasize God's love most strongly, viz. Hosea and Jeremiah, are also most vehement in their description of the divine wrath. In Hos. v. 12, 14, Yahweh says: 'Therefore will I be unto Ephraim as a moth, and to the house of Judah as rottenness;... For I will be unto Ephraim as a lion and as a young lion to the house of Judah: I, even I, will tear and go away, I will take away, and none shall rescue him'. One of the harshest descriptions is found in Jer. xiii. 12–14: the prophet is told to go to a group of inhabitants of Jerusalem who are drinking and to say to them: 'Let all the bottles be filled!' The others answer jestingly: 'Of course, that is what they are for!' But then he must also say what his words, a terrible oracle, mean: 'Yah-

[1] R. Schärf, *Die Gestalt des Satans im A.T.*, doctorate thesis Zürich, in C. G. Jung, *Symbolik des Geistes*, 1948, pp. 151ff.; A. de Bondt, *De Satan*, n.d.; von Rad and Foerster in *Th. Wb. z. N.T.*, II, pp. 71ff. s.v. διάβολος.

weh will fill all the inhabitants of Judea, high and low, with the draught of His wrath, so that they are inebriated by it; and then He will dash them together and break them like bottles, so that only sherds remain.' In His wrath Yahweh invites the people to a drinking-bout, ending in a dance of death. This cup of wrath Yahweh also gives the nations to drink in Jeremiah's prophecies of judgment (Jer. xxv. 15ff.). Horrible is the description of the divine wrath in Isa. lxiii. 1–6, where the garments of Yahweh are red with the blood of the slain heathen, like the apparel of one who treads the winepress with his feet. The day of the Lord, which in Israel is looked forward to as the day of salvation, is depicted by Amos (ch. v) and Zephaniah (ch. i; ii) as a day in which God shall pour out the vials of His wrath over the sinful people. Even obduracy may be described by the prophets as a judgement of Yahweh: this happens not only to Pharaoh in the story of the Exodus, but also to the people in Isa. vi. 9f.[1] It is even possible that Ezekiel (xx. 25f.) represents the law of Exod. xxii. 29 (28) as a temptation by Yahweh, by which He prepared the people for judgment. Such things are said by the prophets, who have a thoroughly moral conception of God! Behind the severity there is the great inward alarm and indignation at the sins of the people; their message of the divine wrath is at heart rooted in their consciousness of the offended holy love of Yahweh, the God of the covenant.[2]

According to the prophets the worst of all is that in their wicked self-conceit men say that God cannot be angry (Amos ix. 10; Isa. v. 18ff.; Mic. ii. 7; Zeph. i. 12). This is a denial of the majesty of God, as is also the derision of those who think that there is an escape from God's punishment (Isa. xxviii. 14ff.). In the emphasis they lay on God's wrath which pronounces judgment upon sin, the Scriptural prophets are the exact opposite of the so-called false prophets, who only speak of peace (salvation) (Mic. ii. 11; Jer. vi. 13f., cf. viii. 11; xiv. 13; xxviii.).[3] The sharp contrast between these nationalist 'prophets of peace' and the preachers of penitence whose writings have survived, is found with all the pre-exilic prophets; it almost cost Jeremiah his life (cf. ch. vii and xxvi). Only the words of the great preachers of penitence have been preserved for posterity, because their prophecies were borne out by the catastrophe of the downfall of the nation (cf. Deut. xviii. 21f.). It is clear, therefore, that there was also in Israel a nationalistic tendency which could connect with God only the idea of the expectation of

---

[1] This demonstrates once more that we should be cautious in ascribing demonic traits to Yahweh, which was done repeatedly on the ground of the 'hardening' of Pharaoh's heart; cf. F. Hesse, *Das Verstockungsproblem im A.T.*, 1955.
[2] *Th. W. z. N.T.*, V, p. 404.
[3] See above, p. 82.

salvation for the people; but this trend was consciously opposed and abandoned, because in it the true faith in God as the Holy One had been lost.

In His wrathful chastisement God does not, however, show His ill-will against man in himself; on the contrary, He does not rejoice at the death of the sinner, but seeks his conversion, his righteousness and his life, as Ezekiel (xviii) says emphatically. And that this is the meaning of the whole of the Old Testament appears, among other things, from the story of the Flood. The relationship between God and mankind in the Babylonian narrative of the Flood (upon which the story of Genesis depends) is quite different in character from the Biblical narrative. In the former the gods wish to destroy mankind, in the Bible the desire to save predominates: before Yahweh executes His judgment he decides to save Noach and thus to save mankind; in doing all this God is not driven by wrath only but He also *repents* of having created man (Gen. vi. 6). Even at this most terrible moment in the history of the world God's pitying love an His desire to save are manifest; the judgment He brings upon mankind because of His righteousness by no means detracts from His love.

In His wrath and chastisement God reveals nothing but His righteousness, and in this righteousness He proves Himself the Holy One (Isa. v. 16; x. 22; Zeph. iii. 5).

From the first of these verses it is clear that the notion of God's holiness in the Old Testament is closely linked to the idea of the righteousness of God, i.e. the moral conception of God.[1]

We have already established clearly that the idea of holiness originally formed a category in itself; for this reason it is never absorbed in the category of righteousness, though the two are connected again and again, and very closely. In Israel's conception of God, together with the ideas of holiness, majesty and exclusiveness, some other ideas also become prominent: not only universalism, so that in the course of history the strange gods entirely fade before His splendour, but also righteousness and other moral qualities. His actions are guided by the will to bring righteousness. This is very strongly marked in the prophets; from Amos onwards it is clear from their preaching that the moral and spiritual demands are of paramount importance.[2] Amos

[1] Righteousness *(ṣedaqah)* is not a static but a dynamic conception, like all Hebrew words. Righteousness results in justice. As such the word is ambivalent, it has a positive meaning (restoring justice), an indication of the bringing of salvation, as well as a negative meaning of judgment. The positive meaning dominates the negative to such an extent that we may doubt if we should not do better to place the notion of righteousness in the next section along with mercy. It may therefore be used as a transition to this quality. See also below p. 311.
[2] Cf. Ch. VIII, III, and Vox Theologica 1949: *Het ethisch karakter van de oudtestamentische profetie.*

fights social injustice; according to his preaching God cannot accept a cult if injustice is not suppressed in the life of the people (ch. v, cf. also Hos. iv. 1f., vi. 1–6; Mic. iif., vi. 8ff., vii. 1ff., Isa. v. 8ff., x. 1ff.; Jer. vii; etc.). When the prophets are confronted with the choice between the cult and morality, they choose the latter; for the right attitude towards God manifests itself first and foremost in morality. That the holiness of God is closely linked up with the demand for justice in the priestly literature as well, appears most emphatically from Lev. xix. The demand: 'Ye shall be holy, for I am holy' is the introduction to, and the conclusion of, a great number of commandments, mostly moral in character; while also in Psalms xv and xxiv the right attitude to life of the man who comes to worship God in the temple is defined in exclusively moral terms; here all ritualistic demands are dropped. It is of the utmost importance here that the Decalogue (Exod. xx) with its religous and moral demands (and not the so-called cultic decalogue of Exod. xxxiv and Exod. xx. 23ff. and xxiii. 14ff.) ranks first in the narrative of the revelation in Mount Sinai. This attitude did not spring up after the appearance of the major prophets but is it of much earlier date (Hosea iv. 1ff. certainly refers to it already).[1]

When Hosea depicts the new covenant of love between Yahweh and the people we find righteousness and law mentioned there as the primary foundation-stones of this covenant (ii. 21; English versions ii. 19). The future Kingdom of God in the new Israel is depicted as a kingdom of righteousness (Isa. ix. 6; xi. 4f., ii. 4, xvi. 5; Jer. xxiii. 5). In the oldest stories, too, the moral element plays an important part; remember especially Nathan's judgment upon David's sin and the king's repentance, (2 Sam. xii), a history which serves as an introduction to David's domestic tragedy: David even takes the curse of Shimei upon himself as a chastisement by Yahweh (2 Sam. xvi. 11). Elijah's behaviour towards Ahab because of the injustice done to Naboth also bears witness to the connection between religion and righteousness. From this close connection the prophets even derive the courage to take action against the kings; a phenomenon not found anywhere else during the whole of ancient oriental history.

For that reason divine chastisement is meted out on the principle

[1] On the question of the Decalogue we shall give only a selection from the vast literature on this subject: B. D. Eerdmans, *Alttest. Studien*, III, 1910, pp. 131ff.; S. Mowinckel, *Le décalogue*, 1927; L. Köhler, 'Der Dekalog', *Th. Rundschau*, I, 1929, pp. 161ff.; P. Volz, *Mose und sein Werk²*, 1932; A. Alt, *Die Ursprünge des isr. Rechts*, 1934; my 'Litterair-historische vragen aangaande de Dekaloog', *N. Theol. Studien*, 1939, pp. 2ff., 34ff.; J. J. Stamm, 'Dreißig Jahre Dekalogforschung', *Th. R.* 1961, pp. 189ff., 281ff.; id., *Der Dekalog im Lichte der neueren Forschung²*, 1962; H. Graf Reventlow, *Gebot und Predigt im Dekalog*, 1962; G. Fohrer, 'Das sogenannte apodiktisch formulierte Recht und der Dekalog', *K.w.D.* 1965, pp. 49ff.

of retribution. In the oldest J-narrative Jacob, who had cheated his brother of the blessing due to him as the first-born (Gen. xxvii), is himself cheated by Laban who gives him first-born daughter instead of Rachel. The righteousness of God is also revealed in the correspondence between His judgment and sin. This is pronounced very clearly in one of the early psalms (xviii. 26); again and again the prophets, too, see in Yahweh's chastisement the application of the retaliation[1], Isa. iii. 10f., xxx. 16; Jer. ii. 5, 17, 19; Obad. 15, etc. This, however, does not warrant the conclusion that the idea of righteousness in the Old Testament is to be taken first and foremost in the juridical sense (see below *sub* IIIc), for it is moral in character, though it is influenced strongly by the conception of the covenant and the laws of the covenant. The covenant itself, however, is not merely a juridical institution either, but it creates a communion which has clearly moral traits (see above pp. 168ff.).

This double aspect – the traits of holiness and morality – is particularly evident in the idea of *truth*, or rather *trustworthiness*, which is connected with God, so that He may even be called *the God of the Amen*. (Isa. lxv. 16).[2] In Hebrew the word for truth is connected with a stem meaning 'to steady', 'to hold out'.[3] The Hebrew word for faith is also connected with this: *he'emin*, i.e. to regard God as steadfast, trustworthy. God is the God of true faithfulness (Pss. xxx. 10; lvii. 11); His *chesed we'emeth*, His true or faithful love is assumed again and again in the historical narratives, in the Psalms, and by the prophets. It is God who offers His *'emunah*, His faithfulness, to Israel (Hos. ii. 22; English versions ii. 20). In His faithfulness or truth Yahweh is the reliable God; truth is a word used in the relationship between man and man, and between God and man; it lacks, therefore, the intellectual and uncharitable tang which it may have in the western languages. Yahweh's trustworthiness is also apparent from the fact that the Old Testament always warns against vanity, i.e. deceit and falsehood.[4]

[1] We should bear in mind that, as appears from the *ius talionis*, the idea of retribution was one of the most fundamental elements of ancient Eastern criminal law, and in Israel as well (Exod. xxi. 23ff.). This idea of a religious concept of retribution is opposed by K. Koch, *Gibt es ein Vergeltungsdogma im A.T.?*, ZThK, 1955, pp. 1ff. Von Rad, *Theology* I, pp. 383ff., largely agrees with him. He also emphasizes the 'sphere of action which creates fate'; according to him Israel's faith in Yahweh as the 'universal cause' delivered Israel from this part of the ancient oriental conception of life. Though there is no denying that it was felt in Israel that sin carries its own punishment, this view is not the predominant note in the O.T. The views of the two scholars mentioned above leave the law of the covenant out of account too much.
[2] Cf. on the word 'Amen' in St. Paul, 2 Cor. i. 15–24. W. C. van Unnik, 'Reisepläne und Amensagen', in *Studia Paulina*, 1953, pp. 215ff. (Festschrift J. de Zwaan).
[3] See above, Ch. IV, pp. 99 and my *Geloven en Vertrouwen*, 1957.
[4] It remains therefore to be seen whether L. Köhler's remark, referring to the Deca-

We feel, therefore, completely justified in maintaining that the ethical element in Yahwism has full justice done to it and that God, the Holy One, is also known in Israel as the morally perfect or rather absolutely Moral God[1], who will not compromise with anybody in any province of life when justice and truth are at stake. The prophets knew themselves to be His representatives and so sharp were their attacks on all sorts of sacred things and men – even the patriarchs (Hos. xii: Jacob!), the cult (Amos, Hosea, Isaiah, Jeremiah, Deutero-Isaiah), the king (Nathan, Elijah, Hosea, Isaiah, Jeremiah), the priesthood and the prophecy of their days (all prophets of the 7th and 8th centuries) – so clearly did they state and identify the sins of their contemporaries, high and low, priests and politicians (cf. Mic. iif.; vif.), that it is impossible not to acknowledge that to them God is a Holy Being and for that reason they know Him to be perfect righteousness and truth, and take truth seriously.[2]

God has revealed Himself to Israel as the Holy One, i.e. the Unapproachable, wholly Other God, as the glorious Majesty, the Ruler over all powers in heaven and on earth, the God who vindicates His honour, who judges in His wrath, and who is also absolute in righteousness and in truth. The full glory of Yahweh's holiness ranges itself behind His demands for righteousness and gives a character of inevitability to the moral standards. The giving of the law on Mount Sinai is the first sign of this revelation and the prophets are its most conspicuous proclaimers. They were never conscious of saying anything new about Him; they knew they were speaking in the name of Him who had revealed Himself to His people in the deliverance from Egypt and in the miracles in the desert. This idea of the later prophets must in its

logue: 'The fact that there is no clause, "Thou shalt not lie", in the biblical decalogues raises all kinds of reflections', (*Theologie*, p.239, n.80) should not be regarded as an insinuation; see now M.A.Klopfenstein, *Die Lüge nach dem A.T.*, 1964, pp. 321ff.
[1] The words *tam, tamim* and *shalem*, which express the idea of perfection, are hardly ever used to denote God Himself (cf. 2 Sam. xxii. 26, i.e. Ps. xviii. 26); the words that are used are: *yashar*, 'upright', and *ṣaddiq* 'righteous'. That the words denoting perfection were not applied to Yahweh may be best explained from the fact that the ideas that fundamentally meant 'sound', 'complete', were not considered elevated enough to denote the holy God. God is rich in (ethical) virtues, but transcends the human ethical standards. Cf. N.H.Snaith, *Distinctive Ideas*. Ch. III, and the article, already mentioned above, in the March number of *Vox Theologica*, 1949; C.Edlund, *Das Auge der Einfalt*, 1952. The same is true of *chakam* (wise), that only once is applied by Isaiah (xxxi. 2) to God, cf. *Wisdom in Israel and in the Ancient Near East*, presented to H.H.Rowley, *Suppl. to V.T.*, III, 1955, p.232 (art. of M.Noth, Die Bewährung von Salomos "göttlicher Weisheit"). The term *chakam*, (wise) is also used only occasionally to denote God (Isa. xxxi. 2), cf. M.Noth, *Die Bewährung von Salomos göttliche Weisheit*, in Rowley Festschrift, Suppl. V.T., III, p.232.
[2] This remains so, even if the white lie does occur a few times in the O.T. (for instance, Jer. xxxviii. 24ff.), cf. Klopfenstein, *op. cit*, pp. 325ff.

essence already be completely present in the revelation to Moses even if certain elements only became more explicit later on. Some historical evidence for this is to be found in the great writings prior to those of the 8th century: J, the original Saul-David story, the song of Deborah,[1] the oldest laws, such as the Book of the Covenant, and, ultimately, the Decalogue.

3. *Yahweh is merciful and gracious*

In the foregoing we have seen one aspect of the nature of God according to the Old Testament revelation: His holiness, His being the wholly Other One. The distinctive characteristics of this holiness are His transcendence, glory, omnipotence, jealousy, unapproachableness, wrath, truth and righteousness. There is, however, also another aspect: He is not only transcendent, exalted above this world, but also turns Himself towards this world, including it in a *communion* with Himself. Some of the qualities of God discussed under His transcendence could be included here as well: jealousy, wrath, and especially truth and righteousness; they are, however, so closely bound up with the idea of holiness that they cannot very well be separated from it. Indeed, the qualities we shall now discuss cannot be considered apart from His holiness: they, too, find their foundation in the holiness of His Being.[2] God is not double-faced in the Old Testament, as some heathen gods are: He is not a double but a single Being (Deut. vi. 4). Yet that side of His nature which goes out to man and to the world constitutes another aspect, so much so that in our rational system of ideas we must distinguish it from those qualities which we include under holiness (cf. Jer. xxiii. 23).

In Ch. VI we stated as our starting-point that God is transcendent but also enters into a relationship with the world. Yahweh as the holy, absolute God stands in a direct relation to the world, not only because He has created the world but also because all creatures live by His power and because He has intercourse with man in many ways: He is the giver of life, He is loving and merciful. In the next few pages we shall discuss this latter aspect, turned towards man, of which love, mercy, grace and forgiveness are the chief elements, or speaking dogmatically, 'attributes' of God. Once more we must state emphatically that the Old Testament gives no theology in the sense of a list of divine attributes systematically arranged in reflected ideas, a list which would give a complete description of this Being. The Old

---

[1] Cf. also M. Buber, *Der Glaube der Propheten*, 1950 and my *Religion of Israel*.
[2] In Jer. xxxi. 37 the certainty of Yahweh's mercy on Israel rests on the inscrutability of Yahweh's Being as evident from the inscrutability of the Creation. Cf. Hos. xi. 9; Isa. xl. 21ff., 27ff.

Testament word, particularly in the prophetic writings and in certain of the Psalms, was written from a direct spiritual experience of God.

The 'attributes' of God are no clearly separable conceptions but rather symbolical, partially overlapping indications.

When the prophets speak of knowing God this is, as we have stated above, not an intellectual knowledge but a knowing with one's heart, with all one's soul, which particularly implies communion with God.

The greatest and most distinctive element of Old Testament religion is not that the holiness of God was thought to be so absolute that the naturalistic conception of God was broken and the conception of God was raised to a truly spiritual plane, but that the idea of the spiritual sublimity of God has deepened rather than weakened that other conception of communion between God and man. The relation between the pious Israelite of the Psalms and God is closer than any that is to be found in the ancient Semitic world. Man can address himself to God directly: 'My God', and knows that he has been admitted into communion with God, who hears him. It is not necessary to come to Him with great ceremony as happens in most of the Babylonian psalms: man has immediate access to the King of Kings and the God of gods!

There can be no natural intercourse between God and man (the transcendence of God prevents any natural relation), but nevertheless communion can be complete. For this God is merciful and gracious, long-suffering and abundant in love (solidarity, i.e. *chesed*) and truth (Exod. xxxiv. 6).[1] The holy, powerful God desires to have intercourse with man. The words of Exod. xxxiv cited above are repeated in many connections and are applied to God again and again in various shades of meaning. Merciful (*rachum*) is really the word used to denote the relation between mother and child and for that reason its stem is also used in Isa. xlix. 15, where the love of God for His people is called more steadfast than a mother's love for her child. God is gracious (*chanun*) as the one who reveals His high favour to man; the word favour (*chen*)[2] expresses the great benevolence of the superior towards the inferior. One who is long suffering is strictly speaking one who postpones his anger for a long time and has great patience. 'Abundant in *chesed*'[3]: this word, here rendered by love, indicates a firmly established relation: there is a close bond of union between God and man. This union (or faithfulness) is typified by the relation between Abraham and God (Gen. xxiv. 27). The Old Testament is full of this word; in the A.V. and R.V. it is usually rendered by 'lovingkindness', and that is,

[1] See R. C. Dentan, *l.c.*, and above p.294f.
[2] W. F. Lofthouse, 'Chen and Chesed in the O.T.', *Z.A.W.*, 1933, pp. 29ff.
[3] See below, pp. 387f.

indeed, part of the meaning; the most important element is, however, faithfulness (hence R.V.S. renders it 'steadfast love'). The words *chesed* (union) and *'emeth* (faithfulness, steadfastness)[1] are found together again and again and often constitute one single idea: a firm, faithful union which is indissoluble. The same words that are used in Exod. xxxiv are found over and over again in the prophets and the Psalms (cf. e.g. Hos. ii. 21, A.V. 19, where the word *chesed* is strengthened by the addition of *rachamim*, pity, and also Jer. ii. 2) and also in the wisdom-literature[2]. Isaiah is so certain of the faithful love of God that it is a perfect safeguard in life to him and that in the most difficult moments of his life (when the enemy is approaching) he extols faith[3] as precious beyond anything (Isa. vii. 9*b*; xxviii. 16 and xxx. 15). On the ground of this love of God the relation between Him and Israel can exist (Hos. xi. 1); only this makes His covenant with the people possible (Exod. xix. 4ff.). So that Amos can say: 'You only have I known of all the families of the earth: therefore I will punish you for all your iniquities' (Amos iii. 2, cf. Ezek. xvi. 8; Jer. xiii. 11, etc.). The prophets conceive of the covenant with Israel the token of God's love (Hosea, Jeremiah and Ezekiel). The relation between God and man in the Old Testament rests on this idea of a relationship with man entered upon by God. The J-narrative of Gen. ii and iii sees this intercourse as something original that existed between God and man in Paradise though there is no question of a covenant-relation there (the only text to which reference might be made to support the idea that the relation between God and the first man was a covenant-relation is Hos. vi. 7, but this text is probably corrupt)[4]. At any rate it is certain that the author of the Paradise-story, who considers this relation between God and man to be a most intimate communion, looks upon it as essentially surpassing the Covenant, because of its directness; God walks in the garden in the afternoon in the cool of the day; man lives there near the tree of life and the tree of the knowledge of good and evil, which are divine trees; there exists an immediate intercourse between God and man, and when the latter has sinned and hides himself God calls him: 'Where art thou?'

Elsewhere, when Yahweh sees how corrupt man has become upon the earth He feels deep sorrow (Gen. vi. 6), and therefore God will not destroy mankind by the Flood without saving Noah. And after the Flood He resolves not to destroy mankind again (in Gen. viii. 21ff.,

---

[1] See above, p.309; cf. Snaith, *op. cit.*
[2] R. C. Dentan, *op. cit.*
[3] *He'emin*, to declare that God is true, that God 'holds out', see above, p. 309.
[4] We must probably read here 'in Adam' (a place-name), instead of 'as Adam'; see among others my *Paradijsvoorstelling bij de oude semietische volken*, 1937, p. 231.

J, as well as in ix. 1 – 16, P). The ultimate aim of the call of Abraham (Gen. xii. 1ff.) is that all generations of the earth shall be blessed in him. It is remarkable that in one of the very oldest books of the Old Testament (J) this thought is brought out with so much emphasis.[1] This idea of the merciful intentions of God for the whole world is only found again at the heights of prophetic proclamation. So the nations are also (if only occasionally) involved in the salvation of Israel (Isa. ii. 2ff.; Mic. iv. 1ff.; cf. Isa. xi. 9f.); even the animal kingdom is to participate in this glory (Isa. xi; Hos. ii.20, A.V. 18).

Though the message of salvation is in the Old Testament mostly limited to Israel and though God is mainly concerned with His chosen people there are, however, also other voices to be heard throughout the Old Testament,[2] e.g. in the words of the Judean farmer from Tekoa who says neither more nor less than that Yahweh cares for Philistines and Nubians as well as for Israel (Amos ix. 7). The books of Jonah and Ruth also show this tendency and proclaim that other nations of the world than Israel also live under God's goodness. The one prophet, however, who understood better than all the others how all-embracing God's grace must be, is Deutero-Isaiah, the unknown poet of the Exile, who in many respects may be counted among the greatest prophets (Isa. xl.ff.); he stresses this point in ch. xlii. 1 – 7 and xlix. 1ff. He has understood that God's mercy only has its fullest revelation when the heathen participate in God's gift of salvation, and for that reason he knows of Israel's missionary call.[3] It is only the very greatest men of Israel who by the strength of the Spirit of God broke through the nationalistic limitations which, then as now, held the nations captive. This spiritual victory was due to a faith in God that knew God not only in His greatness but also in His love and knew that in this way He stretched out His hands towards the whole world.

In ethics, too, love penetrated as a command; most deeply in the well-known word of Lev. xix. 18, which are given a central position in the New Testament by Christ: 'Thou shalt not avenge, nor bear any grudge against the children of thy people, but thou shalt love thy neighbour as thyself: I am the Lord'. In the ethical field the religious relationship with God is reflected on the plane of everyday life. The neighbour in this text is the fellow-countryman. Love of one's enemy

---

[1] See a.o. A. Alt, 'Die Deutung der Weltgeschichte im A.T.', *Z. f. Th. u. K.* 1959, pp. 129ff.

[2] It is remarkable that in the prophetic writings the patriarchs play such a subordinate part, or even no part at all (Abraham). The message of the prophets emphasizes God's mercy, not the noble descent of the people (see K. Galling, *Die Erwählungstraditionen Israels*, 1928, and my *Die Erwählung Israels*, pp. 78f.).

[3] Notwithstanding P. A. H. de Boer, 'Second Isaiah's Message', *O.T.S.*, XI, 1956, pp. 8off.

is not mentioned in the Old Testament, though an attitude of loyalty and readiness to help is in a way expected (Exod. xxiii. 4f.). The 'stranger' (the *ger*, i.e. the foreigner who has been admitted to the country and is considered a guest) should receive the same treatment as the Israelite; we even find the words, 'Thou shalt love him as thyself', repeated in this connection (Lev. xix. 34). That perfect love which finds expression in the love of one's enemy was not formulated absolutely until the New Testament; it was discovered by Him who knew no sin. That one should hate one's enemy (Matt. v. 43) is apparently a late Judaic popular interpretation that was finding acceptance in the days of Jesus, but not an immediate datum of the Old Testament.[1] Hatred of one's enemy is, it is true, accepted as natural in the Old Testament, and feelings of hatred and revenge are sometimes given free rein (even by Jeremiah), so that from this point of view the Old Testament can be held responsible for the conclusion which Jesus attributes to the Jews.

Besides the personal motive for hatred there is another, a religious motive in the Old Testament, expressed most clearly in Ps. cxxxix. 21 f. It plays a part in the historical books (e.g. 1 Sam. xv; 1 Kings xviii. 40; the Deuternomist, e.g. in the book of Joshua). This very complicated phenomenon, of a cultic rather than religous and ethical nature, will not be discussed here (see below III, p. 401).

One other point must be dealt with here: the Old Testament knows of God's love, mercy and grace, and there are examples where the heathen are not exluded from these. But, we may ask, does not the Old Testament contradict itself regarding its doctrine of Love? Do we not find, time and again, evidence that Yahweh is also seen in another light, so that it seems that He is arbitrary in the distribution of His love and His hatred? Are not the rejection of Cain's sacrifice, the rejection of Esau (cf. Mal. i. 2f.), the hardening of Pharaoh's heart, and other things, too, at variance with the belief in God's mercy? Is not there much that must be called arbitrary, particularly in all that has been summed up in the word election?

We must admit that certain stories were viewed in a particularist light, especially perhaps the contrast between Esau and Jacob; on the other hand we should not forget that in these stories there is also the unwarrantable attitude of Esau towards his right of primogeniture; the hardening of Pharaoh's heart, an act of God, is also due to his guilt; that God punishes sin with sin (i.e. the hardening of the heart) also applies to Israel (see pp. 305ff.).

And as for 'election', there is no question of arbitrariness, of chance sympathies and antipathies; even when the words love and hatred are

[1] See, for instance, Strack-Billerbeck, *Kommentar z. N.T.*, I, p. 353, and below, p. 400.

used in this connection they are not to be taken in the affective sense; the Hebrew word for 'to hate' often means to scorn, or to rank something lower than something else (cf. Deut.xxi. 15) while 'to love' may mean to choose something and rank it higher than something else.

Election itself is a manifestation of the majesty and holiness of God and implies the right to take decisions that transcend man. There are two things to be considered: election means first of all that some one who is to perform a task is called upon and designated; to be elected implies special responsibility; it does not merely mean to be loved. The idea of being loved may, indeed, be connected with it (as is clear from Deutero-Isaiah, but also as early as Deuteronomy), but the emphasis really rests on the call, the task.[1]

In the second place, rejection is somehow practically always placed in an ethical and religious light. The fact that Cain's sacrifice is not accepted is given a certain ethical aspect in Gen.iv. 7; we have already dealt with the stories concerning Esau and the Pharaoh of Egypt.

But the main point is that the Old Testament proclaims first and foremost God's absolute power to act according to His holy will.

Remarkable is the occasion when this principle of God's absolute power is stated: when Moses asks God to reveal Himself to him (Exod. xxxiii. 18) and when God does so, in so far as He can reveal Himself, He says: 'I will be gracious to whom I will be gracious and will shew mercy on whom I will shew mercy'. God's grace is infinitely abundant, but He Himself decides who shall be admitted to this grace. It is not to be wrung from Him. More than once we find in the prophets (Amos v. 15b; Joelii. 14; Zeph. ii. 3) the idea that God may forgive; for them, too, Yahweh remains the only one who can dispose of His favour. Yahweh may, therefore, decline a prayer of penitence (Amosvii. 7f., viii. 1f.; Hos.vi. 1ff.; Jer.xiv. 10ff.), or accept it (Amos vii. 1ff.; Joelii. 18ff.).

Here God reveals Himself as the Holy One, who in His majesty has the right to decide. It is realized quite clearly in the Old Testament that there is a great tension between God's love and His Holy Being. This tension is sometimes even transferred to God, for however clearly the Old Testament may proclaim Yahweh's omnipotence and accepts all its consequences, it never makes Him an arbitrary despotic Ruler but always regards Him as a God who sympathizes with man; this is depicted most profoundly in the hesitation of Yahweh, who takes counsel with Himself on what is to be done in Hosea (vi. 4; xi. 8), and in the fact that Yahweh repents of certain deeds. On the other

---

[1] H.H.Rowley, *The biblical doctrine of election,* 1950, *passim;* and my *Die Erwählung Israels, passim.*

hand this tension makes itself felt in human life and its problems, particularly the problem of suffering.

Most profoundly it is realized by Job who appeals to God his Redeemer, against God whose hand has struck him (Jobxix.21ff.). This problem of life will always remain for the faithful who live before the Holy One, with God who is Goodness. As long as the holiness and the love of God are the central conceptions in faith there must be insoluble spiritual conflicts in thought and life. Even Jesus Christ, when He suffered on the Cross, spike the words: 'Why hast Thou forsaken me?'

4. *Yahweh is the living God*

The Old Testament does not give us any sharply defined conception of God: it does not set out to teach either religious philosophy or dogmatics. It speaks of God as He has revealed Himself in history and in the life of believers. Though occasionally a figure is hinted at (p. 184 f.), the Old Testament will have none of a representation of God: God cannot be depicted, either in stone or wood, or in thoughts or ideas[1] – not only because He is the Holy One, who transcends all human beings, but also because He, the Living God, cannot be caught in a static conception. Not only is there originally a fundamental objection against images, but also against the fixed house of God, the Temple. He is as much the God of the heavens as the God of the earth, and reveals Himself in many places. He does not stand committed to one time or place.

God is a living God. The Old Testament speaks of His activity and His self-revelation, His works in nature and history, of His chastisement and His salvation, of His miracles and His mercy. But it bears witness to Him only in the language of faith.

This remarkable unsystematic speaking about God, this seeing of His revelation in the most different forms, the experience of His intervention in the most divergent situations, all these things indicate that the living Being of God is a fundamental idea in the Hebrew conception of God.

That God is alive rests essentially on the fact that God is a person, – He is not a force, nor a Power, but a personal Being (1 Sam.xvii.26, 36). This explains why in so many ways Yahweh is a living God; He is alive because He moves and is moved, in His life-giving power, in His love which grants communion (Pss.xlii.3; lxxxiv.3).[2]

---

[1] See also above p. 296. Maimonides was the first to give a summary of Israelite dogmatics in 13 articles; see H. Schrade's *Der verborgene Gott*, 1949, which should, however, be read critically.
[2] Cf. J. Hempel, *Gott und Mensch*², pp. 30ff.; H. Gollwitzer, *op. cit.*

This also explains why all phenomena of life could be ascribed to Yahweh, and why He, originally the God who intervened in history and in private life, could also become the God of the land, the God of fertility, adopting all the functions of Baal.

There is an element of truth in Buber's idea that Yahweh was originally the *melek*, the *guiding* God of the nomadic tribes, though the idea cannot comprise the full reality of the conception of God in Ancient Israel.[1] As such He is also the *fighting* God[2] who marches at the head of the hosts of the Israelites (Num. x. 35f.) and who inspires the heroes of the age of the Judges by the Spirit (Judges vi. 34; xiv. 6, 19; xv. 14; 1 Sam. xi. 6).

Man is seized by the *ruach Yahweh* and made a leader, *shofet*. In this experience of His *ruach* Yahweh proves very clearly to be a Living God. In Judges vi. 34 it is said that the Spirit of Yahweh 'puts on' somebody like a garment, i.e. pervades him; it is also said that the Spirit 'comes mightily upon' someone (*şalach*, Judges xiv. 6, 19, etc.).[3]

According to the ancient Hebrew idea (2 Sam. vii) Yahweh will not have a temple or be tied down to a particular place. He is guiding, leading His people by the Ark, His holy symbol; it is kept in a tent. There is a restless activity in Yahweh's work which keeps urging Him to new acts of revelation.

But this element of activity in itself does not constitute the full or central content of His Being, but only a way in which it reveals itself, a way rightly brought out by Buber and Söderblom.[4] But God is more. He is the very fulness of life. All life in this created world springs (see p. 339f.) all that lives and gives life; from Him comes the vital energy of men and animals.[5]

[1] *Op. cit.*; the opinion that this idea underlies the word *melek*, seems to me to be mistaken (see p.438).
[2] Cf. H. Fredriksson, *op. cit.*; Pedersen, *Israel*, III-IV, pp. 1ff.; G. von Rad, *Der heilige Krieg im alten Israel*, 1951.
[3] This is, therefore, a description of *inspiration*, or rather of *enthusiasm* (Procksch, *Theologie*, pp. 461–2), which is of a temporary nature; we must not speak here of mysticism, or of *unio mystica*, cf. also Köhler, *Theologie*[3], pp. 98ff. We never hear that Yahweh Himself descends upon man and dwells in him. In the O.T. it is always the Spirit, or the hand of Yahweh which is upon anyone. The Israelite religion always was on its guard against that mystical union between God and man which would wipe out the difference. This is also very clear from general usage in the Bible, for instance in the text, already mentioned above, of Isa. lvii. 15; 'I dwell in the high and holy place, with him also that is of a contrite and humble spirit'. There is no question, properly speaking, of any indwelling of God in man (cf. Ps. lxxiii. 23ff.), God lives in the sanctuary which is to be found in the midst of the people. The Old Testament usage does, therefore, clearly limit the communion between God and man, so that it never becomes indwelling or union. See for the word *ruach* A. R. Johnson, *The vitality*[2], 1961, pp. 31ff. and above pp. 211ff.
[4] *Op. cit.*
[5] W. W. Graf von Baudissin, *Adonis und Esmun*, 1911, pp. 450ff., and above pp. 215ff.

Wherever there is life, it is His gift. He, and He only, also gives the goods of nature (Hos. ii; Pss. xxxvi, lxvii, civ.) Hence life with Him means to Israel prosperity and abundance of natural goods (Deut.). The Old Testament belief in God is certainly not spiritual in an abstract sense; on the contrary, it sees God wherever there is abundance and salvation. We might call Yahweh Life, as in the New Testament God is called Love (cf. Pedersen: *Israel* I–IV, who proceeds from this conception rather one-sidedly).

In Israel the name of Yahweh is connected with the verb *hayah* – to be (Exod. iii). Hos. i. 9: 'I shall not be for you', may be read together with Exod. iii. 14. That God is, has not the abstract meaning of an immovable being that is the prime cause of moving[1], as in Greek philosophy, but rather that of being present. According to Alt this idea is even to be found in an Egyptian formula[2] where one of the Pharaohs uses a similar expression, with a menacing undertone: 'I also am'. In the Old Testament the being of God indicates that His Being is personally concerned with the world. That is why in the Old Testament God is praised over and over again and most emphatically as the Living God (Ps. xviii. 47; Hos. ii. 1)[3], to mention only the oldest texts; especially in the literature of the period of the later kings the expression 'the Living God' occurs repeatedly. Oaths are sworn by the living God: 'as truly as Yahweh (God) lives'. This emphasis on God's being alive is striking in Israel and the best explanation is perhaps a certain antithetic parallelism with the Canaanite belief in the gods of the vegetation-religion who die and then rise again from the dead.[4] It is Elijah, the great opponent of Baalism, who fights for Yahweh as the Living God who reveals His power in this world.

This living, personal character of Yahweh is apparent from the many *anthropomorphisms* and *anthropopathisms* of the Old Testament, never abandoned completely, not even when the development of theological thought started and these phenomena came more and more to be rejected. An author like J, though proclaiming that God is the God of the world, can represent Him as entering into direct contact with man. Yahweh comes to Abraham in the shape of a man and speaks to him; we also hear of a direct meeting between God and Moses.

[1] In the above we particularly have in mind Aristotelean philosophy, which had such a profound influence on Christian dogmatic thought. This qualification of the immovable does not apply to Plato's conception of God, cf. C. J. de Vogel, *Antike Seinsphilosophie und Christentum*, 1958. We might define more fully: the O.T. does not think of the being of God, it does, however, presuppose without further preface His existence (Gen. i. 1); but it lives by faith in God, who reveals Himself *in actu*.
[2] *Z.A.W.*, 1940–1941, pp. 159–60. See however, *Festschrift Bertholet*, 1949: '*Ehje'ašer 'ehje*; see further pp. 342ff.
[3] Translations 1. 10.
[4] W. W. Graf von Baudissin, *op. cit.*

More particularly, however, the narratives about prehistoric times tend to be very anthropomorphic, notwithstanding their profound spiritual and ethical character: Yahweh walks in Paradise, speaks to Cain, comes down to see what is happening in Babylon where the tower is being built. These are expressions, which lend support to the idea that God was, in fact, conceived in human shape by Israel, in spite of the fact that He cannot be depicted. Even in the exalted visions of Isa. vi, Ezek. iff., Dan. vii a certain shape is attributed to Yahweh. These traits must not be neglected in favour of the spiritual conception of God: the latter does exist but finds many times its representation in the anthropomorphical image. The fact that man was created in God's image also presupposes that to some extent God is thought of as being human in shape.[1]

Another category of anthropomorphisms is rather of a linguistic kind: they mention God's hand, face, nose, eyes, ears, feet, etc. They are not so clearly relevant from a theological point of view as the ones mentioned before. Not all of them are intended to attribute a human shape to God, they rather indicate an activity.[2] They are more symbolical than the former. The same applies to the category of the anthropopathisms, in which all kinds of human emotions, like repentance, anger, hatred, sorrow, are attributed to God. Yet these two 'literary' anthropomorphisms may be linked up with thinking about God. Even though these symbols denote motives and functions rather than concrete representations, the fact that the Old Testament speaks so widely of God in this sense must somehow be connected with experiencing God in images familiar to man. In part this may be due to the fact that ancient Eastern people expressed themselves more visually and less abstractly than modern Western man does, so that a unity of form and essence is experienced to a greater extent.[3] On the other hand it

---

[1] Cf. J. Hempel, *Gott und Mensch*[2], pp. 265ff.; and especially 'Gott, Mensch und Tier', *Z.f. syst. Theol.*, 1931, pp. 211ff., see above pp. 184f.

[2] J. Barr, *Theophany* etc., Suppl. VT, VII. p. 31, thinks that these are not to be linked with the previous ones. We may consider his views essentially correct.

[3] This should always be borne in mind in reading the O.T.; because the O.T. has a different psychological orientation, a non-abstract, concrete range of ideas, derived from the visual, the O.T. vision is also fundamentally different. From words such as *shpk* (both to pour out and to heap up), *haga* (to murmur and to think of), *chamad* (to attempt to seize and to desire), *yaṣa'* (to arise and to go out), *nafal* (to fall, to decay), *ruach* (draught, current of air, wind, spirit), *nefesh* ('movement of life', 'self', 'soul') etc., it is evident that especially the movement itself of things, action, and things in their functions are considered. For that reason things are not known as abstractions. That makes it so very difficult to approach the O.T. 'dogmatically'; Old Testament ideas are much more fluid in all directions than we realize at a superficial reading and with a western-theological range of ideas and complex of problems. Literature: J. Pedersen, *Israel*, I–II; Th. Boman, *Das hebräische Denken im Vergleich mit dem Griechischen*, 1952; my *Erwählung*, pp. 38ff.; M. E. Chase, *Life and language in the O.T.*, 1956 (popular). See also especially the criticism on Boman and Pedersen by J. Barr in *The Semantics of biblical Language*, 1961.

must also spring from the fact that God is indeed recognized and experienced in human representations. These naive and realistic ways of thinking and feeling were partly caused by the immediate relationship with God. A faith such as Israel's on the one hand forbids the depiction of God and denies the possibility of beholding God,[1] on the other hand it speaks of Him in terms that are strongly anthropomorphic. Apart from historico-religious backgrounds this could only be explained from the fact that the conception of God is very personal in character. Thus we may take it that both these categories of anthropomorphisms in the Old Testament bear witness to a recognition of the personal nature of Israel's God. After all, no one who speaks of God as the living God can escape using anthropomorphisms.[2] The very fact that we speak of God as 'He' (even if, like the Christian Scientists, we were to call Him Father-Mother!) proves that in our speaking of God we cannot get away from our human conceptions. In the Old Testament Ecclesiastes almost succeeds in this respect: for him God is God, and beyond that he can hardly say anything about God. On the other hand, there is hardly any trace of a personal relation between this God and Ecclesiastes: the two elements, the personal and the anthropomorphic, are always closely connected. But wherever there is immediate communion with God, all reserves imposed by reason are abandoned, consciously or unconsciously, and human feelings and a human shape are attributed to God without any hesitation.

The anthropomorphisms are evidence of the inadequacy of human speech about God, but they also bear witness to the living relation to Him.[3] It is not true that, on the ground of anthropomorphisms, certain parts of the Old Testament may be considered as standing on a particularly low level. There is no such strong contrast between the parts of the Old Testament as was often construed in the last century on the

[1] It also excludes from the image of God various representations (sexual elements, representations of the deity dying, animal representations). See J. Hempel, *Die Grenzen des Anthropomorphisms im A.T.*, ZAW 1939, pp. 75ff. and W. Baumgartner, *Ugaritische Probleme und ihre Tragweite für das A.T.*, ThZ 1949, esp. pp. 96ff.
[2] See, for instance, G. van der Leeuw, *Anthropomorphismus* in *Reallexikon für Antike und Christentum*, I, p. 449: 'The one-sided opposition to anthropomorphism is always a sign of rationalism and religious decadence'.
[3] M. A. Beek, 'De vraag naar de mens in de godsdienst van Israël', *Vox Theol.*, 1952, pp. 69ff., says: The faithful Israelite lives by the humanization of God, which also determines the whole of his anthropology' (p. 75), and with Michaeli (cf. also Vischer and Horst, see the literature quoted above, p. 162, n. 1) regards this anthropomorphism of the O.T. as the basis of the Christian doctrine of the Incarnation. Rather than regarding the antropomorphisms as the basis of the Incarnation I should prefer to emphasize the communion between God and man, of which anthropomorphism is a certain consequence. That the Incarnation in the Cristian sense of the word can be taught only on the basis of the Biblical religion is certain and is also corroborated by the history of religion.

ground of this notion. Certain authors, such as E, it is true, make God reveal Himself by means of angels and dreams rather than by personal apparitions. Yet these authors, in spite of their deeper theological reflection on the Being of God, are not more profound or more spiritual than the ancient J-author; there are rather texts where the reverse is true (see pp.57ff.).

It is especially in the prophetic revelation, in which Yahweh speaks directly to the prophet and even enters into a discussion with him[1] (Jer.xv. 15–21), that Yahweh proves to be the Living God, who enters into personal contact with man. God and man address and answer each other, and that directly, without any intervention of a priest who belongs to the oracle, as in the pagan world. This living contact is essential for the relation between God and man in the Old Testament: this encounter with man has existed from the beginning in Paradise (Gen.ii.f.); God enters into contact with the prophet, but also with the faithful who can address themselves to God in their prayers and who know that God answers (Pss.xx. 7 and xxii. 22; the final words of the latter verse, after the complaints are 'Thou hast heard me', followed by the thanksgiving; cf. Pss.vi. 10; xl. 18).

The fact that there are in the Old Testament several prophets who definitely did not belong to the priesthood (Amos, Micah, Zephaniah, and Haggai certainly) indicates that communion with Him is not inseparably linked to the cult; cf. the story of Num.xi. 24ff., which proves that even in later times (probably during or after the Exile) Israel remained conscious of the fact that the Spirit of God is not tied to the sanctuary but entirely free (cf. Jer.xxxi. 31ff., Exek.xxxvi. 25ff. and Joel ii. 28ff.).

The living nature of God in the Old Testament is shown not only by His direct revelation to man, but also, and principally, by His works in history and nature; indeed, these two things go hand in hand again and again. In His actions Yahweh wrote His name clearly legible for Israel, the name which the prophet learned to interpret.

This idea dominates the historical books as well as the prophecies. The conception of the personal guidance of God in the Old Testament is an integral part of the revelation of God in the Old Testament, however much this may be doubted in Israel (Judges vi. 13) and however loudly the thought that God does not hear or see may be expressed among the people (Isa.xxix. 15; Ps.x.4, 11). This sceptical outlook is opposed most strongly by the prophets. God intervenes not only in history but also in the life of nature; the natural phenomena (thunder, Ps.xxix. the natural process of growth, Hos.ii) are the work of God. He grants the rain (Deut.xxviii. 12), all things come from Him; He

[1] See M.A.Beek, *Het twistgesprek van de mens met zijn God*, 1946. See, however, p. 160.

can, therefore, withhold fertility, rain, and dew (Amos, Hosea, Deuteronomy, Haggai, Joel). He has at His command the wind and the waters of the sea (Exod. xivf.; Ps. cvii), the stars in their courses (Judges v), and the sun and the moon (Josh. x. 12ff.; Isa. xxxviii. 7ff.). He is the God who performs miracles, who creates new things that have never been before (Isa. xlii. 8ff.). No thing is too hard for Him (Jer. xxxii. 27). What Yahweh says is done; this is emphasized so strongly that the prophets use the *perfect tense* for their divine message, as if the future things spoken of by Yahweh had already become facts of the present; to the prophets they are already coming to pass, indeed. There is no essential difference between the future and the present in the word of God, any more than in the New Testament where the Kingdom of God is represented as still to come and already present, all at the same time. These two ideas may seem distinct to us; to the faithful Israelite they are one. The background to all this is to be found in the certainty of the living Being of God, who performs what He has spoken.

5. *Yahweh is One God and a Unique God*

Unity and uniqueness are not the same. The Old Testament teaches both: God as *one* Being and God as a *unique* Being.

That God is one is emphasized in the book of Deuteronomy. In the famous words of Deut. vi. 4–7, which became part of the Jewish *Shemaʿ*-prayer, the unity of God is stressed.[1] It is difficult to give an exact translation of this text, but in all probability it should be: 'Hear, Israel, Yahweh, our God, Yahweh is one (a unity)'.[2] And because Yahweh is one in Being (we might also say 'single') the demand follows that Yahweh must be loved with all one's heart, with all one's soul, and with all one's might (literally 'multiplicity'). The oneness of God's Being demands the heart, the entire being of the faithful. This word is one of the most profound of the Old Testament; no wonder that it became the introduction to the Jewish evening-prayer, and that Christ derived from these verses what He called the first and greatest Commandment. In 2 Kings xxiii. 25 it is said of Josiah that he served God in that perfect manner that is demanded in Deut. vi. 5. This is asserted after we have been told that he had put away all idolatry. And in Deut. vi. 14, too, the demand is associated with renouncing

---

[1] Joh. de Groot and A. R. Hulst, *Macht en Wil*, pp. 41ff. 299ff.; see above p. 294.

[2] The same grammatical construction is to be found at the end of Exod. xxxvi. 13: 'so that the tabernacle became one (a unity)'. Cf. also the Ugarit-text II AB VII 49, where Baal says: *'aḥdy dymlk 'l 'lm*, i.e. only I (I am the only one who) bear sway over the gods (see G. R. Driver, *Canaanite Myths*, pp. 100ff.; Aistleitner, *Texte aus R. Schamra*, 1959, p. 45).

other gods. The Unity and the Uniqueness of God are, therefore, quite clearly related.[1] The Unity indicates that God is not divided. His uniqueness means that Yahweh alone is God. The Israelite religion arrived at this doctrine because for a long time Yahweh was worshipped in various places and in somewhat different ways and because Yahweh was apparently called the God of various cultic places – as was the case with Baal–, e.g. Yahweh as the God of Hebron, of Jerusalem,[2] etc. To this the Deuteronomist opposes the affirmation that God is One. And this is the point of view from which the Deuteronomist demand of ch. xii must be understood, that God must be served in one cultic centre only, which He chooses for Himself, viz. Jerusalem. All possibilities of differences within Yahwism and dissension in religious life are to be avoided; it is not only necessary to abandon the worship of the pagan gods, but also the worship of Yahweh in various places with distinct cultic forms of their own and apparently distinct conceptions of God. There is only one way to speak of God and to serve Him. There is no pluriformity of faith, confession, or cult. Deuteronomy is the introduction to an orthodoxy that rejects both syncretism and divergent ways of thinking. In the struggle against Baalism things had come to such a pass that, in order to maintain the unity of the faith, all the ancient holy places were rejected, even if it was Yahweh who was worshipped there. Here the last, extreme consequences are drawn from the belief in the unity of God. Deuteronomy does not intend to teach monotheism[3] but presupposes it and only draws the extreme consequences of monotheism: the Being of God is absolutely One and has only one actual place of revelation. Here all possibilities of differentiation as to the knowledge of God and the cult are done away with. This is the birth of Hebrew orthodoxy, and for that reason the words of Deut. vi became the startingpoint for Hebrew dogmatics. Owing to this strict monotheism the Jews in the days of Jesus could not help being offended by Christ who knew that He was one with the Father. And on this ground the Jews could not but consider the Christian doctrine concerning God as tritheism and as the rejection of true monotheism.

That the Deuteronomist arrived at his thesis has for its profound spiritual background the struggle against paganism and the fact that fundamentally different conceptions of Yahweh were springing up

---

[1] In Deut. vi. 4 both *unitas* and *unicitas* are to be found, cf. S. R. Driver in *Deuteronomy* (I.C.C.) and E. König, *Das Deuteronomium*, 1917, loc. cit. We should not sacrifice unity to uniqueness, as is done by P. A. van Stempvoort, *Eenheid en schisma in de gemeente van Korinthe*, 1950 (doctorate thesis Amsterdam), pp. 8ff.

[2] Cf. the text found at Lachish, see my *Jahwe en zijn stad*, pp. 4f.

[3] See, for instance, Eerdmans, *Godsdienst van Israël*, I, pp. 147, 151ff.; *The religion of Israel*, p. 96.

within Israel.[1] This latter possibility also had to be rejected definitely. The great spiritual gain yielded by this 'orthodox' attitude in Israel is that, in the moral field too, it meant the end of all temporizing because the heart is claimed entirely for the worship of the one Yahweh. Life in its entirety is focused on God.

We cannot but admit that here the prophetic ideas have been expressed most succinctly; indeed, the entire introductory sermon of Deuteronomy rests on prophetic ideas; cf. e.g. Deut.x. 12ff.; and cf. verse 12 with Mic.vi.8; and Deut.x.16 with Jer.iv.4. Words like these are in complete agreement with the ideas of Jeremiah, and if the people will repent in this manner, Jeremiah is also willing to accept the Deuteronomist reformation (certainly alluded to in Jer.iii. 21–iv.4 and in Jer.xi).[2]

As regards this side of the conception of God (viz. monotheism) the Deuteronomist verdict represents the end of the development of the religion of Israel. A verdict clearer and more rigid than this brief statement is not to be expected from the ancient oriental world with its general tendency towards syncretism. This doctrine means greater rigidity as well as greater depth, as it binds Yahweh to one place; this results in stronger nationalism and stricter cultic rules; these end in the pretension God can only be truly worshipped in Jerusalem (Johniv.20).

This unity of God is rooted in the *Uniqueness* of the Being of God, in the recognition that Yahweh alone is the true God. For this acknowledgement Elijah fought, as we are told in 1 Kingsxviii.[3] This does not mean that Elijah was the first to conceive this idea but rather that it attained full maturity with him; he draws the conclusions from the exclusivism which was connected with Yahwism from the beginning; moreover, he carries through this confession among the people and demands its acknowledgment in the presence of Ahab; the death of the priests of Baal is its confirmation. This leads to a conflict between Jezebel and the prophet, a conflict that continues and afterwards meets with a response in the army, resulting in the bloody revolution of Jehu and the terrible downfall of the house of Omri. That religious motives play a part in all this appears from the activity

---

[1] A comparable phenomenon in the Christian Churches is the christological struggle fundamentally also a struggle to maintain the unity of faith in Christ.
[2] See now H.H.Rowley, 'The prophet Jeremiah and the Book of Deuteronomy', in *Studies in O.T. Prophecy*, pp. 157ff.
[3] L.H.K.Bleeker, 'De betekenis van den Profeet Elia voor de geschiedenis van Israëls godsdienst' (*Theol. Studiën*, 1910, pp.415ff); H.Gunkel, *Elias, Jahwe und Baal*, 1906; J.J.P.Valeton, 'De strijd tussen Achab en Elia'², in *O.T. Voordrachten*, 1909; A.Alt, 'Das Gottesurteil auf dem Karmel', *Festschr. G. Beer*, pp. 1ff.; K.Galling, 'Der Gott Karmel und die Ächtung der fremden Götter', *Festschr. Alt*, 1953; O.Eissfeldt, *Der Gott Karmel*, 1953; G.Fohrer, *Elia*, 1957.

of a prophet (2 Kings ix. 1ff.) and of the Rechabite (a very strict nationalistic Yahwistic sect) Jehonadab ben Rechab (2 Kings x. 15ff.).

The origin of this conflict is bound up with the awakening of the
consciousness that in the days of Ahab and his successors the essence of
Israel's religion was at stake. This religious revolution caused mono-
Yahwism to be acknowledged in Israel as the state-religion, neither
more nor less.

The recognition that Jahwe is unique did not originally include the
doctrine that there were no other gods.[1] There are several indications
that during a long period the uniqueness of Yahweh had not yet been
thought out theoretically. There are various data to justify the conclusion that to a certain extent gods of pagan peoples were recognized
(cf. e.g. Judges xi. 23f.)[2] It was only during the long struggle against the
paganism into which the people relapsed again and again, that these
very last remnants of polytheism were swept away. A student of the
history of religion who comes to understand how hard ancient religious ideas and observances are to kill will have to admit that the
existence of a monotheistic Yahwism on the one hand, together with
the existence of pagan remnants on the other, is perfectly possible.[3]
In this respect Christianity and the religion of Israel do not differ
very much. Ever so often we find that the Old Testament Laws warn
against witchcraft (already in the Book of the Covenant we read that
witches must be killed: Exod. xxii. 18), against spiritism, etc. Yahwism has disposed of magic and belief in the spirits of the dead, but yet
these things survived for centuries and among the post-Biblical Jews
continued to flourish. The parasite plant of superstition continued to
thrive, however often it might be cut off at the root.

That the prophets should be the creators of monotheism, a view
which is still maintained quite wrongly, is impossible. The writings of
the prophets nowhere justify the conclusion that these men looked
upon themselves as introducing a new doctrine. On the contrary, they
always referred to things already known to the people; they only demanded that the people should adhere to Yahweh, whose will was
already known to them.[4] It is certain that the earliest of them, Amos
(ii. 1ff.; ix. 7) already presupposes monotheism, though the first place
where we find it expressed clearly, is Jer. ii. 5, 11. Neither Amos nor
Jeremiah, however, introduce this conception as something new. We
may go even further: the story of David, and even the Song of Deborah, are incomprehensible without the recognition of the belief in

---

[1] See pp. 32ff.   [2] Cf. pp. 32f, 302 and 338.
[3] H. Th. Obbink, *Survivals*, 1929.
[4] This is rightly emphasized by Joh. Pedersen, *Israel*, III–IV; it remains, therefore,
to be seen if the word 'reactionary' describes them adequately.

one God whose word is decisive in Israel and in the world. When, for instance, the stars are represented as fighting against Sisera this cannot mean anything but that the heavenly host is subjected to the will of Yahweh and therefore fights against Israel's enemy.

There is, therefore, nothing to stand in the way of a recognition of a monotheistic Yahwism given by Moses, though not pursued by him to its ultimate consequences. It is true that in the first of the Ten Commandments the existence of other gods is not exactly denied but it is practically done away with in the words: 'Thou shalt have no other gods except Me'. Yahweh here detaches Israel from all forms of polytheism. The fact that Yahweh never had a female counterpart is of great fundamental value. The Hebrew language does not even have a native word for goddess! To the Israelite mind this idea must, therefore, have been an intrinsic contradiction. The uniqueness of Yahweh may be considered as the central dogma of Mosaism. Only this doctrine is in harmony with the holiness, majesty, and jealousy attributed to Yahweh.

It is, therefore, as unacceptable to explain the plural form of Gen. i. 26 as evidence of polytheism as to explain it from the dogma of the Trinity. As to the latter idea, we need not add anything to what has been said above about Deut. vi. 4. Is is necessary, however, to devote a few words to the possibility of a polytheistic survival in Gen. i. 26. The whole atmosphere of Gen. i, where God is recognized as existing before all other things and where all present existence is traced back to His Word only, is so anti-polytheistic that the very idea of polytheism is out of the question. Yet God says in i. 26: 'Let us make man in our image'. The plural form is used here; the same phenomenon is found in Gen. iii. 22, and also in Isa. vi. 8, where *I* and *us* are used alternately. This last text should put us on our guard against rashly concluding to polytheism on the ground of a grammatical plural form. In Isa. vi it becomes clear that Yahweh cannot only say *I* but also *We*, because He is surrounded by angels whom He includes in His speaking.[1] The conception of a host of angels or heavenly beings surrounding Yahweh is always present in Israel; cf. 1 Kings xxii; Job if. People could not conceive Yahweh in another fashion. This explains why in the Psalms the *bene'elim* (xxix. 1 :sons of god, divine

---

[1] A 'corporate personality' (H. Wheeler Robinson, The Hebrew conception of Corporate Personality, in *Werden und Wesen des A. T., Beith. Z.A.W.* 66, 1936, pp. 49ff). can always speak of himself in the plural as well as in the singular; the two forms may even occur within one sentence; cf. the Hebrew text of 2 Sam. xxi. 4; see also A. R. Johnson, *The one and the many in the conception of God*, 1942. Moreover the possibility of a 'plural of deliberation' must always be kept in mind as well as the possibility of a *plural of majesty*. Cf. K. Budde, *Jesaja's Erleben*, 1928, loc. cit., and Gesenius-Kautzsch, *Hebr. Gr.*[28], pp. 416/7, N. 3.

beings; the R.V. wrongly reads 'sons of the mighty') are called upon to praise Him; why in Ps. viii. 6 it can be said that man was made a little lower than the *'elohim*, divine beings; why in Ps. lxxxii. 1 we hear of God who stands in the congregation of the mighty and judges among the *'elohim*, divine beings[1] (cf. Ps. lxxxix. 8: the assembly of the saints: holy beings), and how we also find in Ps. lxxxix. 7 the *bene'elim*, the divine beings who cannot be likened unto the Lord (cf. Gen. vi. 1f.). The conception of God includes, therefore, the idea of a heavenly host, of a mighty army of divine beings surrounding Him. Even if they are not even mentioned in Gen. i and iii, yet they are there in the author's mind, and speaking of God he can suddenly pass from the singular to the plural, thus giving us the idea that God addresses His holy attendants. This idea of beings surrounding God by no means detracts from the uniqueness of God; on the contrary, these divine beings rather emphasize His uniqueness; He is the God of gods, their God, too; and they praise His Holiness (Isa. vi). *Far from clashing with monotheism this conception lays the greatest stress on the Majesty of Yahweh.*[2] Yahweh is a unique God, but He is not alone. The question of the *'elohim* surrounding Yahweh is to be considered apart from that of the recognition or otherwise of the pagan gods. Considered from the point of view of the history of religion these two questions have a common background but it was recognized as little in Israel as we nowadays are conscious of the polydemonic background of our mourning customs.

The uniqueness of God is proclaimed most impressively by Deutero-Isaiah (xl. 12ff.; xliii; xliv, etc.): 'I am the first and I am the last; and beside Me there is no God' (xliv. 6); 'I am the Lord, and there is none else' (xlv. 5f., 14, 18, 21), but this does not mean that we are justified in regarding him as the first true monotheist.[3]

6. *Yahweh is an Eternal God*

The eternity of God[4] is presumed in the Old Testament, though not pronounced very often *expressis verbis*. That in Gen. i and ii. 4b ff., both dealing with the creation of this world by God, there is a God, before and above the world, is quite clear.

In the Old Testament here is no allusion to any genealogy of God or to a theogony, a birth of God, elements that exist in practically every

---

[1] Like Ps. 29 this Psalm clearly shows an original polytheistic *background*, cf. J. Morgenstern, '*The Mythological Background of Ps. 82*' (*H.U.C.A.* 1939, pp. 29ff.); see also the various commentaries. Generally speaking the origin of these representations cannot be reduced to the same denominator. See now P. A. H. de Boer, *De Zoon van God in het O.T.*, 1958, and G. Cooke, *The sons of the Gods*, ZAW 1964, pp. 22ff.
[2] See, for example, also V. Maag, *Jahwäs Heerscharen*, cf. above p. 298, n. 3.
[3] S. A. Cook, *The O.T.*, *A Reinterpretation*, 1936, pp. 142ff.
[4] See E. Jenni, *Das Wort 'olam im A.T.*, doctorate thesis Basel, 1953, pp. 53ff. (also *Z.A.W.*, 1952 and 1953); O. Eissfeldt, 'Ewigkeit im A.T.', *Th.St.u.Kr.*, 1947, pp. 25ff.

non-biblical religion. Their absence is, therefore, significant; it proves unmistakably that there is no place in Yahwism for any such ideas. The world has a beginning, God has none. There is no time when He did not exist. The idea that God could have been born seems absurd to Israel; the Old Testament does not even argue against it. It must have been thought no better than a pagan myth about which one had better keep silent. This silence is one of the strongest arguments in support of the entirely different nature of Israel's conception of God.

It is true that the two accounts of the Creation, Gen. i and ii. 4bff., both presume the existence of a chaos before the Creation. (Gen. i. 2, which is to be taken as an independent parenthetic clause,[1] reminds us of Babylonian as well as of Phoenician data; Gen. ii represents the chaos as an arid desert without rain, rather in the Palestinian-Israelite fashion.) This chaos is, however, not antithetic to God, as in the ancient oriental mythologies; the representation has lost[2] its mythological character entirely and is no more than a *survival*, not yet abandoned because at that time complete nothingness could not yet be conceived.[3]

A few places in the Old Testament still give us a glimpse of a struggle between Yahweh and the chaos-monster, or even express such an idea (cf. Pss. lxxiv. 13ff.; lxxxix. 11; Isa. xxvii. 1; li. 9), but these passages are clearly symbolic in meaning. Already in Amos ix. 3 we read that Yahweh can command the serpent in the depths of the sea (this may be the serpent of ancient creation-mythology which was banished there); it is, therefore, completely subjected to Yahweh (cf. also Ps. civ. 26). Essentially the chaotic condition in Gen. i. 2 and ii. 4bff. preceding God's creative activity has no meaning but that of a survival, even if the chaos is the mass that is at the disposal of God in which He creates order according to His will.[4] This is not only a fundamental

[1] See i.a. P. Humbert, *Trois notes sur Gen. I*, Mowinckel Festschrift, 1955, pp. 85ff., and his discussion with W. Eichrodt in ZAW 1964, pp. 121ff.; cf. Eichrodt, *In the beginning*, Muilenburg Festschrift, pp. 1ff.
[2] On the relationship between the O.T. and the mythological thought of the ancient oriental world see the fundamental article by J. Barr, *The meaning of 'mythology' in relation to the O.T.*, VT 1959, pp. 1ff.; B. S. Childs, *op. cit.*; J. Hempel, *Glaube, Mythos und Geschichte*, ZAW 1953, pp. 109ff. and B. J. v.d. Merwe, *Pentateuchtradities*, pp. 205ff.
[3] The chaos, *tohu wabohu*, became, in fact, *a nothing* because it had lost its living mythological background; cf. Isa. xl. 23, where the word *tohu* runs parallel with *'ain = not to be!* After the process of de-mythologization the chaos did not become eternal primeval matter, as in Greek philosphy, but it shrank into nothingness when confronted with the conception of God. See now Ph. Reymond, 'L'eau, sa vie, et sa signification dans l'A.T.', *Supp. V.T.* VI, 1958, p. 172.
[4] The fact that God creates by separating (in the first days of creation of Gen. i) strengthens the view of i. 2 that the material substrate of the world was present at the Creation. On the other hand it is quite evident from i. 3 that the author means to say that God called forth all things by the Word. Gen. i shows how difficult it was for the Israelite to find an adequate expression for his conception which was peculiar to him.

victory over the ancient conception of chaos but also means that God is supposed to be eternal.

The eternity of God is emphasized in the later literature of the exile[1] and after.[2] In the magnificent words of Ps. xc. 2 the post-exilic poet (cf. verse 15) gives expression to the eternal glory of God: 'Before the mountains were brought forth or ever thou hadst formed the earth and the world, even from everlasting to everlasting, thou art God'. Deutero-Isaiah very clearly lays a connection between God's eternal existence and His creative power (Isa. xl. 12ff., 28). In Israel's conception of the Creation the idea of God's eternal existence was already implicit; in Job xxxviii ff. and Prov. viii. 22ff. God's eternal existence is certainly presupposed. The idea is quite clearly present and is expressed more and more emphatically (Jer. x. 10; Isa. xxvi. 4, xxxiii. 14; Deut. xxxiii. 27; Dan. xii. 7).

God's eternal existence is particularly stressed in the Old Testament by the comparison with the Canaanite-Phoenician conception of the Being of God.[3] Ras Shamra has furnished evidence that Baalism was a typical vegetation cult, deriving its conception of God from the natural force which comes most to the fore in agriculture, viz. that of life springing up and decaying. The god of life Baal was conceived and depicted in the cult as a god who dies and rises again from the dead. The God of Israel, on the other hand, is not renewed in the cult, as Pedersen has shown[4]; He is the Living God, who exists and who is also present among His people under all circumstances; He transcends life and death. In this connection we shall also deal briefly with a related question, the problem of the feast of Yahweh's enthronement. Mowinckel's opinion[5] that in Israel, as in Babylon, a feast of Yahweh's enthronement was celebrated on New Year's Day, as if He renewed His Kingship of His people every year, must rest on a misinterpretation. This conception can only be understood against the background of a vegetative or astral-mythological range of ideas.[6] The fact that not a single cultic text in the Old Testament refers to

---

[1] In the earliest literature Gen. xxi. 33 is especially notable. Procksch (*Theologie*, p. 50) takes it, that Gen. xxi. 33 demonstrates that Abraham confessed Yahweh as the 'God of eternity' and that this was the beginning of his new religious creation. A more cautious view is that of Jenni (*op. cit.*, pp. 53ff.), who finds in this text the testimony to God as an unchangeable power, and to God's constant activity.

[2] Cf. also Pss. ix. 8; x. 16; xxix. 10; xxxiii. 11; xcii. 9; xciii. 2; cii. 13a; cxlv. 13; cxlvi. 10a. Some of these texts are certainly pre-exilic.

[3] It is true that El, too, is called eternal in the Ras-Shamra texts, cf. J. H. Patton, *Canaanite Parallels in the Book of Psalms*, Baltimore, 1944, p. 16.

[4] *Acta Orientalia*, vol. 18, pp. 1ff.

[5] *Psalmenstudien*, II, 1922. Mowinckel interprets *Yahweh malakh* in the Psalms as: Yahweh has become king; see however L. Köhler in VT III, 1953, and now A. S. Kapelrud, VT XIII, 1963, pp. 229ff.

[6] On the Marduk-religion see B. Meissner, *Babylonien und Assyrien*, II, 1925, p. 98.

such a feast is fatal to Mowinckel's theory; if this feast had really been of central importance in the religion of Israel, as he supposes, one would expect it to be mentioned more clearly in the Old Testament. The so-called feast of the ascension of Yahweh to the throne is an unfounded modern hypothetical construction which is confusing rather than clarifying.[1] Yahweh's life is not renewed, neither is His Kingship. The eternal element in Yahweh's Being is presupposed in the Old Testament and so is the eternity of His rule.[2]

The Jews are accustomed to paraphrase the name of God 'Yahweh'. which is not pronounced, by the title 'the Eternal One'. The Septuagint paraphrased it as: Kyrios, the Lord (English versions, LORD).[3] As we said before, it is extremely improbable that the name Yahweh should be taken to mean originally *He Who Is*, because *being* in the Old Testament must not be taken in a philosophical and ontological sense. Therefore the later Jewish rendering according to the substance is unacceptable. It is founded on the interpretation of Exod. iii. 14; 'I am that I am', which was strongly influenced by Hellenistic thought. Cf. also pp. 179, 319, and 342ff.

7. *God as the Creator, Saviour, and Maintainer*

That Israel should have honoured its God as the Creator, as the other ancient oriental peoples did, is to be expected *a priori*. Yet belief in the Creation is not of such paramount importance in the religion of Israel as might be expected from a superficial reading of Gen. i. In the historical books the work of Creation seldom comes to the fore,[4] and the same applies to the prophetic books. It is only in Jeremiah, and particularly in the prophecies of Deutero-Isaiah, that God is pro-

---

[1] See especially O. Eissfeldt, 'Jahwe als König', *Z.A.W.*, 1928, p. 81; Mowinckel's views have also been combated by N. H. Snaith, *The Jewish New Year Festival*, 1947, but here, besides many excellent remarks, various doubtful hypotheses are expressed; cf. H. J. Kraus, *Die Königherrschaft Gottes im A.T.*, 1951; A. R. Johnson, *Sacral Kingship in Ancient Israel*, 1955; also L. Köhler, *V.T.*, III, 1953 (Syntactica).

[2] The Old Testament scholar from Copenhagen A. Bentzen, whose premature death was a great loss to Old Testament scholarship, did not agree with this passage (*Studia Theologica*, III, 1951, p. 154). In his opinion it may be supposed that Israel adopted all kinds of Canaanite cultic forms in Canaan, and that the New Year Festival was one of these, as reminiscences of this festival can be found in the Psalms. In reply to this criticism we must say that in our opinion the latter has not been proved and that the former must, of course, be considered correct, generally speaking, but that in this case the form in which the Scandinavian scholars express their view is most improbable. With respect especially to such an important and primitive nature-festival very strong opposition might be expected among Israel, and at any rate at least a fundamental modification. In my opinion it may be presumed that there was a New Year festival in ancient Israel, and that this festival may have celebrated Yahweh's kingship, but not His *ascension to the throne*.

[3] See further p. 344.

[4] Gen. xiv. 19, 22, cf. P. Humbert in Festschrift Bertholet, pp. 259ff.

claimed as the Creator.[1] This is so striking that it gave rise to the supposition that the belief in the Creation arose in Israel only under the
influence of Assyro-Babylonian culture. This conclusion must, however, be rejected as it rests too one-sidedly on the *argumentum e silentio:*
because belief in the Creation is not demonstrable in the available literature before the 8th or 7th centuries it is said not to have existed at
all before that period. The belief in God as the Creator is not only
apparent from the historical and prophetic books, but also from the
Psalms, cf. Pss. viii; xix; xxiv; xxxiii; civ. These cannot be dated with
certainty, so that they cannot be adduced as decisive evidence for the
age of belief in the Creation.[2] Nevertheless we may suppose that Israel
worshipped its God as the Creator at quite an early date: first of all
on the general ground that all religions consider their principal god to
be the Creator and that therefore belief in the Creation must be admitted to have existed as an integral element in the conception of
God in Israel; secondly because, when Israel's belief in the Creation
does appear, it immediately shows a character of its own by completely
ignoring the idea of a theogony or any form of dualism (see pp. 327,
328f.); and lastly because the account of the Creation in Gen. i,
which may date from the days of the later kings, certainly must have
been preceded by older accounts.[3] But the fact remains that in the
Old Testament belief in the Creation is only stressed at a later period
and only developed into a more prominent element during the
period of the later kings. It is not unlikely that this happened on
account of the conflict with the Assyro-Babylonian philosophy of
life of the eight and seventh centuries. The confrontation with the religion of this world-power made Israelite Yahwism more conscious of
this point, just as in the Christian Church the dogmas were formulated
after the confrontation with Gnosticism and Neo-Platonism. Belief in
the Creation is in the Old Testament an idea which lay dormant for
a long time and was only brought out at a fairly late date. This may
be explained by the fact that the belief in God the Creator is as much
a matter of philosophy of life as of the personal religious relation with
God, for the latter is in Israel wholly dominated by the message of
salvation by God in history (the Exodus). Israel's God is a God of
salvation, a Saviour (see p.335). This may be the reason why the
idea of Creation – as soon as it comes to the fore – is used not only

[1] See Dr. H. Brongers, *op. cit.*, and above, pp. 162 and 337.
[2] Pss. xxiv and civ may certainly be pre-exilic.
[3] As is evident from the structure of the chapter itself and also from Gen. ii. Compare
especially the parallel stories collected by Gunkel in his commentary on Genesis
(4th ed. 1917, pp. 120ff.); cf. also F.M.Th. de Liagre Böhl, *Opera Minora*, 1953,
p.2–3, and G.Lambert, 'La création dans la Bible', *Nouvelle Revue Theol.*, 1953,
pp. 252ff.

with respect to the creation that took place once in prehistoric times, but also with respect to history, and even to the present, as becomes abundantly clear in Deutero-Isaiah.[1] The idea of creating, applied only to God, implies the idea of the miracle, of something new.[2]

The belief in God as the Creator emerges when people begin to think more consciously about this world and its origin, and when belief in God is connected with the question of the origin of things.

In Israel a *philosophy of life* was developed only rather late under the influence of the wisdom-literature, at any rate the evidence for a separate religious philosophy of life is of a fairly late date. The Israelite world-*picture* is clearly similar in character to that of the ancient oriental peoples; the earth is a plane, surrounded by the ocean,[3] resting on the waters below, covered by the dome-like starry sky. Above this dome the ocean of heaven is supposed to lie, and above that the heaven of heavens, where the world-god lives. From the point of view of 'natural philosophy', the Old Testament offers little that can be called new, little that the other nations did not have already.[4] It would, therefore, be absurd to attempt to maintain this world-picture as an element of revelation in the Old Testament: it is wholly derived from the ancient oriental world-picture and it has no independent value as a revelation of God. It is no use trying to protect this 'Biblical' world-picture against modern scientific conceptions. Yet, unfortunately, such attempts are still made only too often, even in these days, to say nothing of former times (Galilei).

The important new element introduced by Israel is that it came to see this world as given by the one holy and loving God; it applied its conception of God, its belief in the God of salvation and grace, to the ancient oriental conception of the world and in this way it arrived at a novel description of the Creation of this world. How extremely difficult this task must have been appears from the fact (already alluded to, see pp. 329f.) that Israel had so much difficulty in finding a solution for the mystery of the chaos, which was represented either as the primeval ocean (Gen. i; Ps. xxiv. 2; Ps. civ. 6f.) or as a desert (Gen.

[1] See Procksch, *Theologie*, p. 274; Rendtorff 'Die theologische Stellung des Schöpfungsglaubens bei Dt.-Jesaja, *Z.f. Theol. u. Kirche*, LIV, pp. 3ff.
[2] Procksch, *op. cit.*, p. 455–6. See further Böhl, 'Bara', in *Alttest. Studien*, Kittel-Festschrift, *Beitr. Wiss. A.T.*, 1913, pp. 42ff.; P. Humbert, 'Emploi et portée du verbe bârâ', *Theol. Zeitschr.*, Basel, 1947, pp. 401ff.
[3] Cf. O. Eissfeldt, 'Gott und das Meer in der Bibel', *Studia Orientalia-J. Pedersen*, 1953, pp. 76ff. demonstrates that the ocean can be strongly ambivalent in the Old Testament; that it can be both God's creature and God's enemy. See also A.J. Wensinck, *The ocean in the literature of the Western Semites*.
[4] G. von Rad, *Aspekte alttest. Weltverständnisses*, Ev. Th. 1964, pp. 57ff., wrongly opposes this distinction between *worldpicture* and *philosophy of life*. On p. 58 the terms *Weltbild* and *Weltverständnis* are in fact used synonymously.

ii. 4bff.). Proclaiming the One, Holy and Merciful God as the Creator of the world became, however, of the utmost importance to the Israelite and Christian conceptions of the world; this made it possible to see nature as an entity, to know the world as the perfect work of God, to recognize a close relationship between God and the world, to proclaim the unity of mankind, of husband and wife, and even of God and man who is made in God's image. Considered in this light the world can never be a power hostile to man, the natural gifts and powers in this world can never be condemned in themselves. There can be no sin in the nature of things as such, but only in the will of man. This cuts off every tragic outlook upon life, every tragic way of thought, at the root. This dogma also opens up the possibility of viewing suffering in this world from the aspect of guilt (Gen. iif.), thus overcoming fundamentally all dualism and demonism. This linking together of Israel's faith in the God of Salvation and the Creation of the world gives to the Old Testament philosophy of life a clarity, tranquillity, warmth, and grandeur not to be found outside the Bible. After all, the sublimity of the prophecies of Deutero-Isaiah rests first and foremost on this view. And Christian belief in God will always continue to rest on it in its own philosophy of life.[1]

When compared with Gen. ii or Ps. civ, the account of the Creation in Gen. i shows to how great an extent it rests on reflection, theological and cosmological.[2] Theological: the idea of the Sabbath dominates the conception of the Creation; moreover, behind the Creation of the celestial bodies on the fourth day lies also a protest against the ancient oriental astral religion. Cosmological: the world is built up in 2×3 days, in correspondence with each other (the eight acts of creation may be a reminiscence of an originally different arrangement consisting of 2×4 creative acts); the number 3 is clearly predominant: this is evident from the number of days: 2×3; also from the 3 kinds of plants, 3 kinds of animals on the fifth day (vs. 21), 3 kinds of animals on the earth (24); 3 kinds of celestial bodies (sun, moon, and stars). A clear distinction is made between the acts of the first period of three days and those of the seond; the first series rests on cosmological speculations, according to which creation is the introducing of order and the separating of light and darkness, the upper and the lower

---

[1] See G. von Rad, 'Das theologische Problem des altt. Schöpfungsglaubens' (*Werden und Wesen des A.T., Beih. Z.A.W.*, 66, 1936), pp. 138ff., who speaks of 'this soteriological understanding of the work of creation'; L. Köhler in his *Theologie*[3], pp. 69ff., goes still further, but perhaps even too far, by speaking not only of a 'declaration of the meaning of human history', but even of an 'eschatological conception'.
[2] In his above-mentioned article in *Th. Zeitschr.* (and earlier also in *Revue d'hist. et de Phil. relig.*, 1935) Humbert emphasized the liturgical and cultic character of Gen. i; this view was opposed by H. Ringgren in *Svensk exegetisk Arsbok*, XIII, 1948.

world, sea and land; the second (including the creation of the plants) shows how the views on vegetative, animal, and human life developed. That man is looked upon as a very special creature appears from the doctrine of the image of God as well as from the dominating position granted to man. In vegetative and animal life, too, order is clearly observable. There is a tendency towards a rational structure of the world; there is something of a conception of creation of ever higher planes of life, though we cannot speak of evolution in the account of the Creation, not only because the origin of all these things is described as being due to the activity of God alone, but also because the parallelism between the two triads of days is too evident. Gen.i shows marks of profound reflection in the field of religion as well as in that of natural science, and cannot simply be regarded as a naive, adopted, ancient mythological conception: it represents a deeply considered philosophy indeed. It certainly is the most 'modern' of all accounts of the Creation known from the ancient East. But its real meaning is to be found in the attempt to place cosmology wholly in the light of the beliefe in the One God.[1]

Israel's belief in God itself did not, however, originate in these reflections, but it preceded them, for it was born from the spiritual experience of God's activity directed towards the people and the individual; *Israel met its God as a Living God*, who revealed Himself *in the history* of the people and in the life of the individual; Israel came to know God as *the Saviour* and *the Leader, the Redeeming God*. Israel did not derive its knowledge of God first and foremost from nature, as the ancient oriental peoples did, but from the acts of God in the history of the people as they appeared in the light of His revelation to Moses and the prophets. So Israel's faith sprang from two sources, closely connected with each other and even essentially one: a spiritual and a historical source. God is not a mode of being, but a personal Power who consciously works salvation in this world (cf. p. 192). This belief in God is fundamentally different from that of the great popular religions of the ancient Near Eastern world.[2]

On reading the writings of the prophets of the 7th and 8th centuries we are struck by the fact that they always refer to the revelation of Yahweh in the deliverance from Egypt and the miraculous preservation of

---

[1] See Böhl, *op. cit.*, Gunkel in *Die Schriften des A.T.*, I, 1, pp. 108ff.
[2] A.Bertholet, *Die Eigenart der alttest. Religion*, 1913, pp. 23ff.; *Der Beitrag des A.T. zur allgemeinen Religionsgeschichte*, 1923, pp. 18ff.; R.Bultmann, *Das Christentum als orientalische und als abendländische Religion*, 1949, p.15; *Das Urchristentum*, 1949, pp. 17ff.; W.Eichrodt, 'Offenbarung und Geschichte im A.T.', *Th. Zeitschr.*, Basel, 1948, pp.321ff.; J.Lindblom, 'Zur Frage der Eigenart der altt. Religion' (*Werden und Wesen des A.T.; Beih. Z.A.W.*, 66, 1936, pp. 128ff.); J.Hempel, *A.T. und Geschichte*, 1930; my *Religion of Israel*.

Israel during the years in the desert. The primeval religious phenomenon of Israel's religion is the experience of being saved by Yahweh.
H. Wheeler Robinson is certainly quite right in saying: '... the revelation consists in a redemption, not the redemption in a revelation –
which is what the ascription of a whole and complete legislation to Sinai is apt wrongly to suggest'.[1] This redemption has left its mark on religious life, it may even be called the focal point of the life of the people.
Israel as a people was born in the desert after the deliverance from
Egypt: there the Hebrew tribes, fairly loosely linked by ties of blood,
were welded together into a people under the leadership of Moses.
From the outset Israel was a religious community rather than a national unity founded on consanguinity; certain groups of tribes left
Egypt, mixed with all sorts of foreign elements (Num. xi. 4; older traditions speak of a Kenite streak: Exod. iif.; xviii; of Moses' marriage to
a Kushite woman; cf. Ezekiel's remark on the mixed origin of Jerusalem, xvi. 3). That Israel came into being is due only to the faith of one
man, whom Hosea (xii. 14) justly calls a prophet: Moses. No wonder,
then, that all collections of traditions describe him as a hero of faith,
for that was what Israel knew him to be. It did not depict him as a
national hero or a leader of the people, but first and foremost as a
prophetic figure, who as such succeeded in fanning the spark of national
consciousness in his people. All the prophets bear witness to this one
fact that it was Yahweh who made Israel into a people. It will never
do to deny or under-estimate the religious element in the Mosaic-
Israelite movement, in the teeth of this predominant tradition. Whatever use should or may be made of the stories of Exodus and Numbers
historically, this one thing may be considered incontestable, that Israel
as a national unit was born from a religious movement: Mosaic Yahwism.

This is confirmed by the subsequent history of the people: when
reformatory movements spring up among the people they emanate
from this same spiritual force, Yahwism; apparently the movements
that brought the people to a new awakening were always Yahwist
movements. The historians see Israel's struggle as a holy war, Yahweh
is a 'warrior', their 'ban' (*cherem*)[2] is a sacred act. That religious and
national motives coincide in the holy war, exactly as the starting-
point of the history of Israel – though in the later (Deuteronomistic)
conception of history the character of a holy war may have been
stressed too one-sidedly – indicates that the movement from which
the national unity of Israel sprang was the result of religious mo-

---

[1] *Redemption and Revelation*[3], 1944, p. 88.
[2] C. H. W. Brekelmans, *Heren in het O.T.*, 1959.

tives.[1] In this respect Israelite historiography is rather more reliable historically than many scholars have been willing to admit in the last few decades.

In this way Yahwism was born and strengthened, in distress and redemption, in struggle and victory; and in this way Yahweh and Israel were united in a communion. This gave to Israel's faith in God its warmth and its profound consciousness of mercy and fidelity; this is the reason why the expectation of salvation was linked particularly with the conception of God; it also explains why power and 'jealousy' are among the predominant components of the conception of God.

No wonder, then, that the concept of the Creation is not originally inherent in Israel's religion and does not rank first in the message of the prophets.[2] Not until Deutero-Isaiah who lived in the time when Israel, almost destroyed, lay between the great world-powers, did the greatness of Yahweh as the Creator and His omnipotence come to be of central importance in the message of the prophets. The God of Salvation is then at the same time the God of the world, and as such He brings salvation to all the nations.

With the conception of God as the Bringer of Salvation is closely connected the idea of God as the *Maintainer* even more then the Creation.

Owing to the historical starting-point of the conception of God His Providence is first and foremost related to the history of the people and to the maintaining of life in the country where His people dwell, and only in the second place to the world of the nations and to nature in general – though the idea is already present in the words of the earliest Biblical prophet (Amos ix. 7; ii. 1ff.)!

Yet He also rules the world of the nations; this is evident not only in the Passover-stories of Exod. i–xv but also in the story of Joseph and in the history of primeval times (the narrative of the Flood; the story of the tower-building at Babylon); further in the prophets (the texts of Amos cited above; Isaiah's teaching concerning Assyria, Isa. x etc.; the prophecies against the nations in Amos, Isaiah, Jeremiah and Ezekiel; Deutero-Isaiah who speaks of Cyrus as the man called by Yahweh; Daniel); the idea is emphasized more and more. It can hardly be maintained that the idea only arose in the period of the great prophets, even if the first definite statement that can be dated

---

[1] Cf., for instance, Max Weber, 'Das antike Judentum' (*Ges. Aufsätze zur Religionssoziologie*, III, 1923).

[2] The fact that in Israel with its ancient Oriental religion the idea of Creation lags behind the idea of salvation to such an extent may even be regarded as one of the most striking proofs of the speicial origin of this religion.

with any certainty is not found until Amos: this does not justify the conclusion that he was the first to form this idea, for it is implied in the living faith in Yahweh, as is proved e.g. by J (Gen.xii.3; xviii).

The fact that Israel's belief in God was born from the miracle of the deliverance from Egypt, gives us *a priori* a right to suppose that with the action of Yahweh against Egypt the belief is given that He has power over the nations. Even if to the conscious mind of the Israelite the gods of other nations continued to exist, at any rate to a certain extent (see p.326) and even if, for that reason, the doctrine of Yahweh's dominion over the world long remained latent as a general conception, yet it is implicit in the preaching of the deliverance from Egypt; Yahweh is the God of gods, not only as the *primus inter pares*, but because He has proved to be the true, living God; and for that reason He transcends the other gods completely in His holiness as the Incomparable God (Ps.lxxxix. 7, 9), Whom all powers must adore: even the divine powers (Pss.xxix; lxxxii; ii; cx)[1]. These cultic texts clearly show that this representation is not late, but early Israelite (cf. also Judges v). The message of salvation of the prophets, and particularly Messianism, could not be understood without this conception. This is a particular application, within the framework of prophetic teaching, of the faith in God Who leads history and guides it towards its final goal: His Kingdom upon earth. The Kingdom of God may be considered the essential content of the message of salvation. Yahweh is King (Ps.xciii etc.) and will one day reveal His Kingship in all its fulness.

He does not only guide the history of Israel and of the nations, but also what we call nature and what the Old Testament calls 'the world and all that is in it'. Because He is often connected with nature Yahweh has often been regarded as a nature-god, especially as the God of the wind, the tempest, and the thunderstorm (Exod.xix; Pss.xxviii; xxix), natural phenomena with which He is often associated (see above, p. 214). As the ruler of nature He is described as acting and revealing His power in it. There is, therefore, no contrast between God and Creation; there is communion as well as distance in His relation with man, and the same is true of the relation between God and nature. He is the Creator; that means distance; He is also the Maintainer, and that means communion.

Everything in nature exists through God; He gives of His Spirit (= breath of life) to man so that he lives (Gen.ii. 7). That also applies to the animal world; indeed, to all that exists (Ps.civ.29f.). This Spirit returns to Him again at death (Eccles.xii. 7). All life is from Him and in Him. We might even say that what we call creative

[1] See C.J.Labuschagne, *op. cit.*

natural force is to the Israelite – God.[1] Therefore, wherever in nature exceptional forces reveal themselves God is seen acting. He speaks in the thunder and reveals His strength in the tempest, His life-giving power in plants and animals. Nature is the revelation of the fulness of His Being. But in spite of the fact that all is from Him and has received life and existence from Him, we cannot speak of *Deus sive Natura*, or of an affinity between God and nature or God and man. The essential objection which in our opinion must always be raised against Pedersen's *Israel* is that God and the force of nature or that of the life of the people are considered identical.[2] Certainly it is true that all these things are from Him, but this does not make man or nature divine. They live through Him; it is His strength that enables man to breathe and move, and yet as the Holy One He is absolutely greater than these forces and quite distinct from them. We should bear in mind how cautiously Hosea (ii. 20ff., Hebrew text 24ff.) uses the verb '*ana* (to answer, to hear). The prophet seems to say that heaven receives the prayer of intercession from the earth and passes it on, while the earth receives the prayer of the corn, and the corn the prayer of Jezreel, and that Yahweh finally hears this prayer. There are contacts, but the whole world stands praying before God expectantly.

He is not absorbed in them, He is the Lord of all. He rules the sea, from the waters of the chaos and the Red Sea to the mighty ocean (Pss. xciii; xcv; cxiv; cvii),[3] as well as the land and the animal world (the miracles in Egypt), and the fertilizing powers of nature (Hos. ii; Ps. civ). He gives all creatures what they need; to the animals He gives their food (Pss. xxxvi. 7; cxlvii. 9; cf. lxxxiv. 4), to the land the rain (Deut. xi. 11ff.; 1 Kings xviif.), to the poor justice and deliverance (Pss. cxiii; cxlv; cxlvi), and to those who hope in Him His favour (Pss. xxiii; xxxvi; xxxvii; ciii, etc.), He is the God of the living and of the dead (Ps. cxxxix.8; especially in later literature, Isa. xxvi. 19), the God of heaven, of the earth, and of the nether world.[4] All the epithets that are applied to various pagan gods are concentrated in Him, so that it is impossible to regard some heathen gods as the origin of the Israelite conception of God; we find all sorts of images, used for cer-

---

[1] H. Wheeler Robinson, *Inspiration and Revelation in the O.T.*, 1946, p. 1.
[2] Joh. Pedersen denies on principle the right to explain the religious life of Israel in a different way from that of the other peoples, and thinks that ideas such as 'paganism' are of no use in understanding the religion of Israel; see his article 'Die Auffassung vom A.T.', *Z.A.W.*, 1931, pp. 161ff., esp. pp. 180–1.
[3] Beside the above-mentioned essay by O. Eissfeldt see also Ph. Reymond, *op. cit.*, pp. 239f.
[4] On the other hand, the kingdom of the dead is in many cases regarded as withdrawn from the influence of Yahweh, the God of life, for instance, Ps. cxv. 17; Job. xiv. 9ff.

tain gods in the Canaanite world, employed to denote Him (e.g. He that rides on the clouds: Ps.lxviii.5, R.S.V.4); even hymns destined for the worship of other gods may be adopted and adapted for the worship of Yahweh, as has been supposed of Ps.xxix!

Yahweh is, therefore, the Lord of all life. It belongs to God; it is a power to which He has a right. For that reason man may not shed the blood of his fellow-man (Gen.iv; ix.5f.; Exod.xx.13); animal life, viz. the blood (the seat of life, Gen.ix.4; Lev.xvii.10ff.) is sacred, too[1], and must be devoted, given back, to Yahweh (Gen.ix.1ff.; Lev.xvii. 10, 12ff.); hence various commandments in the law concerning the killing of animals and the flesh of animals torn by wild beasts (Exod. xxii.31; Lev.xvii.12ff.; xxii.8; Ezek.xliv.31). These religious observances were taken over by the first Christians (Acts xv) and are still observed strictly by the orthodox Jews who keep the law. Behind these ideas and laws lies a most profound respect for life and its mystery, which is known to God alone![2]

The vegetative life of the plants is not brought into immediate connection with the divine forces of life; we may take this to be a protest against the ideas of the Canaanite world which thought that divine life was to be found in the grain. The goods who died and rose again from the dead returned to life in the vitality of the whole of nature, so that natural life as such was looked upon as an immanent divine force. In Israel vegetation is a gift of God (Hos.ii), but certainly not a revelation of divine life itself. In the account of the Creation in Gen.i the plants are brought forth by the earth at the command of God (i.11ff.), while the animal world is brought into existence by a particular act of creation (i.21ff.) and man is created in a very special manner (i.26ff.). A special *berakhah* (blessing) of God creates in the animals and in man their reproductive faculty (i.22, 28), which is not the case in the vegetable world; there the production of seed is the purpose of the existence of the plant, in order that man and animal may feed on it (verse 29).

Animal and human life are, therefore, seen very clearly as coming from God. Reproduction, and so sexual life, too, are a special gift to them (Gen.i.22f., 28f.). For that reason everything connected with sex is looked upon as sacred, and this is also evident from many laws and stories in the Old Testament. Children are a special blessing of Yahweh. Sexual life especially is governed by very strict laws. In the Canaanite world we find the exact opposite: there the natural in-

---

[1] According to Gen.i.29f. (cf.ix.1ff.) animal life *originally* was not given into the power of man.
[2] This remains true, even if the opposition against the use of blood etc. should be regarded as a combating of animist views. In any case these laws brought this respect with them.

stinct as such was considered sacred, and this gave rise to many forms of lechery; even the most unbridled lusts of the gods were celebrated in hymns.[1] In the Babylonian and Assyrian laws the worst forms of sexual crime (incest with daughter or mother and pederasty) are condemned, it is true, but the Israelite laws go much further in this respect (Lev. xviii; xx).

Yahwism, however, never becomes reactionary so as to condemn sexual life as such, as some later purist sects in Greece did. In Israel there is a certain balance between the natural and the spiritual element in sexual life; this is only possible owing to the fact that in Yahweh power over nature and moral being were completely fused. He is as much the Wholly Other, Holy God as the God who has turned Himself towards the world and binds His people morally in the natural revelation and communication of His power.[2]

Yahweh supports life and maintains the laws of life, He guides the forces of nature and history. The knowledge of His Providence springs from the experience of salvation granted by Him and is not a consequence of theories about the Creation. No wonder that it is particularly employed in the preaching of salvation: in the past (Hos. xi) as well as in times to come (Hos. xiv; Amos ix; Isa. ii; ix; xi, etc.). Especially for Isaiah (ch. xi) the message of salvation takes the form and colour of a representation of Paradise. In the historical books the Providence of God is depicted most splendidly in Gen. xxii, Abraham's sacrifice, and in the history of Joseph. The latter story rests entirely on this idea (Gen. l. 20). In the more recent literature it plays a part in the books of Ruth, Esther, and Daniel. Among the prophets it is Isaiah, and Deutero-Isaiah, too, by whom this idea is emphasized most strongly. But in their works this faith never becomes a generally optimistic conception of life, as is found in the wisdom literature of the Proverbs, and, predominantly, in the 'false prophecies'; Isaiah knows only too well that Yahweh is the Holy God and recognizes only too clearly that destruction and ruin may be used by God as a means to accomplish His design with Israel, even if this means that only a remnant will participate in His salvation.

---

[1] See Albright, *From Stone Age to Christianity*[3], 1946. pp. 176, 178. Cf. Lev. xviii; xx; Num. xxv; Gen. xix; Judges xix; Exod. xxii. 19; Deut. xxvii; the prophets *passim;* 2 Sam. xi etc.

[2] Cf. Prov. viii and Job xxviii, where wisdom, created by God, is the pre-existent foundation of the Creation; see Procksch, *Theologie*, pp. 477ff.; afterwards the Law comes to occupy this place in Hebrew theology (cf. W. D. Davies, *Paul and Rabbinic Judaism*, 1948, pp. 168ff.) and in the N.T. the Logos which has become flesh.

8 The Names of God[1]

The real Israelite name for God is Yahweh, in compound proper names *Jeho-*, *-jahu*, *Jo-*, *Ja-*, *-ja;* sometimes also used by itself as a name of God: *Jah*.[2]

The problem of the original meaning and form, source[3] and distribution of this name (problems on which opinions are divided and for which a satisfactory scholarly solution will probably never be found) belongs to the history of religion, not to theology. Even if, for instance, the origin and meaning of the English word 'God' are not known, it is none the less very well possible to define the meaning of the word for the Christian churches in England. The same applies to the name of God in Israel. Theologically important is what the Israelite meant by the name, what the name meant *to him*.

[1] J. de Groot and A.R.Hulst, *op. cit.*, pp.74ff.; Sellin, *Theologie*, pp.3ff.; König, *Theologie*, pp.141ff.; Eichrodt, *Theologie*, I, pp.86ff.; Köhler, *Theologie*[3] pp. 17ff.; and *Lexicon in V.T. libros*, s.v.; Procksch, *Theologie*, pp.50, 64, 72, 436ff.

[2] On the name Yahweh there is an enormous amount of literature, of which we mention a number of titles here; besides the Theologies (see n. 1) the dictionaries and encyclopaedias of the Bible may be consulted (Herzog-Hauck; *R.G.G.*[2]; *Enc. Judaïca; Dictionnaire de la Bible; Reallexicon der Vorgeschichte; Th.W.z.N.T.*, III, s.v. κύριος; etc.; further: B.D.Eerdmans, *Religion of Israel*, pp.14ff.; *O.T.S.*, V, 1948, p. 1ff.; in these same *O.T.S.*, G.J.Thierry, 'The pronounciation of the Tetragrammaton', and B.Alfrink 'La prononciation "Jehova" du Tétragramme'; G.R.Driver, 'The original from of the name J.', *Z.A.W.*, 1928, pp. 7ff.; O.Eissfeldt, 'Jahwe-Name und Zauberwesen', *Z.f. Missionskunde*, 1927, pp.161ff.; 'Neue Zeugnisse für die Au sprache des Tetragrammatons als Jahwe', *Z.A.W.*, 1935, pp.59ff. (cf. id. 1936, r. 269); 'Ba'alšamem und Jahwe', *Z.A.W.*, 1939, pp. 1ff.; *Sanchunjaton von Beirut*, 1952, p. 32 (cf. Bauer in *Z.A.W.*, 1933, pp.81ff. and R. de Langhe, *Un dieu J. à Ras Schamra?* 1942); A.J.Wensinck, 'Oorsprongen van het Jahwisme', *Semiet. Stud.*, 1941; J. Hänel, 'Jahwe', *N. Kirchl. Z.*, 1929; W.Vischer, *Jahwe, der Gott Kains*, 1929; Kuhn, '*Jw, Jh, Jhw, Jhwh*' in *Orient. Stud. Littmann-Festschr.* 1935; Vincent, *La religion des Judaeo-Araméens d'Eléfantine*, 1937, pp.25ff.; P.Dhorme, 'Le nom de Dieu d'Israël', *R.H.R.*, 1952, pp. 1ff.; O.Grether, *Name und Wort Gottes im A.T.*, 1934; W.W. von Baudissin in *Studien z. Sem. Relig. Gesch.*, 1876, and *Kyrios als Gottesname*, I–IV, ed. by O.Eissfeldt; a number of articles in *J.B.L.*: 1933, Schmökel, 'J. u. die Keniter' (pp.212ff.), 1943 and 1944: Morgenstern and Montgomery; 1948: Albright (pp. 319ff., see also his *Stone Age*[2], 1946, p.197); 1949: J.Obermann (pp.301ff.); R.A. Bowman, 'J. the Speaker', *J.N.E.S.*, 1944, pp. 1ff.; Lukyn Williams in *Z.A.W.*, 1936, pp.262ff. and A.Schleiff in *Z.D.M.G.*, 1935, pp.372ff.; Alfrink and Kuhn in *Theol. Zeitschr.*, Basel. 1949, pp.72ff.; S.D.Goitein, *Yhwh, the passionate*, VT 1956, who thinks of a verb meaning 'to love'; J.Lindblom, *Noch einmal die Deutung des Jahwenamens*, Annual Swedish Theol. Inst. III, 1964, pp.4ff., translates in Exod. iii.14, as other scholars also do, I am, who is; G. von Rad, *Theology* I, pp.20f., 27f., 181ff.

[3] Many scholars regard the name as not originally Israelite, but either as Kenite (Eerdmans, Vischer), or as Ugaritic (Bauer), or as generally Semitic; but according to Eissfeldt the name is proper to Israel. In that case the Biblical tradition of the Mosaic origin of the name can be upheld. The name Ja'ubidi from Hamat (8th century) would then have to be of Israelite origin, cf. Noth, *Personennamen*, pp. 110f. (for further title see below) and Hehn, *Bibl. u. Bab. Gottesidee*, 1913, pp.245ff. (an entirely different opinion is held by Eerdmans, *O.T.S.*, V); see also my *Religion of Israel*, p.108.

First of all we may state that the name Yahweh is for Israel a *proper name* borne by God as the God of Israel. The fact that God has a proper name implies that Israel knew that Yahweh was a personal Being and wished to distinguish Him from other gods. In various traditions the name Yahweh is connected with the revelation to Moses (Exod. iii. 13f.; vi. 2); only in Gen. iv. 26 it is considered as a primeval possession of mankind. Here we have, therefore, two distinct traditions, a fact which leads to the supposition that in Israel different opinions regarding the origin of the holy name existed already. From the use of the name Yahweh in connection with pre-Israelite history it is evident that Yahweh cannot simply be regarded as a popular name of God, as e.g. G. F. Moore or J. Wellhausen a.o. say.[1] This view proves untenable when we bear in mind the Yahwist and Amos ix. 7. The Israelite mind can also conceive Yahweh as the God of the world; theologically this is highly important. Among other things it means that the preaching of Yahweh's relationship to Israel is also applied to His relationship to the world outside Israel.

Israel clearly understood by the name Yahweh *the being of God* (see p. 179f.; Exod. iii; Hos. i. 9), in the sense of a personal presence. Whether the explanation given by E in Exod. iii. 14 is also historically the original meaning of the name, can no longer be ascertained, but yet it must definitely be considered possible. More important than the correctness of the etymology is the fact that in the faith of Israel, at any rate as expressed in the Old Testament (Exod. iii) the name Yahweh had this meaning.[2]

As a primary religious feeling the name Yahweh called up the idea of *the living, awe-inspiring presence of God*. This may make it likely that the shortened names of God in personal names, Jahu, Jeho, Ja and Jo, were meant as weakened forms of the name of God: the full name was not pronounced in daily life; in cultic or prophetic texts it was, however, retained.[3]

The holiness of the name of Yahweh is already evident from the Third

[1] See above p. 291
[2] For a more detailed discussion of Exod. iii see pp. 179f.; we may also refer to Isa. lii. 6, which proves that to Deutero-Isaiah knowing God ranks with God's speaking: see, here I am. Kierkegaard (*Begriff der Angst*, ed. Schrempff, p. 83) already pointed out that the Latin 'praesentes dei' meant that the mighty gods are near as man's helpers.
[3] Other shortened names of gods also occur in the ancient East, cf. the name Had (-da, -di) for Hadad (see R. de Langhe, *Textes de R. Schamra-Ugarit*, I, 1945, pp. 64–5), especially in personal names. In personal names the Name is never found in its complete form, only as Ja-, Jo-, Je-, Jeho-, -jahu, or -ja; see M. Noth, *Die isr. Personennamen im Rahmen der gemeinsemitischen Namenbildung*. The complete form of the name is already found in the stone of Mesha and in the Lachish-letters. The tetragrammaton is the correct original form of the name, see the above-mentioned essays by Eissfeldt and Thierry, and L. Köhler, *Lexicon*, p. 368.

343

Commandment and from the later Jewish custom of not pronouncing the name at all. Hence in later times 'adonai was read instead of Yahweh, and for the same reason the Greek text used the translation κύριος (on this see the above-mentioned book by Baudissin, and also above p.331). Baudissin argued that the name κύριος denotes Yahweh as the Lord of a certain group. In that case the rendering κύριος to translate Yahweh would be well-chosen indeed.[1]

A longer form is *Yahweh Ṣebaoth* (see p.298), which emphasizes even more strongly the majesty of Yahweh.[2]

The compound *'Adonai Yahweh*, my Lord Yahweh, (English versions, 'the Lord GOD'), occurs, often used as a vocative, but also employed generally to denote God. Ezekiel uses it most frequently, though he also employs the name Yahweh by itself.[3]

There were many other ways of denoting the God of Israel; particularly *'El* with its (dialect) subsidiary form *'Eloah*, and the plural *'Elohim*. *'El* is a general word for god in the Semitic world, the meaning of which is not clear (not unlikely it is 'power', 'sphere of authority').[4] This word is used especially in compound forms to denote God, but is also applied to Yahweh. *'Elohim*, which is to be taken as a plural of intensity, can have many meanings (see pp.33f.): gods, godhead, spirit (1 Sam.xxviii), the heavenly beings around the throne of Yahweh; but also 'Godhead', 'God'.[5] Applied to Yahweh it only has this last meaning. He is *'Elohim*, God. There is no question of polytheistic remains in the use of this word with relation to Yahweh (cf. also how already in the Canaanite world a plural form may be used in the sense of 'mighty god', as appears from the El-Amarna letters, where the Pharaoh is sometimes addressed as *ilaniya*, 'my gods', i.e. my god).

The use of *'El* to denote God is a feature of the patriarchal period; it emphasizes the greatness and sublimity of God, which emphasis is perhaps found even more strongly in *'El Shaddai* (see below); *'El* is already used in the Canaanite-Phoenician world as the absolute ruler

[1] The Semitic word for Lord as the possessor is *ba'al;* for Lord as the absolute Sovereign *'adon*. W.Foerster, *Herr ist Jesus*, 1924, emphasized the meaning of Kurios as Ruler; see also W.S. van Leeuwen in *Het oudste Christendom en de antieke cultuur*, I, 1951, pp.575–6.
[2] For particulars of this usage see Köhler, *Lexicon*, s.v., and *Theologie*, pp.31. It is used frequently by Amos, the first Isaiah, Jeremiah, Haggai, Zechariah and Malachi, while Ezekiel uses very often *Adonai Yahweh*.
[3] See von Baudissin, *Kyrios*, I, pp.481ff., II, pp.58ff.; Köhler, *Lexicon*, p.11.
[4] *'El* usually is an appellative in the Semitic languages, and always in Hebrew; outside Israel *'El* is found as the name of a god; see O.Eissfeldt, *El im ugaritischen Pantheon*, 1951; Quell, 'El und Elohim im A.T.', *Th.Wb.z.N.T.*, III, pp.79ff.; see also the various Theologies.
[5] Also in Exod.xxi.6 ('Elohim – God or temple), see i.a. H.A.Brongers, *Nederlands Theologisch Tijdschrift*, 1948/9, pp.321ff.

of the pantheon; if and to what extent a movement which aimed at monotheism could be said to have existed there as early as the seond millennium B.C. we cannot be certain.[1]

Sometimes God is referred to by *periphrasis;* as such may be regarded the names: *'Elyon*[2] (the Most High; a shortened form of which may occur in the name of god *'Al,* Hos. xi. 7) and *Shaddai*[3] (perhaps 'the mountain', a widespread Semitic word for God, denoting the stability of the divine; cf. the image of God as a *Rock* in the Old Testament). Other periphrases are: *Ba'al* (lord, possessor), a title which during certain periods was also used as a name for Yahweh but was rejected afterwards (Elijah; Hos. ii); *'adon* (lord, ruler); and *melek* (king; cf. Isa. vi. 5); especially in the Psalms the conception of the kingship of Yahweh plays a great part. Yahweh is the ruler of Israel (Judges viii. 23; 1 Sam. viii), which accounts for the late rise of kingship in Israel and the objections raised against the institution of kingship in the time of the first kings.[4]

A study of the names of God in Israel leads to the conclusion that they lay particular stress on the Majesty of God's Being: *'elyon, shaddai, 'adon, ba'al* and *melek* as well as *'elohim.* Behind the multitude of these names there is, of course, also a long history which shows how Israel's belief in God developed in its contact with and protest against non-Israelite conceptions of God. These attributes were partly derived from the non-Israelite world and applied to Yahweh on the ground of the conviction that He was the Ba'al, the Melek. But precisely these names wich were used in the heathen world were rejected again afterwards.[5] In the Deuteronomic period, for instance, the name Yahweh was preferred emphatically to the general description Elohim, as is evident from the Israelite cylinder-seals.[6] This means that the recognition of the special revelation of God in Israel, beyond the general revelation in the Creation and in Nature, comes to the fore. Yahweh represents the *revelatio specialis,* El the *revelatio generalis.*[7] This is not to say that the faithful Israelites were always conscious of this distinction,

[1] See Eissfeldt, *El im ugaritischen Pantheon,* 1951, pp. 69ff.; Eichrodt, *Theologie,* I, p. 86.
[2] Could this be connected with the *'Elyon* – worship at Jerusalem before David's time? H. Schmid, *Jahwe und die Kulttraditionen von Jerusalem,* ZAW 1955.
[3] Used in Job over 30 times; further also in various early or archaizing texts; cf. i.a. M. Weippert, ZDMG, 1961, pp. 42ff.; 'Gott der Flur'.
[4] See Buber, *Königtum Gottes;* A. Alt, *Kleine Schriften,* I, pp. 345ff.
[5] Cf. for example on *melek* O. Eissfeldt, 'Jahwe als König', *Z.A.W.,* 1928, pp. 81ff., who regards *melek* as an ancient Semitic predicate of the deity. After the Exile the name *Melek* came to be used more frequently again. The name *Ba'al,* on the other hand, disappeared completely after Elijah's fight against syncretism.
[6] A. Reifenberg, *Ancient Hebrew Seals,* 1950, p. 167.
[7] As O. Eissfeldt, *Ba'alšamen und Jahwe, Z.A.W.,* 1939, p. 31 once expressed it very clearly.

for this can be seen from the use of the names in the texts. Sometimes the names are found combined: *Yahweh 'Elohim*, but this happens fairly seldom and may probably be explained in part from liturgical usage.[1]

II. THE FORMS OF THIS COMMUNITY

1. *Introduction*

The community of God of which we hear in the Old Testament assumed many forms, closely bound up with all kinds of historical and social conditions. As we observed before, it started with a patriarchal phase, but when it manifested itself independently for the first time it was a Yahweh-league; afterwards it developed into a tribal union, then into an independent nation with a government of its own and finally it lost this independent form and became a religious community (a congregation), though without losing its sense of nationality.

From this brief summary of the history of the community of God two things are immediately apparent:

a) Its national character is a form of life acquired in the course of history and cannot be considered vital to the existence of this community. In history this was proved repeatedly by the fact that when independence and sovereignty were lost the community of God survived.

b) The community of God as it appeared in history owed its actual origin and survival to its faith in Yahweh. This faith gave it a character all its own, so much so that it could hold its own as an independent community in the midst of surrounding related and hostile groups.

Yet ethnic relationships always played their part, too; from of old people were aware of the bonds of family relationship and common descent. In many respects this ethnic connection, expressed in genealogies, may be uncertain, yet it does play an important part (see below p. 370). The ties of blood are nearly as strong as the bonds of faith. We should therefore tread warily and not emphasize the latter unduly as the only factor (see below p. 384 n. 1).

It would of course be impossible to enter here into the details of the social development of the religious community which is depicted in the Old Testament. On this subject one should turn to such authors as Max Weber,[2] A. Causse,[3] J. Pedersen[4] or now R. de Vaux.[5] The

---

[1] So in Gen. ii and iii where the names must be taken either as alternative readings, or as a stylistic transition to the following Yahwist part.
[2] *Das antike Judentum.*   [3] *Du groupe ethnique* etc.   [4] *Israel* I–IV.
[5] *Les Institutions de l'A.T.*

346

social systems themselves cannot be dealt with at length here; they can only be mentioned in so far as they are essential to our understanding of the faith of the community of God itself.

2. *The social systems* (from a historical point of view)

a. The family relationship of the patriarchal age and religious life.

Though we may hesitate to accept the family relationships of the patriarchal age as historical[1] we may think the description of the social life of the clans in the pre-Canaanite patriarchal period fundamentally reliable.[2] More important from a theological point of view is the fact that the religious form characteristic of the period of these patriarchal clans was apparently supported mainly by an awareness of communion with the God who made Himself known to their ancestors. The clans called this Deity by the name of the patriarch to whom He had revealed Himself first of all: God of Abraham. All this was dealt with by A. Alt in his *Der Gott der Väter*. Though many aspects are still obscure and Alt's views are frequently combated it is the likeliest scholarly approach to the earliest pre-Israelite patriarchal religion so far.[3]

These views also enable us to establish a connection between this form of religion and that of the Mosaic period: according to Exod. iii. 6 Moses knows that Yahweh who called him is the god of his father. Though he witnessed a new revelation of God he was at the same time given to understand that this God was the God who had already entered into a relationship with his ancestors.[4] So. O. Eissfeldt is prepared to admit that this history is of vital importance from a religio-historical point of view.[5] It is clear, at any rate, that the early narrator of Exodus (J) accepts this connection, thus integrating the Yahweh-revelation into the ancient Hebrew faith, according to which God had already established a relationship with the ancestor. This revelation to the ancestor makes the clan itself into a religious community that is aware of an immediate communion with the God of the fathers.

b. Moses and the Yahweh-league

If Moses understood the revelation of Yahweh to have this meaning, as Exod. iii. 6 has it, the early relationship to the father-God is actualized and intensified again in this text. For, again according to Exod. iii, Moses looks upon the name of God, Yahweh, as a proclamation of the

---

[1] Cf. e.g. *History of Israel*, or *Überlieferungsgeschichte des Pentateuch* by M. Noth.
[2] R. de Vaux, *Die hebräischen Patriarchen und die modernen Entdeckungen*.
[3] See i.a. my *Religion of Israel*, ch. IV.
[4] This identification is also made by P in Exod. vi. 2, though in a different manner.
[5] Eissfeldt, *Jahwe, der Gott der Väter*, ThLZ 1963, pp. 481ff.

347

communion with God; Yahweh assures him of the fact that He is there.

(Exod. iii. 14, see above pp. 343 and 179f.). Yet the conception of God entered upon an absolutely new stage in his days. Yahweh did not merely identify Himself with the God of Moses' father, but He also revealed Himself as the God of battle and victory, of wind and storm, intervening in nature and history. So He proves to be more than a mere family- or clan-god; He is the mighty God and as such He becomes the absolute Lord of the groups of slaves that have been delivered. These unite into a Yahweh-league. The members of this league are no longer certain consanguineous families only, but also relatives (Jethro) and all kinds of hangers-on (Num. xi. 4; compare also the Kushite woman of ch. xii). From the outset the community of Yahweh was not merely a family-group, but also a community linked with each other and with Him by the deliverance they had experienced. Probably only certain clans or tribes or tribal groups formed part of it. It was stamped as a lasting community by a proclamation by Yahweh, who makes His will known. In this proclamation Yahweh's saving act of revelation is made the starting-point; underlying it we find the demand that Yahweh and He only shall be worshipped (the first few verses of the Decalogue: Exod. xx. 2–4a. Moreover, a second series of commandments (the so-called second table of the Decalogue) proclaims the basic civil law. This, too, comes under the protection of Yahweh and is united with the former to constitute a whole which afterwards became known as the Decalogue (Exod. xx and Deut. v).[1] This twofold legislation (cultic and moral-social) comes to be the basis of the community of God as it originated in the desert and penetrated into the land of the fathers (Palestine-Canaan).

c. Amphictyony

There the third stage of the community of God develops, because the Yahweh-league in Canaan achieves an alliance with other, still half-nomadic tribes of the patriarchal period. From the outset certain Canaanite cities (Gibeon, Shechem) may have been admitted on special conditions. The ancient principles of justice received in the desert become the basis of life in this community and the starting-point of the administration of justice. As A. Alt has demonstrated[2] there exists a connection between the demands of the Decalogue and criminal law (though this connection cannot be shown literally in the texts).

[1] See i.a. my *Religon of Israel*, p. 147f; G. Fohrer's article: *Das sogenannte apodiktisch formulierte Recht und der Dekalog*, KuD 1965, pp. 49ff.; Gerstenberger, *op. cit.*
[2] *Die Ursprünge des israelitischen Rechts.*

Thus the new, extended community of Yahweh was governed from the beginning by a covenant; beside the confession of Yahweh as God there is the strong link of collective law. W. Zimmerli rightly pointed out that in the Old Testament law is an integral part of the spiritual community.[1] So this community takes the form of a community of law;[2] it is dominated by *shofeṭim*, judges, who in some cases also take action as military and political leaders, consequently as liberators and rulers.[3]

This legal basis keeps dominating the Yahweh-community during the further course of its history, though it undergoes various changes. We shall revert to this ground-plan of the legal community in the next section. This new community of Yahweh or this covenant (called amphictyony by M. Noth) is the core of the later people of Israel; it was not long before it took this name, known from early traditions that told of the *heros eponymos* of one of the oldest tribes of Central Palestine: Israel, who was indentified with the figure of Jacob of other traditions. The name of Israel as the name of a people also had a clear religious connotation.

d, e. The people of Israel; Israel as a temple congregation

Two times this development was to be modified drastically: first when the desire for national unity led to the institution of a monarchy and the formation of one state, the second time when after the destruction of the state (fall of Jerusalem) the temple with the high priest becomes the centre of the community of God instead of kingship with the temple. How great the influence of kingship was, how it had originated and disappeared, will be explained more fully in § 4.

f. Desintegration

Finally, after a long period of national subjection and degeneration of the hierocracy the community of God desintegrated owing to the activity of the sects which developed more and more.

3. *The structures of the community*

a. The legal community

After the patriarchal way of life, in which family relationships predominated, the structure of the *legal community* (see above) became of decisive importance to Israel's spiritual and religious life. From this

---

[1] *Das Gezetz und die Propheten*, 1963.
[2] L. Köhler, *Die hebräische Rechtsgemeinde*, 1931.
[3] The problem of the place of the *judges*, a matter on which M. Noth's views differ widely from those of other scholars, cannot be discussed here. See Noth, *Das Amt des 'Richters Israels'*, Bertholet Festschrift, 1950, and against him: W. Richter, *Zu den 'Richtern Israels'*, ZAW 1965, pp. 40ff.

a religious life and thought developed in which proclaiming and obeying the divine commandments were considered vital to all spheres of life in the community of God. The most impressive witnesses to this are the classical prophets of the Old Testament, but it is also borne out by the earliest collection of canonical writings which was most important to the community of God: the *Torah*. Its central part is dominated by a series of *laws* (Exod. xx – Num. viii and Deut.). *In principle* this element of Israel's faith cannot be considered late, though it is true that a great deal of late material was incorporated in the collections as we have them.[1]

It is evident that this connection between law and religion was of paramount importance in Israel's faith; it even gave this faith a wholly new turn, for in the periods about which we have historical information the belief in Yahweh was dominated completely by righteousness (*ṣedaqa*) and communion (*chesed*). This connection gave Israel's conception of God, which was determined by Yahweh's intervention in nature and history, a strong moral character, and ultimately it tended to make the structure of Israel's religion rather one-sided and legalistic.

It cannot be said, however, that this legalism had been present from the outset. The carrying through of legal standards in the community of God was not so much intended to serve a political purpose nor was it primarily meant to strengthen the external forms of the community; its aim was rather to maintain the strong communal sense that had existed in the community of God from the beginning, also when after the settlement of Canaan the Yahweh-league expanded into a group of tribes joined together by a treaty.

Not without truth H. J. Boecker[2] says of the legal order in Israel that it, 'so paradox es klingen mag, nicht eigentlich juristisch zu verstehen ist, sondern von dem eigentümlichen Begriff von Gemeinschaft her, der so wichtig für das hebräische Denken ist".[3] The need of rules of law, particularly those of criminal law, became considerably stronger after the tribal alliance had come into existence, but the purpose of these rules remained essentially the same as in the pre-Palestine pe-

---

[1] In this respect I cannot agree with J. Wellhausen, who looked upon the whole of the cultic laws as late anyhow, nor with G. von Rad, who seems to attribute the rise of the legal element in Israel's faith particularly to the activity of the prophets (*O.T. Theology*, II). Pedersen (*Israël*) rightly pointed out that in their preaching of penitence the prophets appealed to the *early* theory of law; cf. also W. Zimmerli, *op. cit.*, who on account of the amphictyony emphasizes the juridical structure of the Israelite religious community.

[2] *Redeformen des Rechtslebens im A.T.*, 1964, p. 16.

[3] See in particular Köhler, *Rechtsgemeinde*, p. 9: 'im Hebräischen sind "Richten" und "Helfen" Parallelsbegriffe"; and also B. Gemser, *The importance of motive clauses in the O.T. law*, Suppl VT, I. 1953, pp. 50ff., who drew attention to the connection between law and wisdom on the ground of the warnings attached to the legal formulae.

riod. Law bears upon the community and its members as such in a religious and social sense, both as a whole and as individuals.

Now that the word Covenant has been used a few times we think it advisable to say a little more about it in this connection (on certain important general theological implications see ch. VI).

In the Old Testament itself the whole of Israel's saving history ever since Moses is viewed in the light of the covenant (Exod.xxiv; according to P since Abraham, see Gen.xvii and above pp.62f.). W.Eichrodt's *Theology of the Old Testament* was built up entirely on the conception of the Covenant. In the last few years more and more light has been shed on the problem of the part played by the Covenant in the Old Testament. The study of this problem was stimulated particularly by the contribution made by G.E.Mendenhall.[1] Up to now opinions have been divided. R.Kraetzschmar[2] and many others who followed the line of thought traced out by Wellhausen supposed that the concept of the covenant did not arise in Israel until the Deuteronomic period, and they had good reasons to think so because it was the Deuteronomic literature that emphasized the covenant so strongly. On the other hand, the covenant was already mentioned by Hosea and, even more important, the ancient traditions frequently showed the influence of this conception, even if the term itself is not used.

It is impossible to bring up the whole of this controversy here (see McCarthy, *Treaty*)! We cannot be certain that the communion between God and the people was considered from the outset as a *covenantal* communion. The question arises whether this relationship was looked upon as a communion entered into freely on God's part (as E imagines for instance in Exod.xxiv. 11, cf. 2 Sam.ix), or as an alliance concluded formally and confirmed by both parties (as in the Deuteronomic part of Exod. xxiv, vss. 3–8), or in some other way.

There are many kinds of treaties: a) those concluded by two equal partners, b) the treaty between a sovereign lord and his vassal[3] (both these kinds are also found among the Hittite treaties), c) treaties between two parties under the guidance of some high-ranking official;[4] then also a treaty concluded by the king with his people.[5] J.Hempel speaks of four kinds of treaties,[6] thinking first and foremost of e) the social communal relationship which is found generally with the Semitic tribes.[7]

---

[1] See above p.166 n.1.   [2] *Die Bundesvorstellung im A.T.*, 1896.
[3] Cf. J.Begrich, *Berith*, ZAW 1944, pp. 1ff.
[4] See M.Noth, *Das alttest. Bundesschliessen eines Maritextes*, see Ges. Studien, pp. 142ff. This is found in the O.T. in 2 Kingsxi. 17 and Joshua xxiv. 25.
[5] G.Fohrer, *Der Vertrag zwischen König und Volk in Israel*, ZAW 1959, pp. 1ff.
[6] RGG³ I, p. 1514 (s.v. *Bund, im A.T.*).
[7] And about which J. Pedersen always writes.

It seems that in the Old Testament the relationship between Yahweh and the people came to be looked upon more and more as a covenant, but that this covenant was viewed in a different light every time. Some authors (P) strongly emphasize the fact that it was God who instituted the covenant; with them God is the sovereign Lord and Israel the vassal. In the Deuteronomic theology the independence of the people as the vassal is still recognized in that it is asked to assent to the terms of the covenant (Deut., Exod. xxiv. 3ff.), as also in the Assyrian and western Semitic treaties.[1] J. Hempel[2] rightly pointed out, indeed, that this adherence to the independence of the partners in the covenant is, in fact, merely a formal matter.

Over and above these, however, there are many less formal types of covenants, thus the covenant described by E (Exod. xxiv. 9ff.) is marked by a communal meal eaten before the face of the Lord. We may wonder if the author did not have in mind a royal pact (though the word covenant is not used), at which the God of Israel, enthroned in high heaven, prepared a ceremonial meal for the elders of Israel (for such a ceremonial meal see Isa. xxv; also 1 Kings i. 9ff. and 2 Sam. ix).

In Exod. xixf. there is no ceremonial meal nor any other ceremony that reminds us of a covenant, while the word itself is not used either. Here Yahweh appears on Mount Sinai amidst thunder, lightning and smoke and proclaims His law. This way of representing things may be connected with the decrees promulgated by monarchs at their accession. It cannot be proved that kingship is implied in the form of the Sinai story because a) the word King is not used there (though 'kingdom' is found in vs. 6 in the Deuteronomic part of the text), and b) one can hardly attribute any kingly traits to this appearance of Yahweh.[3]

From a historical point of view it is most probable that the formal link between the covenant-concept and the relationship between Yahweh and the people was forged in the tribal alliance (amphictyony) at Shechem, which aimed at the worship of Yahweh as the Lord of the covenant (Josh. xxiv.). This view is also held by a great many scholars in this field. This covenant-concept must have attained a dominant position in the E-tradition and thus have been incorporated into the Sinai-tradition. Afterwards it was given a wholly new form in the Deuteronomic theology, which strongly underlined the juridical element; in this way the community of God was in some degree given the character of a community held together by a treaty.

[1] In his article *The vassal treaties of Esarhaddon and the dating of Deuteronomium* (OTS, XIV, 1965, pp. 122ff.) R. Frankena pointed out the strong affinity between the Deuteronomic covenantforms and the Assyrian treaties of the period of Esarhaddon.
[2] RGG³, I, p. 1514, art. *Bund II, Im A.T.*
[3] One might rather consider this to be true of the initial verses of the Decalogue.

This juridical element becomes even stronger in the post-exilic period owing to the theology of P, in which the law-giving on Sinai comes to dominate the whole of the Yahweh-revelation, and ultimately owing to the codification of the Pentateuch, which makes the *Torah* as the codification of the law predominant in the religion of Israel.

b. The community of God as a state

The amphictyonic bond developed by the tribes in Canaan, probably under the leadership of the Yahweh-league, may be thought to have prepared the way for the state, which developed afterwards. It is mainly a cultic and legal community centred round a sanctuary and is intended to maintain the collective relationship with Yahweh and therefore the mutual bond rather than the defence against the outside world. For that reason it did not have a pronounced political form. Consequently we find no actions of the amphictyony against the outside world in the Old Testament (cf. Judges v); an example of action taken within the amphictyony (against Benjamin) is afforded by tradition in Judges xx.

The leadership of the tribes rested with charismatic figures who are described as prophets (the prophetess Deborah) or as judges (the major judges) rather than with the amphictyony (where apparently there were certain officials who administered justice). On the strength of the evidence it may be assumed that for some time certain parts of the country were under the leadership of such judges (who therefore governed these territories) and that during the last period of the judges the priesthood at the sanctuary of Shiloh played a prominent part. After the destruction of the sanctuary at Shiloh by the Philistines the need of a stabler form of government made itself felt strongly, particularly the need of a concentration of political and military forces. The Yahweh-lague and the amphictyony had had their day; a more comprehensive unity was required if the tribes of Israel were to hold their own against the invading Philistines and other tribal groups. No wonder, then, that the desire for a central leadership was growing and that this could be guaranteed best by kingship. For Israel, which had hardly outgrown the semi-nomadic period yet was getting acquainted with agricultural conditions, kingship was an innovation. It formed part of urban civilization. In the ancient Eastern countries it had already existed for a long time, and in Canaan too, though there it had failed to develop into a very influential institution owing to the division and dependence of the country (on the kingship itself and its importance in religious life and the state see also below). In spite of the opposition of some old social and religious groups against this desire for a king, the idea of kingship won through, even if at first charismatic figures only were invested with this dignity.

The first man designated to hold this office, Saul, though originally called in the charismatic manner, fell short of the expectations people had cherished about him. But his successor, David, did come up to these expectations and most unexpectedly and impressively he made kingship in Israel into an institution that was valued very highly and accepted fully; to such an extent even that the succession to the throne was solemnly given to his dynasty for all time (2 Sam. vii). David was not only called to the throne by the southern tribe of Judah from which he had sprung, but he was also accepted as king by the northern tribes. This is how during David's lifetime the state of Israel came into being, comprising all the old Hebrew tribal groups as well as many ancient Canaanite cities that had submitted and were incorporated into the new kingdom in one way or other.

What interests us in connection with the theology of the Old Testament is not the subsequent history of this state, but its importance in the development of the community of God which Israel was in essence.

This importance was very great. The state as a new form of government meant a radical change in the position of the tribes of Israel. It confronted them with the surrounding nations in a way totally unknown so far; ancient civilized states such as Egypt and Phoenicia were beyond their horizon no longer. At home a new form of civilization sprang up: urban civilization. People began to live in and with the ancient Canaanite cities and within a short time many new Israelite cities were constructed as well. The semi-nomadic and agricultural civilization was gradually being complemented by urban culture.

The influence of all this on religious and spiritual life was very great. When people began to be interested in the international scene they came to familiarize themselves with and appreciate foreign wisdom; ancient Canaanite religious notions and practices became known and gained in influence. All this widened the spiritual horizon but also caused grave tensions. On the one hand, it led to syncretism (cf. 1 Kings xii), on the other hand, as a reaction, people began to concentrate more and more on their own spiritual values. This gave rise to the need to collect the ancient traditions (J) and to adapt them, as well as to the tendency to take a stand against these new influences (Gen. ii–xi).

The new royal temple in Jerusalem is a clear case in point. It was built in a 'modern style' which is in many respects reminiscent of structures of the western Semitic architectures.[1] On the other hand it also expresses the will to maintain the ancient Yahwism: the Ark

[1] See i.a. A. Parrot, *Le temple de Jérusalem;* R. de Vaux, *op. cit.*, II.

which had already been transferred to Jerusalem by David, the secret palladium of the Yahweh-league, was placed in the cella of the sanctuary which thus became the 'Holy of Holies'.

In religious thought Wisdom becomes of unprecedented importance, but on the other hand the cultic element is also stimulated strongly. The philosophy of life becomes an element of religion: God is proclaimed as the Creator-God (cf. Gen. xiv. 18ff.); through genealogical registers (Gen. x) the history of Israel is fitted into the history of the world and linked up with traditions of the primeval history (Gen. iiff.).

In the social field the way is paved for great changes; as Israel is being drawn into the life of the nations by trade and politics the old simple social relations are interfered with. A 'money-economy' comes to dominate social and economic life, the ancient social rules are going by the board. The protests of the prophets who call upon the people to maintain the ancient ways of life for Yahweh's sake try to stem the tide of this social disorganisation. Classical prophetism brings out clearly Israel's growing awareness of the imminent social, cultic and religious dangers. By this spiritual struggle Israel's faith was focused upon the vital problems of life and in this way Israel arrived at a (practical) theological reflection all its own.

Through these tensions Israel's faith was deepended and enriched (see ch. II, pp. 26f.). A very great part of the Old Testament came into being during this period and is marked by it, both the collections of historical traditions and the prophetic, cultic (many Psalms) and wisdom literature,

c. The community of God as a cultic community

In virtue of its nature the community of God as it appears in the Old Testament was always a cultic community, too. There was always some form of communal worship of God round whom the community developed. This was the case in the patriarchal period, but also in the Mosaic period, the age of the Judges and the Kings and in the postexilic period. In each of these, however, the form of the cultic community was different. The Old Testament gives fairly detailed information about the cult, but it has been handed down to us in the *Torah* as one whole without any historical connection; the later priesthood of the second temple in Jerusalem lumped them all together and ascribed them to the Mosaic period. By consulting the historical writings it is possible to gain a deeper understanding of the real situation as it presented itself in the course of history, even though this insight may be called very fragmentary and in places even insufficient, because the nature of the sources compels us in many respects to make shift with hypotheses. The brief outline of the cultic community in the course of history given here is of a very tentative character; for further material see now especially R. de Vaux's *Les Institutions de l'Ancien Testament* II, which we have already mentioned repeatedly and which gives a fairly complete survey of the literature on each separate subject.

The earliest form of the cultic community was the family grouping. Like all corporate life (see pp.370f.), cultic life also had a strongly marked family character. This remains perceptible throughout the course of history. In principle the father appears as the sacrificer, though it is the priest who set the sacrifice upon the altar (see 1 Sam. i–iii, and cf. Levit. 1); the paschal offering was killed and eaten in the family circle.

This must have been true *a fortiori* of the patriarchal period, when the cult was aimed first and foremost at the worship of the *theoi patroioi*, but on that period we lack evidence that can be dated with any degree of certainty. We are justified in supposing that the various Hebrew tribes or clans, several of whom worshipped the *theos patroios* under a name of their own (called after the ancestor), must have differed with respect to the cult.

These differences must have become more pronounced in Canaan where the clans or tribes settled, as each of them sought to associate itself with existing sanctuaries so that distinct cultic traditions must have formed within the different tribes.[1]

A strong impetus towards unity was, however, given by the Yahweh-league that had formed around Moses and played a prominent part in the Yahweh-amphictyony (see above, p.348). It made the Yahweh-worship of central and exclusive importance among the tribes that had joined it, thus greatly promoting the unity of spiritual life (cf. Joshua xxiv and such texts as Exod. xxxiv. 14, xx. 3, etc.). This exclusive worship of Yahweh entailed all kinds of prohibition of cultic practices (Exod. xxii. 20, xxiii. 18ff.), of magic (Exod. xxii. 18) and divination (1 Sam. xxviii) and of the use of names of deities and the abuse of the name of their own God (Exod. xxiii. 13[b] and xx. 7). Yet we may assume that the differences of the older period could not be cleared away all at once. Certain sanctuaries with which people had associated themselves carried on their old traditions, so that even after the tribes of Israel had come under the influence of Yahwishm different cultic traditions continued to exist. Such traditions could suddenly come to life again in later times, as appears from the story of the restoration of ancient cultic practices at Bethel and Dan in the days of Jerobeam (1 Kings xii) and from the fact that the prophets felt called upon to protest vehemently against the cult at sanctuaries at

[1] See i.a. my *Religion of Israel*, pp. 160ff.

Bethel, Gilgal, Beersheba, etc. (Hos. iv. 15, vi. 9, ix. 15; Amos iv. 4, v. 5). Yahweh was worshipped as the God of Israel nominally rather than actually. In point of fact various ancient non-Yahwistic practices survived at some sanctuaries; others (such as the ancient Shiloh) probably did not permit them or only to a lesser degree. No wonder that the opposition against the syncretistic sanctuaries became stronger and stronger, culminating in the legislation of Deuteronomy. This legislation was largely founded on ancient anti-Canaanite cultic laws we have mentioned above (the Book of the Covenant, Exod. xxi–xxiii, may be considered to form the nucleus of Deuteronomy), but particularly on the tradition that had developed in the temple-cult at Jerusalem since David and Solomon.

For that reason this temple (see above, pp. 247f.) became highly important for the community of God in Israel. The cult at this temple certainly did not escape pre-Israelite Canaanite influences, but it was based essentially upon the ancient Israelite tradition which the temple-cult was to incorporate, as is proved by the fact that the ark, the ancient-Israelite nomadic palladium (see above, p. 354) became the real sacral centre of the sanctuary. Instead of associating itself with the patriarchal religion (as was done at Bethel in the days of Jeroboam) Jerusalem adopted the old Mosaic tradition.[1] This became of immense importance in the religion of Israel and the message of the Old Testament as a whole.[2] This is the historical foundation of the link between the Mosaic tradition and the temple at Jerusalem, stated so emphatically by Deuteronomy and the Deuteronomic history. No wonder, therefore, that both in the Deuteronomic history (2 Sam. vi) and in the Chronicles (1 Chron. xv) the history of the state is introduced by the story of the preparation of the foundation of the temple.

Though we must be careful not to over-rate the importance of the temple at Jerusalem in Israel's spiritual life, we must certainly recognize its existence. The clearest proof of this may be the fact that after Israel became independent Jeroboam felt called upon to promote two sanctuaries at Bethel and Dan to the rank of royal temples to counteract the influence of Jerusalem. Everywhere and at all times the temples were the centres of spiritual life, as the priesthood did not only discharge cultic duties but also influenced education, legislation, etc.

The importance of the royal sanctuary at Jerusalem was detracted from by many sanctuaries (the 'high places') and (after the kingdom was split up) especially by the two royal temples in the north we mentioned just now.

[1] Cf. beside the books mentioned above, p. 195, n. 2 and 3, R. E. Clements, *op. cit.* and J. Schreiner, *Sion-Jerusalem.*
[2] For the importance of the temple see above, p. 248.

Not always did the temple at Jerusalem remain faithful to the worship of Yahweh: there were periods of decadence (Athaliah, cf. 2 Kings xi; Ahaz, 2 Kings xvi; Manasseh, 2 Kings xxi), but also periods of restoration (Hezekiah, 2 Kings xviii; Josiah, 2 Kings xxiif., cf. Jer. xxii. 15). Throughout the course of history the kings accepted the ancient holy places outside Jerusalem (only the Deuteronomic reformation in the days of Josiah attempted to abolish them all), and some of them even tolerated the worship of other gods on behalf of their wives who were of foreign extraction (1 Kings xi; xv. 1f.; cf. vs. 13 and elsewhere).

That is why the kingship and the royal sanctuary of Jerusalem did not always strengthen the community of God by any means, but on the contrary often affected it unfavourably. They frequently caused dissension, because the priests of the royal sanctuary had no other choice but follow the monarch. Solomon and Ahab are attacked by the prophets; in later times the priesthood is criticized severely by the prophets at every turn; the cult of the sanctuary at Jerusalem is opposed openly by Isaiah (i. 10ff.) and Jeremiah (vii; xxvi). The community of God and the cultic community do not always coincide by any means; on the contrary, they are drifting apart to an even greater extent. According to Isaiah it is only a 'remnant' that constitutes the community of God, and in his message the contrast between the two stands out clearly. This does not justify the conclusion, drawn by some scholars,[1] that the work of the prophets was individualistic; we should bear in mind that in their opinion the faithful who remained loyal constituted the true Israel. They looked upon 'the remnant that returns' as Israel, the Israel that has a future before it, whereas the rest of Israel was heading for destruction. And in this way Isaiah could proclaim to Israel both judgment ('this people') and salvation ('my people').

The fact that he is aware of the approaching separation between those who have faith (Isa. xxviii. 16) and those who have not (xxviii. 7 ff.) does not make Isaiah an individualist. Even if there are only few people who understand his message (Isa. viii. 16ff.), these few represent the people of Yahweh (Isa. xiv. 32) even if they are only the poor of the people. The community of God does fall apart, but not along personal or social lines, but on the ancient – Israelite moral and religious lines implied in the covenant-relationship. According to Isaiah the cultic community must be dominated by loyalty to Yahweh alone, by righteousness and justice; it must not be governed by national, political or ethical ideas. Some of the prophets even seem to

[1] Cf. A. Causse, *Du groupe ethnique.*

reject the whole cultic form of the community of God as it had developed in the course of history (Jer. vii. 22f.; cf. xxxi. 31ff. and iii. 16).

Whereas Ezekiel thinks in collective terms (he looks upon Israel as a unity, both in judgment and in restoration) in spite of ch. xviii, Deutero-Isaiah shows greater differentiation: in the first few chapters he addresses the people as a whole, but from ch. li. 1 onwards he calls them more frequently the faithful (denoting a plural). With Ezekiel the temple ranks high in cultic importance; this is hardly the case with Deutero-Isaiah. From the days of the major prophets there always remained a tension in Israel within the cultic community concerning the importance to be attached to the external cultic acts performed in the temple. Those who, like Jeremiah (vii), did not think the temple and its cult of central importance but rather the loyalty to Yahweh and the keeping of His commandments take a different view of the cultic community from those who thought the sanctuary and the sacred acts indispensable. To the former the destruction of the temple (Micah, Jeremiah, perhaps Isaiah too[1] did not seem to be an irreparable disaster but an inescapable divine judgment. To the latter it became the token that God had rejected His people (cf. Jer. xxxiii. 23, Isa. xlix. 14, xlii. 18ff.). The Lamentations show affinity with the message of the prophets rather than with the latter, because they describe the downfall as God's judgment (cf. i. 18).

In Deuteronomy we find an attempt to unite the two: the cultic and the ancient-Israelite prophetical elements. The divine law is emphatically proclaimed in the spirit of the prophets, but at the same time the cult is concentrated in the purified temple-worship in Jerusalem.

The Deuteronomic reformation attempted to reform the state, the temple, the laws and the life of the people by the creation of a theocratic state with at its head a king who, like his subjects, is fully amenable to the divine law which is preserved by the priesthood (Deut. xvii. 18ff.). Though Deuteronomy itself constituted the law of the country for a short period only (621–609), it exercised great influence on the development of the cultic community. As the summary of the words of Yahweh it continued to dominate the life of the community of God, because it was not only the starting-point for the development of a whole literature that may be called the Deuteronomic history[2] (as was done by M. Noth), but even became the nucleus of the collection of canonical writings that have been handed down to us in the books of Genesis to Kings. For that reason Deuteronomy is

[1] See my *Jahwe en zijn stad*.
[2] See above, p. 60.

the starting-point in the development of the canon, which gave the cultic community of Israel such a strong support in the 'sacred book'. This development linked the cultic community permanently to the 'sacred book'. Just as in the pre-exilic period the community of Yahweh was guided by the sanctuary and by prophecy, this is done after the exile by the temple and the canonised book. We shall go into these two subjects a little further.

First of all the temple, which after having been destroyed for 70 years, was rebuilt in Jerusalem (Haggai, Zechariah, Ezrah). Because it became the focal point of the renovated Yahweh — community after the exile, it got a quite different aspect. Now it really became a cultic community; its right to exist was the restoration and execution of the templeworship in Jerusalem (E zek.i, cf. 2 Chron.xxxvi.22f.), and this also gave it coherence. Haggai (ii. 11ff.) states that the new temple-community must be ritually pure and must not contain any elements that were not originally Israelite.[1] For that reason the foreigners (especially foreign wives) must be expelled (Haggai, Ezrah ix, Nehemiah xiv.) Some voices were raised in protest (Isa.lvi; Ruth), but they were in the minority though a prophet like Zechariah cannot have been very much out of sympathy with these protests: he does not think observing the fast essential, but he does emphasize the old prophetic demand to abide by the word of God, (vii.2ff.).

Soon the organization of the community of God was left completely to the high priest. As appears from ch.iii and vi Zechariah hoped that a secular leader would take his place by the side of the high priest, but these hopes were not realized: it seems that the two leading figures of the initial period (Zerubbabel and Joshua) were not present at the consecration of the temple; they are not mentioned in Ezrah vi.16ff. As the priesthood, led by the high priest, became the leaders of the community, the renewed community of God became truly hierotheocratical in character; the priests were the representatives of the community of God. The temple and its cult dominated religious life. Liturgical manuals on the temple-cult (Levit.i–vii) and other cultic and ritual tracts rouse the general interest. This makes it necessary for the Deuteronomic canon, which had already been generally accepted, to be extended with information about the cult. This was done by combining the collection of cultic narratives and laws, known as the Priestly Code,[2] with the Deuteronomic code. In this way the series of writings came into existence which we now have in Gen.i–2 Kings xxiv. The first part of this, from Genesis up to and including Deuteronomy, became known under the name of *Torah* as an inde-

[1] Cf. K.Elliger, *ad. loc.* in *Haggai*, ATD 25, 1951, pp.89ff.
[2] For this see the *Introductions to the O.T.*

pendent corpus consisting of five parts and as such it was considered Mosaic. Whether this collection was given its present form by Ezrah or soon after him cannot be established with any degree of certainty. Owing to the acceptance of the *Torah* the hierotheocracy that is predominant in the post-exilic community of God is determined more than ever before by this book. We might even say that it develops into a nomocracy. The spiritual life of the community is embedded in the *Torah*, which is looked upon as the unalterable written Word of God and from which the guidance of God could be received by study and interpretation. In this way the living word of God of the prophets was replaced by the book of revelation. Instead of the prophecy the study of the law became of ever greater crucial importance (Ps.i, cxix). Thus the community of God as a cultic community gained two centers; the temple and the law. They should not be contrasted, for they are thought to be in an even line theologically; the temple is the bearer of the law, and the law is the word that God gave to Israel from the sanctuary.

Historically and actually, however, the community developed in two directions, because it was dominated by two factors. The law was given its own institution in the synagogue that was established in every congregation and where the *Torah* was read and studied. It is true that the synagogue cannot be compared with the temple which retained a value all its own as the cultic meetingplace of God and the people, yet in many cases it was the principal spiritual educational institution in the community of the faithful. So a community of faith focused on the *Torah* develops beside a temple-community focused on the cult. The two communities often had widely divergent interests. The priests who were the leaders of the temple-community often held opinions (conservative in the theological field, progressive in civil life) that differed widely from those of the Scribes, who came particularly from the other group and often held opposite views. The tensions between the Sadducees and the Pharisees that are referred to again and again in the New Testament were partly due to these different developments which led to ever greater contrasts.

Besides, through and sometimes against these two main trends some few prophetical influences make themselves felt, as appears for instance from the book of Jonah and some Trito-Isaian prophecies. The influence exercised by apocalyptics was greater, as is evident from some parts of the Old Testament but particularly from the apocryphal writings (see p.455). Moreover, the wisdom continues to make itself felt, now opposing the ancient traditions, then adapting itself to them more and more (Jesus Sirach).

In the last few centuries of Israel's existence as a nation the cultic

361

community comes to present ever more differentiated and in part even confused characteristics. In spite of the fact that the outward appearance of unity was maintained under the leadership of the temple-priesthood and by the authority of the canon of *Torah, Nebi'im* and (in large part) the *Kethubim*, an authority which was generally accepted, the disintegration of the cultic community continued. The sects flourished, the gulf between the leading groups widened, the common people did not know the law so that the community of God, proclaimed and expected so emphatically, could hardly be effected to any appreciable extent. The formal attitude of the priesthood and the rigidity of the scribes could not check this disintegration. In a period when the community of God stood in desperate need of a spiritual leadership they failed dismally. More than ever before it became apparent that the cult and the law, the temple and the tradition, however important to the community they might be, could not take the place of the living Word of God that had been accorded to Israel for centuries. The failure of the community of God as a cultic community caused hopes to spring up of the fulfilment of the prophecy that held out the prospect of a recreation of the community of God.

4. *The pillars of this community*[1]

a. The importance of the *patriarchs* in Israel's faith is valued very highly in the Old Testament. Abraham in particular is the great champion of the faith (Gen. xii; xv. 6; xxii). It is clear that this view of the patriarch was influenced theologically by later ideas, and that these ideas clearly show the hand of the authors of the first half of the period of the Kings (J and E; cf. above pp. 56ff.), authors who show great affinity with the prophets and the wisdom-literature.

The type of faith we find in the figure of Abraham is that of the authors rather than that of the patriarch himself. To them he is the ideal figure in whom they depict the relationship between Israel and Yahweh, Israel's God.

Any reconstruction of the historical reality can only be hypothetical. It is clear, however, that Abraham did not know Yahweh, as we read that Yahweh first revealed Himself to Moses. It is therefore extremely difficult to determine the historical importance of the patriarchs for Israel's faith. A. Alt's study *Der Gott der Väter*[2] may not be the definite solution but up to now it is the likeliest hypothesis concerning the faith of the patriarchs and has not been superseded in spite of strong criticism.[3]

[1] Cf. M. Noth, *Amt und Berufung im A.T.*, 1958.
[2] 1929; see i.a. my *Religion of Israel;* V. Maag, *op.cit.*; M. Noth, *Traditionsgeschichte des Pentateuch.*
[3] For this discussion cf. esp. B. Gemser, *Vragen rondom de patriarchenreligie*, 1958.

In this study the patriarchs are looked upon as the mediators of revelation for the *theoi patroioi* who are called after them: the God of Abraham, the Fear of Isaac, the Mighty One of Jacob. The deity who had revealed himself to them remained the God of the family and afterwards of the tribe, the God with whom the descendants of the patriarchs retained the bond. In the Father-god religion we find therefore: the elements of the revelation, the charismatic receiver of this revelation and the personal bond between the deity and the patriarch with his family. All these are elements that are to play a dominating part in the later religious life of the Old Testament. So from the outset the tribal community must have had a religious basis, and this would go to show that there was a great measure of continuity in the different phases of the belief in God as is depicted in the Old Testament.

b. Moses

Here, too, the historical data at our disposal do not allow us to solve the problem of a historical continuity between the faith of the patriarchs and the faith of Moses. From the traditions of the Old Testament we do get the impression that the God who was revealed to Israel through Moses, Yahweh, was a deity quite different in character from the Father-gods of the patriarchs. O. Eissfeldt may be right when in his interpretation of the story of Exod. iii[1] he says that Moses already laid the connection between the faith in the God of the fathers and the faith in Yahweh, thus causing a change of crucial importance. With Eissfeldt we may assume (cf. Exod. iii. 6a) that Moses lived in the tradition of the Father-god and that he discovered the God of his family in the God who revealed Himself to him as Yahweh (cf. besides the J-tradition in Exod. iii.6a, also the P-tradition in vi. 2). It is this linking of the Father-god, the god of the community with the God of thunder and lightning of Mount Sinai who had also revealed Himself in history as the deliverer-god, which causes the belief in Yahweh to develop as He is proclaimed in the Old Testament, the majestic God of the personal communion who reveals Himself to be the Saviour-god by His actions. In the name borne by this God widely different 'qualities' are hinted at paradoxically: actualness and transcendence, power and saving intervention (see above, p. 181f.). The tribal groups were associated with this God who is – in religio-historical terminology – both Family-god and High-god, and this association was qualified by legislation, contained in the Decalogue.[2] In this way the tribal

---

[1] O. Eissfeldt, *Jakobs Begegnung mit El und Moses' Begegnung mit Jahwe*, OLZ 1963, pp. 325ff. esp. 331.
[2] See below, p.395.

groups, their descendants and those who associated themselves with these groups afterwards came to have a type of faith all their own, which set them apart for ever in their ways of life and thought from the nations that are their contemporaries. As the mediator of revelation Moses is the central figure in the community of faith, the Yahweh-league which was founded by him. His work prepares the way for the faith of the subsequent generations. The association with Yahweh inaugurated by him made the Yahweh-community the magnet that drew the tribes in Canaan and even other non-Hebrew elements towards Yahweh, so that the amphictyony could develop in Canaan. His task was unique, even if we do find figures in the Old Testament who held more or less the same manysided functions, such as Samuel, who was both prophet and judge.

c. The Judges

The community centering round a sanctuary did not play the most important 1ole in the development of the community of God, though it may have been of great importance for some time. About the history of the amphictyony we know so little, in fact, that we cannot even establish with certainty what sanctuary was its centre. Several sanctuaries emerge in succession from the mists of history which seem to have been central in the life of the tribes at certain times (Shechem, Gilgal, Bethel, Shiloh).

More important than the amphictyony, which appears to have fallen into decay soon, were certain Judges in whom the old spirit of the Yahweh-league came to life again. It is remarkable that in the book of Judges the title of *shofetim*, judges, is used to denote two wholly different types of figures that appear in history. On the one hand there are the so-called 'minor judges' (cf. Judges x. 1ff. and xii. 8ff.), on the other the so-called 'major judges' (Gideon, etc.). They are so widely different that they can hardly be said to belong to the same category; as M. Noth did we may look upon the minor judges as the holders of the amphictyonic office of a judge and the major judges, on the contrary, as charismatic heroic figures, as were Saul and David in the early period of the age of the kings. In that case these two types of judges[1] would represent two of the most important elements of the ancient-Israelite community: the charismatic type and the type that preserves the tradition particularly respecting the divine will in matters of law.

[1] In Hebrew as well as in Phoenician, Punian, Ugaritic and in the Mari-texts the word *shofet*, 'judge' can have a twofold meaning: 'ruler' and 'judge', in the sense of the man who upholds the law, who draws up the laws and administers justice (cf. beside M. Noth, *op.cit.*, and W. Richter, *op. cit.*, now also K. D. Schunck, *Die Richter Israels und ihr Amt*, in Suppl. V.T., Geneva, 1966, and elsewhere).

As appears from the description of the earliest kings the charismatic element still plays an important role after the period of the judges, which is proof of the decisive importance of this element for the religion of ancient Israel; the most important aspect of the kingship is, however, upholding the law (see also above, pp. 349ff.: the legal community).

d. The Kingship

Like the 'major judges' the first kings were charismatic figures. It would therefore be wrong to assume a contrast between kingship in Israel and the charismatic judges and to account for the original Israelite kingship by means of Canaanite and Egyptian influences only, or to look upon the king as a characteristically cultic figure. These elements do come into the picture, but they do not dominate the picture.

Quite soon the kingship in Israel changed in its aspects: the original peculiarly Israelite type was distorted, on the one hand into an oriental despotism (Solomon), on the other into a military dictatorship (Baasha, Zimri, Omri, Jehu, etc.). In spite of that the original charismatic element occasionally manifests itself in the way in which some monarchs were invested with their office. Several of the kings were anointed by prophets (Jeroboam, Jehu), others deliberately chose the line of the Yahweh-tradition (on Josiah cf. 2 Kings xxiii. 25f.) and they were therefore truly kings 'by the grace of God'. Anointment implies 'sanctification', being dedicated to God.[1]

Though the form in which the kingship arose in Israel[2] gave it a character all its own, adapted to the way of life of Israel and to Yahwism, it is in fact an institution which Israel adopted from the world around it, especially the Canaanite and Phoenician world, with its city-kingships.[3] Kings like Saul and indeed David, too, at the beginning of his reign (at Hebron, afterwards in Jerusalem; cf. also Jeroboam at Shechem, Omri at Samariah) and others show some traits of the city-kingship. Soon other influences came to play their part, as well, especially in the days of Solomon; then it adopted strong Egyptian traits and developed into despotism. This form soon decayed, because both the religions and the social conditions were lacking in Israel. In fact Israel always remained a tribal community based on the semi-nomadic life of the clans, in which the family and the oldest

[1] M. Noth, *op. cit*, pp. 15ff., Kutsch, *op. cit.*
[2] Cf. i.a. the article by A. Alt and H. Donner, *Königtum in Israel*, RGG³ III, pp. 1709ff.
[3] The Egyptian kingship also exercised some influence, a. through the Jebusite kingship and b. through the contacts in the days of Solomon.

members of the community continued to occupy a prominent place, and for that reason Israel rejected the kingship Egyptian style which was a divine kingship. The few formulas in the Old Testament that might remind us of such a conception of kingship are never to be interpreted in a literal sense.

The character of the Israelite kingship is a subject that has been very much in the limelight in the last few decades. On the ground of theories of the so-called *Myth and Ritualschool*[1] some Scandinavian scholars[2] developed the theory that the kingship in Israel as God wished it to be was of a sacral character, so much so that the king was looked upon as a sacred and even divine figure. They did not draw a distinction between the kingship of the ancient oriental world as a whole and that of ancient Egypt; they took the line that there was 'one cultural (and cultic) pattern' dominating the ancient Eastern world as a whole, a pattern to which Israelite life conformed, too.[3] It has become more and more evident that this theory is untenable, not only because ancient Eastern life in all its aspects was much more varied and complicated than the above-mentioned scholars thought, but also because within that complex whole Israel proves in many respects to have structures that are all its own.

As we said, the clan or tribe remained for a long time the form assumed by the community, and it was greatly strengthened by the religious links with the one God, Yahweh; and the combination of these two motifs made the idea of the community exceedingly strong.

The kingship did not break through this idea, but rather helped to strengthen it even more. Originally at any rate it did not affect the tribal community; the oldest members of the tribes made their influence felt at the election of a king (2 Sam. v. 3, cf. 1 Sam. xi. 12ff.,

---

[1] The name derives from the title of a book published in 1933 by some scholars, among whom S. H. Hooke (followed by *The Labyrinth*).

[2] G. Widengren (*Ps. cx*, 1941), but in particular I. Engnell, *Studies in Divine Kingship in the Ancient Near East*, 1943; cf. also A. Bentzen, *King Ideology* etc., St. Th. III, 1951, p. 142; *Det sakrale kongedømme*, 1945, and *Messias, Moses redivivus, Menschensohn*. On Egypt see: H. Kees, *Das Priestertum im ägypt. Staat*, 1953.

[3] This idea was rejected not only by the O.T. scholars, but even more strongly by the orientalists. To Mesopotamia this pattern does not apply at all; variously widely different forms of sacral kingship existed there which were only occasionally divine in character (see i.a. W. von Soden, *Königtum, sakrales*, RGG³ III, pp. 1712ff.), and are not, therefore, comparable with those of Egypt. Sharp criticism was levelled at this school by M. Noth, *Gott, König und Volk im A. T.*, ZThK, 1950, pp. 157ff. Many advocates of the Myth and Ritual School afterwards warned against unproven conclusions, cf. S. H. Hooke c.s., *Myth, Ritual and Kingship*, 1958. The fundamental ideas remained influential: A. R. Johnson, *Sacral Kingship in Ancient Israel*, 1955. Besides M. Noth other critics were: H. Frankfort, *Kingship and the Gods;* C. J. Gadd, *Ideas of divine Rule*, 1948; J. de Fraine, *L'aspect religieux de la royauté israelite*, 1954; K. H. Bernardt, *Das Problem der altorientalischen Königsideologie im A. T.*, 1961; W. Schmidt, *Königtum Gottes in Ugarit und Israel*, 1961.

366

and 1 Kings xii; 2 Kings xxi. 24f., xxiii. 1f., 30); in later times, however, it attempted to affect the tribal community unfavourably (1 Kings xii), and it certainly did so again and again in the days of the military dictatorships in the north.

The Old Testament data show that there existed great tensions concerning the kingship again and again. Though on the one hand this institution was accepted, also spiritually[1] (prophets anoint kings), it is on the other hand not adopted without great hesitation because it was rightly considered to be non-Israelite in origin[2] and was therefore rejected on religious grounds. The communion with God as King was thought to be endangered by an earthly king (1 Sam. viii). This objection was apparently overcome by the activities of David; he is called 'a man after God's heart' and can afterwards even be denoted as 'man of God' (2 Chron. viii. 14), and thus he became the symbol of the messianic hope of salvation. As the earthly kingship begins to weaken this notion of the messianic kingship becomes more and more prominent (Amos, Hosea?, Isaiah) and particularly when the former is played out altogether the appeal of the latter to the spiritual life of Israel becomes greater and greater.

From certain texts in the Old Testament that might suggest a divine kingship is evident that the dangers involved in kingship were not imaginary. First of all there is the adoptionformula of Ps. ii. 7 and cx. 3 (emended text), but this concerns the investiture with the royal office: the king himself is not made into a God but he is looked upon as the son of God, thus participating in the communion with Yahweh, who takes him under His protection in all things and allows him to share in His power (Ps. ii. 7ff., cx. 3ff.).

Ps. xlv. 7 is frequently taken to be proof positive of the existence of a divine kingship in Israel. In my opinion the word *'elohim* is to be connected with the throne rather than with the king, so that the text speaks of 'thy divine throne'.[3] In 2 Sam. vii. 13 the words *for ever* need not to be taken absolutely; what we have here is the promise of a lasting hereditary kingship. Certain formulas such as those of Ps. ii and cx may have been influenced by the ancient orientel terminology connected with the kingship. Such an influence would be quite conceivable in Jerusalem which was taken by David. The city had been

---

[1] The fact that Nathan accepted the royal house of David to such a degree that he was allowed to prophesy its lasting existence, certainly became of the greatest importance for the development of kingship in Judah (2 Sam. vii).

[2] M. Noth (*op. cit.*, pp. 174ff.) rightly points out that Israel did not have a king at all originally and that it was more than two centuries before this institution was adopted.

[3] For similar constructions see Ps. lxxi. 7; lxix. 5; 2 Sam. xxii. 33; Hab. iii. 8b (Levit. xxvi. 42); Noth (*op. cit.*, p. 157) and others translate: thy throne is (like that) of God.

under the influence of Egypt for centuries and its court-ceremonial must have owed a great deal to Egyptian ceremonies.

In the period of the kings the communion with God in which the people participates was centred not only in the sanctuaries but especially in the relationship between God and the king. That is why the king in this capacity may discharge priestly duties; he intermediates between God and man; he may be looked upon as a life-giving force (Lam. iv. 20) and as endowed with exceptional, supra-normal wisdom (2 Sam. xiv. 17, 20; 1 Kings iii, x; Solomon as a wisdom poet in the later tradition), and more particularly he is the great dispenser of justice, rescuing the poor and the destitute (Ps. lxxii).

In Israel the king is of central importance in religious life (indeed, *mutatis mutandis* this applies to all Eastern monarchs). He is absolutely bound to the laws of the Yahweh-community and in all respects he is its most prominent exponent. While with other people this is expressed especially in cultic and ritual ceremonies, in Israel it becomes evident in moral and social relationships (2 Sam. xi, Hos. vii. 3ff., Isa. i. 23, Jer. xxii).

Though the notion of a theocratic kingship in the sense that the earthly king is viewed as the representative of God's kingship on earth is hardly found, if at all, it must be admitted that the kingship of the Old Testament approaches this idea very closely. The only places where there is a direct link between earthly and divine kingship are the well-known texts of Judg. viii. 23 (where the two are contrasted) and 1 Chron. xvii. 14 and xxviii. 5. In the last two texts it appears that the Chronicler did indeed see the kingship of David in a theocratic light (see ch. ix).[1] They bear witness to a clearly theocratic view of the Chronicler, in that he looks upon the kingship of David as immediately representing the kingship of Yahweh Himself. As to Judges viii. 23, that is a different story altogether. M. Buber[2] thought this verse the earliest evidence of the occurrence of the concept of theocracy (cf. also Num. xxiii. 21). An unsolved problem is the question to what period the text belongs; it is difficult to prove that a text such as this one does indeed date back to the period of the early Judges.[3] There is, however, another point that should be considered: in Judges viii human rule is *contrasted* with that of God, and on account of the existence of the latter the former is even considered altogether impossible. So the connection is different from that in the Chronicler's theocratic

---

[1] 1 Chron. xvii. 14 runs parallel to 2 Sam. vii. 16, from that part of the history of David that was revised by the Deuteronomist; the text in Samuel does not yet have the theocratic wording!
[2] *Königtum Gottes.*
[3] See i.a. W. Beyerlin, *Geschichtliche und heilsgeschichtliche Traditionsbildung im A.T.*, V.T. 1963, pp. 1ff., and B. Lindars, *Gideon and Kingship*, JThS, 1965, pp. 315ff.

theology. If the word theocracy is to be used in both senses, to denote the statement of faith: Yahweh is a king[1] as well as the recognition (which springs from this faith) that the king of the house of David in Jerusalem sits on the throne of Yahweh, it is possible to do so on account of the meaning of the composite word theocracy, though it is rather confusing. One should keep in mind that the word has a two-fold meaning and distinguish clearly between the two. It was at any rate a long way from the belief in God's rule over Israel to the theological and political statement that the king of Jerusalem was the deputy of God as King.

e. The priesthood

In the Old Testament, or at any rate in the *Torah*, the priesthood gives the impression of unity; it is represented as belonging to one family (Aaron) and has a clearly settled hierarchy (high-priest, priests, Levites). This notion is due to the organisation of the priesthood in the post-exilic Jerusalem which was projected back into the past.

Actually the priesthood was greatly divided for centuries, as appears from the historical books. Ancient sanctuaries had and maintained their own priesthood, which was hereditary within a family. The priests served at a sacred place where God was known to have revealed Himself and which was therefore looked upon as a place where God and man could meet (see above the discussion of the meaning of the sanctuary, pp. 245ff.). They were above all the keepers of that place and also intermediaries between God, who had revealed Himself in that place, and those who came to the sanctuary (because the priests knew the rites and could proclaim the will of the deity by imparting an oracle, and because they could assist at the sacrificial cult which was pleasing to God; see above p. 240 on the function of the priests).

As there were many sanctuaries spread all over the country the priests could hardly appear as representatives of the whole people. There were only some priests who did, such as, according to the tradition, Eli and the priests Jehoiada and Hilkiah in Judah (2 Kings xi and xxiif.). Not until the Deuteronomic centralisation of the cult in Jerusalem did a situation arise which made a stronger central priesthood possible. Its influence already makes itself felt clearly in Deut. xviiff. The priests are mentioned before the king and it seems that they reserve for themselves a place in the administration of justice beside the judges.

Their position becomes entirely different again when the monarchy has disappeared; then the only central body that is left is the priest-

---

[1] On theocracy in that sense see below ch. IX and O. Plöger, *Theokratie und Eschatologie*.

hood at Jerusalem with the high-priest at its head. Quite rightly it
has been pointed out frequently[1] that the high-priest adopted certain
insignia in his robes of office, insignia which originally belonged to
the king.[2] Moreover the anointment that forms part of the consecra-
tion-rites of the kingship is transferred to the (high-) priesthood as
well.

While in the days of Zechariah (cf. ch. iiif.) there are still hopes of a
twofold government (monarch and high priest), a wordly monarch is
never heard of again afterwards. In certain matters the high priest
takes over his function and becomes of central importance in the community of God. This development had many important consequences,
the principal of which are: the fact that the *cult* and the *torah* came to
play a decisive role in Israel's spiritual life to an ever-increasing extent. As the monarchy disappeared owing to external circumstances,
the charismatic gift was more and more thrust into the background by
this internal development so that prophecy in its earlier free form
disappeared. The provision of oracles became more and more merely
cultic in character, and the prophetic gifts found expression in the
psalms, and another outlet was the apocalyptic dream-world.

5. *The community of God in the world*

a. Introduction

The structure of the social thought of the ancient Israelite world (as
also of the whole Semitic world, from of old up to now) is in fact
determined entirely by the family. People felt inclined to view all
interhuman relationships in terms of the family; not only the social
relationships within a national community, but also the national and
international. On this ground the Old Testament looks upon universal
history as a family-history; the authors of the earliest sources in particular think of the relations between the nations as family relationships.
Hence the great importance attached to genealogical registers in the
Old Testament; the genealogy is the way in which Israelite and Semitic thought express the communal relationships (see especially
Gen. iv, v, x, xi, xxii. 20ff., xxv. 12ff., xxix. 31ff., xxxv. 23ff., xxvi,
xlvi. 8ff. etc.). The word brother (*'aḥ*) is not only used to denote the
real brother, but it can also be used broadly of anyone belonging to the
clan or the people (Levit. xix. 17); other words, too, that denote family
relationships can be used in a much wider context (father, mother,
sister).

The family (the father's house) and the clan are the social units in

---

[1] See i.a. M. Noth, *op. cit.*, pp. 12ff.
[2] Noth mentions: the mitre (Exod. xxviii. 4, cf. with Ezek. xxi. 31, (R.V. 26)); the
breast-plate and the flower on the headband, cf. *op. cit.*, OTS 1951, pp. 18ff.

and from which the individual lives. This social structure of life was strengthened by the influence of Yahwism that authorizes it particularly strongly. It cannot be said that Yahwism adjusted itself entirely to this structure. Yahweh did not primarily become a Father-God, He remained a High-God and identified Himself especially with El. He did not arise from the life of the people and did not indentify himself with it (see above, p. 291), Yahweh is the God of Sinai and of the exodus from Egypt, the God of salvation and history. It is true that occasionally Yahweh is seen in a historical perspective with the God of the Fathers, as we said above (Exod. iii. 6 and vi. 2), but He is not absorbed in this relationship; in the Old Testament He is the God of the Covenant rather than Father-God (see pp. 166 and 173ff.), and this presupposes both distance and relationship.

The authorisation by Yahwism of the concepts of social structures becomes particularly clear in the absoluteness with which patriarchal authority is maintained in legislation, not only in the period before state-authority existed (the Book of the Covenant, Exod. xxi. 15, 17) but up to the end of the period of the monarchy (Deut. xxi. 18ff.). In both these laws the deathpenalty is emphatically demanded in the case of the son who rebels violently against parental authority; this is remarkable for it is found nowhere else in Eastern laws. The parents are looked upon as the authority appointed by God; they are in the first instance the spiritual and temporal authorities. Hence the Decalogue places the demand for reverence, for veneration *(kabod)* of one's father and mother immediately after the commandments with respect to Yahweh.[1] For that same reason children are brought up very strictly in ancient Israel, and the recommendation not to spare the rod is found again and again in the Book of Proverbs (Prov. xiii. 24; xxii. 15, xxiii. 13f., xxix. 17).[2]

The family as the constitutive element in tribal and national life is given theological recognition both by J (Gen. ii) and P (Gen. i) when they emphasize that the creation of man is only complete when the husband-wife relationship has been created. Gen. ii is even clearer on this point than Gen. i.

In contrast with the Creation-narratives of other ancient peoples the Old Testament does not hold that towns and temples (i.e. the original *states*) or certain peoples were created. The nations are taken to form one great family; their dispersion is the result of a divine

---

[1] In Levit. xix. 3 even in a reverse order; here the word "to fear" is used; probably this text was a "children's catechism".
[2] A. Klostermann, *Das Schulwesen im A.T.*, 1908; L. Dürr, *Das Erziehungswesen im A.T. ind im antiken Orient*, 1932; Schürer, *Geschichte*, II, pp. 491ff.; Moore, *Judaism*, I, pp. 308ff.; S. Krauss, *Talmudische Archäologie*, III, 1912, pp. 199ff., and Vriezen, "Opvoeding en Onderwijs in Israel", *Herv. Theol. Studies*, 1949, pp. 20ff.

chastisement (Gen. xi), but they are all looked upon as having sprung from only one ancestor, Noah. We shall afterwards have to recur to the unique importance and particular value of this idea (pp. 375ff., cf. also p. 171): the Old Testament is the only ancient Eastern work in which we find this universal outlook, as far as we know; in Mesopotamia, but especially in Egypt, foreigners and foreign nations are simply looked upon as barbarians[1].

There is no essential difference in the Old Testament between the family and the nation: the nations are, as it were, large families and are often called by the name of their ancestor.

b. The national existence in Israel's faith

The word for people ('am) was originally used to denote the connection between kinsfolk,[2] then for the people of Israel as one great whole, and also frequently for other peoples.

Israel knows it owes its existence as a people to God; He spoke to to Abraham: 'I will make of thee a great nation'. God made this promise come true miraculously (the birth of Isaac and afterwards or Jacob). He delivered Israel from Egypt and made it possible for it to become a people (cf. the liturgy in Deut. xxvi. 5–10. Indeed, He made it His people by the Covenant and thus made it unique among the nations (Deut. xxvi. 16–19). Precisely this spiritual view, the recognition that the people of Israel did not spring from a *contrat social* nor merely from a natural consanguinity, but from a spiritual relationship between worshippers of Yahweh, is the best historical explanation of its origin.[3]

The belief that Yahweh had miraculously made Israel a people has three important implications:

In the first place, Israel here proclaims that it is a religious communi-

[1] On Egypt cf. B. H. Stricker, *Brief van Aristeas*, 1956, p. 32.
[2] See Pedersen, *Israel*, I–II, pp. 54ff.; cf. also in English: "his people" = "his relatives" (cf. "folks" = parents); the word is used to denote the tribes of Israel, but also for the nations of the world in general, and it may even be applied to animals. The same applies to *goi*, which is, however, used first and foremost of non-Israelite peoples, afterwards with the meaning of heathen, but also several times of Israel. See besides the Hebrew concordance and dictionaries: *Th. Wb. z. N.T.*, II, pp. 362ff. (G. Bertram) and IV, pp. 32ff. (Strathmann); L. Rost, *Die Bezeichnungen für Land und Volk* (Festschrift Procksch, 1934) and *Die Vorstufen von Kirche und Synagoge*, 1938; N. Dahl, *Das Volk Gottes*, 1941.
[3] Cf. J. Hempel, *Das Ethos des A, T,*. 1938, pp. 77ff.; see also the theory of the amphictyony-relationship as the basis of national unity, held by M. Noth, *Das System der zwölf Stamme*, 1930, and *History of Israel*; also H. J. Kraus, *Prophetie und Politik*, 1952. An allied problem is that of the holy war, the wars of the Lord, cf. G. von Rad, *Der heilige Krieg im alten Israel*, 1951; H. Fredriksson, *Jahwe als Krieger;* Pedersen, *Israel*, III–IV, pp. 1ff.; on the problem as a whole and its consequences for missionary questions see J. C. Hoekendijk, *Kerk en Volk in de Duitse Zendingswetenschap*, (doctorate thesis Utrecht), 1948, pp. 230ff.

372

ty, linked together not only by ties of blood but first and fore-most by God; in this way Israel is made to realize God's Covenant and the certainty of its election by God becomes possible, in which it knows of its special place and task in this world (Amos iii. 2; Deut. vii and elsewhere; Isa. xli. 8ff., xliv. 1ff. and elsewhere, cf. above i. a. p.315f.);

Secondly, the belief that God gave being to the people of Israel could become the foundation-stone of Israel's hope of salvation, even when every thing pointed to destruction. The prophets believed that God would destroy the people as a state but that He would not leave it in this disastrous situation. He was the God of love, who had called the people into being and, being a faithful God, He would not forget His mercy but continue to manifest it to all eternity and lead His people back from ruin to a new existence (Hos. xi. 8ff.; Jer. xxiii. 6; Ezek. xxxvi. 22ff.; Isa. xliii. 25);

Thirdly, Israel was really preserved when its existence as a people was destroyed. In spite of their popular religion the ancient Eastern nations could not survive; their gods perished together with the people. Israel, which was doomed to destruction as a people (although indeed it was a community related by consanguinity) could keep on functioning as a religious community. That it did survive in this sense is due to the preaching of the prophets, who, – by predicting the downfall of the state and the destruction of the national existence as being the will of God – made Israel preserve its communion with God. In this way Israel could become a congregation, denoted as *qahal* ('men called up' in the Deuteronomist works and in Chronicles) or as *'edah* ('the congregation of the people', gathering round the tabernacle, *'ohel mo'ed*; the word is taken from the Priestly Code)[1]; Israel considers itself the congregation of those who have been called up by the Word of God, or as a cultic community gathered round the cultic centre. After the exile Zechariah is assured that Israel as the people of God shall no longer be a state: Jerusalem shall be as an open city, protected by Yahweh alone (ii. 8, English versions ii. 4). Nehemiah is indeed working on a new state by restoring the walls of Jerusalem, but the result is merely a church-state; politically it is entirely dependent on the Persians whose suzerainty is acknowledged. Yet in Chronicles the Jewish community is upheld against the Samaritans as the revelation of the Kingdom of God.[2]

It has often been thought that Isaiah already had this idea of the

[1] For the linguistic research see the literature mentioned above p.372 n.2; and also W. Hertzberg, *Werdende Kirche im A.T.*, 1950 pp. 18ff.; O. Plöger, *op. cit.*, pp. 37ff.; in the Septuagint and the N.T. *qahal* and *'edah* were rendered respectively by ἐκκλησία and συναγωγη.

[2] I Chron. xviiff.; cf. R. H. Pfeiffer, *Introduction to the O.T.*, p. 790; O. Plöger, *op. cit.*, pp. 51ff.

congregation in mind; we can only say, however, that he prepared the way for this idea, by connecting the expectation with a remnant: 'a remnant shall return'. On the other hand, however, Isaiah considers the remnant of the old people as the basis of the new Israel (cf. e.g. ix. 1f.); in his work the remnant and the people cannot be contrasted without more ado. Already in Deutero-Isaiah (and also after him among the Jews) it appears that the congregation of salvation and the people cannot be considered identical; there is and remains a gulf and especially in Trito-Isaiah it becomes apparent in the distinction between the people and those (individuals) who are chosen (Isa. lxv. 8ff.).

c. Israel and the world of nations

When Israel proclaims that it was placed in this world by God, this implies a conviction of a divine calling; or the reverse might even be true. Anyhow, the two ideas are closely bound up. It is at any rate remarkable that from the early beginnings of theological thought (to be found in J and his precursors) these two go together. Abraham is called and simultaneously attention is drawn to the world of nations (Gen. xii. 1–3, cf. also Amos iii. 2). Fundamentally this openness towards the outside world, the other nations, rests on the fact that this early theology was essentially theocentric in character. This quality enabled authors such as J and prophets like Amos, Isaiah, Micah, Deutero-Isaiah and others to avoid a narrow ethnical and nationalist way of thought. In part this was certainly also due to the confrontation with the world of nations in the days of David and Solomon, during the world-dominion of Assyria and Babylon and during the exile. Because Israel was confronted with the other nations again and again it was forced continually to decide on its attitude towards them and trained in a more universal way of thinking. And Israel could do this because of its faith in God. This necessity of taking a stand resulted in two kinds of reaction: on the one hand, a defensive attitude, directed against the religious, magic and cultic ideas of these nations, but on the other hand also the grateful acceptance of various cultural and spiritual values that enriched Israel's own life and thought (architecture, wisdom, art, hymns). Even in prophetical circles a purely reactionary way of thought did not come to prevail (at least the Rechabite tendencies never became predominant and hardly come into the picture in the O.T.).[1] Nor did the opposition against the threat of syncretism betray the great theological interpreters of Israel's faith (the prophets) into sectarianism of fundamental particularism. On the contrary, their faith caused them rather to include the world of nations in the

[1] See i.a. my *Hosea profeet en cultuur*, 1941.

374

communion between Israel and Yahweh. The community of God which they proclaimed was in their view based wholly on the will of Yahweh[1] and was looked upon as an act of grace (cf. Hos.xi; Deut. vii. 6ff.; ix. 4ff.; Jer.xxxi, Isa.xliii. 22ff.; li. 1ff.; lxv. 1ff.). The belief in Israel's calling and election as proclaimed in the books of the Old Testament is fundamentally viewed in the light of God's activity; it is God from whom the word proceeds every time. The recognition that the election of Israel is a matter of grace makes it possible to accept the relationship with God without turning into something absolute or fundamentally particularising it.

The root of the universalism of the Old Testament is to be found in the confession that Yahweh Himself in universal.[2] A man who knows himself to be under God's protection leaves room for relationships between God and the world outside Israel. This universalism in Israel's faith which caused ancient authors like J[3] to describe the nations as men who had sprung from a common ancestor (see p. 372) and to relate Abraham to their world also gave the prophets a new insight into God's activity among the nations (Amos ix. 7; cf. 1. 3ff. and ii. 1ff.), so that they could even welcome the nations, the enemies of their own country, as sharing in the revelation of Yahweh (Isa. ii, Micah iv and elsewhere).[4]

In Israel's hopes of the future the nations come to play a more and more important part, cf. beside the two texts mentioned last[5], also Zeph. iii; Zech. ii. 7; Isa. xix. 19ff., xxv. 6ff. These notes are also struck in the Psalms (Ps.lxxxv), as well as in the missionary message of Deutero-Isaiah (xlii, xlix; see p. 449) and the propaganda for Judaism in the Hellenist world.[6]

This spirit is also found in the book of Jonah, and perhaps in Ruth too; though Jonah does not intend to set Israel a missionary task, it fundamentally rejects particularism and dares to proclaim that God can also send his messenger to the enemies of Israel and even to the

[1] For Deuteronomy see O. Bächli, *Israel unter den Völkern*, 1962.
[2] H. Donner, *Israel unter den Völkern*, Suppl. VT, XI, 1964, pp. 171ff.
[3] On J see H. W. Wolff, *Das Kerygma des Jahwisten*, Ev. Th. 1964, pp. 73ff.
[4] The question if the willingness to adopt hymns (such as Ps.xxix, civ) into Israel's own liturgy orto use wisdom-proverbs (Prov.xxii. 24ff. and xxxf.) in teaching could also be reduced to this theological root is a problem in itself, which cannot, in my opinion, be answered affirmatively without more ado; tradition and fashion may also have played a part. Yet these things may be looked upon as important phenomena, perhaps even as phenomena attending the theological process described above. As is so often the case, it is not simply possible to distinguish between cause and effect here. Cf. also Gen.xiv. 18ff, the mutual recognition of Abraham and Melchizedek.
[5] At this point we cannot enter into the question whether the two passages were independent or used independently; see the *Introductions*. At any rate it is clear that this prophecy played a prominent part in the literary tradition.
[6] see E. Lohse, *Mission* in RGG[3] IV, pp. 972ff.; ThW, VI, pp. 727ff.; G. F. Moore, *Judaism* I, pp. 323ff.; see also Matth. xxiii. 15.

perverted city of Niniveh to warn them that judgment is coming and to convert them.

The author of the book of Job went so far as to make non-Israelites state the problems and give the testimonies to be read in the chapters iii–xxxi; but he could only do this because he was convinced that the non-Israelites, too, have to do with God and His revelation.

Of some importance is still the place occupied by foreigners in the Israelite and Jewish society in the days of the Old Testament.[1] Unlike what we find in Egypt, where the foreigners were looked upon as barbarians,[2] in Israel the foreigner – though not in the possession of full civil rights – was accepted in social life. Because from a juridical and social point of view the foreigner belonged to the weaker stratum of society he was safeguarded by protective provisions incorporated in the laws for his sake (Exod.xxii.21; xxiii.9; Levit.xix.33 and elsewhere). In certain cases and on certain conditions they can be admitted into the Israelite community (Deut.xxiii.7f.). There is though, as we pointed out on pp.374f. above, a difference in attitudes. Ezrah and Nehemiah absolutely refuse to accept foreigners, others, however, advocate their admission (Isa.lvi).

In this way various testimonies are given within the community of God concerning the relationship between the world of nations and Yahweh. The Old Testament does not give a simple answer to the problem of this relationship, certainly not a negative answer. Though the idolatry of the other nations and of the Canaanites in particular, was condemned strongly, a relationship between Yahweh and these nations is not denied (cf. Amos ix.7, certain prophecies and some of the Psalms). The book of Job and Gen.xiv.18ff. really go even further by taking seriously the present knowledge of God of non-Israelites as well; in both the vital issue is the belief in God the Creator: apparently the concept of creation, which is also found outside Israel, is acknowledged to the common property.

[1] On this see A.Bertholet, *Die Stellung der Israeliten und der Juden zu den Fremden;* F.Horst, *Fremde,* RGG³ II, pp.1125ff.
[2] B.A.Stricker, *Brief van Aristeas, loc. cit.*

1. *Motives*

A. The foundation of all action: the religious nature of morality

In all religions the relation between man and man is fundamentally determined by the *relation between God and man.*[2] Always and everywhere religion and ethics are bound more or less closely together.[3] In Israel this connection becomes very evident; there is a strongly developed consciousness that the foundations of the moral laws rest in Yahweh. To prove this we need only remember two things:

1. the Old Testament teaches that a summary of the basic moral principles in the ethical Decalogue (Exod. xx; Deut. v) was given by Yahweh at the beginning of His revelation to Israel;

2. the wisdom-literature (wisdom is a more pedagogical expression of the moral element in religion, different from that given by the laws; fundamentally the laws are looked upon as received directly from God by revelation, while wisdom is a sit were the human reflection of this) proclaims that the ground of true wisdom is the fear of the Lord (Prov. i. 7; ix. 10; Ps. cxi. 10; Job xxviii. 28, Prov. iii. 5ff.).

Considered from a historical and material point of view morality has, of course, also a natural background in social life and this manifests itself still very clearly in various relations (for instance, slavery, polygamy,[4] but this should not prevent us from doing full justice to the religious connection. In the whole of ethical ideas religion and morals have merged.

It will probably always remain very difficult to effect a clear distinction between the religious and the natural factors in this merging of religious and ethical elements,[5] but one thing is certainly wrong: to make it appear as if the whole of the religious and moral ideas had sprung from only one of these two elements. For both these lines of

---

[1] W.S.Bruce, *The ethics of the O.T.*[2], 1909; W.A.L.Elmslie, 'Ethics', in H.Wheeler Robinson, *Record and Revelation*, 1938, pp. 275ff.; J. Hempel, *Das Ethos des A.T.*, 1938; W.Eichrodt, 'God and man', *Theology*, II, pp. 231ff.; N.W.Porteous, 'The basis of the ethical Teaching of the Prophets', in H.H.Rowley, *Studies in O.T. prophecy*, dedicated to Prof.Th.H.Robinson, 1950, pp. 143ff.; also J.Pedersen, *Israel*, I–II.
[2] Procksch, *Theologie*, pp. 677ff.; E.Jacob, 'Les bases théologiques de l'Ethique de l'A.T.', *Supp. V.T.* VII, 1959, pp. 38ss.; J. v.d. Ploeg, *Mens tegenover mens in het O.T.* (oration), 1960.
[3] On Egypt see S.Morenz, *Ägyptische Religion*, 1960, pp. 117ff.; on Mesopotamia W.G.Lambert, 'Morals in Ancient Mesopotamia', *Jaarbericht E.O.L.* 15, 1957/8, pp. 184/6; idem, *Babylonian Wisdom Literature*, 1960.
[4] Of course the wisdom-literature gives many examples of human behaviour in daily life.
[5] Cf. N.W.Porteous, *op. cit.*, p. 155.

thought find their adherents among Biblical scholars, but both are one-sided and hence incorrect. In the former case (namely when the ethical values in the Old Testament are simply looked upon as inspired by God) the morality of the Old Testament is made into something completely absolute; in this way it seems possible to solve all moral problems, even those of our days, with the help of the Old Testament, a point of view that must be considered extremely dangerous to Christian ethics. In the latter the Old Testament morality becomes an entirely fortuitous social phenomenon that has only historical importance and can no longer have any fundamental meaning for us; from a theological point of view this latter notion is no less contestable than the former; it arose from the denial of the spiritual background of Israelite morality, or rather from the denial of the fact that this religion rests on divine revelation and that this religion is part of the basis of these moral ideas.[1]

Theology admits the value of the ethics of the Old Testament for the present, too, on the ground of its confession that the revelation of God in the Old Testament was fundamentally confirmed in Jesus Christ; but theology will also always assert the necessity of extending these ethics further, particularly in those fields where the New Testament brought a renovating influence: monogamy; the love of one's enemy; the recognition of the mercy of God for every sinner who repents; the following up of the prophetic victory of the moral element over the cultic motif in religion; equality of all men before God, who regards neither race, nor people, nor any particular initiation rite, etc., but only the heart.[2]

Old Testament morality is therefore not autonomous, but quite the contrary; in this respect it is diametrically opposed to Greek and modern philosophical ethics, which attempt to build up a morality on the basis of human reason[3] starting from an *idea of the good.*

The Old Testament is conscious of the fact that its moral demands were given by Yahweh. He it is who knows what is good. See Prov. iii. 5ff.: 'Trust in the Lord with all thine heart; and lean not unto thine own understanding. In all thy ways acknowledge Him, and He shall direct thy paths. Be not wise in thine own eyes: fear the 'Lord and depart from evil'; cf. also Micah vi. 8. He it is who has taught Israel in the Law what is good and what evil.

That God alone knows what is good also emerges in the Paradise-

---

[1] Fundamentally this seems to be the attitude of J. Pedersen (cf. 'Die Auffassung vom A.T.', in $\mathcal{Z}.A.W.$, 1931, pp. 180f.; and *Israel*, I–II, p. 310).
[2] Compare also H. van Oyen, *Christelijke Ethica*, 1946, p. 63.
[3] The virtues are known by φρονησις, cf. D. Loenen, *Eusebeia en de cardinale deugden*, 1960, pp. 85ff.

378

narrative: man must leave the knowledge of good and evil to Him. The idea of the knowledge of good and evil is used in a very general sense but may also imply the ethical values. With respect to ethics, too, it is God who has true insight and from whom man receives His knowledge; for man is entirely dependent upon Him.[1]

For that reason the conception of 'conscience' is never, or hardly ever, to be met with in the Old Testament.[2] Here and there the word *leb* (heart) might perhaps be translated in this way (1 Sam. xxiv. 6; 2 Sam. xxiv. 10). *At any rate the human conscience is not the starting-point of the knowledge of good and evil.* The words of St. Paul 'I had not known sin, but by the law' (Rom. vii. 7) are also quite true of the Old Testament. In the Paradisenarrative that which we call conscience is 'awakened as soon as the commandment is broken and the consciousness of the nearness of God has also become a living awareness': 'Conscience has been awakened as the "Innewerden eines positiven Sichverfehlens gegen Gott" ("the realization of a positive transgression against God")'.[3] When the Old Testament makes a theological statement it appears that it is only God to whom the knowledge of good and evil may be ascribed.[4]

On the ground of the dependence of ethical knowledge upon God we must therefore say that the morality of the Old Testament has more affinity with the ethics of the ancient Eastern world than with those of Greek and Western civilization. In ancient Eastern ethics the deity was also known as the giver of the rules of law,[5] for instance Shamash, the sun-god, gives Hammurabi the code of law he is to enact, and is therefore ultimately looked upon as the legislator. In the Babylonian world the deity is also found as the protector of law and justice, particularly Shamash, the sun-god and Sin, the moongod;

[1] Cf. also C. v. Leeuwen, 'God, de Koning en de armen in Ps. 72', *N. Th. T.* 1957, p. 29f.
[2] Indeed, it is not frequently met with in the N.T., either. Cf. H. van Oyen, *Christelijke Ethica*, 1946, pp. 18ff. Conscience, in the meaning of the autonomous sense of justice inherent in man, it the product of an a-religious humanism: see also Van Oyen's contribution to *Wending*, 1950. In later times the Jews do not know the concept of conscience in the western sense of the word, cf. R. I. Zwi Werblowsky, *Das Gewissen in jüdischer Sicht*, in: das Gewissen (Studien Jung-Institut VII), 1958.
[3] J. Hempel, *Das Ethos des A. T.*, 1938, p. 191.
[4] Sometimes the O.T. speaks popularly of the popular custom as the standard of good and evil ('such a thing is not done in Israel', cf. Gen. xxxiv. 7, II Sam. xiii. 12, both times in a case of rape, which was apparently considered a very grave offence in Israel; the man must marry the girl and is no more allowed to divorce her, Deut. xxii. 28f.). We can hardly attach any theological importance to this statement. According to Prof. Dr. J. H. Semmelink, J. J. P. Valeton held that this wording, which apparently presupposes customary law as the basis of morality, proves that the *Torah* (as God's commandment) had been incorporated wholly in the life of the people. That would, of course, put quite a new face on the matter (see E. Gerstenberger, *op. cit.*).
[5] Cf. Lambert in J. E. O. L., 15, pp. 191.

but other deities, too, protect law, which is often to be put on a level with order, world-order; among the Babylonians we even find deities such as *Kittu* and *Misharu*, Law and Justice; in the western Semitic world there probably also was a God *Ṣedeq* (justice, righteousness; cf. Malkiṣedeq: 'my king is *Ṣedeq*'). But besides these there existed also other notions; for instance, that the gods deceived each other or committed other vices and even brought iniquity among mankind,[1] so that Roth's statement[2] is not incorrect: 'Polytheism involved a variety of standards, that is to say, no standard at all; monotheism substituted the principle of unity, one Judge of all the earth with one law for all.'

It is this last element (its absolute validity), that makes the ethics of the Old Testament transcend fundamentally the ethics of other ancient Eastern religions. For there is one will, that of Yahweh, that dominates the whole of life and is valid among all circles of the community.[3] This is not merely a formal principle but rather an element that has immediate implications for practical life. The whole people forms a community around Yahweh and each is equally bound to Him, the king as well as the lowest subject. David is bound to the prohibition of adultery as well as any of his subjects, and Ahab dare not interfere with Naboth's proprietary rights, even if he is the king. Jezebel does this without any scruple, though she does seek a legal form to save an appearance of justice. As regards adultery, it appears from the first tablet of the Gilgamesh-epic that ancient Eastern kings applied a different morality to themselves from that which they applied to their subjects.

The fact that among Israel the moral code applies absolutely, from high to low, is most clearly evident from the activity of the prophets who proclaim their judgment irrespective of persons; and in the laws, too, it is pointed out frequently that people must act thus (for instance Exod. xxiii. 2ff.; Lev. xix. 15; cf. also Deut. iv. 8ff.). The absoluteness of law and justice is therefore an established fact in the Old Testament, because both have been given by the one God. Compare, for instance, how in the so-called Code of Holiness, Lev. xvii–xxvi, the words: 'Ye shall be holy, for I the Lord your God am holy' are repeated again and again to emphasize the law. The laws, and particularly also the

---

[1] See for example the discussion between the believer and the doubter, *Jaarb. E.O.L.*, 1935, p. 106: 'the gods have given man lies and untruth for ever'. Cf. also W.B. Kristensen, *De goddelijke Bedrieger;* A.H. Edelkoort, *Zondebesef*, pp. 72ff. and A. van Selms, *Babylonische termini*, pp. 97ff.

[2] *The Legacy of Israel*, p. 434, quoted by Elmslie in *Record and Revelation*, p. 280.

[3] Compare also Porteous, *op. cit.*, p. 152; J. Kaufman, *Toledoth Ha'emoena Hajisraelieth*, on the legislation on Mount Sinai (quoted in *Ned. Irs. Weekblad*, May 15 1953, p. 8); Lambert, *Jaarb. E.O.L.* 15, pp. 186f.

moral laws (Lev. xviii–xx) are the expression of Yahweh's holy will; thus the demand arises for the sanctification of man's life.

This awareness is found not only in these later laws, taken to belong to the exilic period, but also in Deuteronomy; the earliest parts of the Old Testament, the Decalogue and the Book of the Covenant already show the close connection between the moral and the religious element, though we don not find here a sanctification of life in general.

This may also explain why in the Old Testament moral and cultic laws are found side by side again and again; the two fields can never be separated entirely. Yet it is, on the other hand, not quite right, either, to say that in the Old Testament the two fields are entirely mixed up. On a superficial view this may seem to be the case, but it is not true, certainly not of the later laws. When for example in Lev. xix we suddenly find cultic commandments in between the commandments of 3f. and 11f. (which certainly belong together) this may be accounted for by literary criticism; the verses 5–10 disturb the original connection. In the same way a passage such as Exod. xxiii. 1–9 must also be looked upon as an originally independent part, etc.[1]

Following the line of this literary criticism we find that in many respects the Old Testament has already classified the moral, cultic and juridical laws. This becomes even more evident when we pay attention to the preaching of the prophets, which often even oppose the moral demands to the cultic commandments (Amos v; Mic. vi; Hos. vi; Isa. i; Jer. vii); and also from the fact that the wisdom-literature does not really make any cultic demands!

It may therefore be considered an established fact that on the one hand the Old Testament makes a distinction between these various fields; it is theologically no longer so naïve in these things as many other ancient Eastern writings are; cf. for example this quotation from a Babylonian treatise on morals:[2] 'He who touches a passing menstruating woman, shall be unclean for six days. He who does not honour his father shall perish soon. In whose stove a fire has been lit, for him the blessing of God has been provided'. In the Egyptian book of the dead and other ancient Eastern wrtings we also find all sorts of things jumbled together in the same way.

On the other hand we must also admit that in the Old Testament the prophetic and 'wisdom' range of ideas did not come to dominate absolutely and that for that reason the moral element did not become all-important in religion. The cultic and ritual element (clean and unclean) was also retained, and is frequently connected directly with

[1] See my *Literatuur van Oud-Israël*, l.c.
[2] B. Meissner, *Babylonien und Assyrien*, II, p. 421.

the ethical and social element (cf. the book of Deuteronomy).[1] Thus cultic, ritual, and moral commandments together form the expression of God's will in the Old Testament. To a certain extent the first-mentioned were placed last; cf. that (ultimately at any rate) it was the ethical Decalogue (Exod. xx) and not the cultic Decalogue (Exod. xxiii. 12ff., and 34) that came to be of central importance and was connected with Mount Sinai. This is a confession! But on the other hand the multitude of cultic and ritual commandments predominated over the ethical and religious commandments, at any rate in the period after the exile and of the origin of the New Testament.

For that reason the fact that Jesus Christ established the two commandments of the love of God and of one's neighbour as the summary of the law (Matt. xxii. 36ff.) remains of great importance. In doing this, He both maintained and kept together the religious as well as the moral element (cf. Deut. vi. 5 and Lev. xix. 18) and thus placed them together in the centre of religious life. This in contrast to some old rabbis who only praised the love of one's neighbour as the most important element.[2] It is sometimes asserted by Jewish scholars that in the field of morality Jesus did not create anything new. But in its absoluteness, its limiting and combining recapitulation this word of the New Testament must in fact be looked upon as something new: by bringing together exactly these two from the mass of the Old Testament moral, religious and juridical commandments, Christ brought out in what way religion and ethics must support and pervade each other. And by doing so He crowned the work of the prophets and brought all at once the renovation of religion which had already been prepared by them.

B. Two guiding principles of ethical action: sense of community and individual responsibility

Already in the Old Testament the central motive of moral life is the *sense of community*.[3] Social, historical and religious motives all combine here in a remarkably felicitous manner. The strong social connection between the Semitic tribes which are divided into clans and families, a connection which rests on real or supposed consanguinity, plays an important part in Israel; it is nor necessary to adduce evidence for the view that the ideas of blood-relationship and community are very

[1] Noth generally opposes the separation of these fields and thinks that 'noch jedes Lebensgebiet seine Beziehungen zu kultischen Begehungen hatte', *Die Gesetze im Pentateuch*, Ges. Studien, p. 68.
[2] For example Hillel in a negative form: 'Do not do to thy neighbour what is unpleasant to thyself. That is the whole of the Torah, the rest is its interpretation'. Cf. Strack-Billerbeck, *Kommentar z.N.T. aus Talmud und Midrasch*, I, p. 907; cf. also pp. 353ff.
[3] See also W. Eichrodt, *Krisis der Gemeinschaft*, Rektoratsrede Basel, 1953, p. 3.

much alive among Israel, for they are found ready to hand in the narrative literature of the Old Testament. In his above-mentioned book *Israel*, I–II, Pedersen has set out completely this structure of Israelite life.[1] This natural bond of connection is strengthened by historical and particularly by religious motives. The tribes of Israel are bound together not only by bloodrelationship, but also, and actually probably even more, by their common history. Generally speaking we may say that a people is welded into a unity by its history. With respect to Israel this may also be considered an established fact, though it is impossible to estimate quite correctly the part played by history in this process in itself. This is as difficult as weighing accurately and according to the standards of scholarship the importance of the social factor for the origin of Israel's community against the other factors. But if from a historical point of view there is one thing that we may look upon as an established fact it is that on the one hand a common descent played an important part in Israel but that on the other hand various foreign elements met in this people.[2] From the earliest times a historical common destiny linked the tribes together (Kenites); and afterwards, even in the period of David and afterwards, a considerable number of Canaanites (and probably also of other groups such as the Philistines) was received among the Israelites by conquest and intermarriage – the population of the towns of northern Israel (cf. Judges i) which only became Israelite at a later date, particularly Shechem (Judges viiif.) All these also formed part of the Israel that existed in history between the years 1000 and 600 B.C., the Israel among which the sacred books mainly originated.

But besides the social and the historical factors there is still a third element that interest us particularly from a theological point of view, and that is the religious factor. For it was Yahwism that advanced most strongly the development of Israel into a people, to an even greater extent than the other factors, and at certain moments at any rate, decisively. We may think here of Moses, of the prophets and of the period of the exile; so that we may indeed say that it was Yahweh who called Israel into being and maintained it.[3]

This religious factor must be separated most emphatically from the social element. That is why the connection between Yahweh and the people cannot be taken to be so immediate as was done by Pedersen. On account of the revelational character of this religion Yahwism

---

[1] Cf. M. Weber, *Das antike Judentum*, and A. Causse, *Du groupe ethnique à la communauté religieuse*, 1937; S. Nyström, *Beduinentum und Jahwismus*, 1946.
[2] On this problem viewed, for example, from an anthropological point of view cf. C. U. Ariëns Kappers and L. W. Parr, *An introduction to anthropology of the Near East*, 1934, ch. IV, pp. 43–73.
[3] Compare, for example, Hempel, *Ethos*, pp. 77ff., see also above pp. 372ff.

became a binding power. Yahweh, the divine Saviour who proved to be *the Power* on earth, placed Himself in communication with the people by the intermediation of Moses and thus made His spiritual demands at the same time. This relation entered into with Yahweh (see pp. 167ff.) bound the tribes together into a religious community in a way unknown in the ancient polytheistic East.[1]

The faith in the one God of the Covenant gave the social and historical factors already uniting the tribes of Israel their sanctification and therefore their absolute confirmation; it advanced this unity so particularly because the belief in God of Yahwism was so exclusive and made any other religious ties impossible. It was in this atmosphere of the spiritual community that the demands made not only in Deuteronomy and in Lev. xix, but even as early as the Book of the Covenant, could spring up. We should fail to do justice to the spiritual nature of Israelite ethics if we were to agree with Pedersen's remark: 'The commandment to love is thus not a dogmatic invention, but a direct expression of the character of the soul and the organism of family and people'; or again that 'the basis of all Israelite ethos is the common feeling, love, and according to the nature of the compact it must, in its innermost essence, be a family feeling'.[2]

Here Pedersen has not done justice to the fact of revelation, nor, in fact to the importance of religion in general in Israel.[3] When Lev. xix. 18 concludes a series of social commandments by the words: 'Thou shalt love thy neighbour as thyself', these words are followed by: 'I am the Lord'. In other words: this commandment is transmitted and known not only in a social but in a religious and theological connection.[4] This is equally true of the commandment to love the

[1] To state it again quite clearly: the fact that Israel outgrew the status of the small Canaanite peoples which were continually at war with each other, or of the groups of tribes East and South of Palestine, is due to the moral and religious power of Yahwism. This remains true, even if from a historical point of view it would have to be admitted that the 'tribes of Israel' did not enter Canaan simultaneously. For the group of tribes that originated around Moses must be looked upon as the spiritual and 'national' core of the people. On the other hand this does not mean, however, that one may establish a contrast between Israel as a people and as a community and say that Israel is a community and not a people (thus J. C. Hoekendijk, *Kerk en volk in de duitse zendingswetenschap* (doctorate thesis Utrecht), 1948, pp. 234f.).
[2] *Israel*, I–II, pp. 310, 309; cf. also *Z.A.W.*, 1931, pp. 180f.
[3] The parallel from the history of religion that may be referred to, the linking together of the Arabian tribes by Mahomet, suffices to prove that it is impossible to exclude the element of revelation. Mahomet's influence is inseparable from his prophecies!
[4] The general form of this word is clearly *theological* in character, the reference to Yahweh is religious. In The *Vassal Treaties of Esarhaddon* (edited by D. Wiseman, 1958, ll. 49f. and 266ff.) we also find the demand that the vassal shall love his king as himself (as his life). Here the demand is focused on a special person, the king. This is not the kind of world in which general moral rules are found. *What applied to the relationship between vassal and suzerain in Assyria was made the basis of the whole of social relations in Israel.* J. Pedersen is right in stating that the demand that in certain cases a

stranger as oneself (Lev. xix. 34), which is followed by the words: 'for ye were strangers in the land of Egypt: I am the Lord your God'. This statement very emphatically refers to the history of salvation; and thus this commandment as handed down to us really appears to be qualified 'dogmatically' or at any rate 'religiously and theologically'.

Because of the conviction that Israel was a national community as well as a community of faith Israelites could recognize each other as brothers and the words brother and compatriot could be considered real synonyms.

For that reason the struggle against the suppression of the poor by the rich, against the unequal distribution of riches (Isa. v. 8; Mic. ii. 2; Amos) was conducted in the name of Yahweh. In the ancient times of the Judges we read of a divine judgment of the tribes against Benjamin in connection with moral offences (Judges xviiiff.), from which the moral character of the link that held the tribes together is apparent. In this connection we must also point to several moral religious regulations that were included in the earliest laws, particularly the 'apodictic' laws[1] in the Book of the Covenant (Exod. xxiff.).

The ethico-religious nature of verses such as Lev. xix 18 and 34 does not, therefore, stand alone and is, indeed, quite apparent in the words of this whole chapter. We may moreover remark that the absolute form in which the commandment is given: 'Thou shalt love thy neighbour as thyself', also deserves our full attention. To love *as thyself* is the greatest demand that can be made, it is love pure and simple. An Oriental with his concrete way of expressing things could not express the idea of absolute love more clearly than this.[2] The absoluteness and universality of brotherly love could only be worded

---

man should be willing to lay down his life for a member of his tribe (when for example a relative or chieftain is in danger in battle) fits in with the social structure of the nomadic world. But this demand is inconceivable in the ancient nomadic world as a *general* commandment with regards to every compatriot. See my paper on Levit. xix. 18 read at Berne on Nov. 28th, 1964, included in ThZ (Basel) 1966, pp. 1ff.

[1] Cf. A. Alt, *Die Ursprünge des irs. Rechts*, 1934; E. Gerstenberger, *op. cit.*

[2] Of Jonathan it is said once or twice that he loved David as his own soul (I Sam. xviii. 1, xx. 17), and David, too, loved Jonathan (11 Sam. i. 26) and for a long time kept feeling a strong bond with him (11 Sam. ix). In *Zwei Glaubensweisen* (p. 69) Buber thinks on account of the construction with *le* that the verb *'ahab* of Levit. xix has a more general meaning: to be affectionate to. W. L. Moran, *The Ancient Near Eastern Background of the Love of God in Dt.* 1963, pp. 77ff., looks upon the demand to love as a demand to maintain the covenant-relationship; he emphasizes the meaning: friendship rather than: love. He is right in so far that the emotional aspect of the word 'love' should not be emphasized.

It is comical (or worse!) that moral theologians should frequently and in all seriousness have taken the words 'as thyself' to mean a restriction! In the sense of: not more than thyself! See also St. Paul in Eph. v. 29. For this problem as a whole see ThZ (Basel) 1966, pp. 1ff.

in this way on the basis of the knowledge of the greatness of God's love which includes the whole national community. This demand is only made of those who belong to the community of God.

In the foregoing pages we have pointed to the communal sense as an element of ethical life. This element is qualified spiritually, religiously. The Old Testament law of revelation (*torah*) knows that man must live for the community with God from which he derives life.

For that reason it does not clash with another element that also takes up a very prominent place in Israel, namely the idea of individual responsibility. Often these two spiritual elements are opposed to each other in the description of Old Testament ethics: it was made to seem as if the individual element did not come to the fore in the spiritual life of Israel until a late period (Jeremiah) and the collective element remained predominant until the exile.[1] But on the contrary these two elements, the social and the individual, pervade and streng then each other. We may even say, indeed, that the demand 'thou shalt love thy neighbour as thyself', in this form (2nd person singular!), remains unaccountable if the individual responsibility of one man for the other had been unknown in Israel.[2]

The view that personal responsibility was originally unknown in Israel cannot therefore be considered correct; and a reference to the history of 2 Sam.xxiv, where the people are punished because of David's sin, is no proof, either; for 2 Sam.9ff., which is at least as old and probably older still, makes it very clear (in 2 Sam.xif. and also in xvi) that David is certainly punished individually, too, for his personal sins! The king, too, is personally responsible for his acts. That we read something different in 2 Sam.xxiv and in Joshua vii (Achan) does not prove that individual responsibility was unknown in Israel but that it also knew of a broader, social responsibility besides this individual responsibility. When David sins *as king*, as in 2 Sam.xxiv, and therefore as the representative of the people, the people may be punished with him. And Achan sinned as head of the family and hid the stolen objects in his tent and for that reason all those who lived in the tent (and were, in a sense, accessories) were punished.

This collective responsibility implies that a man may be held responsible both as an individual and as a member of the community,

---

[1] Compare above pp.418ff.; and D.Klein Wassink, *Persoonlijke religie in Israël*, doctorate thesis Groningen, 1918 and now N.P.Bratsiotis, *Die Stellung des Individuums im A.T.*, 1962 (German summary of the New-Greek book).
[2] M.Löhr, 'Sozialismus und Individualismus im A.T.', *Beih. Z.A.W.*, X, 1906; E. Gerstenberger, *op. cit.*, pp.95ff., strongly emphasizes the educative nature of such proverbs; the adolescent young man is taught them so that he may profit by them in later years.

even if he is not directly guilty personally.[1] What we find in Ezekiel xviii is apparently no new doctrine but serves to combat the tragic view of life, the self-pity of the exiles, a notion that may spring from a one-sided moral collectivism and prevents true consciousness of guilt. Ezekiel wants to establish the message of God's absolute justice, even with respect to the individual; it must rather be considered in connection with the pastoral duty of the prophet than as an innovation.[2] The fact that these 'collective' and 'individual' elements go together is in our opinion quite evident from the opening words of the book of Deuteronomy. Von Rad[3] thought that the variations of subject (plural or singular in the address to the people) were connected with a weakening of the awareness of the unity of the people, viz. the singular form of address would denote the people as one whole, the plural as a group of individuals. Even if this may be true from the point of view of grammatical form, the fact that the two sources were very soon united proves in our opinion that there is here no question of a fundamental change of view-point – the two may be put on a level: the people may be considered as a unity and the individual members together may be addressed with a plural form. When we see how free Deutero-Isaiah is in this respect – namely that he (almost like a modern preacher) now includes himself among the people and speaks of 'we', then again uses 'they' and at the same time also 'it' (cf. ch. xlii. 24f.) – this feature no longer astonishes us. The people forms a *corporate personality* (H. Wheeler Robinson) and as such it may be looked upon both as a unity and as a multitude.

The 'individual' element in Israel is strongly based on the doctrine of the image of God. Though in this form this doctrine may be of late date (P), it is certainly admissible that the idea behind it should be much older. We may remember here the strongly personal depiction of the figures and their relation to God in the earliest Israelite stories (for instance the history of Abraham in J), in which Yahweh is not only interested in the patriarch but also in the Egyptian slave Hagar, (ch. xvi) and in the 'righteous' men at Sodom (ch. xviiif.).

C. The atmosphere: the 'humanitas'

The Old Testament has a strongly developed sense of the peculiar nature of the humane. The cosmos is geocentric, the earth is anthropocentric, as we might put it for a moment, without, however, losing sight of the fact that the anthropocentric view can only exist as the

[1] On this problem in contemporary ethics see H. van Oyen, *Verantwortungsgefühl im modernen Denken*, Basel, 1948, esp. pp. 14f.
[2] Cf. now also W. Eichrodt, *Krisis der Gemeinschaft*.
[3] *Das Gottesvolk in Dt.*, 1929; see J. H. Hospers, *De Numeruswisseling in het boek Dt.*, 1947, pp. 101f.

consequence of a truly theocentric theology. In the narrative of the Creation and in Ps. viii this emerges very clearly: man is nothing, a mere creature but yet – wonderful mercy of God – he is invested with the highest authority on earth!

The idea of man's self-respect in Israel becomes very apparent when we compare the appreciation of man in his relation to the animal world and to the demon world as found elsewhere (see pp. 426ff., 422ff.). The latter, the demon world has almost entirely been lost sight of, because of the theocentric range of ideas; and, in contrast to the rest of the Eastern world, the animal world has become altogether infra-human. Thus man is thrown on God alone and, further, on himself! This gave the world as Israel knew it an almost modern character; by Yahwism man was delivered from all fear of the infra-human and the demonic. Men are closely linked together. The Old Testament might be called the most humanely minded book of the ancient world.[1] The strongly anthropomorphic and anthropopathic nature of Yahweh may be adduced to prove this. This 'humanism', however, is wholly religious in nature. The relation between man and man is dominated by the relation between man and God (see A); as Yahweh lives in a community with man, man is also linked with his fellow-man by *chesed* (faithfulness). Men linked together by Yahweh are brothers. Israel is a community of brothers (see above, B). Within this community men must help each other as much as lies in their power. And, like the relation between God and man, that between man and man is also personal throughout. The background of the words 'faithfulness', 'righteousness' and 'justice', without which the Israelite community cannot exist, is the idea of the Covenant. Lofthouse[2] remarks: 'The Hebrews, like most of the ancients, lived in a world of covenant, not of contract. It is true that they had only one word, *b'rith*, for the two English expressions. But it is still truer that they did not understand the idea of contract at all. Every bargain was to them a matter of covenant, of personal relations'. For the Israelite justice pure and simple ('*summum ius*') is no justice at all.

Hence communal sense (*chesed*) is the principal moral conception.[3] The first demand that results from it, is the maintaining of law (*mishpat*) and justice (*sedeq or sedaqah*), i.e. to give somebody his due, to do justice to somebody. Justice is something positive; it aims at

---

[1] Cf. also J. Hempel, *Das Ethos des A.T.*, 1938, pp. 194ff.; O. S. Rankin, *op. cit.*, pp. 1ff.

[2] W. F. Lofthouse, 'Chen and Chesed in the O.T.', *Z.A.W.*, 1933, pp. 29ff.

[3] See N. Glueck, 'Das Wort chesed im alttest. Sprachgebrauch', *Beih. Z.A.W.*, 47, 1927; Lofthouse, loc. cit.; N. H. Snaith, *The distinctive Ideas of the O.T.*, 1944, pp. 94ff. ('The covenant love'); see further literature in H. H. Rowley, *The biblical doctrine of election*, p. 22 n. 2.

restoring the law that has been infringed first of all by saving the one who had suffered by this violation of the law and on the other side by punishing the one who had made somebody else suffer. The king who judges his people, the righteous king, helps the poor (Ps. lxxii. 1 ff., 12f.); the truly righteous man who puts on righteousness (Job xxix. 14) is the man who delivers widows and assists the blind (verse 12ff.).[1] The word-stems denoting justice, both *ṣdq* and *šfṭ*, though they are both used most frequently in juridical and political life do not have a theoretical or exclusively forensic, juridical meaning, starting from a given law, but denote the task of the king and the judge who have to restore justice (which, as we remarked above, implies aid as well as judgment); they procure the *ṣedaqah*, i.e. they cause justice to prevail; thus each man gets the share to which he has a right, and Yahweh is honoured (Jer. xxii. 16).

Ṣaddiq is somebody or something that is as he or it should be; the meaning of the word is '*real*', 'pure', 'true',[2] that which agrees with the end to which it has been created, that which inwardly, fundamentally corresponds to its external appearance, and therefore actually fulfils the function for which (he) it exists. In *mishpaṭ* the idea of the established norm is more prominent, particularly in the later laws; but the original meaning is rather use and wont, custom, especially that which is in keeping with a certain relationship in life and therefore that which is proper.[3] Maintaining 'law' and 'justice' is therefore to take care that the true relations are not disturbed (*mishpaṭ*) and that the integrity of each man in the community is maintained fully (*ṣedaqah*). Only thus is the demand of the *chesed* done full justice, and can the Covenant-relation in the people continue to exist.

For that reason every relation is truly humane. In this community a slave, for example, is not a commodity but a human being, too. There are several traits that show how the humane element plays a special part in the Old Testament laws (see pp. 420f.), though this does not mean that it broke through and re-created the ancient Eastern social strata.[4] Not only was the slave admitted to the communion of the cult but it is emphasized that he must also share in the

[1] Cf. J. Hempel, *Das Ethos des A. T.*, pp. 151–162; H. van Oyen, 'Liefde, gerechtigheid en Recht', *Ned. Th. T.*, 1946, pp. 27ff., *Evangelische Ethik*, 1952, pp. 31f.; Leivestad, *Guds straffende Rettfertighed*, 1946; C. van Leeuwen, *op. cit.*, pp. 212ff.; see also his *Sociaal besef in Israël*, passim.
[2] Compare, for instance, K. H. Fahlgreen, *Ṣedaqa*, 1932; B. D. Eerdmans, *Godsdienst van Israël*, II, p. 86; N. H. Snaith, *op. cit.*, pp. 51ff.; Dr. W. ten Boom, *Oud-Testamentische Kernbegrippen*, 1948, pp. 36ff., and my contribution on Semasiology in *Vox Theologica*, 1950; besides it F. Rosenthal, 'Ṣedaqa, charity', *H.U.C.A.*, 1950/1, pp. 411ff.; C. v. Leeuwen in *N. Th. T.* 1957/8, p. 25.
[3] See J. Pedersen, *op. cit.*, I, pp. 348ff.
[4] See Prov. xiv. 31, xvii. 5, xxii. 2; cf. Hempel, *Ethos*, pp. 202, 268.

rest on the Sabbath (Exod. xxiii. 12; Deut. v. 14f.). The author of the book of Job can even make Job say that he has not despised the cause of his manservant or maidservant, even in a quarrel with himself (Job xxxi. 13); this means complete equivalence of lord and servant as human beings. Of course, this does not mean that here equality is recognized! In the wisdom-literature poverty, for instance, is still considered as something intended by Yahweh. In this respect, too, the break-through was not really effected until the New Testament (Acts ii; iv) – though the Christian Church very soon lost sight of it again completely!

D. Man's disposition

In the teaching of the Old Testament, in the first place by the prophets but also throughout the rest of the Scriptures, wisdom and historical literature, man's disposition, the heart, is again and again considered to be of decisive importance for man's activity.

It would, however, certainly not be correct to say that Israel was the first to discover the importance of the heart, one's inner self to human life; for in the non-Israelite wisdom-literature this importance was understood. We have in mind here especially the splendid Babylonian Proverbs of Utnapishtim.[1]

Nor can we simply say that the morality concerning man's inner self entirely dominates the Old Testament, for it is exactly the sinful act that is considered as sin. Generally speaking this is the case particularly in the Proverbs and in the historical literature.

But nevertheless the emphasis upon man's disposition remains so great in the Old Testament, especially with the prophets, that we may say that the spiritual message of the Old Testament is primarily moral. The emphasis upon truth and justice, the claiming of the heart of man for the service of God, forms the basis of this teaching.

But this should not, as is sometimes done, be taken in a modern mystical sense, as if the pious Israelite thought in terms of the heart as man's 'Eternal Self', the special nature of which should be preserved – for the heart of man is as it should be only when it listens to *the Commandments of the Lord* (Deut. vi. 6). For we must not expect to find an autonomous morality concerning man's disposition (see A).

We may add here some statements to throw light upon the first paragraph above. One of the most striking examples is the well-known text from the later, post-exilic parts of Proverbs (from the

---

[1] See a translation of this in B. Gemser, *Spreuken*, II, etc. (Tekst en Uitleg), 1931, p. 51; Gressmann, *Altorient. Texte z.A.T.*², pp. 291ff.; on Egypt see: S. Morenz, *op. cit.*, p. 142; on Mesopotamia: Lambert, *op. cit.*; also S. du Toit, *Bybelse en Babilonies-Assierische Spreuke*, 1942.

introduction to the book): 'Keep thy heart with all diligence; for out of it are the issues of life' (Prov. iv. 23). The heart is here considered as the centre of life; it should certainly be taken in the moral and spiritual, not in the physical sense here. The life meant here is life in the fullest sense of the word, comprising life on this earth, joy, happiness, and peace with God. The poet of the Proverbs is here of the opinion that true life is only possible if man keeps his heart, his inner self; i.e. if man takes care of it (the verb *naṣar* – 'to guard'!), if he does not allow it to go the wrong way. For that reason, as Gemser[1] rightly remarks, these verses should not be separated from the preceding verses, where the words of life are mentioned (20–22), the words of wordly wisdom, founded on tradition and revelation. Out of the heart are the issues of life, but this life is guaranteed in the fulfilment of God's will – this is the short summary of the outlook on life of the Old Testament.

In a quite different manner it becomes evident that the prophets look upon the heart as the only thing that counts in life. Not what man does is in the first instance decisive for man's action, but in what spirit something is done, the attitude of the heart to things; cf. Isa. xxix. 13f. 'Forasmuch as this people draw near me with their mouth and with their lips do honour me, but have removed their heart far from me, and their fear toward me (= their religion) is taught by the precept of men (verse 14), therefore, behold, I will proceed to do a marvellous work among this people, even a marvellous work and a wonder: for the wisdom of their wise men shall perish, and the understanding of their prudent men shall be hid.'

An acquired religion (however correct it may be) is nothing;[2] the only thing of importance is that the heart should serve God (cf. Deut. vi. 5). We should also think of Mic. vi. 8. In Jer. iv. 4 (Deut. x. 16; xxx. 6) the demand is made, as emphatically as possible, to dedicate one's heart to God before the sanctification of the body by circumcision. In spiritual and moral life it is the heart that matters. And therefore Ezekiel xxxvi. 26 speaks of a new heart, and Ps. li. 12 of the renewal of the spirit.

Finally we recall to memory the well-known verse, Gen. vi. 5 and viii. 21, where every imagination of the thoughts of man's heart is called evil from his youth.

All this proves that there is no doubt that man's disposition plays an important part in the Old Testament, and that man's actions are

[1] *Op. cit.* p. 106, interpretation of iv. 22f.
[2] This is one of the few clear texts from which it is evident that the prophets oppose not only the illegitimate religions, paganism and syncretism, but also a legitimate but outward spiritual life. This is straight opposition against the dead orthodoxy of those days; cf. also my *Essentials of the Theology of Isaiah.*

also partly judged by man's disposition. This becomes very clear in Lev. xix. 17: 'Thou shalt not hate thine brother *in thine heart*'. God is a God who sees through man's heart: even before man has uttered one word Gods knows everything concerning his life (Ps. cxxxix. 4), and even his fleeting thoughts (id., verse 23f.).

God is concerned with man's inner self (Prov. xxiv. 11f., 17f.), as is also evident from the well-known text 1 Sam. xvi. 7: 'man looketh on the outward appearance (as it seems to the eyes, so "at the outward appearance"), but Yahweh looketh on the heart' (as it appears to the heart, 'starting from an inward evaluation').[1] In our opinion it is stated here emphatically that God applies a spiritual standard by which He judges man.

Some have denied this moral element in the Old Testament. Eerdmans wrote in the *Theologisch Tijdschrift* a remark which has not yet lost all its influence,[2] in which he denied the existence of a morality concerned with man's disposition. He thought that the Old Testament only spoke of actually committed sins. This was said in connection with an interpretation of the tenth commandment: 'thou shalt not covet'. Eerdmans denied[3] that the verb *chamad* used here could mean 'to covet' in our sense of the word. On the ground of Exod. xxxiv. 24 he takes it to mean 'to appropriate'. Bleeker, who opposes Eerdmans' views in general, admits this point[4] but emphatically denies that the Old Testament otherwise lacks a morality of man's disposition. Others (Beer, *Exodus*)[5] maintain the meaning 'to desire'. An examination of the idea *chamad* leads us to agree with the results of Hermann: *chamad* is 'to covet' *and* 'to try to obtain'; *chamad* is 'to desire' with the express, concrete aim to appropriate something at the expense of someone else. Eerdmans' translation 'to appropriate' goes too far as a general

---

[1] This text has been dealt with, for instance, by B. D. Eerdmans, *Theol. Tijdschr.*, 1905, who thought that this verse does not mean 'The Lord looketh on the heart', but 'God looks with the heart', i.e. He penetrates deeper than man who looks with his eyes. Ehrlich, *Randglossen*, ad loc. cit., takes the text to mean 'to select after His own heart'.

[2] *Op. cit.*, 1903, p. 25: 'It is well-known that O.T. morality does not go into the matter of man's disposition. It is the act that constitutes sin, not the motives from which the act has sprung'. Eerdmans' view was already opposed in *Z.A.W.*, 1904, pp. 17ff. by J. C. Matthes, 'Der Dekalog'.

[3] Also *Godsdienst van Israël*, I, 1930, p. 44, and the English edition of 1947, *The Religion of Israel*, p. 31.

[4] *Zonde der gezindheid*, p. 18; cf. also J. Herrmann, *Sellin Festschrift*, 1927, *Das Zehnte Gebot: chamad* = 'to desire' and 'to attempt to satisfy this desire'. Similarly L. Köhler in *Theologische Rundschau*, 1929. In his valedictory lecture (*Het objekt van het zedelijk oordeel in het O.T.*, Homiletica en Biblica, 1961, pp. 1ff.) B. Gemser proves to be a true disciple of Bleeker. Cf. especially the statement of the Egyptian Amenmope: Be not greedy after a cubit of land, do not encroach upon the boundaries of a widow. (ANET, 422b, trans. Wilson).

[5] Handbuch z.A.T., ed. by Eissfeldt, 1939, p. 103.

meaning. Nor does Exod. xxxiv. 24 demand this meaning: the word may best be translated by 'to cast a look at', or 'to stretch out one's hands towards': 'No man shall stretch out his hands towards thy land when thou shalt go up (to the sanctuary), thrice a year to appear before the face of Yahweh'.[1]

To desire means here, therefore to cast a look at something and attempt to obtain it. The Hebrew words denoting spiritual functions always contain a concrete element; the Hebrew hardly thinks in *abstract* spiritual terms. There is a great deal of truth in what J. Pedersen says[2] (though he puts the matter too radically) :'For the Israelite ... the soul is a unit. But no more are the action and the result to be distinguished from each other or from the mental activities; they are implied in the actual mental process. This is to be attributed to the fact that the soul is wholly present in all its works'.[3]

We must therefore agree with Eerdmans when he says that the Israelite *did nit know of sins in thought*[4] but we must emphatically oppose the thesis that 'Old Testament morality does not penetrate as far as man's heart' (see above). It appears to me that in this discussion both Eerdmans and Bleeker have paid too little attention to the distinction between sins of thought (in the abstract sense) and sins of the heart.[5]

From his 'no sins of thought' Eerdmans drew the conclusion: 'and therefore no morality of man's disposition, either'; from 'there exists a morality of man's disposition' Bleeker concluded that there must therefore be sins of thought, too. In my opinion the primary findings of both these scholars are correct, but their conclusions from these data too rigid! If one wants to do justice to somebody over against others there is no greater danger than that of drawing logical conclusions from certain words of the other man and putting them into his mouth.[6] In this case these facts are true: there are no sins of thought in the Old Testament and there exists a morality concerned with man's disposition. In other words: Israel lacked the pure (dogmatic) abstraction, 'sin of thought', but Israel only lacked it in the strictly

[1] This verse is certainly a Deuteronomic interpolation in this context.
[2] Cf. *Israel*, I–II, pp. 123–131.
[3] According to modern ethnologists, we cannot deny the ancient Israelite all powers of abstraction; cf. G. W. Locher. *De anthropoloog Lévi-Strauss en het probleem van de geschiedenis*, 1961, pp. 201ff., who strongly opposes Pedersen's statement, referring to Josselin de Jong (Forum der Letteren, 1961, pp. 201ff.).
[4] In the sense that 'the Israelite did not separate the *thought* from the *act*', *Theol. Tijdschr.*, 1905, pp. 308ff.
[5] Bleeker, *op. cit.*, even puts the two on a level.
[6] This is the main danger threatening every dogmatic system that attempts to arrive at a completely balanced view (in our Western eyes), even if it is built up in the most logical manner on the basis of the Bible. On the dangers of logical deduction in exegesis see above, p. 128 n. 3

formal sense of the word, not because Israel was wanting in moral insight, but because Israelite psychology was less abstract and analytic in its examination of human action than our western scholarly world is; in the East we do not find the theoretical distinctions provided by more recent psychology, distinctions which the Oriental will perhaps never take over from us.

The story of Cain (Gen. iv) is the clearest case in point; on the one hand the author refers back to Cain's disposition from which the evil arose, but on the other hand Cain is not considered guilty until the moment when the crime happened. The same is true of 'the sin in Paradise' (Gen. ii.f.). Just as with Cain it is the sinful act that is here looked upon as sin. So in the narratives man is not judged by his attitude towards the general commandment 'thou shalt not covet', but by the transgression of a concrete commandment. Coveting in itself is not applied as a standard for judgment, but in Gen. iv. 5ff. and iii. 1ff. the desire is depicted clearly as the *beginning* of sin (and as such it has therefore implicitly to do with sin).

Thus we find that the Old Testament – as well as Christ, for instance, in Mark vii. 21 – knew that the origin of evil lies in the heart, and that the heart is frequently and emphatically denoted in this sense; cf. for instance Ps. xiv. 1, where the sin of the fool is depicted as originating in his heart, in his notion that there is no God; cf. Ps. x. 4, 11, 13.[1]

To recapitulate, the best way to formulate our conclusions may be: in the tenth commandment man is warned against indulging the desire that leads to sin, just as in the narratives of the Old Testament the sinful act is traced as far as man's disposition, as far as the inner notions of his heart. Further in some places the heart, man's disposition is also mentioned emphatically (cf. Lev. xix. 17f.). But the *judgment* on sin can of course only be given *on the ground of the act itself*. By the act the sin became manifest and the commandment is transgressed.[2]

[1] We must also emphasize the importance attached to the *intention* by the Jews; see A.J.Wensinck, *De intentie in recht, ethiek en mystiek der semietische volken*, Semietische Studien, 1941, pp. 6off., esp. 67ff.

[2] Although the acts are differentiated according to their motives; in jurisdiction not every act in itself is made punishable, because the conception of involuntariness, of unintentional crime is accepted (not every case of manslaughter is a case of murder). The cultic acts, the expiatory offering can only take place if they are performed for sins committed *bi-shegagah* (see p. 263). This does not imply, of course, that every act is judged by its origin in man's disposition. Indeed, our own administration of justice has not attained this stage yet, either, though motives are taken into account in arriving at a verdict; there was a time, and not so long ago either, in our own administration of justice when the verdict in the law-court depended solely on the letter of the law.

In Israel the element of unintentional offences was limited strictly to certain well-defined cases; but this already made it possible to form a clearer idea of the offence and to consider from an ethical point of view the motive for the offence.

In religious and moral judgment, too, the deed becomes the starting-point (*doing* well or *doing* wrong remains the basis for punishment), although the Israelite knows that the life of the mind precedes the act, and though with the act man's disposition is condemned, too. We may conclude that the Old Testament teaching, also in the field of morality, is directed entirely towards practical life; it is sober, simple, it does not lose itself in theory, but it is certainly also justified spiritually and psychologically because it includes the heart in its considerations.

E. Material Ethics

It is not our intention to discuss the rules of life in the Old Testament themselves at great length after the general theological outline given above. We cannot, however, dispense with a short summary, including particularly a reference to the principal textual material.

There are in the Old Testament several summarizing moral texts. The bestknown of these are the so-called ethical Decalogues (Exod. xx and Deut. v); but besides these there have been others that were used in the cult (Pss. xv and xxiv; Ezek. xviii); there were also ethical rules for certain categories, for instance for judges (Exod. xxiii. 1ff.), as well as more general social and ethical collections (Lev. xix. 12ff.). Moreover we find many ethical rules of life in the books of wisdom, particularly the Proverbs, Ecclesiastes and Job. The teaching of the prophets is full of it, too; it frequently makes use of summaries in the spirit of the Decalogues (Hos. iv. 2 and Jer. vii. 9).

The principal of these is the (ethical) Decalogue, which has come down to us in two versions.[1] We shall not deal with the differences between them here. This Decalogue has received the central place in the revelation of God at Mount Sinai. It starts with the formula of selfrevelation: 'I am Yahweh, thy God, which have brought thee out of the land of Egypt, out of the house of bondage';[2] Yahweh, the

[1] Properly speaking there are three, cf. besides Exod. xx and Deut. v, Lev. xix. 3f., 11f.; see also Hos. iv and Jer. vii. We can only mention here some recent outlines and studies: L. Köhler, 'Der Dekalog', *Th. Rundschau*, 1929, pp. 161ff.; S. Mowinckel, *Le Décalogue*, 1927, and 'Zur Geschichte der Dekalogen', *Z.A.W.*, 1937, pp. 218ff.; P. Volz, *Mose²*, 1932; my 'Litterair-historische vragen aangaande de Dekaloog', *N. Th. St.*, 1939, pp. 2ff., 34ff.; now particularly the surveys of literature by J. J. Stamm, *Th. Rundschau* 1961/2, pp. 189ff., 281ff.; E. Gerstenberger, *op. cit.*; see above p. 308.
[2] A similar formula is also found in the introduction to the Code of Hammurabi, who at the beginning introduces himself as the king designated by the gods, thus indicating the legal title of his code. G. E. Mendenhall, *Law and Covenant in Israel and in the Ancient Near East*, 1955, thinks there is a special affinity with the ancient Hittite treaties; on the discussions see my *Religion of Israel*, pp. 145ff.,| 299; cf. W. Zimmerli, *Ich bin Jahwe, Geschichte und A.T.* (Alt Festschrift, 1953, pp. 179ff.), K. Elliger, *Ich ben der Herr*, K. Heim Festschrift, 1953, and my 'Exode xx, 2', *Recherches bibliques* VIII, n.d., 35ff. In the subordinate clause Yahweh's right to His people is vindicated by a reference to the deliverance from Egypt, a view on which all prophetic preaching is based.

Saviour of Israel, is Israel's God and He lays down the law for the people. This linking together of provisions of the law and an theophany of the deity is something extraordinary in the ancient Eastern world, which clearly shows how remarkable Israel's religion of revelation is.[1]

The content of the laws demonstrates that Yahweh, Israel's God of salvation and Legislator, is an absolute God and a moral God. The first commandment states the recognition of the exclusive nature of Yahweh as the basis for all spiritual life in Israel. The second commandment[2] forbids the making of images, referring to Yahweh's exclusiveness ('I, Yahweh, thy God am a jealous God') : Yahweh, who absolutely transcends all things of this earth, cannot be tied down to images wrought by the hand of man and so drawn into the sphere of influence of man. The third commandment states the holiness of Yahweh's name, which He revealed to Israel as the greatest possession of His people; that name is not to be used in connection with anything unworthy.

The fourth commandment proclaims the holiness of the seventh day, the day that is proclaimed as the social day of rest (Deut. v) or as the day sanctified at the Creation (Exod. xx). The seventh day is the end of the week (known only in Israel), and the transition to the new week.[3] In the Sabbath it is fundamentally the whole of life and work that is dedicated to Yahweh, in an ever-recurring rhythm independent of nature and given at the Creation[4]. The commandment to keep the Sabbath is of very great social importance particularly because of the demand that it should apply to all : the free and the slaves, man and the animal.

To the so-called second table of the commandments belong those which demand reverence for one's parents; for life[5] that is given and taken by Yahweh alone; for the married state that was instituted by Yahweh (Gen. ii); for property; and for the absolute purity of man's

---

[1] See Zimmerli, p. 208.
[2] See W. Zimmerli, 'Das Zweite Gebot', *Festschrift Bertholet*, pp. 550ff.; A. Kruyswijk, *Geen gesneden beeld*, 1962, p.208.
[3] There exists a very extensive literature on the Sabbath; besides the above-mentioned studies on the Decalogue in general we mention: Hehn, *Siebenzahl und Sabbath;* B. D. Eerdmans, 'Der Sabbath', *Festschrift Marti*, 1925, pp. 79ff.; my 'Kalender en Sabbat', *N.Th.St.*, 1940, pp. 172ff.; N. H. Tur-Sinai, 'Sabbath und Woche', in *Bi. Or.*, 1951, pp. 14ff.; E. Jenni, 'Die theologische Begründung des Sabbathgebotes im A.T.', 1956, *Th. Studien*, 46; J. H. Meesters, Op zoek naar de oorsprong van de Sabbat (doctorate thesis Amsterdam), 1966.
[4] See pp. 63 and 261.
[5] On the sixth commandment see for example J. J. Stamm, 'Du sollst nich töten', *Theol. Zeitschr.*, Basel, 1945, pp. 81ff. T. Canaan, ZDPV, 1964, pp. 85–99, points out that up to this day murder and adultery are punished by death among the Bedouins.

testimony in the administration of the law; and finally striving after something at the expense of someone else is condemned.

The great importance of the Decalogue is that it places all spheres of life under the absolute rule of Yahweh.

In a shortened form, either in this or in a slightly different composition these commandments, the origin of which cannot be established with certainty,[1] may from their origin have formed part of the spiritual property of Yahwism.

It is, at any rate, clear that they form the spiritual foundations of the whole of Israelite life. They are the basis of Israelite criminal law;[2] transgressing them is liable to be punished by death (except in the case of theft); to what extent they form the basis of moral thought in Israel is proved by Nathan's appearance before David, after his adultery with Bathsheba, and David's reaction to his appearance;[3] they lie at the root of the teaching of the prophets, as appears from Hos. iv. 2 and Jer. vii. 9.

Besides this summary of moral action – probably also in imitation of it – there are several other similar series of rules of life, of which the 'mirror for judges' in Exod. xxiii, and the series of ethical and social commandments in Lev. xix. 13–18 are finest examples.

Besides such series of rules of life there are certain 'forms of confession' or 'catalogues of sins', also presupposing a system of duties, and particularly used in the cult, cg. Deut. xxviii. 15ff., Ps. xv and Ezek. xviii. The moral element plays an important part in the cult, therefore, which confirms the view, also in agreement with the Scriptural tradition, that the link between the law and the revelation of God is of central importance in the Israelite cult.[4]

In the literature of wisdom – just as outside Israel – the moral element is emphasized; we know the description of the 'civil and moral' ideas in the book of Job (xxix and xxxi), which in this form, too, runs true to the high Israelite character (cf. xxxi. 13, where the right of the slave is recognized even in a conflict with his lord).

In the book of Proverbs,[5] too, we find unmistakably the moral religious mark of Yahwism besides general moral ideas which Israel shares with other nations, and besides typical popular wisdom: the fear of the Lord, the warnings against the strange woman, the emphasis on justice, the reverence for one's parents, and also the

---

[1] See above p.40.
[2] See A. Alt, *Die Ursprünge des israelitischen Rechts*, 1934, and in *Kleine Schriften*, I, 1953, pp. 1ff.   [3] See p.380.
[4] See above pp. 223ff. and 238f.; the instruction given by the priests must therefore have been largely moral in character (cf. Hos. iv. 6).
[5] See for example, J. C. Matthes, *De Israëlietische wijzen*, 1911; W. A. L. Elmslie, *Studies in life from Jewish proverbs*, n.d.

warnings against covetousness (xviii. 1).[1] The pedagogical ethical literature also confirms the importance of the Decalogue in the life of Israel; it is to be observed throughout the Old Testament in very widely differing gradations. But apart from Exod.xx and Deut.v not a single literal doublet of the Decalogue has come down to us, which proves how 'personal and individual', as we might say, the moral tradition was in Israel. In this respect the fact that the Decalogue has been handed down in a shortened form in Lev.xix.3f. and 12f. is so interesting; it seems to have been drawn up for children (xix.3 begins with the demands of respect for the parents, in which the mother is mentioned first!).

11. *Limitations*

In respect to morality, too, the Old Testament has its limitations – the spiritual main issues that we can trace are partly also the culminating-points. In many places various typical nationally limited or general ancient Eastern elements come to the fore. In morality, too, the Old testament reaches out above itself for its fulfilment as it was given in Jesus Christ. Very briefly we shall mention some of these unfulfilled elements.[2]

a. The Old Testament is *historically limited,* also with respect to the history of culture and spiritual life; in spite of the fact that it bears witness to the living revelation of God, it is also borne by the life and ideas of the time when it came into being; even the greatest treasures can only be offered in earthen vessels; those who received and reproduced them belonged to their own period.

This becomes apparent on several occasions also in the relation between man and man. We shall mention two instances here: *slavery* and *polygamy.*

However much the humane element may stand in the foreground, under the influence of the idea of man as the image of God, the recognition of a personal vocation and the awareness of belonging to a community of God – yet slavery continued to exist. We must, however, remark here that among Israelites it could only exist because of debt, and therefore for a *limited time* (legally defined with an ultimate term of six years; only voluntarily could it be translated into slavery for life; cf. Exod.xxi.1ff.; that people did not adhere to it is apparent from Jer.xxxiv.8ff.).[3] We may maintain, therefore, that *fundamentally,*

---

[1] Unless a different reading should be accepted.
[2] See J. Calvijn, *Institutio* II, ii and the commentary on this by R. Bijlsma, *op. cit.,* pp. 358f.
[3] Cf. M. David, *The maunmission of slaves under Zedekiah,* OTS V, 1948, pp. 63ff.

according to the law, no real slavery of the members of the people itself was tolerated. Behind this lies the idea of the Covenant. There were, however, slaves from other nations. To them the already mentioned humane slavery laws certainly applied, too (see pp. 420f., 389f.). The principle of humanity had therefore not yet been carried through completely, as it clashed with the national principle.[1]

A stronger violation of the essential principle of humanity is *polygamy*. The equivalence of man and woman, which was recognized fundamentally, for instance in Gen. iif., is not maintained in practice or carried through in preaching. Woman remains subordinate to man; this position is considered as a just and permanent punishment in Gen. iii. Not the fact that woman is looked upon as the help-mate of man or in the first place as the mother, the one who gives birth, should be called a token of weak spiritual insight, but the practice of polygamy and its toleration in the Old Testament was degrading for woman, for in the stories polygamy is continually presupposed without criticism.

b. Further there are *national* limitations
The protective legislation applies to the 'neighbour',[2] i.e. the compatriot. This limits its ethical importance; though we may be convinced that in ancient Eastern society a different notion was inconceivable. With respect to the non-Israelites only few provisions are known.[3] We must make a distinction here between the stranger *(ger)*, i.e. the non-Israelite who had established himself in Palestine, and the foreigner; and among the latter between those foreigners who were allies of Israel and those who did not have this relation. As a matter of fact the latter are always the enemies, unless of course they live too far away for any contact to take place. The 'strangers' *(gerim)*, the non-Israelites residing among the people[4] have a protected position and are ultimately included under the commandment of love on the same footing as the members of the people themselves (Lev. xix. 34, see also pp. 376 and 385). To real enemies of the people the Israelites

[1] It was more than 18 centuries before the practice of the Christian nations rose above that of Israel!
[2] Cf. J. Fichtner, 'Der Begriff des "Nächsten" im A.T.', *Wort und Dienst* 1955, pp. 23ff., particularly pp. 39f. and *Th. Z* (Basel) 1966, pp. 1ff.
[3] Moreover the various books contain widely different views and opinions concerning certain peoples. Compare, for example, the opinion about the Moabites, Ammonites, Edomites and Egyptians that appears from the provision of Deut. xxiii. 3–8 and those expressed in the prophetic and historical writings; compare also the different views on the Moabites within the book of Deuteronomy itself (ii. 29 and xxiii. 3). Further the different views on the Edomites in Deut. xxiii. 7 and, for instance, Obadiah, Isa. lxiii. 1ff., Mal. i. 2f.! The best illustration of the historical limitations of certain laws is afforded by Deut. xxiii. 3ff.
[4] In contrast with the *nokriyim*, the foreigners who did not maintain relations with the people.

showed but little mercy (see p.420f.), and the laws concerning the 'stranger' were certainly not applied to them; that is why Jesus' parable of the good Samaritan is so unprecedented, so entirely different from what the Old Testament taught (Luke x). It is true, though, that in Deut. xxi. 10ff. a treatment worthy of a human being is demanded for a female prisoner-of-war who had been made a slave.[1]

A different case is the demand of the *love of one's enemy* (*in a personal sense*) as made by Jesus in Matt. v. 44. This demand is also unknown in the Old Testament.[2] Exod. xxiii. 4f. does not demand the love of one's enemy, for here nothing more (or less!) is said than that one may not make one's hate felt in such a way that it might make the personal enemy lose his valuable property or that an animal would suffer by this hatred. So the Old Testament here sets bounds to man's personal hatred. It remains surprising that the Old Testament gives no general statement on this matter (the love of one's personal enemy), even though we may think it implied in Lev. xix. 15–18 (see n. 2), whereas the Babylonian Proverbs of Utnapishtim do contain such a statement.[3] We wonder why in Israel the aversion is not spiritually

---

[1] On this whole question see the still very valuable work of A. Bertholet, *Die Stellung der Israeliten und der Juden zu den Fremden*, 1896. Further M. Preisker, *Die Stellung der Nichtisraeliten zu Jahve*, 1907; H. J. Schoeps, *Jüdisch-Christliches Religionsgespräch in 19 Jahrhunderten*, 1937, pp. 16ff., and particularly M. Guttmann, *Das Judentum und seine Umwelt*, 1927.

[2] At any rate not literally in this form. See Strack-Billerbeck on Matt. v. 43, in this case against the majority of Jewish authors; also Beer, *Exodus*, p. 119, quoting Bousset, Weiss and Holzmann. Beer thinks that it is possible to speak of love of one's enemy in view of Exod. xxiii. 4f., and that Matt. v. 43 wrongly imputes to Judaism that it preached the hatred of one's enemy. As far as Exod. xxiii. 5 is concerned, it is probably rather a question of protection of animals than of hatred of one's enemy (on the former cf., for instance, Deut, xxii. 6ff., xxv. 4). It is remarkable that in Deut. xxii. 4 the brother's ass is mentioned in the same connection as the enemy's ass in Exod. xxiii. 4. It is likely that for the Deuteronomic legislator the brotherhood of the people was of such central importance that he neglected the personal contrast presupposed in Exod. xxiii. On these grounds it can also be maintained that in Lev. xix. 18 (cf. also the preceding verses) the demand of the love of one's neighbour already meant the love of all compatriots in such a sense that it also implies the love of one's personal enemy (see especially xix. 17).

It is indeed a fact that neither Judaism nor the O.T. teach positively that one should hate one's enemy. But this does not make Matt. v. 43*b* slanderous; we may agree with Strack-Billerbeck (I, p. 533) that the word may be a popular summary expressing briefly the customary view of life of the average Israelite of Jesus' days; or perhaps the word 'to hate' may here be taken in the weaker meaning of 'to avert oneself from' (cf. Luke xiv. 26 and elsewhere, see *Theol. Wb. z. N. T.*, IV, pp. 689, 694f.). In any case this shows that Judaism did not demand the love of one's enemy in Jesus' days. See now the very well-considered and frank observations of M. Buber in *Zwei Glaubensweisen* (Eng. trans., 1952), pp. 68ff. who considers Jesus' word as a statement sprung from Jewish ethics but rising above it, and to be explained from the eschatological and enthusiastic way of representing things in the Gospel; cf. also J. Klausner, *Von Jesus zu Paulus* (Eng. trans., 1944), pp. 23, 559 and his *Jesus von Nazareth*.

[3] 'Do thy adversary no harm; return good to him who does thee evil; do justice to thy enemy' (cf. Gemser, in *Spreuken*, II, p. 52, Tekst en Uitleg, 1931; F. M. Th. de

overcome so clearly, while otherwise the humane element comes to the fore more strongly in Israel and particularly the idea of faithfulness and love to one's neighbour is expressed so unambiguously. On considering this matter, there can, in our opinion, be no other answer than that in the Old Testament there are always two lines, now running parallel, then again crossing, which were inseparable because they were both founded on the will of God: the line of the social and moral connection between Israelites and that of the moral and religious demand of justice, of necessary judgment and retribution (which can be made strongly personal, too, cf. Ps. cix; cxxxvii. 8; see above p. 315)[1]. Outside Israel wisdom could arrive at a doctrine of a general love of mankind before the demand of the love of one's enemy was made in Israel, because in Israel religion and ethics were closely bound up with each other and with the life of the people, and also because Israel's religion was exclusive. The syncretism of polytheism, always inclined towards tolerance, could create a basis for the idea of the love of mankind as taught in the Stoa.[2] The love of one's personal enemy was checked in Israel by the idea of justice, which was maintained strictly and according to which man must *expiate* his *sin individually according to the law*. First of all the last two of these ideas must receive attention; but further the idea of sin is also of importance here, for the harm done to someone else (from which enmity springs) is a sin against God and an offence against the brother, and for that reason doing evil ultimately demands expiation. This led Israel on a legalistic track in moral judgment, and in the course of time this legalistic

Liagre Böhl, *Opera Minora* 1953, pp. 316ff.; W. G. Lambert, *Babylonian Wisdom*, pp. 98ff.). The tone here is very pure, a purity equalled and surpassed only in the N.T., for there this idea breaks through all religous and national contrasts (Luke x). Such religious and national contrasts are unknown in the syncretism of the Eastern world; hence there is no motive either for what has been called 'religious hatred'. It is therefore difficult to compare statements springing from such widely different spiritual atmospheres correctly. There is nothing in the O.T. that can be placed beside the proverbs of Utnapishtim as an exact parallel. There are some texts that come quite close to it, Prov. xxv. 21f., xxiv. 17f.; the former text is quoted by St. Paul in Rom. xii. 21; it is, however, not absolutely possible to define the moral level of the motivation because this expression: coals of fire may also imply inward satisfaction (Gemser on this text); this consideration becomes particularly striking when Prov. xxiv. 18 is compared with this text; Procksch (*Theologie*, p. 695) gives a very positive appreciation of Prov. xxv. 21f. Prov. xvii. 9 may also be mentioned in this connection (Procksch), but the point of this text is different. For the bearings of this question on the history of religion and theology see also: H. H. Rowley, 'The Chinese Philosopher Mo Ti' (*Bulletin John Rylands Library*, vol. 31, no. 2, Nov. 1948); A. Bertholet, 'Parallelen der Religionsgeschichte', in *H.U.C.A.*, XXIII, 1950–51, pp. 561ff., especially p. 568; now also S.V.T. XVII, 1969 p. 12
[1] H. A. Brongers, *Die Rache- und Fluchpsalmen im A.T.*, OTS XIII, 1963, pp. 21ff. emphasizes the latter.
[2] On natural tolerance and ethical relativism in naturalistic polytheism see H. Kraemer, *De wortelen van het syncretisme*, 1937, p. 23, and *The Christian Message*, 1938, pp. 154ff. We should also bear in mind the relation of the Stoa and the N.T.

tendency became stronger and stronger.[1] It is true that in the wisdom-literature we find the less rigorous text: 'He that covereth a transgression seeketh love' (Prov. xvii. 9a). but here is meant only the maintaining of friendly relations. It is a word that exhorts to an attitude of true forgivingness, and for one moment points towards 1 Cor. xiii. 7a and Rom. xii. 21: 'Overcome evil with good'.[2]

What the Old Testament could attain is the word also quoted a few times in the New Testament: 'Vengeance is mine; I will repay' (Deut. xxxii. 35; Rom. xii. 19; Hebr. x. 30), i.e. man surrenders his revenge to Yahweh. This also happens frequently in prayers (Jeremiah, the Psalms). Only from the starting-point of Isa. liii, transcending this and proclaiming the self-sacrificing love of the 'Ebed, can the demand of the love of the sinner, and also of one's enemy in general, be made. But this consequence did not strike a responsive chord in Israel until the coming of Jesus Christ.

The New Testament is different in this respect, spiritually stronger, in that it fully accepts the guidance of God's love, which desires that man should live, even in the relation between God and the sinner.[3] This predominance of God's love is, indeed, also found in the Old Testament (Exod. xxxiv. 6f.), but there is applies to the people of the Covenant[4], and does not dominate morality as a whole. In the New Testament this predominance is absolute, so that it becomes there simply: God is love and consequently the direct demand to live by the love of God is made. But thus the sacrifice, the cross, also becomes the fundamental idea of any Christian ethics.[5]

c. Connected with the preceding are the *legalistic limitations* of Old Testament morality, to which we have already referred. The idea of revelation as it is found in the Old Testament (*torah*, 'teaching') and particularly its codification in writing, for which Israel was justly very thankful (Deut. iv. 6ff.) involves spiritual dangers. It may make man

[1] Cf. H. van Oyen, 'De Joodsche Geest en de ethiek', in Prof. Dr. H.J. Pos, *Antisemitisme en Jodendom*, 1939, pp. 97–100.
[2] One should now also read *DSD*, X 26–XI2.
[3] Cf. van Oyen, *op. cit.* and *Th. Z.* (Basel), 1966, pp. 10f.
[4] Exceptions are Hagar (Gen. xvi), the runaway slave who had become proud and was yet heard by Yahweh, and especially the book of Jonah, which proclaims God's will of salvation for Nineveh. In this way the special meaning of this book becomes very clear indeed.
[5] We may also point to the doctrine of sin, which bases the willingness to recognize the solidarity in guilt with others on Christian theology and strengthens the desire to grant forgiveness. This ground alone would, however, lead to a passive attitude rather than to an attitude of active love; in my opinion the passive attitude dominates in *DSD* XI. The characteristic element of the teaching of the N.T. is active love (cf. also A. Schweitzer, *Die Weltanschauung der indischen Denker*. With Buddha we also find the demand of overcoming evil by good, but we do *not* find active love, pp. 74ff.).

spiritually proud (because he becomes so well-informed) and rigid (the necessary rules of life have been prescribed with the greatest exactitude); this results in an atmosphere of subjection to observance which is something different from moral obedience from love, but becomes a slavish following of certain fixed rules. The Pharisaism of the New Testament is a very clear case in point. But this legalistic tendency is also promoted by the negative form of the commandments. That is why the Old Testament needed fulfilment and why this form of religion, in which *the law*, a book mainly containing prescriptions, had become predominant, had to be broken through in order that the personal relation to God in perfect love and surrender could be realized so that in this way the revelation could become wholly spiritual. In this manner all obstacles between God and man, and also between men themselves, were removed, in order that man should be able to serve the God of love in freedom by the Spirit of Jesus Christ (Rom. viii).

d. In spite of the spiritual understanding found in the Old Testament – viz. concerning the heart, man's disposition as the mainspring of moral life – it is the *sinful act* by which man is judged, even by God (from Gen. iii. iv, etc.). This involves the danger of the consciousness of guilt becoming a matter of outward show. Here, too, all kinds of consequences did not fail to make themselves felt in later Judaism because this trait of Israel's religion led to *casuistry* in ethics. This is not yet the case in the Old Testament. Yet the catalogues of sins (Ezek. xviii; Pss. xxiv. xv, etc.) and the Decalogues were, indeed, influences that contributed to make the consciousness of sin an outward show. This objection is mainly to be traced back to the preceding. Essentially casuistry is a certain form of legalization of the moral (and particularly the cultic and ritualistic!) vital principles.

e. In a certain sense connected with this, is a *eudaemonistic* trait, which is not to be denied altogether and is attributed, among others, by B. Gemser,[1] particularly to the Old Testament wisdom-literature. 'The idea of retribution, the false hopes of reward, the pointing out of evil consequences and of the approval and disapproval of one's fellow-men are the most customary means of persuasion. This gives the Proverbs an utilitarian and eudaemonistic tone, as if riches and honour and a long life were the greatest good and the highest aim in life'. On the other hand this should not be emphasized too strongly, which, indeed, Gemser does not do, for he admits that also in the Proverbs the principal emphasis is laid on God's law and justice! Yet something that may be called eudaemonism is found through-

[1] *Spreuken*, I (Tekst en Uitleg), p. 27.

out the Old Testament; cf. for example various promises in the opening words of Deuteronomy and the motivation of the fifth commandment ('that thy days may be prolonged in the land which the Lord thy God giveth thee'), which also shows Deuteronomic influences.[1]

The realism of the Bible that knows God as the Living One, Present here and now, and that restores the direct contact between God and man, did not only sanctify all things earthly and material, but was also, at times, the reason why too great a value was attached to material things. There is a tendency in the Old Testament to value material blessings especially highly[2] and to think that these are inseparable from divine blessings (final verses of Job xlii).

IV. MAN IN THE COMMUNITY OF GOD[3]

1. *General Observations*

As we did with other subjects (cf. above on the worldpicture, p.331ff.) we have to emphasize at the outset that on the one hand the doctrine of man in the Old Testament does not form a unity from the point of view of systematic theology, so that we cannot speak of a theological anthropology; and on the other hand that Israel's faith dominated the conception of man to such an extent that a special light is shed on this concept so that we can say that (as compared with the ancient Eastern world) the Old Testament does have an anthropology all its own. The Egyptians[4] and the Babylonians[5], and probably the Phoenicians, too, looked upon man as born of the gods; in the whole of the ancient Eastern world, as also in Greece, man was taken to be of divine origin,[6] and therefore the conception of man was 'idealistic'.

In the Old Testament the conception of man is closely bound up with the belief in the holy God and with living in communion with God. As a result there is *a priori* a fundamental distinction between God and man. Man does not spring from God but is *created* (Gen. i) or *formed by God out of the dust of the earth* and made a living being by

[1] This idea was also known in Egypt. Thesis III, doctorate thesis of Dr.J.Zandee, *De hymnen aan Amon van Papyrus*, Leyden, I, p. 350, 1948.
[2] Compare for example J.Lindblom, *Israels Religion²*, 1953, p. 273, cf. above p. 100 n.4.
[3] W.Zimmerli, 'Das Menschenbild im A.T.' (*Theol. Existenz heute*, N.F. 14), 1949; L.Köhler, *Hebrew Man* (Eng. trans.), 1956; G.Pidoux, *L'homme dans l'Ancien Testament*, 1953.
[4] See H.Kees, *Der Götterglaube im alten Ägypten*, 1941, pp. 3–4, and G. van der Leeuw, 'Egyptische Eschatologie' (*Med. Kon. Ak. van Wetensch.*), 1949.
[5] See my *Paradijsvoorstelling bij de oude semietische volken*, 1937, p. 100.
[6] While the gods, on the other hand, are always looked upon in a 'naturalistic' light; e.g., cosmogony is theogony, etc. On the contrast between the idealistic thought of the Greeks and Biblical thought, see for example. J.N.Sevenster, *Leven en dood in de Evangeliën*, 1952.

the breath of God (Gen. ii)[1] or he comes into being by procreation under the miraculous guidance of God, as the description of the chokmah has it, which is much more realistic.[2]

By this anthropology all demigods, intermediate forms between God and man, in other words, all the mythological figures of the ancient world, are ruled out from the start. Only in Gen. vi. 1ff. do we find an allusion to the existence of such figures, but there the existence of these giants, the offspring of sons of gods and mortal women (see pp. 54f.) is looked upon as the worst sign of sin upon earth. They disappear as unexpectedly (at the Deluge?) as they spring up. Only the king was said to have been begotten by God (see p. 367) in imitation of ancient Eastern which had crept in through the court-ceremonial at Jerusalem, representations, but this was certainly not to be taken literally.[3] In consequence of God's absolute holiness in contrast with the world, the Old Testament considered man therefore as a being fundamentally different from God.

This radically theistic starting-point implied, on the one hand, the absolute dependence of man upon God (the man as is *created* being), on the other hand the recognition of the high place given to man by God in His world-order, because God is known as the God who has communion with man.

The Scriptural doctrine of creation rejects once and for all the ancient oriental mythical notion that the world was an originally undifferentiated, chaotic, material-spiritual mass, from which sprang gods, men, animals, plants, stars and matter and looks upon the world as a *cosmos*, called into being by God in the beginning. And therefore man may be thought of as a being with a quite distinct character, created by God in a very special way. Thus it also became impossible that man should be represented as having lived originally in a close relationship with the animal world. This view is not so strange in the ancient Eastern conception (cf. the beginning of the epic of Gilgamesh, and the representation of the gods in the shape of animals and animal symbols, and also occasionally of intercourse between gods and animals).[4] From the outset man ranked above the animals, as is stated emphatically in Gen. i, but also presupposed in Gen. ii by the statement that Adam gives the animals their names. The relationship between man and the animal may be very friendly (by no means strange in a semi-nomadic, semi-agrarian civilization such as formed

---

[1] The breath of God is not the spiritual, immortal part of the human being, but the life-giving, vital element in man (see pp. 407f.).
[2] In Job x. 8ff. (Ps. cxxxix. 13ff.) the two ideas are mentioned side by side.
[3] Cf. H. Frankfort, *Kingship and the gods*, pp. 6, 337ff.
[4] See J. Hempel, 'Gott, Mensch und Tier im A.T.', *Z. f. syst. Th.* 1931, now also in Apoxysmata, 1961, pp. 198ff.

the background of the author of the narratives of primeval times), yet it is a clearly established fact that there was no real communion between man and animal in primeval times.[1] In accordance with God's intention man bears sway over the animals, and, according to Gen. i, ii, even over the whole of the world (cf. also Ps. viii).

The Old Testament message of God's holiness and love makes man truly human, an independent being with a task of his own on behalf of the world and all that is in it. The pure, Biblical belief in God does not destroy the value of man but brings it out properly and absolutely, and not only his value as a member of the community but also as an individual.

Nowhere in the ancient Eastern world do we meet such profound ideas on the nature of man as in the Old Testament, even if some important epic and wisdom poems of Babylonian literature in particular do contain some reflections on the nature of man (of which Gen. i–xi reminds us in various ways). It is remarkable that whereas in Babylonian literature the various reflections on the state of the human being are demonstrated in all kinds of half-mythological figures, the Old Testament gives in Gen. iiff. observations on *ha-'adam*, on man as such (*ha-'adam* is not used here in a collective sense but as a general description of man). Though in a concrete historical form, we are yet given here a more or less general theoretical reflection on human nature and human life as such which reminds us of what the *Chokmah* has to say about man (see above p.244).[2] Very often it is exactly the author of the primeval narratives who proves to be able to state general fundamental problems, in spite of his ways of representing things which still remind us of ancient Eastern mythology. When the Church refers in her dogmatics to Gen. iiff. and Gen. i for her anthropology, this is quite justified, for these narratives are no confused myths, but a well-considered elaboration of Israel's philosophy of life on the basis of prophetical Yahwism, even if the author derived his images and expressions for the greater part from the ancient Eastern (mythological) way of representing things.

2. *The man as being, created by God; mortality and death; man and woman*

Man has been created by God and is fundamentally different from his Creator. In Gen. ii. 7 the creation is described as a being formed by God out of the dust of the earth and animated by the breath of life that comes from Him. In Israel man is an animated body, or rather a

---

[1] Man is alone, and finds no fitting helper among the animals (Gen. ii. 18ff.).
[2] For that reason the modern conception of 'Urgeschichte' is not to be rejected entirely, notwithstanding Köhler, *Theologie*[3], p. 167; see now also H. W. Wolff, 'Das A.T. und das Problem der existentialen Interpretation', *Ev. Th.* 1963, pp. 1ff.

body to which life has been given, and not, as in Greek philosophy, an eternal soul, enclosed in the body (an incarnate soul.) With respect to the doctrine of man the Old Testament is very realistic.

Man is called *dust*, and also *flesh*. Both these words denote that man is transitory; the former does so most clearly, but the word flesh (*basar*, which has a quite neutral meaning and denotes the matter out of which man was made) can denote something transitory again and again[1] in the Old Testament (Isa. xxxi. 3; xl. 6). The body returns to the dust from which it was taken (Gen. iii. 19; Eccles. iii. 19f.; xii. 7). God infused breath (*neshamah*) into the material form, and in this way man became a living being (*nefesh chayyah*), Gen. ii.

This infusion of breath by God does not mean that man has received a divine soul or spirit. The notion that the human spirit is something divine is not to be found in the Old Testament; but the spirit (*ruach*) or breath returns to God who gave it (Eccles. xii. 7), so that life itself is seen as God's gift and the miraculous element in life itself is experienced.[2]

The breath or spirit exists in all that lives on the earth, also in the animal world as appears from Gen. vi. 17, so that generally speaking breath or spirit does not denote the souls as a higher, eternal principle, although the word *ruach* may, indeed, have a higher meaning: the whole of the spiritual sentiments that animate man. Thus the conception *nefesh* (mostly translated by soul) may quite often be taken in the sense of personality, the individuality,[3] but never in the sense of an independent element in man which possesses eternal life in its own right (the Greek 'soul' or 'spirit'); the *nefesh* is the vitality that animates the body and it is inconceivable that it should exist independently outside the body.

The Old Testament does not give a psychology properly speaking. The words soul, spirit, and heart are often used side by side or promiscuously. The main distinction that can be drawn between them is that the *soul* (*nefesh*) is man in his being alive, or rather in his activity;[4]

[1] Particularly in the more recent literature, cf. H. Wheeler Robinson, *The Christian Doctrine of Man*, 1911, p. 25, see W. D. Davies, *op. cit.*, p. 18, A. R. Johnson, *The Vitality*[2], pp. 37ff.
[2] See pp. 320 n. 3, 338f., Procksch, *Theologie*, pp. 456, 459. Compare also that the verb *bara'* in Gen. i. 21 and 27 is used particularly to denote the creation of the living beings; cf. also Ps. civ. 29a.
[3] See also J. N. Sevenster, *Het begrip psyche in het N. T.*, Assen, 1964, and J. Th. Ubbink's criticism of this work in *Nederlands Theologisch Tijdschrift*, 1947, pp. 49–51; Pidoux: *op. cit.*, p. 17.
[4] J. H. Becker, *Het begrip nefeš in het O. T.*, 1947, p. 116 (doctorate thesis Free University, Amsterdam); but blowing, breathing, the gasp of breath, rather than breath, should be considered the fundamental idea; D. Lys, *Nephes̆*, 1959; idem, *Ruach, le souffle dans l'A. T.*, 1962; on *ruach* also: J. H. Scheepers, *Die Gees van God en die gees van die mens in die O. T.*, 1960, and my *De heilige Geest in het O. T.* (mentioned above).

it is the motor impulse in his life, physically as well as psychically; he has *spirit* (*ruach* i.e. wind, the moved air itself, air, breath, coolness, space, spirit) in so far as this living existence also has a content, in so far as he is inspired by certain ideas and feelings; the *heart* (*leb*) is man's inner being, from which spring his will and action; it may also mean reason.[1] It is not necessary to go further into this Old Testament 'psychology'; one remark, though, is of importance: in the Old Testament we find neither a trichotomy, a division of man into soul, spirit and body, nor a dichotomy, a division into soul and body, for these various functions are not considered as distinct notions.

Because he is an earthly being man is mortal. In many cases death is looked upon as something natural; there is a good death, dying 'old and full of year's, but also an evil death, when man dies a miserable and untimely death (Jer.xxii. 18f.). We hear of the 'death of the righteous', which is desirable (Num.xxiii. 10*b*), and of a 'death of the uncircumcised' (Ezek.xxviii. 10); the former is a blessing, the latter a judgment; this should probably also be borne in mind in the interpretation of Ps.lxxiii; in vss. 17–19 the evil death is depicted, and in vss. 23–24 the honourable death of the righteous man,[2] who, moreover, also knows of God who remains his heritage even in death (25f.).

Nowhere in the Old Testament do we hear of the immortality of the soul,[3] or of man being incorruptible after death. But in daily life – in accordance with the notions of the ancient Eastern world – people evidently do take account of a continuation of life after death in the underworld; a typical ancient Eastern element is also that this spirit life is even taken to be more or less bodily; when in 1 Sam.xxviii the witch of Endor makes the spirit of Samuel rise from the earth he is described as an old man wrapped in a robe. There is, therefore, such a thing as a survival in the *She'ol*, the underworld, in the religion of Israel (cf. also Isa.xiv). On the other hand God may also take a man to Himself, but here, too, both body and spirit are involved, man as a

[1] On the psychology of Israel see Pedersen, *Israel*, I–II; H.Wheeler Robinson, 'Hebrew Psychology' (in *The People and the Book*, 1925, pp. 353ff.); and A.R.Johnson, *The vitality of the individual in the thought of ancient Israel*, 1949; on *leb* see F.H. von Meyenfeldt, *Het hart* (*leb, lebab*) *in het O.T.* (doctorate thesis Free University, Amsterdam) and Edelkoort's criticism of this book in *Ned. Th. T.*, 1951, pp. 308ff.; Pidoux treats all these questions, very briefly, in the light of theology.
[2] Also Suttcliffe, *The O.T. and future life*, 1946, see *Bi. Or.*, 1951, p. 102; and Chr. Barth, *Die Errettung vom Tode*, 1947, pp. 160ff.
[3] Besides the literature mentioned in the last note see also P.Torge, *Seelenglauben und Unsterblichkeitshoffnung*, 1909; A. de Bondt, *Wat leert het O.T. aangaande het leven na de dood* (doctorate thesis Free University, Amsterdam), 1938; my *Paradijsvoorstelling;* C.V.Pilcher, *The hereafter in Jewish and Christian Thought*, 1940, pp. 133ff.; E.S.Mulder, *Die Teologie van die Jesaja-Apokalipse*, pp. 94ff.; R. Martin-Achard, *De la mort à la resurrection dans l'A.T.*, 1956; from a systematical point of view, G. van der Leeuw, *Onsterfelijkheid of Opstanding;* F.W.A.Korff, *Onsterfelijkheid*, 1946.

living being, as he exists here on earth (Enoch; Elijah). Yet these two notions are not emphasized in the Old Testament and the belief in a continued existence in *She'ol* is even more or less suppressed, as is evident from the wisdom-literature, which looks upon death as the absolute end (Job xiv; Eccles. iii. 18ff.). This is partially due to the fact that the Law absolutely forbids man to seek contact with the spirits. The notion of being transfigured and taken up by God occurs so sporadically that it could not become the basis of a general religious conception. No reference is made to it therefore in the teaching of the prophets.

Neither in its conception of the soul (*nefesh*) nor in that of life after death is the Old Testament one-sided. Apparently we have on the one hand the ancient popular belief (where the spirits and *She'ol* are referred to), and on the other hand the theology of Yahwism (when the decay of the body and the return to God of the breath of life are emphasized). This latter conception may be due to the fact that Yahwism always had to combat the ancient Eastern belief in spirits, the worship of the dead and the raising of spirits. This conflict also accounts for the fact that the Old Testament speaks only very little about life after death; this is, in fact, one of the important elements where the Old Testament clamours for its 'fulfilment' by the New Testament. The reaction against paganism in the heathen practices on the one hand, and the strong sense of reality in Yahwism on the other made this ground, as it were, *terra incognita*.[1]

Yet this lack is scarcely felt as a hiatus in the Old Testament. For the belief in the God of Israel, as the One who governs life and history, is focused so strongly on the present, on life on this earth, that it leaves hardly any room in religion for speculation on a life after this life. We may conclude: *The faithful in the Old Testament at any rate in after times leave life in the hereafter entirely to Yahweh, who is the Lord with whom he lives in communion and whom they cling to even in death* (Ps. lxxiii).

Faith in God as the Lord of life, who performs miracles and rules everywhere, even in She'ol, was the root from which afterwards the

[1] Not until the later apocalyptists do we find victory over death and the resurrection from the dead (Isa. xxv. 8; xxvi. 19; Dan. xii. 2, see p. 454); the resurrection of the body is the only possible form in which the Israelite faith can give adequate expression to the individual, eternal hope of salvation. The unity of body and soul, so clearly manifest in Israel's anthropology, makes itself felt again in this expectation of salvation. However primitive it may seem, this physical and psychical unity of human nature offers, though, a most important point of view, which is also of great importance for a Christian anthropology in its totalitarian tendencies. See A.T. Nikolainen, *Der Auferstehungsglauben in der Bibel und ihrer Umwelt*, I–II, 1944–6; W. Eichrodt, *Theologie*[5], III, pp. 346ff.; for the Judaism D. S. Russel, *The method and message of Jewish apocalyptic*, 1964, pp. 353ff.; G. F. Moore, *Judaism* II, pp. 279ff.; W. Baumgartner, 'Der Auferstehungsglaube im Alten Orient' in the collection of essays *Zum A.T. und seiner Umwelt*, 1959, pp. 124ff.

belief in the resurrection of man could spring (Isa. xxvf.). The question in how far Persian influences are at work here may remain unanswered: the possibilities for this belief are already implicit in Israel itself; but if we wished to or were compelled to assume Parsee influences they are no more than the occasion for this religious conception, and certainly not its deepest cause, for it fits completely into the picture of the spiritual life of Israel as a later phase of development.[1]

There is one part of the Old Testament where we find further statements concerning the nature of man with respect to life and death: Gen. ii and iii. These chapters, which may belong to (later?) Yahwist historiography, present a wholly independent conception of the life of man. They do not state that man is immortal but something that resembles is, namely that man was originally placed in Paradise near the tree of life, without being forbidden to eat of its fruit. In other words, Gen. iif. states that according to the will of God, man was initially granted the possibility of eternal life by means of the fruit of the tree of life.[2] While everywhere else in ancient Eastern literature the tree of life is represented as standing in a place inaccessible to man, the author of Gen. ii.f. says that it was in (the middle of) the garden of Eden which was assigned to man as his original dwelling-place. The author further says that man was removed from this tree of life because of his sin: he desired to acquire divine knowledge (the fruit of the tree of the knowledge of good and evil) and become the equal of God.

According to the author of this chapter man was therefore deprived of the possibility of reaching the tree of life on account of the sin of disobedience or rather high-handedness, hybris. Death is the punishment of the sin of man who had originally received from God the possibility of eternal life on earth, even if he was mortal and earthly in origin. In a rather complicated way these chapters give answer to the problem of the nature of man from the standpoint of Old Testament belief in God; we may take this to be the work of a prophetic spirit who contrasted the purely Yahwistic ideas with ancient Eastern conceptions. Here it is not the deity who is the cause why man must die, as in Babylonian literature, but man himself, that is to say his sin, his desire to be the equal of God, his high-handedness. Man would not live with God as His child, but wanted to face God as an equal, and this original sin brought death on him. But man himself, made from the dust of the earth, is already mortal; the fact that he *must* die is due to the punishment of sin inflicted by God, because that is the reason why he must leave the garden of Eden with the tree of life. Hence St. Paul

[1] See A. T. Nikolainen, *op. cit.*, though this author is not sufficiently critical.
[2] N.B. We are here not concerned with *the immortality of the soul*, but with a continuation of man's life on earth, as he was created, in his corporeal existence!

is quite right in saying that the wages of sin is death. This profoundly spiritual view, springing from the conflict between the Yahwistic and the other ancient Eastern conceptions, and to be read and explained from those ancient Eastern conceptions, is one of the greatest statements of the Old Testament on anthropology, but it stands quite alone in the Old Testament. This conception is scarcely referred to (except in Ps. xc. 3 and perhaps in Job xv. 7), and the same may be said of Isa. liii. Only in the New Testament are these two culminatingpoints of the Old Testament message taken up again and done full justice.[1]

At the creation the two *sexes* were created, too: 'male and female He created them' (Gen. i. 27). God grants man sexual life, and fertility is granted by a special *blessing* of God (Gen. i. 28).[2] Here Yahwism reveals its pure consciousness of natural values. That is why in Israel the conception of children was always considered a sign of God's grace (see pp. 340f.). Nowhere in the Old Testament do we find the view that one might dispose of one's children, a question to which an affirmative answer was given without more ado in the ancient Arabian and classical western world. The respect shown in Israel to the miracle of reproduction, received as a divine gift, should not be regarded as a primitive element but rather as a spiritually purified element of Yahwism. These views also help to account for the struggle against the Baal-cult. The chastity of the love-poetry in the Old Testament (especially the Song of Songs) is a result of this appreciation.

If in Gen. i man and woman are put on the same footing as regards their sexual differences, in Gen. ii we find a certain social trait in the account of the creation of woman: here woman is said to have been created as the helpmate of the man, as his complement and partner.[3] She was taken from the first man, so fundamentally his equal, but secondary, although man, as a social being, cannot do without her; God gave her to man who recognized her as 'bone of his bones and flesh of his flesh';[4] she is the *'ishshah* (woman) beside him as the *'ish* (man). Love is the original relationship between man and woman

[1] On the exegesis of Gen. ii.f. compare P. Humbert, *Études sur le récit du paradis et de la chute dans la Genèse*, Neuchâtel, 1940; and my *Onderzoek naar de Paradijsvoorstellingen bij de oude semietische volken*, 1937.
[2] We must be careful not to understand this blessing as a law with respect to the sexual act in marriage; Gen. i is not concerned first and foremost with marriage, but with sexuality in general; both here and in verse 22 the meaning of the blessing as giving power is clearly evident.
[3] It cannot be maintained that Gen. ii. 18 stresses the *mutual assistance* of husband and wife, as is done in the *Herderlijk schrijven van de Synode der N.H. Kerk over het huwelijk*, 1952, pp. 11ff. This text should particularly not be applied to the sexual problem without more ado, and even less may we contrast Gen. ii. 18 with Gen. i. 28.
[4] This indicates the close family relationship; in ii. 24 the words 'one flesh' point to the unity of the family (Köhler, *Lexicon*, s.v.) or to the physical union of husband and wife (Gunkel, ad loc., and my *Onderzoek naar de Paradijsvoorstelling*, pp. 163, 171).

411

according to God's intention; she was made for him and he will cleave to her.

In this respect, too, the author of Gen. iif. presents a most spiritual conception of the relationship between man and woman, by which he stands out from the current views of his days. He believes monogamy to be the original relationship between man and woman; this is confirmed by the fact that in ch. iv bigamy is first ascribed to Lamech, one of the descendants of the cursed Cain and the man who song the hymn of the blood-feud. This proves that bigamy (polygamy) was to be condemned according to the author of Gen. ii.ff. and we may, therefore, attribute to him the above-mentioned idea of monogamy.

This social relationship between two people who were different from the outset, was, however, transformed by the influence of sin: woman's dependence upon man is a punishment of sin. This punishment also includes the fact that pregnancy and child-birth become a heavy and painful task for woman (Gen. iii. 16). The former punishment must allude to the patriarchal relationship between man and woman in Israel in which woman is allotted only a minor rôle in marriage; so this rôle is represented as willed by God: the wife is the possession of her husband (the be'ulah) and belongs to her husband's household.[1] Even in the New Testament this idea can be discerned (1 Tim. ii. 11ff.), but essentially[2] it may be considered as set aside in Christ. In Christ all human beings are wholly equal, and in Him there is neither male nor female. The stress on the fact that woman was tempted first (cf. 1 Tim. ii. 14) may also be connected with the late Israelite estimation of woman as the morally (sexually) weaker vessel.[3]

[1] This does not mean that the wife may be looked upon as the husband's property; the husband does not buy a wife by means of the dowry and he is not allowed to sell her. Marriage is not a marriage by purchase (an opinion held by J. Benzinger, *Hebr. Archäologie* and the *Herderlijk schrijven*), see for example J. Pedersen, *Israel*, I–II, pp. 63, 69 on *ba'al*, also von Baudissin, *Kyrios;* M. Burrows, *The basis of Israelite marriage*, 1938; further M. David, *Vorm en Wezen van de huwelijkssluiting naar de oud-oosterse Rechtsopvatting*, 1934; also F. Bloemhof, *Het vraagstuk der bewuste geboortebeperking*, 1953, pp. 101–2, where also further bibliography; J. Schoneveld, *Huwelijk en huwelijksrecht in de wereld van het O.T.* n.d. (1952?); B. Maarsingh, *Het huwelijk in het O.T.*, 1963; cf. also J. Leipoldt, *Die Frau in der Antike und im Urchristentum*, 1962 (in this book also a chapter about 'Die Juden').

[2] It is doubtful, though, in how far woman ranked below man in ancient Israel. From a juridical point of view this was apparently the case, but not in religion; woman stands in a personal relation to God just like man (Hannah, Hagar, etc.), she may also attend the cultic festivals, and prophesy (Deborah, Huldah); she is not allowed to serve in the cult or to offer up sacrifices (owing to anti-Canaanite tendencies), compare particularly M. Löhr, *Die Stellung des Weibes in Jahwe-Religion und -Kult*, 1908, who opposes the thesis held by Wellhausen and others that Yahwism was a man's religion. This was much more true of later Judaism than in ancient Israel.

[3] See J. Sirach xxv. 24: With a woman sin originated, and for her sake we all die

3. The State of Man; the image of God, innocence, suffering and sin

Man was originally created *in the image of God* (Gen. i).[1] We have dealt with this most important idea in ch. VI so that we need not dwell on this subject at greater length; it denoted man in his peculiar relationship to God, in his vocation to be God's vice-regent on earth but most of all to reflect in his nature the nature of God, just as the child is the image of the father. Besides the expression 'the image of God' we also find 'the likeness of God'. This latter phrase is a further definition of the former, it does not add a new element. Those dogmatics which have founded certain speculations upon this view are therefore on the wrong track; the expression 'after our likeness' is no more than a further explanation of the words 'in our image' (i. 26; v. 3).

Man as the image of God is set over the animal world. This does not mean that man's being in God's image only means that he rules the animal world, the latter is, in fact, the important consequence of the former: because man stands in a special relationship to God he is entrusted by God with dominion over the world.

The *image of God* in man was not lost, nor yet mutilated; at any rate this view is not found in the Old Testament. Gen. ix. 6 speaks of the image of God in man as well as Gen. i. Even if the priestly author knew the story of the lost paradise, it did not lead him to abandon the idea of the image of God in man after Gen. iif., or even after the Flood.[2] This proves that the image of God in man does not indicate his state of rightness, but the special relationship with God *in* which He has placed man, in contrast to the relationship between God and the animal world; it is man's fundamental vocation to be God's child, and this is not lost – not even by sin, because it rests upon God's will and is, therefore, founded upon the Creation.

It is clear that the author of Gen. iif. originally meant to say that man lived in perfect peace with God; there was perfect harmony in Paradise. God associated with man and walked in the garden of Eden, He sought man. The relationship was one of childlike attachment.

This is not to say that the state in which man and his wife are depicted originally is childlike, nor is it a state of cultural poverty (as the other Eastern peoples pictured primitive man, living with the animals and naked, which was intended to depict him as a being

(trans. Matter-Dyserinck, 1908). On the appreciation of the position of woman in the Bible and Christianity see G. Huls, *De dienst der vrouw in de Kerk*, 1951. We must also bear in mind the prayer in the Talmud, 'Praised be He that He did not create me as a heathen, as an ignorant man, or as a woman' (cf. Strack-Billerbeck, *op. cit.*, III, pp. 611 and 558B).
[1] On the relationship between God and man as the relationship between a father and his child, see pp. 172f. and 413; on literature about the image of God, pp. 170 and 171.
[2] Nor was this done in later Jewish theology; cf. Moore, *op. cit.*, I, p. 479 and Davies, *op. cit.*, pp. 33ff.

413

without culture). This is not the leading idea of Gen. iif., though it is certainly related to these ancient Eastern notions. For man had to cultivate and maintain the garden, which means that some degree of culture is presupposed; indeed, in Gen. ii man is also superior to the animals, no less than in Gen. i.

The state depicted in Gen. iif. might better be called the *state of innocence*, in terms of religion, a life in a pure childlike relationship with God, a life also reflected in the relationship between man and woman. It is, therefore, a perfectly natural harmony between them and also perfect harmony with nature. In this state of spiritual innocence the purity of natural life is still possible; this finds expression in the fact that man and woman do not feel shame in spite of the fact that they are naked. This does not exclude their consciousness of being man and woman, as is clearly apparent from the narrative; sexual consciousness is accepted as quite natural in this state of innocence. Hence in Gen. iii it is impossible to consider sin itself as the awakening of sexual consciousness. The consequence of sin is, however, that not only the relationship with God is broken (man hides from Him) but also the pure natural harmony between the sexes: man feels shame.[1]

Because man has eaten the fruit of the forbidden tree of the knowledge of good and evil the natural harmony between one human being and another suffers immediately.[2] This manifests itself in shame before each other and at the same time also in the disharmony between man and God. The cleavage in the original harmonious relationship between God, man, and woman (and ultimately the animal world, too) was caused by reaching out for the fruit of the one forbidden tree – the tree of the knowledge of good and evil, the symbol of higher divine knowledge. Sin is man's desire of independence, his *hybris*,[3] the desire to shake himself free of the childlike relationship with God, free of true innocence. And the punishment for this cleavage is the rupture of the relationship between man and the animal world, man and woman, man and the earth, it means suffering for woman and for man, and ultimately this punishment is death (symbolized in man's expulsion from the garden of Eden with its tree of life). Here God recognizes the fact that the harmony between Himself and man

---

[1] On the value attached to the element of sex in the Paradise story see my *Onderzoek naar de Paradijsvoorstelling*, pp. 142ff., 177, 181; a completely different view is held by J. Coppens, *La connaissance du Bien et du Mal et le Péché du Paradis*, 1948, reviewed by P. Humbert in *Bi. Or.*, V, 1948, pp. 140ff. (cf. also IV, pp. 46ff.).
[2] It might perhaps be said that man discovers that he is different from his partner.
[3] P. Humbert, 'Démesure et chûte dans l'A.T.', in *Maqqel shaqedh*, Festschrift W. Vischer, 1960, pp. 62ff., particularly pp. 68ff. and 79f., also my articles 'Sünde' and 'Sündenvergebung', *R.G.G.*[3] VI.

has been broken. Man who wanted to be himself, must fend for himself on this hard earth and in this hard life. The only sign of grace that he is given on his wanderings through life is the coat of skins he receives from God.[1]

In Gen. iv; viff. the author continues his reflection on the state of man. Instead of being innocent, as God intended him to be, man is a sinner and this fact makes itself felt more and more. When man in his high-handedness is left to himself he goes from bad to worse: Cain commits fratricide, his descendant Lamech sings the praises of revenge, hatred and war. In ch. vi. 5 and viii. 21 (cf. ix. 18ff. and xi. 1ff.) we see how sin poisons the human heart. Especially in vi. 5 this is stressed very clearly: '*every imagination* of the *thoughts* of his heart was *only* evil *continually*'. A more emphatic statement of the wickedness of the human heart is hardly conceivable. This is emphasized once more because in viii. 21 the same judgment is pronounced on humanity after the Flood; indeed, in ix. 18ff. and xi. 1ff. both Noah and his descendants prove to be wicked.

We cannot but conclude that the Yahwist author of Gen. ii–xi was a man who fathomed the depths of the sinfulness of the human heart and gave expression to his spiritual conviction of the depravity of the human race throughout his history of primeval times. The contention that this doctrine was not yet known in the Old Testament must, therefore, be incorrect,[2] though it would be as incorrect to assert that this view is found in the Old Testament as a whole.[3] The priestly author, for example, in ch. vi represents Noah as a righteous and honest man who is saved on account of his righteousness, and with him the doctrine of the author of the history of primeval times found but little response. In some of the Psalms (for example, Pss. xviii. 21; xxvi; xli. 13; cxix. 101ff.) and in the books of Job and Proverbs we also find the notion of the righteousness of the pious man (though not all the texts mentioned are relevant from a theological point of view[4].

[1] See the remarkable article by E. Peterson, 'Theologie der Kleidung', *Universitas*, III, 1948, pp. 1409ff.
[2] We should also think of the sins discovered by the authors J and D and by the prophets in the patriarchs and in the people in the desert; cf. for instance Deut. ix; Hos. xii; Ezek. xvi; xx; xxiii; Isa. xliii. 27; Pss xiv. 1–3; li; cxliii. 2; Eccles. vii. 20.
[3] It should be borne in mind what we said about sin in Ch. II, pp. 31f. On the hesitations of later Judaism compare Davies, *op. cit.*, pp. 20–34: it finds a twofold tendency within the human heart, one towards good, the other towards evil, cf. F. Weber, *Jüdische Theologie*[2], pp. 209ff.; and below pp. 285f.
[4] The idea 'righteous' already has a nomistic foundation in Proverbs (or is used popularly). In various Psalms (such as xxiv and xli) we cannot attach any theological importance to this protestation of innocence; the speaker protests his innocence against those who slanderously accuse him of evil. Job does not protest against the idea of sinfulness in general (xiv. 4) but against the view that his great suffering was caused by his great sins.

If we may take it that the Yahwistic narratives of Gen.ii–xi are by the same hand there must be a connection between the views of this author in Gen.vi.5, viii.21 and in the Paradise-narrative. This must lead us to the conclusion that the Christian interpretation of the Paradise-narrative as the story of man's fall (already taught by St.Paul in Rom.v and afterwards elaborated into the doctrine of original sin) is not unsound.[1] Is it true that the connection between human misery and sin is in the limelight in Gen.iif., but the continuation of the story in Gen.iv makes it clear that human sin, which started with the first man, continued in his descendants and revealed the corruption of his nature; for Gen.iv. is the immediate sequel to Gen.ii f.: fratricide, the worst of all sins, is already committed by the first child of the first human couple. The author is fully aware of the fact that, once man has admitted sin into his life it spreads rapidly and is transmitted from one generation to the rest.[2] He has, therefore, come very close to the conception of original sin.

This does not mean, however, that all men are equally bad sinners; the author of Gen.iif., too (cf. pp.55f.), seems to admit the existence of a line of righteous men who continue to glorify God, side by side with the line of the sinners (Seth, Enos, Noah, Gen.iv.25f., v.29).

For that reason we cannot say that the author of Gen.iif. teaches a general doctrine of *original* sin (the doctrine according to which the compulsion to sin impels all generations of man inescapably), however near he may have come to it. The fact that these two views mentioned above go together is one more indication that the Oriental is slow to arrive at a general doctrine, which draws abstractions from the particular and pronounces judgments on the whole with absolute validity. In other words, there is no question in the Old Testament itself of a dogma of original sin in the sense which the term has in Christian theology. It was St.Paul who, taught by the Spirit of Christ,[3] drew this radical conclusion as a doctrine from Gen.iif.

Nor did the Old Testament arrive at a systematic doctrine of sin, as is manifest from the many aspects of sin in the Old Testament. The dynamistic aspect we have already dealt with (pp.31f.), but we may add here something on the general moral and religious aspect. Generally speaking one may say: the commonest word for sin, both with respect to its linguistic use and its content, is *cheṭ* or *chaṭṭath*, derived from a root meaning 'to miss', so that it denotes sin as an *error*; the

---

[1] See Davies, *op. cit.*, p.33–4.
[2] Similar statements are also to be found in the Wisdom literature: Prov.xx.9 and Eccles.vii.20; cf. also 1 Kings viii.46 from one of the latest parts of Kings.
[3] And – we must add with respect to the formal point of view – living in a new atmosphere of thought (of the Hellenistic world), which tried to reduce general truths to formulas. See Davies, loc. cit.

moral aspect of sin is shown in the word 'awon, wrongness, while the religious aspect is denoted by the word pesha', which means sin as a revolt against God; God is the Lord to whom man owes obedience and who has expressed His will in His commandments; the transgression of these commandments is sin.[1]

But sin considered as an error also has a religious aspect; when Potiphar's wife wishes to seduce Joseph he says: 'how then can I do this great wickedness, and sin against God?' Adultery is a sin against God because God's commandment forbids adultery. At the back of the fact that sin is especially looked upon as a revolt there lies the belief that man stands committed to God, the Lord, and to His Revelation.

Like death, suffering (in the form of the pains of childbirth for the woman and the sorrows of everyday work for the man) is viewed as a consequence of sin in Gen. iif. This narrative may be looked upon as a spiritual document as highly important for the religious thought of Israel as the epic of Gilgamesh for that of Babylon. It connects suffering with sin, but this is not a direct, automatical connection, as if sin should involve suffering as a kind of fate.[2] For it is Yahweh who punishes sin with suffering. Suffering does not come upon man without His will,[3] as it does not happen without the will of the gods in the non-Israelite world either. There are, however, differences: in the Babylonian world there is no fundamental connection between suffering and sin but it can be brought about by the gods without any cause; moreover many demons make man suffer without reason, and when suffering is represented as punishment, this is done especially for cultic or ritual reasons.

The notion that there is a connection between suffering and sin is not only found in Gen. iif., but is also one of the underlying ideas of the wisdom of Proverbs (Prov. xii. 2 1, xxviii. 18ff.) and here, too, they are connected because it is the will of Yahweh (and the converse is true, as well).

That does not mean that this point of doctrine, which is an established fact for Israel, provides the solution for all problems. Like all other nations, Israel experienced again and again that happiness and faith, suffering and sin do not always go together (the opposite often proves to be the case). This leads to the question of the why and where-

---

[1] See Quell in Theol. Wb.z.N.T. I ἁμαρτανω; L. Köhler, 'Archäologisches', Z.A.W. 1928, pp. 213ff., Theologie[3] 1953, p. 158; Vriezen, R.G.G.[3], 'Sünde'; R. Knierim, Studien zur isr. Rechts- und Kultusgeschichte, cht' und chms, 1957; idem, Die Hauptbegriffe für Sünde im A.T., 1965, arrives at a different definition on the ground of a different method.

[2] In this direction think G. von Rad, Theologie I, p. 382, and Koch, op. cit.

[3] H. Donner, 'Leiden' II, R.G.G.[3] IV, p. 295. See further J. J. Stamm, Das Leiden des Unschuldigen in Babylon und Israel, 1946; and my De overwinning van het tragische levensgevoel, etc.

fore of suffering, a question which occupied many faithful believers (Ps. xxxvii; lxxiii) the above-mentioned psalm, reference is made to the fact that appearances are deceptive; one should mark the end of the wicked; in other cases suffering is thought to have a pedagogical end (Lam. iii. 25ff.; Job xxxiii. 36). The two most profound answers are found at the conclusion of the book of Job and in Isa. liii. They are widely different, but not contradictory; the former springs from the views of the *chokhmah*, the latter from the prophetic vision. The book of Job ends with the proclamation of the glory of God, who at the Creation wrought many things that are incomprehensible to man and for whom nothing is too wonderful. Thus man is thought to accept the greatness of God's majesty as the guarantee of the justice of divine rule, even if it should lead to things that are wholly unacceptable to man. In Isa. liii the Servant of the Lord effects atonement and renewal of life through his guiltless suffering. Whereas in Job suffering which is not understood finds it solution in the praise of God, in Isaiah liii it operates in the world as an atoning force.

All this made it impossible for a tragic view of life to develop in Israel such as came to prevail in literature in the ancient Eastern world and in Greece (cf. p.278). There are only occasional passages in the Old Testament that suggest such a view of life. When we attempt to reconstruct the earliest source of the life of Saul we get the impression that Saul is actually represented as a tragic hero rather than as a man who is conscious of his guilt. And from a story such as that of Jephtah (Judges xi. 30ff.) it becomes clear, too, that the tragic view of life was not altogether lacking in Israel. But in the Old Testament the expression of such a view was eliminated entirely in certain sources. Israel's faith in God radically put an end to this pessimistic and aesthetic view and depiction of life.

4. *The individual and the community.*

In very many respects, and particularly with respect to social relationship, the Old Testament bears strong ancient Eastern traits so that evidence for the special significance of Yahwism is not found ready to hand. Indeed, it is nowhere easy to demonstrate the importance of religion in the *social life* of the people, in present-day Christianity, either in its Protestant or in its Roman Catholic form, any more than in Israel.

In respect to the position of woman, family life, the connection between individual and community, and the relationship between the sovereign and his subject, the ideas and opinions of Israel are ancient Eastern through and through. These relationships should therefore be dealt with in a history of Israelite civilization rather than in a history of Israel's religion, let alone in a theology of the Old Testament. For an outline of these relationships we may refer to the splendid works by Max Weber, *Das antike Judentum*, and J. Pedersen, *Israel*, I–IV. Some features may, however, be pointed out that are particularly characteristic of Israel and justify the supposition that they are connected with the peculiar nature of Yahwism. It is these elements that should receive prominence in a theology of the Old Testament.[1]

The first important element that should be considered here is the way in which the Old Testament stresses the personal *responsibility* and personal *value* of man. The importance of personal life is emphasized very strongly in Israel, so that we may even say that here the full conception of personality was born.[2]

The personal element may be considered from three aspects:

a. as the indication of the individual as opposed to the social element.

b. as an indication of the value of human life, the human element as opposed to the infra- and supra-human.

c. as the idea of man's absolute responsibility as a spiritual being, i.e. as a human being who has been called by God. This last feature is characteristic of Israel; because he believes in God, the Holy One, who enters into relationship with man, the pious man who lives before the face of the Lord knows that he has a duty to Him.[3]

In all these respects the personal element in the Old Testament is done justice. In Israel the apprehension of the spiritual nature of human life lies at the root of all that is individual and humane. This may also be the reason why the other two forms of the conception of the personal element came to develop so early in Israel. Here, too, it would be better not to go back to a psychological explanation (see p.408), but to refer to the basis of Old Testament theology: faith in God (see p.406).

a. That the idea of the individual developed early in Israel was stated, for example, by Hempel,[4] against the views of most scholars for whom Israel's collective thoughts and ideas are an established dogma;[5] according to them individualism only came after the preaching of the prophets, and Jeremiah (xxxi. 29f.) and Ezekiel (xviii. 20)

---

[1] Very successful in this respect is W. Eichrodt, *Das Menschenverständnis des A.T.*[1], Zürich, 1947.
[2] See a.o. N. P. Bratsiotis, 'Der Monolog im A.T.', *Z.A.W.*, 1961, pp. 30ff., cf. p. 294 n.2.
[3] R. Bultmann, *Das Christentum als orientalische und als abendländische Religion*, pp. 16ff.
[4] *Gott und Mensch*, 1936, pp. 189ff.; *Das Ethos des A.T.*, 1938, pp. 41ff.; Eichrodt, *Theology*, II, pp. 238ff.; also found already in M. Löhr, *Sozialismus und Individualismus im A.T.*, 1906.
[5] For instance Joh. Pedersen, *Israel*.

were the first witnesses to it.[1] This is only correct in so far as it must be considered an established fact that individualism developed strongly during the age of the major prophets, which was also the age of spiritual conflict and political downfall. But this does not mean that individual experience did not exist before. This is evident, for instance, from the fact that in the earliest Israelitic book of law (the Book of the Covenant, Exod. xxi–xxiii) the death penalty is only inflicted on the offender himself, never on any one else, either a slave or a child, to take the place of the person guilty of the death of a third party,[2] as against certain cases in the Code of Hammurabi; in other words, the offender himself is responsible for his actions (cf. also Deut. xxiv. 16; 2 Kings xiv. 6). In practice the traditional collective punishment continued, in certain cases, to be inflicted for a long time (2 Sam. xxi; 2 Kings x).[3] See Ch. VIII, III.

It is remarkable that the Hebrew seals practically always contain the proper name of their owners, whereas this is only seldom the case with the Babylonian and Egyptian seals.[4] Names of women also occur on Hebrew seals.[5] Many of these seals are as early as the eighth century. This is a most welcome corroboration by archaeology of what could already be concluded from literature.

b. That the humane element was prominent in Israel at an early date is evident from the same code of law, which protects the slave against his master, even in contrast with the other ancient Eastern laws; a parallel to a provision such as that of Exod. xxi. 10 will be looked for in vain in ancient Eastern law (cf. also Job xxxi. 13).[6]

Indeed, the fact that the Book of the Covenant (Exod. xxi) *starts* with the demand for the release of the Hebrew slave after six years,[7]

---

[1] Compare A. Causse, *Du groupe ethnique à la communauté religieuse*, 1937, pp. 106–113; J. de Fraine, 'Individu et société dans la religion de l'A.T.', *Biblica*, 1952, pp. 324ff., 425ff. and H. Cazelles, 'A propos d'une phrase de H. H. Rowley', *Suppl. V. T.*, III, 1955, pp. 26ff.
[2] Eichrodt, *Menschenverständnis*, p. 8.
[3] In 2 Sam. xxi the demand is made by the Gibeonites; in 2 Kings x the issue concerns a royal house; in Deut. xiii. 12f. it is a question of collective guilt.
[4] A. Reifenberg, *op. cit.*, p. 9.
[5] Reifenberg, p. 14, who draws the conclusion that in ancient Israel women were 'persons from a juridical point of view'.
[6] Cf. Br. Meissner, *Babylonien und Assyrien*, I, 1920, pp. 375ff., who maintains that in antiquite slaves were not looked upon as human beings. They are particularly dealt with in the ancient Babylonian laws in so far as they were the property of a free citizen. Afterwards conditions improved to some extent.
[7] Meissner, *op. cit.*, p. 376, points out that in Babylon slaves for debt had to be released after three years (in the fourth); this is certainly connected with the greater value of labour in Babylonian society (which was much more complicated than the agrarian economy of Israel) rather than with more humanitarian motives; cf. also that according to the Code of Hammurabi § 118 a slave for debt could also be sold to others.

speaks volumes. The legislator is anxious to protect the *liberty* of those who are socially weak.[1]

The fact that for crimes against property[2] the death-penalty is never demanded in Israel's laws as against the other ancient Eastern laws is also a proof of the high value attached to human life. The opposite case, that a murder can never be atoned for by a gift of money, also points in the same direction.

The human element is also evident in provisions such as that of Exod. xxi. 10f., in which the Hebrew bondwoman is assured of all those rights of man that are due to him (according to the ideas current in those days).

The human ideals are expressed particularly strongly in the book of Deuteronomy, which emphatically asserts the rights of strangers and slaves (cf. especially Deut. v. 14 and 15).[3]

For all the severity of the laws of war operative in Israel (e.g., in the ban)[4] we do not find in the Old Testament certain cruelties found in later Assyrian military history (severe mutilations, flaying people alive, etc.). The Israelite kings are called merciful kings by the Aramaeans (1 Kings xx. 31).

c. The spiritual task man has before God was put first and foremost by the Yahwist in his historical narrative where he relates the personal calling of Abraham; indeed, the still older history of David also reminds us again and again of the way in which David was chosen personally by God (2 Sam. vi. 21).

The prophets in particular emphasize this feature of Israel's religion and point out man's personal task (cf. for instance, Mic. vi. 7f.). They themselves had been called directly by God and so they tried to make others realize this vocation, too, by their demand for repentance and spiritual obedience.

The book of Deuteronomy with its appeal, 'thou shalt love the Lord thy God with all thine heart, and with all thy soul, and with all thy might' (ch. vi. 5), is one of the most profound testimonies to the awakened consciousness of personality. The love of God becomes the dominating idea of life; the emphasis on the heart of man proves that the author demands man's absolute personal surrender in religious life.

[1] The possibility that this sense of freedom is in fact connected with the deliverance from 'slavery' in Egypt (Deut. xv. 15) deserves serious consideration; cf. C. van Leeuwen, *Le développement du sens social en Israel*, 1955, pp. 12ff. though he goes rather far in making all social consciousness dependent on this sense of freedom.
[2] Eichrodt, *op. cit.*, p. 9.
[3] See B. Maarsingh, *Onderzoek naar de Ethiek van de wetten in Dt*, 1961.
[4] We may also remind the reader of David's retaliations in 2 Sam. viii. 2. We do not read of mutilations in the O.T., except Judges i. 6f. as a pure act of revenge. The act of Menahem (2 Kings xv. 16) is mentioned with abhorrence, cf. Amos i. 13.

All this does not mean that the sense of community lags behind in the Old Testament; on the contrary, in various respects the Old Testament is strongly dominated by a collective consciousness which often strikes us as truly naive and 'natural'. But apart from this there are also traces of a quite consciously purified and spiritual sense of community, particularly in the teaching of the prophets and in the Paradise narrative.

In the latter we read how man was first created alone but that he could not be happy in this way of life. He then had to choose a partner, and for this purpose Yahweh first created animals; but man could not find a helper equal to himself among them; he does not find this helpmate until God creates woman out of one of his ribs (i.e. out of himself) and therefore his equal. On beholding her he exclaims, rapt in admiration: 'This is now bone of my bone and flesh of my flesh'.

It is God who gives the woman to man. And only in this fellowship does man find the fulness of life. Thus the author of Gen. iif. rejected individualism and acknowledged man to be a social being.

According to the author of Gen. iif. the creation of man was not complete until the fellowship between husband and wife, a relation considered as a *family community*, which implicitly includes the family, and therefore the children too. In this respect Gen. ii and Gen. i start from exactly the same conceptions (for Gen. ii cf. ii. 24 and the curse that falls upon the woman, which presupposes the child; see further pp. 411f. above).

5. *Man and the world (nature)*

The idea of nature as such is as foreign to the Old Testament as the notions of *cosmos*, world, and so many other abstractions. There is a heaven and an earth (Gen. i. 1) which together form the universe; we do find some general terms, such as *tebel*, the earth as land, and *cheled*, that which is, a word that may be applied to the term of life and to that which is spatially, the world, but these expressions are not intended as abstractions. In this sense the latter word is found twice in the Psalms (xvii and xlix); the former several times in the Psalms, the Wisdom-books and some Prophecies.[1] We come very close to an abstract wording when the term *kol*, all, is used in the sense of universe (Isa. xliv. 24). The more general notions belong to the poetic style and probably derives from the wisdom-literature.

Generally speaking, the Israelite does not live in a universe, nor in nature (which is a concept of Greek origin),[2] but under the wide open

[1] The word *'olam* only got its meaning of world in a spatial sense in later, non-Scriptural Hebrew.
[2] See von Rad, *Aspekte*, etc.

skies in his coutry in the midst of the things in their concrete existence, all of which are looked upon as the creation (Ps. civ. Job xxxviiiff., Gen. i). He clearly distinguishes between the various life-forms: there are trees, seed-bearing plants and grasses, but there is no word for plants in general. It is true that the Old Testament certainly knows gradations of life-forms, as is apparent from the Creationnarratives such as Job xxxviii, Ps. civ, but especially Gen. i: there is a difference between the inanimate cosmic phenomena (first and fourth days) and the living beings; vegetation is classed among the things of the earth; animate life begins with the animals.

There is also a certain gradation in nature. It is clear from Gen. i, and that is the point at issue, that man was called into being as the last and highest creature. A separate act of creation is needed (i. 26); whereas at the creation of the animals sea and earth are ordered (i. 20, 24) to bring forth fishes and animals, God performs the last act of creation Himself. The narrative of Gen. ii.4bff. is an antiparallel, for there man, as the principal creature, is created first and the animals afterwards.

In the narrative of creation there is on the one hand a direct connection between man and nature (the earth and the animals), on the other hand there is also a great distance. Man stands, as it were, on the border-line between two worlds: with regard to the matter from which he was taken he is linked closely to the earth, but on the other hand he stands at God's side, as the image of God, in accordance with God's will and is appointed to rule the earth (i. 26ff.; in Gen. ii. 19f. the fact that man gives the animals their names is a token of his power over the animal world).

This does not mean that the faithful in the Old Testament are not confronted with problems in nature, and that they see nature rationally. On the contrary, to the Israelite the world remains a miracle of God, in his eyes various natural phenomena are miracles (Ps. xxix, cvii. 23ff. the sea); this is emphasized particularly strongly in Job (xxxviiiff.). The idea of miracle is, as it were, implied in God's creative activity.[1] The earth is Yahweh's, in the full sense of the word (Pss. xxiv, civ, cvii); man can never fully understand Him and His work. There is, indeed, some degree of tension between two elements: that of the Creation-hymn Gen. i, in which the creation is subjected to man, and that of the Old Testament religious poetry where the miraculous element in nature is brought into prominence. This tension is, indeed,

[1] See pp. 333 and 407. – The conception of the miracle is still naïve, though; it is not concerned with breaking the laws of nature! See a.o. C. J. Mullo-Weir 'Some thoughts on O.T. Miracles', *The Annual of Leeds University Oriental Society* I, 1959, pp. 25ff. The words denoting miracle are: *mophet*: sign, symbol; *'ot:* sign distinguishing mark, stamp: *pele':* the miraculous.

realized, as is manifest from Ps. viii. On the one hand nature is viewed as a miracle because it is known as the mysterious work of God, but on the other hand it is withdrawn completely from the mysterious and terrifying atmosphere of the demonic; the terror experienced by primitive man, and also by the civilized man of antiquity, when confronted with nature which is in a sense hostile to man and civilization,[1] has been removed; with Eichrodt we may speak of the 'Entgötterung der Natur', which puts an end to the 'mythopoeic fantasy which binds man closely to the dark, instinctive life of the plant and animal world'.[2]

The Israelite belief in God, as it takes its birth from the history of salvation, in its transcendence and at the same time in its belief in the communion between God and man, delivers man from his fear of nature and lifts him from the state of a primitive being.

So, although man has sprung from the earth and is a creature, like the animals with which he must share the earth, he stands wholly at God's side and is an independent, spiritual being; he as it were executes God's will (Gen.i. 26ff.; Ps. viii). What this conception implies becomes clear when we think of some conceptions of the ancient Eastern world, where primitive man is represented as living with and like the animals;[3] of this idea we only find a reminiscence in Israel in Gen. ii. 18ff., but there, too, man is depicted precisely in his essential difference from the animal world (there is no helpmate for him among the animals; he must give the animals names).[4]

That is not to say that the Old Testament leads to dualism and contrasts man as a spiritual being with the earth and the animal world, represented as earthly. On the contrary, the first notion remains that man, too, is dust and is connected with the animals and the earth. *As far as matter is concerned man is merely material but because he has been called by God and stands in communion with Him he is a different being;* this is stated in the confession that God imprinted His image upon man and set him the task to rule over the earth and the animal kingdom.

The relationship between the faithful Israelite and the earth and the animals is therefore not antithetical. On the contrary, the earth and the animals have sprung from God's creative work and were also found very good by Him (Gen.i.31). The earth and the fullness thereof belong to Him (Ps. xxiv. 1) and praise His glory. Hymns such as Ps. civ and Job xxxviiiff. show how God rejoices in the creation.

---

[1] For instance, the sea; see above p.334, and cf. O. Kaiser, *Die mythische Bedeutung des Meeres in Ägypten, Ugarit und Israel*, 1959.
[2] W. Eichrodt, *Das Menschenverständnis des A.T.²*, 1947, p. 30.
[3] See my *Onderzoek naar de Paradijsvoorstelling*, pp. 47, 93, 97, (122) and above p.405.
[4] On the relationship between man and animal see now: M.L. Henry, *Das Tier im religiösen Bewußtsein des altt. Menschen*, 1958.

Man may also make full use of all these things; they were placed at his disposal. The Old Testament is anything but hostile to the world; it is well aware of the value and importance of beauty and the things of this earth. There is no estrangement from the world in Old Testament theology;[1] on the contrary, some Christians even find it difficult not to consider it heathen and eudemonistic. The joy that dominates the Old Testament was, however, also experienced by Jesus Christ: He, too, rejoiced in the splendour of nature to the full, such an intense joy over the life of birds and flowers as Christ appears to know in Matt. vi. 26–30 is unparalleled in antiquity. In this respect, however, Christ only repeats in even more splendid language, the fundamental mood of the Old Testament, as already found in Gen. i, Ps. civ, Job xxxviii and Prov. viii.

The joy about the world in the Old Testament is essentially joy about God's Creation; it cannot, therefore, be rendered without more ado by the maxim of Nietzsche: 'remain true to the earth', which springs from naturalism as such. Nor is the joy of the Old Testament equivalent to the joy to which the Russian author Dostoyevski bears witness in *The Brothers Karamazov* when he makes his hero kiss the earth – we may suppose a mystical naturalism at the back of this, connected with the idea of Mother Earth rather than with the Biblical appreciation of nature.[2] Nevertheless the Bible speaks with great appreciation both of life in this world and of the world itself.

In this light we must also see the hope of the future in the Old Testament. Here the same joy over nature and its abundance is found again (Amos ix, last verses; Hos. ii); here, as in paradise, the animals are man's companions (Isa. xi. 6ff.; Hos. ii. 17). Perhaps we can find it in the tradition of Christmas that the ox and the ass stand near the manger.[3]

---

[1] With only a very few exceptions. In the primitive stories of Gen. ii–xi we find an anti-cultural (not anti-natural) tendency (see p. 55), but this tendency is hardly to be found anywhere else in the O.T., not even in the work of the prophet Hosea, where this tendency was often supposed to exist; see my *Hosea, profeet en cultuur* (address 1941). Cultural elements were opposed by Hosea, Isaiah, and others only when, and in so far as, they led to a false reliance upon the powers of man or of the state. In the same way the prophets may stand out against the military institutions when they are the cause of pride among the people and prevent the people from relying upon Yahweh alone.

That is also the reason why it would be wrong to say that some prophets or psalms attach a greater value to the state of poverty, though as a matter of fact riches and injustice are often looked upon as closely linked, to such an extent even that sometimes the rich man is put on a level with the oppressor and vice versa (Isa. liii. 9; Amos ii. 6f.; Isa. i. 23; Pss. xlix, lxxiii). There also exists a certain parallelism between the ideas 'ani = poor and 'anaw = humble, but probably the text has not been handed down to us correctly in all these cases. The dangers of riches are enlarged on again and again in the O.T. (Hos. xiii. 6; Deut. xxxii. 15).

[2] Cf. above pp. 281f.   [3] The animals derived from Isa. i. 3.

It is no wonder, therefore, that the animals are also protected in Israel's legislation (cf. Exod. xxiii. 5; Deut. xxii. 6f., xxv. 4 – though St. Paul refuses to accept the literal meaning of this text in 1 Cor. ix. 9; in 1 Tim. v. 18, too, he uses the word in a symbolical sense). From the fact that not until Gen. ix. 2ff. is man allowed to use animals as food (in contrast with Gen. i. 29f. where man is given tree-fruits to eat while the animals are given herbs) it appears that the priestly author – like so many poets of antiquity who describe the golden age – was acquainted with the conception of peace among the animals at the beginning of the world.

At any rate this fact and the respect for the blood of slaughtered animals, which must always be given back to Yahweh (cf. Gen. ix. 4), reveal a profound respect for the miracle of life, even where the animal world is concerned (see p.340).

On the one hand the love of animals is by no means unknown in Israel (we could hardly expect anything else from an agricultural and pastoral people) and is even prescribed by the law so that it is a religious demand made by God. On the other hand Israel resists most strongly any form of sodomy for which in Lev. xviii. 23f. the Canaanites are reproached. From other sources, too, similar practices are known.[1] In Israel such things are invariably punished by death (Exod. xxii. 19; Deut. xxvii. 21; Lev. xx. 15f.).

6. *Man and the spiritworld*

It is important from a theological point of view that throughout the Old Testament the secondary religious world was almost entirely thrust into the background. Whereas in Babylonia and Assyria the literature of exorcism plays an important part (*shurpu-* and *maqlu-* texts) there is no trace of these things in the Old Testament, and already at an early date it was forbidden officially to perform any exorcism, sorcery or interrogation of the spirits (Exod. xxii. 18; 1 Sam. xxviii; Deut. xviii. 9ff.; Lev. xix. 31, xx. 27). In Mesopotamia magic and demonology assumed ever greater proportions,[2] especially in the tenth century B.C., while in the Old Testament only traces of this are found. This does not mean that in the practice of Israel's religion as it lived among the people demonology did not play any part at all. Not only do the repeated prohibitions point that way but other things too;

---

[1] On Egypt see Herodotus II, 46. In Hittite law the king may grant pardon in case of a death penalty (wich was not demanded in all cases).

[2] Landsberger, 'Der kultische Kalender', *Leipz. Sem. Stud.*, VI, 1, 1917; yet the sorcerers were repeatedly condemned in the Assyro-Babylonian laws, but apparently this applied rather to the unofficial ones.

in periods of syncretism magic and the consultation of the dead came to the fore again and again.[1]

The theological value of the ban on intercourse with spirits and demons in any form becomes particularly clear when we bear in mind that the people certainly always believed in the existence of such beings; this appears, for instance, from 1 Sam. xxviii, where the spirit (called *'ob* or also *'elohim*, deity, spirit) of the dead Samuel appears; and from Lev. xx. 27 where we read that the spirit of a dead man may take possession of someone.

People did not only believe in magic (think of the sorcerers at the Egyptian court!) but also in a world of spirits and demons. We find, for instance, Azazel (Lev. xvi. 8), the desert-demon, Lilith (Isa. xxxiv. 14), a post -exilic female night-demon adopted from Babylonia; the *se'irim* (A.V. satyrs, Isa. xiii. 21, xxxiv. 14; devils, Lev. xvii. 7), desert-demons; and the *shedim* (Deut. xxxii. 17; Ps. cvi. 37. A.V. devils), known from Babylonia as tutelary deities. People also believed in 'guardian angels' (cf. Acts xii. 15).

There are, therefore, various conceptions of all sorts of earthly and subterranean spirits but Yahwism forbids man to enter into contact with them and to worship them. The fact that the whole of this demonic world could be overcome in official Yahwism clearly demonstrates the peculiar spiritual strength of the belief in Yahweh. In this connection we must also bear in mind the difference between the Babylonian views concerning the various days and seasons of the year with respect to demonology, as we have found it in Assyro-Babylonian hemerologies, and the Biblical conception of the festivals and the Sabbath.[2]

Besides all kinds of spirits and demons of the earth and the underworld, there are also – as in the Babylonian religion, which clearly distinguishes between the gods of the underworld and those of the upper world – spiritual figures connected with the heavenly spheres; the sons of gods or angelic beings. Except when these appear as the angels revelation (*mal'akh Yahweh*, see pp. 209f.) the faithful have hardly any contact with them. Though the 'spirits', sons of gods and angels, belong to the divine world, they do not play an independent role but are only ministering spirits. These three all belong to the category we generally call angels although they are of quite different origins: the 'spirits' are probably connected with personifications of Yahweh's spiritual activity; the 'sons of gods' are rather figures of ancient popu-

[1] J. Th. de Visser, *De daemonologie van het O.T.*, doctorate thesis Utrecht, 1880; H. Duhm, *Die bösen Geister im A.T.*, 1904; E. Langton, *God and evil spirits*, 1942.
[2] On the hemerologies see R. Labat, *Hémérologies et ménologies d'Assur*, 1939, and my 'Hemerologieën', in *Jaarbericht E.O.L.*, 6–8, 1939–1942, pp. 114ff., 417f.

lar religion and are, therefore, polytheistic in origin; the 'angels' are messengers of God.

In the immediate relationship between God and man there is hardly any room for heavenly intermediaries, except in a later period when God is envisaged as more and more transcendent. It is true that in the practice of religious life the mediation of men, prophets or priests, was frequently invoked for prayers of intercession,[1] but here quite different factors play a part. The stars, which probably reprensented the heavenly hosts, could fight on Israel's side, too (Judges v. 20). Not until the post-exilic prophet Zechariah did an angel appear occasionally in behalf of man as intercessor (Zech. i. 12), as defender (iii. 1ff.), but in ch. i this figure is probably the guardian angel of the people, a function fulfilled by Michael and Gabriel in Daniel xii. 1 and x. 13ff.;[2] such a figure also appears already in 'the captain of the host of Yahweh' (Joshua v. 13ff.). But that an angel can be *called on* by man to intercede for him we find only in the Book of Job, and especially in xxxiii. 23–26 where in this connection the *mal'akh meliṣ* (i.e. the interpreter-angel) is mentioned (cf. also Job v. 1). In later post-Biblical Hebrew literature this phenomenon occurs repeatedly, because by that time the distance between God and man had become so great that heavenly intermediaries begin to appear. This interceding angel of Job and Zech. iii may have been introduced as the counterpart of the accusing angel, the *saṭan* ('he who accuses') whose duty it is to denounce the sins of the world.[3] This latter angel is one of the spirits who surround Yahweh's throne and was originally and in himself not the enemy of man, and even less the enemy of God. It is, at any rate, most remarkable that it is precisely in the book of Job (i.f) and in Zech. iii that the Satan plays an important part, and that it is precisely in the work of these two authors that we find the counter part of the Satan: a defending angel.

Both the possibility of the suppression of the demonic figures and the fact that there are no intermediary beings between God and man (none at all in the pre-exilic texts, and practically none in the post-exilic works) bear witness to the absolute personal and spiritual nature of the true worship of Yahweh. Consequently the divine beings were

---

[1] See N. Johansson, *Parakletoi*, 1940; P. A. H. de Boer, 'De voorbede in het O.T.', *O.T.S.*, III, Leiden, 1943.
[2] Cf. Deut. xxxii. 8 in the reading of the LXX, usually held to be the original one (according to which the nations were allotted to certain gods, cf. Deut. iv. 7 and Daniel x. 20); the Masora is defended by G. F. Moore, *Judaism*, I, pp. 226–7; see also H. S. Nyberg in *A.R.W.*, 35, 1938, p. 366. The LXX reading is now confirmed by a Hebrew fragment from Qumran (see *BASOR*, Dec. 1954, pp. 12ff.). Procksch (*Theologie*, p. 489) connects these heavenly powers with Ps. lxxxii and Isa. xxiv. 21.
[3] Cf. above pp. 304f.

eliminated from nature (see p.424) and the space between God and man was cleared completely of all intermediaries, thus remaining free. Yahweh's all-dominating majesty and the immediate relationship with Him proved victorious in both, though in popular beliefs many survivals remained and though, as in the later Christian churches with their adoration of saints, heavenly mediators, pleading man's cause with God, spring up in the work of prophets and teachers of wisdom after the exile. This last element heralds a new development which made great progress in Judaism with its angelology, but does not come within the framework of Old Testament theology.

CHAPTER IX

The prospect of the community of God

God, man and the world in the present and the future

A. INTRODUCTION

Yahweh's intervention in history dominated the faith of the Community of God in Israel and of its members, so much so that He was known first and foremost as the God who is actually Present; that is why the faithful believers in Israel more and more came to see Him not only as the God of the present but also as the Lord of the past and the future (pp.178ff.). In the living communion with Him the whole existence of man and the world was encompassed.

In the preceding chapters we spoke at length of Yahweh as the God of the community in the present and in history (pp.188ff.), but the prospect of the future was only hinted at tentatively (p.204f.). This is the moment to revert to this subject.

This aspect of Israel's belief in God calls for separate consideration: it is one of its most important elements. In the hardest times of Israel's history ever greater value was attached to this aspect; it was this prospect that gave Israel's faith its invincible strength, that guided the community of faith in days of distress and safeguarded Israel's existence as a people through the ages; it is this prospect, above all, that the New Testament takes as its starting-point (Mark i.2, 15).

To this prospect Israel could always cling, but it is even more important that Israel's hopes of salvation were permanently renewed. In the melting-pot of suffering the expectations of the future were purified and sanctified more and more and truly focused upon God Himself to an ever greater extent. In every-day life and especially during the critical periods of history these hopes were put to a severe test. More perhaps than any other aspect of faith it was the subject of fierce controversies between believers and unbelievers, in which one prophet strongly opposed the other's views. The great struggle to understand the will of Yahweh in the present and the future frequently reshaped the message of these hopes of the future completely and caused these hopes to be reborn ever and ever again. This is true of both the individual and the national and universal hopes of salvation. This continuous reorientation of the perspective of salvation makes

God Himself and communion with Him of vital importance to an evergreater extent (Jer. xxxi, Ezek. xxxvif., Isa. xl, xlix, lii). In days of great distress when God seems to be hidden in darkness, these hopes of the future made faith spring up again. Some clear examples are: the Exile, when the prophets Ezekiel and Deutero-Isaiah proclaimed their message of salvation looking forward to the future; the Persian period, marked by the appearance of prophets like Joel, Deutero-Zechariah, etc.; the days of the Maccabees, when the faithful cling to the message of the book of Daniel, or the period of the Essenes,[1] who in post-Maccabean times apply the words of the prophets to their own days; and last but not least the message of John the Baptist, of Jesus and St. Paul in the New Testament and in the early Christian Church.

From the point of view of universal history there is hardly any element of the Old Testament that had such a strong and renovating influence on the philosophies of life of later days.[2]

This is not to say, however, that we should view the message of the Old Testament wholly in the light of the hopes of the future. For these hopes are founded upon the belief in Yahweh who revealed Himself as the living God of the community. There is a tendency in present-day theology to over-emphasize the element of the promise, the expectations of the future,[3] nearly always at the expense of the communion. Recently H. Berkhof rightly pointed out that the hopes of the future should not be allowed to supersede the certainty of the presence of God.[4] The hopes of the future cherished by the eschatological movements mentioned above are inconceivable without the certainty of communion with God, a certainty which is deeply rooted in faith. It is quite clear, for instance, from the hymns of the Qumran-sect that the perspectives of hope of this sect rest upon the certainty of communion with God. Something comparable in the New Testament is the relationship between the present and the future regarding the expected second coming of Jesus Christ. In my opinion O. Cullmann and others are right in rejecting all alternatives and look upon the Kingdom of God as both present and future in Jesus Christ.[5] In the Bible these two aspects of the belief in God cannot be divorced, neither in the Old Testament nor in the New. The hopes of the future are based upon the certainty of the belief in the actual relationship to God, and

---

[1] See i.a. A. S. van der Woude, *Die messianischen Vorstellungen der Gemeinde von Qumran*, 1958.
[2] Cf. K. Löwith, *Weltgeschichte und Heilsgeschehen*, 1953.
[3] G. von Rad, *Theology;* cf. his *Offene Fragen*, ThLZ, 1963; see also Moltmann, *op.cit.*, e.g. pp. 88ff.
[4] *Over de methode der eschatologie*, pp. 480ff., NTT, 1964/5.
[5] See his *Das Heil der Geschichte*, 1965, pp. 18ff.

presuppose such a certainty; conversely the belief in God would become impotent without this prospect of the re-creation of man and the world.

This does not mean that we must not differentiate between the belief in the Kingdom of God in the present and in the future in the Old Testament. We shall be doing so in the following sections of this chapter. V. Maag, however, stated that we should not distinguish in the Old Testament between the Kingdom of God that is and the Kingdom that is to come.[1] On the strength of his sociological approach to Israel's religion he thinks that the promise had played such a predominant role in Israel's faith that this is the focal point of the whole of Israel's religion;[2] in his opinion Israel's faith is fundamentally and wholly based upon the prospect of history. However varied in its presentation, this view is too one-sided owing to its sociological starting-point. It seems indisputable to me that there was not only a belief in God in Israel that was focused on the hopes of the future but also another form, orientated towards the present, on account of the contrast between the beliefs of the so-called 'false' and 'classical' prophets as well as on account of the tensions that are found after the exile between two types of faith, the one 'theocratic', the other 'eschatological'.[3] In the following sections we shall discuss: the rule of God in the present (B) and the Kingdom of God in the hopes of the future (C).

B. THE RULE OF GOD IN THE PRESENT

In the Old Testament the rule of Yahweh in the present bears on God's activity on behalf of His people (Ps. ciii. 6–19) as well as on His providence regarding all creatures (Ps. cxlv. 10–16), so it is concerned both with history and the creation. It can be referred to Israel in particular (Ps. xxiv, 1 Chron. xvii. 14 and xxviii. 5f.).[4] Yet the notion of Yahweh as King mostly testifies to a universal view (cf. Isa. vi. 1–6, Ps. xxix. 10). In Ps. xxiv the notion of Yahweh's kingship is linked expressly with the concept of His universality (cf. xxiv. 8 and 1); the Yahweh-King-Psalms all have a strong universal tendency (Ps. xlvii. 3, 7f.; xciii; xcvff.). This is not surprising when we consider that the transference of the dignity of the kingship to Yahweh must be

---

[1] *Malkuth JHWH*, Suppl. VT., VII, 1959, p. 130.
[2] *Op. cit.*, p. 140.
[3] On this last contrast see O. Plöger, *Theokratie und Eschatologie*, 1959. On the other hand one should not over-emphasize the contrasts, as if the two types had nothing in common. In this observations on the prophets *(Theology* II*)* von Rad errs in that direction.
[4] In Dan. vii. 27 this is viewed in an eschatological light.

connected with the fact that Yahweh came to take the place of El, the king of the gods and the creator of the world.[1]

More than anything else the conception of Yahweh as King demonstrates the two-sided character of the belief in Yahweh. Again and again universal and particularistic ways of thinking coincide here. The cosmic and universalistic traits must be emphasized here, because we so often find a one-sided universalistic and nationalistic view of the Old Testament.

In various ways this universalism penetrated into Israel's religious thought and was adopted. One of these ways was being introduced to so many other nations and their religious ideas, especially their wisdom-literature; but the most important impulse towards universalism must have come from Israel's experiences during the period of David and Solomon, when Yahweh opened the whole world to Israel, as it were, and revealed His power over the nations.

One of the most important motifs that may have made a strong impression in that period is the concept of creation (Gen. xiv. 18f., cf. also Gen. ii. 4bff.). Though this notion was incorporated into their message by the last of the pre-exilic prophets only (cf. Jer. xxxi. 35ff.) we may take it that the idea had already been integrated in Israel before that time and that it ready been integrated in Israel before that time and that it played an important part particularly in the cult (Ps. xix. 2; xxiv. 2; xxxiii. 6, 9; civ).

The period immediately preceding and during the exile was the time when the concept of creation was given its regular place in theological thought. One may maintain that the history of creation that underlies Gen. i was elaborated in those days for the benefit of the worship of Yahweh in the temple-cult. It is Deutero-Isaiah's message in particular that bears testimony to the fact that in those days the creation-motif had been incorporated into Israel's faith both spiritually and theologically.

This concept, which Israel elaborated for its cult in such an impressive manner (Gen. i), – together with the wisdom-literature[2] – constituted a considerable contribution to the genesis of the notion of the unity of the world, the conception of a certain order in nature and of the connection between the various parts of the world-order, in other words, the genesis of the idea of order, of the cosmos,[3] and in a sense also of a development in accordance with God's plan.[4] This theological

---

[1] See my *Religion of Israel*, pp. 33ff.
[2] For wisdom see above, p. 244f.; it might also be one of the sources for the conception of the Creation, see below.
[3] Compare with this the element of making a separation at the Creation.
[4] We think here of the structure of the Creation narrative, in which there is a

conception of the Creation was and is (as we observed above, p.333f.) of tremendous importance for the whole of Israel's view of life and of the world, and indeed not only of Israel but also of the Christian world up to this day. In this 'hymn', intended to magnify God, a complete view of life is contained.

In the 'creation-theology' Israel found a new means to proclaim the glory of God; it was therefore taken up immediately by the prophets, by Jeremiah, but especially by Deutero-Isaiah. The latter, particularly, realized and made people realize what it means even for a believer to think in terms of the cosmos, to know that God not only dominates the history of the nations, but that He has also created and still rules the universe, that He has appointed the courses of the stars, of the sun and the moon. This realization strongly supports Israel's faith, based on experience and revelation, and does not fail to make its influence felt throughout the whole of spiritual life. It is particularly to this connection of the preaching of salvation and the preaching of the Creation that Deutero-Isaiah's message owes its sublimity and its influence (xl. 12ff., 26f.; xliv. 23ff.; xlv. 6ff., 18f.; xlviii. 12ff.).

Israel's prophets had always known that the living God revealed Himself in His strength in the world, and also in nature; but now this message was given a very special accent because it came to be proclaimed that the whole of the world was entirely dependent upon Him, because He and He alone was the Creator. This made the Old Testament message concerning God even more urgent. Particularly so, because the faith in God as the Creator of the world did not place the Creator Himself outside the world but also realized His connection with the world; in Jeremiah (xxxi. 35ff.) the Creator remains the God of history whose activity continues up to this day, and even more in Deutero-Isaiah's message where he puts first and foremost the affirmation that Yahweh is going to create something new in the world (xlii. 9ff.; xliii. 19ff.; xlviii. 6ff.; lii. 15). By this the creation becomes a *creatio continua;* creation is not only a historical or a cosmological but a downright topical theological idea. This is, of course, connected with the whole of Deutero-Isaiah's view, according to which the world is passing through a period of transition towards the kingdom of God.[1]

For that reason I cannot agree with Eichrodt[2] when he considers

progress from inanimate to animate nature, and of the creative power that is attributed to the earth (Gen. i. 11f. and xxiv) and to the word of God.
[1] See below pp.450ff., 457.
[2] *Theology*, II, p.154; cf. L. Köhler, *Theologie*, p.73: 'The creation is not a declaration in the field of natural science, but of human history'. See p.334.

the doctrine of the creation as a transition from an anthropocentric to a cosmic philosophy of life and thinks that in this latter view nature is considered for its own sake. It is true that the doctrine of creation also has a 'scientific' aspect,[1] but it is equally true that it is much more than that and, apparently, that this is not even its most important element. Indeed, the creation-narrative is not merely cosmic; on the contrary, man is the crowning glory of the creation (cf. particularly Ps. viii, and also Ps. civ.); the whole story might as well be called anthropocentric as cosmic. The best solution of the problem will be to say that it is theocentric; from God both the world and man are viewed in their comparative independence – but what surpasses this is the fact that man, the world, and God are considered as connected with each other, while He is and remains the Only One from whom everything springs and to whom everything points.

There is a close connection of Gen. i with the old prophetic view of nature, but also with the nature-psalms (viii, xix, xxix, civ, cxlviii; Pss. viii and cxlviii are more recent than the other three). In such Psalms as viii, xix, and civ elements of wisdom emerge; in the beginning of Ps. xix, in xxix and civ we may recognize memories of ancient nature-myths; there is certainly a literary connection between Ps. civ and the Egyptian hymn to Aton; but in spite of all that all these psalms became truly Israelite hymns celebrating the glory of Yahweh. In the theology of the creation man is assigned a place of honour by God (Gen. i; Pss. viii, civ), entirely in agreement with the doctrines of Yahwism.

If, therefore, the creation-narrative of Gen. i cannot be looked upon merely as the expression of a cosmology, this theological conception may promote the idea of the independence of the world beside God, so that the directness of the relationship between God and man tends to be lost. This happens particularly when not God Himself, but a hypostasis of God, Wisdom, is looked upon as the Creator of the world; but this only becomes manifest in the apocryphal literature.[2]

The theology of the Creation has certain definite limits; it owes its value for religious life only to its connection with the history of salvation. When this connection is lost sight of and the theology of the Creation alone remains, the Creator Himself becomes an unknown Being without any distinctive qualities, which can no longer be

[1] One might suppose that the theology of the Creation was also influenced by Wisdom; but the former did not come to the fore until Israel had been overwhelmed by the nations and learned to look up to Yahweh as the omnipotent Majesty. Isa. vi. 3 ('the whole of the earth is full of His glory') might be looked upon as one of the first prophetical utterances pointing this way.
[2] This correct view is held by Gemser in his commentary on Prov. viii. 22ff. in *Tekst en Uitleg*.

known. This happens in the book of Ecclesiastes, in which no trace is to be found of the idea of the Covenant or of the history of salvation which gave the prophetic message its colour and warmth. The theology of the creation stood firm when confronted with ancient Eastern and Hellenic wisdom, but in itself it lent only slight support for the every-day practice of religious life. It is no wonder, therefore, that Ecclesiastes should waver when confronted with the problems of life, in spite of the fact that his relationship with God remained intact. From a rational point of view he could make out a strong case, but from a religious point of view he is a border-figure in the Old Testament message, whose value lies in his exposure of the weakness of all human security.[1]

Thus the theology of the creation in itself remains of secondary importance compared with the knowledge of God founded on revelation and on the history of salvation;[2] it is an ultimate consequence of this knowledge and widens our view, but it does not offer a starting-point for faith.[3]

There is another field in the Old Testament where universalism finds expression: in the relationship between Israel and the world of nations.[4] In this respect a spiritual growth in history is clearly to be observed, though this development was interrupted again and again. In point of time it is probably anterior to the cosmological views[5] (as far as we can judge on the grounds of literary criticism). This is not to be wondered at, though, for because of the starting-point of its religious life (cf. the preaching of the prophets) Israel orientates itself mostly towards history. It experienced God's hand particularly in His guidance of the nations of the world, by His deliverance of Israel from the power of the Egyptians.

At all events the Old Testament view of the world of nations actually reached its widest outlook as early as Isaiah. To him it becomes clear how God meant the relationship between Israel and the nations to be and how it will be one day: the nations will share

---

[1] On Ecclesiastes compare my 'Prediker en de achtergrond van zijn wijsheid', *Ned. Theol. Tijdschr.*, 1946, pp. 3ff. and 65ff.

[2] Against the non-Biblical religions where the belief in the creator-deities plays a much more important part, apparently owing to their 'naturalistic' character.

[3] Köhler (*Theologie*, p. 71) calls the Creation an eschatological conception; by this he means that the idea of Creation places God there where He 'spans all time, appointing its goal and completing it, while He dominates and forms all times'. See above, p. 334.

[4] See besides A. Bertholet, *op. cit.* (above p. 376 n. 1), now R. Martin-Achard, *Israël et les nations*, 1959.

[5] Here, too, we find the influence of the foreign wisdom that was very popular in Israel during the reign of Solomon and reached Israel mainly from Egypt. This wisdom, which represents a kind of 'religious humanism', certainly helped to widen Israel's range of ideas at an early period.

with Israel in the knowledge of God; the whole world is included in God's mercy: the nations, too, are admitted to the mount and the house of the Lord, and will receive His *torah!* (Isa. ii). Here the preaching of the Old Testament has gained its greatest tension.

This happened in the period, which became of the utmost importance to Israel, when the northern kingdom, Ephraim, was led captive to Babylon and when Jerusalem, too, was threatened by the all-conquering Assyrians but Yahweh once more saved the city dedicated to Him and delivered it by a miracle from the power of the mighty enemy hosts. In this period when faith had to stand a severe test and the prophet Isaiah came to his profound pronouncements on faith as the sole ground of vital strength and salvation (ch.vii; xxx), in this period when Israel was confronted with the sternest reality by the world-powers and when the question concerning the relationship between God and these nations was raised with great emphasis (think, for instance, already of Amos ix.7), Isaiah replied in faith that God uses the nations of the world in His service to perform His will, and, indeed, even to execute that will concerning Israel! The preaching of Amos and Isaiah brings the nations of the world within the religious horizon of Israel; in prophetic preaching they are considered as guided by Yahweh: even the world power of Assyria is a rod in God's hand. In these tensions which arise within Judah and in which the prophets share to the full, a new universal conception springs up in which the nations are also included in the world-order directed by Yahweh. And this means that they come to be seen in the light both of God's holiness and God's love. Judgment is pronounced upon them, too (Isa.x. 5ff.; xxxvii. 2ff.), but they also share in the expectation of salvation (Isa.xi. 10; ii. 2ff. = Micah iv. 1ff.) Light and darkness are not distributed in such a manner that all the light falls upon Israel and the world of nations stands in utter darkness, or vice versa; on the contrary, both Israel and the world of nations get their share of light as well as darkness. In this period of the severest afflictions the Spirit made it clear to the prophet and assured him that God is and remains God for all men; that He continues to rule, as the God of holiness and love, over all the world. In this very period the danger of the nationalization of Israel's faith in God (the danger of particularism, which assumed serious proportions after Elijah's struggle against syncretism) was overcome and the broad conception of God's relationship with the world arose, in which even the enemies of Israel on earth share in the knowledge of God and in communion with Him!

This view of Isaiah's is the broadest we find in the Old Testament; which does not mean to say that after that period no new elements were introduced in the relationship between Israel and the nations –

on the contrary. For it is evident that in Deutero-Isaiah (ch.xlii) such a new element is introduced; the expectation of the salvation of the nations (which he shares with Isaiah) leads him on to the message that Israel must bring the *torah* to the nations; it brings him to a new, missionary understanding of Israel's calling; but this point will be dealt with at greater length in the latter half of this chapter (see p.452).

Faith in Yahweh's rule is expressed in the statement that He is *King*.[1] This kingship of Yahweh was already taught by Israel at a very early period (Judges viii. 22f.) and bears first and foremost upon His communion with the people; it comprises the idea of His rule as a power and a blessing for His people.[2] But Yahweh is also denoted as king in general, to indicate his power over the present and the future for Israel and the whole world. From the original idea of Yahweh's kingship over Israel the conception of the absoluteness of Yahweh's rule has sprung. He is honoured as the king par excellence especially in the so-called psalms of accession to the throne (xlvii; xciii; xcv-xcix); Yahweh is glorified in the cult as the Lord of the world to such an extent (Ps.xxiv; xlvii), that it is not to be wondered at that in later psalms (than these)[3] Yahweh is celebrated as the King in an eschatological sense.

While the book of Isaiah emphasizes the universal character of Yahweh's kingship (cf. Isa.vi.5 with iii; especially Deutero-Isaiah thinks in these terms, xliii.14f.), with the Chronicler the idea of the real kingship of God comes to the foreground (1 Chron.xvii.14; xxviii.5; xxix.23 etc.): he speaks of the *malkuth Yahweh*, the kingdom of Yahweh, when he means Israel.[4] This theology, which directly

---

[1] G. von Rad: *Melek und malkut im A.T.* (s.v. βασιλεύς), *Th.Wb.z.N.T.*, I., I, pp. 563ff.; id., 'Erwägungen zu den Königspsalmen', *Z.A.W.*, 1940, pp.216ff.; O. Eissfeldt, 'Jahwe als König', *Z.A.W,.* 1928, pp.81ff.; M.Buber, *Königtum Gottes*, 1932; A.Alt, 'Gedanken über das Königtum Jahwes', *Kleine Schriften*, I, pp.345ff.; H.J.Kraus, *Die Königsherrschaft Gottes im A.T.*, 1951; V.Maag, *malkut JHWH*; J.Hempel, 'Königtum Gottes im A.T.', *R.G.G.*[3] and the book of W.Schmidt mentioned on p.366; W.Eichrodt, 'Les rapports du N. et de l'A.T.' in *Le Problème biblique*, ed. J.Boisset, 1955, pp.105ss., especially pp.121ss.

[2] The fact that the development of the word *malakh* was different in the various languages (Akkadian and Aramaic 'to advise'; Hebrew 'to rule'; Arabic 'to possess') points to the various functions connected with being *melekh*, that of powerful wisdom probably being the earliest; otherwise W.Schmidt, *op. cit.*, p.55, and H.Wildberger, *Eigentumsvolk*, p.86. Buber connects with it the idea of leading the way. It is a question whether this idea is not rather connected with the conception of the king as *shepherd*, a symbol used in all the ancient Semitic languages and also frequently met with in the O.T.; in any case the idea of the shepherd expresses the relationship between king and people much better. Cf. also J.Boehmer, *Der alttestamentliche Unterbau des Reiches Gottes*, 1902, pp.31ff. (Under Aramaic influence the word *malakh* is used once in Hebrew in the meaning of 'to consult', Neh.v.7).

[3] It seems most probable to me that in the Yahweh-King-Psalms we should distinguish between an earlier and a later group (later: Ps.xciii; xcvff.).

[4] See above p.368f., and particularly O.Plöger, *Theokratie und Eschatologie*, 1959.

438

identifies the kingdom of God with the empiric post-exilic Israel,[1] is on the one hand a consequence of the expectation of salvation as inaugurated by Deutero-Isaiah (see below, pp.450ff.), on the other hand it comes dangerously close to Israel's conceptions of the period before the great prophets in which Yahweh's kingship assured Israel of its own unassailable position and its dominion over the nations (cf. Num.xxiii.20ff. and the other prophecies of Balaam). Here the same thing happens as in the case of the idea of being called: the later Judaic conception in a way returns to the naturalistic notions on Israel as the people of God, already opposed by the prophets.[2]

The expression *malkuth Yahweh* is used frequently in the New Testament, but there it is understood particularly in a universal and eschatological sense. Especially universality, already connected with the idea of Yahweh's kingship in the Psalms, made the expression *malkuth Yahweh* a term that could very well be used in an eschatological sense (Dan.vii.27).

C. *The kingdom of God in the expectation of the future*[3]

The belief in the kingship of Yahweh, which was expressed especially in the cult but which also formed the basis of the preclassical prophetic predictions, raised high hopes in Israel of blessing and prosperity in a national sense; because contemporary theology in which Israel was looked upon as the people of God, assured the people of communion with God, they also thought they could rest assured that Yahweh would continue to reveal His acts of salvation (*ṣidqoth Yahweh*).

People had set their hopes on the final acts of revelation of God, who would destroy all Israel's enemies, an expectation expressed in many Psalms, particularly in the King-Psalms (ii; xx; xxi; lxxii; cx). This day of reckoning was looked forward to as the great day of salvation; it would be a day of light, the day of the Lord, the *yom Yahweh* (Amos v.18).[4]

This hope was destroyed entirely by the classical prophets (Amos v.18; Isa.ii.6ff.; Zeph.ii); in strict contrast to the hope of salvation which had become customary, they proclaimed the day of God's revelation as a day of darkness and ruin. This put an end to an opti-

---

[1] In *Theology of the Chronicler*, JBL, 1963, pp.369ff., R.North opposes to this view that the Chronicler wants to represent David instead of Moses as the true Chosen one.
[2] See my *Erwählung Israels*, p.110, n.4 and above pp.59 and elsewhere.
[3] For further literature see the end of this chapter.
[4] On the day of Yahweh there exists an extensive literature; cf. L.Cerný; W.Cossmann; H.Gressmann, *op. cit.*; S.Mowinckel, *Psalmenstudien*, II; P.A.Munch, *The expression bajjom hahu*, 1936; A.Lefèvre, 'L'expression "en ce jour là", dans le livre d'Isaias', *Mél. bibl. A. Robert*, pp.174ss.; H.Wheeler Robinson, *Inspiration and Revelation*, pp.135ff.; G. von Rad, 'Der Heilige Krieg', *Theologie* II, pp.133ff.

mistic, uncritical religious conception founded on a naïve expectation of a communion between God and the people which as it were continued to exist of itself.

Procksch[1] has justly emphasized that it is incorrect to identify the belief in Yahweh's kingship and the belief in the kingdom of God in the eschatological sense.[2] The former had been professed in Israel from early times, while the latter was the fruit of the preaching of the prophets. It is true that the former may be considered the basis and deepest content of the latter, for the prophets, no less than the rest of their people, were convinced of the fact that Yahweh ruled as king; but they had come to understand by the Spirit of God that this kingship in itself did not mean that Israel as a state and a people would always and in all respects be victorious without more ado. On the contrary, they were convinced that Israel would be broken down and would first have to pass through the severest judgments in order to be prepared for the true kingdom of God.

The hope of salvation took widely different forms; in the various writings of the Old Testament they are found in a very unsystematical order; often all kinds of different types are found together in one collection (Zech. ix–xi; xii–xiv; Joel iv [English text iii]). It is therefore not easy to discover the connections between them. We shall first sketch the various conceptions themselves and then we shall see how these occur successively in the writings of the prophets and in what succession, to finish up these observations with an indication of the connection of these conceptions with the New Testament.

a. The various forms of the hope of salvation

In order to be able to survey the field we shall first have to make some distinction between the specifically messianic expectations and the expectations of salvation in general. Usually they are all lumped together in theology and all expectations are subsumed under the term messianic. It is clear that this does not occur in Jewish theology,[3] probably in deliberate contrast with Christian theology; there are many among the Jewish theologians who include messianic belief entirely under the general hopes of salvation and do not give the Messiah a central position;[4] there are even some who have wholly

---

[1] *Theologie,* p. 591.
[2] Cf. also G. von Rad, *op. cit., Th.Wb.z.N.T.,* I, pp. 566ff., against this V. Maag, *Malkut JHWH,* see above p. 432.
[3] Strack-Billerbeck, *op. cit.,* IV 2, 858.
[4] Strack-Billerbeck, *op. cit.,* IV 2, p. 817; R. Aqiba brings the days of the Messiah back to 40 years, so that the Messianic period is merely a short transition period (cf. also *Bab. Talmud, Sanhedrin,* XI, I, II, fol. 99).

abandoned the idea of a Messiah as the personal saviour.[1] This latter view, however, was emphatically rejected by the Jews in general.[2]

The fact that it is necessary to distinguish between those expectations of salvation which are phrased in more general terms and whose fulfilment is dependent upon God and those in which the figure of a saviour (Messiah) plays a part should not make us assume a *contrast* between these expectations.[3]

Even the use of the words Messiah and messianic' is already problematic in this connection. What must these words be taken to mean – any expectation of salvation in which a person occupies a central position, or only those hopes which centre upon the figure of a king? If the latter should be the case, the question arises if we can only consider as messianic expectations those hopes which are connected with the house of David; if the former should be correct, we must ask ourselves if a figure like the *'ebed Yahweh*, the Servant of the Lord, may also be looked upon as a messianic figure. On this point it is difficult to reach a decision that is satisfactory in every respect, because the word *Messiah* (the anointed)[4] is nowhere in the Old Testament used in connection with the figure of the saviour! The latter is indicated in various ways, but never as the Messiah;[5] the name king is not applied directly to him, either.[6]

Because the word Messiah is so little defined, so 'mehrdeutig', the word messianic could readily be applied to all those prophecies that place a person in the limelight as the figure of salvation. We need not make an exception for the Servant of the Lord; even if on account

[1] In olden times for example R. Hillel (3rd century), *Sanhedrin*, fol. 98b; compare also Strack-Billerbeck, I, p. 70b. There are also modern Jewish theologians who defend this view. In certain Jewish circles it is the custom to call the national deliverance of Israel of our times the Messianic age; there are many who say deliberately that the Messiah has come. Many of the orthodox Jews, however, absolutely reject this view.
[2] Compare *Sanhedrin*, fol. 99, R. Joseph against R. Hillel; Maimonides included the expectation of the Messiah in his 13 articles of faith as the 12th point of doctrine; see M. Friedländer, *Die jüdische Religion³*, 1936, pp. 18, 124ff.
[3] H. W. Wolff, 'Herrschaft Jahwes und Messiasgestalt im A.T.', *Z.A.W.*, 1936, pp. 168ff.
[4] The word Messiah, the anointed, is used to denote certain functionaries, particularly kings (Isa. xlv. 1); it was the custom for kings and priests to be anointed; on one occasion the patriarchs are called anointed and prophets (Ps. cv. 15), and there is also one text where the people is said to be anointed (Hab. iii. 13). Cf. for later Judaism A. S. van der Woude, *Die messianischen Vorstellungen der Gemeinde von Qumran*, 1957, pp. 244ff. (dissertation Groningen). O. Eissfeldt, Christus I (Messias), *R.A.C.* 2.
[5] See for example A. H. Edelkoort, *De Christusverwachting in het O.T.*, p. 6, A. S. van der Woude, *Messias* in B.H.H. II, 1964, p. 1197.
[6] Cf. Jer. xxiii. 5; see Eichrodt, *Theologie*, I, p. 271; Edelkoort, *op. cit.*, pp. 123f., 291; G. von Rad, *Th. Wb. z. N.T.*, I, p. 566; H. W. Wolff, *op. cit.*, p. 197; Ezekiel uses the name of king to denote the Davidic figure of the future xxxvii. 22, 24), but in ch. xlff., for example, he avoids this title; on this problem in the work of this prophet see E. Hammerhaimb, 'Ezechiel's view of the monarchy', in *Studia Orientalia*, Joh. Pedersen, 1953, pp. 130ff.

of the word Messiah we were to conclude that the Messiah must be an anointed figure and that he must bear an office (king, prophet or priest), the *'ebed Yahweh* could not be excluded because after his suffering he, too, is given kingly power (Isa.lii.13, 15; liii.12). Moreover, the word *'ebed* also denotes an office, though a subordinate one; it is true that no mention is made of his being anointed, but the same applies to the figures whose appearance is proclaimed in Isa.ix, xi or Jer.xxiii.

Either of these groups should be differentiated as to content.[1]

Within the messianic expectations there are differences between, on the one hand, those hopes which allude directly to the house of David (Gen.xlix; Num.xxiv), or even call the messianic figure by the name of David (for instance, Ezek.xxxiv.21ff.), some of which emphasize rather the national character of the salvation brought by the house of David (Num.xxiv) while others stress the moral and spiritual element (Isa.xvi.5; Jer.xxiii); and, on the other hand, those expectations which do give the house of David a place in the background but do not without more ado give it a place of central importance (Isa.xi; Mic.v; Amosix.11), and finally those in which the royal house is no longer considered (Isa.liii), or in which at any rate the house of David is no longer mentioned (Zech.ix.9).

Among the general hopes of salvation there are some which offer very concrete representations whereas others speak most emphatically of a hope of a spiritual salvation. In the former we find again and again general ancient Eastern conceptions, while the expectations of the latter group express the hopes of those prophets who have passed through the severest afflictions. Directly material are the expectations of exceptional prosperity (Amosix.13; Joeliv.18, A.V.iii.18) or of peace among the animals (Hos.ii.20; Isa.xi.6ff.; Ezek.xxxiv.25ff.; Isa.lxv.25); they are characterized by supra-normal and sometimes mythical conceptions which remind us of all kinds of mythological conceptions of the ancient Eastern world.[2]

Besides these there are also expectations which transcend contemporary life on earth without being mythological; they speak of the salvation that will come to Israel, surpassing all that has ever been: Israel will rule over the nations, the nations will serve Israel (Mic. iv.13; vii.10ff.; Isa.lx–lxi; Obad.17ff.). Sometimes these hopes are

---

[1] On the various forms see H. Gressmann, *Der Messias*, 1929.

[2] On account of this a certain connection between ancient Eastern and Biblical representations cannot be denied, but this connection should not cause us to trace back the eschatology of the O.T. itself to the ancient East, as was done, for example, by Gressmann, for there is no such thing as an ancient Eastern eschatology, as has rightly been emphasized by Mowinckel in several of his works.

more universalistic: the nations will come to know Yahweh (Isa. ii; Mic. iv) and share with Israel in the salvation of the Lord (Zech. viii. 20ff.); they will also have peace among themselves (Isa. ii; Mic. iv).

Finally there are the expectations of spiritual salvation which is to fall to the people in future. This aspect, too, can be viewed in quite different lights: we may find that emphasis is laid upon the fact that the people will serve Yahweh with all their heart (Jer. xxxi. 31ff.; Ezek. xxxvi. 26f.), or that Yahweh will dwell in Israel (Ezek. xxxvii. 27; xlviii. 35; Zech. ii); or that the Spirit of the Lord will descend upon all flesh, Joel iii (ii. 28ff.); or that all the nations will partake of God's feast (Isa. xxv. 6ff.).

b. The historical connection

It is clear that these conceptions cannot be lumped together or fitted together exactly, so that their theological relevance could be understood by applying the method of the greatest common measure or the least common multiple.

The only way to gain a true insight into the meaning of these conceptions is to consider them in their proper historical milieu, in their context, and thus to place them in a certain perspectival connection. This is not to say that the historical perspective always agrees with what might be called the perspective in an ideal sense.

The hopes of salvation in the Old Testament are very closely bound up with the history of Israel's religion. In all their diversity they show how Israel was driven along from one hope to another. In whatever circumstances the people might find itself, it could always retain its hopes, because it was allowed to keep its faith in the communion with God, in spite of and through all judgments. So Israel could keep looking forward to Him in faith, and all kinds of visions could appear to the eyes of faith, some of which were lasting, others of a more transitory nature. The living operation of God's Spirit caused new insights to spring up while old conceptions are dropped. In all this it is clear that certain fundamental aspects come to the fore to an ever greater extent, particularly those of the community of God itself as the central element of these expectations (Jer. xxxi. 31ff.; Ezek. xxxvi. 26f., xlviii. 35; Isa. lii. 7ff.; Zech. ii. 4ff = Hebrew text 8ff.; Joel ii. 8ff., Hebrew text iii), though the other aspects, political and national, naturalistic and cosmic are still found as well.

The basis of all expectations of salvation is therefore faith in Yahweh, i.e. *He who is*,[1] faith in the actual presence of the Holy God, who is also the God of salvation. With Procksch we may say: 'Israel's faith

[1] See p. 179f.

443

in God embraces the future'.[1] The promise with respect to the future lies in the *actuality* of Yahweh and in His community-relationship with His people, both of which are implicit in the name Yahweh (as is also the case with His holiness.[2] They remain the basis of all further relationships, even of the most diverging, and even contradictory hopes. This security is found in its purest state in the prophetical hopes of salvation mentioned above which bear the mark of the Spirit of God in the fullest measure, which look forward to the day when Yahweh shall be Israel's God and Israel shall be Yahweh's people, or, to put it in a different way, the time when God shall dwell among His people. In this way we can find the basis of the security of salvation repeated again and again in those prophecies which express most adequately the hopes of salvation in the Old Testament.[3]

That does not mean that the hope of salvation contains only this spiritual element; because Israel believed in God as a God who grants life and abundance, including material earthly abundance, its hopes were also always directed towards earthly blessings, towards freedom and material plenty, towards victory over Israel's enemies and towards peace in Israel. Even in the words of those prophets whose thoughts are most spiritual such elements are to be found again and again; with Deutero-Isaiah, for instance, who emphasizes the expectation of God's kingship in Jerusalem so strongly (lii. 7ff.), this kingship does not only represent something spiritual, but also earthly reality. This even applies to the *'ebed Yahweh*, of whom it is said that after his humiliation and suffering unto death he will be feared as an irresistible royal majesty; therefore the song of the suffering servant even begins with the jubilation of his glorification (lii. 13).

Yet it is, on the other hand, unmistakable that there are profound differences, gaps even, between the earliest expectations of salvation and the later hopes of classical prophecy;[4] as a matter of fact, a strong

---

[1] *Theologie*, p.582; see also my *Die Hoffnung im A.T.*, p.580; cf. Bleeker, *op.cit.* Pidoux, *op. cit.*, and C. Westermann, *Das Hoffen im A.T.*, in Ges. Studien Forschung am A.T., 1964, pp.219ff., e.g. p.264: (Die Hoffnung) gründet sich auf das Dasein Gottes für sein Volk und hat darin ihre unbedingte Gewissheit. Westermann finds its literary origin in 'dem Bekenntnis der Zuversicht in den Klagepsalmen' (p.265).
[2] In my opinion H. Berkhof (*Over de methode der Eschatologie*, NTT, XIX, 1964/5, pp. 48off., cf. pp.450ff., 46of.) rightly opposed the ideas of J. Moltmann (*Theologie der Hoffnung*) by emphasizing that the Biblical hopes cannot be divorced from that which has already been granted by God in faith.
[3] Cf. Berkhof, *op. cit.*, p.485. We may say that in the light of the above a central element of Baumgärtels *Verheissung* must be considered to be correct, though of course many objections must be raised against the framing of this point and the consequences involved.
[4] This led Von Rad, *Theology* II, to suppose that the prophets had definitely broken with the belief in Yahweh as the God of salvation in the sense of the ancient Israelite tradition.

tension also springs up afterwards between these critical prophetic expectations and the latest expressions of Israel's hope, which, in spite of great differences in their way of representation, turn back again in part towards the earliest expectations.[1]

The gap is clearly visible between the earliest expectations of salvation, on the one hand, which are wholly political in character and are founded on a naïve optimism which at once turns God's grace for Israel into material earthly hopes of prosperity and power, and on the other hand the classical prophetic pronouncements which in contrast with the former could be called critical and realistic and which may only predict ruin for the near future and see the time of salvation only in the distant future for a remnant which has survived and has been renewed inwardly and spiritually.

The reason for this contrast is not only to be found in different political or economical situations, it is not only to be explained from the fact that the earliest expectations arose in a time of political progress, the latest hopes in times of national downfall. For Amos' first prophecies, proclaiming the downfall of the northern kingdom of Israel, were pronounced before the great changes in the field of politics abroad made themselves felt (by the appearance of the Assyrians under Tiglath-Pileser); the kingdom of Jeroboam II was even at its height still (p.69). The cause lay deeper: it came to be realized that God's favour to Israel was not something to be assured of once and for all, as had often been done on traditional and cultic grounds, but that it had to materialize in the Community of God: the communion between Yahweh and His people makes the highest demands upon Israel, both in the religious and in the moral field (see the attacks against Israel by Amos, iii.2, Isaiah, ch.i, or Jeremiah, ch.vii). Transgressions against God's commandments, given to maintain the communion, were looked upon as disloyalty towards Yahweh Himself which could not but be followed by chastisement. The perturbation at the immorality, the social abuses and the hollow piety caused the prophets to protest that there was no question of a real community of God any longer and that there was fundamentally no difference between Israel and the nations which God had destroyed before the eyes of Israel (Amos ii.6ff.). Amos understood that a general belief in Yahweh's providence formed a basis too unstable for a life in communion with God as He had revealed Himself to Israel.

And for that reason the time had come to destroy the ancient hopes of salvation; it is Amos in particular who was called upon to turn against the ideas that had arisen in Israel concerning God's saving

[1] Cf. O. Plöger, *op. cit.*

activity and especially against the hope for the approaching day of the Lord as a day of salvation (Amos v).

In fact, Amos here takes a stand against the average piety as it had taken form on the ground of the ancient hopes of salvation and of the cult with its Psalms on Yahweh as king (Ps. xlvii); hence he and the other prophets, who proclaimed the same message after him, aroused such opposition among the priests (Amos vii) and among most of the other prophets ('false' prophets, see p.59 and *passim*), who clung to the ancient promises and the theology of providence and covenant which sprang from these promises. The prophets' views were disputed hotly. The only ground for Amos' preaching was the 'roaring of the lion': the fact that 'Adonai Yahweh spoke (iii. 8, cf. i. 2). From certain visions of his handed down to us (vii. 1–9; viii. 1ff.; ix. 1ff.) it becomes apparent how he came to realize that Yahweh had decided irrevocably upon the destruction of the people.

Now that we have indicated the break in Israel's hopes of salvation we must speak of the ideas that lie on either side of this break. We shall first deal very briefly with the prophecies from the time before Amos. They are to be found in the collections of Gen. xlix, Num. xxiiif. and Deut. xxxiii. It is clear that they are strongly influenced by 'political' considerations, by ideas dating from the period of the Judges and from that of David and Solomon. The question arises here whether these expectations may be called prophetic – even if they occur in a context of prophetic statements. Part of these, especially those collected in the blessings of Jacob and Moses are 'sayings' rather than prophecies (Gen. xlix. 13ff.). In these expectations the national and political element plays as important a part as the religious element: they express a firm belief in the indestructible relationship between Yahweh as the Lord with His people Israel, while the spiritual nature of this covenant and the religious and moral demands implicit in it are hardly mentioned at all (only in the Levi-proverbs of Deut. xxxiii).

Related to these political and national expectations is the prophecy of Nathan which predicted for the house of David and enduring (hereditary) kingship in Israel maintained by the grace of God ('I will be his father, and he shall be my son', 2 Sam. vii. 14),[1] and the 'last words' of David in which Nathan's prophecy is alluded to but also the religious and moral nature of this kingship is emphasized. (2 Sam. xxiii. 1ff.). Unfortunately the original form of these two texts is difficult to ascertain, for 2 Sam. vii was rewritten in a Deuteronomic manner and 2 Sam. xxiii. 1ff. is a corrupt text. This prophecy had a great influence upon the whole of Israel's range of ideas; thus the

[1] See A. Cacquot, *La prophétie de Nathan*, Suppl. VT, 1963, pp. 212ff.

dynasty of David was linked with the covenant between God and His people.

This will serve to explain not only why so much attention is paid in the books of Samuel and Kings to the period of David and the succession of Solomon, and why the Chronicles even take David and Solomon as the starting-point of a completely new period (it is even stated that David and Solomon occupy the throne of the kingdom of Yahweh in Jerusalem, and that they are His viceroys, 1 Chron. xvii. 14; xxviii. 5; xxix. 23), but also why the Davidic dynasty keeps on playing a part in the prophetic predictions of salvation, from Amos ix. 11 (and Hosea iii. 5, if the words 'and David their king' are authentic) until the latest parts of the Old Testament (Zech. xii. 1off.) and until the New Testament. But, as we remarked above, especially in the classical prophecies from Isaiah and Micah this expectation, connected with the house of David, was also judged critically; this may already be the case in Amos ix. 11 where Amos speaks of the tabernacle of David that is fallen (or falling); but this is certainly true of Isa. xi, where the prophet says clearly that he no longer expects anything from the reigning branch of the house of David but that he hopes that salvation will be brought by a new shoot that will spring from the trunk that was cut down entirely (cf. also Micah v. 1f.).

The message of the classical prophets is characterised by the new turn given to the hope of salvation. In their preaching the Scriptural prophets have indeed accepted various elements of the ancient popular expectations, the Davidic and political hopes[1] as well as the naturalistic expectations, but nevertheless they place the whole of the hope of salvation in a new light, the light of the judgment, the cleavage in the community, the sin of the people and the holiness of God. From now on Israel is given to understand that the judgment is not only to fall upon the enemies of the people; not upon the man in the street, but first of all upon the king, the priest, the prophet and the wise man.

In the classical prophets the work of God's revelation, coming to them through visions, words and events, awakened a sense of the all-overpowering certainty that God would not allow the people with which He had entered into communion to exist in its empirical reality, but that He would cause it to perish. This appears most impressively from the vision of Isaiah's call (vi), which proclaims absolute ruin,[2]

[1] The fact that the eschatological hopes of the pre-exilic prophets are historical and 'diesseitig' is emphasized (as appears from a short survey in ZAW 1960, p.87) again by J.H. Grønbaek; see also E. Rohland, *Die Bedeutung der Erwählungstraditionen für die Eschatologie der a.t. Propheten*, 1956, and R.E. Clements, *Prophecy and Covenant*, 1965, pp. 103ff.
[2] This message is not mitigated either by the last few words of the Hebrew text of Isa. vi. 13, which should be considered as a gloss (cf. my *Prophecy and Eschatology*,

but fundamentally the same is true of Amos, of Micah, of Hosea, Jeremiah, and Ezekiel; Jeremiah could even think bad news characteristic of the truthfulness of the prophetic message.

In spite of all this the prophets did not deny the belief that God loved Israel; on the contrary, it was exactly on the ground of this belief that the prophets announced the coming judgment (Amos iii. 2); therefore they adhered to their belief that Yahweh would renew Israel through judgement and suffering. They proclaimed the coming of a new Israel which would glorify God with all its heart in the midst of the world. Several of the prophets think this renewal so overwhelming that the whole of the world becomes involved: the Kingdom of God is viewed in a universal, and sometimes even in a cosmic light.

There is a difference in insight among the prophets on the relationship between judgment and salvation; with Amos the message of salvation comes at the end of his book, quite abruptly (*unvermittelt*) after his proclamation of judgment; the passage looks either like an addition by a later hand or like a message from the prophet which he passed on in the circle of his disciples; This message is more traditional than in his message of judgment; but it occupies a wholly different position with him from that which it occupies in ancient piety: the salvation he expects comes only after the judgment, not until after the complete downfall of the house of David.

Hosea sees a closer connection between downfall and restoration – the downfall will lead to repentance (Hos. ii. 17, R.V. 15) and Israel will again love Yahweh.

In Isaiah's work downfall and restoration are not quite in a direct line; he emphatically stresses God's miracle[1]; he speaks of this restoration in paradoxical terms (ix. 1; vii. 10–17; viii. 5–10).[2] Isaiah expects complete ruin and after that full salvation.[3] The new Kingdom of God will be brought about by a prince of salvation who is described as a 'Wonderful Counsellor, the mighty God, the everlasting Father,

---

p. 210); Isaiah did believe, indeed, that there would be a remnant that was to predominate, but this remnant would be very small and would only escape by a miracle of God and form a new people; ch. vi does not speak of this remnant; this was afterwards felt to be an omission, which resulted in the addition of the gloss.

[1] See *Prophecy and Eschatology*, pp. 207ff.

[2] In viii. 8 Immanuel should be translated by 'God be with us', but in viii. 10 by 'God is with us'; *she'ar yashub* may imply a promise as well as a threat; in him the 'strangeness' of God's activity becomes evident (28f.). The Immanuel prophecy predicts the birth of a son to the young, newly-married queen who is not aware as yet of her pregnancy. In this prophecy it is particularly the name which the mother will give her child in view of the political circumstances that is of fundamental importance (the name implies a prayer as well as an eulogy). Cf. also J. J. Stamm, 'Die Immanuel-Weissagung', *Vetus Test.*, IV, 1954, pp. 20ff.

[3] See my *Jahwe en zijn stad.*

448

the Prince of Peace', (ix. 5), and who, according to a later prophecy (xi. 1ff.), will be led in all things by the Spirit of Yahweh.

He believes that not merely Israel but the whole world will benefit by this salvation (xi. 9; ii. 2ff.); it will even bring about a cosmic change (peace among the animals, xi. 6ff.). The very fact that Isaiah uses mythological images demonstrates that the salvation expected by Isaiah transcends historical reality. Isaiah no longer sees the restoration on the historical plane only, but in a supra-historical light.[1]

The last Isaian hopes of salvation have therefore been transposed to a different key, salvation has become universal even if it is Israelite and even if it is received via Israel. Salvation will be given in a wholly spiritual manner, not brought about by victories gained by the sword, although the king of salvation is also the victor. Salvation does not result in the powerful state of Israel, but in peace in the world, even among the animals: one might feel inclined to say with quote St. Paul: God shall be all in all, when Isaiah's hopes are summarized in the verse: 'for the earth shall be full of the knowledge of Yahweh' (xi. 9).

On account of this transposition of the hope of salvation Isaiah may be called the first preacher of the eschatological expectation; he sheds a purely eschatological light upon this salvation – he is clearly concerned with the 'last things'. He looks upon the downfall of Israel as the dawning of the day of the Lord (ii. 10–18), and as the harbinger of the destruction of Jerusalem. The old state of things will not return (ii. 4; xi.6ff.). That which is to come is more than a restoration of the historical even if it is to be enacted on this earth –, but it is a complete renewal of the world. All this gives us the right to consider Isaiah in particular as the creator of eschatology in the true sense of the word (although Hosea is not far behind Him).

The prophets after Isaiah did not have much to add to his prophecies; the prophet who reminds us most of Isaiah is Micah; he alone proclaims the downfall of Jerusalem even more directly than Isaiah did (iii. 12). The prophets after Isaiah until the exile do not soar so high as the prophecies of Isaiah. Universal traits are not wholly lacking (Zeph. iii. 9), but yet we get the impression that the struggle to save the spiritual life of Israel itself is so hard that the preaching of the prophets must concentrate more and more and must therefore centre on the judgment and the salvation of Israel. It is true that religious life tends to become more and more inward (cf. Mic. vi. 8; Zeph. iii. 12; Jer. xxxi. 31ff.), Ezek. xxxvi. 26ff. Jeremiah's messianic expectation (xxiii. 5) bears some traits closely related to Isa. xi. 1ff. (*Yahweh ṣidqenu*, 'Yahweh our righteousness', or 'our salvation', is the name of the 'righteous Branch'). Both with Ezekiel and with Jeremiah a universal

[1] As against Buber: *Der Glaube der Propheten.*

449

hope is lacking. The most profound expression of hope of these two prophets is: 'Ye shall be my people, and I will be your God'. In the work of Ezekiel, who apparently experienced the downfall at an earlier age than Jeremiah, the expectation of restoration comes to the fore again (ch. xxxiv, xxxvi, xxxvii, xl–xlviii), but here, too, this restoration is seen absolutely in the light of the miracle granted by God (the resurrection in ch. xxxvii).

Deutero-Isaiah represents a new stage in the prophetic expectation of salvation; with him the high hopes of Isaiah return, though they are here placed in a different light. Whereas Isaiah expected a complete renewal of the world after the judgment which was to come and of which he and his people were only experiencing the beginning, Deutero-Isaiah proclaims that Israel has passed through the judgment and that definite salvation has come very near. *Deutero-Isaiah's ardent faith expects the emergence of the last things in a very near future.* From various terms and images used by the prophet it appears that to him the salvation he expected was an event that far transcended the historical plane; cf. the repeated use of the verb *bara'*, to create,[1] which proves that the salvation of Israel was no less than a new creation; he sees new things come to pass that have never been before (xli. 20; xliii. 7, 19; xliv. 24; xlv. 8; xlvi. 9f.; xlviii. 6f.); the deliverance may be compared with the creation (li. 9ff.), and with the deliverance from Egypt;[2] Yahweh shall be glorified in the presence of all and unto Him every knee shall bow; Yahweh reigns again in Jerusalem (lii. 7f., cf. xl. 9). There will be an everlasting covenant which will reveal all the faithful acts of grace granted to David, so that all the nations will run unto Israel which is His witness (lv. 3–5); Israel is called to be 'a light to the Gentiles' and a 'covenant of the people' (*berith 'am*)[3] to teach the world the *torah* and the *mishpaṭ* (xlii; xlix). *In this latter* a missionary task for Israel is implicit; the awareness of this task arises from the conviction that the fulfilment of the prophetic expectations is approaching (near eschatology). The missionary character of Deutero-Isaiah's message has often been denied and it was thought that the hope that Israel was to be a light to the Gentiles would concern the deliverance God would accomplish for Israel;[4] the miracle of God's deliverance accomplished

---

[1] 16 times, cf. Humbert, *bârâ*, and my *Prophecy and Eschatology*, where the reader will find further literature and documentation.

[2] See B.J. van der Merwe, *op cit.*

[3] The meaning of '*am* (in Isa. xlii. 6) as mankind, or men in general, is based on the use of the word in the preceding verse.

[4] For example W. Zimmerli: παῖς θεοῦ, *Th. Wb. z. N.T.*, V, pp. 653ff., and P. A. H. de Boer, 'Deutero-Isaiah's Message', *O.T.S.*, XI, 1956, pp. 8off.
R. Martin Achard, *op. cit.*; see the review by H. Cazelles in VT 1960, pp. 91ff., who, in opposition to him defends the missionary character.

for Israel, would be the light itself. This view does not, however, do full justice to Isa. xlix. 5–6, where the deliverance of Israel is represented as an easy task in comparison with the greater and ultimate task that Israel should be a light to the Gentiles so that God's salvation might spread as far as the ends of the earth. The missionary élan must, therefore, have been born in the circle of those who believe that ultimate salvation is near; the same has always been the case in the early days and also during the further history of Christianity.[1]

Many attempts have been made to explain the expectations of the prophet of the exile from the fact that he was a poet[2], but his pathos is not merely that of the poet but especially that of the visionary who sees the birth of a new world. This must certainly have been the reason why Israel, but most clearly early Christianity, reverted to the message of Deutero-Isaiah again and again, as is evident from the Gospel according to St. John and the Epistles of St. Paul.

The prophet's high hopes require the application of counterpoint; through the high notes of rejoicing at deliverance and salvation we hear the sonorous sounds of the theme of the suffering servant of the Lord. This daring harmonizing of two contrasting scales has brought many scholars to the conviction that this work was not composed by one man but that here the work of several authors was mixed up.[3] This view seems to us to be absolutely incorrect: if Deutero-Isaiah had only spoken of deliverance and salvation he would not really have proclaimed the word of God but would have not done much more than renew the ancient hopes of salvation on the ground of the belief in providence and revive the ancient nationalistic hopes. But this hope is in fact sustained by the pure faith in Yahweh's covenant with Israel, which is addressed by him again and again as *bachir*, 'elect', or as *'ebed*, 'servant'; the two words supplement each other: the chosen one is essentially the servant.[4] In his preaching all the elements of the faith in Yahweh play a part: Yahweh's holiness, His majesty which is apparent in the Creation, His intervention in the history of His people and of the world. Deutero-Isaiah is convinced that he stands at the end of the period of the judgment of his people (xl. 1f., li. 17ff.) and at the beginning of the period of salvation (xl. 3ff.; xlviii. 20f.; liv. 1ff.). But while he was proclaiming this salvation he came to understand

---

[1] Cf. Th. C. Vriezen, 'Zending in het Oude Testament', *Hervormd Teologiese Studies*, 1954 or Heerbaan, 1954.
[2] For example J. Lindblom, *The Servant Songs in Dt. I.*, 1951, p. 88, who goes very far in this respect.
[3] See the survey given by Volz in his commentary *Jesaja II*, and C. R. North, *The Suffering Servant in Deutero-Isaiah.*; R. Preis, *Der Gottesknecht im A.T.*, ZAW, 1955, pp. 68ff., J. Hempel, *Vom irrenden Glauben*, now in Apoxysmata, 1961, pp. 189ff.
[4] See my *Die Erwählung Israels*.

ever more deeply that his people is unbelieving, blind and deaf (xl. 27ff.; xli. 11–14; xlii. 18ff.; xliv. 8; xlviii. 7ff.; xlix. 14ff.; l. 1ff.; li. 12f.), especially because of the great spiritual disappointment he had met with on the part of his people because they did not believe in the realty of Yahweh's power.[1] And in his preaching he joins battle so violently that the sharpest contrasts spring up and he is not spared suffering (l. 4ff.); He endures this suffering for the sake of God and on behalf of his people and thus he arrives at the understanding that the true deliverance of his people and of the world and therefore the fulfilment of salvation can only come to pass through the suffering of the true servant of the Lord. Thus he is inspired to the conception of the figure of the suffering servant[2], through which figure he proclaims that future salvation can essentially only be realized through atonement for sin, through the purification of the people by the struggle and the suffering of the guiltless servant whom God calls to this task. Deutero-Isaiah expects the salvation of God for his people, no less at the end of his appearance than at the beginning, but more than at the beginning he then links the realisation of it to a spiritual purification. In his initial message (xl. 2) he thought that the sins of his people had already been atoned for by the suffering during the exile, but afterwards it appears that he is aware that it is not merely the outward participation in the judgment, but only the inward sharing of suffering because of sin that can prepare the way for the renewal of life.

Just as the pre-exilic prophets consider the judgment as a part of the expectation of the future, the suffering servant is an integral part of Deutero-Isaiah's message of salvation. This figure is also comparable to the messianic figure of the pre-exilic prophecies, but it has changed a great deal: it is, as it were, the negative of the pre-exilic figure. Yet, as we have already remarked above (p.441f.), the messianic element of the victorious king is not lacking in Deutero-Isaiah's work; on the contrary, both the beginning and the conclusion of the pericope (Isa. lii. 13–liii. 12) speak of him as an invincible prince.[3]

The new world which Deutero-Isaiah predicts for his people, and therefore for all the nations, is characterized by this atoning suffering. A few elements of this message are also found again in the book of Zechariah: it is, at any rate, remarkable that his message begins with a call to repentance and that in his opinion salvation can only be realized by the Spirit of God; moreover the king of salvation in

---

[1] In his most valuable book *The Servant Songs* J. Lindblom (like J. Hempel) emphasizes too strongly the disappointment experienced by the prophet in his hopes of Cyrus.
[2] On the problems connected with the collective or individual interpretation of the 'ebed see particularly (beside Volz and North) H. H. Rowley, *The servant of the Lord.*
[3] For further literature see p.77n.1; further also W. Zimmerli, J. Jeremias, παῖς θεοῦ, *Th. Wb. z. N. T.*, V.

Deutero-Zechariah bears the character of the *'ani*, the humble one (cf. xii. 9ff.)[1] message may also be connected with that of the exilic prophets (cf. Zeph. iii. 12 with Zech. ix. 9); in the same way Zech. i refers to the earlier, apparently pre-exilic prophets.

Besides Zechariah we may further mention Lamentations iii, which also strikes notes similar to those of Isaiah liiff., but this chapter is not eschatological in content. Generally speaking the songs of the *'ebed Yahweh* found but very little response in Israel. It is true that the Jews did not deny completely the statement that by the suffering servant of the Lord the Messiah was meant; there are a few texts in the Testament of Benjamin and the book of Enoch which prove this; the latter book also associates the *Son of Man* with the *'ebed Yahweh*. This relationship is found again in the New Testament in Jesus' consciousness of His being the Messiah.[2]

Though the message of the suffering servant found only little response during the post-exilic period, the hopes that the coming salvation would be brought about soon inspired especially the first period. There are some indications, especially in Haggai (ii. 21ff.) and Zechariah (iii f.) that the formation of the state of Israel was expected soon. Some (Haggai and Zerubbabel) probably also wanted to put this expectation into practice in 521–520 during the difficult period for the Persian Empire.[3] This hope was not only national and political, but also universal and cosmic (Haggai ii. 6–9); Jerusalem would be the city of God, the metropolis of the world (Zech. ii. 5–9, 10–17; viii. 20ff.) after Yahweh had conquered all the nations (ii. 1–4). The representations in the last part of Isaiah (Trito-Isaiah) rather one-sidedly place Jerusalem in the limelight (lx–lxii)[4] but in the last few chapters (lxvf.) they contain universal and supra-historical elements; especially in lxv. 17ff. there are various traits that are elaborated in later apocalyptic works (a new heaven and a new earth; the long term of life of men as in the period before the Flood, the Isaianic paradisiac peace). Here we have come to the last period of the expectation of salvation in the Old Testament, in which people revel in the signs of

[1] Cf. K. Elliger, *op. cit.*, on this text (ATD).

[2] J. Jeremias, *op. cit.*, pp. 685ff., further literature p. 654; the relationship between Jesus and the *'ebed Yahweh* in the N.T. is doubted by J. N. Sevenster, NTT 1958/59, p. 27; see also F. Hahn, *Christologische Hoheitstitel*, pp. 54ff. On this question see further G. Sevenster, *Christologie*; Cullmann, *op. cit.*, J. Coppens, *l'Espérance messianique*, R. Sc. Rel., 1963, pp. 40ff.

[3] Compare R. Kittel, *Geschichte des Volkes Israel* III, 1929, pp. 454ff. and e.g., the 2nd edition of J. M. Powith Smith: *The prophets and their time*, 1940, pp. 240ff.; also my *Religion of Israel*, pp. 253ff.

[4] N. W. Porteous, *Jerusalem-Zion, the growth of a symbol*, Verbannung und Heimkehr, Rudolph Festschrift, 1961, pp. 235ff.; also A. Causse, *La mythe de la nouvelle Jerusalem*, R. H. Th., 1938, pp. 377ff.; K. L. Schmidt, *Jerusalem als Urbild und Abbild*, Eranos-Jahrbuch 1950, pp. 207ff.; G. von Rad, Theology II, pp. 147ff., 292ff.

future salvation (cf. Zech. viii. 4f. with Isa. lxv. 20). In this late prophetic period the cosmic element is emphasized more and more (Isa. xxivff.; Joel iii) and besides that also personal salvation (the expectation of resurrection from the dead, Isa. xxvi). We are here on the borderline between prophecy and apocalyptic[1]: salvation is seen in a transcendental light. Besides that, however, people emphatically cling to the reality of the salvation inherent in Israel, as appears from the theology of Chronicles which apparently in opposition to the Samaritans emphasized the fact that Israel was the kingdom of God (see p. 438).

That the hope of God's salvation in the near future was turned into a transcendentalizing expectation of salvation in apocalyptic may be explained from the disappointment and the feeling of insecurity which took possession of many people in the years after the exile. After the high hopes of Deutero-Isaiah the Jews who had returned to Jerusalem soon began to feel disappointed. Something of this is already noticeable in Haggai and Zechariah (cf. also Ezra iii. 12ff.), but it completely dominates the background of the message of Malachi, who starts out with emphatically combating the view that God no longer loves Israel (i. 2); the same disappointment may lie at the back of ii. 17; and Malachi opposes to it the message of the reality of the day of Yahweh and of the judgment and the salvation this day will bring with it. A similar feeling of disappointment is expressed in Jer. xxxiii. 34ff., where the doubts concerning Israel's calling are answered with the words of Jer. xxxi. 35ff.

In post-exilic Israel there was, therefore, a profound dissension concerning the eschatological hope: some, who held theocratic views, continued to cling to the reality of the salvation received, to the belief that in Jerusalem, in the restored temple, salvation had come and would continue to come if only the people remained faithful (Mal. iii. 6–12); others were dissatisfied and no longer expected anything, others, finally, thought that salvation would come in other ways – that the realization of salvation could only come about in a future world; they first expected the destruction of this world and did not think salvation could be realized in this world unless it descended to earth from heaven; thus the time of salvation was moved to a new world, to the 'olam habba'.[2]

It is impossible for us to deal further with the development of the expectation of salvation in apocalyptic, for this no longer belongs to the field of Old Testament theology; here the most widely differing

[1] See E. S. Mulder, *Die teologie van die Jesaja Apokalipse*, 1954.
[2] Compare particularly O. Plöger, *op. cit.*

elements, of widely different origins, come together.[1] If its roots are to be found in the eschatological prophecies,[2] it owes its transcendental framework to the fact that the *parousia* failed to come, and its literary form apparently to many, often non-Israelite influences such as the dualistic Parseeism, the ancient oriental wisdom, popular ancient mythological elements, early gnostic views, etc.

In the Old Testament itself the following elements are also of importance:

a. first of all the hope, expressed in Joel iii. 9ff.; Zech. xiii and Ezek. xxxviiif., of a final battle of the nations which is to be fought before the definitive coming of salvation; we may wonder if Isa. xxiv–xxvii was also written from the point of view of this conception; in such texts the views of the more theological groups and the apocalyptic ones appear to have merged;

b. The computation of the time when the salvation will be realized; it is best known from Daniel (Dan. ix. 27ff.), but also lies at the back of the chronology of the Old Testament (Gen. v, xi), based on the doctrine that the world was to last 4000 years[3]; this doctrine was probably elaborated in the later MSS. of the Hebrew text; the Samaritan text contains other and probably more ancient numbers.[4]

Finally the doctrine of the son of man in Daniel (vii. 13),[5] which plays an important part in the New Testament; in Daniel vii. 13 dominion is given to 'one like the Son of man' at the end of time; in verse 22 this kingship is associated with the people of Israel, at any

---

[1] On this compare (see p.46 n.2): M. Friedländer, *Die religiösen Bewegungen innerhalb des Judentums*, 1905, pp. 22ff.; Bertholet, *op. cit.*, pp. 435ff.; E. Schürer, *Geschichte des Volkes Israel*, II⁴, pp. 579ff.; Volz. *op. cit.*; W. Bousset, *Die Religion des Judentums*³, 1926, pp. 202ff.; M. J. Lagrange, *Le Judaisme*², 1931, pp. 70ff.; G. F. Moore, *Judaism*, II, 1932, pp. 323ff.; J. Bonsirven, *Les idées juives*, 1934, pp. 136ff., and *Le Judaisme Palestinien*, 1950, pp. 140ff.,; C. Steuernagel, *op. cit.*; M. A. Beek, *Inleiding in de Joodse Apocalyptiek van het oud- en nieuwtestamentische tijdvak*, 1950; D. S. Russel, *Between the Testaments*, 1960, and *The method and message of Jewish apocalyptic*, 1964.

[2] G. von Rad, *Theology* II, pp. 303ff., fundamentally denies this connection (see, however, p. 308) and looks upon apocalyptic as essentially a form of *gnosis*, because its chief aim is the unveiling of the mysteries of the scheme of things. An important aspect of this conception is that it gives the "wisdom-element" in apocalyptic its due. On the other hand it neglects aspects that are important for an understanding of apocalyptic, such a complicated subject in itself. Moreover, it rests too much on earlier, non-Biblical texts (von Rad, *op. cit.*, pp. 305ff.). Compare now O. Cullmans well-considered views in: *Heil als Geschichte*, 1965, pp. 61ff.

[3] Cf. for example L. Köhler, *Theologie*³, pp. 72, 238 n. 70.

[4] Cf. Dillmann, *Handbuch z. A.T.* on Gen. v and xi; also Acts vii. 4, which presupposes the reading of the Samaritan text, as was already observed by P. Kahle, *Th. St. u. Kr.* 88, 1915, p. 400 (*Untersuchungen zur Gesch. des Pentateuchtextes*); the Book of Jubilees also has the figures of the Samaritan text, cf. Dillmann in *Sitzungsber. Kön. Preuss. Akad. v. Wiss.*, Berlin, 1883, I, p. 323.

[5] See besides Russell's books, J. Coppens, *Le messianisme sapientiel et les origines litteraires du Fils de l'homme daniélique*, Suppl. VT, III pp. 33ff.; L. Dequeker, *Le fils de l'homme et les Saints du Très Haut*², 1961.

455

rate with a plural entity, 'the saints'; this term may refer to a special category, namely the pious men among the people.[1] Nevertheless there is no denying that in a later period (in the books of Enoch and IV Ezra and in the New Testament) the son of man means the Messiah. The question arises whether in the book of Daniel, too, a singular figure may have been intended; it is possible[2] though by no means certain[3] that the bearer of the kingship at the time of salvation in Dan. vii must be taken to be Israel's king of salvation, the Messiah; in that case the prince would be called the bearer of the royal dignity, and in verse 22 the people[4]; both, however, have the same function.[5] This figure is, at all events,[6] represented as the bearer of the kingly dignity of the eschatological kingdom; he is here already the heavenly figure (in contrast to the animals, which represent the chaos and the 'nether world'), though not yet the pre-existent figure of later eschatology.

c. Summary and survey

In order to obtain a satisfactory survey of the development of the idea of salvation in the Old Testament the best plan will be to distinguish four periods:

1. pre-eschatological
2. proto-eschatological
3. eschatological with reference to the near future (or in the process of realization)
4. transcendental-eschatological.[7]

The first period is the period before the appearance of the classical prophets. In those days there is the expectation of a *yom Yahweh*,[8] which, as appears from Amos, is looked upon as the day of salvation, when by His victorious deeds[9] Yahweh shall reveal Himself anew as

[1] M.Noth, *Die Heiligen des Höchsten*, Ges. Stud. pp.274ff., who looks upon the 'saints' as angels, is opposed by C.Berkelmans, *The Saints of the Most High and their kingdom*, OTS, XIV, 1965, pp.305ff.
[2] So Steuernagel, *op. cit.*, p.482; cf. also A.Bentzen, *Daniel² (Handbuch z. A.T.)* 1952, p.63; J.Muilenburg, *The son of man*, JBL1.
[3] See for example H.W.Obbink, *Daniel* in *Tekst en Uitleg*.
[4] Compare a similar transition in v.28 and vi.1 (so also Steuernagel).
[5] In that case this would be a parallel to the problem in Isa.liii; there we also find a singular being described who can represent a collective idea; in this connection we may think of the reference in Dan.xii.3 (plural) to Isa.lii/liii (liii.11; singular); cf. R.Martin-Achard, *De la mort à la résurrection*, 1956, pp.116ff.
[6] Cf. Bentzen, *op. cit.*, p.65, who quotes with approval J. Hempel, *Die Mehrdeutigkeit der Geschichte als Problem der prophetischen Theologie*, 1936, p. 43; cf. also Bentzen, *Messias*, p. 72.
[7] In the following pages we shall give the concluding pages of our lecture *Prophecy and Eschatology*.
[8] For literature on the *yom Yahweh*, see above, p.439, n.4.
[9] Compare von Rad, *op. cit.*; so we should not relate this conception to the cultic theophanies, as Mowinckel does.

the Lord for the sake of Israel (see above, pp. 190ff. on the epiphanies of Yahweh) and shall bring Israel to its full glory by restoring it to the position of authority it once had in the time of David. The future is seen to a great extent in the light of the past, the idealized age of David; people live at least as much in the grip of the past as in the grip of the future, though the latter element was not entirely lacking in Israel even in the days before the classical prophets (the Yahwist in Gen. xii. 3). In this pre-eschatological period Israel's hopes are, as far as we can ascertain, mainly political and national (Gen. xlix; Num. xxiv; Deut. xxxiii; the earliest Yahweh-King-Psalms?), though moral motives were not lacking. This form cannot really be called eschatological, because this expectation is not concerned with the renewal of the world but with Israel's greatness.[1] Its tendency is much rather expansive and nationalistic than looking out spiritually for a new world created by Yahweh; moreover it is, in fact, directed to the past rather than to the future. Yet this period may be called pre-eschatological, in the sense that even in this period there were elements that are found again in the next period and themes on which this next period rests. We especially think of the certainty of Israel that it is God's people, a certainty the background of which lies not only in the cult but especially in history.[2]

The second period is that of Isaiah (Amos to Jeremiah): it is the period in which the vision of a new people and a new kingdom is beginning to play a part, a kingdom that will embrace the whole world and that rests on spiritual forces that spring from God. I would call this the period of *awakening eschatology*; this kingdom certainly is an eschaton, *'acharith*, (though it appears in history).

The third period is that of Deutero-Isaiah (and Ezekiel); its influence was felt for many centuries afterwards in various movements (see above, pp. 450f.). The kingdom of God is not only seen coming in *visions* but it is *experienced* as coming. The world is going to be changed: Israel is now called upon to be a light to the world and the nations are called upon to share in the glory of Zion.

This period is the precursor of the fourth period, the apocalyptic period during which a *dualistic eschatology* springs up. Owing to various causes, first and foremost because of the disappointment after those high hopes and owing to the influence of a growing sense of distance in

---

[1] A view such as the Yahwist's on the moral and spiritual call of Abraham and his importance to world history should not be looked upon as a national hope related to the one just mentioned; he is rather a precursor of the major prophets.

[2] Mowinckel, *Psalmenstudien* II, considered the cult of central importance but also admitted the importance of the historical factor, though he underestimated or at any rate did not elaborate it, p. 295f.

religious life, but also under the influence of Persian dualism[1] and Hellenistic thought, the eternal world of God above and reality on earth below, which is doomed, are separated; the divine is transcendentalized and this implies not only that the world is secularized, but also that this world is demonic; God and the world are separated. The difference between this period of eschatology and the preceding is not only that the latter is actualized within the framework of time and the former is not, but there is also a difference in scene of action and in person. We might almost say that in the time of the classical prophets (also, therefore, during the first period after the exile) there still is a unity of place and time (this world) and action (person; it is God who truly works). In the apocalyptic period this unity is broken; the place where the new kingdom is to be realized is different, for the world is to be destroyed and a new world is to come; the time is different, for we enter into eternity here;[2] and the action is different, too: there is not merely the activity of God through the Messianic figure, but there are many figures who take action, who do preparatory work, while the Messiah (Messiahs) become(s) the bringer of salvation.[3]

d. Conclusions

The eschatological vision is an Israelite phenomenon which has not really been found outside Israel – as has rightly been maintained by Mowinckel against Gressmann etc.; but it is not the wishful thinking of a people that had become tired of its cult (Mowinckel), it must be accounted for by a truly genuine Yahwism, purged from nationalistic, wordly and secularized expectations by the religious prophetical criticism.

[1] It is very probably that this influence should be recognized. We must bear in mind the remark of H. Gressmann, *Der Messias*, p. 352, that this was the influence of popular religion. It is rather improbable, however, that this influence should already have made itself felt at the time of the generation of the exile. The influence concerns mainly the form of the representations and may perhaps be traced back to Parseeism in a negative sense, for at the first contact with Parseeism (during the period of the exile, cf. Isa. xlv) dualism was taken up; Deutero-Isaiah opposed it fundamentally on monotheistic grounds, but as regards the form he used the dualistic terminology. Cf. J. H. Moulton, *Early zoroastrianism*, 1913, pp. 186ff.; B. Reicke in RGG³, s.v. *Iran IV*, also H. H. Rowley, *The relevance of apocalyptic;* D. S. Russell, *Method*, p. 19; G. von Rad, *op. cit.*, (German ed.⁴, 1965, 328).
[2] We can agree entirely with Buber, *Der Glaube der Propheten*, when he calls the end of time 'history's coming to a standstill'.
[3] We may again point out here that this apocalyptic attitude to life was not the only one to develop during the Persian period. Other (eschatological) conceptions also survived; we may suppose that particularly in the congregation at Jerusalem, which held rather strong theocratical views, a view came to predominate according to which the renewed temple-congregation of the holy city was for the time being the fulfilment of the promised salvation, which only awaited its ultimate fulfilment by a messianic figure or by the intervention of God that would really make Jerusalem the metropolis of the world, dominating everything. This view is also found in later times.

458

Eschatology did not arise when people began to doubt the actuality of God's kingship in the cult, but when they had to learn in the greatest distress to rely, in faith alone, on God as the only firm basis of life and when this realism of faith was directed critically against the life of the people so that the coming catastrophe was looked upon as a divine intervention full of justice and also so that it was confessed that the Holy God remained unshakeable in His fidelity and love to Israel. Thus the life of Israel in history came to have a double aspect: on the one hand judgment was looked upon as near at hand and the re-creation of the community of God as approaching. In this way the classical prophetic religion brought about a tension completely different from the tension that dominates the cultic religion. People begin to think in terms of near future and a more distant future[1] – the latter indicates the limits of the horizon and must therefore, from the point of view of the prophet, be final; for him it is essentially an *'acharith* in the sense of an *eschaton*. Eschatology is a religious certainty which springs directly from the Israelite faith in God as rooted in the history of its salvation.

The eschatological vision was *possible* because Israel knew its God as the living Lord, who is near, who in His holiness does not abandon this world and goes on working in history; this vision became *reality* because the prophets, penetrating into the knowledge of God's holy Being, more and more experienced the discrepancy between what was and what should be. The final break in the ancient Israelite philosophy of life, with its totalitarian tendencies, which attempted to weld together God, the world, the people and the compatriot[2] into an unbreakable unity, is the point where eschatology breaks through; and eschatology is the form in which the prophets' critical realism of faith maintained its confession of Yahweh, the Lord of the World. This basic content of eschatology is the prophetic word of God that Jeremiah as well as Ezekiel impress upon their people in their greatest distress: 'Ye shall be my people, and I will be your God'! Justly Gemser[3] repeats the remark of Franz Delitzsch that the principal point of the hope of salvation in the Old Testament is not the Messiah, but the *parousia*, the coming of Yahweh in the near future.[4]

It was not national optimism or mythical thought that led to the hopes of salvation, but only the certainty of reality of God, of that

---

[1] H.H.Rowley, *The Growth of the O.T.*, 1950, pp.83f.
[2] Cf. J.Pedersen, *Israel;* in my opinion, however, there is no justification for his view that this totalitarian vision is at the basis of the whole of the Israelite-Yahwistic conception of life.
[3] *De Psalmen*, III, 1949 *(Tekst en Uitleg)*, p.103.
[4] Cf. Edelkoort, *Christusverwachting*, p.60; Köhler, *Theologie*, pp.224, 230f.; compare also A.M.Brouwer, *Wereldeinde en wereldgericht*, 1928, pp.17ff.

God who had from the beginning linked Himself with the people as the holy God of the Covenant, of that God who carries His work into effect in spite of the sins of mankind. By this faith[1] Israel's greatest prophet, Isaiah, not only saved Jerusalem from disaster at one of the most critical moments in the history of Israel, but also brought about that turn in the religion of his people by which it learned to think eschatologically,[2] on the ground of the grace revealed by God in the Covenant and affirmed by Him in the course of history; so that even in the midst of the most terrible catastrophe the people learned to place the future, too, entirely in God's hands.

Thus the message of the future kingdom of God was born *from faith alone*, the kingdom God would reveal in Israel for the sake of the whole world. This message sprang from faith, and could only be assented to in faith. It came to be actualized by the author and finisher of our faith, Jesus Christ (Hebr. xii. 2), and through Him faith expects this promise to be fulfilled completely.

The revelation of God's salvation in history was the starting-point of the faith underlying the preaching of the Old Testament, the renovation of the whole of this earth into the kingdom of God became its ultimate hope.

God called Israel to great things; the greatest of which is that He gave Israel visions, that through the prophets He made Israel behold *new* visions. The greatest of these visions are the coming Kingdom of God, and the servant of the Lord who gives up his life to atone for sin.

The latter expectation was fulfilled in the coming of Jesus Christ; the former began to be realized in Him but awaits complete fulfilment in His second coming.

Eschatology is the expression of the belief that God holds history in the hollow of His hand, and that He will make the history of the world end in complete communion between God and man, so that He will come as King; or, in other words, so that He may be all in all.[3]

It became of the utmost importance in the history of Israel,[4] for it is certainly above all due to this vision that the hope of restoration was preserved in Israel and that this people did not perish like so many

---

[1] See C. Westermann, *op. cit.*
[2] That does not mean supra-temporally, for in the O.T. the Kingdom of God remains something of this earth; here, too, the realism of Israel's way of thinking manifests itself again, in which psychic and spiritual things cannot be separated from physical things. That is why the 'eschatological' element does not cancel out the national element but gives it a far wider meaning, that of universality.
[3] E. Brunner, *Das Ewige als Zukunft und Gegenwart*, 1953.
[4] J. H. Moltmann, *op. cit.*

460

small nations in those days. This clearly demonstrates the tremendous importance of this faith even for every-day life.

Eschatology gave the history of the world a goal, because this history is enacted 'in a significant connection'.[1] Eschatology can give the history of the world a perspective[2]; something which neither the ancient Eastern nor the ancient Western world could attain,[3] because there world-history was looked upon as consisting of an (infinite) chain of cyclic periods, of which the beginning and the end are practically the same (like the yearly cycle in nature). Compared with this cyclic world the Biblical philosophy of life might be called linear,[4] though it is preferable to keep to the idea of perspective. This perspective in world-history has been preserved in the Jewish-Christian world in widely different forms, from the most remarkable apocalyptic and adventist forms to the most secularized forms in philosophies and social views of life.[5] All these have no other foundation than the Biblical-religious basis; where this faith is lacking the perspective itself is lost, too. The only reason therefore why the Biblical faith can see that a future dawn will break for this world is because it believes in God, or rather because it faithfully hopes for the *parousia* of of God, for His coming; it lives in virtue of the fulfilment of its hopes[6]; in this hope placed on God and His kingdom it gained the victory over the myth of eternal repetition.[7] And on account of this faith the believer lives in the world of freedom, as God's child,[8] for God reigns as king and as such He will make His dominion perfect.

[1] Bultmann, *Das Christentum als orientalische und abendländische Religion*, p. 15; Brouwer, p. 17.
[2] G. van der Leeuw, *Historisch Christendom*, 1919, p. 193; G.J. Heering, *De verwachting van het Koninkrijk Gods*, 1952, pp. 217ff.
[3] On the West (Greece) compare Bultmann, *op. cit.*, and *Das Urchristentum; J.N. Sevenster, *Leven en dood in de Evangeliën*, 1952, pp. 31ff.; B.A. van Groningen, *In the grip of the past*, pp. 115ff.
[4] As Cullmann did in his *Christ and Time;* one must be careful, however, not to elaborate this view as *the* Christian conception of time, for God is, according to the belief of the Scriptures, the God of the miracle and there cannot really be question of a rectilinear view. In his latest book *Heil als Geschichte*, 1965, IX, Cullmann is prepared to modify this image; here he speaks of a 'Wellenlinie' rather than of a 'Linie'.
[5] Cf. K. Löwith, *Weltgeschichte und Weltgeschehen*, 1953.
[6] Van der Leeuw, *Historisch Christendom, loc. cit.*
[7] When this hope disappears, the myth immediately rears its head again, as is demonstrated quite impressively by Sartre's *Huis Clos*.
[8] M. Eliade, *La mythe de l'éternel retour*, 1949, p. 238; G. Van der Leeuw, *Urzeit und Endzeit*, 1950 (*Eranos-Jahrbuch*, 1949); K. Löwith, *op. cit.*; G. Pidoux, *Le Dieu qui vient*.

Some further literature:

History of Religion:
H. Gunkel, *Schöpfung und Chaos in Urzeit und Endzeit*, 1895.
A. J. Wensinck, 'The Semitic New Year and the Origin of eschatology'. *Acta Orientalia* I, 1923, 158ff.
M. Eliade, *Le mythe de l'éternel retour*[6], 1949.
G. van der Leeuw, *Urzeit und Endzeit*, Eranos-Jahrbuch 1949.

Philosophy of Religion:
K. Löwith, *Weltgeschichte und Heilsgeschichte*, 1953.

Systematical Theology:
J. Moltmann, *Theologie der Hoffnung*[2], 1965.

Old Testament:
B. Duhm, *Die Theologie der Propheten*, 1875.
W. Nowack, *Die Zukunftshoffnungen Israels in der assyrischen Zeit*, Theologische Abhandlungen 1902, pp. 33ff.
H. Gressmann, *Der Ursprung der israelitisch-jüdischen Eschatologie*, 1905.
B. Duhm, *Das kommende Reich Gottes*, 1910.
W. Baumgartner, *Kennen Amos und Hosea eine Heilseschatologie?*, 1913.
W. Cossmann, *Die Entwicklung des Gerichtsgedankens bei den alttestamentlichen Propheten*, 1915.
W. Eichrodt, *Die Hoffnung des ewigen Friedens im alten Israel*, 1920.
L. H. K. Bleeker, *Over inhoud en oorsprong van Israëls heilsverwachting*, 1921.
E. L. Dietrich, *Schub Schebut, die endzeitliche Wiederherstellung bei den Propheten*, 1925.
G. Hölscher, *Die Ursprünge der jüdischen Eschatologie*, 1925.
A. M. Brouwer, *Wereldeinde en Wereldgericht*, 1928.
H. Gressmann, *Der Messias*, 1929.
G. Ch. Aalders, *Het herstel van Israël volgens het O.T.*, 1933.
A. H. Edelkoort, *De Christusverwachting in het O.T.*, 1941.
G. Pidoux, *Le dieu qui vient*, 1947.
L. Černý, *The day of Yahweh and some relevant problems*, 1948.
A. Bentzen, *Messias, Moses redivivus, Menschensohn*, 1948.
A. Hempel, *Worte der Propheten*, 1949, 237ff.
O. J. Baab, *The Theology of the O.T.*, 1949, pp. 156ff.
M. Buber, *Der Glaube der Propheten*, 1950.
S. Mowinckel, *Han, som kommer*, 1951 (cf. review by A. Bentzen in Dansk Theologisk Tidsskrift, 1952, pp. 112ff.), English translation by G. W. Anderson: *He that cometh*, 1956.
Th. C. Vriezen, *Prophecy and eschatology*, Suppl. V.T. 1953; *Die Hoffnung im A.T.*, Theol. Litt. Zt., 1953, pp. 577ff.
J. van der Ploeg, *L'espérance dans l'A.T.*, RB pp. 481ff., 1954.
O. Plöger, *Theokratie und Eschatologie*, 1959.
G. Fohrer, *Die Struktur der a.t. Eschatologie*, ThLZ, 1960, pp. 401ff.
D. S. Russell, *Between the Testaments*, 1960; *The Method and Message of Jewish Apocalyptic*, 1964.

462

H.H.Rowley, *The Relevance of Apocalyptic*[3], 1963.
J.Coppens, *L'espérance messianique, ses origines et son développement*, Rev. Sciences Relig., 1963, pp. 3ff.
A.Herrmann, *Die prophetischen Heilserwartungen im A.T.*, 1964.

Jewish eschatology:
A.Bertholet, *Biblische Theologie des A.T.*, vol. 2: *Die jüdische Religion von der Zeit Esras bis zum Zeitalter Christi*, 1911.
P.Volz, *Die Eschatologie der jüdischen Gemeinde*, 1934 (1st ed.: *Jüdische Eschatologie von Daniel bis Akiba*).
C.Steuernagel, *Die Strukturlinien der Entwicklung der jüdischen Eschatologie*, Festschrift Bertholet, 1950, pp. 479ff.
J.Klausner, *The messianic idea in Israel*, 1955.
A.S. van der Woude, *Die messianischen Vorstellungen der Gemeinde von Qumran*, 1958.
D.Rößler, *Gesetz und Geschichte:* Eine Untersuchung der jüdischen Apokalyptik und pharizäischen Orthodoxie, 1960.

Further the great works by Moore: *Judaism;* Schürer: *Geschichte des jüdischen Volkes;* Bousset: *Die Religion des Judentums;* Lagrange; *Le Judaisme* and further handbooks about the Jews in the early centuries of our era; also RGG[3] IV, pp. 901ff.

Abraham, (historical approach hardly possible) 26, 39; (with J) 56f. 165, 314, 421, 457; (with E) 58, 303f.; (with P) 62f., 170; (with the Chronicler) 66; (with St. Paul) 95

Achiqar 244

Ain Feshkha (findings at ≈) 47, 121f.

Allegorical exegesis, see Exegesis

Altar, (in the earliest period) 36, 246, 255; (in connection with ceremonies of atonement) 266ff.

Amphictyony 38, 290, 348

Angel, (of the Lord) 209f.; (angels) 298, 322, 327f., 427; see also index of Hebrew words: *malakh, bene 'elim* and *'elohim*

Animal (world) 62f., 388, 405f., 413ff., 422ff.

Anointment 365, 370, 441

Anthropology 170ff., 404–429 passim; see also Image of God

Anthropomorphisms 155, 183ff., 319ff., 388; (in the history of primeval times and with J) 161f., 319f.; (in the cult) 267ff.

Anthropopathisms 319ff., 388

Anti-cultural tendencies, (in Gen. ii–xi) 54f., 284, 425; (to some degree with Amos and Micah) 55; (generally not found with the prophets) 87, 284f., 425; (in the Nazirate and among the Rechabites) see Nazirate and Rechabites

Apocalyptic writings 35, 38, 46, 77f., 84, 229, 408f., 428, 453ff., 457

Apocrypha 435; (in the N.T.) 13 n. 5; (in the Septuagint) 86; (R.C. and Reformation) 16

Ark 36, 146, 187, 210, 240, 247, 318, 354, 357

Atonement 261f., 264ff., 274f.,; (dynamistic background) 31, 64; (≈ in connection with the Passover) 36f., 262, 265; (≈ and the prophets) see Prophet (and cult); (Day of ≈) 262

Attributes, see Qualities of God

Baalism 330; (influence of and struggle against ≈) 44, 70, 158, 319, 324ff., 411

Babylon, see O.T. and the ancient oriental world

Background (study of ≈ and the theology of the O.T.) 28ff.

Ban 336, 421

Battle (Yahweh as God of ≈), see Yahweh

Blessing, (God's ≈) 340, 411; (man's ≈) 30

Blood, (as the force of life) 265, 269, 340; (belonging to Yahweh; not to be used) 62, 340, 426; (at circumcision) 304 n. 1; (≈ manipulations at the various sacrifices) 261–267

Blood revenge 54, 269

Body and soul 406ff.; (unity of ≈) 407ff.

Breath (of Life) 338, 404f., 406f.

Calling 56, 64, 80, 374, 419

Calvin 17

Canaanite religion, see O.T. and ancient oriental world

Canon 12ff., 53, 67, 85, 86f., 149; (Judaism) 12ff., 86, 116; (early Christian Church) 12ff.; (Reformation and R.C. Church) 15

Casuistry 403

Chaos 29f., 329, 333

Chassidism 58

Children 192f., 340, 411, 422

Chokhmah (literature of wisdom) 84, 87, 242ff., 377, 381, 390, 397f., 403f.; see Wiseman

Christ and the O.T., see Jesus Christ and the O.T.

Christian Church and O.T. 11–20, 91–141; see also Jesus Christ and the O.T., O.T. and N.T., Word of God

Circumcision 62f., 304

City(state) (attitude to the ≈) 54f., 284f., 365, 371f.

Clean – unclean, (in connection with the conception of sin) 31f., 275; (≈ and ethics) 381f.

Code of Hammurabi, see O.T. and ancient oriental world

Collectivism, see Individualism

Communion between God and man, (in J) 313; (in P) 63; (in the Torah) 64; (in general) 154ff., 166ff.; passim; 177ff., 216f., 220f., 224f., 277, 311ff., 321f., 336f., 447; (≈ with man and God's Holiness) 64f., 87f., 155ff., 160f., 164, 170, 172, 174, 178f., 258, 311ff., 404f.; (not a natural relationship)

Exclusiveness 34f., 303, 307, 325, 384, 396, 401
Exegesis, (allegorical and typological) 15ff., 23, 96; (typological) 137; (allegorical)112, 127f., 140; (historical and philological) 130–134, 139f.; (hermeneutical) 128ff., 134f.; (systematical and theological) 130, 135ff.
Exodus (tradition of the) 192ff.
Expectation of salvation 68–79, 82, 123, 195f., 204, 286, 373, 436–461; (connection with the Covenant) 66, 337, 444; see also Day of the Lord, Messianism, Remnant
Expiatio 270–275, 401

Faith 94, 121, 166, 309; (in Isaiah) 71, 164, 313, 437; (in Habakuk) 73
Faithfulness of God, see index of Hebrew words: 'emet
Family (also ≈ of Nations) 370ff.
Fate 202
Father, see Parents
Father – child relation between God and man 172f., 288, 413f., 461; (king as son of God) see King; also: Parents
Fathers (God of the) 41
Fear of the Lord 155, 287, 377; see also index of Hebrew words: Yir'at Yahweh
Feasts 36f., 259ff.
Flesh (man as ≈) 71, 407
Forgiveness 196
Freedom (liberty) (social) 421; (spiritual) 287f.
Fulfilment, see Promise

Gilgamesh-epic, see O.T. and ancient oriental world
Glory 207f., 248
Gnosis, 455
Gnosticism 15
God, (no doctrine concerning God) 156; (historical development of faith in God) 39ff.; (content of the testimony concerning God) 291–346; (of O.T. and N.T.) 105f., 157; see further Holiness, Love, Unity, God of the Fathers (see Fathers), etc.
Gods, (polytheism in Israel?) see Polytheism; (gods of other nations) 32f., 43, 302f., 326ff., 338
Grace (mercy) of God 43, 70, 203, 312; (history of earliest times) 55; (J) 58; (D) 60

Hands, see Imposition of hands
Hardening of the heart 219, 305ff., 315
Hatred (cf. also Enemy and Psalms of revenge) 315f., 400ff.
Heart 390ff., 408, 421; see index of Hebrew words: Leb
Heathendom (Israel and ≈), see Nations

Hemerologies 427
Historical criticism, see Criticism
History and revelation 188ff.
History, (God's activity in ≈) 39, 87f., 161f., 271f., 317f., 322, 460f.; (with J) 56ff.; (with D) 59f., 271f.; (with P) 62, 64; (with the prophets) 68f.; (with Ecclesiastes 155; see also Creation and history, Egypt
History of tradition, see Traditionsgeschichte
Holiness of God 233, 299–311, 316f.; (with Ezekiel) 75f.; (with Isaiah) 43, 71f., 164, 297ff., 341; see also index of texts Isa. vi; (with Deutero-Isaiah) 76f.; see also Communion between God and man
Holy Communion see Lord's Supper
Homiletic use of the O.T. 138–142; (homiletics and exegesis) 138f.
Humanity 387ff., 398f., 419f.
Humility 287f.
Hymns (temple ≈, ≈ of praise) 38, 46, 86
Hypostasis 435; see also 209f.

Image of God (God not to be depicted) 155, 317, 319ff.,; (man as ≈) 63, 170ff. 387ff., 398, 413f., 423; (≈ in man not lost nor mutilated 413
Immortality 408, 410f.
Imposition of hands 263, 273
Incarnation (basis of doctrine of ≈ in the O.T.) 321 n. 3
Individualism (and collectivism) 385ff., 419ff., 422
"Infallibility" of Holy Scripture 17, 99, 116
Inspiration (of prophets), see Prophets; (≈ of the Holy Scriptures)17, 116, 119
Introduction of the O.T. and O.T. Theology 50
Ius talionis 309
Intercession, see Prayer

J 51f., 54, 56ff., 64, 311, 319, 322, 338; (≈ and the prophets) 51, 79f., 166
J-narrator, (in Gen. ii–xi) 54ff.; see also index of texts; (relation to J) 54f.; (relation to the prophets) 55f.
Jealousy of God 302f., 337
Jerusalem, (temple at ≈) see Temple; (destruction of ≈) 51, 71f., 74, 84; (place of ≈ in hopes of the future) 72, 75–78, 444, 453
Jesus Christ and the O.T., (attitude, to and use of the O.T.) 11ff., 17, 19, 89, 99ff., 126, 382, 400, 425, 453; (God's revelation in the O.T. and in J.C.) 19, 23, 26f., 47f., 89f., 93ff., 99f., 114, 122ff., 141, 152, 204, 289, 378, 402f., 460f.

Hebrew words

473

yir'ath Yahweh 160, 179, 287
yom Yahweh 191, 439, 456

kabod 207f., 248, 299, 302, 371
kafar; cf. s.v. kipper 262
kethubim, see General Index s.v.
kipper; cf. s.v. kafar 63, 262, 264, 268
kum (hi) 169
kol (hak-) 422

leb 379, 408

machah 262
malakh (verb.) 438
mal'akh (-Yahweh) 209f., 427
(-melis) 428
malkut Yahweh 438f.
maṣṣoth 260
megilloth 84
melekh 318, 345, 438
midbar 55
minchah 37, 265
mishpaṭ 71, 388f., 450
mophet, 423

nabi' 230
(nebiim rishonim: cf. General Index s.v.)
naṣar 391
nathan 169
nefesh 320, 407, 409
(nefesh chayyah) 407

neshamah 407
nokriyim 399

'ob 427
'od 169 n.3
'ohel moced 373
'olah 36f., 265
'olam habba' (-hazzeh) 35, 454
'ot 423

padah 196, 275
pele' 299, 423
pesha' 55, 417

qahal 373
qanna' 302 (cf. s.v. el qanna')
qdsh (qadosh, qodesh) 297f.
(Qedosh Yisrael) 71

ra'ah 227
(ni. en hi.) 185, 188
(ro'eh) 231
rachamim 313
rachum 312
raṣah (ni.) 262, 264
raṣon (le-) 262, 264ff.
reach nichoach 31; 264, 267f.
ruach 212, 320, 407
(-Yahweh) 210, 211ff., 318

ṣalach 318
Seba'oth 71, 298
ṣdq 389
(ṣaddiq) 63, 310, 388f.

(ṣedaqah) 63, 307, 388 f.
(ṣedeq) 380, 388f.
(Yahweh ṣidqenu) 449
(ṣidqoth Yahweh) 439
satan (cf. General Index s.v.)
se'irim 427
semikhah 263
sim 169
sukkot 260
shabbath (cf. General Index s.v.)
shabu'ot 260
shaddai 345
shalem 310
she'ar yashub 448
shedim 427
shelem 37, 264f.
shem 208
shema' 294, 323
she'ol 408
shfṭ 389
(shofeṭ) 364

tam (tamim) 63, 310
tebel 422
tehom 215
terafim 33
todah 86
tohu wabohu 329
torah: (cf. General Index s.v.)

'urim (and thummim): (cf. General Index s.v. 'urim)

zaraq 264
zebach 37

474

Authors

Cossmann, W. 439
Cramer, J. A. 17
Cramer, K. 298
Cullmann, O. 42, 453, 461
Cumming, C. C. 257

Dahl, M. 45, 372
Daube, D. 193
David, M. 33, 81, 247, 398, 412
Davidson, A. B. 67
Davies, W. D. 93, 94, 286, 341, 407, 416
Delitzsch, Fr. 19
Denton, R. C. 146, 153, 295, 312, 313
Dequecker, J. 450
Dhorme, P. 343
Diestel, L. 95, 125
Dillmann, A. 33, 247, 304, 455
Dinkler, E. 14, 130
Dodd, C. H. 125, 126
Doeve, J. W. 127
Donner, H. 236, 365, 375, 417
Driver, G. R. 257, 323, 342
Driver, S. R. 324
Dubarlez, 179
Duhm, B. 67
Duhm, H. 427
Dupont-Sommer, A. 47, 122
Dürr, L. 117, 371
Dusseaud, R. 36
Dijk, I. I. A. van 165

Ebeling, G. 120, 129, 130, 150
Edelkoort, A. H. 258, 380, 441, 459
Edlund, L. 310
Eerdmans, B. D. 32f, 45, 278, 282, 308,
    324, 343, 389, 392f., 396
Ehrlich, A. 301, 392
Ehrlich, E. L. 187, 229, 250
Eichrodt, W. 38, 57, 70, 80, 97, 114, 124,
    137, 144, 146, 151, 171, 212, 221, 231f.,
    297f., 329, 335, 343, 345, 351, 382, 387,
    409, 419, 421, 424, 434, 438, 441
Eissfeldt, O. 26, 50, 66, 83, 100, 111,
    144f., 148f., 278, 299, 304, 325, 328,
    331, 333, 339, 342ff., 363, 438
Eliade, M. 461
Elliger, K. 77, 304, 360, 395, 453
Elmslie, W. A. L. 377, 380, 397
Engnell, F. 251, 366
Erasmus, 130

Fahlgreen, K. H. 389
Falkenstein, A. 258
Fascher, E. 32
Fensham, F. L. 30
Fichtner, J. 242f., 399
Flüsser, D. 105
Foerster, W. 47, 344
Fohrer, G. 233, 294, 308, 325, 348, 351
Fraine, J. de 366
Frankena, R. 296, 352
Frankfort, H. 165, 167, 366, 405
Frederiksson, H. 42, 298, 299, 318, 372

Freedman, D. N. 52
Freud, S. 34
Friedländer, M. 47, 441, 455
Fry, R. 67

Gabler, J. G. 144
Gadd, C. J. 366
Galling, K. 56, 314, 325
Gaster, Th. 37
Gemser, B. 26, 117, 242, 243, 288, 300,
    362, 390, 392, 435
Gerleman, G. 14, 118
Gerstenberger, E. 225, 348, 379, 385,
    386, 395
Gese, H. 242
Gispen, W. H. 242, 279
Gloege, G. 17
Glueck, N. 388
Goistein, S. D. 343
Gollwitzer, H. 297, 317
Goppelt, L. 137
Gottwald, N. K. 85
Gray, G. B. 250
Gray, J. 37
Gressman, H. 257, 390, 439, 442, 457
Grether, O. 343
Greijdanus, S. 125
Grolle, J. H. 283
Grønback, J. H. 447
Groningen, B. A. van 114
Groot, Joh. de (zie Hulst), 22, 39, 128,
    294, 323, 343
Gross, K. 67
Grossouw, G. 122
Guillaume, A. 27, 228, 231
Gunkel, H. 117, 257, 325, 332, 335
Gunneweg, A. H. J. 66
Gunning, J. H. jr. 125
Gutbrod 226
Guttman 400

Haag, H. 115, 187
Hahn, F. 274, 453
Haitjema, Th. L. 134, 145
Haldar 234, 250
Hammerhaimb, E. 441
Hänel, J. 297, 343
Haran, M. 12
Harnack, A. von 15, 120
Häussermann, F. 230
Hebert, A. G. 48
Heering, G. J. 461
Heiler, F. 92
Hehn, J. 298, 342
Hempel, J. 30, 56, 76, 118, 145, 164,
    317, 320, 321, 329, 335, 351, 352, 372,
    377, 383, 388, 389, 405, 438, 451
Henri, M. L. 424
Henssi, K. 119
Herbert, A. S. 251
Herrmann, J. 262, 268, 392
Hertzberg, W. 373
Heschel, A. 163, 223, 232

477

478

Information

STUDIA BIBLICA ET SEMITICA

THEODORO CHRISTIANO VRIEZEN

QUI MUNERE PROFESSORIS THEOLOGIAE PER XXV ANNOS FUNCTUS EST,

AB AMICIS, COLLEGIS, DISCIPULIS DEDICATA

CONTENTS

M.A. BEEK, Amsterdam: Zeit, Zeiten und eine halbe Zeit / P.A.H. DE BOER, Leiden: 2 Samuel 12:25 / H.A. BRONGERS, Utrecht: Die Zehnzahl in der Bibel und in ihrer Umwelt / J. COPPENS, Louvain: L'espérance messianique royale à la vieille et au lendemain de l'exil / O. EISSFELDT, Halle-S: Israels Führer in der Zeit vom Auszug aus Ägypten bis zur Landnahme / W. FOERSTER, Münster-W: Die Irrlehrer des Kolosserbriefes / G. FOHRER, Erlangen: Die Sprüche Obadjas / R. FRANKENA, Utrecht: Einige Bemerkungen zum Gebrauch des Adverbs *'al-ken* im Hebräischen / CH. T. FRITSCH, Princeton-N.J.:TO 'ANTITΥΠON / G. GERLEMAN, Lund: Bemerkungen zum alttestamentlichen Sprachstil / W.H. GISPEN, Amsterdam: Genesis 2:10-14 / F. HESSE, Münster: Erwägungen zur religionsgeschichtlichen und theologischen Bedeutung der Erwählungsgewißheit Israels / J.H. HOSPERS, Groningen: A hundred years of Semitic comparative linguistics / A.R. HULST, Utrecht: Bemerkungen zum Sabbatgebot / E. JENNI, Basel: Distel und Zeder: Hermeneutische Überlegungen zu 2 Kö 14:8-14 / J.L. KOOLE, Kampen: Quelques remarques sur Psaume 139 / H.J. KRAUS, Hamburg: Glaube und Politik bei Martin Buber / C.J. LABUSCHAGNE, Pretoria: The emphasizing particle *gam* and its connotations / F.M. TH. DE LIAGRE BÖHL, Milsbeek-Limburg: Blüte und Untergang des Assyrerreiches als historisches Problem / B.J. VAN DER MERWE, Pretoria: Joseph as successor of Jacob / J. MUILENBURG, San Anselmo-Cal.: A liturgy on the triumphs of Yahweh / H.W. OBBINK, Utrecht: On the legends of Moses in the Haggadah / J.P.M. VAN DER PLOEG, Nijmegen: Réflexions sur les genres littéraires des Psaumes / N.W. PORTEOUS, Edinburgh: The relevance of the Old Testament as a rule of life / G. VON RAD, Heidelberg: Das Werk Jahwes / N.H. RIDDERBOS, Amsterdam: Psalm 51:5,6 / W. RUDOLPH, Münster-W: Eigentümlichkeiten der Sprache Hoseas / A. VAN SELMS, Pretoria: A forgotten god: *laḥ* / J.J. STAMM, Bern: Elia am Horeb / W.C. VAN UNNIK, Utrecht: Der Ausdruck 'ΕΩΣ 'ΕΣΧΑΤΟΥ ΤΗΣ ΓΗΣ (Apostelgeschichte 1:8) und sein alttestamentlicher Hintergrund / W. VISCHER. Montpellier: Erste Eindrücke von Jerusalem und seiner Umgebung / C. WESTERMANN, Heidelberg: Jesaja 48 und die 'Bezeugung gegen Israel' / A.S. VAN DER WOUDE, Groningen: Der Gerechte wird durch seine Treue leben. Erwägungen zu Habakuk 2:4f / G. ERNEST WRIGHT, Cambridge-Mass.: Reflections concerning Old Testament theology / W. ZIMMERLI, Göttingen: Der Mensch und seine Hoffnung nach den Aussagen des Alten Testaments

406 pp.   cloth Dfl. 39,50   papercover Dfl. 36.-   postage+packing Dfl. 1,50

Publisher H. VEENMAN & ZONEN N.V. WAGENINGEN (THE NETHERLANDS) 1966

ISBN 90 278 0004 9